# The child as thinker

The study of children's thinking is an extremely lively area. An enormous number of studies are being produced, and new ways of understanding the findings are proliferating. *The Child as Thinker* provides an informed and accessible overview of this whole area.

After a brief discussion of the nature and subject of cognition, Meadows reviews children's thinking in detail. She discusses the ways children remember and organise information in general, the acquisition of skills such as reading, writing and arithmetic, and the development of more complex reasoning as children grow to maturity.

As well as studies that typically describe a generalised child, Meadows also reviews some of the main areas relevant to individual differences in normal cognitive development, and examines three major models of cognitive development. In outlining the work of Piaget, information-processing accounts and neo-Vygotskian theories, she also evaluates their different explanations of cognitive development and their implications for education. Finally, the book examines biological and social factors that may be involved in normal and suboptimal cognitive development.

Meadows provides an important review of the crucial issues involved in understanding cognitive development and of the new data and models that have emerged in the last few years. Her book brings together areas and approaches that have hitherto been independent, and examines their strengths and weaknesses. *The Child as Thinker* will be required reading for all students of cognitive development and psychology.

**Sara Meadows** is Lecturer in Education at the University of Bristol.

# The child as thinker

## The development and acquisition of cognition in childhood

Sara Meadows

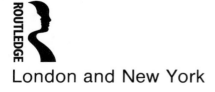

London and New York

First published in 1993
by Routledge
11 New Fetter Lane, London EC4P 4EE

Simultaneously published in the USA and Canada
by Routledge
29 West 35th Street, New York, NY 10001

Typeset by Witwell Limited, Southport
Printed and bound in Great Britain by Biddles Ltd,
Guildford and King's Lynn

*British Library Cataloguing in Publication Data*
A catalogue record for this book is available from the
British Library.

*Library of Congress Cataloging in Publication Data*
Meadows, Sara.
    The child as thinker : the development and acquisition of
cognition in childhood/Sara Meadows.
    p.   cm.
    Includes bibliographical references and index.
    1. Cognition in children. 2. Human information pro-
cessing in children. I. Title.
    BF723.C5M383 1993                          92–40457
    155.4'13—dc20                                   CIP

ISBN 0–415–01142–6
      0–415–01143–4 (pbk)

*In memory of my father, and with gratitude for his contributions to the development of my cognition during my childhood*

# Contents

# Figures and tables

# Chapter 1

# Introduction

The study of cognitive development is one of the major areas of child psychology – the only one to monopolise almost one volume of the 1983 *Handbook of Child Psychology* – and even livelier now than it was up to the early 1980s. Currently there are a number of interesting shifts in what cognitive development is thought to be, and this book is intended to review the field and, as far as possible, suggest answers to the issues involved. There is relevant research in several different areas; these have tended to be isolated from each other and from other approaches. Workers in each field could be better informed about each other's progress. Recent work has generated new data and new explanatory models which I want to juxtapose. The aim of this book is to provide an informed and accessible overview of the area.

Here, in the first chapter, I will present, briefly, some of the issues which will surface for closer examination elsewhere. The first is the question of what is 'cognition'. This may seem to be capable of a clear answer, but in fact there are a number of problems in the background, stretching right back to psychology's unresolved tension between its two definitions as 'the science of mental life' and 'the science of behaviour'. At one level cognition is what people can be observed to do when they have to think, learn, remember, understand, judge, use concepts and so forth; at another it is the system behind these different abilities. Researchers focus on one level rather than another, just as they differ on whether they attend to the formal properties of a cognitive system or to the material it is made of, when seeking to explain why it works as it does. Here different researchers are using different allied disciplines; the user of the latest neurophysiological research is probably not dealing with quite the same question about cognition as the users of the latest advances in artificial intelligence or in educational programmes. I am going to argue that there would be more progress in the study of cognitive development if practitioners who differed in their focus on the subject nevertheless took into account the illumination that other focuses provided. The study of reading processes in childhood and adulthood seems a shining example of the advances that arise when different disciplines, in this case experimental cognitive psychology, developmental psychology and cognitive neurophysiology, are brought together intelligently.

Another uncertainty stretching back to the early days of psychology is about what the limits of cognition are in the sense of what is not 'cognitive'. Virtually every human action involves some thinking, learning, use of concepts, and so forth, and is therefore cognitive. The traditional division of psychology's subject-matter was into 'affective' (or emotional), 'conative' (or motivational) and 'cognitive' (or intellectual). The problem with this division is that it underplays the links between cognition, emotion and motivation, and they have been largely neglected in research, which as I show later is regrettable. Nor does it easily accommodate the social dimension of behaviour, and here another problematic issue about cognitive development is relevant: is it a matter of each individual constructing his or her own individual cognitive system, or are cognitive systems constructed within and by social interaction? The explanatory models in the literature tend to focus on one without giving the other adequate consideration, and many of the descriptive studies do not help with the problem because they seek to describe a generalised child and do not examine the variation between individuals with different powers of construction or different experience of social interaction. Work which did take on the problem of different pathways through cognitive development would clarify how individual construction and social construction are balanced. The theoretical models which make individual construction pre-eminent tend to focus on very general abstract cognitive processes instantiated in behaviour on problems which are not part of the usual educational curriculum, such as conservation, or solving the problems of the Tower of Hanoi, or of the Cannibals and Missionaries who want to cross a shark-infested river. The social constructivist theories are more likely to look at cognition in socially valued areas, such as school achievement or becoming a skilled craft worker.

A further problem about cognition is whether it is general, a matter of a few processes which dominate cognitive behaviour in all disciplines and all domains, or whether it is 'domain-specific', with each area of subject-matter having its own specialised ways of thinking. Again, it must be both, but we need to say how the two work together in development. A parallel debate to this one is concerned with whether there are universal cognitive processes which are the same for every normal individual, or at least a level of description where universals may be used, or whether there may not be more than one normal way of solving the same problem. The two very important developmental versions of this are whether the successful solution processes of children might differ from the successful solution processes of adults, and whether there might not be distinctly different pathways from early childhood to adulthood for different individuals or groups. I argue that some attention to the possibility of differences between individuals in their cognition may illuminate both what cognition is and how it gets to be as it is.

A whole set of even more unresolved issues arise about the parallel question of what 'development' is: I am not going to address them here, partly because I do so in considerable detail in the rest of the book and partly because to have too many problems brought up in the introduction might demoralise the reader. I do hope readers will be able to enjoy a bit of uncertainty as they use this book: years of immersion in the field has taught me that very little indeed is firm scientific certainty, but there are enough fairly firm tussocks in the marsh of our ignorance to keep us from getting wet much above the knees!

There are, I think, three good reasons for studying the development and acquisition of cognition in childhood. First, it is there, interesting in itself and providing a good excuse for some pleasant time with children. Second, understanding it is going to make a major contribution to understanding human cognition: as J. M. Baldwin (1895) said 'the study of children is often the only means of testing the truth of our mental analyses'. Third, understanding it should illuminate our activities as formal and informal educators of children; I think we can already draw ideas from the field about how to facilitate their cognitive development, and about what could impede it, even though we are some way from a rigorous understanding.

The plan of the book is as follows. It begins with a review of what children's thinking is like in a number of different areas, beginning with the ways that they remember and organise information in general and with the generally applicable cognitive skills of reading, writing and arithmetic and going on to what may be less general areas such as drawing, spatial reasoning and ideas about socio-economic systems. This long chapter addresses the 'what' of cognitive development in childhood: what do children do when they remember, draw maps, act as naïve psychologists or physicists, or whatever; what changes and what remains the same as they grow to maturity? The studies reviewed in this chapter typically seek to describe a generalised child: they say '5-year-olds do this, 10-year-olds do that' and variation amongst children of the same age or stage is rarely focused on, and may be explicitly consigned to the separate study of 'individual differences'. I think that this is unfortunate, for reasons developed throughout the rest of the book, and therefore Chapter 3 reviews some of the main areas relevant to individual differences in normal cognitive development. As it happens, much of the work on intelligence, creativity and cognitive style has been assertively non-developmental, insisting that many of these individual differences are to a major extent innate; my discussion of them focuses on how this has impoverished the research and how it could be enriched by a developmental perspective.

Having discussed the 'what' of cognitive development I move towards the 'how': Chapter 4 reviews the three major current models of cognitive development. Here Piaget's work, Information-Processing accounts, and neo-Vygotskian theories are each outlined and evaluated. Each has a different set of answers to the question of how cognitive development occurs, and different descriptions of its causes and of the role of education. Chapter 5 examines some of the areas in mainstream psychology that might contribute to our understanding of the 'what' and 'how' of cognitive development. The first part is predominantly biological and medical, drawing on research on genetics, brain development and brain damage for what they can tell us about both normal and suboptimal cognitive development. The second part looks at social influences on cognitive development, focusing first on demographic variations in cognitive achievement and then on the effect of social interaction in the family and in school on how well cognitive development proceeds. The final chapter raises some of the pervasive problems and omissions of the field, and indicates where I think progress is likely.

# Chapter 2

# Descriptive studies of children's cognitive skills and knowledge

This chapter contains reviews of some of the knowledge and the cognitive skills that children develop and acquire during the years of childhood, including reading, writing, arithmetical computation, remembering, reasoning, drawing, metacognition, categorising into concepts, and their ideas about music, persons, socio-economic systems, science, stories, maps and so on. I provide here only a brief outline of each topic with references to the material from which my outline is derived; readers must consult these references to get anything like a comprehensive picture. I have not attempted to integrate the separate bodies of research which have produced the descriptions I summarise here, nor to go beyond description to explanation. Nor have I dealt with every skill or area of knowledge which has appeared in the literature. Particularly in the section reviewing studies of children's concepts of this, that and the other, I have focused on areas where there was a reasonable quantity of work of reasonable quality, which I found relevant to the concerns of the rest of the book, and have omitted some areas because I found too high a proportion of atheoretical and insensitive description. Some research of high quality and great importance is omitted because it has generally been thought of as outside the category of 'cognition', and to have included it would have widened the topic beyond what I could justify. Children's spoken language is the main body of work I would have dealt with if I had been able to be comprehensively inclusive, but I did not because there had to be limits to what 'the development and acquisition of cognition in childhood' included, and the language literature and the cognition literature have been to a considerable extent separate. Finally, the selection of material has necessarily been dependent on what I came across: doubtless there have been many brilliant studies which I simply failed to notice, and some I failed to understand, which are therefore not dealt with here.

I would not want to draw a strong distinction between skills and knowledge, being persuaded by the evidence that they are so interdependent as to be inextricable. However, there is some difference in the descriptions of children's behaviour in this chapter which maps on to the skills –

knowledge distinction. In some areas what is described is what children *do*, and these areas are on the whole more skill-like (reading, writing, reasoning and so forth), while in other areas the description is of what children *say* about a topic, and here the focus is perhaps knowledge (of people, socio-economic systems, music, etc.). There are some intermediate areas, metacognition for example, where the interplay between skill and knowledge is most conspicuous. Many would argue (see e.g. Brown *et al.* 1983, Meadows 1986, Meadows and Cashdan 1988, Siegler 1986) that knowing enough about your cognitive skills to apply them consciously, deliberately and flexibly is a major part of cognitive development, perhaps *the* major part so far as cognition acquired through education is concerned. How far knowledge about one's 'declarative' knowledge (of persons, countries, sub-atomic particles or whatever) affects either that knowledge or one's 'procedural' knowledge (skills such as remembering, understanding and reasoning) is not clear (see e.g. Carey and Gelman 1991, Chi and Ceci 1987); but certainly differences in the efficiency of such cognitive procedures will affect one's access to and use of one's knowledge. An ability to remember information or to recognise that there is a contradiction between two 'facts' will no doubt be necessary for using knowledge satisfactorily. Some aspects of the procedural knowledge – declarative knowledge distinction are discussed later in this book. The distinction functions here only as the reason why the contents of this chapter are presented in the order that follows: roughly, 'skills' before 'knowledge'. This structure separates some sections which are linked, and deals with some topics several times, from somewhat different angles. Readers will find that the text does contain some cross references, but it would be advisable to use the index too. It is essential, rather than advisable, that readers should not believe that any section contains all that is to be said about its subject!

## READING

Reading is one of the delights of my life and many other people's, a source of information, a way into new worlds, a tool of my profession, one of the means I have to extend and deepen my understanding and my empathy. For those who are being educated, reading is one of the most basic, essential and central skills, permeating most of what goes on in school, required for almost all school tasks, absolutely necessary for succeeding in the educational system, thus politically sensitive (e.g. Chall, Jacobs and Baldwin 1990, Olson and Torrance 1991). It is also a self-evidently complex structured set of cognitive processes, occupying a central place within cognitive psychology, and interestingly affected by brain functioning. Uta Frith called it a 'complex and astonishing accomplishment' (Frith 1980a), and the more we examine reading and how children come to be able to read, the more profound our agreement must become.

Analysis of exactly what readers do when they read has produced many interesting insights but not yet agreement on a complete model of how reading is done. Researchers agree that many perceptual, attentional, linguistic and cognitive skills are involved, but not yet how they fit together in either the skilled reader or the novice, nor which are to be emphasised. Work in experimental cognitive psychology has done a great deal to illuminate the basic processes which decode visual information into a verbal form. It seems that skilled readers have three distinct 'routes' into extracting meaning from a written word (Marshall 1987a, 1987b). These are a 'phonic' route, a 'direct' route and a 'lexical' route. In the 'phonic' route the phonological representation of written units smaller than words (letters, syllables, morphemes) is conjured up prior to accessing meaning, so that for example 'cat' might be spelled out as '| c | | a | | t |' means 'cat' means 'a small furry purring animal'. In the 'direct' route the pronunciation is assigned directly to the whole word, and in the 'lexical' route meaning is attached directly to the written word before its pronunciation is arrived at. I understand the meaning of 'flaccid', for example, but would have to check its pronunciation (to 'rhyme' with accident rather than with acid).

Ellis (1984) suggests that skilled readers have met most of the words they have to read many times and know their meaning and pronunciation very well. Visual recognition of such words at once activates their meaning in a semantic representation system, and their pronunciation can be retrieved from the phonemic word production system either directly from the semantic system or through one-to-one correspondences between units in the visual word recognition system and units in the phonemic word production system (Figure 2.1). For example, when I see the word 'Byzantine' I recognise it and can access its meaning (belonging to the capital of the Eastern part of the Roman Empire, the city of Byzantium or Constantinople (now Istanbul); or to its art or architecture; or to its politics, hence a more general use describing social relations or systems which are complex and sinister, with conspiracy, murder and all sorts of nasty things going on under a smooth social surface). My pronunciation derived from grapheme–phoneme correspondences in English so that until very recently my phonemic representation was incorrect, as I read the initial 'By' as | bai | (as in by-road) not as | bi | (roughly as in bit), which the word's Greek origins makes the correct version. If the word encountered has not been seen before, its component letters have to be identified. The letter sequence may be close enough to a familiar word to be accepted as a version of it, particularly perhaps if it is being read from material where misprints are likely. If it is not close enough, it may be possible to guess it from the context or to use familiar letter sequences to assemble a possible pronunciation. The word 'dispauper', for example, breaks down quite easily into three pronounceable syllables or two morphemes, and the latter analysis suggests its meaning (to deprive of the privileges of a pauper, for example,

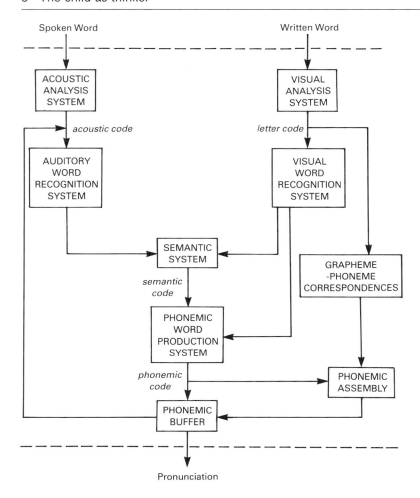

Spoken Word

Written Word

*Figure 2.1* A model for both the direct and the phonically mediated recognition, comprehension and naming of written words.
*Source*: Ellis 1984: 33

to disqualify from suing without payment of fees: an early piece of evidence (1631) for the existence of a legal aid system under threat, perhaps!). If the unfamiliar word is phonemically irregular, however, the reader may not be able to do much more than guess at a pronunciation and will have no access to meaning other than the context or resource to a dictionary.

Being able to read a sentence or a longer passage involves more than the sum of reading each individual word. Knowledge about language becomes more important at this level, though it has been helpful even at the single word level (as in reading 'dispauper'). Readers use their knowledge of syntax (for example word order or inflections) and of story scenarios and the real world.

Winograd (1972), commenting on attempts to program computers to interpret English correctly, emphasises the amount of world knowledge that we bring to bear on tasks like finding the referents of pronouns in sentences such as 'The city council refused to allow the protesters to hold a demonstration in the main square because they advocated violence' or 'The city council refused to allow the protesters to hold a demonstration in the main square because they feared violence'. This sort of processing for deep implicit levels of meaning has implications for other levels of reading. Skilled readers who are reading aloud, for example, give their sentences appropriate emphasis, intonation and phrasing, even if the sentence is long and even if getting to the end of it requires turning over a page. The eyes run ahead of the voice so that the interpretation of the sentence can run ahead of having to express that interpretation. Skilled musicians reading and performing music manage the same feat. *Hearing* what is being read does not seem to be necessary for understanding its meaning except when subtle meanings or minor linguistic anomalies and changes have to be detected (Baddeley and Lewis 1981).

Visual processing, phonological analysis and the use of contextual information, then, contribute jointly to reading. Adults seem to have three main routes available to them. The dominant one in skilled readers is probably the recognition of whole words, a processing of the overall shape and pattern of a familiar unit which is fast and does not need all the graphemic information available (hence the difficulty people find in detecting graphemic errors in proof-reading, for example). The second route is via the analysis of individual graphemes in their spatial order, a slower process of conjuring up grapheme–phoneme correspondences which may still be underway while the faster lexical recognition has reached the right answer. Matching grapheme to phoneme can be complicated by spelling irregularities and inconsistencies of symbol–sound correspondence.

These difficulties are somewhat reduced in the third route between written word and meaning described by analogy theory (Patterson and Morton 1985). The processing here involves finding a known word that contains the same orthographic sequence as the word being read, for example a sequence such as 'are' or 'tion', retrieving how it is pronounced in the known word and assuming that it sounds similar in the word to be read. Symbol–sound correspondence works here through analogy with examples rather than through abstract phonic rules. My earlier discussion of the pronunciation of 'flaccid' used analogy to illustrate what I had looked up in dictionaries and found written in terms of phonemes. Such a process would avoid some of the problems of inconsistent spelling as, despite the existence of notorious exceptions such as 'ough', grapheme strings have fewer irregular pronunciations than single graphemes, and this might make up for having a more complex unit for analysis.

This very brief account of what experimental cognitive psychology is suggesting about reading processes does not do justice to the field's achievements. Interested readers should go to sources such as introductions by Ellis (1984), Eysenck and Keane (1990), Oakhill and Garnham (1988), or more technical accounts such as Beech and Colley (1987) and Henderson (1982). It does however make the point that 'reading' includes many different activities at different perceptual, linguistic and cognitive levels, and that these may well operate in different ways as the reader tackles different tasks. In some ways it may be misleading to call all instances of 'reading' by the same name. What we do when we recognise 'cereals' in a supermarket is probably simpler than what we do when we see it in a newspaper article on the government's farming policy, and that 'reading' might be different from meeting the same string of letters in a scientific article or a poem. For our present purposes, the most interesting question is how the various components of skilled reading co-occur and interact as the child progresses from its pre-school innocence of literacy to advanced reading skills.

**Development in reading processes**

Since 'reading' involves visual processing of a visible text, I will start my discussion of reading development with visual processes. Unless the amount of text we have to deal with is very small (10 or 12 letters or spaces), we have to move our eyes over the text. This is not normally problematic; the saccadic eye movements which produce rapid changes in fixation that relocate targets from the periphery to more sensitive foveal vision are functional, within limits, at birth, and babies 3 months old can manage fairly smooth eye movements following a moving object or along an informative shape. They can also discriminate between shapes like *b* and *d* (Banks and Salapatek 1983). The *uses* to which visual processes are put may well change as development proceeds, but the basic capacities are functional very early. Nor does there seem to be much evidence for there normally being a general visual processing problem even in poor readers (Beech and Colley 1987, Bryant and Bradley 1985) except the inexperience which is the result of their reading less; that is, they do not read worse because they cannot distinguish letters, they distinguish letters worse because they read less.

In the earliest stages of 'reading,' most words which the child can read are in fact probably dealt with by recognising either their shape or their standard sequence of letters; many children are taught very early on to recognise their names, for example, and the environment has many emphasised written patterns such as 'STOP' or 'EXIT'. Throughout later stages of learning to read, the presence of a particular letter or combination of letters which distinguishes a particular common word may be taken as a sign that the present word is the known one, even if the other letters in it are not quite right: the combination 'll' meant 'yellow' to at least one child learning to read, even if the actual word present was, say, 'taller'. Bryant and Bradley (1980, 1985) found children who could read certain words whose spelling was irregular but whose shape was distinctive (such as 'school' or 'light') very well; but if they were asked to spell these words they could not. Conversely, there were words which could be spelled correctly but not read, even when produced for reading in the child's own handwriting. *These* were phonetically regular words such as 'bun' and 'mat': and children did better at reading them after a brief training in reading words phonologically letter by letter. There would seem to be quite strong evidence here for a discrepancy between a phonological spelling strategy and a reading strategy which chunked letters into complete familiar words or familiar parts of words.

Children learning to read English do of course often encounter words where there is a problematic relationship between sound and letter. Some languages, for example Italian, have a nearly consistent relationship between the two: the spelling of the word conveys its pronunciation unambiguously in most cases. While this is the case for many English words also, there are others which break the normal correspondences between grapheme and phoneme. Stubbs (1980) goes into these in some detail, and Gelb (1963) provides a very useful history of different writing systems. For our present purposes, there are two main points to be made. It is somewhat easier to learn symbol–sound correspondences which are consistent, hence the usefulness of regularised alphabets such as the initial teaching alphabet (Downing 1979). However, spelling reforms like such alphabets do not provide a totally unproblematic solution. If later reading has to be done with the conventional alphabet and spelling system, then the reader has to transfer his or her ITA skills to more complex material. The regularised alphabet does not allow for regional pronunciation differences, so that the same symbol would be associated with different vowels in, say, Yorkshire and Sussex. Most important, and this is the second point I want to make, the conventional English spelling system contains, and the regularised alphabets do not, a great deal of lexical and syntactic meaning which is of great use to the reader. For example, conventional spelling indicates the plural of many words by adding an 's' to the singular form: for example 'cats', 'cows', 'horses'. The way in which the 's' is sounded, however, is slightly different for each of these: in 'cats' it is | s |, in 'cows' it is more like | z |, and in 'horses' something like | iz |. If the words were spelled phonetically with a regularised alphabet the morpheme indicating the plural would be different in each case and the syntactic regularity would be obscured. Another problem would arise with homophones, that is, words which have the same sound but different meanings, and are spelled in different ways so that the spelling can show which meaning is intended.

There are nine such words in the preceding sentence (only one of them put in deliberately!); 'would', 'which', 'but', 'two', 'or', 'more', 'so', 'their' and 'be' could not be distinguished, if sound and spelling correspondence were regularised, from 'wood', 'witch', 'butt', 'to', 'too', 'awe', 'ore', 'maw', 'sew', 'sow', 'there' and 'bee', except by syntactic rules and lexical probabilities. Readers would probably in the end be certain what was meant, but losing the visual distinction means that an additional cue to meaning is lost. A further sort of information present in conventional English spelling but not in regularised alphabets is at the lexical and etymological level. 'Sign' and 'signature' or 'bomb' and 'bombardment' look similar because their meanings are related; regularised spelling would obscure such relations. It would also disguise the origins of the many words which English has borrowed from other languages, preserving the spelling even if the pronunciation is somewhat mangled.

All in all, it is very plausible that, as Stubbs (1980) has argued, the English spelling system is extremely informative for a native speaker who knows its phonological and morphological rules and something of its history: that is, it is better suited to adult fluent readers than to children learning to read.

For all that I have been saying about the uncertain route to identification of words which phonemic analysis provides, it is fairly clear that an ability to discriminate between different sounds is an important component of learning to read. Bryant and his colleagues (Bryant and Bradley 1985, Goswami and Bryant 1990) provide convincing evidence that there is a causal association between insensitivity to phonemic differences and difficulties in learning to read. They tested 400 non-reading 4- and 5-year-olds on a series of rhyming and alliteration tasks, such as identifying the odd word out in sets like 'bun hut gun sun', 'hug pig dig wig' and 'bud bun bus rug', also giving them verbal intelligence and memory tests. Scores on the rhyming tests did predict how well the children were reading and spelling three or four years later, even when intelligence differences had been partialled out; they did not predict success in mathematics. In further studies, they trained children on the categorisation of words by their shared sounds, and found here that such training improved reading and spelling. This combination of evidence from longitudinal and training studies supports an important role for sensitivity to the sounds of words and an ability to categorise them by sound in learning to read. Phonemic analysis is quite hard to learn, and young children and illiterate adults find it almost impossible to segment words correctly into phonemes, though relatively easy to segment them into syllables (Liberman *et al.* 1977) or, as more recent and very precise research has shown, into onset and rime (e.g. c-at, thr-ead) (Goswami and Bryant 1990, Goswami 1991, Hansen and Bowey 1992, Marmurek and Rinaldo 1992, Masterson, Laxon and Stuart 1992, Naslund and Schneider 1991, Thorstad 1991). Experience of playing with contrasting sounds, as in nursery rhymes and as in many of the 'poems' and monologues young children often create for themselves (Bryant and Bradley 1985, Bryant *et al.* 1989, 1990, Chukovsky 1976, Dowker 1989, Kirtley *et al.* 1989, Stuart 1990) looks like a very possible facilitator of phonemic awareness and learning to read. Experience of reading also facilitates the child's awareness of both letter–sound or letter-group–sound correspondences. Becoming able to 'sound out' words successfully is one of the important breakthroughs in the early stages of reading. Sounding-out reduces dependence on recognising the visual patterns of words (and hence is particularly useful for the less distinctive patterns of words like 'bun' and 'leg') and supplements the reader's knowledge of likely meaning. It also makes it possible to read regularly formed non-words, such as 'vib', which readers without phonic skills typically refuse to read (Campbell and Butterworth 1985). However, because of the irregularities of letter–sound relationships, the existence of homophones, and the problem of blending separate phonemes into a word, phonics alone cannot be enough for skilled reading.

Corroborative evidence on the roles of different ways of reading comes from studies of 'retarded' readers. These are people who have problems learning to read which cannot be accounted for by general intellectual impairment, specific sensory impairments, lack of education or emotional or motivational problems. Their reading attainment is much lower than would be expected from their age and IQ. The survey of a national sample of 10-year-olds carried out by the Child Health and Education Study (CHES) (Rodgers 1983) showed that poor readers tend to have problems in other school subjects (these might well require reading, of course); to be regarded by their teachers as more anti-social, inattentive, clumsy and anxious, and having parents who were not very interested in the child's education; to be boys rather than girls; and to attend schools with a high proportion of children from poor housing, with parents of non-UK cultural groups, and with parents in manual occupations (see also Chall *et al.* 1990, Snow *et al.* 1991). Some of these differences may be causes of their poor reading; many might, rather, be consequences of it. This direction of causation problem complicates what we can draw from the research literature (Ellis and Large 1987). Studies which compare poor readers with normal readers of the same age (comparable with the CHES data) and find they differ on some diagnostic task cannot differentiate between three possibilities. The first is that the diagnostic task does indeed measure a cause of the reading difficulty, for example that the reading difficulty is caused by poor short-term memory, or poor phonological awareness, or poor shape recognition skills. The second possibility is that, on the contrary, poor performance on the diagnostic task is caused by not having learned to read; if the shapes or sounds to be recognised or remembered or analysed are graphemes and phonemes the good reader is likely to have had more experience with them than the poor one, and the greater experience may be the cause of the difference. Thirdly, both poor test performance and poor reading may have the same underlying cause, such as neurological immaturity; the underlying deficit causes two problematic areas of performance but these two areas may not affect each other.

We can reach clearer conclusions on the causes of reading retardation if we combine research designs to decide between these possibilities. As well as comparing poor readers with normal readers of the same age, we can compare them with a control group matched for reading age and IQ but younger, that is reading at a level appropriate for their age. These controls will have the same absolute level of reading skills as poor readers, and their use and experience of reading will thus differ from the poor readers less than would the same-age controls. If the reading age controls differ from the poor readers on some measure, the difference is less likely to be due to differences in experience and more likely to be related to the cause of the poor reading. However, lack of difference on a measure does not mean that it is irrelevant to the cause of the reading problem in the older children: they may be suffering from a development lag in some process, remaining at an immature state which the younger children will grow out of. Longitudinal studies help here. The first measures are taken before the children have started to learn to read. Poor performance on a measure at this stage cannot be due to the effects of failing to learn to read, and should therefore, if it does predict later reading performance, show possible causes of reading failure. Longitudinal studies however are expensive and in this case have to be done on a large scale because severe reading retardation is quite rare and there would be only a few children likely to become very retarded readers in any sample chosen before reading began. They cannot rule out the possibility that the diagnostic difference found does not itself cause the reading problem but is another symptom of some underlying cause.

The best way out of the problem of interpreting the causes behind correlations such as those between poor reading and poor scores on other tests is to do training studies. If training memory, visual skills or whatever improves performance on the criterion task *and* on reading, this is quite strong evidence that initial deficits in the trained skill contributed to the reading problem. It may also show what might be a useful remedial programme for poor readers, though not all deficits may be amenable to remediation.

Given these caveats about research problems, what can we say about the causes of reading retardation? It seems probable, first, that poor readers are the tail of a normal distribution, showing deficits on skills which work better in better readers, rather than a special group whose reading processes are different in kind from those of better readers (Ellis and Large 1988, Rodgers 1983). Hulme (1987) provides a useful review of where their problems may lie. He suggests that the clearest difficulty shown by retarded readers is in their word recognition skills. Typically this difficulty is not due to visual problems such as abnormal eye movements or abnormal lateralisation of visual function, though a small minority of poor readers may indeed have these problems. Slower processing of visual information presented for a brief period of time may be a sign of an underlying neurological problem which also causes difficulties with normal reading, but is unlikely to be the cause of reading retardation itself; in normal reading, after all, the material to be read can be looked at for as long as the reader wishes. Short-term memory difficulties leading to problems in 'blending' separate phonemes such as | c | | a | | t | into the word 'cat', and in holding partially decoded words in mind while comparing them with pronunciations retrieved from long-term memory, may characterise some retarded readers. The evidence is a little inconsistent on the direction of causation (see e.g. Bryant and Bradley 1985, Ellis and Large 1987, Gathercole and Baddeley 1989a, Naslund and Schneider 1991) and Hulme asks for training studies, but difficulties in holding material in the correct order in short-term memory may contribute to reading retardation. Differences in long-term memory have received less attention from researchers but may contribute to reading problems. Awareness of speech sounds is now known to be closely related to learning to read. Here, the evidence comes from studies involving the range of designs discussed earlier. Various tests of phonological awareness such as the ability to segment words into the correct number of phonemes predict later reading ability (Liberman *et al.* 1977). Bryant and Bradley showed that the ability of 4-year-olds to categorise sounds predicted their reading three or more years later (Bradley and Bryant 1983) and that training on sound categorisation plus letter–sound correspondences, spread over two years, produced a significant advance in reading compared with control groups. Phonological awareness is obviously necessary for the development of phonic skills, and it seems that retarded readers have particular difficulty in using phonic rules, for example an inability to read non-words, that is, letter strings which are pronounceable but happen not to be meaningful words.

## Learning to read in a literate environment

The cognitive psychology studies of reading single words and the research on children learning to read and retarded readers all suggest, then, that there are several ways of decoding a written word into its meaning. Beginning readers, and skilled readers reading familiar words, probably rely heavily on sight vocabulary, going direct from visual image to meaning without necessarily needing the sound of the word. Linking sight and sound is, however, necessary for expanding the sight vocabulary and dealing with unfamiliar words. Sensitivity to sounds and an ability to make and use grapheme–phoneme correspondences are important here. However, the research summarised in the last few lines has centred on reading isolated words or small units of text. As we saw in discussing models of reading earlier, skilled readers probably use both sight vocabulary and phonic analysis within a more contextual way of reading. In text comprehension the information given in a text is integrated with the reader's prior knowledge of the topic, which may itself have been gathered, of course, from earlier encounters with text. Beginning readers lack both general knowledge about topics and knowledge about the general characteristics of text.

These may be very important parts of learning to read. In the socially representative sample of children whom Gordon Wells studied in his research on language development (e.g. Wells 1981b, 1985) there were significant positive correlations between parents' and children's interest in literacy, particularly the frequency with which stories were read to the child, during the pre-school years, and the child's progress in learning to read. Children who learn to read early and easily (Clark 1976) have generally acquired very early a good understanding of what reading is about in general, and about such specific aspects as that you go along the lines from top left to bottom right, that the message is in the text though the pictures may provide clues, what things called 'words' and 'sentences' are, and so forth (Elley 1989, Rice 1989, Rice and Woodsmall 1988, Tunmer, Herriman and Nesdale 1988). Precocious talkers are not especially likely to learn to read early; instruction by parents, parents' reading to children, and, especially, the child's engagement in being read to, are better predictors of early reading (see also Crain-Thoreson and Dale 1992).

Hall (1987) reviews the evidence on 'the emergence of literacy'. He compares it with the development of spoken language and its use, which he sees as a matter of child construction within parent facilitation, not parent instruction. In the latter, oral language is used for non-linguistic ends (including developing meaning and understanding the world, and participating in social interaction). He argues that literacy, like spoken and heard language, is used to create meanings and to allow communication between people. Many early experiences relevant to literacy are embedded in a social interaction, for example discussion of a shopping list (Tizard and Hughes 1984). Such interaction carries information about literacy – for example that writing can be used to organise information and plan events, that it can be stored and amended, that it can be translated by reading into spoken language – incidentally to the social purpose of feeding the family. It may be more powerful, intellectually, therefore, than 'purer' literacy activities such as reading storybooks. Possibly, Hall argues, the child could learn about literacy as 'naturally' as he or she learns to talk and to listen.

Children growing up in literate cultures are likely to have a great deal of writing around them in the form of 'environmental print': shop signs, advertisements, slogans on T-shirts as well as books, newspapers and letters. Many young children show much interest in this print and make good use of it. Hall argues that such use is an intrinsic part of becoming literate. It develops along with experience of being read to, which is known to show a high correlation with learning to read well (Wells 1985). Parents reading stories may discuss such text-based concepts as 'word' and 'letter' as well as modelling reading behaviour. Stories also provide experience with 'literary language' and with settings beyond the child's daily life; again these can be discussed, and children can reflect on text and experience. The whole constellation of seeing text, being read to, using written and spoken language, and discussion with more expert users, may lead to 'emergent' literacy well before reading and writing are formally taught in school. Hall argues that formal teaching must respect the knowledge and understanding that learners already have, and the variety of uses literacy may be put to.

## Skills and stages in learning to read

Reading involves the co-ordination, then, of a number of different skills. Some of these are particularly strongly implicated in the difficulties of poor readers; others, though just as necessary for reading, are less relevant to their problems. If patterns of reading skills differ for more and less skilled readers, if there are a number of different 'routes into reading', might there be *developmental* differences in the course of learning reading skills? Might the nature of 'reading' change as it is acquired by the child? Are there 'stages' in the development of reading?

Examination of longitudinal data is necessary to answer such questions. Ellis and Large (1988) studied forty children, from their first signs of reading ability at the age of 5, to the age of 8, by which time some were expert readers and some were less skilled. They were given tests at twelve-month intervals on a variety of measures, including tests of reading, spelling, vocabulary, short-term memory, visual skills, auditory–visual integration ability, auditory and language abilities, language knowledge, rote-ordered knowledge (days of the week and number names forwards and backwards) and the full Wechsler Intelligence Scale for Children (see Ellis and Large 1987, for details of the tests). Scores on these tests were used to provide a profile of each child's skills, and correlations between tests were examined to discover what skills were most associated with reading ability at each age, and which predicted reading at later ages.

The skills correlated with reading ability at 5 involved knowledge of the alphabet, verbal short-term memory and vocabulary tests involving word recognition. At 6 reading was also associated with processing language sounds and associating them with written symbols: phoneme segmentation, auditory short-term memory, and spelling were beginning to be correlated with reading. At 7 even more of these skills were associated with reading, and knowledge of vocabulary, of syntax and of rhymes, among others, were added to the correlates of reading. These results suggest that the 'nature of reading skill changes rapidly in the first 3 years of its acquisition' (Ellis and

Large 1988: 52). Initially the information-processing skills involved are an undifferentiated mixture of phonological awareness, visual short-term memory for symbols, and knowledge of the alphabet; the first two of these are the most important skills by the age of 6 (when almost all children have sufficient alphabetic knowledge). Seven-year-old good readers are using symbol–sound correspondences based on units larger than a single letter, and analysing letters in terms of their sequences within a word: the beginnings perhaps of a direct access to meaning via the orthographic route described above (see Goswami 1991, Hansen and Bowey 1992, Marshall 1987a, 1987b, Masterson, Laxon and Stuart 1992, Thorstad 1991); though phonological skills are still important in their reading, it is not segmentation of words into sounds or knowledge of language sounds that these good readers have thoroughly mastered, but skills such as sound blending and auditory short-term memory.

Mastery of a succession of skills is necessary, therefore, for learning to read. 'Reading does not develop in isolation . . . but rather it grows from a number of different tributaries of skill' (Ellis and Large 1988: 61). Recognising letters (a predictor from kindergarten) is the ubiquitous entry point to the acquisition of reading; phonemic awareness develops interactively with learning to read and to spell, each facilitating the others and resulting from them at different times. Visual skills determine reading ability briefly between the early stages of learning to recognise letters and the development of a phonological style of reading; holistic skills predict it while children are using a 'logographic' reading strategy of recognising whole words from their working sight vocabulary, and visual order skills later when good readers at 7 are beginning to use non-phonological routes to meaning. Ability to learn sound–symbol correspondences becomes associated with reading only after the early stages, seeming to be most important in the proficient 7-year-olds when their reading ability is clearly affecting their sound–symbol linking abilities as well as vice versa. Reading predicts auditory short-term memory, as if it developed the child's ability to attend to, process and remember the sounds of words and sentences, though in the earlier stages STM itself benefits reading as well as the reverse. Early reading seems to make little use of grammatical context, but thereafter grammatical knowledge and reading skill develop in a mutually supportive fashion. Other, general, knowledge also develops with reading, but perhaps grows from reading skill more than it contributes to it in these early years.

How do the accounts of reading outlined above, drawn from cognitive psychology and information-processing examinations of children learning, well or poorly, to read, fit together into a developmental picture? What recommendations can we draw from this work for helping children to become readers? It is clear, first, that once we get down to detail there is no one universal way to learn to read, a conclusion that might have been inferred from there being several different ways to read and from 'reading' being in any case a somewhat varied activity. Thus any picture we draw of 'developing readers', any prescriptions we make about how to facilitate reading in its early stages, will have to admit many exceptions (Stuart and Coltheart 1988). However I will risk some generalisations. Children who make some use of the print which is available to them well before formal 'learning-to-read' starts may gain useful information from this about the shapes, names and sounds of letters, about the functions of reading and writing, about the nature of books and stories; and they may be motivated (especially perhaps by enjoyable story reading) to use them more (Clark 1976, Hall 1987, Tizard and Hughes 1984, Wells 1985, Crain-Thoreson and Dale 1992). They may have become used to talking about language as well as using it. Possession of such experience and knowledge predicts later reading skills (Crain-Thoreson and Dale 1992, Wells, 1985); lacking them completely is characteristic of children who have problems learning to read and to cope with school tasks generally. A sense of 'what reading is about' helps in learning to read. It is harder to learn to do something which makes no sense in itself and which you cannot link to your other experience than something part familiar whose purpose you can appreciate. When the 'senseless something' is as complex and artificial as learning to read, it may be the best you can do to do it slowly, weakly and by rote, as some of the children described in a sensitive case-study (Francis 1982) did.

From such experience and from, perhaps, some deliberate efforts to teach and to learn, come not just general understanding but a 'sight vocabulary' of words which they can recognise when they see them written (the child's own name may be the commonest such word) and a knowledge of the sounds of the alphabet. The latter predicts reading development over the first year of schooling (Ellis and Large 1987, 1988, Stevenson *et al.* 1976), but the first step made in learning to read often does not use phonic knowledge but rather a strategy of 'glance-and-guess'. A few words are recognised by shape, but unfamiliar words are guessed using the context as a guide. Their graphemic or phonemic characteristics are relatively unimportant in the guess: errors make sense in the context (e.g. 'rocket' for 'space capsule') but look different and sound different from the correct word. Unfamiliar words without context cannot be read at all, even if they are phonemically simple and regular. Such early 'readers' as these may not yet be clear about certain concepts related to reading, such as knowing what 'word' and 'letter' mean, distinguishing between numbers and letters, knowing that the words in the book, not the pictures, tell the story. Adults' discussion of reading may be confusing: there is a touching (but perhaps apocryphal) little story of a child who became convinced she was deaf because although her attention was directed to what written words and letters 'say' she could not hear them make any noise at all, even with her ear very close to the page!

A second step, of 'sophisticated guessing' (Ellis 1984), comes with increased sight vocabulary and an improved guessing strategy. Unfamiliar words can now be dealt with in terms of their visual similarity with familiar words, particularly perhaps using visual cues from the beginnings of words rather than those in the middle or end of words. Context is also used in guessing, but for the first time the child can attempt to read unfamiliar words without context.

Having a fairly good grasp of visual and contextual cues and what reading is about seem to precede using phonic cues. However if children are to extend their sight vocabulary there are really only two ways to do this. One is by rote memory, which is shown by the experience of children learning the logographic writing system, Kanji, in Japan to be extremely slow. Japanese learners of Kanji go on acquiring new word symbols into adulthood, though they have mastered other writing systems that use a simple correspondence between written symbols and the pronunciation of spoken syllables in the very early years of school or even before (Oakhill and Garnham 1988). The other method, potentially faster and more generalisable, is to analyse the constituent parts of words in terms of sounds. Knowing that spoken words are made up of sounds, and written words are made up of letters, and having a writing system with a fairly simple correspondence between letters or groups of letters and the sounds they represent, enables the reader meeting an unfamiliar written word to make a good guess at how it should be pronounced, and then to recognise it and access its meaning from the way it sounds. To do this the child has to recognise letters or letter groups and know what sounds are associated with each. As we saw earlier, English has grapheme–phoneme correspondences which are not 'fairly simple' but distinctly complicated, so even this first step may be problematic. Further, the sounds of individual letters (or of sub-groups of letters) have to be 'blended' to produce the word as a whole. Analysis of 'dog' into | d |,| o |,| g |, has to be followed by blending into the single-syllable word, not into the trisyllable 'duh-o-guh'. Unfortunately young children have great difficulty in analysing sounds; children who are particularly poor at phonemic awareness tests in pre-school and the reception class are especially likely to have difficulty learning to read (Bryant and Bradley 1985, Ellis and Large 1987, 1988). Even better readers may rarely use phonic attack skills until they have developed a degree of competence in the use of visual contextual cues. In the study by Francis (1982) her quicker readers used 'sounding out' unfamiliar words largely to supplement an analysis of graphemes and context which was not quite adequate for succeeding in reading the word. As we have seen, the complexity of grapheme–phoneme correspondence rules is considerable, and they may not be equally used (or useful) to all readers. It seems possible, for example, that some children may use phonological rules when spelling but not when reading (e.g. Bryant and Bradley, 1980, 1985, Cataldo and Ellis 1988). Adult readers may read unfamiliar words using analogy with known ones rather than sounding them out letter by letter (Oakhill and Garnham

1988 and p. 8 above). Nevertheless phonic strategies combine with visual and contextual ones to extend reading. Realising the possibility of letter–sound correspondences seems to be one of the crucial insights of learning to read.

As children become more and more skilled readers, passing beyond the early stages which have been described in detail, they combine a number of reading strategies in a flexible repertoire. Reading itself contributes to these strategies, for example increasing sight vocabulary to the point where expert readers rarely encounter a word they do not know, and enriching context by the growth of world knowledge. The purposes of reading also develop, as Chall (1983: 85–7) and Meadows (1986: 80) suggest.

## The teaching of reading

Reading is an instrument for knowing, heavily influenced in its development by what the child's 'ecosystems' provide and demand (Bronfenbrenner 1979, Tierney *et al.* 1989). In particular it is required for school achievement and is taught in schools. How should this be done?

Briefly, it has become clear from decades of research on reading instruction that no one method is clearly best: all methods studied worked well for some children, less well for others. Some reading programmes are clearly more relevant to the visual skills of reading, others to phonological analysis and learning about grapheme–phoneme correspondences. They may be most applicable at different stages of learning to read. The 'look and say' method, where children are taught to recognise a pool of words which make up most of the text of their earliest readers, enables them to read and gather meaning from text without having to do difficult grapheme–phoneme analyses. However, although this may get the novice reader off to a good start we have seen that more analytic reading skills will be necessary sooner or later. 'Phonics' approaches to teaching reading emphasise such analyses. Children learn more general reading skills such as 'sounding out' letters in words in order to 'decode' from written word to sound and meaning by the 'phonic' route. Chall (1967, 1983) concludes that an early emphasis on phonics leads to better reading aloud and reading new words by fourth grade, with no difference in comprehension as compared with children whose teaching had emphasised 'meaning'. 'Language experience' methods combine learning to read with learning to write, stressing that the function of both uses of language is to communicate meanings. These methods tailor materials to individual children's interests, vocabulary and language capabilities. In the 'Breakthrough to Literacy' scheme (Mackay *et al.* 1970), for example, children have their own folders or dictionaries of words, some from basic reading books and some from the child's own vocabulary, which they use to compose written sentences about events which mean something to them; thus the children use words as writers as well as meeting them in their reading. The motivating effect of dealing with meaningful text is emphasised by writers such as the Goodmans and Frank Smith, who argue that children should learn to read by reading (e.g. Goodman and Goodman 1979, Smith 1973). They see learning to read as being as 'natural' as learning to talk and recommend immersion in interesting, motivating reading matter. Children who want sufficiently to understand this material are expected to pick up whatever rules of reading they need in the course of 'making sense' of the text. Certainly some children do learn to read in this way, particularly perhaps children who teach themselves to read before they start school (e.g. Clark 1976, Torrey 1979). This sort of approach is probably best combined with explicit teaching of phonics skills; even motivating literature may be more easily dealt with if some relevant techniques are well to hand.

Oakhill and Garnham (1988) encapsulate a sequence of methods for facilitating the development of efficient word recognition.

> A general procedure based on what we know about beginning readers' capabilities and limitations would be to start them reading with a limited vocabulary of sight words, and to introduce phonics only gradually, once they are able to read and understand simple stories and have some confidence in their ability to read. Such training could start by pointing out the visual similarities of words that sound the same, to show that parts of words correspond to sounds and that there is some regularity in this correspondence. Phonemic segmentation and blending could then be taught, using first compound words, then syllables and finally phonemes, as suggested by Rozin and Gleitman (1977). However, word recognition in itself is not reading: whatever approach is used, it should be supplemented by instruction to develop comprehension and other language skills. A curriculum rich in language activities seems to foster the development of linguistic awareness skills which, as we saw above, are so important in early reading. Thus, reading to children and giving them opportunities for writing and playing word games etc. can all make an important contribution to the development of early reading.
>
> (Oakhill and Garnham 1988: 101–2)

### Understanding what you read

My discussion of reading has concentrated so far on the processes used to recognise written words and on the early stages of reading. However even once word recognition has become skilled and fluent much further development in reading is possible. My next concern therefore is with the cognitive skills necessary for comprehending text. Oakhill and Garnham (1988, ch. 2) provide a clear account of what is known about the processes involved in text comprehension, from use of sentences, syntactic structure to constructing 'mental models' of what a text is about and using the information from the model to go beyond what is merely implicit in the text. This last sort of cognitive activity is of particular interest. Even apparently simple and straightforward texts may require readers to import knowledge from the outside world if they are to make sense of what is written. The sentences I quoted earlier from Winograd (1972) about the city council refusing protesters permission to hold a demonstration because 'they advocated [or feared] violence' is an example: the two different verbs imply different referents for 'they', but only a reader who knew that city councils rarely advocate violence, but more often fear it, could get the referents right. Similar inferences may be needed to sort out connections between sentences, or to discover what their full implications are. Consider the following sentences:

> Tybalt hated Romeo. He loved Juliet and felt that the young man's love for her was outrageous. The feud between the Capulet and Montague families ended in tragedy.

Only some knowledge of the whole story makes clear which is the 'he' and which 'the young man' talked about in the second sentence, or indeed whether the love felt for Juliet is cousinly or passionate (assuming, genteelly and pre-Freudianly, that it would not be both). If the passage ended after Juliet the 'he' would be completely ambiguous; spoken, an unstressed 'he' would mean Tybalt and an emphasised one Romeo, but the written text does not present such cues. The relevance of the third sentence has to be assumed unless the reader knows that Tybalt and Juliet were members of the Capulet family and Romeo a Montague.

Some inferences are *necessary* parts of understanding a text. Oakhill and Garnham (1988: 21–2) quote a children's story:

> Jane was invited to Jack's birthday party.
> She wondered if he would like a kite.
> She went to her room and shook her piggy bank.
> It made no sound.
> Jane frowned.

This only makes sense in the light of knowledge about birthday parties, birthday presents, buying things with money, saving money in piggy banks, and so forth. Without it Jane's musings and her actions would be completely incomprehensible. However readers with the relevant knowledge seem often to make necessary inferences as they read without much difficulty, and often with so little awareness that they are inferring information rather than simply reading it that they later believe the implied information had actually been explicitly presented (Paris 1978, Paris and Lindauer 1978). Similarly there may be inferences which *elaborate* the text. If we read 'Mary cut into the pudding' we have, from linguistic necessity, to infer that she used some instrument to do so. We might suppose that the instrument was a knife, since knives are strongly associated with cutting, but it could be a spoon if the pudding was of a soft consistency or even a fork if the pudding was Mary's own individual portion and, perhaps, she is a slightly greedy or at least a vigorous eater. Readers probably make inferences about possible referents and possible implications by using the knowledge which they have accumulated into 'scripts' or 'memory organisation packets' (see the section on 'scripts' later in this chapter), though exactly how this is done we do not know. Obviously children may have problems with inferences because they do not have the necessary information.

Text also involves links which integrate its various parts. 'Scripts' integrate large sections: adjacent sentences will be linked by *anaphoric* devices such as pronouns (such as the 'he' in the second sentence of the 'Romeo and Juliet' example given earlier) or certain noun phrases beginning with 'the' (such as 'the young man' in the same sentence). These sorts of expressions take their meaning from other parts of the text and do not stand alone. They are very common in written text, and children often have problems with them (for a summary see Oakhill and Garnham 1988: 56-8). Work by Annette Karmiloff-Smith (1986, 1988) suggests that they also use them in an immature way when narrating stories.

**Understanding the structure of a text**

Readers may approach a text with an idea in mind about its overall structure. Attempts to describe text structures in ways analogous to sentence grammars, in terms of a hierarchy of goals and subgoals, are problematic (Garnham 1983). However even children as young as 4 use their world knowledge to understand stories, and have 'story grammars' in the sense they have 'scripts' of familiar events in their lives (Mandler and Johnson 1977, Wimmer 1980). Four-year-olds' narration about a set of pictures is primarily descriptive but if the pictures tell a story the narration includes details derived from their understanding of the story (Poulsen *et al.* 1979). Although their initial retelling of stories contains mainly surface events, probing with 'why' questions elicits many inferences about the characters' motives and intentions (see also the section on 'children's theories of mind'). This is particularly the case if the story is a familiar, interesting and profound one. In an innovative nursery school curriculum, Christianne Hayward introduced serial readings of books such as *Watership Down* by Richard Adams; she linked it with activities such as puppet rabbits and a 'burrow' for imaginative play, and materials based on the story for early mathematics work. Children who had had this experience were able to produce elaborate and sophisticated retellings of the text, as is shown by this verbatim example of part of one child's retelling, using a book of pictures from the film of *Watership Down* (see also Hayward 1980).

And they were chewing the rope so that the ahh boat or something could move out, and by the time that they come they were, they just finished off so that . . . and they were all ready in the boat except for the one that was chewing the rope and then he, and then the boat nearly rushed off, and he gave a great big leap so that he could get on the boat, and he just about finished ahh, didn't get in the boat. And then General Woundwart nearly went in the water. And then they were all in the boat sailing off and Kehaar flew and they got across the water, and then they rested and they fell asleep. And then Fiver, Fiver said there was something going wrong again. And then they find Hazel to talk to Woundwart and then they're trying to get in the burrow where there's Bigwig and Hazel [before the relevant frame] and then they found it [before the relevant frame]. And then Bigwig finds something, some mud to cover him over with [predicts] and they're about to get in, and they were chewing the rope so that the dog could get out. And ahh, ahh except for the cat and then General Woundwart finds the little one an( as he was walking, Bigwig jumped and bit him and they fighted and the dog was chasing one of the rabbits and that looks like they're killing each other [pointing]. And the dog's coming and he [points to Woundwart], and he scratched him just there, like that [points to own face above eye] and then they were both all scratched and then the dog was coming to get the rabbits and was going to eat it and he did. He got the rabbit in his mouth. And General Woundwart is covered in blood, he is, even his teeth. I still can see he hasn't got an eye there 'cause something pulled his eye out before. Bigwig doesn't die.

(Meadows and Cashdan 1988)

As they grow into older and more experienced readers children also become more able to identify the more important and less important ideas in a text (e.g. Brown *et al.* 1983, Yussen *et al.* 1980). Even the youngest children are likely to remember more important points than unimportant ones, but picking them out explicitly or even rating them as 'very important' or 'very unimportant' is hard even for children of 10 to 12. This might make it harder to study texts effectively: we do know that children's efforts may be inappropriately directed in memory tasks. Increasing knowledge of texts and of the world, and better metacognition, will both be involved in the developmental advance that children make.

The comprehension of written text, then, involves a wide range of cognitive skills, including word recognition, use of syntactic knowledge for processing sentences and larger units of text, inferences derived from the text and from world knowledge external to it. It will also involve decisions derived from knowledge about the nature and purposes of a text, such as the likely characters and motives of fictional personages or the relative import-ance of items of information in a factual text. It will perhaps be necessary not just to comprehend the text but to monitor one's comprehension, that is, to check whether the text is being understood, to be aware of breakdowns in understanding and to take some appropriate action to remedy them. Very many of these comprehension skills are deployed simultaneously, so it is necessary for some of them to become automatic as otherwise the cognitive overload would result in failure to comprehend. One of the reasons why beginning readers may decode a text into recognised spoken words but fail to understand it is that they cannot manage to decode and to comprehend simultaneously, and slow effortful decoding leads to the forgetting of earlier text and its information. Children may in any case have difficulty in integrating bits of text into a consistent whole (e.g. Garner 1987, Markman 1979, Robinson and Robinson 1983). In her work Markman assessed children's ability to spot ambiguities and omissions in instructions about how to play a game, and logical inconsistences in texts. Even 10-year-olds quite often judged that texts which had gross internal contradictions, like the one which follows, were perfectly satisfactory.

*Ants*
Everywhere they go they put out a special chemical from their bodies. They cannot see this chemical, but it has a special odor. An ant must have a nose in order to smell this chemical odor. Another thing about ants is they do not have a nose. Ants cannot smell this odor. Ants can always find their way home by smelling this odor to follow the trail.

(Markman 1979)

Obviously failure to recognise that there has been a comprehension breakdown means that it is impossible to take appropriate action to correct it. Forewarning children about possible problems means that they are more likely to recognise them (Markman 1979); however, problems such as incomplete instructions and unfamiliar vocabulary, for which the criteria for comprehensibility are explicit, are easier to detect than internal inconsistencies like those in the 'ants' passage, where each word and individual sentence would pass comprehensibility tests. Older children do better than younger ones, and good readers better than poor ones (Baker 1984). No doubt further experience of texts as a result of having done more reading is a contributor to this development, but explicit instruction has also been shown to be helpful, as Markman's and Baker's work shows (see also Garner 1987, Marton *et al.* 1992, Masterson *et al.* 1992).

Having detected a problem, the next question is of course what to do about it. Possible strategies include ignoring the uncomprehended words or passages; waiting to see if the meaning becomes clearer later; guessing, the guess being confirmed or disconfirmed later; re-reading the immediate problem passage or the larger part of the text in which it occurs; seeking outside help, from peer, teacher, dictionary or another text; or combinations of these. Which of these strategies the reader uses will depend, amongst other things, on task requirements and the available resources; casual reading is likely to use the simpler strategies at the beginning of the list, while detailed mastery of difficult text requires much more re-reading, analysis and comparison of different sources. Which strategy is used will also depend on the characteristics of the reader, and in the case of very young readers on how they are being taught to read. Experience of reading, how expert one is at it, will affect one's strategies for coping with comprehension. Even the most novice reader will however have used skills somewhat like these in trying to understand spoken language. The most obvious skill which is more applicable to written language than to spoken language is re-reading, both because spoken words are much more ephemeral and because requests for the repeating of an uncomprehending utterance would often produce, in normal discourse, a rephrasing of what was said, not a verbatim repetition. Guessing, ignoring and seeking outside help are, however, well-practised strategies, and children have little difficulty in applying them.

## WRITING

Like reading, writing is an activity which integrates many different processes – physical, linguistic, cognitive, even social and affective – in different ways according to the writer's age, experience and purposes. Scardamalia (1981) lists the interdependent skills involved, among them the physical production of text through handwriting or typing; spelling and punctuation (these may be avoided through dictation, which delegates them to someone else, but involves other skills); considerations of content, word choice, syntax and textual connections (which must be at least minimally included); and considerations of overall purpose, intended effect, organisation, clarity and euphony (which may be optional or subjective). Each of these skills is itself of course highly complex; each shows developmental change in what is done and in what is expected. Some writing skills, but not all, are intensively taught; some remain the area of expertise of comparatively few writers.

Two aspects of writing, its nature as a physical skill and the 'ecology' of its use, I will only mention briefly, concentrating my discussion on the cognitive skills of writing. Writing involves the use of fine muscle movements in varied but co-ordinated patterns, with visual monitoring, at a speed (in experienced writers) far faster than the brain can send messages to the hand and receive feedback, though more slowly than thinking or speaking. As Thomassen and Teuling (1983) remind us, the human hand is an extraordinarily intricate and delicate mechanism, controlled by a large number of muscles. During writing, movements in fingers, wrists, arms and shoulders, plus movements of the eyes (and perhaps head) for monitoring writing, have to be co-ordinated. These muscle movements have to be small, quick and precise, and because the speed of transmission of neural control messages along the length of the arm is relatively slow, the brain cannot wait for one movement to be completed before the next is begun. Even at this level the brain must plan ahead to get the hand in the right position at the right place at the right time.

To do this, we write not in single letters but in larger units. As an example, compare the ease of writing 'written backwards' with the difficulty of writing 'sdrawkcab nettirw' and note where the pauses and breaks in writing came. 'Units' may occur over longer strings than single words: we pause more between clauses than within them, for example. 'Over-uniting' may produce errors; I planned the second sentence of the last paragraph, 'Writing involves the use of fine muscle movements' etc. as it is now printed, but wrote 'final' instead of 'fine', conflating 'fine' with the sound at the end of 'muscle' rather than making a semantic error. Motor skills of the highly complex sort involved in writing fluently are acquired mainly through practice. Children's fine motor co-ordination continues to develop throughout childhood (Laszlo and Bairstow 1985) and maturation may limit the neatness of their handwriting. Nineteenth-century pedagogy did successfully force several generations of children to write (and sew) neatly, as witness surviving copybooks and samplers sewn by what now seems remarkably young girls. However accounts in biographies and novels testify to the pains of being made to conform to strict standards of neatness, and casual observation today will show that a high proportion of people never really learn to write neatly!

Given a piece of paper and a pencil, a child in the second year of life will enjoy making marks on the paper. Initially these line and dot scribbles are probably not unsuccessful attempts to write or draw, rather they are successful attempts to make marks on the paper where there were no marks before. 'Writing' usually follows attempts at drawing representations of objects. Vygotsky (1978b) points out that writing is a second-order symbol system: the letters stand for the spoken word, which itself stands for the object. Drawings and idiosyncratic pictographs are, like spoken words, in a first-order symbolic relation to the object they represent. Such an account of writing's symbolic relations obviously implies that writing will develop after drawing has begun: writing is a special sort of drawing which represents language. As children experience written language by being read to (or reading for themselves), they learn that 'writing' consists of particular sorts of patterns arranged on the page in particular orientations, in English, horizontal lines from left to right of the twenty-six letters of the alphabet. Young children may 'write' in a scribble or string of letters running horizontally across the page, or accompanying a picture as an adult might produce a caption. Kamler and Kilarr (1983: 187–9; see also Meadows 1986: 89–91) provide a fascinating observation of a child just under 5 as she composes a 'story' to accompany a picture. She writes horizontal 'words' using a limited set of letters. Her first word is written at the top of the page, the second nearly at the bottom, the third, fourth and fifth words are fitted in between them, and the sixth is a late addition at the bottom of the page. She composes in bursts, and reads what she has written from top to bottom of the page. Thus when she first wrote it, 'Kioe' at the bottom of her page was her second word and meant 'sat', but when she next rereads from top to bottom it is the third word and means 'mat'. She has considerable difficulty in being consistent in her matching of written word to thought-of word. Kamler and Kilarr comment that the child may be making her 'random clusters of letters' first and only later attributing meaning to them, like the child artists who seem to decide what their drawing represents after they have produced it. The demands of making the movements and marks which produce the written words are themselves considerable and may make coherent composition virtually impossible. Smith (1982) advocates writing practice which is free from demands for correctness in spelling, punctuation or composition, demands that may distract from establishing automatic motor patterns. It is important to point out that children do not normally write letters untidily or incorrectly because of inadequate visual processing, but because of production difficulties: letters have to be precisely formed in direction, size, joins, spaces and so forth, and the motor control needed for this is very considerable. Practice gives a fluent production system, but children who lack one make the sort of errors and attempt the sort of solutions that they do in drawings (Freeman and Cox 1985). There is a complex interaction of the purely motor and the cognitive skills in the apparently simple making of written symbols.

Writing is embedded in a social context, and can serve a variety of purposes. Where a reader is essentially concerned with extracting meaning from a pre-existing text, with or without increase in enjoyment or knowledge, a writer may have any of a wider range of purposes, for example to inform, to entertain, to persuade, to criticise, to record, to express something personally felt, and so forth. This list is obviously similar to one listing the functions of spoken language: recording is the major exception, as generally it is better done by writing than by speaking, and indeed some theorists suggest that writing was invented largely for record-keeping purposes (records of property and liability for taxes, regrettably; see e.g. Goody 1977, Goody and Watt 1968). Children's spoken language will have been used for most of these functions by the end of the pre-school years (Wells 1985, Meadows 1986), but they may not have experienced all these functions expressed in writing. Although most adults write sometimes, studies of the 'ecology' of writing (e.g. Griffiths and Wells 1983) show that the main functions of writing at home are in response to social or mnemonic requirements: domestic messages, family letters and shopping lists. When adults do write to express themselves, to tell stories or to record their own experience they mostly do so privately or at least away from the interruptions of pre-school children, who will thus have little writing activity to observe that involves anything other than notes of information or domestic letters. Adult literacy is positively correlated with children's literacy (Wells 1981b, 1985), perhaps because the children of literate parents have both more opportunities to observe literacy and more formal and informal teaching from their parents. Tizard and Hughes (1984) describe some mothers teaching their daughters to write, sometimes as a session of letter forming or copying words, sometimes as part of an activity such as writing a letter to grandparents. The latter is probably a fairly common real-life experience for quite a lot of children. Parents may encourage (or require) children to write letters to grandparents or to people who have given presents or hospitality; thus there is a real social purpose to writing. Most available examples from young children seem to be conventional rather than expressive. There are clear rules for beginning and ending the text of letters, and since there is often a specific interpersonal reason for writing the letter, at least some of what it must contain is also specified. A thank-you letter from $Z$ to $X$ acknowledging a gift, $Y$, must include at least phrases equivalent to 'Dear $X$,' 'Thank you for the $Y$', 'from $Z$'. Collerson (1983) collected the letters his daughter Juliet wrote between the ages of 5 and $9\frac{1}{2}$; they show an increase in length via the inclusion of informative or expressive material beyond the minimum demanded by the formal letter scheme, and an increasing tendency to use written language as a means to a continuing dialogue with people who are known but too far away to speak to. The child 'learns that letters can be a means of reporting and interpreting experience, a device for exchanging information, and a method of maintaining social interaction among friends' (Collerson 1983: 92).

This list of the functions served by children's letters is not unlike the functions of spoken language listed by Halliday (1975) and other linguists. Writing and speaking have both similarities and differences. It may appear that writing is simply written-down speaking, a pen and ink record like a tape recording, or a pen and ink production instead of a lips and larynx enactment. However this is not the case. Stubbs (1980) points out that the relationship between written and spoken language differs for different writing systems, different authorial purposes, and different cultures, but one consistent difference is that the written text has to convey its meaning more independently of paralinguistic context than spoken language has to do. The writer must construct the text without the assistance of signals from the recipient about whether the meaning is being understood, whether more or less information is needed, whether jokes are being appreciated or persuasive arguments are having the desired effect. The reader has to get meaning from the text in the absence of many of the signals that accompany spoken language: cues from the speaker's 'body language', pitch, intonation, speed of speaking, facial expression and so forth are not available in conventional written text, though devices of punctuation and typography may be used to make up for some of this loss. Writers and readers interact much more distantly than speakers and listeners. Writers cannot, alas, monitor their readers' understanding. If they wish to be effective, they must therefore compose and review their writing more carefully than most speakers need to do, lest problems in their choices of words and syntax and the overall organisation and clarity of the text, or adverse reactions by the readers to the writer's purpose and assumptions, should prevent satisfactory communication. They also need to appreciate some of the conventions that differ between spoken and written language. The text must create its own paralinguistic context, so the writer must assess what knowledge can safely be assumed and what information must be incorporated into the text. The writer must also assess what is the best order for pieces of text and present each piece unambiguously and explicitly. It may be easier for the reader to go back and read text again than it is for the listener to recall speech in order to re-examine it, but the writer cannot adjust content, order or emphasis, as the speaker can, in response to the reader's cues of understanding or failure to understand. In short, effective written language normally needs careful thought in the composing.

Given this need, and given the high importance placed on being able to compose effectively (at least at the level of writing applications for jobs), it is not surprising that a considerable amount of research has been done on composition. Martlew (1983) reviews some of the errors that poor or inexperienced writers make: they write as they speak, leaving their writing dependent on a context which the reader may not share; they plan poorly, if at all, and prepare themselves for writing too briefly to be able to produce clearly organised text; they rarely review or criticise what they have produced, and what review and self-criticism occur almost never lead to improving the text. Some of these inadequacies no doubt arise because the whole task of considering the adequacy of the text *plus* spelling correctly *plus* writing neatly *plus* producing the right amount to satisfy the teacher overwhelms young writers. Some, however, probably stem from their uncertainty about what to do in composition, and how to do it. Frederiksen and Dominic suggest that important cognitive resources 'include the writer's knowledge, the already established strategies and procedures for constructing a meaning and expressing it, and the general characteristics of their cognitive systems such as processing capacity and both the automaticity and efficiency of component processes' (Frederiksen and Dominic 1981: 4).

Very young writers often find problems simply in generating content. They frequently produce the equivalent of one utterance on the subject, and then stop, claiming that that is all they can think of to say. Carl Bereiter and Marlene Scardamalia (1982) demonstrate that devices of various sorts increase the amount produced. Instructions to produce a large amount, the opportunity to speak or to dictate the text instead of having to write it, instructions to continue composing leaving aside questions of difficult spelling, the provision of simple prompts such as 'on the other hand' or 'also', all increase both the number of words and the number of ideas expressed, as well as the children's satisfaction with their writing. On their own, children have clearly not really reached the limits of what was available on the subject. They welcome prompts and appreciate their effects. Learning to provide prompts for yourself is part of the development of writing skills.

Although not generating enough material is a problem in writing, the optimum solution is not simply to generate more irrespective of its quality, truth, relevance, suitability and so forth. It is preferable that the writer should think what to say, stay on topic, produce a coherent and intelligible whole appropriate to the audience, and to do this involves co-ordinating searches of memory for useful material with the various physical, linguistic and cognitive processes which I mentioned earlier. To do this may be comparatively straightforward when writers are recounting personal experiences or dealing with routine scripts and stories. It becomes more problematic when the task is one of making an exposition of a subject. Scardamalia and Bereiter (Bereiter and Scardamalia 1982, 1987, Scardamalia 1981, Scardamalia and Bereiter 1983, 1986) suggest that the predominant and 'natural' strategy is what they call 'knowledge-telling'. It is 'natural' because it uses skills developed in normal language competence and learned through ordinary social experience, but it does not go beyond them. It starts with the writer constructing a mental representation of a writing task, identifying topic and genre. The writer has some relevant knowledge on the topic (Piaget's theory, say) and on what the genre (an exam question calling for 'evaluation') involves (a tabulation of positive and negative points). The mental representation of topic and genre call up from memory an item of content, for example the experiments which assessed children's understanding of conservation. As this is relevant to the topic and to the demands of the genre it is expressed in language suitable for the essay, for example 'Piaget did experiments on conservation where he asked children if spacing out a line of counters changed the number of counters and young children said the number did change. However Margaret Donaldson did the experiment with a naughty teddy messing the line up and her children said the number was still the same'. This then serves as a probe for a further search of memory so perhaps an account of other variations on the conservation situation is produced. This alternation of finding a relevant idea and expressing it continues until a sufficient quantity of text has been constructed, or memory yields no more material, or time runs out. One of their students, aged 12, summarised it thus:

> I have a whole bunch of ideas and write down until my supply of ideas is exhausted. Then I might try to think of more ideas up to the point when you can't get any more ideas that are worth putting down on paper and then I would end it.
>
> (Bereiter and Scardamalia 1987: 9)

The 'knowledge-telling' strategy for composition is comparatively rapid and automatic, and it does not involve much reflection on what is produced; the results of each probing of memory are juxtaposed like beads on a string, independent of each other and invariant in order. However, knowledge-telling lacks goal-related planning and significant revision, and the pouring forth of what is known is only minimally adjusted to the precise demands of the task or to the characteristics of the reader. The text is not interconnected but made up of unrelated passages produced one after the other without reference forward or, more particularly, back. It may therefore contain repetitions and contradictions; there is evidence from reading comprehension studies (Brown *et al.* 1983, Markman 1979, 1981) that children seem to have difficulties in spotting such problems in other people's writing as well as in their own. On the other hand, knowledge-telling does guarantee a fairly easy generating of text that is on topic and does fulfil the minimum demands of the genre, and it usually leads to a quantity of text sufficiently large to satisfy task requirements. It fits, in fact, many novice writers' needs and beliefs about what writing involves. Knowledge-telling followed by rigorous revision and ruthless discarding of weak material is a perfectly respectable technique of composing. However, inexperienced writers are very unlikely to do such revision: they normally limit themselves to proofreading, word choice and checking the 'mechanics' of spelling, punctuation and grammar (e.g. Nold 1981, Brown *et al.* 1983).

Knowledge-telling is a serviceable strategy, and may persist because of that, as it is conspicuously difficult to give up strategies and theories which work well within limits in favour of a more complex strategy or theory which has greater potential but also higher 'running costs' (Brown *et al.* 1983, Karmiloff-Smith and Inhelder 1974/5, Van Geert 1991). Scardamalia and Bereiter (1986 and Bereiter and Scardamalia 1987) describe another writing strategy which is distinctly more complex and distinctly rarer. In it knowledge-telling is a subordinate process within a far more radical questioning and reorganisation of both content and genre. Memory search is not simply a matter of taking whatever item comes next, but involves personal elaboration of the connections and implications of items and thus the construction of reformulated representations of what is known, a heuristic search of memory (Newell and Simon 1972) not just a mechanical probing of it. Similarly the writing task itself is represented in a more complex way, with explicit considerations of the goals involved, the probable effect of the text on the expected reader, and so forth. Content and topic can influence each other: for example, if a passage seems unclear, the effort to achieve clarity may be translated into a need to examine whether the ideas to be expressed have really been fully understood; or thinking of a new item of content may change the direction of the argument or the possible conclusions to be drawn. This strategy is therefore called 'knowledge transforming'. It involves far more integration of procedures for composing, monitoring and revising, consideration of the text in terms of its overall structure, gist, and goals as well as at the microlevels of spelling and so forth, and, especially, far less automatic production of text and more self-regulation. It is harder work, more problematic, but also more rewarding. It is also, perhaps, an important means to better thinking not just better writing (Scardamalia and Bereiter 1986, Palincsar and Brown 1984) – at least *some* authors have occasionally felt that they only knew what they thought when they read what they'd written!

Bereiter and Scardamalia present a variety of material in their description of writing strategies, but asking writers to think aloud as they write is one of their central methods. They found that young and inexperienced writers 'rehearse' their text as they think aloud, repeating out loud (with trivial variations) what they are about to write down. Good writers are more verbose and provide more commentary on their activity and more attempts at clarifying and solving problems, so that much less of what they say is part of their eventual text. Similarly the written revisions of inexpert writers tend to remain at the level of addition and rephrasing, while experts may make revisions that transform the essay and the information which it contains. Training programmes designed to improve children's planning and revision of their text have had some success, both in the research by Bereiter and Scardamalia (Bereiter and Scardamalia 1982, 1987, Scardamalia and Bereiter 1983), and in 'real world' programmes such as the National Writing Project. The latter seems to have been a very positive experience in British classrooms (and has got its aims incorporated in the National Curriculum) (Czierniewska 1992, Henn 1987, Morgan 1989, Styles 1989). It is of some relevance to the models of cognitive development discussed elsewhere in this book that while Bereiter and Scardamalia insist on the individual nature of writing and are interested mainly in the internal processes of the autonomous writer, the National Writing Project has made very successful use of collaboration (both between teacher and pupil(s) and between peers), thus using a more socially-based approach to developing writing.

One issue here is the nature of the relationship between oral speech and writing which I raised earlier in this section. It has been believed for a long time that the 'autonomous text' (as in, for example, a scientific essay) is the highest point in the shift from speech in context to the expression of facts in such a way that there is an exact correspondence between text and meaning and no ambiguity, and no need for implicit inference between writer and reader remains (e.g. Olson 1977, Olson and Torrance 1991). Bereiter and Scardamalia, by focusing on the genre of short expository essays and by rejecting the value of exercises focusing on improving awareness of the audience, seem to be using this view of the best text being the most autonomous. But it is questionable whether text can ever be substantially autonomous, for even the purest scientific text has to be related to the alternative ways of making the same statements, such as graphs, formulae or reworded text, and to the replicatable phenomena of the experiments described, and exists in the context of other texts on the same subject which it questions, refutes, amplifies, extends or otherwise revises. Even here, but more obviously in the texts of the humanities literature, there is the phenomenon of 'intertextuality' (Kristeva 1986), the implicit or explicit presence of other, antecedent, texts in the present text. Except perhaps in the case of text produced by a writer who has never before encountered any text whatever – if such a production could be found, let alone made – any text must be a response, reply, reflection, remembrance of earlier texts. Readers need to share the earlier texts to some degree if they are to understand the present one; shared knowledge of earlier texts is as necessary for understanding written language as shared knowledge of earlier dialogue is for understanding oral language. Shared, intersubjective discussion of texts may be essential to understanding them and to producing better ones.

This seems to be one of the main pedagogic assumptions now embodied in the National Curriculum. It is assumed that all children should, by the age of 11,

> begin to revise and redraft in discussion with the teacher, other adults, or other children in the class, paying attention to meaning and clarity
>
> (DES 1990: 12)

and this emphasis on discussion and revision and on the context of reading and writing pervades the Key Stages.

Redrafting partnered by discussion seems likely to facilitate not only the production of a clearer or more elegant or more copious text but also the clarification of thought that 'knowledge-transforming' writing produces. An educational ambience which encourages revision and successive improvements rather than perpetuating the demoralising myth that writing involves producing a single perfect draft is desirable. Calkins (1983) describes various classroom strategies directed to this end.

## Maths

Having discussed the development of reading and writing, I want now to look at 'the third R', children's arithmetic. A considerable amount of work has been done on children's understanding and use of mathematics in recent years, as psychologists have increasingly focused their attention on cognitive skills that are related to school learning. A 'psychology of mathematics' is perhaps beginning to emerge. It includes fine-grained task analyses, but goes beyond defining what knowledge is necessary for success on a task to examine the cognitive processes and knowledge which must go on in the student's mind, whether or not the task is successfully tackled. There is thus a growing body of work on students' incorrect strategies (e.g. Brown and Burton 1978, on 'buggy algorithms'), and some on individual differences in solution strategies (Siegler 1988). Mayer (1985) provides introductions to the field and its educational implications: among useful collections of papers are books edited by Brainerd (1982), Ginsberg (1983) and Lesh and Landau (1983). I will discuss here some aspects of early number concepts and their role in children's handling of addition and subtraction, how children represent mathematical problems, and some of the cognitive processes which make up competence in the use of written mathematical symbols. Throughout I will try to bring together task analytic approaches, ecological work on children's spontaneous mathematics (since there is beginning to be documentation (e.g. Carraher *et al.* 1985) of what mathematical goals children set for themselves, both in school and outside it), and considerations of mathematical language (see also Davidson 1987).

One basic and very early aspect of using numbers is knowing number words, their names. Observations of pre-school children at home and in settings such as playgroups show that they quite frequently encounter number words and number word sequences in nursery rhymes, songs, conversation and games (see, for example, Tizard and Hughes 1984, Davie *et al.* 1984). Saxe *et al.* (1987) document the number-related activities of 2-year-olds and 4-year-olds in Brooklyn; more than 70 per cent of these children engaged in such activities as counting toys, reading number books, playing games and so on at least three times a week, and both mothers and children showed a high level of enthusiasm for number play. Most had invented their own number activities, but television and commercial games which taught number or used it in the course of some other activity were also used. Thus adults often make use of opportunities to use numbers. Parents may deliberately teach their children to 'count' in the senses both of reciting number words and of applying those words in finding out how many objects there are. As Saxe *et al.* (1987) describe in an analysis of the levels of the goals involved in number activity, the former is conceptually much simpler and appears earlier in development. Many 2-year-olds use number words in a consistent order in what appears to be a form of denotative reference, saying 'one, two, four' and so forth while gesturing in a sweeping way at a set of objects, but they show little evidence that they are counting in the sense of linking words to the corresponding objects, or that they are using the last word they say as a representation of the number in the array. Young children's number lists do not always use the conventional number sequence: they often are idiosyncratic, with an initial conventional and correct sequence such as 'one, two, three' followed by an unconventional portion – 'five, eight, nine, eleven' – which is used consistently, and a final non-stable portion which varies from occasion to occasion. However knowing number words is one useful component of later mathematics. Such number lists gradually develop towards the correct form; Fuson and Hall

(1983) showed that a majority of children can count to twenty or so by the time they are 5, and most can count to one hundred by the age of 6 given moderate practice in school.

In English (though not in all other languages) numbers are regularly structured from the teens onwards, with a units part, a 'decades' part and a hundreds or thousands part as appropriate. Thus 1992 is 'one thousand, nine hundred, ninety, two' (or 'nineteen hundred, ninety, two'); 41 is 'forty, one'; and so on. The number names up to the teens have to be learned more or less by rote, as do the names of the decades; the rest can be generated by rule. Children's learning of number names seems to be initially by rote. It is usually after they have learned to recite the sequence to beyond twenty that they realise there is a repetition of 'something-one, something-two' and so, and after they have grasped the sequence to one hundred that they can really generate numbers iteratively *ad infinitum* (Siegler and Robinson 1982). Many children find this exciting and set themselves the number goal of counting to some enormous figure, like the 4-year-old who could not leave the playground to take part in a research project because she was 'very busy counting to a million', and seemed to be only marginally discouraged that it was taking a very long time. Understanding infinity (and zero, negative numbers, fractions, etc.) comes of course later still, though we may underestimate what children can do here (Siegal 1991).

Knowing the number words is not, as Piaget (1952) pointed out, the most important part of number concepts. As I said earlier, number words have to be matched to countable objects if the child is to 'count', that is, to be able to answer questions involving 'how many'. (The exception occurs when the set contains very few items. Adults can produce the cardinal number for small sets (up to four) and very well learned larger sets (such as the configurations on playing cards and dominoes) very quickly and without observable counting. This capacity is known as 'subitising'. It is possible that young children can also subitise small sets of two or three items, possibly even as neonates (Antell and Keating 1983, Starkey 1992, Starkey and Cooper 1980, Strauss and Curtis 1981). It is, however, hard to define what subitising consists of, even in adults, given the problems of distinguishing between pattern recognition and very rapid covert counting (see e.g. Fuson and Hall 1983: 59–61, and Gelman and Gallistel 1978: 64–8, 219–25). Thus it is not at present clear what role subitising plays in the development of counting. Using number to represent a single set is level 2 in the hierarchy of number goals described by Saxe *et al.* (1987). It requires an understanding that correspondence between number word and object in a count can lead to the identification of 'how many' objects are present. By the age of 3 or 4 most children do use number words as signs to the numerosity of small arrays, for example reporting the last number name in the sequence that has been matched to the objects as the answer to 'how many?' questions. The analysis made by Gelman and Gallistel (1978) shows how complex an activity this is.

Number words have to be matched to countable objects if the child is to 'count'. Accurate counting requires that each and every object must be tagged with one and only one number word. To do this, objects and words have to be kept in step, and objects have to be accurately divided into 'already counted' and 'not yet counted' groups, with this division being continually updated in step with the counting. Children often use pointing or touching or moving objects to help themselves do this; rhythms in the counting or orderliness in the array may also help, though Saxe *et al.* (1987) suggest that young children may not be able to use spatial order (such as arrangement in lines) to help their unsystematic counting. There is quite a lot of evidence that children's counting (Fuson and Hall 1983, Wynn 1992) does mainly allocate one number to one object; it is less clear whether they regard this as a necessary principle of counting. Unsystematic organisation of what to count next leaves a real possibility of double counting or skipping items, and the rate at which number names are generated may get out of step with the touching of objects. Smaller sets make successful counting more likely for young children because there is less scope for these errors to arise.

To find out how many objects there are in a set, one should count them using the one-number-name-to-one-object principle and the stable-order (of names) principle described above, and then report the last number name used, which by the cardinality principle gives the numerical value (or cardinal number) of the set. Young children often fail to report the last number, but when they have counted the set aloud they may be expecting the experimenter to realise that the last number said while counting is intended as the answer. It is perhaps somewhat disingenuous of the experimenter to require further telling. It appears that most middle-class children do repeat their last counting word with added emphasis to indicate that it is their answer, by the age of 4 (Fuson and Hall 1983). They also appreciate that counting is related to addition and subtraction, and that spatial rearrangement of a single *small* set does not change its number (Gelman and Gallistel 1978). However, appreciating that you would get the same cardinal number for any correct count of the objects in any order is a rather later achievement, as Piaget pointed out long ago, and both Fuson *et al.* 1982 and Saxe *et al.* 1987 show that even 4-year-olds have a shaky grasp of this principle. It is of course an achievement which depends on accurate counting: if your procedure for counting is imperfect, you might get a different numerosity each time and not realise the source of the variation. Detecting counting errors, and avoiding them by the use of more systematic counting strategies, may form a major part of the development of 3- to 5-year-olds (Saxe *et al.* 1987, Wynn 1992).

Although there are possible comparisons of numbers implicit in producing strings of number names and in counting a single set of objects, once there are two (or more) sets there are inevitably comparisons of numerosity to be made. Terminology such as 'more', 'less', 'fewer', 'same', 'equal', 'greater than', and so on, becomes involved. Siegel (1978) reviews studies of children's problems with these terms. One source of confusion is that comparatives are correlated in the natural world: in comparing sets of the same objects, for example, the longer line does more often than not have more in, or the taller heap contain more objects. Sorting out the dimensions of the comparisons, deciding that 'less' is not a synonym for 'more' (Donaldson and Balfour 1981), and sorting out exactly which entities are being compared (Siegel *et al.* 1978) seem to be among the harder preliminaries to making a comparison.

Ecological studies suggest however that activities at this level are common in the day-to-day lives of children. As well as the discussions of who's got more and is it fair which are prevalent in later childhood, pre-schoolers are frequently involved in activities such as setting the table with equal quantities of plates, glasses, knives and so forth. Efforts to do tasks like this are a bit laborious to begin with. Commonly, if 4-year-olds are asked to put out as many plates and glasses as there are children they will count all the plates, then count all the children, recount the plates and unsystematically add or subtract plates until the right number is arrived at, then work out the number of glasses in the same trial and error way. A 6-year-old is much more likely to use the streamlined strategy of counting the people and then counting out that many plates and glasses from sets which do not need to be counted further. A number of different strategies will reach the final goal though they may vary in their cost effectiveness. Up to a point, perceptual comparison strategies may give quite successful results. If numbers are small, or if there is a big difference between the sets to be compared, or if an approximate answer will do, relative judgements work quite well, and young children use them quite readily (Bryant 1974, Sophian 1988). They work less well with exact comparisons between larger sets or sets nearer in size, and do not work at all, of course, on number symbols: 71 is not obviously larger than 48. New strategies therefore have to be developed, and the old ones relegated to the tasks for which they are adequate. One possible strategy is matching each item in one set with an item from the other: if a set has one or more items left over after this procedure it has more items. The evidence reviewed by Fuson and Hall (1983) suggests that if children have perceptual cues like touching, moving and linking with drawn-in lines (techniques which also help with counting, as I described above), they can use matching to establish relative numerosity by the age of about 6. If matching is perceptually harder fewer children use it (Brainerd 1979). One-to-one correspondence remains a useful strategy in tasks such as table-laying where it is highly desirable that each person's setting should contain one of each sort of implement or container, not just that the table as a whole should have the same number of each, less systematically distributed (see any etiquette book!).

Another possible strategy for establishing relative numerosities is of course counting. If the cardinal numbers of two sets are the same, they are equal in quantity; if not, the *order* of the cardinal numbers in the sequence of number words shows which set has more and which fewer items in it – at least to someone who knows the number sequence and that if number *a* comes before number *b* then number *a* is smaller than number *b*. This is level 4 of the hierarchy in Saxe *et al.* (1987), an arithmetical function of a high order. Exactly how children make these judgements is still controversial (Fuson and Hall 1983: 93–8; Siegler and Robinson 1982: 267–86). They are probably easier to make if the smaller number is very small and the gap between the numbers is large: Siegler and Robinson suggest that young children do not view numbers as a scale with even intervals but categorise the number sequence into smallest, small, medium and big numbers. Pre-schoolers judge nine to be a big number in all contexts: adults judge it to be a big number in the context of one to ten but not in the context of one to a million. (Adults, however, have difficulty in appreciating the very large or very small numbers involved in such things as geological time, nuclear physics, and religious conceptions of the life after death (Gould 1987, Joyce 1916).)

Counting may be of two separate sets existing simultaneously, or of one set before and after a transformation. In the classic number conservation test, both comparisons are involved. It is a well-replicated finding that children who have counted both sets before the transformation, and agreed that they are equivalent, will deny the same equivalence when one set of counters is spread out, even though they may count again and reach the same numbers. Nevertheless, counting does help in conservation of number tasks (Klahr and Wallace 1976, Siegler 1981). It is presumably *not* used as the best cue to numerosity in conservation when the child has a strong perceptual strategy and a low level of confidence in his or her own ability to count accurately. A conviction that spatial extent is a good cue to numerosity, and the knowledge that your counting techniques are shaky, would both make counting do badly in a cost-benefit analysis. As we have seen elsewhere children (and adults) find it difficult to give up a 'good enough' strategy in favour of a perfectionist one (Karmiloff-Smith and Inhelder 1974/5, Siegler 1988).

I have discussed using numbers to find the numerosity of a set or the relative sizes of several sets. Numbers can also be used to describe relative positions within a set: I am the fourth of my parents' children, the second tallest woman in my department, an inhabitant of the seventh largest city in England. Children do learn ordinal words such as these, but some time after they have learned the conventional counting sequence, and probably the ordinal number sequence becomes systematic and iterative through school practice. Using the ordinal words to refer to the correct items of an ordered set – indicating the third, fifth or whatever item – is also difficult. Putting items in order of size or some other physical quality is something pre-school children enjoy doing, though as Piaget's seriation experiments show they may stick at comparisons of pairs of objects and not systematically complete an ordered set (Piaget 1952); they may deal with equipment such as nested cups by trying to fit them by brute force, not by taking out the small cup which has been misplaced in a large one and prevents the insertion of a medium-sized cup. How ordinal number development is related to cardinal number development is not known: ordinal number may lag behind because it less frequently occurs in children's everyday activities (though ordinal numbers are used daily in the calendar) or because its vocabulary is acquired later, or for both reasons.

In contrast to the comparatively small amount of research done on the development of children's ordinal number concepts there has been a great deal of work on children's strategies for adding and subtracting numbers. Among useful reviews of this area are Carpenter et al. 1982, Carpenter and Moser 1983, Ginsburg 1977, Levine, Jordan and Huttenlocher 1992, Resnick 1983, Siegler and Robinson 1982 and various papers in Hiebert 1986. Children's most basic strategy is to construct sets of objects or fingers to represent the two numbers to be added, move the two sets together and then count all the joint set from one to the total. A more sophisticated (and quicker) strategy is to count on from the cardinal number of the first set through the members of the second set to the total number of the combined set. More efficiently still, the child may count on from the larger number through the smaller set to the total: the counting-on (min) algorithm.

Reaction time evidence (Groen and Parkman 1972) suggests that in their first year of school children use the counting-on (min) algorithm, as it took longer to reach the correct answer if the minimum addend was two than if the minimum addend was one, and so on. The mean response times for 1 + 6 and 6 + 1 were identical and over a second shorter than the mean response times for 3 + 4 and 4 + 3, for example. Children's verbalisations also often mention counting-on from the larger number (Ginsburg 1977). The main sums that were exceptions to the reaction time pattern were 'double' sums such as 1 + 1 and 4 + 4. These were particularly easy, as Figure 2.2 shows. It may be that these short solution times reflected a fourth strategy for coping with addition, that is, the memorisation of number facts. Ashcraft and Fierman (1982) suggest that there is a transition from counting strategies in addition to retrieving number facts from memory, for their samples at about the third grade (10 years old). Resnick (1983) also suggests that adults do most of their addition and subtraction by using mental short cuts such as using memorised number facts with little or no overt counting. Siegler (1986, 1988) points out that it may be most useful to have a number of different strategies to call on to solve addition problems. What is needed is not a single 'hierarchy' of strategies which children are assumed to pass through in sequence, discarding each as they grasp the next, but analysis of what range of strategies a problem-solver uses, how they are brought to bear

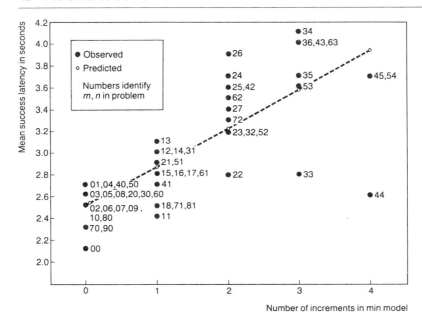

*Figure 2.2* Graph showing that response time depends on the number of increments required in the min model. Number pairs represent the two numbers to be added, e.g. 13 means 1 + 3.
*Source*: Groen and Parkman 1972

on different problems or on different occasions, and why there is variation. He reports a study of overt strategy use by pre-schoolers and found that there was a correlation of 0.91 between error rate and use of overt counting strategies such as reciting number words aloud or putting up fingers. Thus these young children were more likely to use an overt strategy on the harder problems, while on the easier ones they more often answered without having shown any sign of counting. Using overt counting strategies increased the children's chance of getting the right answer on almost all the sums. It was much slower than remembering the relevant number fact, so only counting on difficult problems, not on easy ones, saved time over all.

Siegler (1986, 1987) suggests that the child's information-processing system contains number facts (or pseudo-facts) associated to varying degrees with sums, for example if the sum was '2 + 1' the answer '1' would be associated with it at a strength of 0.05, the answer '2' with a strength of 0.05, the (correct) answer '3' with a strength of 0.79, and the answer '4' with a strength of 0.05. The system sets a confidence criterion for accepting a number fact as stateable, for example it might be decided that only if the associative strength was greater than 0.75 would an answer be stated. A limit on how many searches for number facts will be made is also set. Then the system begins to work on a problem, say '2 + 1 = ?'. An answer from the stored number facts is retrieved: as '3' has by far the highest associative strength it is the most likely to come up, in fact the figure of 0.79 here means that it would be expected on 79 per cent of trials of '2 + 1'. The '3' has an associative strength higher than the confidence level of 0.75, and is therefore stated. If '2', with its low associative strength of 0.05, had been retrieved, it would not have passed the confidence criterion and so another search would have been made. If the pre-set number of searches has been made without retrieving a satisfactory answer, the child has to try another strategy, perhaps imagining the sum mentally or using fingers, or counting, or both.

Siegler suggests that this model explains the relationships between overt strategy use, percentage of errors, and time required to reach a solution. Underlying them is the distribution of associations linking problems and answers. A very well learned fact, such as '2 + 1 = 3' means a peak of associative strength at the right answer, '3', and very low associations with other possible answers: a less well learned sum will have a flatter and wider distribution of answers so that none would reach a high confidence criterion but several might reach a low one. In this case it may be necessary to count, or, for comparatively sophisticated arithmeticians, to decompose and recompose numbers into ones where the relevant facts are known (for example 18 + 23 can be turned into 18 + 2 + 23 - 2). Adults do this often: so, particularly, do professional arithmetic calculators (Smith 1983). Siegler suggests that distributions are built up as a result of accumulated practice: children associate whatever answer they state with the problem to which they state it. Correct answers probably receive reinforcement from outside the child and so become somewhat more strongly associated, but errors may also become linked with the problem they have seemed to answer, and thus receive an increase in associative strength which may make them hard to get rid of. Siegler suggests this sort of model may underlie much non-arithmetical problem-solving, for example reading or spelling (see earlier sections in this chapter).

A similar variety of strategies for doing simple subtraction is described by Carpenter and Moser (1983). A strategy involving concrete objects is *separating from*: making a set of the larger numerosity, separating the smaller number off from it spatially, and counting the remainder. This is an enactment of phrasings such as '5 take away 3', which Conroy (1984) and Coleman (1982) found to be the preferred and easiest phrasing for children. There is a parallel counting strategy called *counting down from*; the child counts backwards, starting with the larger number, for as many number words (in sequence) as the given smaller number. The remainder is the correct answer. Other strategies include starting with the smaller number and *counting up* until the larger one is reached, noting how many names have been added as that is the answer. Again, children by the age of 8 or so seem to combine strategies to use the minimum of counting, so that if the sum is '8 - 2' they will count down from 8 but if the sum is '8 - 6' they will count up from 6, in each case using the quickest strategy. As in the case of addition, using number facts supersedes these counting strategies to a considerable extent.

A new set of problems arise as children become required to do more complex addition and subtraction with larger numbers. Although *counting-on*, *counting-down-from* and the other strategies continue to be capable of giving the right answer they become cumbersome and thus slow and inaccurate. Imagine using a counting strategy to solve 10,543 - 6,975, for example. Number facts that will solve the problem in one step will also be less likely to be usable. One aspect of the complication of later arithmetic is that it may involve competence with written mathematical symbols and with representing the structure of problems, topics which I will discuss later. One strategy is using 'derived facts', for example 'the solution to 14 - 8 may be found as follows: '7 and 7 is 14; 8 is one more than 7; so the answer is 6' (Carpenter 1986: 116–17). Decomposition into 'hundreds, tens and units' and the computation of each of these using number facts or counting strategies makes up a useful procedure for the addition and subtraction of large numbers, but it is far from unproblematic. It has to be a decomposition that uses the possibility of transforming 'tens' into 'tens and units', for example, as 10,543 – 6,975 shows: '3 take away 5 you can't', so 43 has to be decomposed into 30 and 13, and 5 subtracted from the latter. Then, of course, '3(tens) take away 7(tens) you can't', so the hundreds column also has to be decomposed. Decomposition has to be done in the correct order and the columns kept in step; all in all, it is a complex task. Not surprisingly, children's attempts to solve problems like 10,543 - 6,975 often contain 'bugs', erroneous procedures which lead to systematic errors (e.g. Brown and Burton 1978, Resnick 1983). One very common bug is to subtract the smaller number in a column from the larger, irrespective of which is actually on top. This bug's solution of 10,543 - 6,975 would look like this:

$$10543$$
$$-6975$$
$$\overline{16432}$$

– blatantly wrong, but systematic! Buggy procedures seem often to arise from learning procedures without understanding them (Davis 1986, Hiebert and Lefevre 1986, Hiebert 1988), that is, there is a dislocation between conceptual and procedural knowledge.

Carpenter (1986) argues that it is important to examine the relationship between knowledge of step-by-step procedures and rich knowledge of a network of concepts, capable of more flexible access and use. Children enter schools, as we have seen, with considerable experience of arithmetic and highly developed informal arithmetical systems. By holding up fingers or

Glasgow University Library
Checkout / Renewal Reeceipt

Customer name: **JOICE, TREVOR**

Title: The child as thinker : the development and
acquisition of cognition in childhood / Sara
Meadows.
ID: 30114005477396
**Due: 05-03-10**

Total items. 1
15/02/2010 10:30

Please keep This Receipt For Your Own Records.
All Borrowed Items Are subject to recall, Which
may Mean Earlier Due Dates

pointing out objects, or mentally, they can directly model quantities named in a problem (if they are small quantities), perform actions on these models which reflect arithmetical manipulations, and enumerate sets to get the answers to problems. Thus they can cope with problems such as 'Sally has 5 candies. She bought 8 more candies. How many candies does she have altogether?' or 'Sally had 13 candies. She ate 5 of them. How many candies does she have left?', though a non-canonical form such as 'Sally had some candies. She ate 5 of them. Now she has 8 candies left. How many candies did she have to start with?' is harder to solve, no doubt because of the difficulty of modelling the unknown initial quantity, or because the solution requires reversing the sequence of actions described in the problem. This procedural knowledge in young children uses semantically accurate representations of the problems, but lacks the flexibility of older children's behaviour. With a richer conceptual base, more practised and efficient procedures, and better links between concepts and varied procedures which can be used to check up on each other, much greater flexibility and efficiency become possible.

The relationship between conceptual and procedural knowledge in arithmetic is likely to be complex. A number of different emphases can be found in the literature: Riley, Greeno and Heller (1983) characterise procedural advances as stemming very largely from advances in the representation of concepts and problems, while Carpenter (1986) points out that more advanced procedures may be constructed not only because they reduce the demands of cognitive processing but also because they represent knowledge more fully (see also Chapter 4, on mechanisms of cognitive development as described by information-processing theorists). Children do often invent arithmetical procedures that reduce information-processing demands: however some of these are inefficient because they give the wrong answer (as in the subtraction 'bugs' mentioned above) and others because they depend too much on the availability of outside help (as in relying on a calculator or a clever neighbour). Conceptual knowledge is often local before it can be broadly applied, and initially there may be a limited range of linked procedures and representations of problems. With increases in both conceptual and procedural knowledge, children will become better able to recognise that 'this is another problem of this sort, which usually worked with this procedure', a recognition (or problem representation) that seems to be important in understanding mathematical and scientific problems. A lack of links between conceptual and procedural understanding, such as may arise in an educational programme which emphasises one at the expense of the other, can lead to superficial analysis of problems with consequent gross errors. Carpenter (1986) quotes the answers given to the problem '*Estimate* the answer to $12/13 + 7/8$. You will not have time to solve the problem using paper and pencil.' Over half of 13-year-olds chose 19 or 21 as the best estimate of the sum of these two fractions, and almost as many 17-year-olds made the same error as chose the correct answer, 2. It should have been obvious that the sum of two fractions each slightly less than 1 would be nearly 2, but these teenagers simply added the numbers which were numerators or denominators of the fractions without thinking how their answer made conceptual sense.

Similar problems arise in coping with alternative forms of writing arithmetical problems equations. Learning the formal code of arithmetic is part of the whole endeavour. Hiebert (1988) proposes a model for the development of competence within written mathematical symbols. Competent use involves *connecting symbols with referents*, for example, 75 could be represented with seven 10-unit Dienes blocks and five single-unit blocks, while ÷ represents partitioning an initial unit into a number of smaller equal groups. Both numbers and actions can be more or less helpfully represented, as the work mentioned above illustrates. As in all such translations, different symbol systems have different advantages and disadvantages. Dienes blocks are cumbersome but make it quite clear that the 7 represents 7 large items, while the written 75 makes the difference between large and single units far less obvious. Children do indeed have difficulty in grasping the principle of place notations, and hence have problems in the second aspect of competent use of written mathematical systems, which is *developing symbol manipulation procedures.* They may learn by manipulating the referents of the symbols first and then parallelling this action with action on the symbols. To use Dienes blocks again as an example, blocks representing 75.1 and 12.84 can easily be added together by combining blocks of the same size, and in the same position relative to the decimal point. To do the same with written symbols involves the rule 'line up the decimal points', size no longer being transparently mirrored in symbols. Manipulations of symbols have to preserve what is true in the referent world; as said earlier, procedural knowledge is best backed up by conceptual understanding, lest mistakes like the fraction 'addition' ones arise.

Children first apply written symbols to comparatively simple referents, such as small numbers and concrete objects. However, symbol manipulation rules can be analysed and elaborated so that they apply to new or more complex tasks. These more complex tasks may be much more easily performed using written symbols than concrete objects or other non-written symbol systems, as the example of what it would be like to solve five-figure subtraction tasks using a counting-down strategy will have made clear. Similarly, understanding the use of regrouping or recomposition of numbers, discovered in addition sums such as '43 + 29', may be applied to subtractions. The history of mathematics includes many examples of inventions of new ways of representing quantities and actions which allow a dramatic extension of the possibilities of computation: the algorithm for long division, the slide rule, logarithms and computer programs, to name parts of just one progression. There is a move away from attention to the concrete referents and towards reflection on the symbols and rules themselves, and on the consistency of the results produced by these different procedures, not just on whether what they produce is true in the concrete world ultimately referred to, as this is less easily checked, and in some advanced mathematics is unknowable except through its symbolisations. High level mathematics can manipulate even imaginary entities (for example, the square root of -1) to useful effect. James Hiebert quotes the physicist and mathematician Poincaré: 'It is by separating itself from reality that [the symbol system] has acquired this perfect purity. The power of mathematics lies in this purity, this abstraction from particular situations', and the philosopher and mathematician Whitehead: 'By the aid of symbolism, we can make transitions in reasoning mechanically by the eye, which otherwise would call upon the higher faculties of the brain' (Hiebert 1988: 341). Thus the third aspect of competent use of written mathematical symbols is *analysing and elaborating symbol manipulation rules*. This includes extending a simple algorithm to deal with more complex problems; for example a child might learn to manipulate written symbols to add small numbers (which he or she can also efficiently add by using concrete objects) and extend the written procedure to larger numbers where the concrete objects would be more cumbersome. The realisation that the written addition algorithm can be used for *any* numbers demonstrates its power and the usefulness of analysing and elaborating techniques for manipulating symbols. Similarly, a subtraction procedure might be developed from an addition one, or vice versa. The relationship between procedures becomes increasingly important, for example two different addition procedures should produce the same answer, or the result of the 'buggy' subtraction procedure discussed earlier is seen to be wrong because the 'answer' and the number to be subtracted do not add up to the number from which the subtraction was made: $6{,}975 + 16{,}432$ does not equal $10{,}543$, as $6{,}975 + 3{,}568$ does! Consistency is an important feature of mathematics: rules that are extended to new contexts must not contradict rules that apply to the old familiar context.

Mathematical procedures, like other cognitive procedures, may develop because they are analysed and reflected on, but they also have to be run efficiently, and becoming automatic and routinised may be the means to maximum efficiency under normal circumstances. Automatic procedures need less mental effort so that cognitive working space is freed for other processes. Much school mathematics aims at routinisation of procedures, for example acquiring a large stock of 'number facts' such as '5 x 7' in the primary school. Evidence collected by Smith (1983) suggests that expert calculators have particularly extensive knowledge of such facts, for example that they have memorised the square roots of many large numbers. Increasing use of electronic calculators may make such knowledge less useful (except of course as a check on whether the machine has worked properly). It is worth noting that the amount of time spent on school mathematics appears to underlie both cultural and gender differences in achievement (e.g. Raymond and Benbow 1986, Song and Ginsberg 1987, Stevenson *et al.* 1986, Stigler *et al.* 1987).

The final aspect of competence with written mathematical symbols described by Hiebert (1988) is building more abstract symbol systems, either by mapping a familiar symbol system on to new, more abstract, referents and rules, or by creating symbols of the patterns and consistencies between earlier symbol systems. Again, this is very much a feature of creative high level mathematics, but it is in some ways similar to Hiebert's first process, when the meaning of concrete referents is transferred to a first system of written symbols; here meaning is transferred from one symbol system to another, and through a chain of related symbol systems contact can ultimately be made with the concrete world.

Studies of children's early use of written mathematical symbols suggest that they are interested in producing written symbols and do so quite successfully. Hughes (1983) gave 5- to 7-year-olds the task of showing on paper how many bricks there were on the table. They found this easy, drawing the objects or an equivalent number of tallies or writing the appropriate conventional number. They were then asked to show what happened when a few more bricks were added or subtracted. Most just drew the final number of bricks. There were a few attempts to represent initial number, final number and what had been added on or subtracted, for example by showing hands adding bricks or putting bricks away in the box, or the ingenious if slow strategy of drawing a line of British soldiers marching from left to right to represent added bricks, and a line of Japanese soldiers marching from right to left to represent subtracted ones. Not one of the seventy-two children tested used the conventional operator symbols of + and -, although they were using them regularly in their arithmetic lessons, and although, as shown in further work by Hughes, even younger children could use these symbols in a number-guessing game.

Work by Thomas Carpenter and his colleagues (Carpenter 1986, Carpenter and Moser 1983, Carpenter *et al.* 1982) suggests that many children in the early years of school may manipulate written number problems with little or no connection of them to the world of real objects. Instruction which refers to concrete situations and actions which children have experienced and understand well is particularly helpful. Children are able to develop procedures for manipulating symbols (Hiebert's second level of processes), recognising that these procedures parallel procedures they have already used on concrete referents, but instruction which does not highlight this recognition may lead to symbol manipulation which lacks understanding and hence cannot lead either to insightful use or to elaborated procedures. Written mathematics must not lose its attention to what the symbols mean until the aspirant mathematician has progressed far through the stages Hiebert describes (Davis 1986, Gelman and Meck 1986), and even then translation from one symbol system to another or to concrete referents, as appropriate, may still be a useful aid. It will be essential in coping with algebraic story problems such as 'If one man digs a ditch in three days, how many days would two men take to dig the same ditch?', which can easily be misrepresented (Mayer 1982a, 1982b). Children need to understand the 'reality context' of the calculation, its mathematical structure and the appropriate representations and algorithms, and to relate all these, if they are to work successfully. This is an important field for collaboration between psychologists, mathematicians and educators (see e.g. Davis 1986, Hiebert 1988, Mayer 1986). Studies of mathematics learning outside school will also be illuminating (Saxe 1988, Saxe *et al.* 1987), as will examination of what happens in classrooms (Brissenden 1988, Desforges and Cockburn 1987, Mellin-Olsen 1987).

## MEMORY

### Introduction

It is obvious that remembering of some sort is necessary for virtually any human cognitive activity. Whatever stimulus or whatever problem we encounter, we are likely to deal with it using some comparison with situations met earlier in our experience. Even a novel situation must evoke some review of our memory if we are to be able to say 'I've never seen one of those before'. It is hard to believe in the possibility of an intelligent organism that does not store, recall and use at least some of the information it has encountered. All the major models of cognitive development discussed in Chapter 4 include memory processes, conspicuous in the information-processing model which underpins much of the work I discuss in this section but implicated also in Piaget's model of assimilation and accommodation. Almost all cognition, perhaps all, involves some sort of memory. Conversely, the use of memory is rarely an isolated intellectual skill of 'pure' remembering. It is affected by people's language skills, knowledge, judgements and inferences, for example, as well as by various cultural influences. Early memory researchers found it necessary to concentrate on memory for meaningless materials such as nonsense syllables because this was the only way to control for differences in other aspects of subjects' cognition (see, for example, Baddeley 1990). Memory development, therefore, is likely to be both important and multifaceted.

There have been four main suggestions about what develops in the improvement of children's memory from infancy to adulthood. They are, first, an improvement in basic capacities such as memory size or the speed of simple memory processes; second, development in memory strategies, which might for example diversify and be used more often, more effectively, more

External input

Decay of and loss
from sensory register ← Sensory register

Attention

Displacement and loss
from short-term store ← Short-term store
(Working memory)

Mnemonic activity

Decay, interference and
loss of strength in
long-term store ← Long-term store

*Figure 2.3* The multi-store model of memory.
*Source*: adapted from Atkinson and Shiffrin 1968

deliberately, or with more flexibility; third, changes in children's knowledge about their own memory such that they can regulate their remembering more appropriately; and, fourth, an increase in the amount of knowledge other than about memory available, which could make remembering related information easier and mean that fewer situations are completely unfamiliar. Obviously there could be developmental changes in more than one of these areas. We will examine them in turn, after first setting up a simple model of what memory is.

### Developmental changes in basic memory capacities?

There are various accounts of the basic structure and processes of memory (derived mainly from work on adults), but a distinction between sensory store, short-term memory, and long-term memory (e.g. Atkinson and Shiffrin 1968) provides a useful framework. Their memory system would look something like Figure 2.3.

Information enters the system through the sensory register, and persists there for a short time after the end of stimulation, but much never passes beyond it. If it proceeds, information then enters the short-term store and, perhaps, passes thence to the long-term memory store. At each point of entry some information may be lost, in part because both sensory register and short-term store are seen as being limited in size and in how durable the information they contain is, and all three stores need time to execute basic processes. Each store uses control processes on the information it contains; for example, rehearsal, or repeating items to be remembered over and over again, is an important control process in the short-term store where its use stops material being lost. The examination of associated information and inference contribute to the storage and recall of information in long-term memory, because such examination is associated with the semantically-based processing of information which produces a more durable and accessible memory trace.

Control processes affect whether information is lost or transferred from one store to another. They also affect the organisation of information within each store, and thus are important in affecting functional capacity, since better organisation and ready transfer can transcend the stores' limitations of size and processing speed.

The sensory store is the entry point to the memory system. If young children could not take in as much sensory information as older ones, or if they could not take in certain sorts of sensory information, or if they took in sensory information more slowly, the sensory store could be a cause of developmental differences in memory. Not much is known about the sensory store in infancy, though research on perception suggests that babies are capable of perceiving information very much like adults do (for a summary see Meadows 1986: 47–54, and for details see papers in Haith and Campos 1983). There is evidence that the capacity of the sensory store does not change in childhood. In an experiment by Morrison, Holmes and Haith (1974) 5-year-olds and adults briefly saw a set of geometric figures. One twentieth of a second later they were asked to say which figure had been at a particular position in the array. The children's performance under these conditions was very much the same as the adults'. Thus children probably can take as much information into the sensory register as adults can. Differences in the sort of sensory information they can take in are also unlikely to account for children's poorer memory performance; adults would be more likely to suffer from poorer sensory acuity (they would be worse on very high pitched auditory stimulation, for example), though children's inhabiting of an adult-sized world might reduce their access to some sensory information which is, for example, literally 'over their heads'. However children do seem to be somewhat slower in forming a sensory representation of what they see (Hoving et al. 1978) although there is some controversy about this (Anderson 1989a, 1992, Nettelbeck and Wilson 1985). This slower speed of taking in information might restrict learning and memory. We do not know why children are slower, or why the speed of representation increases. There is some association with IQ though there is disagreement about exactly what. Anderson's model of intelligence and cognitive development (Anderson 1992 and Chapter 3 this volume) sees speed of information processing as the non-developing core of intelligence.

Nettelbeck and his colleagues see it as subject to developmental change (Nettelbeck and Vita 1992, Wilson and Nettelbeck 1986, Wilson *et al.* 1992).

The next possible source of developmental changes is the short-term store. Here information from the immediate environment (via the sensory register) and information from past environmental encounters (via the sensory register) and information from past environmental encounters (via retrieval from the long-term store) are combined as required for the current problem-solving situation: here is the consciously accessible 'working memory' part of the cognitive system. As in the sensory register, development could be due to changes in speed or capacity or to how they are used. Some theorists, for example Pascual-Leone (1970), believe that children's capacity is more restricted than adults', that because their working memory or 'M-space' is smaller they are subject to severe limitations in their information-processing. A task might require more information-processing capacity than is available, and in this case the child would fail on it. An increase in M-space is necessary for successful performance and transition to a more advanced stage of development. As children grow older their M-space grows with them so that they become able to operate more programmes or processes at one time. Thus their cognitive performance is markedly improved. However it is not clear how we can distinguish between growth in M-space and development in processing. As we shall see, it is clearly the case both that people's repertoires of cognitive processes and strategies increase with age and that the members of the cognitive repertoire may become slicker, more automatic and more efficient, thus taking up less of the resources of working memory. Children's performance on any task will be a function of the cognitive processing used, the demands that processing makes on M-space and the size of M-space itself. We know the first two of these develop with age: attempts to use performance to measure M-space have to hold processing and processing demands constant if they are to distinguish between changes in the size of M-space and changes in the way a stable-sized M-space is used. Let us suppose that the task in question is that of making a transitive inference, of inferring from the two pieces of information 'Grandpa is older than Mummy' and 'Mummy is older than Baby' that 'Grandpa is older than Baby'. We might arbitrarily hypothesise that this would require four units of processing space: one each to store the pieces of information, 'Grandpa older than Mummy', 'Mummy older than Baby', one to store the information that 'older than' is a transitive relationship as opposed to one such as loving, which is not ('Tybalt loves Juliet' and 'Juliet loves Romeo' do not combine transitively into 'Tybalt loves Romeo', the reverse is true), and one to make the inference. Children may come to be able to deal with the transitive inference task by developing an M-space of four units. They may also come to be able to do it by having their inferential strategy use up less space, for example by learning the relative ages of Grandpa and Mummy and of Mummy and Baby so well that they only require half as much storage space. Or they could be able to deal with the task by using a non-inferential strategy which requires less M-space, for example 'reading' the answer off a visual image or simply memorising the known familiar answer. Only very precise experimental analysis of tasks, of learner activities, and of the interdependencies between strategies and processing can clarify the relative importance of capacity and its use.

At present, researchers differ in their views about developmental changes in short-term memory capacity: it seems a reasonable guess that structural changes are less important than usage changes, that development is due not to an increase in the total size of working memory but to an increase in the proportion of working memory which is free from the demands of basic operations and so can be used for more complex information processes and storage. Case takes this view (Case 1985, and see also Chapter 4 this volume). Prenatal exposure to pollution can be detrimental to short-term memory and sustained attention (Jacobson *et al.* 1992, and Chapter 5 this volume).

Capacity changes in long-term memory are not thought to be a source of cognitive development, as for all practical purposes long-term memory seems to have no effective size limitations, at least until extreme old age when the deterioration of the senile brain might result in holes in its memory as well as literal holes in its structure (Mayes 1988, Squire 1987). However control processes in both short-term and long-term stores are very convincing candidates for developmental change. As the research emphasis has been on strategic control of memory, these developments will be discussed in the next section. Recognition, which is not structural capacity but is not strategic either, will be dealt with here however. Infants show an ability to recognise objects remarkably early, as their habituation to repeated events and their preference for particular faces and voices show (e.g., Fagan and Singer 1983, Kagan *et al.* 1978, Mehler *et al.* 1978, Papousek 1967, Wetherford and Cohen 1973). Infants' rate of habituation and capacity for sustained attention may be amongst the best predictors of their intelligence, incidentally (Anderson 1989a, Bornstein and Sigman 1986, Fagan and Singer 1983, Rose *et al.* 1988). Infants who attend to and recognise objects and events about them, particularly if they don't sleep much during the day, are presumably giving themselves many more opportunities to learn about all sorts of aspects of the world!

The main development of recognition is not in the ability to do it at all but in the complexity of what is taken in and later recognised. Young infants recognise simple or very salient stimuli over surprisingly long periods of time (Bachevalier and Miskin 1984, Rovee-Collier and Hayne 1987): older ones remember more information about the stimulus and can therefore discriminate smaller differences between the familiar stimulus and the novel one, and do so over a longer period of time (Kagan *et al.* 1978). Similarly, pre-school children recognise pictures of simple objects about as well as adults but do less well on recognising pictures of complex scenes, where adults can make more use of their interpretations of the meaning of the scene and are more likely to examine it thoroughly (Nelson 1971, Nelson and Kosslyn 1976, Newcombe et al. 1977); that is, strategies can make a marked difference to performance.

To summarise, the basic structure of memory is not thought to change during childhood, though possibly the size of working memory stores may increase. Basic speed of processing may be developmentally stable (Anderson 1989a, 1992). Recognition and learning too seem to be basic processes that are present from very early in life and are refined by experience rather than changing radically (Bachevalier and Mishkin 1984, Rose 1981). However, the use of structure and processes often involves strategies. We will now discuss what develops in this area.

**Developmental changes in memory strategies?**

There is a great deal of evidence now that there are marked changes in the use of memory strategies as children grow older, changes so marked that some researchers have seen this as the major developmental shift in memory (and in other cognitive areas, see e.g. Baron 1978, Brown et al. 1983, Schneider and Pressley 1989, Siegler 1986). Strategies are deliberate controlled mental or behavioural activities used so as to enhance memory performance by improving the encoding, the storage or the retrieval of information. A variety of memory strategies are discussed in the psychological literature (e.g. Pressley, Borkowski and O'Sullivan 1985). A sophisticated learner will know about a number of strategies, for example the following: single item repetition, that is, repeating material over and over, one item at a time; cumulative rehearsal, repeating material over and over in a cumulative fashion, rehearsing new items along with old ones; meaningful organisation, looking for and remembering meaningful relationships between items such as common categories or syntactical rules such as 'they're all opposites'; imagery elaboration, making up a memorable image in which the items to be learned interact, such as a scene in which a tiger in a boat eats a bun; verbal elaboration, making up a sentence or story including the to-be-remembered items such as 'The tiger in the boat is eating a bun'; differential allocation of effort, for example deciding which items are most important and studying those first, or putting more effort into studying material which has not yet been memorised; and complex combinations of these such as the SQ3R study method. In this, material is first surveyed, then learners question themselves, and then read the material to learn it, recite it to test memorisation, and review whether the important information has been learned (e.g. Robinson 1946). Professional mnemonists (see e.g. Luria 1969, Ericsson et al. 1980) can perform extraordinary feats of memorisation as a result of bringing such techniques to a high degree of expertise. Children under 7 or so are rarely seen to use memorisation strategies that would be appropriate to memory tasks. There is little spontaneous use, for example, of the simple and quite effective technique of rehearsal. Where older children and adults would repeat such material as a telephone number or the words they have to speak in a play over and over to themselves, under the age of about 7 there is little rehearsal, and what there is rudimentary and inefficient, for example repetition of isolated items or only part of what is required. Older children and adults are more likely to rehearse several items and to adapt their rehearsal strategy to the particular demands of the task, for example giving more rehearsal time to items they have not yet remembered adequately and less to material that has already been memorised. Subtle improvements such as this contribute to a steady improvement in memory performance over childhood.

A similar result is found with the organisation of material. It is frequently helpful to the learner to reorganise material into categories and rehearse categorised material as such, using the information about what categories were included to summon up and recognise the actual instances involved: if we notice that four words in the list were animals, for example, we can use 'animal names' as a cue to help us remember whether 'cat', 'pig', 'fly' and so forth were in the list. Young children are less likely to divide a list according to stable and helpful categories, or to search categories systematically. They are also less likely to use helpful elaboration techniques. These create a connection between the items to be learned by, for example, juxtaposing them in a vivid visual or verbal image, or associating them with an already learned string of items or some other memorable structure such as rhyme or a tune. 'One, two, buckle my shoe' does this job for number words (or alternatively for the items which rhyme with the overlearned number list). These strategies too are rarely spontaneously used until quite late in childhood, and are more often found in schooled than unschooled cultures (Hasselhorn 1992, Moely 1977, Pressley, Borkowski and O'Sullivan 1985, Rogoff 1990, Schneider and Pressley 1989).

Why do young children rarely show a use of memory strategies? One explanation would be in terms of a 'mediational deficiency', that young children do not rehearse, organise or elaborate because they cannot effectively regulate their behaviour through internal mental processes mediating between the task stimulus and the response. This explanation suggests that the deficit is irremediable, that training could not produce the radical shift of behaviour which is required. It is thus effectively countered by the considerable amount of evidence that children can be taught to use memory strategies such as rehearsal, categorisation and cue-based search (e.g. Kail 1990, Lange and Pierce 1992, Pressley, Forrest-Pressley, Elliott-Faust and Miller 1985 for reviews). Even children as young as 6 or 7 have shown themselves perfectly able to use the mnemonic strategy they had been trained in while the experimenter required them to use it. So *inability* to use mediating strategies of rehearsal, categorisation, cue use and so forth is clearly not their main problem. However strategy use is not so effective in the hands of trained young children as it is for older children (e.g. Flavell, Beach and Chinsky 1966) and they may not continue to use the strategy later, when not explicitly instructed to use it (e.g. Hagen *et al.* 1973, Keeney *et al.* 1967); the pre-school subjects of Lange and Pierce (1992) showed an increase in strategic activity even as late as three days after training, though improvement in memory achievement was less marked. The most likely explanation for both the failure to produce strategic memorising behaviour initially and the failure to continue to employ a useful strategy after the instruction has ended, or to transfer its use to a new task, lies in the child's poor knowledge about memory problems and how to transcend them. For a full discussion of this, the role of 'metamemory' in memory development, see the next section.

Two points remain to be made about memory strategies *per se*, however. First, they typically show further development in how effectively they are used for some years after their first appearance. These developments include more complete and polished performance of the different components of a memory strategy. For example, Pressley and Levin (1980) showed that although both 6-year-olds and 11-year-olds could be taught to generate and use an elaborative imagery strategy to memorise words, the 6-year-olds had to be reminded to think back to the images they had thought up earlier when they were trying to recall the words; the 11-year-olds did this without being reminded. Development also includes an improvement in fitting the strategy to the task; for example Naus, Ornstein and Aivano (1977) found that 11-year-olds remembered more items in a list than 8-year-olds even when all used rehearsal, because the younger children over-rehearsed the first items in the list while the older ones continually changed the items they rehearsed, thus learning more items well enough to recall them. This sort of strategy adaptation may be one cause of a related development; younger children may find the adoption of a strategy provided by the experimenter is more helpful than using a strategy they have devised for themselves, because their strategy is not maximally efficient, while older children who can devise particularly helpful strategies may find the experimenter's less effective for them than their own (e.g. Siegler 1986: 237). Familiarity with the material to be remembered will also affect strategy use: helpful clustering of well-known material, such as the names of classmates, may be used where there is no sign of clustering of less familiar material (e.g. Bjorklund and Zeman 1982, Hasselhorn 1992, Marmurek and Rinaldo 1992). This of course means that an apparent failure to use a strategy on one material does not mean that the child is incapable of using the strategy on any material.

The second point about memory strategies is that although they ; ae rarely seen in the performance of young children it is very evident that young children can and do remember. Improvements in the use of strategies probably account for many of the developmental changes in memory performance during the school years, but babies' and pre-schoolers' memories may be impressively accurate. Rovee-Collier and Hayne (1987) investigated 3-month-olds' recollection of mobiles suspended over their cots, for example, and found that they remembered how to move the toy for as long as eight days. My own daughter at the age of 16 months remembered the actions which went with a nursery rhyme she had last heard two weeks earlier. Forbes (1988) reports on his slightly older child's feats of recollection. We do not know how these children remembered; presumably they did not consciously and deliberately set out to memorise, but behaviour such as repeatedly requesting recitations or namings may facilitate recollection – rehearsal with the parent as the stand-in who does the work for the child!

**Developments in knowledge about memory: 'metamemory'?**

'Metamemory' is one of the major components of 'metacognition'; it was in fact the first metacognitive area studied (Flavell 1971). It is one's knowledge of memory, one's awareness of what memory behaviour is happening at the moment, and one's understanding about task difficulties, one's own skills, abilities and deficits, and strategies that will enable one to perform a task satisfactorily, just as metacognition in general is such awareness and knowledge of a range of cognitive procedures. It is assumed that someone with mature metamemory will recognise when a task requires deliberate memorisation and that there is a range of mnemonic techniques suitable to different tasks, that there are individual differences in memory skills and variation within individuals on how well they remember in different situations, and that monitoring memory will often be useful in the performance of memory strategies. A mature memoriser will know about the value of a strategy, the range of tasks it applies to, and how best to execute it appropriately. It is assumed that such metamemory knowledge is associated with better memory performance (see Schneider 1985 for a comprehensive review) and that young children's worse performance is associated with their less complete metamemory.

It is not clear whether 'metacognition' and 'metamemory' are really unitary things; in particular the relationship between knowledge and action has not been clearly conceptualised (Robinson 1983). It seems fairly clear that one could have relevant knowledge and not be able to put it into action, or one could act appropriately without being able to give an account of one's understanding. Given this complexity, it is perhaps not surprising that the review by Wolfgang Schneider (see also Schneider and Pressley 1989) finds that the relationship between metamemory and memory behaviour varies. It is more likely that there will be a positive relationship for young children when memory monitoring and the recall or recognition of small quantities of information are concerned, and there is at best a weak relationship when more demanding tasks involving a combination of complex strategies are employed. Older children show closer relationships between metamemory and memory, but these are still task related, with more positive links when memory monitoring is considered and weaker ones when metamemory knowledge is linked to recall tasks. Metamemory knowledge predicts how well children transfer a taught strategy to another task and their use of elaborative and organisational strategies.

This intricate pattern of results suggests several important points. First, it is not easy to measure 'metamemory', and a variety of assessment methods may be needed. In particular, children may have less to say about their metamemory when asked before a memory test than they can report having just done the test, with a very recent experience to reflect on and describe. Similarly they may show more knowledge about performance on a real task than on a hypothetical one (Thorpe 1988). Second, we need a more complete theory of how and why metamemory and memory behaviour affect each other at different ages and in different tasks. Children's knowledge about memory clearly increases as they go through the school years. They know more stateable facts about memory and they know more memory strategies. Particularly during the early stages of development, some of this knowledge may be only loosely related to the monitoring and regulation of memory activities, which only become linked to factual knowledge late in childhood. This dislocation of knowledge and action characterises the early stages of many skills. It is an interesting area for training studies. In the memory area, training which combines facts and procedures relevant to memory is maximally effective if it involves explicit use of children's metamemory activities. Thus Whittaker (1983) suggested that showing children that their memory was significantly improved by their use of mnemonics increased the extent and effectiveness of their mnemonic behaviour, and children who attributed their success to a particular mnemonic technique were more likely to use the same strategy in a different appropriate situation. Continued use of mnemonics is more likely if the demonstrated improvement is large, as if the mnemonics have to be seen to be cost-effective. Here knowledge of specific strategies and specific tasks may be involved, that is, knowledge of when and where the strategy can be used, its usefulness on a task compared with the usefulness of other approaches, how the strategy may be modified to suit task demands, whether it is suitable in the general task context and so forth. (A consideration of the social context may be relevant here, for example using a calculator to get the result of multiplying 9 by 7 may not be acceptable in a school curriculum which expects children to 'learn their tables', and reciting the multiplication table from the beginning may not serve in a school which expects 'number facts' to be well learned and instantly retrievable.)

Children's metamemory knowledge about tasks develops during the school years (Brown *et al.* 1983, Kail 1984, Wellman 1983, 1985b). Pre-school children know that, all other things being equal, familiar lists are more memorable than unfamiliar, and long lists are harder than short ones. They do not appreciate that a homogeneous set of items which show a consistent relationship may be very easy to learn irrespective of its length, thus they predict that a short paired associate list where there are arbitrary pairings will be easier to learn than a longer paired associate list where all the pairs are common antonyms. By the age of 9 or 10 children (like adults) judge that the antonym list is easier to learn, and if asked to generate a list which will be 'easy to remember' invent one with highly related items. Pre-school children know about the rapid decay of short-term memory, so that they will advise that one should use a telephone number directly after looking it up and not stop and do something irrelevant to telephoning; they tend to agree with adults that recognition is easier than recall. It is not until the age of about 10 that they say it is harder to remember word for word than to paraphrase and 'tell you in my own words'. These results suggest that although children have achieved some understanding of the demands of memorising by the time they enter school, they can only gauge task demands accurately after considerable further experience of memorising. Young children frequently overestimate their memory capacity (Cavanaugh and Perlmutter 1982); being over-confident about remembering would probably reduce the amount of special effort to remember, while a realistic appraisal of the difficulty of remembering would show that extra effort was needed for success. Failure on a memory task is peculiarly hard to judge. One may know that one has not remembered everything one meant to get at the supermarket but feel that only one item has been forgotten; back home with the list one initially forgot to take out to the shops one all too often finds that several items have been listed and then forgotten without the list as an *aide-mémoire*. Over-confident children may do badly on memory tasks but not notice their deficit. Unlike shoppers, young children may only rarely have their failure made visible to them, as adults probably take much of the responsibility for remembering things. A child who goes to school, on the other hand, is having to live in two microsystems, 'at home' and 'at school', which will involve both relatively spontaneous reporting of school events at home and vice versa, and the deliberate carriage of information from one to the other. No longer can one caretaking adult take all the responsibility for the child's remembering: it is only the child who inhabits both microsystems and knows all their details. The school microsystem, what's more, requires the child to memorise larger and larger quantities of information, for more formal testing, and may model mnemonic strategies and even, occasionally, discuss them.

Teaching memory strategies for a specific task has been effective in improving performance on that task (see Brown *et al.* 1983 for a review and also elsewhere in this volume). Other researchers have shown that providing explicit information on the usefulness of the strategy increases generalisation to similar tasks, and children who have learned to make their own evaluations of their strategy use may perform even better (Pressley, Borkowski and O'Sullivan 1985). However, although training improves performance, most children's performance improves without training as they move through the school years. They know more about memory and they remember better, but the extent of any causal relationship remains unclear.

### Developmental changes in knowledge?

It is so obvious that children acquire more knowledge as they grow older that psychologists have shown little interest in knowledge growth until recently (Chi and Ceci 1987). However, what we remember and how we remember are inextricably tied in with our relevant knowledge. Once information has progressed beyond short-term memory it becomes mixed up to some degree with information we have acquired at other times. This was why the psychologists who studied memory early in the history of psychology deliberately set their subjects to learn unfamiliar meaningless material such as nonsense syllables. It is (generally) much easier to remember information if we already have related information. Older children's greater quantity of stored information might account for much of their better remembering. Chi's elegant experiments with chess players illustrate this particularly neatly (Chi 1978). She compared children (average age 10) with adults on two tasks: immediate recall of a string of digits, and immediate recall of stimuli placed within an eight by eight array. The adults performed better than children on the digit list, as expected; but the children remembered more about the stimuli in the eight by eight array. This unusual finding of better performance by children is explained by the fact that the children were experienced chess players and the adults were not, and the 'stimuli placed within an eight by eight array' were chess pieces in a mid-game position on a chessboard. This array was meaningful and thus memorable to a chess player, meaningless and difficult to someone ignorant about chess. It is worth noting that chess players did not find the array easier to remember if the pieces were put on at random, but only if they were in positions that they could legitimately have reached in the course of a genuine game.

Familiar and meaningful information is more easily remembered, and may show use of mnemonic techniques which are not evident in the handling of unfamiliar material (for example Bjorklund and Zeman 1982 found clustering in young children's recall of their classmates' names though not in their recall of less familiar lists of words). There will also be associations between the familiarity of material and the sort of memory errors which are made. In familiar material, errors often consist of substituting one plausible element for another related to it, or drawing inferences which go beyond the information that has been given (Myles-Worsley *et al.* 1986). Memory for information which is familiar and meaningful can use reconstruction and inference rather than the rote learning and recall of every detail. Experience and familiarity both highlight the salient points and so make understanding and remembering easier (Brown and De Loache 1978, Lorch *et al.* 1987), and aid recall through allowing association, inference and other active reconstruction processes. It seems that there may be an interaction between knowledge of the material to be remembered, the strategies that can be used, and the capacity of short-term memory (Huttenloch :r ande Burke 1976, Kobasigawa 1977). Well-known information may need fewer attentional resources in short-term memory, and thus leave more mental working space for other items or for demanding strategies. Children, who know most pieces of information less well, have to use up more resources on remembering each piece and would thus both remember fewer items and be less able to work through a complex memory strategy. Strategies may first be used effectively on comparatively familiar material (e.g. Bjorklund and Zeman 1982, Chi and Ceci 1987). Practice with using strategies might lead to their becoming automatic and using fewer resources, and then being applicable to content that is less familiar and more demanding.

Thus some of the development of children's memory must be associated with increases in their knowledge base. General knowledge, the information already stored in long-term memory, facilitates the remembering of new information in several different ways. It provides a network within which new information can be placed (see Chapter 4 this volume for discussion of the structure of such networks). It facilitates the drawing of inferences, and serves as a check on the plausibility of particular events, associations and instances ('Caracas wasn't on the list because they were all towns in North America'). It makes important information, or the hard-to-remember, stand out from information which needs less attention. It may reduce the demands made on working memory, thus facilitating deeper and strategic information-processing. There may be some minor costs, however, particularly in the form of more errors in recall due to implied information being inferred and so judged to have been explicitly presented. Prior knowledge can interfere with memory as well as help it. Sir Frederick Bartlett, one of the British pioneers of memory research, asked subjects to retell a strange little folk-tale about how some North American Indians encountered a party of ghosts (Bartlett 1932). The successive retellings gradually Anglicised the story, losing or changing details which had significant meaning in the Indian mythology but had none to Cambridge minds. The children's party game in which a whispered message is passed from one person to another round a circle of players illustrates the same phenomenon. Memory is normally holistic and inferential, and while in most cases this is advantageous it can contribute to errors and distortions of information.

## Summary

This review of what develops in memory development has been long and perhaps not memorable. I will therefore recapitulate some of the conclusions that are being drawn at present, before moving on to two areas of research and theorising which have somewhat different messages about memory.

First, it seems unlikely that the structure or the capacity of children's memory stores changes with development to any developmentally significant extent, though the efficiency with which memory capacity is used increases as cognitive operations are executed more quickly, more effectively and more automatically. There may well be differences between individuals in the speed or capacities of their memories, as shown in such measures as digit span and speed of habituation. Second, there certainly are developmental changes in the use of memory strategies, with a major increase in the frequency and the efficiency of their use over the school years (though younger children are sometimes strategic in well-understood tasks such as hide and seek games, and adolescents and adults will quite often fail to use strategies). Third, children acquire knowledge relevant to their memory performance in two ways: they come to know more about themselves, tasks and possible memory strategies, and they acquire more knowledge about things other than memory, which lends more meaning to what they have to remember and so improves encoding and recall.

Integrating these different areas of memory development is hampered by a lack of empirical data on how they interact in development. As my discussion of whether memory capacity develops will have indicated, there must be interaction but it is hard to tease different components apart (see e.g. Hasselhorn 1992, Marmurek and Rinaldo 1992, Naslund and Schneider 1991). Age by age, rather than memory component by memory component, the picture would look something like this: The basic brain structures of memory have developed to something much like the mature form by the end of infancy, or at the latest by the age of 5. Babies and young children are learning an enormous amount during this period, and can remember some quite complex events over quite long periods of time; but they show little use of strategic memory outside a few well-learned contexts such as hide and seek games and nursery rhyme repetition. They provide incorrect answers to many questions about memory and the variables which affect it, tending to be wildly optimistic about what they will remember, for example. They are not good at monitoring memory performance and so may remain unaware of failure to learn or to remember.

During primary school, more memory strategies and more awareness of memory develop, as does the knowledge base. Children are more likely to use effective input and retrieval strategies and to judge their performance more accurately. They have more information at their command and so can reconstruct memory actively as well as retrieving it passively. The cultures they live in, and in particular the schooling they take part in, require them to remember and provide mnemonic techniques (Rogoff 1990, Schneider and Pressley 1989). These sorts of development continue through adolescence into adulthood, though few adults reach the highest levels of memory skill.

## Memory for events in childhood

Two consistent phenomena crop up in the literature on memory for events in childhood. First, most people's 'earliest memory' dates from their fourth year of life, or later: it is rare to remember anything about the period of one's life before one's third birthday, and there are comparatively thin recollections of the period from 3 to 5. This is the phenomenon which Freud (1973, 1977) called 'infantile amnesia', and he attributed memory loss either to repression of the unacceptable sexual and aggressive impulses of early childhood, that is, to a later blocking of memories with too strong an emotional tone, or to an initial failure to create a fully formed narrative memory for an event and a later difficulty in translating the fragments of incoherent early memories into a form reportable by the grown-up person (Pillemer and White 1989), explanations which we will look at a little later. Second, young children have great difficulty in answering questions such as 'What did you do at school today?', despite their rapid learning over the pre-school years of immense quantities of material such as names of objects, nursery rhymes, and even generalised 'scripts' of events such as what one does in school (Fivush 1984, 1987, Fivush et al. 1992).

In deciding between the competing theories of (1) emotional blockage, (2) failure to encode the data to be memorised, (3) failure to translate material remembered earlier into a form which is retrievable later and (4) the effects of brain maturation (Bachevalier 1992), a number of recent studies well reviewed by Pillemer and White (1989) are relevant. The emotional blockage theory seems the least likely of the four (though perhaps relevant to the minority engaged in Freudian psychoanalysis), given findings which suggest that the emotions which accompany memories of early childhood are very similar to those accompanying memories of other periods of life (Davies 1987, Kihlstrom and Harackiewicz 1982, Pillemer et al. 1988).

Failure to encode data to be memorised remains one possible source of childhood difficulties in remembering, but this is not a total failure. Anecdote and careful observation of children's spontaneous conversation and behaviour document many instances of data being registered, retained for some time, and recalled. My own daughter, for example, recalled at the age of 20 months a unique sight from two months earlier. She had first visited my sister's house just before she was 18 months old, and had seen there balloons hanging from the curtain rail in the sitting-room (it was my sister's birthday). We next visited the house nine weeks later; when she re-entered the sitting-room through the french windows to the garden, my daughter looked up at the curtain rail and said 'balloon'. No one had mentioned those balloons to her at any time in the intervening period, and she had not played with them during the birthday party. Her 'balloon' and look upwards demonstrated a memory for an earlier feature of the room. A. R. Eisenberg (1985), Farrar and Goodman (1992), Fivush *et al.* (1987), Forbes (1988), Nelson (1988) and Perlmutter (1980), similarly report excellent memory appearing in young children's everyday talk. Nelson (1990) documents a 2-year-old using bedtime monologues to construct a memory and an understanding of her day's activities. However, these verbal expressions of memory for specific events are not yet documented as being frequent, and they may generally consist of only a few ideas rather than a coherent narrative. Specific cues from adults may elicit more information, as may relevant non-verbal context (Morton 1990, Wilkinson 1988). Adults who are familiar with the child's life are able to confirm the accuracy of the child's reports, but such prior knowledge is often essential if the people, places, events and so forth implied in the child's 'loose and disorganised' narrative are to be identified correctly (A. R. Eisenberg 1985).

As we know that young children often have difficulty constructing a narrative about material that is in front of them, it could be argued that this problematic construction of narrative may handicap them in their accounts of remembered material, even if they actually have a well-formed memory of it. Young children can re-enact a game learned two weeks earlier better than they can describe it in words (Morton 1990, Smith *et al.* 1987), and there is evidence of toddlers showing associations between places they knew much earlier and the events or activities they had gone through there. However, verbal memories of pre-verbal baby experiences seem to be both anecdotal and concerned with repeated experiences and so, perhaps, with general knowledge rather than specific event memories (Pillemer and White 1989). Nelson (1986) suggests that children have difficulties with memory for individual episodes because they automatically build up 'General Event Representations' (GERs) in which repetitions of the same type of event are fused into a generalised schema or script. Having a rapidly-formed and accurate general script of 'what you do in school', the child has, Nelson supposes, little or no access to the specifics of 'what you did in school today', and with increasing time since a particular event, GERs will increasingly dominate (Myles-Worsby *et al.* 1986).

Certainly, unique events do seem to be remembered more specifically and more accurately than any particular instance of a routine event, but part of the difference is due to the sort of question asked. Open-ended questions are harder to answer than direct questions about specific parts of events; indeed when adults search their memories for information on 'what they did yesterday afternoon' they are likely to attempt several direct probes (Morton 1990: 6 provides an example). It seems likely that young children's recollections of specific events are more often expressed in conversation with other people than in monologue, particularly during episodes when an adult is trying to elicit recall narratives from the child. Pillemer and White (1989) argue that this builds up a socially addressible memory system which is added to the less communicable and predominantly non-verbal, affective and image-based memory existing from birth. This 'social memory system' is what is used when an intentional, purposeful search of memory and a narrative-like recall are required, and thus is what is typically needed to answer a researcher's request for verbal recall of an earlier event. If it is not operational until the age of 3 to 5, little from before that age will be recalled except events which are non-verbal, affective and image-based (of which my own earliest memory, of pride in and the look of a new pair of socks, would be an example; they were red, white and blue socks, in Coronation year). When we remember such events or images as adults, they may become overlaid with information from later memories and later-developed skills: my image of my Coronation socks, for example, is something I can describe verbally in ways which I certainly did not command at the time, and this description and the image of other, later, socks tend to intrude on the memory.

Pillemer and White argue that language is the basis of the later memory system which builds up over the primary school years. Another development is an increasing ability to provide one's own memory probes, perhaps through the use of increasingly elaborated scripts. The social sharing of memory experiences both teaches what must be included when you recount a past experience and establishes it as a rewarding activity: Mummy asks what you did at the childminder's today while she was at work, and is interested in discussing why one of the other children cried and what was done about this. It might be expected that a memory system so dependent on language and on the understanding of 'scripts' and narrative would develop rapidly from about 3 onwards, and so might account for the developmental changes in memory for events in childhood.

A recent paper (Morton 1990) provides a more formal model of these memory systems, which also distinguishes between memories used to act on, and those used for narration. Memory consists of a number of separate 'headed records'. Each has a 'heading', containing elements which contribute to retrieving the 'record', much as 'key words' indicate the contents of a scientific paper. The record will contain information not in the heading; the heading may contain information not in the record, and it is the headings which are searched through when we try to remember something, as we attempt to match our 'description' of what we are looking for. Thus if we had a description 'Developmental psychologist who smoked' we would try to match this to headings such as 'Development psychologist' and 'Smoker' and if we were successful this might conjure up our records on Jean Piaget and Sigmund Freud. But if Piaget's heading lacked 'Smoker' or Freud's 'Developmental psychologist' we would not retrieve their records. In that case we would have to formulate a new description, think of a new way to search our headings.

The problem for adults seeking to recall childhood memories is, in part, that they now automatically formulate descriptions that have been useful in recalling their adult memories, for example descriptions such as 'Coronation' or 'Feelings of patriotism' or of 'anti-monarchism'. These may conjure up all sorts of records but would not be part of the heading which at the age of 2 I linked to my special socks. The young child's headings (Socks, Looking Nice, Something Special Going On, Being Admired) come less readily to the adult as potentially useful cues, and no doubt are now inadequate in so far as there have been so many subsequent years with occasional Socks, Looking Nice and Being Admired events to have records of. The headed record which the young child used to interpret the world and guide action is not an efficient tool for much later narration by the adult, nor is it efficient for the child who has little practice of being a narrator and is being interrogated by an adult, particularly if that adult uses open-ended questions ('What did you do in school today') rather than more specific ones which suggest a useful heading ('Who nearly caught Peter Rabbit in his garden?'). The whole process of communicating what one remembers may become quite emotionally fraught. My daughter and I had a long conversation when she was 3½ trying to select the videotape she wanted to watch. She initially listed the following distinctive features: 'he's in the snow, there's a monster, there's a robber lady'. I considered these cues, and offered *The Snow Queen* which has snow, robbers and some odd if not monstrous characters; this was turned down. So were *Toad's Winter Sports* (snow, wicked weasels who steal Toad's snow goggles) and *The Snowman* (snow but no other relevant features). These were very firmly rejected, and a further cue offered: 'the robber lady steals some bananas'. I am afraid my reaction was 'we haven't got a tape like that, you've got it mixed up', and the discussion got so fraught we had to look at every tape in her collection and identify what was in it. This exhaustive search produced what she wanted: a tape on which two Charlie Chaplin films were recorded: *The Gold Rush* (he's in the snow, there's a monster in the shape of wicked prospectors in enveloping furs threatening the little tramp's life), and *Modern Times* (the waif steals bananas to feed her orphaned sibs). Anne's memories of the tape were correct, but her headings were not accessible to an adult, who was in any case operating on the assumption that the headings might be slightly wrong, an assumption probably all too commonly made by adults.

Schneider and Körkel (1989) link memory to the general store of knowledge relevant to the domain in question, and suggest that the latter is the more important determinant of recall. Brainerd, Kingma and Howe (1985) point out that an asymmetry between forgetting and acquisition characterises memory in both childhood and adulthood, even on memory tasks less embedded in the subjects' daily lives. They argue that acquisition and forgetting processes seem to obey different laws and to develop partially independently. Retrieval processes are more problematic for the young and for learning-disabled children (Howe *et al.* 1985, Howe *et al.* 1989). This description may account for problems in memory for events in early childhood.

## CHILDREN'S REASONING

There is an enormous literature on 'reasoning' in general and on children's reasoning in particular. Exactly what 'reasoning' is taken to be varies. 'Going beyond the information given' (Bruner 1957) or 'searching through a problem space' (Newell and Simon 1972) are wide definitions, while other writers centre their attention on, for example, induction of a rule from an initial set of assertions (Wason and Johnson-Laird 1972) or deduction from an initial general and abstract rule to the particular case (Holyoak and Nisbett 1988). Galotti (1989) proposes a definition which takes the middle ground: reasoning is

> mental activity that consists of transforming given information (called the set of premises) in order to reach conclusions. This activity must be focused on at least one goal (but may be focused on more than one). The activity must not be inconsistent with systems of logic when all of the premises are fully specified, although there may not always be an applicable system of logic to govern specific instances of reasoning. The activity may or may not be self-contained; that is, people may implicitly or explicitly add to, subtract from, or otherwise modify any or all of the premises supplied. When original premises are modified, the final conclusions must be consistent with the modified premises. The activity may, but need not, involve the breaking of mental set. The conclusions may, but need not, be startling or nonobvious at the outset of the activity. The conclusion may, but need not, be deductively valid.
>
> (Galotti 1989: 333)

This definition would include solving syllogisms, assessing probabilities, doing analogical reasoning tasks, and similar laboratory or psychometric problems; it would also include many more 'everyday' tasks such as evaluating arguments, testing hypotheses, and deciding between the balance of merits of two different soap powders, places to go on holiday, or economic policies. (It excludes one-step mental processes such as simple memory retrieval, 'gut reactions' or flashes of insight.) Galotti is very much interested in the relationship between 'formal reasoning', and 'everyday reasoning'. Formal reasoning is used in certain domains and problems; all the premises are supplied, there is only one correct answer, there are rules about how to move from premises to answer (including the rule that no information should be added to or subtracted from the premises, which are taken as read) (see Smith *et al.* (1992) on the psychological reality of rules of reasoning); such reasoning seems to be a somewhat artificial and abstract activity (cf. Braine and Rumain 1983). On the one hand, 'everyday reasoning' uses less specified information, can reach a more open-ended range of goals, and is typically far more embedded in one's normal context of interests and values. Developmentally, the latter seems to emerge much earlier than the former, which is what we will concentrate on here.

Braine and Rumain summarise a substantial amount of work on propositional logic and predicate logic and suggest a considerable resemblance between the reasoning of children just entering school and the reasoning of older children and adults. Even very young children find some logical problems very easy, and those which they find hard tend to be solved incorrectly or inefficiently even by adults. Children and adults make the same sort of errors. Premises are often inadvertently altered, for example 'All *A* are *B*' is taken as meaning that *A* and *B* are identical, so that 'All *B* are *A*'; world knowledge is allowed to intrude, sometimes helpfully, sometimes damagingly; negative premises, such as 'No *B* are *A*', are dealt with less successfully. Some of the possible interpretations of a premiss, and some of the ways of combining premises, may not be thought of, particularly if to do so would mean allowing contradiction of one's initial beliefs. Reasoning is subject to a 'confirmation bias' (Wason 1977), and reasoners are often over-confident about the reliability and validity of their judgements, a failing which may be associated with their tendency to draw firm incorrect conclusions to logical problems which have no deductively valid conclusion (Baron 1985, 1988). Despite these general similarities between young children and older people, at least in schooled cultures, skill in formal reasoning increases over the school years. Young children are more likely to use 'pragmatic processing' (Bucci 1978) in reasoning about logical problems, that is, to determine meaning using facts they knew previously about the domain rather than restricting their interpretation to the grammatical relations between the words used in the premises. Thus they may reason more accurately on fantasy-content problems than on problems where they know about the domain (Hawkins *et al.* 1984). They are also more likely to define terms within the problem incorrectly, for example misunderstanding 'some', 'more', and 'less' (as Piaget pointed out long ago).

In particular, children are likely to take 'If *A*, then *B*' as also meaning 'If *B*, then *A*', the biconditionality problem in syllogisms (Russell 1978, 1982). Children may also develop an increased awareness that there may be not one possible solution to a given problem but more than one, or no valid solution at all (Acredolo and Horobin 1987, Braine and Rumain 1983, Johnson-Laird *et al.* 1986); this may perhaps be because of a developmental trend towards more exhaustive processing and the avoidance of premature conclusions, or perhaps because of increasing recognition of multiple possibilities and ambiguity. Developmental increases in working memory or short-term storage space (Case 1985) might underlie these improvements, if indeed these increases actually happen (see section on memory earlier in this chapter): as the cross-cultural evidence suggests that literacy or schooling, or both, may be necessary for competence in formal reasoning problems (Laboratory of Comparative Human Cognition 1983, Olson and Torrance 1983), the goals and comprehension skills of the reasoner may be more important. A number of school programmes have sought to teach reasoning, with some success (Coles and Robinson 1989, Resnick 1987b, and see section on teaching thinking later in this volume).

### Children's analogical reasoning

It has been suggested (e.g. Bryant 1974, Crisafi and Brown 1986, Siegler 1989b, Sternberg 1985, Vosniadou and Ortony 1989) that the use of analogy is both the core of intelligent cognition and one of the most important mechanisms of cognitive development. Analogical reasoning is seen as critical in bringing existing knowledge and skills to bear on new information and tasks, as central to the processes of learning and transfer and to the construction of mental models. It facilitates cognitive development by allowing poorly understood situations to be reconceptualised in terms of better understood ones, both in the course of cognitive development and in the course of any novice's becoming expert in a domain. Using analogies appropriately is thus believed to be definitively intelligent. It is also a skill whose development in the child has been studied with somewhat different conclusions being drawn.

Exactly what 'analogy' is and is not remains a matter of debate. Most researchers agree that it is a 'fuzzy concept' (De Jong 1989), but it would seem that essentially it involves a correspondence between two things (or subject areas) which are alike not so much in themselves as in the relations between two or more elements, attributes, properties and effects. The familiar examples from so many tests of intelligence and reasoning illustrate the classic Aristotelian type: 'cat is to kitten as dog is to (puppy, kid, collar)'. Metaphors (Glucksberg and Keysar 1990) may use analogy to offer the possibility of understanding one thing in terms of another: 'Shall I compare thee to a summer's day?'; No, because you are more lovely, yes, because your beauty is similarly vulnerable to time and rough weather as the day's is, but it can (like the day's) be immortalised by a poet's praise. Similarly, in the analogy which compares atomic structure to the solar system, the relationship between sun and planets in the forces acting between them and in size and movement relative to each other is transferred to the atomic nucleus and the electrons: enormously different in scale but taken as similar in their relations. Analogy may also be used in problem-solving tasks (e.g. Johnson-Laird and Wason 1977), where a solution worked out for one problem can be extrapolated to another where the relational structure is the same. The classic example is Duncker's radiation problem: the patient has an inoperable malignant tumour which could be destroyed by massive radiation focused on it, but healthy tissue around it should not be damaged. The analogous (and previously solved) problem involves getting attacking forces to an enemy citadel whose approach roads are defended against major (but not minor) forces; this is done by splitting up the army and sending parties of soldiers too small to set off the defences along each of the roads that converge on the fortress. Similarly, the tumour deep in the body can be attacked by converging many narrow and weak rays on it so that only there at the tumour is the radiation strong enough to destroy tissue.

Much of cognition and learning depends on identifying the relevant knowledge which the learner already has in existing memory so that this knowledge can be used as a starting-point for learning what is new. Having no starting-point, or an unnecessarily distant one, or a starting-point from which one sets off in the wrong direction, will hamper learning and reasoning; so will an unwillingness to deal with a starting-point from which the end-point is not obviously within reach. Finding, using and evaluating analogies may therefore be one of the most important aspects of successful cognition. At least three sorts of processes are involved: finding an appropriate source domain to provide the basic analogy; mapping some of the information we have about the source domain on to the elements of the target domain; and producing from the success or otherwise of this new mapping a new representation of the target domain (which may in its turn have implications for how the source domain is represented in future). Various papers in Vosniadou and Ortony (1989) present models of the stages of analogical reasoning. Rumelhart (1989), for example, discusses how the 'parallel distributed processing' mechanism, which he believes the human mind to be, would cope with reasoning by similarity and analogy. Anderson and Thompson (1989) and Gentner (1989) present 'structure-mapping' computer simulations of the mapping stage and less thoroughly instantiated accounts of the other stages. Johnson-Laird (1989) argues that analogies vary more than the purely 'structure-mapping' models allow, and in particular that the computational models cannot account for profound and creative analogies. He insists that analogies cannot rest entirely in structural relationships; rather, matters of fact and meaning must also be taken into account. These semantic considerations will be crucial at the point when the relationships which *could* be mapped from source to target have to be evaluated. Thus the more knowledge individuals have of the source and target domains the more likely they are to find and use appropriate analogies. Knowledge may be an essential prerequisite for creativity (see Chapter 3 this volume), and for the intelligent use of analogies. This is an important point for developmental studies of analogical reasoning and I will return to it later.

Researchers from a number of theoretical backgrounds have studied children's analogical reasoning; Goswami (1991) provides a very useful review. A large number of studies, including Piaget's work and experiments by various Piagetians, suggested that pre-adolescents were unable to reason by analogy because it was only during adolescence that an ability to recognise and reason about 'higher order' relations was developed. Thus 9-year-olds were unable to solve analogies such as 'Bird is to air as fish is to?', while 12-year-olds and 15-year-olds were quite successful (Levinson and Carpenter 1974). However Levinson and Carpenter also demonstrated both that the younger children could solve what they called 'quasi-analogies' such as 'A bird uses air, a fish uses ?' and that there was a transfer effect in that children who were given quasi-analogies first and true analogies second solved more of these analogies at all ages. Thus making the relevant relation between the elements and the nature of the analogical exercise improved performance significantly. Recent work by Brown and her colleagues (1989, Crisafi and Brown 1986, Goswami and Brown 1990b) has shown that young children may use analogy to solve problems particularly well if a causal principle which they understand is involved. Children as young as 3 or 4 could solve problems such as 'instant coffee granules is to mug of coffee as soap power is to soapy water', or 'half circle is to half rectangle as quarter circle is to quarter rectangle' (Goswami 1991). Again, there was positive transfer if the child had previously solved analogous problems, and performance was enhanced if the principles common to the problems were highlighted by explicit discussion or if children had to recount the story in which a problem was solved to another person before they went on to a new problem which could be solved analogically. This work shows that children can solve classical analogies and problem-solving analogies well before adolescence, if they understand the nature of the task and the relations on which the analogies are based. They can do this even when the target and source are not obviously similar perceptually. This success is contrary to the long-held theory that young children are 'perceptually-bound'. It was for a long time assumed that transfer and analogy occurred most readily when the perceptual characteristics – shape, colour, size and so forth – are identical in the situations involved, and that such perceptual identify was a *sine qua non* for young children. Gentner (1988, 1989) suggested that 'surface' similarity, that is, similarity based on perceptually similar attributes, is the basis for young children's analogical solution strategies, and is superseded by 'relational' similarity in which surface appearance is no longer important and higher-order relations are preferred. (This would no doubt be analogous to the characteristic-to-defining shift in children's use of the properties of concept members which Keil (1989) suggested.) Among Gentner's evidence for this use of perceptual similarity were two studies (Gentner and Toupin 1986). In one children who were told a story about animals such as a chipmunk, a robin and a horse were more willing to transfer the story to perceptually similar animals such as squirrel, bluebird and zebra than to dissimilar ones (elephant, shark and cricket), In another, children preferred attribute-based similes such as 'soap-suds are like whipped cream' to relational ones, such as 'a cloud is like a sponge'. Brown (1989) argues that physical similarity of stimuli, problem and situations is indeed an important criterion for whether children consider them to be alike, either as members of a concept or as material for analogies and metaphors, but it is also important for adults. Given the right circumstances, children too can override perceptual similarity and go beyond it. She proposes that children rely on appearance as a fall-back option when there is no other basis for them to use. That is, children are not perceptually-bound, but, like adults, they organise their experience on the basis of appearance if they have no other theory about how it should be organised. Lacking knowledge, they are forced back on surface perceptual similarities, and may fail to transfer an appropriate solution from one situation to another because it does not look sufficiently similar. Lack of knowledge may prevent them finding relational similarities or even noticing ones that are presented unless they are strongly highlighted by discussion, repetition or other emphasis. The traditional ways of investigating children's analogical reasoning did not contain these facilitating conditions, the experimenter never giving any indication that transfer might be appropriate. Children are faced with what might well be a 'now for something completely different' experience, and so treat each test as a new one. This may be a problem which spreads beyond analogy-finding. Karmiloff-Smith (1988) suggests that children may treat successive instances in her block-balancing task as being independent problems, working out how to balance each successive block *de novo*. Such behaviour would make transfer and analogy-finding much less likely, but it may not be entirely inappropriate for beginning learners, who do not have enough experience and knowledge to link successive experiences appropriately, to proceed instance by instance rather than by carrying through one solution too optimistically to the next problem. Children's willingness to make analogies when they know the course and target domains and when they understand the relational principles involved makes a telling contrast with their failure on abstracted artificial tasks. Perhaps a certain amount of knowledge is required before any deliberate use of similar content or structure can contribute to analogical reasoning.

I will point out here, parenthetically, that an interesting case has recently been made that an innate drive for 'coherence' and a high level cognitive mechanism for producing it are at the heart of human cognition, and that 'autism' is caused by a failure to develop the latter. Uta Frith (1990) argues that the central cause of autism is a physiologically-based inability to see and develop coherence between different but analogous events and rules. The autistic person cannot 'see the wood for the trees', each of which is uncontrollably novel, mysterious and demanding. This handicap leads to characteristic behaviours such as the compulsive ordering of objects into rigid patterns, facility in analysing complex shapes into the components and failure in synthesising them into a reassembly, repetitive and stereotyped language which does not develop into the normal give and take and implicitness of conversation, absence of pretend play, and a failure to develop a 'theory of mind' (see the last section of this chapter). A full consideration of autism and of Frith's account of it is outside the scope of this volume, but this view does provide an interesting sidelight on analogy in normal cognition, suggesting that it is indeed central and has effects on many different cognitive areas.

Reviewing the literature on the development of analogical reasoning, then, it would seem that even pre-school children can display analogical reasoning in both Aristotelian analogies and in story problems *if* they understand the sort of relations on which the analogies are based (Brown 1989, Goswami 1991), though they may not display it unless given hints or instructions which highlight the underlying relations. Older children and adults are more likely to show analogical reasoning even without supportive conditions, though as both the classic and the modern problem-solving literature show, they may need hints to succeed in analogy tasks (e.g. Holyoak and Nisbett 1988, Johnson-Laird and Wason 1977). This difference in the facility of analogical reasoning might be associated with differences in the development of the conceptual bases of source and target domains (Vosniadou and Ortony 1989), or to differences in metacognitive skills which mean that young children cannot yet consciously reflect on the nature of analogy or analogical reasoning strategies (Goswami 1991). These two possibilities are not mutually exclusive, and neither is adequately documented. They need to be linked to the points made at the beginning of this section about the successive processes involved in using analogies.

The developmental literature and the traditional test paradigms centre on understanding (or even perhaps merely recognising) an analogical relation set up by the tester, and have much less to do with finding an appropriate source domain for a particular target domain, let alone creating new domain representations or evaluating analogies. They do not go far beyond the 'structure-mapping' focus which Johnson-Laird (1989) criticises. To elucidate the development of this wider range of analogical reasoning it may be necessary to search the literature on language development for instances of child-generated analogies, and for the ways in which adults present analogies to help children structure new information, as in the 'links' and 'world links' which mothers present to their 2-year-olds (Meadows and Mills 1987, Mills and Funnell 1983, Chapter 5 this volume).

## CHILDREN'S USE OF METAPHORS

Metaphorical language (such as 'Anne is a flowerbud') has been of interest to philosophers, students of rhetoric and of literature, and psychologists from Aristotle onwards. Exactly how it works is still a matter of debate. A *topic* ('Anne') is linked with a *vehicle* (a 'flowerbud') by an implicit unstated relation (the *ground*), so that the statement is literally false but figuratively true. Aristotle concentrated on metaphor as an implicit comparison between the topic and the vehicle which conveyed some sort of esoteric poetic or rhetorical truth through the analogy it set up. Another view is that the vehicle is simply an ornamental substitute for literal language, such as 'Anne is young and beautiful and will be still more beautiful when she grows up.' A richer description is that the topic and the vehicle interact so that *each* acquires some of the constellation of meaning of the other: Anne's youth, tenderness, vulnerability and potential unfolding are emphasised, and flowerbuds become more associated with brightness, liveliness and freshness, and with the need for protection. Metaphor allows the reinterpretation of topic and vehicle in terms of each other, thus extending their meaning. This is the view of metaphor which I find most useful. It involves the use of some perceptible similarity between topic and vehicle (a sentence like 'Anne is a tin of baked beans' might be a metaphor if the child was particularly cylindrical in shape or ate nothing else, perhaps, but is otherwise anomalous), and they must belong to different conventional categories ('Anne is a pretty baby' is not a metaphor but a literal (if bald) statement). Many metaphors have become absorbed into language (or 'frozen') so that their non-literal origins are no longer obvious: the sentence 'Anne is sweet' is not literally true, though we have no difficulty in perceiving its intended meaning as directly as if it were. Metaphors must also be distinguished from other non-literal sorts of language such as sarcasm and hyperbole ('Anne is the most beautiful thing in the world') and analysts of language have traditionally distinguished them from similes ('Anne is *like* a flowerbud') where the fact that a comparison is being made is explicitly indicated.

The remarks I have just made about the characteristics of metaphor should suggest that they are not linguistically or psychologically altogether straightforward. I want to draw two points from this before I describe the literature on children's use of metaphors. The first is to raise the question of why we use metaphors if they are so complex and so problematic. While they can have a number of simple functions such as avoiding undue repetition ('Anne is a flowerbud, a treasure, a peach, an enchantress, a honey, an angel') three major functions suggest themselves. They may allow the expression of ideas which the speaker could not otherwise express because his or her language lacks suitable terms. English uses temperature-linked terms ('hot-blooded', 'a cold fish', 'a sunny temperament') to describe personality traits, for example, and wine buffs have imported phrases from other semantic areas to describe the nuances of their gustatory experiences. This function is obviously an interesting one developmentally since children, comparatively lacking in specialist literal terminology, might resort to metaphor to express their meaning (we will examine this possibility later). A second major function of metaphors is their communicative compactness: all the applicable characteristics of the vehicle are implied through the naming of the vehicle itself and do not have to be listed. Conversely, of course, a metaphor may suggest the application of inappropriate character-istics and so be misleading or disturbing or incomprehensible. One example from the research literature, 'hair is like spaghetti' (Billow 1975, 1981) seems to me to run into this problem (besides being a simile, not a metaphor). The third important function of metaphors which I want to raise is perhaps a consequence of their usefulness for expressing the inexpressible and for conveying meaning compactly. This function is the use of metaphorical models drawn from one domain to facilitate our understanding of another: we have tried to understand brains in terms of computers, for example (see Chapter 4 this volume, and Boden 1987), or to understand the polity in terms of a body ('the head of state', 'communism/Fascism/materialism/liberalism/political apathy is a cancer in the body politic'). Such metaphori-cal 'mental models' as these are widespread and may be our normal way of getting a grasp on highly complex subject-matter (Johnson-Laird 1983 and see my discussion of analogy elsewhere in this chapter). They can of course get us into trouble if we breach the applicability of the vehicle by transferring its inappropriate qualities to the topic, or if we forget that it is a metaphor that is involved, not a literal description. It may be necessary to look at what we understand to be the limits and the strengths of a particular metaphor as well as of metaphor in general. What is and what is not a metaphor may also be ill-defined and disagreements may arise. These may be particularly acute when *children's* use of metaphor is being discussed.

Even pre-school children produce utterances which look like metaphors or similes (see e.g. Billow 1981). Piaget (1962) recorded his daughter Jacqueline, aged between 3 and 4, saying that a winding river 'is like a snake' and a caddis worm in its stone coat in a stream 'is an insect in its cage'. He did not believe that utterances like these are true metaphors, however. Essentially this was because he believed that such young children think in 'preconcepts' based on symbolic images and action schemas and not in terms of true concepts 'defined by the objective qualities of the objects themselves'. Metaphor involves a deliberate violation of concept boundar-ies; as Piagetian young children lack the concepts they cannot violate them and produce true metaphor. Recent work (see my discussion of concepts elsewhere in this chapter) suggests both that young children do have an ability to classify items into conceptual groupings with clear boundaries based on similarity and contrast, and that not all concepts fit the classic type which Piaget centres on. Thus his dismissal of early 'proto-metaphorical' utterances is not sound: very young children are able to construct systematic classes and thus may be able to make comparisons across class boundaries in the awareness that they are metaphorical. It could be argued that what changes is not the possibility of metaphor but the knowledge on which metaphor is based (Palermo 1989). Thus in a well-understood domain even 4-year-olds may understand metaphor correctly (Johnson and Pascual-Leone 1989, Waggoner and Palermo 1989).

It may, however, be difficult to distinguish between metaphor and more literal comparisons (Mandler 1983, Vosniadou 1987). My daughter aged not quite 2 watched her tights being put on, the flaccid pale pink woolly length swelling out as her leg went down it, grinned with delight and said 'Pink balloon'. Should she be credited with a metaphor or only with a sharp bit of observation? A child (or indeed an adult) may use a term not normally applied to an object to pick out a perceptual similarity without necessarily intending a metaphor, as in some of the 'overextensions' discussed in the literature on early language development, or as in pretend play where objects are renamed in terms that suit their role in the 'pretend': a chair is renamed 'my castle', is used as a castle and in a sense 'becomes' a castle. Metaphor requires a marking of perceptual similarity between objects from different conventional categories in a non-literal comparison (Vosniadou 1987: 874). Its development is probably associated with the development of classification skills and of symbolic play. Evidence from children's spontaneous productions needs to be supplemented by their response to production tasks and comprehension problems.

In one study, Vosniadou and Ortony (1983) asked children aged 3 to 6 to choose between pairs of statements in a comparison task ('A is like X') or a categorisation task ('A is the same kind of thing as X'). In the categorisation task the pair contained a metaphor and a literal statement, such as 'Rain is the same kind of thing as tears' and 'Rain is the same kind of thing as snow'. Children over 4 selected 'Rain is the same kind of thing as snow' as the better alternative significantly above chance level. In the comparison task they chose the better of all three pairings of a metaphorical statement (e.g. 'Rain is like tears'), a literal statement ('Rain is like snow') and an anomalous statement ('Rain is like a chair'). Even 3-year-old children chose this last nonsensical statement least, and there was no preference for literal or metaphorical statements as comparisons. These results (since replicated several times) suggest that an early distinction was made between comparisons that made no sense and comparisons that picked up similarity, and that by the age of 4 literal and non-literal similarity were beginning to be distinguished as possible bases for comparison and categorisation. Vosniadou regards this latter distinction as analogous to the appearance-reality distinction investigated by Flavell and his colleagues (Flavell 1986, 1988, Flavell *et al.* 1986 and see the section on 'theory of mind' later in this chapter).

Tests of children's comprehension have produced conflicting results: success by pre-school children in work by Gardner (1974), Gentner (1977), and Waggoner and Palermo (1989), or even babies (Marks *et al.* 1987), failure by children younger than 14 (Winner *et al.* 1976). One source of the differences was the use of different tasks. Gardner's young subjects were asked to match adjectives to items from the same domain, for example 'quiet' and 'loud' to sounds differing in volume, and also to other domains such as colours and faces, where sound words might be used metaphorically (grey is a 'quiet' colour, scarlet a 'loud' one). Winner *et al.* asked for paraphrase or explanation of sentences such as 'The prison guard was a hard rock', or 'Summer's blood is ripe blackberries'. The differences between such tasks makes comparison of results difficult, though it does make conspicuous something that some of the literature fails to emphasise, to wit that since metaphor can involve a wide range of language forms, concepts and comparisons, its successful use may not be an all or none affair but rather something which is achieved over a period of years. Failure to comprehend a metaphor may arise because of a failure to realise that an implicit comparison and not a literal one is intended, as in James Thurber's recollection of

the enchanted private world of my early boyhood . . . . In this world, businessmen who phoned their wives to say that they were tied up at the office sat roped to their swivel chairs, and probably gagged, unable to move or speak, except somehow, miraculously, to telephones . . . then there was the man who left town under a cloud. Sometimes I saw him all wrapped up in the cloud, and invisible . . . . At other times it floated, about the size of a sofa, three or four feet above his head, following him wherever he went . . . . There were many other wonderful figures in the secret, surrealist landscapes of my youth: the old lady who was always up in the air, the husband who did not seem to be able to put his foot down, the man who lost his head during a fire but was still able to run out of the house yelling, the young lady who was, in reality, a soiled dove.

(Thurber 1953: 23-4)

Another source of failure would be to fail to see the similarity between the metaphorical vehicle and the topic (this is my problem with 'summer's blood is ripe blackberries', where colour, function, location and every other perceptual and conceptual characteristic seem incongruent). Finally, if the comprehension test involves explanation or paraphrase the subject may understand the metaphor but be unable to produce an adequate verbal account (Palermo (1989) discusses this). Tasks and materials appropriate to the child's linguistic powers and knowledge level are needed if metaphorical competence is to be correctly diagnosed.

Recent work has established that very young children show understanding of some metaphors (Mandler 1983, Ortony 1988, Vosniadou 1987), mainly those where topic and vehicle come from fields the child already knows about as distinct domains; children's ability to understand metaphorical language improves considerably during the primary school years. Vosniadou (1987) discusses the variables that affect the comprehension of metaphor. These include the linguistic input, the available context and the child's knowledge base, metacognitive abilities and linguistic skills. Knowledge and understanding interact. A metaphor cannot be properly understood if the relevant conceptual areas are not known about. Which attributes of a vehicle are transferred to the topic may obey some basic conceptual constraints (Carey and Gelman 1991, Keil 1979, Markman 1990). For example, Vosniadou and Ortony told children stories containing an analogy from a more familiar to a less familiar domain; in one the white blood cells (the topic) fighting an infection were compared to soldiers (the vehicle). The children correctly concluded that the white blood cells kill germs but not that they wear uniforms or use guns; but they also attributed human emotions to the blood cells, supposing that they thought the germs were bad and felt frightened while fighting them (Vosniadou 1987: 881). They were not willing to attribute blood cell characteristics to human soldiers, an asymmetry of attribution which Susan Carey also found in children's generalisations about biological characteristics (Carey 1985).

It has, finally, been argued, as I said earlier, that we can usefully employ metaphors drawn from a well-understood area to understand a newer, less familiar, one (Goswami 1991, Johnson-Laird 1983). Knowledge acquisition may require the use of metaphor and analogy, using the existing model of one subject to understand another subject, 'Knowing that they are not quite the same things but slowly figuring out the full range of their differences' (Vosniadou 1987: 882). A conscious and sceptical use of metaphor and analogy may be one of the sources of cognitive development.

## METACOGNITION

'Metacognition refers to one's knowledge and control of the domain of cognition' (Brown *et al.* 1983: 106): 'metacognition refers to cognitions about cognitions or the executive decision-making process in which the individual must both carry out cognitive operations and oversee his or her progress' (Meichenbaum *et al.* 1985: 4–5). It is one's awareness of one's own cognitive machinery and how it works, both in general and at the particular moment. It involves many basic 'on line' metacognitive processes, including: analysing and defining the character of the problem at hand; reflecting upon one's own knowledge (and lack of knowledge) that may be required to solve the problem; devising a plan for attacking the problem; checking and monitoring how the plan helps in the problem-solving; revising plan (and perhaps the analysis of the problem) in the light of this monitoring; checking any solution reached; and, generally, orchestrating cognitive processes in relation to the cognitive contents and objectives involved, in the service of whatever is one's goal. It includes a range of somewhat diverse psychological contents. Among them would be: awareness of present cognitive and cognitive-emotional states, for example that one has understood, that one had forgotten some necessary information, that one was finding this all rather easy, at the present moment; knowledge about the particular task and its difficulties, and of one's own skills in general and in relation to this task (for example that in order to star in a production of *Hamlet* it is necessary to memorise the part, and that this is difficult because there are many words and you know that you find verbatim memory hard, though getting the gist of something is easy for you, so special strategies will have to be thought of and they can't include writing out the words on your shirt-sleeve because Hamlet will be dressed in black); regulation of the execution of cognitive processes such as those listed in the first paragraph of this section; and, importantly, linking the present metacognitive episode with others in the past, so building up a coherent model of oneself as a cognitive person, which is likely to have a significant influence on one's approach to future occasions in which metacognition is involved. A possible mechanism, linking cognition, emotion and personality here, is attribution of credit or blame for success or failure between one's own skill, one's effort, task variables and extraneous conditions (see Hewstone 1989 for discussion of the social psychology of attribution).

In the early 1980s metacognition took a prominent place in discussion of cognition and cognitive development. This was surely in part the result of the growth of information-processing work, where many theorists gave a central status to metacognitive or executive processes. Sternberg's work on intelligence, for example (Sternberg 1985, Chapter 4 this volume) identified 'metacomponents', a number of key, fast acting, decision processes, as an important part of all knowledge acquisition and problem-solving. Case (1985) suggests that one of the three basic types of cognitive building blocks is 'executive schemes', which choose and monitor strategies and deal with their results. The later Piagetian model, too, emphasises cognitive development's roots in what could be called 'metacognition': both Piaget's account of the role of contradiction between schemes of thought and of conflict between different judgements by peers with different viewpoints, and his work on 'reflective abstraction', a sort of pondering about cognition, suggest that awareness and control of thought are important contributors to its development. Research on metacognition has looked at its role in memory (e.g. Kail 1984, Kreutzer *et al.* 1975), reading (e.g. Meyers and Paris 1978), communication (e.g. Markman 1977, Robinson 1983) and other areas (for a useful overall review see Brown *et al.* 1983). Some discussion of its role in these areas appears in those sections of this chapter which takes them as their central topic (e.g. reading). Here, I will focus mainly on some issues common to most metacognition.

The first is the nature of metacognitive experience, the awareness children have of their own cognitive processes. When do children know that they don't know something? What effect does such an experience have? When do they begin to have a notion of themselves as persons with particular cognitive abilities? Where does relevant experience come from? These are real questions, but not ones to which there is a coherent answer. It is clear that even very young children have an awareness of an intended outcome and of whether it is achieved or not: their pleasure or frustration can be very visible (e.g. see Dunn 1988, Kagan 1984). Such awareness obviously does not always bring with it awareness of exactly what is wrong, nor is it always a lasting awareness. Similarly in later thought, children might be expected to be aware that there is a contradiction without knowing what to do about it, and without being able to take appropriate action (Piaget, 1978a and 1978b). However, Piaget's position was that such awareness of an incipient or unsolved problem was unsettling for you, whether it was a contradiction between two of your own ideas or a conflict between one of yours and one of a peer's, and this 'disequilibrium' acted as a pressure towards advances in cognitive development. This is not always a trouble-free progress, since, as we shall see, diagnosing that there is a problem is only the first step in the long path to solving it.

An experiment by Karmiloff-Smith and Inhelder (1974/5) illustrates the usefulness of having a theory, which requires a high level of metacognitive activity, in progressing towards a solution to a problem. They gave children aged from 4 to 9 the problem of balancing blocks of wood on a narrow bar. Some were simple uniform slabs which balanced at the geometric centre, some had a less regular shape, with a conspicuous bar on one end, others had a heavy weight hidden in one end of an apparently uniform block. The children's simplest strategy was to use physical trial and error, nudging the blocks and rectifying any tilt until they found the balancing point; this was slow but successful for all blocks in the end. This purely 'suck it and see' strategy was, however, supplanted by simple theories which worked for some blocks and not for others. One such was to put the block with its geometric centre over the bar, which was successful for uniform blocks but not for those with an uneven distribution of weight. These latter were dealt with by nudging or by an alternative simple theory, so that the child operated two juxtaposed theories without co-ordinating them. Constructing a higher level procedure, which integrated the simpler theories and left no exceptions, was slow and costly in that it gave rise, while being developed, to more errors than its predecessors had done. Simple theories worked perfectly, though with a limited range of blocks; those blocks the theory couldn't cover were set aside as 'impossible to balance', until there was an intolerably large number of exceptions. Kuhn (1962) and other philosophers of science have observed that advance in scientific theory often is achieved in a similarly slow and painful way. Instances which cannot be dealt with by a theory are discounted or hived off; at best the theory is tinkered with to cover them, thus losing its coherence as it is stretched and patched to fit. Only with reluctance is it given up in favour of a new and better theory, perhaps when the results of metacognitive monitoring are too blatant to be ignored any longer.

For scientists, and for children developing metacognitive awareness, disagreement with peers has been suggested as a source of metacognitive conflict and hence metacognitive advance. Conflict with peers was one of the few social factors behind cognitive development which Piaget focused on (Piaget 1983). Experiments by Genevans such as Doise and his colleagues (e.g. Doise 1985, Doise and Mugny 1984, elsewhere in this volume) address this area.

## TRANSFER

When we first learn or develop a skill it is often closely tied to the original situation we used it in, and we may have difficulty using the skill in a different situation. At least one child has been able to add large numbers correctly and easily when the sums concerned her pocket money, but has been seen to have much more difficulty when the same numbers were involved in ordinary content-free two-digit addition sums (Siegler 1986). Or a new task may require a new composite skill in which older skills and knowledge have to be recombined in novel ways. As Brown *et al.* (1983: 142) say,

> development consists in part of going from the context-dependent state where resources are welded to the original learning situation to a *relatively* context-independent state where the learner extends the ways in which initially highly constrained knowledge and procedures are used.

How do we make this move? How do we transfer knowledge from the situation where we first learned it to other relevant situations? What are the cognitive processes involved in bringing the results of past experience to bear on our present tasks? How do we learn to learn? Do individuals differ in their ability to transfer knowledge appropriately? Questions such as these, on the nature of 'transfer', are a crucial part of the study of the development and acquisition of cognition, and have enormous educational importance.

Gick and Holyoak (1987) provide a useful review of the cognitive psychology of transfer. The classic study of transfer compares the performance of a test task by people with prior experience of a related task and people who have no such prior experience. If the group with related experience do better than the no-experience control group, it is said that there is 'positive transfer' from the prior task to the related test task. If they do worse, there is 'negative transfer'; the knowledge they have of the prior task has interfered with their performance of the test task. In a related type of study, people may be tested for the effect of earlier learning on tasks which are related to their earlier experience in different ways, highly similar or more distantly analogous, for example. In this sort of study it may be possible to identify what was learned about the first task and what inferences are carried forward to the new one, and thus to address questions of how general or how specific transfer is and to diagnose what has gone wrong in cases of negative transfer or failure to transfer.

'Transfer' concerns the use of prior knowledge in new situations; thus we need to consider how knowledge and situations are represented. As I discuss elsewhere in this chapter, there are considerable theoretical complexities about how we represent the knowledge we have learned. However, for our present purposes it is useful to adopt the information-processing approach (e.g. Anderson 1983, Holland *et al.* 1986) and assume that knowledge of concepts and procedures is represented as clusters or networks of 'production rules', for example, '*if* something is a furry animal which barks, *then* it is probably a dog', and '*if* something is a dog *then* it should be approached cautiously as it may bite.' We can apply, or transfer, such rules to new possible instances. Small children's vocabulary learning provides many examples (see e.g. Mervis 1987). Gick and Holyoak (1987) suggest that 'overgeneralisation' and 'undergeneralisation' are transfer mistakes; for example a small child whose rule was 'if something is small and has a tail, then it is called "doggie" ' would overgeneralise to a cat, 'a sort of negative transfer', and fail to transfer (or undergeneralise) to a large dog such as a Great Dane. This analysis suggests that failure to transfer may be due to having an inappropriate restriction in the initial rule (in this example dogs are labelled as 'small', which is not always the case), and negative transfer may be due to lack of appropriate restrictions that would show that there should be no transfer to the new instance (in this case an extra condition that would differentiate dogs from other furry animals; 'barks' might be such a condition). Both the existence of such rules and their strength will be relevant to how they are involved in transfer.

We talked initially of transfer to 'related' or 'similar' tasks or situations. The notion of 'similarity' needs some unpacking. Sharing common features and having few different ones is part of the core of 'similarity', and the degree to which two tasks share features, the degree to which they are perceived as the same, will affect the likelihood that transfer will be attempted. If the transfer task bears a close resemblance to the prior task, it will be more likely that the prior task is remembered when the transfer task is attempted. When learning to drive a car I may comparatively often remember earlier road safety lessons but will rarely think of learning to play tennis. Shared features may however be causally related to the desired outcomes or goals to a greater or lesser degree. Attention to the actions of other road users is causally related to the desired outcome of safety for both pedestrians and drivers, and there may be positive transfer here from one to the other. However the advice to make yourself highly visible by wearing light-coloured clothing, armbands of reflective material and so forth, though valuable for pedestrians and cyclists, is less appropriate for drivers. A straight transfer here would only have a positive effect on performance (safety) when the driver was outside the car, though transfer of the abstract principle to make sure that the *vehicle* was visible would be appropriate.

'Similarity' is not just a matter of shared features, then, but involves consideration of which shared features are relevant to the prior task and to the transfer task, and in what ways. This obviously can involve calling on general knowledge or expertise. Novices in physics tasks, for example, treat problems as similar on the basis of shared features such as all involving levers or inclined planes, where experts make use of the underlying *structural* similarities which determine how the problems are best solved (Chi *et al.* 1980). The context of the tasks will also affect transfer, as in the case of the child calculating her pocket money correctly but getting more abstract sums wrong.

Gick and Holyoak (1987) summarise the relationship between similarity and transfer thus:

> The amount of transfer depends on the similarity between the two situations . . . the direction of the transfer depends on the similarity of the two responses . . . .
>
> When two situations are perceived as unrelated, no transfer occurs regardless of response similarity. When the situations are perceived as similar or identical, transfer occurs; the greater the similarity of the situations, the greater the absolute magnitude of transfer. If transfer occurs, it becomes increasingly negative as the appropriate responses become objectively more dissimilar. If the required transfer response is highly similar to the training response (many shared structural components and few distinctive ones), transfer is positive. But as the response appropriate to the transfer task becomes less similar (few shared components and many distinctive ones), overall transfer shifts to the negative side. The structural dissimilarities cause the training response, evoked by strong perceived similarity, to interfere with the new response that must be acquired for the transfer task.
>
> (Gick and Holyoak 1987: 18–19)

This account implicates memory in the possibility of transfer. Prior experience has to be remembered for there to be any possibility of transfer. Thus representation of both initial task and transfer task is important; encoding of the initial task in a way that emphasises its structure rather than superficial idiosyncratic features may be crucial. Presenting a range of varying examples for prior learning may make transfer easier than if only one prior example has been learned. Later, how the transfer task evokes earlier learning may be important: if you are unable to relate it to relevant earlier tasks, positive transfer will be less likely.

The extensive experimental literature on memory and learning provides Gick and Holyoak (1987) with useful data on transfer. Thorough learning of the prior task makes positive transfer to similar tasks more likely than a slighter degree of initial learning does, particularly if the thorough learning involves familiarisation with the rules governing the tasks. Understanding the rules may also lead to the acquisition of general abstract problem-solving strategies so that there is positive transfer to new tasks which require new responses too. Kendler and Kendler (1975), for example, gave children a learning task in which objects which were either large or small and either black or white were associated with a reward on the basis of either size or colour. Once the child had learned that, for example, black objects were always rewarded and white ones never, and size was irrelevant, the reward pattern was changed. Some children were given a 'reversal shift', so that white objects were now associated with the reward, never having been rewarded before: other children got a 'non-reversal shift', so that size became the discriminating variable for reward and colour was now irrelevant. Children over the age of about 7 who had generalised a rule rather than reacting to each individual case found the 'reversal shift' much easier. Younger children showed less positive transfer to the new task, and made more errors based on their old learning: thus they did better on the 'non-reversal shift' where their old response still gave them a success rate of about 50 per cent.

Learning and transfer of rules that are based on the important structural features of a task, not on trivial surface characteristics, will be easier if the learner encounters a range of examples with a common structure and different irrelevant characteristics. Initially variety in examples may be confusing, but if enough moderately varying examples are given the learner can increasingly infer the general principles which underlie them and transfer them to a wider range of examples. It may be best if initial examples are similar and represent typical instances of the concept or procedure, and more variable examples are given later. Including an abstract rule with the examples may also be helpful in facilitating transfer, as this too will make it more likely that enough is learned about the structure of the initial task for it to be identifiable and usable later (Resnick 1987a and 1987b).

Whether past experience gives rise to better performance in the present task will depend on whether that prior experience is thought of, and seen as relevant, at the right moment. This is more likely to happen if the goals of the new task and the old ones are seen as the same, and as capable of being brought about by the same processes. If the goal of the original task is too specialised, there may be no transfer to new tasks that appear to have different goals. School-based skills, for example, are all too often not used outside school because they are not connected to any clear goal other than 'getting school work done', and therefore won't be thought of as potentially useful when a more practical task is at hand outside school. It may thus be helpful to make it clear what sort of range of uses a particular skill or piece of knowledge may have, just as clarifying the effectiveness of an activity such as strategic memorising makes it more likely that young children will continue to use it (see memory section earlier in this chapter). Here too knowledge of results may be important.

Ann Brown and her colleagues (Brown *et al.* 1983, Campione *et al.* 1982, Ferrara *et al.* 1986) see 'transfer' as an inseparable component of learning, and as crucial in the assessment of cognitive status. They argue very strongly against the 'static' assessment of cognition, which seeks only to estimate a person's current independent cognitive achievements. One way to supplement this and discover useful information about a person's *potential* cognitive status is to assess, additionally, what can be achieved with the support of a more skilled person, which is what Vygotsky saw as the upper end of the 'zone of proximal development' (see Chapter 4). Another way we will be concerned with here is to assess how the person's present cognitive skills are transferred to new situations. Some individuals may manage little or no transfer of their skills and others a great deal, and though static assessment might have suggested they were equally competent, Brown *et al.* would argue that the latter, the ready transferrers, are in a much more favourable position cognitively: they have 'learned to learn'. The psychologist is also better off, as what is being assessed is not the hodgepodge of declarative and procedural knowledge resulting from a long, complex and unknowable history of acquisition and development, but cognitive processes in action. These may be far more illuminating about the nature of cognition and the nature of effective instruction.

In a series of experiments Brown and her colleagues have found that although groups who are different in age or ability may perform at similar levels in initial 'baseline' testing, after equal training older or more able subjects perform at a higher level than younger or less able ones, that is, they have got more benefit out of the same training input. Weak students were reluctant to transfer what they had been taught to related, novel, situations, and would only transfer to highly similar tasks. They seemed to require more explicit instructions and to learn to cope only with the particular task they had been trained on, not to take the risk of 'going beyond the information given' as stronger students would do. Brown and her colleagues argue that students should be assessed using measures of learning and transfer which focus on general rules and principles, for three reasons: first, rules and principles that have some generality within the guided instruction programme will resemble normal school learning and hence will predict students' probable school progress better than conventional intelligence tests can do; second, because measures of how well students have learned general rules and principles will diagnose their strengths and weaknesses more accurately; and third, because this improvement in diagnosis and prediction will make it easier to provide appropriate remedies where better learning and transfer are needed (Brown and Campione 1986, Ferrara *et al.* 1986). Their experimental work supports this argument. Ferrara *et al.*, for example, found that children of higher IQ needed fewer prompts to reach learning criteria and needed less assistance in transferring their learning to somewhat dissimilar tasks, that is, they learned more readily and more flexibly. Older children, similarly, did better than younger ones. Learning and transfer were still related when age and IQ were partialled out, and also occurred to similar degrees on two parallel sets of tasks, one where what had to be discovered was the rule governing a series of letters (such as NGOHPIQJ--) and the other involving a matrix completion task. Less able students showed less transfer and needed help with transfer on more similar tasks than abler students did.

It has been argued that an individual's ability to respond to instruction with learning and a flexible transfer of that learning to new tasks is a better index of future progress than static tests of general ability or initial competence. 'Readiness' to learn, too, cannot be measured simply by seeing what skills a child already can deploy, but by examining how these skills can be used or modified on the job. Ferrara's doctoral dissertation (Brown 1988) reports research that documents this assertion in children's early mathematical learning. Mathematics is a discipline in which a rich knowledge base exists and becomes perhaps increasingly important as a person's expertise increases (see Smith 1983), while tests of deductive reasoning, as used in earlier research, involve minimal prior knowledge. However, although mathematical knowledge is relevant to children's potential performance, their propensity to transfer is still extremely important in predicting their capacity to profit from instruction, and learning and transfer efficiency are the most sensitive predictors of growth in mathematical understanding.

> The data from all the experiments converge on the conclusion that if the goal is to distinguish students who are likely to do well within some area from those likely to experience difficulties, estimates of their initial response to instruction and of their ability to make use of newly acquired resources are powerful tools. They also indicate that the most diagnostic indicator is transfer performance. Insuring that new skills have been learned, even to some constant criterion across students, is no guarantee that those skills will be useful subsequently. If we want to monitor progress through a domain, it is essential that we constantly check to see if 'acquired' skills can be used flexibly, or whether they remain 'welded' or

'inert', triggered only by a relatively complete, instantiation of the context in which they were learned.

(Brown and Campione 1988)

Brown and her colleagues emphasise the role of metacognitive processes underlying individual differences in learning and transfer. They believe that students who are good at transfer are inclined to plan problem-solving approaches, seek additional information, search for and use analogies, check their reasoning, monitor their progress, engage in efficient 'fix-up' strategies when getting off track, and so forth. Poorer performers generate solutions more quickly but try them out less systematically, and when working on a new problem they are less likely to refer back to prior problems. What seems to be involved is a difference in the array of general self-regulatory skills, skills which are 'weak' in the sense that they do not guarantee success as a more specific skill might do, but can be applied to a wide range of tasks.

## PROBLEM-SOLVING

William James, in *The Principles of Psychology* (1890), elegantly defines solving a problem as a search that occurs when the means to an end do not occur simultaneously with the establishment of the end; that is, problem-solving is what you do when you work towards a goal but do not have a routine way to get there, or when an obstacle such as lack of skill or of knowledge interferes with a previously possible solution. It is thus an important cognitive activity, at least for those who do not live in a perfectly predictable world. It has been seen as critical to education, especially in mathematics and the physical sciences but also as both an index of how well a pupil has learned and an aid to learning, since active engagement in solving a problem has been regarded as providing better understanding than more passive learning would. There is therefore quite a considerable literature on problem-solving by adults, children and artificial intelligence systems (for an introduction to the last of these see Boden 1988, as it will not be dealt with here). It is clear that many cognitive processes are involved, for example those usually considered as memory, perception, transfer, analogical reasoning, deduction and so forth. In particular, as we shall see, there may be a complex interaction between strategy and declarative knowledge, whose effect may be that problem-solving is more effective in some domains than in others.

Much work on problem-solving has involved tasks like the Tower of Hanoi, in which a graduated set of discs has to be transferred from one peg to another so that they end up in the same order; during the transfer only one disc can be moved at a time, and at no time may a larger disc be placed upon a smaller one. A simple version of this task would use five discs and

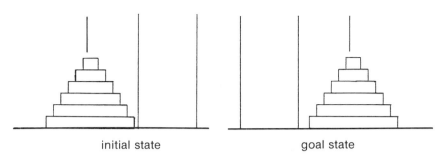

initial state                              goal state

*Figure 2.4* The Tower of Hanoi problem.

three pegs, as in Figure 2.4. More complex versions with more discs and more pegs require progressively longer solutions. Tasks like this have a clearly defined goal state and the problem as given contains all the necessary information: analysis of the problem-solver's performance looks at the successive steps taken towards the goal.

Only a limited range of possible actions are appropriate, and the problem itself strongly suggests what these are (for example it would clearly not be appropriate to seek to solve it by converting the discs into wheels for a vehicle to run from one peg to another, since only one may be moved at a time and they are of different sizes, amongst other reasons). The problem-solver is thus likely to provide comparatively easily analysed sequences of steps to the solution, including some systematic enough to be regarded as evidence of strategy use. One strategy frequently used by adults for well-defined problems is means–end analysis, selecting moves which reduce the difference between the goal state and the current state, if necessary by setting up sub-goals. Less expert problem-solvers may have less sophisticated strategies: for example a 16-month-old often successfully stacked graduated rings, largest first, on a peg, but her 'strategy' was simply to put the nearest ring on the peg first and this only led to a successful solution because her normal 'strategy' for getting the rings off the peg involved tipping them off in a line which often left the largest nearest to hand and the smallest further away. More complex problems may provide a less definite structure, such that the constraints on what can be done, what information is relevant, and even exactly what the goal is may have to be assumed or worked out during the problem-solving. More exploratory activity may be necessary (Vandenberg 1990) and problem-solving will therefore involve much more interpretation and more use of knowledge not given in the problem. Interpretation and possession of relevant knowledge may be crucial, since the solution that is proposed may depend on how the problem is represented. There is obviously a source of developmental differences here, if what the individual knows about the problem and the problem area is important, and if younger individuals know less than older ones.

Another area of developmental differences is the degree of planfulness shown by the problem-solver. My 16-month-old, in the last example, has only the crudest of plans for getting the rings on and off the peg, and the plan is inflexible. The extent to which the effects of the moves made in solving the problem are monitored may also be important, as may be limitations in memory capacity. It is harder to solve problems which require thinking many moves ahead or backtracking, for example.

Information processing analyses of problem-solving suggest four main points (Voss 1989). First, problem-solving involves a wide variety of different cognitive processes, depending on the nature of the problem, the individual's experience with the subject-matter, and other factors such as practical constraints. Second, one crucial aspect is the way in which the problem is understood. The information in the problem statement must be comprehended and a reasonable representation of the problem must be constructed. This involves analysis of what sort of problem this is, which pieces of information have what degree of importance, how the problem resembles or differs from problems met previously, and so forth. Third, skill in dealing with problems involves the gradual build-up of both content-based factual knowledge and procedural knowledge useful to particular sorts of problems: it is thus not quickly acquired. Fourth, the most effective problem-solvers in a domain have typically developed highly abstract knowledge structures which powerfully organise their declarative knowledge and their handling of problem-solving strategies. Expert chess players, for example, use their extensive experience of specific configurations of pieces in selecting and evaluating moves, and they are able to keep very large amounts of information in memory, by 'chunking', which overcomes working memory's limitations, or by rapid accurate access to their long-term memory stores (Chase and Simon 1973).

It is clear that even young children are capable of systematic attempts to solve problems, though their 'strategies' may be crude and relatively ineffective (e.g. Karmiloff-Smith and Inhelder 1974/5), or in some cases may not be put into action because a more expert person is present to do the work (Caplan and Hale 1989, Meadows and Cashdan 1988). They may even show hypothetico-deductive reasoning, controlling variables and experimenting like mature scientists, if they have external help with record keeping, contrary to Piaget's original findings (Inhelder and Piaget 1958, Braine and Rumain 1983, Brown *et al.* 1983). Conversely, some older children and adults are often poor problem-solvers, making invalid inferences and reasoning well only in familiar contexts (e.g. Wason and Johnson-Laird 1972). Thus it is not the case that young children are worse problem-solvers than adults because the former lack even the rudiments of the cognitive skills which the latter can apply regardless of problem-based constraints: rather children have cognitive processes which may be less fluent and may be applied in fewer contexts. Their problem-solving does seem to be more disrupted by increases in the complexity of a task, which might reflect the limitations in processing capacity hypothesised by some information-processing theorists (Case 1985, Scardamalia 1977, but see Anderson 1992). Children may also be less practised than adults at the metacognitive activities that are helpful in problem-solving. They are less successful than adults at identifying the more and less important facts in a passage of prose (Brown and Day 1983, Brown et. al. 1984), and it is noteworthy that novice physicists have similar problems. As compared with experts they tend to rely on superficial features of the problem, not representing it in ways that use the essential information required to develop a solution, and spending an inadequate amount of time in planning how to attack the problem (Chi et. al. 1980, Larkin et al. 1980, Larkin 1983, and see also Spilich et. al. 1979). Expert physicists, given a physics problem to solve, often analyse it by drawing a diagram, and also study the relationship between the variables in the problem. This would lead to categorising the problem as, for example, an 'acceleration' problem, and thence to writing down appropriate equations related to this principle to solve the problem. Novices, on the other hand, focused on a variable and wrote down an equation in which that variable appeared, trying to apply it to solve the problem. This made for a more piecemeal attack on the problem: where experts applied several equations in a coordinated way, novices were more likely to have to backtrack, or to set up sub-goals, and generally produced a less planned performance.

Improvement in planning involves improvement in recognising which features of the problem to consider, and hence in having a more helpful representation of the problem. It thus is inextricably confounded with the role of subject-matter knowledge. Voss (1989) reports that experts' problem-solving in physics will resemble novices', if the expert is given a problem from an area outside his or her area of expertise, or if the novice is familiar with the type of problem (see also Carey 1991, Gelman 1991). Nevertheless, experts and novices differ in how they organise the problem area. Novices sort problems mainly on surface features such as 'being about "colliding objects" ': experts are more likely to sort in relation to more abstract laws and principles, such as the Law of Conservation of Energy, and they also summarise their reading of textbook materials in terms of laws and principles. Part of becoming 'expert', therefore, is developing a structured abstract knowledge of the area of expertise, a conceptual system adequate for solving its problems.

Thus there has been a considerable interest in the conceptual systems which untutored people bring to bear on scientific problems. These are often referred to as 'naïve' or 'intuitive' conceptions. Linn (1986) summarises some of the findings. She suggests that untutored reasoners have constructed a view of natural phenomena from personal experience guided by the use of analogies. For example, they predict that the weight of an object will affect the amount of water it displaces, justifying this (incorrect) prediction by pointing out the importance of weight for momentum, pressure and so forth. Like people did before Galileo, they believe that heavier objects fall faster, and their understanding of movement in space may be pre-Newtonian, or even Aristotelian (Caramazza *et al.* 1981, McCloskey *et al.* 1980) and these beliefs are no easier to modify in the individual than they were in the history of science (di Sessa 1982, 1983).

Intuitive conceptions also arise in the biological sciences (Carey 1985) and social sciences (Voss 1989). Here too experts and novices may represent domains differently and use different strategies. Good representations of problems are particularly important in the highly complex and often ill-defined problems of the social sciences; analysis is the first step in problem-solving, as the major factors of the problem must be correctly identified if a successful solution is to be found. How the problem is represented also affects the evaluation of the solution: experts generate more high level abstract solutions than novices, and also consider what sub-problems their solution would solve and which points would need to be considered if the abstract solution were to work. Experts thus do more to provide arguments for and against components of their problem analysis and their problem solution: evaluation, confirmation and disconfirmation are an intrinsic part of the problem-solving process.

My discussion of problem-solving has emphasised that it requires both good representation of the problem, which involves the use of knowledge that may be specific to that domain (and indeed to that particular type of problem), and problem-solving strategies and procedures, which will also vary in how generally they can be applied. There is debate about whether there are general problem-solving strategies which can usefully be taught, or whether how problem-solving should be done is specific to particular subject domains. There clearly are strategies which can be applied in many different situations, for example analysing a problem into a sequence of sub-problems, seeking to reduce the difference between the present situation and the goal state, systematic testing of variables, finding analogies, and so forth, as well as less general strategies applicable only to a limited range of problems, for example methods for transferring unknown quantities from one side of an algebraic equation to the other without invalidating the equation. Both types of strategy are necessary, though to varying degrees for problems which differ in, for example, the degree to which they are well defined or to which they require the use of information from the domain beyond the problem. While problem-solving strategies can be taught (Brown *et al.* 1983, Resnick 1987b, Voss 1989), it seems to be crucial that they should be taught in those contexts where they are useful. Transfer of learning can be difficult and analogies may be misleading (Gentner 1977,

Gentner and Gentner 1983), because of the crucial role of the knowledge base required for the effective solution of problems. Good performance in solving problems of all sorts and at all levels requires an adequate knowledge base (and in many cases this means a substantial one). This base must be integrated with knowing how to use such knowledge in both strategies which are widely applicable and strategies which are specific to a particular problem. Thus a considerable amount of learning from relevant experience lies behind problem-solving ability.

## CHILDREN'S MUSICAL COGNITION

Research on children's musical cognition presents a sort of microcosm of research on children's cognition in general. It includes an extensive body of work on individual differences in musical ability using psychometric techniques (Shuter-Dyson and Gabriel 1981 review this thoroughly); a body of work on developmental changes in the understanding of the structure of music (see for example Serafine 1988) which is often heavily Piagetian; information-processing and psychophysical studies (Sloboda 1985, Deutsch 1982, Shuter-Dyson and Gabriel 1981); studies of musical taste and preference (see Hargreaves 1986); and observational studies of children singing, dancing, playing instruments, composing and listening to music (e.g. Moog 1976, Hargreaves 1986, Swanwick 1988). It is too heterogeneous and too widespread to be summarised in the space I have available, and interested readers should go to an excellent review by D. J. Hargreaves (1986); Swanwick 1988 is also useful, though more educationally oriented. The existing variety of approaches is hardly surprising, given the heterogeneity of psychology and, more important, the complexity of music, which is obviously open to neurophysiological, psychophysical, cognitive, psychometric, sociological, aesthetic, anthropological and other approaches, all of them legitimate and no one of them comprehensive. Musical abilities also share basic processes, perhaps, with other cognitive skills (Barwick *et al.* 1989).

Much of the evidence on the pre-school years comes from a major study by Moog (1968/76). He carried out 'over 8,000' tests with 'nearly 500 children' and evaluated 'the observations of about 1,000 parents' (the English text was prepared for a music publisher not a psychological one and is intended primarily for practising teachers), and recorded examples of the children's own singing. From these data it seems that babies from somewhat before the age of 6 months (prenatally, even, if mothers' experience of their foetuses' kicking is accepted) start to respond to music with active listening, pleasure and bodily movements, and a little later to indulge in 'musical babbling', sounds of varied and somewhat indeterminate pitch, mostly descending in melody but covering quite a wide range, and not imitations of songs they have heard. Sixty per cent of the 12-month-old babies tested responded to music with musical babbling or singing of their own. At this age babies also showed definite likes and dislikes for Moog's sample material: they reacted positively to songs and rhythmic words, and also to instrumental music, but disliked non-musical sounds (20 seconds each of a vacuum cleaner and traffic at a busy crossroads) and tapped-out rhythms. Unlike adults, some of them positively like cacophonous music (one instrument in a quartet playing a semitone higher or lower than the others, or four different melodies in four different keys played simultaneously).

Between the ages of 1 and 2, more children respond overtly to music, and movement to music in particular becomes important. Babies begin to beat time or clap to music, or to wish to join in musical games such as 'ring a ring of roses'; they spin round to music, make regular stepping movements and eventually carry out dance movements with others. Some children under 2 are able to coordinate their movements with the music for a few bars, or to carry out dance movements with others, and some can manage to sing recognisable songs. Their spontaneous songs commonly contain a melodic phrase which is repeated with slight variations, for example three descending notes repeated at different pitch levels (Hargreaves 1986: 68–77 discusses some examples). They also have versions of standard songs: the earliest versions focus on distinctive words and the correct rhythm and pitch for the song usually come later. Imitating pitch seemed to be particularly hard, the general directions sometimes being followed with reduced intervals, or the imitation only being kept up successfully for a bar or so. Repetitive songs may be performed with the wrong number of repetitions: my daughter could produce a recognisable version of 'Happy birthday' at 18 to 24 months, but sometimes sang 'Happy birthday to you' only once before she got on to 'Happy birthday dear X' and sometimes seemed to get stuck into an unending repetition of the phrase. Songs with similar phrases may be compounded, or a bit of original melody interpolated, in what Moog calls 'pot pourri' songs. The child's spontaneous composing of songs is becoming influenced by the standard repertoire, whose songs are more organised and more easily memorised than spontaneous songs. Hargreaves is among those who believe that children first develop a 'topological' grasp of the song, acquiring its global outline with its words and phrases and underlying pulse first, then its surface rhythm and its approximate pitch contours, with stable pitch and stable intervals following later. Early songs are not structureless, but it takes time for them to develop towards standard songs, particularly to move from 'floating' pitch to accurate reproduction of conventional tonal scales.

Moog's data and the subsequent studies reviewed by Hargreaves (1986: ch.3) show that by the end of the pre-school period children possess many of the basic skills of musical perception and performance. This competence argues against the neo-Piagetian account of musical cognition which bases it on operational thought. Gardner (1973, 1983) has argued that musical intelligence is one of the multiple forms of human intelligence. A child at the beginning of formal schooling will have achieved an elementary understanding of the music of his or her culture, its basic harmonies, cadences, rhythms, and will be able to learn the culture's songs and compose culturally-given motifs into independent ones. Clearly much more musical acculturation and deliberate training occurs during the school years, and the children's musical skills (including motor skills) become more fluent. Hargreaves (1986) and Shuter-Dyson and Gabriel (1981) review development in this period. Musical training, and musical experience, affect the development of musical skills such as singing in tune, discriminating pitches and processing melodies: they also affect preferences for different sorts of music. Studies of musical prodigies (see e.g. Radford 1990) suggest that they usually come from a background where there is a lot of musical activity.

## CHILDREN'S DRAWINGS

Children's drawings are often charming, sometimes beautiful. Producing them is fun for the child artist; interpreting them has been a matter of serious concern for the adult, whether therapist seeking to diagnose the child's inner conflicts and emotional states or more dispassionate psychologist wishing to discover how the child represents the world or how he or she combines perception and drawing to produce a picture. My concern here is to outline current psychological ideas about children's drawing processes as a subset of cognitive skills, and I will not discuss the use of drawings to diagnose or ameliorate children's emotional problems. Thomas and Silk (1990) provide a very useful introduction to psychological theories of children's drawings and their relation to emotional and cognitive development.

The developmental sequence of drawing in childhood seems to be fairly clear. Children begin to show an interest in making marks on paper during their second year of life, becoming absorbed in making 'scribbles' which are not aimless and uncoordinated movements but are frequently positioned so that a degree of visual balance is achieved. Gradually deliberate shape-making merges – lines from side to side of the paper come to be supplemented by dots, circles and zig-zags as the child's motor control improves. These earliest scribbles are probably not intended to be representational; the child is strongly interested in the marks that appear on the paper and may vary them or place them systematically, but they are the result of what Arnheim (1956) calls a 'motor impulse', not of an intention to draw a representation of an object or event. Children's first assertions that their drawings represent something tend to be *post hoc* interpretations: a fortuitous squiggle is pointed out as being, say, 'a rabbit', though no intention to draw a rabbit was announced before the drawing was begun.

The claim to have done a representational drawing sometimes seems to be opportunist, and indeed even if the intention to draw 'a rabbit' was announced early on, the interpretation of the shape that is actually produced may be very flexible (Freeman 1987). Such changes in interpretation are not of course unknown in adults' doodles or other informal drawings, even when the adult is as considerable an artist as Picasso!

Early representational drawings show characteristic problems in achieving a realistic image. Drawings of human figures, for example (Freeman 1988), often appear to be based on a simple formula, initially a 'tadpole' figure where a circle with facial features inside it represents the head or head and body, and dangling lines the legs and arms. Such formulaic drawings are perhaps convenient symbols rather than attempts at realistic representations (Barrett and Light 1976). It has to be noted that the culture's *conventional* representations of objects influence children's drawings from very early on: houses with a central door, four square windows, a gabled roof and a smoking chimney dominate the drawings of people whose own homes look nothing like that.

Children's formulaic drawings have been interpreted as showing how they represent the world mentally, revealing their feelings about and understandings of what they see. Thus the drawer of tadpole figures is accused of having a distorted 'body image'. Norman Freeman (1975, 1980, 1987, 1988) has argued that this is an unreasonable and unnecessary inference. Task demands may get in the way of expressing what one knows. The child's mental representation has to be accessed, and young children may need prompts more than older ones do, as is the case for many of the other cognitive skills discussed in this chapter. The physical demands of producing a drawing are also formidable. Drawings have to be constructed step by step, and decisions at earlier stages affect what can be done at later ones. Thomas and Silk (1990) consider the process of constructing a drawing, and note a number of different problems of planning, positioning and alignment. Both perceptual and performance biases may be of influence. For example, young children typically construct their pictures from a limited 'vocabulary' of forms, notably circles and short lines, while more mature drawers often use an outline which continues round the whole shape to be drawn. Fenson (1985) suggests that outlining avoids artificially segmenting objects into simple component shapes and thus the problem of recombining them, and that it may also make it easier to represent objects from more varied perspectives. Manuals teaching drawing to adults (e.g. Edwards 1979) may seem to contradict Fenson's suggestion, in that they often prescribe drawing by putting together simple shapes rather than using outlining, but the 'simple shapes' have to be based on retinal image rather than on conceptualised formulae.

Watching children drawing reveals a number of biases in their approach to deciding how to do a drawing (Goodnow 1977). They commonly start drawing near the top of the paper and move from left to right (regardless of the direction of writing in their culture), and such preferences as these may go some way towards explaining such phenomena as why the majority of children in the West start their drawings of people with the head (Freeman 1980, Thomas and Tsalimi 1988). Freeman also suggests that children may show a tendency towards 'end-anchoring': the end-items in a series are often recalled better and dealt with better than less conspicuously placed intermediate items, hence a preference for drawing heads and legs over mid-body features such as torso and arms, and for eyes and mouth on faces rather than noses. In tadpole figures the body parts are usually produced in the order head, legs, and finally (if at all) arms, which are more often joined on to the head than the legs. If a body is also provided, tadpole drawers add the arms to the larger of the two: if the head is larger than the body it attracts the arms, if it is smaller the arms are, more conventionally and more correctly in anatomical terms, added to the body. Freeman sees this as an instance of children's problems in organising lines on the page, in handling the interaction between what is already on the page and what is still to come. To produce a representational drawing of even moderate complexity, children have to decide in what order they will draw the component parts, position each so that space remains for later parts, and draw each so that it can be joined on to other elements appropriately. They typically run into problems of not leaving enough space, separating elements completely instead of positioning one appropriately inside the boundaries of another, having to distort a late-drawn item because an earlier one occupies the same space, aligning one element with another rather than with the edge of the sheet of paper, and deciding what to do about parts of an object which are actually hidden by other parts. Freeman (1980, 1988) and Thomas and Silk (1990) see these sorts of production problems as being a major cause of 'childish' drawings of tadpole people, 'object-centred' and 'transparent' pictures where, for example, a man seen in profile has two eyes, failures of scale (Silk and Thomas 1986, 1988), difficulties with occlusion and with representing what the viewer sees as well as knows (e.g. Crook 1984, 1985, Light and Humprheys 1981), and difficulties over depth and perspective (e.g. Ingram and Butterworth 1989, Willats 1977). What children draw rather than leave out is affected by their knowledge of the object or event they are drawing, their interpretation of what aspects of it are important, in general and on this particular occasion, and their capacity to handle the demands of presenting the information (Nicholls and Kennedy 1992). Failure to recognise particularly the last of these has contributed to an underestimation of what information young children can represent. It is now suggested that 'inadequacies' in their drawings should not be attributed to conceptual limitations but rather to difficulties of execution or to preferences for doing particular sorts of drawings. Again, performance is seen as being constrained by experience: drawing may be another cognitive skill where real developmental changes are ultimately mixed up with practice effects, and where education can play an important role.

## CHILDREN'S SPATIAL COGNITION

As in other areas of cognition, there is some disagreement about the child's understanding of the layout and use of the environment, and the sources of whatever competence may be shown. Liben (1981) summarises the contrasted epistemological positions taken by different theorists: the empiricist view that concepts of space are derived directly from experience with physical space and are to at least some degree isomorphic with it; the nativist view that, on the contrary, innate factors such as the organisation of areas of the brain determine how psychological concepts of space are organised (e.g. O'Keefe and Nadel 1978); and the constructivist view that individuals' activity develops their conceptual grasp of space. As in other areas, Piaget and his colleagues (Piaget and Inhelder 1956, Piaget *et. al.* 1960) made pioneering studies which have had a considerable influence on subsequent work.

A number of conceptual and methodological points need to be made before I describe the evidence on the development of spatial cognition. First, we may have to distinguish here (as elsewhere in cognition) between 'knowing how' and 'knowing that', between what Piaget called 'practical' space and Presson (1987) calls 'primary' space use on the one hand, and 'conceptual' space or 'secondary' space use on the other. The former is the capacity to act and move intelligently in space. It guides one's immediate orientation and action within the spatial world: there is incontrovertible evidence for considerable 'primary' competence in infants, chimpanzees, rats, pigeons and insects, who can in their varying ways reach for objects, avoid bumping into them, navigate from *A* to *B* or indeed from *A* to *Z*, and generally cope with living in the three dimensions of the revolving Earth. We have 'primary' space use because evolution has induced in us perceptual mechanisms and processes which specify where we are, orient our actions, monitor our movements and help us to predict their effects. These capacities and our early experience quite rapidly build up our sense of near space to form a working spatial memory for orientation and action. Obviously this primary spatial understanding is refined with more experience, but it is considerable and useful from early childhood or before.

'Secondary' spatial use involves the symbolic representation of an environment by the construction of a 'map' which can be used when one is absent from the actual environment. Competence at this is necessary for the drawing or reading of (literal) maps, and for tasks like mental rotation and perspective-taking. It is dependent on 'primary' understanding but goes beyond it; it appears to be specific to the human species (Presson 1987) and develops, as we shall see, over the years of childhood.

In examining the development of spatial cognition after infancy, therefore, we are mainly investigating children's mental *representations* of the environment. Methodological difficulties are likely to arise. The 'representation' called up when one has to draw a sketch map is likely to be different from what is produced by a request to give verbal directions; the former may display knowledge of spatial relations, the latter of a sequence of landmarks. Obviously different productions make different demands: inefficiency at drawing could make a sketch map a poor concrete representation of the mental representation, for example. Such production problems will (as in other areas) be particularly marked in children, who are less likely to be adequate artists or adequate verbalisers, as well as perhaps less able to make an adequate search and analysis of their mental maps. It may be wise to use several investigative techniques. Cousins *et. al.* (1983), for example, used photograph recognition to assess knowledge about landmarks and routes and a pointer to assess estimates of direction, and also tested actual routes through the area in question.

Using a model environment, asking the child (for example) to assemble a scale model of his or her classroom or neighbourhood may be a useful technique (Weatherford 1982), but using models will itself be affected by the child's experience of models in general (De Loache *et al.* 1991). However, it is likely to present fewer problems for the child than constructing a map by drawing. Matthews (1984, 1987, 1992) investigated children's knowledge of the areas around their homes using either recall mapping, large-scale plans or an aerial photograph. Not surprisingly, the first of these techniques produced much less rich recall than the other two.

'Spatial cognition' is a broad term. Among the phenomena which psychologists have investigated are children's search strategies and their location of themselves and objects in space; children's use of landmarks and directions in their route-finding and knowledge of familiar areas (e.g. Cornell *et al.* 1989, Cousins *et al.* 1983, Gauvain and Rogoff 1986, Hart 1979, Matthews 1992); children's maps, both those they construct themselves and those more formal maps that they meet in school (see Anooshian and Young 1981, De Loache 1987, Matthews 1984, 1992, Presson 1982, Uttal and Wellman 1989); their use of formal map symbols (e.g. Matthews 1992, Somerville and Bryant 1985, Spencer *et al.* 1989); children's knowledge of distant places; and the extent of children's use of their own environment and how well fitted the environment is to such use (e.g. Hart 1979, Moore 1986). Such topics may be very relevant to social and political issues, such as how to provide facilities which will occupy children safely and usefully and so reduce injury and the sort of hanging around on street corners associated with minor delinquency (Coleman 1985, Rutter and Giller 1983), or how to encourage the knowledge and empathy necessary to act sensibly on questions of ecological damage or aid to developing countries, and of course to education. I will not try to cover these diverse areas here, referring the reader to the very useful reviews by Spencer *et. al.* (1989) and Matthews (1992) in the first instance.

However, a couple of general points relevant to the acquisition and development of spatial cognition may be derived from the literature. It is clear that spatial cognition involves a complex variety of mental representations and processes, which may have a wide range of applications or be very task-specific. It has been suggested that there is a developmental sequence of spatial frames of reference, with the child's awareness and skills beginning with body image and body co-ordination and moving outwards to the immediate environment and then onwards to more distant spaces. It seems unlikely that any other direction could obtain: for example, that one could know about distant places if one knew nothing at all about near ones, even if directly-experienced space was not restricted by the comparative immobility of infancy and the chaperonage supplied to children. However, as Pick and Lockman (1981) point out, although there may be an outwards expansion of knowledge of this sort, it is clearly not the case that the more local frame of reference has to be fully mastered before any use or understanding of more distant ones begins. Knowledge and skills even of very close space can continue to be developed throughout life as an individual's tasks demand. One can be a somewhat clumsy person, without a highly sophisticated understanding of one's body's movements, but skilled at activities such as map-reading or orienteering, or vice versa; whether body-centred understanding is useful or a handicap depends on what the task is. Many tasks will require coordination of frames of reference, so that replacement of earlier schemes by later ones must be a matter of addition, not of superseding.

Psychometric studies (e.g. Gardner 1983, Vernon 1972) have suggested that there is a component of intelligence described as 'spatial abilities'. One important 'ability' is 'spatial visualisation', that is, imagining how a pictured object would appear if rotated, inverted or otherwise manipulated, perhaps by mentally manipulating an image in this way. Another is 'spatial orientation', the ability to comprehend the relation between elements in a visual stimulus pattern without being confused by changes in the orientation of the stimulus. These abilities seem to be related to mathematical performance (more closely to geometry than to arithmetical computation, not surprisingly), and are seen as being implicated in sex differences in mathematical and technological performance (Linn and Peterson 1985, Maccoby and Jacklin 1974). It is however clear that there is little difference before adolescence, that the difference on some 'spatial understanding' tests is very small, that cross-cultural differences exist, and that girls and boys are often in receipt of different experience of space, boys being allowed to roam further afield and given more manipulative toys, so no conclusion about the innate superiority of one sex could be supported (see e.g. Matthews 1992). There do not seem to be marked sex differences in algorithms for processing spatial information (Carter *et. al.* 1983) such as one might suppose would be involved if there were brain-based and unmodifiable sources of the sex differences, rather than differences of practice and exposure.

The literature on the development of spatial cognition suggests that young children may show more competence than earlier researchers had concluded. A recent survey by Uttal and Wellman (1989), for example, investigated the development of the ability to acquire integrated knowledge of a space from a map in 4- to 7-year-olds. The children memorised which animal lived in each room of a large playhouse from a map, and then navigated a route through the playhouse itself, during which they named the animal who lived in the room they were about to enter or were to the side of. Children aged 6 or 7 did very well on the task, but even 4- and 5-year-olds succeeded to a degree which allowed the researchers to claim that the children had constructed a representation of the playhouse which captured the two dimensional layout of spatial relations between the rooms. They were not dependent on a single landmark nor on a succession of points on a route, but had what might be called an 'integrated' or 'survey-like' representation (McNamara 1986). Of course in other situations we may use landmarks and route sequences to find the way (Allen *et al.* 1979, Cornell *et. al.* 1989). The test did not demand precise information about quantitative aspects of the space and the children did not display such knowledge. Uttal and Wellman call their subjects' map-reading abilities 'impressive'. Similarly De Loache (1987) showed that children just past their third birthdays were able to draw on their knowledge of where an object was hidden in a model of a room to find an object hidden in the real room; children aged 2½ could not reliably find the object in the real room using a model but could find it if they saw a photograph of the hiding place. This pattern of findings suggests that the 2-year-olds' difficulty with the model, as a source of information about the place it represents, stems from having to treat the model as a representation of another place as well as a real object. Failing to think about a symbolic object (the model) as simultaneously both an object (a miniature room) and a symbol (of the real room), they did not generalise their experience of where hidden objects were in the model to the task of finding a hidden object in the real room. Their more extensive experience of pictorial representations meant that they were able to generalise appropriately from a photograph to the real world. The almost complete success of the 3-year-olds in using the model as a representation suggests a rapid developmental change in the second half of the first year. A recent study (De Loache *et. al.* 1991) examines what characteristics of the model are associated with better performance on the 'finding a hidden object' task, and finds that physical similarity seems to be important. Children here are having to use their mental representation of the model which is a representation of the real room. De Loache speculates that this is a maturational development, and the capacity for such 'metarepresentation' has been linked to the emergence of a 'theory of mind' (see Anderson 1992, Perner 1991a). Spencer *et. al.* (1989) agree that young children have difficulty dealing with models and suggest that toy play may improve their understanding. Perhaps each child should have a dolls' house resembling his or her own, or a model of the neighbourhood and the daily-used routes to shops, swings and school?

## CHILDREN'S USE OF CONCEPTS

My concern here is with recent work on how children develop systems of concepts and how they are organised, with the general issue of conceptual thought in childhood. Work which describes the content of various conceptual areas is dealt with in the next section; the focus here is on structure and process, via philosophical and psychological accounts of conceptual development.

Children and adults alike, we live in a world dazzlingly rich with unique objects and experiences; as the Chinese proverb says, we never step into the same river twice. The pen I am writing with at this moment is similar to other pens, and as far as my normal powers of discrimination go, is identical to the pen lying at the bottom of my handbag, but more exact examination would pick up differences between them besides the obvious one of where they are at this moment. One may have more ink in than the other, or less fluff on its nib, or wear-marks in different places. Normally we would categorise the two as 'the same', both instances of the concepts 'pen', 'thing for writing with', 'long thin objects', etc.: we naturally treat very similar objects, events and experiences as if they were the same, ignoring their uniqueness, because the world would be impossible to cope with if we did not. Without concepts we could not predict, could not remember, could not communicate at all exactly, could not act appropriately with other people. The world which flows by us has to be organised if we are to survive.

The argument begins when we try to specify what sort of concepts we have, and how we get them (for a brief introduction see Eysenck and Keane 1990). The notion I used in the last paragraph was that of similarity. Objects and events are put into categories, as into containers, because they are similar to each other and different from objects and events which belong in different categories. This is the 'classical' theory of category representation: all the instances of a concept share common properties, which are necessary and sufficient for membership of that category. Thus in the world of playing cards, cards belong to the suit or category of hearts because they all bear one or more red heart-shaped symbol and represent a value between the ace and the king. Cards which do not have hearts on do not come into the hearts category, though they may be members of other categories, for example spades, court cards, part of my winning hand, useful bookmarks, etc.

This model of what concepts are has two implications which were for a long time taken for granted but have more recently been questioned (Lakoff 1987). The first is that since categories are defined by properties which all members share, no members are better examples of the category than others – 'a rose is a rose is a rose', perhaps. Second, since categories are defined by properties which are inherent in each member, they are independent of the peculiarities of categorizers: there exists in the real world a 'true', objective category of red things, for example, and my category of red things is a fairly representative sample of the true category while that of a red–green colour-blind person would be a poorer approximation. Concepts are assumed here to be abstract and disembodied, independent of people, eternal, unchangeable, really 'out there' to be discovered, largely by the identification of common properties or similarities.

'Similarity' may seem an obvious and straightforward basis for organising concepts, even a natural one, and in many cases it is. However, closer analysis reveals some philosophical and psychological difficulties. In the first place, any two entities could have an infinite number of properties in common. Take, for example, a beetroot and the *Mona Lisa*. Both weigh more than 1 gram and less than 2,000 kilograms; both contain vegetable matter; both are made up of atoms; I am not going to buy either; I thought of them both a moment ago when trying to invent as dissimilar a pair of entities as possible; and so forth. It may not be obvious which attributes of entities are important; and it might be still less obvious to a naïve observer, such as a child, than to an adult experienced at categorising. Using a combination of *similarity* within instances of a category and *dissimilarity* with non-instances and with members of other categories may help. Rosch *et al.* (1976) call the categorisation level where such similarity and difference are highest the 'basic' level, as they believe it is the core level of the categorisation system. This probably does not resolve the problem completely. In order to use both similarity and difference and end up with cohesive categories there have to be some principles that determine what is relevant and important: we will look at possible principles later.

There are also many concepts where not all members share all the relevant properties. Philosophers have amended the classical theory of necessary and sufficient properties and suggested that properties are *characteristic* of instances, that instances of a concept probably have the relevant properties but sometimes may not. Some instances will have more of the relevant properties and others will have fewer. Take the concept of 'chair', for example. People agree, on the whole, that chairs normally have a seat and back and legs, and can be sat on: some have arms, some cushions, some are made of wood, some of metal, they vary in size and location and comfortableness. There are certain marginally acceptable instances of 'chairs': deckchairs, for example, or stacks of cushions, or car seats, or the coronation chair in Westminster Abbey. It has been suggested that concepts are *probabilistic*: the chair I am sitting on at present has many 'chair' characteristics, having seat, legs and back and being made of wood, and affording, to use Gibson's terminology, 'sitting-upon'; what the driver sits on in a car has fewer 'chair' characteristics: it has no legs, for example, and not is in use in the house, but can count as a 'chair' because of its seat and back and affording sitting. But not everything that we could sit on would be categorised as a chair: it would be eccentric to call a bicycle saddle a chair, and a patch of grass would only be a chair in a rather fey poetic context. Concept members may even have 'family resemblances', such that two particular individual members may have no properties at all in common but each has some of the wide variety of properties which characterise the concept. Games are a good example; some games are competitive, but not all (hide and seek versus ring-a-ring-of-roses), some but not all involve skill (chess versus snakes and ladders), some but not all involve vigorous physical activity (tennis versus Consequences). We might in principle be able to arrange instances of a category according to gradations in their probableness, better instances having more characteristic properties than worse ones. However this suggestion of 'linear separability' seems to be too simple a measure of the psychological structure within a concept: the instance with all four relevant properties is not seen as being twice as good as that with two, or four times as good as that with only one. It is also true that in many cases the relevant properties are not independent and so cannot be simply summed: birds have two legs partly because they have wings, for example, and the feathers, light bones, strong breast muscles and so forth are correlated attributes all necessary for flight. Again we need some sort of principle to explain which attributes are most relevant and important; and again it seems possible that which these are will depend on the context. Most people agree, for example, that car seats could be classified as 'chairs', and that the category of 'chairs' belongs within the superordinate category of 'furniture'; but they would not include car seats as instances of furniture (Hampton 1990).

Considerations like these suggest that there might be better and worse exemplars of categories and more or less 'basic' categories. One major work concerned with basic categories looked at words for colours (e.g. Berlin and Kay 1969). They found that although different languages divided colours in different ways, there were basic colour categories with the same 'best instances', and the terms used for them formed a hierarchy. The simplest basic terminology was to name 'black' or 'cool' colours (black, green, blue and grey) in contrast with 'white' or 'warm' colours (red, orange, yellow and white). The third basic colour term was always the equivalent of 'red', differentiated out from the 'warm' category; yellow, green and blue were equally probable as the next distinction. Boundaries between categories varied from speaker to speaker, but the best or 'focal' colours were the same for all speakers, whatever language terms they habitually used. Thus if the language had only one basic word ('bleen') for the range which English describes as 'blue' and 'green', the focal colour in the 'bleen' range would not be a bluey-green or turquoise but either the blue which English speakers regard as a good blue or the green which they see as prototypical green. Neurophysiological sensitivity seems to underlie these particular foci.

Basic level terminology with non-linguistic roots also occurs in observations of early language development. Roger Brown (1958) describes the actions which typically accompany early labelling: flowers are smelled, balls bounced, pussy-cats stroked. Actions as well as labels differentiate between categories. The basic level for parents' labelling, like that for colours, has the shortest names, is used earliest and most frequently, feels 'natural', and involves distinctive actions. A similar picture arises from studies of biological classification, both folk classification and the scientific classifications deriving from Linnaeus (Lakoff 1987). Psychological discriminability seems to be an important component of our categorisation of the natural world.

The model which develops these findings was first proposed by Eleanor Rosch. She proposed a 'prototype' theory of categories. Some category members are 'prototypes' or 'cognitive reference points'. People consistently rate these as best examples, recognise them and judge them to be true category members particularly fast, produce them more often when asked to think of category members, generalise more readily from prototypical member to non-prototypes than the reverse, and so forth (e.g. Rosch 1978). Both prototypes and less prototypical members are equally truly members of the category – penguins and emus are just as much birds as sparrows are – but there are structural distinctions within categories which are as important as the specific defining properties which classical concept theory picked out.

In these prototype models, instances of a category need not have specific defining properties: the category is represented by examples and new instances are included if they are sufficiently similar to existing members. Unlike the 'classical' and 'probabilistic' theories, this suggests concept learning which could begin with instances whose properties are not clearly defined, as they probably are not for naïve or young learners, but it runs into the same problem of what 'similarity' is, and which ways of being 'similar' are relevant and important.

Characteristics may also differ in their obviousness for different concepts or levels of concepts. Redcurrants are all small, red and globular; fruit, though like redcurrants edible, seed-containing etc., vary very much in perceptual characteristics. In the case of abstract social concepts such as 'justice' or 'liberty' there is such difficulty in either finding sound defining characteristics or comparing each new and unique case with a prototype that we may do better to regard the concept as being comparable to an elaborate theory which is used to explain examples rather than to match them.

We have seen, then, that focusing on similarity as constituent attributes of concepts leads to a lack of attention to questions about how concepts are structured, in their relations to other concepts but also in the internal organisation of elements and their characteristics within the structure itself. I mentioned earlier, for example that characteristics may be correlated or variably important; they may also be in particular specified relations to each other. Medin and Wattenmaker (1987) and Murphy and Medin (1985) address this problem.

Medin and Wattenmaker (1987) and Neisser (1987) explicitly argue for the importance of 'theory' in the acquisition and coherence of concepts, and specify that developmentally the 'theory' is unlikely to be one of matching up perceptual characteristics in any simple fashion. They believe that a great deal of the person's accumulated world knowledge is incorporated and used in ways which fit the immediate context. Thus, for example, Medin and Wattenmaker suggest that only rarely will the characteristic 'inflammable' be linked to money, as money is used in other ways in our usual economic theories. A person who has encountered an eccentric and vulgar tycoon who lights his cigars with spills made of banknotes, or has heard it remarked of a teenager that her first wages are burning a hole in her pocket, may make a stronger link between this attribute and instances of money, but it is not likely to become a central part of the normal theory.

This example may already have suggested that perhaps we would be wrong to assume (as the classical work on concepts has done) that concepts are completely static. Barsalou (1987, 1989) has argued that, on the contrary, concepts are to a considerable degree unstable. The local context affects how a concept is represented: we don't normally think of pianos being heavy until we have a furniture-moving context, to give another example of the 'money is inflammable' type, and we regard robins as more typical birds than swans are if we are Americans reporting our own culture's judgement, but swans as more typical birds than robins if we are Americans reporting the supposed viewpoint of the average Chinese citizen. We can also readily construct *ad hoc* categories to fit the moment's need, for example a category of 'things we must take on our visit to Granny'. Barsalou's view is that concepts have a core of stable context-independent information as well as information dependent on the current context or on recently-encountered contexts, in a comparatively loosely organised system. This sort of reconstitutive conceptual system, with particular bits of information or particular criteria in play or not depending on the immediate context, is roughly what the connectionist models of cognition suggest (McClelland *et al.* 1986, Rumelhart and McClelland 1986).

Theories, like concepts, may be more or less simple and more or less coherent. Simplicity, or 'parsimony', has often been invoked as a hallmark of the good theory, but there are problems here as there were at the level of attributes of concepts. If two theories are equally accurate in their picture of the same data and relate equally well to other theories, then it is reasonable to prefer the more parsimonious; but what if the simpler theory can only cope with a smaller range of data, or if it is discrepant with wider theories of the world? A belief in ESP, for example, provides a simple explanation for a range of phenomena which we otherwise cannot explain; but it fits rather badly into the wider frameworks of physics and of psychology which, though imperfect, probably could provide more complex if less exciting accounts of paranormal phenomena. We do not yet understand very well how people develop or choose between theories. It does seem possible, however, that it has been a matter of evolutionary adaptiveness for successful theories to arise from the interaction of an intelligent and purposive organism with the perceptual world (see e.g. Lakoff 1987). This is a possibility which is more fully considered in Chapter 5: the point I want to make here is that theories and concepts are likely to imply causes, relations and usefulnesses to the organism, not just to map attributes, and to vary according to the context. Developmentally and cross culturally, this suggests a rather different account of children's concepts from the ones which dominated the field until quite recently, an account which does not so much supplement the traditional view as supplement and revalue it.

Young children have been seen by many investigators as being rather inept at concept formation and concept use. The classic work of Vygotsky (1962, 1987a) and of Inhelder and Piaget (1964) was taken as showing that they were unable to form stable and coherent sortings of objects which were consistent in their use of defining characteristics. I will give a brief description of some of the evidence which apparently justified this view, before reviewing recent work showing greater competence in categorisation, and discussing this in terms of the shift in our theories about concepts that I outlined in the first part of this section.

In several pieces of research, children were given objects and asked to sort them out into a number of discrete classes. The central material Vygotsky (Vygotsky 1986, Kozulin 1990) used, for example, was a set of wooden blocks which varied in shape, colour, height and area; Inhelder and Piaget (1964) used blocks varying in shape and colour. Typically young children did not appear to pick out blocks of the same shape, colour and so forth in any systematic way. The youngest children seemed to be arranging blocks in patterns which pleased them, rather than classifying them, so making what Piaget and Inhelder called a 'figural collection', or using some diffuse and subjective feeling of 'these go together'. At a slightly later stage a few blocks were picked in succession which were alike on some criterion, for example colour; but before all the blocks of that colour (say red) had been picked out, the child appeared to switch criteria and pick out a few more blocks which were the same shape as the last red block. After a few chosen by shape, and again before the criterion had been applied throughout the set, they might switch a second time, sorting by a new criterion or reverting to colour. Such sorting seemed to involve 'chain complexes' where one object led unsystematically to the next, and the experimenters' interpretation would be that the child had no overall plan for sorting out the set.

Later still, one criterion might be applied to all the objects so that they were sorted into mutually exclusive groups on the basis of, for example, being the same colour. But there is no abstract rule and the child would not construct groups on the basis of other criteria such as shape, either as an alternative sorting or as subclasses within the different colours. Making a co-ordinated use of the less salient criteria of height and area to sort the Vygotsky blocks, ignoring shape and colour, was quite a late achievement. So is the proper use of negative evidence. In Vygotsky's work, pre-adolescents who might appear to be grouping objects using truly conceptual reasoning (for example sorting by colour) when faced with the revelation that two objects which had been put together because they were the same colour actually belonged to different categories, would react only by tinkering with these objects' place in the sorting, not seeing that this evidence disconfirmed their hypothesis that colour was the correct basis for sorting. Vygotsky said such behaviour involved the use of 'pseudoconcepts', apparently rule governed and often labelled exactly as true concepts would be, but not properly formed, not properly understood and problematic in various ways, not least in the possibility that they are talked about and used parrot-fashion.

Pseudoconcepts have their developmental place, Vygotsky argued, because children who use them, even though they do not understand them, will get positive responses from adults who see the child behaving as they themselves would do and assume that the child's understanding is as advanced as his or her behaviour. The child becomes aware of his or her cognitive operations only after the practice of these operations is 'endorsed' by others: human cognition is a social construction. Adult and child may act alike and talk alike but have different underlying types of concept and conceptual reasoning. The child, being a language learner, develops conceptual complexes which are to a considerable degree predetermined by the meaning particular words already have in the language of adults. Because children need to function and communicate adequately, they seek to understand and to talk as adults do, taking on ready-made meanings without necessarily understanding their conceptual basis.

Children's ability to form and use concepts, it was concluded on the basis of findings like these, was rudimentary until somewhere around school age. Since about 1970 this sort of conclusion has come under an increasingly intense and successful attack in many areas of cognition (as much of the rest of this book shows). In the case of children's concepts, a major contribution was made by work on language development and by changes in theories of the nature of human concepts. If children in their second year could understand and use verbal labels for concepts like 'dog' and 'fruit' in ways which resembled adult usage (though the resemblance was not exact) they were showing some ability to acquire and use concepts in their everyday lives. As cognitive psychology started to examine real-world concepts instead of the tightly defined artificial material which had dominated the field, so theories of concepts which did not go beyond clearly defined necessary and sufficient attributes became more obviously inadequate. Rosch's work on basic-level categories suggests that basic-level categorisation may be easier than superordinate or subordinate categorisations, and early negative conclusions about children's categorisation capacities might have relied too heavily on tasks requiring superordinate-level categorisation (Rosch *et al.* 1976). Instead of looking at attribute-based sorting of objects with low ecological relevance (neither salient in the child's experience nor easily related to other objects which might have been salient), investigators looked at a wider range of behaviour and material. As a result they found competences in young children which had not been obvious in the classic experiments.

Sugarman (1981, 1983), for example, gave children aged between 12 and 36 months a number of tasks involving two groups of small identical objects. She looked at the sequence in which objects were manipulated and the way they were arranged in space. At 12 months the children manipulated items from the same group, selecting them sequentially, though they did not make separate spatial arrangements of groups. Older children did arrange the groups separately, picking out one group by 18 months and by 30 to 36 months being able to shift from group to group while they sorted. More recently (Fivush 1987) Jean Mandler and Robyn Fivush made a similar analysis of what 14- and 20-month-old infants did with objects which were not identical but were groupable in terms of whether they were used when eating or when washing. Here too infants touched objects from the same group sequentially, more than half of even the younger group touching at least three of the four objects from one group sequentially. None of this can be taken as suggesting that infants can categorise like adults, but these and similar studies (see Clark 1983, Gelman and Baillargeon 1983, Smith 1989b) do show rudimentary classification in infants; infants are also quite demonstrably capable of recognising a new instance of an important and familiar category, such as feeding bottles, and treating it as similar to previous encountered instances.

I mentioned earlier that categories can be formed at a variety of levels of specificity and inclusiveness and that it seemed to be useful to think of there being 'basic-level' categories (Rosch and Lloyd 1978, Rosch *et al.* 1976). At the basic level there is maximum similarity within a category and maximum differentiation between categories. 'Chair' seems to be an example of a basic-level category; its subclasses (dining chairs, armchairs, highchairs etc.) are quite similar to each other, and its superordinate class of 'furniture' includes many classes (cupboards, desks, tables) which are internally homogeneous but not (at least perceptually) so similar to chairs. Basic-level categories are relatively easy to recognise, recall and name, using as they do distinctive overall shape and motor interaction, and being at the most general level where a coherent mental image is possible. Classical taxonomic categories, in contrast, involve an 'achievement of the imagination'. Rosch has argued that basic-level categories are early developers, and basic-level object names do seem to be predominant amongst children's early words (Clark 1983, Mervis 1987, Rosch *et al.* 1976), though as Mervis points out these names as used by children do not necessarily correspond to adults' usage. Although adults' talk to young children tends to present basic-level labels, the child does not necessarily pick up what are the relevant criteria or what other instances are members of the same category. Mervis's son Ari, for example, first comprehended the word 'duckie' at the age of 10½ months when he would apply it to live mallard ducks and a variety of model birds, all of them three-dimensional with duck-shaped heads and long bills, but not to two-dimensional pictures of ducks, or to stylised ducks (such as a model Donald Duck), or to model songbirds. At 12½ months he would accept pictures of ducks and slightly later a number of stylised ducks, and by 20 months he had 'goose' and 'swan' categories, though geese and swans were still occasionally labelled as 'ducks'. Throughout, adults had only labelled ducks as such, some of the birds which Ari called 'ducks' being properly labelled as 'goose', 'chicken', etc. Ari seemed to be attending less to adult labels than to criteria of shape and function, though adult labels in conjunction with concrete examples were eventually helpful in the development of adult-type categories.

For Ari, comprehension and production of 'duck' seemed to apply to the same objects. For other children, there have often been more production errors than comprehension errors, especially in the form of 'over-extensions'. Children's over-extensions often apply a basic-level term to instances which are actually from an adjacent class (as Ari did when he called a toy Canada goose 'duckie'). There are usually similarities of appearance, and often the label and the object to which it is not quite applicable are members of the same superordinate category (waterfowl in Ari's case, perhaps, or birds). This sort of usage might be taken as implying that the user 'knows', in some sense, that there is a relationship between the two basic-level categories via the superordinate category; or it might be attributable to the child's sense of the social obligations of discourse, so that he or she uses an over-extension when the correct label is not available but some sort of label is required. Once an appropriate label is available (either the correct basic-level label or a high level general one such as 'thingummy') there will be fewer over-extensions. Young children certainly feel a strong desire to communicate, and this is one of the strongest determinants of language use and development. In so far as basic-level categories really do both pick out correlated attributes that take similar values within categories and differentiate instances from other categories, that is, as they break down the world into really useful units, they will facilitate both the child's communication and his or her understanding and use of information (Waxman and Hatch 1992).

Ari seemed to be developing his 'duckie' concept in part by abstracting common features from the instances he encountered. How could he, how could other children do this? One theory, proposed and then abandoned as not good enough by its author, Eve Clark (Clark 1973, 1983), was the semantic feature hypothesis. This assumed that meanings or concepts break down into combinations of perceptual (and conceptual) units. Children beginning to use words only have parts of the full adult meaning available. The development of meaning involves adding further conceptual units until the child's meaning matches the adult meaning. Thus the theory predicts that children will produce over-extensions (as they do); that if two words share several semantic features the child may confuse them in both comprehension and production (as they do 'more' and 'less', for example); that if one word adds on extra semantic features to another it will be learned later ('boy' should and does precede 'brother'); that children should learn more general semantic features earlier than specific ones and that they will learn combinations of features word by word, not necessarily realising how they apply to related words.

Most of these predictions were borne out by data, but there have been problems which cumulatively have toppled the theory, at least in its author's eyes (Clark 1983). It does not deal with the question raised very early in this section of what semantic features, what attributes, will be salient or decisive. Children seem to prefer contrastive features, those which mark within category similarities and between category differences, as if they assumed that the meanings of different words are contrasted. Nor do children always simply add more attributes or semantic features in their development of a concept; there are, for example, examples of initial 'under-extensions' where 'dog' applies first only to the family's pet but is eventually extended to other canines who lack his particular characteristics of appearance and behaviour. More interestingly, perhaps, there is evidence of conceptual reorganisation where features are reshuffled and reweighted as knowledge grows (see e.g. Carey 1985 and other sections in this chapter). Finally, the semantic feature theory relies too heavily on linguistic evidence, in part because it is emphasising the verbal attributes of concepts, and does not take sufficient account either of the non-linguistic strategies that children use in their communication and language comprehension, or of the embedding of conceptual material in their non-linguistic lives.

My discussion of concepts so far has led to emphasising the place of particular concepts within the person's wider knowledge of the world and how it works. General world knowledge and theories of what is relevant and important to the present particular case seem to influence both the structure and the use of concepts. Ultimately such a view as this leaves cognitive psychologists and philosophers with the impossibly formidable task of describing not just isolateable concepts such as 'furniture', 'peace', 'triangle', and so forth, but entire knowledge systems in more or less flexible use. Fortunately a more manageable task arises for developmental psychology: to examine the possibility that children's concepts arise in considerable part from their direct experience of the working of their own worlds. In particular, there is the more precise hypothesis that children quickly build up mental representations of familiar daily routines and that analysis of these routines leads to formal conceptual achievements such as categorisation into hierarchical concept systems.

A major body of work on this problem has been done by Katherine Nelson and her colleagues (Nelson 1986) under the banner of 'General Event Representation'. They have been concerned with children's generalised representations of 'events' and how such representations develop and interact with other aspects of cognition. An 'event' normally involves people in purposeful activities, acting on objects and interacting with other people in order to achieve a particular result. Events are organised around goals and given conventional labels and conventional boundaries. The event 'grocery shopping', for example, has the goal of buying the groceries which the household needs, and typically includes activities such as writing shopping lists, getting to the grocers', buying the groceries, bringing them home and unpacking them into the appropriate cupboards, but probably does not include menu planning or eating the groceries which have been bought. Representation of the event 'getting married' might include the ceremony itself and the planning beforehand, but would probably not include at least the earlier stages of the courtship, or specificities of 'being married' beyond the generalised 'live happily ever after'; infrequently experienced events may have different sorts of detail and less realism than those which have been gone through daily.

Events, like scripts (Schank and Abelson 1977), normally have a temporal sequence which may be a matter of convention or of logical or pragmatic necessity, and may be more or less strong and specific. In the 'getting undressed' script, for example, there has to be an invariant temporal sequence of taking socks off after shoes, if both are worn; but the script may not specify whether socks should come off before or after trousers, or, more probably, different people's scripts may specify different orders, and doing things in what would be one's own 'wrong order' (trousers off but socks still on, for example) may seem endearingly comic or disturbingly dangerous (as in the dispute between Lilliput where the 'script' (and indeed the law) specified that breakfast eggs should be broken at the small end, and its neighbour Blefuscu, where 'Big Endians' prevailed (Swift 1985). Event representations also enshrine causal sequences ('We needed some bread *so* we went to the baker's') and specify actors, activities and props. These allow of alternative specifications: we would go to a baker's for bread, cake, pies, etc., but perhaps not zip fasteners, electric light bulbs, melons or a daily newspaper. Nelson suggests that experience of these alternative 'slot fillers' leads to categorisation: if two items are alternative props or actors (or, no doubt, activities) at a particular point in a script then they are likely to be seen as in the same category. Similarly, if the script makes two items co-occur, they may be categorised together: a possible source of children's thematic categories.

Many of young children's daily experiences are highly routinised: new instances of the event can be incorporated without changing the general expectation of how the routine goes, but marked deviation from the routine causes distress even in infancy (Dunn 1988, Mandler 1983). Adults clearly teach infants and children to take part in routines ('peekaboo', for example, or 'reading' picture books (Bruner 1983), or going to see Granny), and children learn the script as well as acting in it. By the time children come to use language, they have accumulated a great deal of event knowledge from their daily experiences, and much of their early language use is associated with routines of feeding, playing and so forth. Being able to use language to construct knowledge may be very dependent on being able to relate it to prior experience, including experience which is provided by other people and given a social structure by them. Routines enable children to learn the meanings of words (which mark and comment on the sequence of events) and to engage in a discourse with adults which is more extended than they can manage without the support of a generalised event representation (see e.g. Tizard and Hughes 1984). Within routines they can show advanced skills such as giving informative answers to questions, talking about objects and events that are not present, making causal inferences and so forth. Representations of routine events give children good opportunities of attaching meaning to the routine's constituents and also of comparing this routine with other ones, because the general event representation carries performance and frees the child's attention from maintaining the current activity.

Nelson (1986) suggests that event representations could be the 'basic building blocks' of cognitive development; that from late in their first year children work with generalised event representations (GERs) of whole meaningful events, especially routinised interactions with familiar adults, to come to understand social relations and object categories in the world. The coherent structure of familiar event representations facilitates cognitive processes such as categorisation, analysis of patterns and of cause–effect relations, analysis and synthesis of attributes, specification of what is optional and what is obligatory, and so forth. Using an event representation in a familiar situation to guide both verbal and non-verbal action (and interaction with other people) allows children to make sounder predictions and to organise their own actions and verbalisations more appropriately than would be possible without a GER. As well as helping smooth performance in a routine, GERs support high level cognitive functions such as making and carrying out plans, using logical relationships, extending reality into fantasy, making inferences and so forth. Social and physical knowledge are not so clearly separated as in adult analysis, as objects take part of their meaning from the social interactions and events they are used in, and social interactions often involve or refer to physical props.

As I said at the beginning of this section, we are throughout our lives faced with the problem of achieving some sort of stability in the face of a continuously changing reality. Event representations involve a lifelike picture of elements and relations changing over time and with different details on different occasions. They are generalised and have a structured organisation, but are also specific to particular times, places and persons through the possibility of inserting equivalent specific items as 'fillers' in particular points in the script. They help the child (and the adult) to predict what is likely to happen, to understand what has happened, and to get a grasp on the changing reality of the present. A person who has no available event representation will have fewer cognitive and emotional resources free to deal with the demands of the moment, and may be overwhelmed by the chaos of existence (as, perhaps, in autism; see e.g. Frith 1990, Lewis 1987, Rutter 1983a). Young children seem to need routine as an aid to cognitive stability, and their participation as actors in adult-led routines contributes to their cognitive development.

It may be worth mentioning here a distinction between two types of knowledge representation which has cropped up in several parts of the literature on cognitive development. This is the distinction between procedural and declarative knowledge, between 'knowing how' and 'knowing that'. It is suggested (e.g. Mandler 1983) that the declarative knowledge system, the 'knowing that' system, consists of a data base of facts and a number of very general procedures such as rules of inference for linking pieces of data. Information is stored as units which can be accessed from any part of the system, and new information can easily be added, as a further item on a list of facts or as a new node in a network. Thus we can know who the Prime Minister is or the President of the United States, and after an election we can if appropriate change our information on who is the current premier, relegating the former one to the penultimate position on our list of 'presidents since the Second World War', or whatever. Procedural knowledge is rather different. It consists of sequences of actions designed to arrive at a particular answer; for example as well as (or perhaps rather than) the declarative knowledge that a reef knot is flat and symmetrical, we have the procedural knowledge that to make one we should take the right string over and under the left one, and then the new left string over and under the right one. This sort of routine-based knowledge is very effective for action routines, but specific facts, being embedded in the procedure, may be less accessible and less addable than in the declarative knowledge system. In order to get a piece of knowledge from the procedural to the declarative system, we may often have to run through the procedure and extricate the fact. I expect that almost every reader of this book would be able to identify the sixth letter of the alphabet after F, but in order to do so might well have to recite 'G, H, I, J, K, L'. Having done this often enough, the answer 'L' might become part of the declarative knowledge system, as well as part of the procedure for reciting the alphabet.

It is clear that access to knowledge is important developmentally. As they get older, children get better at accessing knowledge without running procedural routines, early knowledge being heavily procedural rather than declarative (Freund, Baker and Sonnenschein 1990). Having well-established procedures which run smoothly may sometimes make it easier to reorganise their constituents into appropriate places in a declarative knowledge system, though initially constituent bits of a procedure may be too tightly linked to neighbouring parts of the event representation to be easily separated out. Children's tendency to thematic categories, to context-dependent performance and to being unable to describe, explain or modify what they can do might be attributed to good procedural knowledge, a system of declarative knowledge that is less functional, and accessibility problems.

I will mention briefly here another aspect of Vygotsky's work on concepts. He was (as Chapter 4 discusses) very interested in the impact of educational processes on the child's cognition. He therefore compared the development of concepts that the child learned in school with those spontaneously developed through everyday activity. The former were 'scientific' in the sense that they were formal, logical and decontextualised; the latter were experientially rich but unsystematic and very much embed-ded in context. In terms of the coherence and rigour of the concepts, the taught 'scientific' ones were more advanced than the 'everyday' ones, and the children had more reflective control of them; but they lacked the rich base of experience and the connection with other concepts that the everyday concepts had. The two types of concept interacted in development:

> In working its slow way upwards, an everyday concept clears the path for a scientific concept in its downward development. It creates a series of structures necessary for the evolution of a concept's more primitive, elementary aspects, which give it body and vitality. Scientific concepts, in turn, supply structures for the upward development of the child's spontaneous concepts towards consciousness and deliberate use.
>
> (Vygotsky 1986: 194)

For example, the systematic learning of scientific concepts in one field could translate into increased abstraction, awareness and control of thought in other fields, though it will not do so automatically (see sections on transfer and teaching thinking).

Studies of the organisation of knowledge have moved from an almost exclusive focus on attribute similarities within artificial categories to a recognition that we more probably organise our knowledge in many different and more multidimensional ways, as I have indicated above. This gives us a different basis for evaluating young children's knowledge systems. Instead of stigmatising them as immature, inadequate and inferior to adults' ways of understanding the world, recent researchers have been impressed by how much adults and children share in their conceptual systems (for a summary see Mandler 1983, and for recent papers see Carey and Gelman 1991). I will suggest some general points here, while discussion of what children think about within particular areas of cognition may be found, subject by subject, throughout this chapter.

Clearly there are infinitely many different ways of organising what is known, and many of them will be useful, many actually are used. It used to be claimed that children had no capacity at all to use conceptual systems (such as taxonomic classifications), which were the dominant feature of adults' conceptualisation; it now seems that children do show conceptual structures very like adults', and adults have not given up some 'childlike' conceptual structures. Infants show categorical perception in certain domains (hue, speech sounds, faces) within their first six months, for example (see Harris 1983a), and adults can use thematic bases for categories as well as attribute-based ones. Probably learning to use language influences how other children organise their knowledge; indeed it seems unlikely that it should not, but it has been hard to establish specific effects in children (but see Luria 1976 and Cole 1990 for discussion of the effects of becoming *literate*). It is still an unresolved question whether language changes the representation of concepts that the toddler has already acquired, or whether it is 'merely' facilitating their expression and use. It certainly does mark out new and better specified information for the child and allows discussion of concept with other people (at least in so far as they share the same language and concepts and relate them similarly). There is much debate about whether children's concepts are 'incommensurable' with adults', or whether there is merely a gradual elaboration and tidying-up of their concepts as they grow older (see papers in Carey and Gelman 1991). It may be that it is this sort of minor change in flexibility of use and a growth in the amount of information acquired which characterises conceptual development from the pre-school years into later childhood. Where children are knowledgeable and encouraged to discuss their knowledge they seem to have concepts very like those of adults. Chi and Koeske (1983) provide a detailed description of a 4-year-old's dinosaur knowledge; Keil (in Mandler 1983: 470) provides an example of a 5-year-old who thought rocks were alive, the adult-type reasons for his belief being that 'they could have babies (pebbles), grow (perhaps into boulders), and die, as evidenced by their just lying around and being still'. These are perfectly sound criteria for distinguishing the animate from the inanimate (see section on childhood animism later in this chapter); the child's answer is wrong (and charming) because his evidence is poor, not because his concept has a childish structure or his reasoning is poor. It seems that much of the change in thinking over the school years comes from the acquisition of more and more declarative and procedural knowledge, the development of metacognition, an improvement in the accessibility of knowledge, and increased familiarity with a wider range of cognitive and social domains. There is in recent literature an increased interest in domain-specific knowledge, and a recognition that there may be marked dis-crepancies in understanding between different domains. Thus students may succeed on a contextualised version of a logical task but not on an abstract version with exactly the same structure (Watson and Johnson-Laird 1972), or an adolescent may combine high creative achievement as a math-ematician with immature social skills and political awareness. Even if highly abstract concepts are available, both children and adults may in any case prefer more pragmatic thinking and rely on familiar knowledge and procedures.

Thus the current state of opinion seems to be that Piaget was right when he insisted that knowledge and thinking are based on processes which are 'functional invariants' throughout life, but wrong or at least over-simplify-ing when he described qualitatively different structures of knowledge at different ages. Later structures are bigger, more flexible and more easily accessed and reflected on than earlier ones, but not unambiguously different in their organisation and certainly not generalised into a uniform level of competence across different ages. Throughout our lives we use event representations, attribute and functional similarities, contiguities and con-tingencies, sequences and co-occurrences, inferences, and taxonomic classifications to organise our world knowledge. Developmental changes seem to be more a matter of differentiation, elaboration and perhaps integration of knowledge systems rather than qualitative changes in the whole basis of conceptualisation (though there are clearly microlevel changes in limited areas, see sections elsewhere in this chapter). Conceptual development is heavily dependent on experience, and in many domains on instruction, though certainly we go 'beyond the information given'.

## CHILDREN'S CONCEPTS OF THIS, THAT AND THE OTHER

As well as the research on concepts in general which I have described earlier, there are many studies which focus on children's concepts of a particular area. Such areas range from conception (e.g. Goldman and Goldman 1982) to death (e.g. Gartley and Bernasconi 1967, Lansdown and Benjamin 1985, Lazar and Torney-Purta 1991, Orbach et al. 1985, Speece and Brent 1984, Stambrook and Parker 1987), from dinosaurs (Chi and Koeske 1983, Chi et al. 1989) to the threat of nuclear war (Tizard 1986). A substantial proportion of studies of children's concepts of $X$ content themselves with getting age differences in children's answers to leading questions, with attempts at explanation of developmental change being comparatively rare, and often do not consider variations in the answers given that might be associated with the respondents' experience, sample peculiarities, or the form of question being asked. As interviewing children in depth about $X$ can be time-consuming, samples are often small and dubiously representative of 'children in general'.

The major information-gathering technique is the obvious one of asking children to say what they know about $X$, commonly by using the 'Piagetian' clinical interview of core questions and auxiliary probes intended to explicate the child's line of reasoning. This technique is seen by its users as being sensitive and flexible, by its critics as unstandardised, overly verbal and generally unscientific. Piaget's initial account of why he introduced his 'méthode clinique' (Piaget 1929) was that the rigid form of question used in a standardised test might raise the issue in a way which was foreign to the child's conception and thus produce a 'romancing' answer. For example the question 'what makes the sun move?' would be anomalous and hard to answer for a child who imagined the sun was a living being which moved of its own accord (or indeed for a child who knew that the Earth moves round the sun, not vice versa). Varying the questions according to the way the child has appeared to understand earlier questions may elicit a 'truer' picture of the child's concepts. Alternatively, however, such varying of questions may evoke confused responses; children may respond to the repeated questions of an older interviewer with self-corrections elicited by the social structure of the clinical interview, not by their attempt to clarify their account of their concept (see e.g. Rose and Blank 1974 and Siegal 1991 for how easily this can happen even in a conceptually clear situation). Broughton (1978, 1982) argues that variation in the content of questions will produce only variation in the content of answers, not in the form of reasoning those answers reveal. I find myself dubious about this argument; surely the content (which he admits will be affected by the question) may make the reasoning look like one thing rather than another, or even *be* one thing rather than another. Probe questions may offer or close off opportunities for displaying understanding which other questions might have revealed differently. Indeed, understanding may develop during the course of the interview for children who are open to revising their ideas in public, who can say 'Ah. I never thought of it that way before: that would mean . . .'

Categorising children's answers may involve the use of 'stage' models imported from other sources (frequently Piagetian) and of dubious validity, or the use of categories derived from the present field of data and available as a lengthy coding manual available from the authors on request, but not clearly self-evident from the examples given in the published text. Such categorisations may well be entirely justified, but they risk suppressing real individualities in children's concepts to fit them into a rigidly differentiated system, and they tend to work against explanation of how children come to move, as they get older, from one category of answer to another.

Methodologically, the solution is, no doubt, the alternation of flexible clinical interviews with more precisely standardised test methods and experiments, and of categorisation analyses with analyses which allow more continuity in development. Above all, what is needed is a resistance to simplifying development into claims that young children do not and cannot use particular sorts of categories, which older children use to the exclusion of more immature forms, when the data really show wide variation in the use of all sorts of categories at all ages. There may be such variation within an individual's performance; variation between individuals might usefully be examined in terms of the contribution of their experience or other cognitive skills to their concept systems. Finally, studies which extend their investigation of a focal area to other related areas would be welcome, so that we could begin to examine links between distinct but linked topics.

The reader will probably not be surprised to learn that although there are many studies of children's concepts of this, that and the other, comparatively few are going to receive further attention here. To some extent my selection of topics and studies reflects the methodological points I have just made or recent progress in the area, but my subjective feeling that the area studied is conceptually important has also determined my choice. Limits had to be drawn somewhere, and readers have to put up with a writer's limitations!

## Childhood animism

Some of Piaget's early work (Piaget 1929, 1930) showed children attributing animate characteristics, such as independent movement or causal intentions, to inanimate objects, such as bicycles or the moon. Laurendeau and Pinard (1970) and Carey (1985) similarly found young children saying that objects such as cars, fire, the wind, televisions and rocks rolling down hills were alive. Not all young children fail to make a distinction between animate and inanimate objects. Shields and Duveen (1982), for example, asked nursery-school children which of a farmer, a cow, a tractor and a tree could eat, sleep, move by itself, talk, feel angry, and so forth. The children's answers drew a clear distinction between the tractor and the tree, which could not do any of these things, and the farmer and the cow which could. (There was some disagreement over whether cows could talk or have emotions, but children who said they could maintained they talked to other cows or the farmer, extending the meaning of 'talk', but not applying this extension to the firmly inanimate tractor and tree.) Bullock (1985) found 3-year-olds making this distinction, though inconsistently; by the age of 5, judgements were adult-type. Similarly, studies reviewed by Gelman and Spelke (1981:

48–51) suggest that children as young as 2 may make some adult-type distinctions between animate and inanimate objects if the objects are well known to them and if the questions asked are relatively straightforward. Some of Piaget's animistic answers may have stemmed, it is argued, from asking problematic questions such as 'Does the sun know where it is moving?'. In contrast, Keil (1979, 1981b) found the animate–inanimate distinction was fundamental to the ontological aspects of semantic development.

The beginnings of a distinction between animate and inanimate objects, and between people and other animate objects, seems to be discernible in quite young children (Carey and Gelman 1991, Gelman 1990, Gelman and Kremer 1991). It is not entirely clear what the distinction is based on and we do not know how it is built up in the early years of life. No doubt one source of the distinction is differences in the ways persons act on the child and react to his or her actions, compared with the actions and reactions of objects. Such differences would be a better basis for distinguishing the truly animate from the truly inanimate than what children are directly told, given the extensive anthropomorphism to be found in young children's literature, replete as it is with talking animals, toys, trains and so forth. Carey (1985) attributes children's animism to their lack of knowledge of biology. She suggests that only the basic biological functions are good criteria for distinguishing a unified category of 'living things' from 'non-living things'. Children who do not know about biological functions can only apply their general knowledge of people when they try to distinguish between 'living' and 'non-living', and so will be unlikely to have a coherent concept of 'living things'. If their rudimentary 'living things' category is internally hetero-geneous, they will be more likely to include objects which are not actually alive. They might be said to have what is essentially a 'family resemblance' concept rather than a 'defining characteristic' one. For example, the very conspicuous movement of cars and clouds may resemble that of animals enough for them also to be said to be alive. Developmental change might then be largely a matter of elaboration of the knowledge base, and sorting out the factual information from the metaphorical and fictional (rivers which run, trains and rabbits which talk, thunder which is the gods' anger). These changes may of course amount to a substantial restructuring (Johnson et al. 1992, Carey and Gelman 1991).

## Children's concepts of bodies

One obvious but important component of the development of children's concepts of their bodies is an increase in knowledge. Very young children just beginning to talk learn to point to their hands, toes, faces, tummies and so forth, and grazed knees which produce an ooze of blood are also discussed with interest. By the time they start school most know that their bodies contain brain, bones, blood and a heart, and although some seem to believe that their stomachs contain identifiable remnants of their favourite food this is hardly an unreasonable error (Carey 1985, Eiser 1985, Eiser and Patterson 1983). Adults often have poor knowledge about their own bodies and make errors in locating organs when asked to draw them on an outline body; children's degree of informedness does them no discredit. A study by C. Porter of 144 American schoolchildren aged 6–10 (Eiser 1985: 21) found them able to draw organs with accuracy and to scale, and to name, among other body parts, adenoids, bone marrow, cerebellum, cerebrum and cortex, optic nerve, pancreas, pores, schlera and tooth-root.

The naming of body parts can be economically investigated by distributing drawings of bodies to whole classes of children to be filled in or annotated appropriately. Questions about how children's knowledge of their bodies is organised, and what its sources are, and how it is constrained, are harder to provide answers for. A study of children's concepts of the mind and the brain (Johnson and Wellman 1982) raises some interesting issues. Children between 5 and 11, and a group of adults, were asked to judge whether the brain was involved in each of a number of activities. All the children could say where the brain was, and all agreed with adults that it was needed for mental acts such as thinking and remembering. However, there was an age change in the recognition that the brain was involved in sensory-motor acts or involuntary movements such as sneezing. The youngest children denied that the brain was involved in, say, walking: you just need feet. As children got older the involvement of body parts increased beyond the periphery; for example, eating involves mouth and teeth for the youngest children, but stomach, bladder and the rest of the digestive system for older children (Eiser and Patterson 1983). By about the age of 9 children were beginning to show awareness of some of the transformations occurring within the body, for example the digestive process and the circulation of nutrients round the body in the blood. Knowledge of reproduction has been seen to lag behind other areas of understanding, but is also known to be correlated with children's exposure to sex education (Goldman and Goldman 1982).

Knowledge about the anatomy of bodies can be related to knowledge about their functions, about species and about the properties of living organisms (Carey 1985, 1987, Carey and Gelman 1991, Johnson et al. 1992, Keil 1979, 1981b, 1989). Carey claims that an 'intuitive biology' emerges from the young child's essentially psychological understanding. Early accounts of biological functions and organs are in terms of human activities and intentions: activities such as eating, breathing and sleeping are conceptually the same sort of phenomena as playing or bathing. The concept of eating includes information about table manners and about what food appears at what meal as well as the facts that food is put into the mouth (not some other orifice), that it is swallowed, that after eating one's stomach feels fuller, and so on. Eating is explained in terms of intentions: people eat because it is dinner-time or because they want to grow strong. Mature biological theories discriminate between intention and function, between biology and psychology, and have both far more integrated data and more principled explanations, Carey suggests.

She has a variety of different pieces of evidence supporting her claim for the emergence of an intuitive biology from a human-centred psychology (Carey 1985, 1987). One piece shows how people extrapolate information about a particular species to other species. Subjects from 4 years old to adult were taught about an internal organ which was new to them. At all ages those who had learned that humans had, for example, a spleen inferred that other mammals were very likely to have one too, birds, bugs and worms progressively less likely, and that flowers, the sun, clouds, vehicles and tools couldn't be assumed to have one. However, the pattern with which a new organ was 'projected' on to other species differed for children under 10 and older people. Adults and older children who had learned that people had spleens or that dogs had spleens were equally willing to propose that the other species had them too. Younger children would only extrapolate human organs to other species, not non-human ones to either humans or other species. Four-year-olds who were taught that humans had a spleen projected it to other mammals, birds and bugs at a rate above 50 per cent; those taught that a dog had a spleen projected it to other species at about a 25 per cent rate, those taught a bee had a spleen at below 15 per cent, even if the comparison animal was another insect. Carey suggests (1985: 150) that

> only if new knowledge can be integrated into a child's knowledge or humans and human activities will the four year olds project it sensibly to other animals. By age 10, people are only one mammal among many with respect to biological properties, and there is no longer an asymmetry of projection from people and from dog.

However projection from bees remains low.

A second body of evidence that young children structure their knowledge of biological properties such as eating and sleeping in terms of human behaviour is in the asymmetry of their attributing such functions between species. As with the possession of a spleen, young children are much more willing to attribute people-like biological functions to animals similar to people, under-attributing functions such as breathing and eating to animals such as bugs and worms. Older children may make similar judgements but they do so by deductive inferences from category membership or from reasoning about knowledge of biological functions. Thus they can say that worms breathe because they are animals and all animals breathe, or because all living creatures need to burn oxygen for energy and must therefore be able to obtain oxygen from the air. Their knowledge is both greater and more precisely and usefully organised. In particular it involves much more understanding of biological functioning, with a move away from the 'one organ one function' model of the young child. Older children have more awareness of how different organs function together to solve the basic problems of living that confront all organisms. Processes such as death, growth, reproduction, eating and so forth are initially seen in terms of the behaviour of the person, without much knowledge of the mechanisms which mediate between inputs (such as eating too much) and outputs (such as getting fat). Later development may bring about an understanding of the cause and effect relationships here, though the success of the slimming industry suggests that for many people this understanding is incomplete and easily obscured.

### Children's concepts of health and illness

Eiser (1985: 15) claims that 'there is beginning to be considerable evidence that children's beliefs about these issues [the causes and prevention of illness, and their definitions of health and behaviours they think important in maintaining health] develop in a systematic predictable sequence'. She bases this claim very largely on the work of Bibace and Walsh (1981), who describe neo-Piagetian stages in children's concepts of health and illness. They interviewed 24 children at each of the three age levels of 4, 7 and 11, using questions such as 'what does it mean to be healthy?', 'were you ever sick?', 'how did you get sick?', 'how did you get better?', 'what makes colds go away?', 'what is a heart attack?', 'why do people get heart attacks?', 'what are germs?', 'what do they look like?', 'can you draw germs?', 'where do they come from?'.

In the 'prelogical' stage of the youngest children, the main cause of illness was contagion, though God and certain other external causes were cited ('How do people get colds?' 'From trees'). In the 'concrete-logical' stage (7–10) illness arose through contamination by physical contact with the illness, more elaborately by swallowing or inhaling it. In the 'formal-logical' stage illness was seen as caused by specific malfunctioning or non-functioning of an internal organ or process, with psychological and physiological functions ultimately interacting.

Similarly Brewster (1982) found that young children believed that illness was the result of human action and children from 7 to 10 that it was caused by 'germs', while only children over 11 acknowledged that illnesses were the result of interaction between several factors, different for each specific illness. Kister and Patterson (1980) also found lack of differentiation between different illnesses: young children judged that a cold, toothache and a scraped knee could all be explained by contagion (or even immanent justice). Eiser, Patterson and Eiser (1983) describe children's ideas about health. Being energetic, taking exercise and eating good food were increasingly frequently mentioned between 6 and 11 years of age, and were the main components of descriptions of 'health' throughout this age range.

It is not entirely clear that these findings represent children's concepts of health and illness completely fairly (see Harbeck and Peterson 1992, Siegal 1988, 1991). The work stemming from a neo-Piagetian 'cognitive developmental' approach focuses very much on cognition without examining social or cultural influences; it seems very likely that phenomena like the young child's tendency to say that illness is caused by wrong-doing owes something to parental invocations of illness as a consequence of not doing what you're told – 'if you don't eat up your dinner/wrap up warm/wear your boots, you'll get ill'. Neo-Piagetian analyses of such data, focusing on cognitive structures characteristic of discrete stages, will run into the same problems that have brought Piaget's own stage model under question (see Gelman and Baillargeon 1983, Mandler 1983, Meadows 1983). In particular they will fail to account for transition from one stage to another and to acknowledge the existence of individual differences which may be associated with different experiences and cultures. Further, the interview technique used may be insensitive to the understanding of young children, so underestimating their competence. Siegal (1988, 1991) for example, investigated children's understanding of contamination and contagion by asking children to judge other people's (a puppet's or another child's) account of why they got a cold or toothache or a scraped knee. Even 4-year-olds showed a good substantial knowledge of contagion and contamination: they knew that contagion was a good explanation for a cold and a poor one for a scraped knee, and believed that milk into which a foreign body such as a cockroach or a dirty comb had fallen was no longer really safe to drink. Further research using more ingenious techniques such as these, or examining children's scripts (Eiser 1988, Eiser and Eiser 1987) may uncover more understanding in young children and more variation at a particular age than Bibace and Walsh (1981) found.

In particular, it is essential that alternative theories of why cognition develops about health and illness should be considered, both for the improvement of accounts of cognitive development and for the improvement of the care of chronically sick children who need explanations of their illness to allay their fears and increase their co-operation with treatment (Eiser and Eiser 1987).

## Children's concepts of death

Having looked at studies of children's concepts of life, and health, I will briefly survey the literature on children's concepts of death. The literature is predominantly descriptive and the findings described are not entirely consistent – not surprisingly, given that there is variation in method and samples. However the general picture emerging is that the idea that death is final, inevitable and universal is not expressed until somewhere around the age of 8 or 9 (Gartley and Bernasconi 1967, Lansdown and Benjamin 1985, Lazar and Torney-Purta 1991, Speece and Brent 1984, Stambrook and Parker 1987). Children under 5 are said to lack appreciation that death comes to us all and means an irreversible end to all bodily functions. Thus they may deny that they themselves will ever die, or say that a dead person would return to life if only the correct measures were taken, or that life continues on a reduced, less active level – 'she is not dead, but sleepeth', to use a phrase that I remember hearing in Sunday School at a somewhat later age. Alternatively it is claimed that such young children 'know about but deny' the fact of universal irreversible and inevitable death, an obviously untestable hypothesis.

Slightly older children may recognise that death is inevitable and universal, but believe that unless an external agent or event is involved death only happens to the old. (No doubt some parental input intended to reassure them contributes to this.) Death may also be personified, not surprisingly given the long cultural tradition of doing just this. By about the age of 9, the account of death starting to predominate is of an internal biological process operating according to natural laws, universal and final and meaning the complete cessation of body functions, and thus not like sleep or a temporary separation; with an increasing and perhaps compensatory belief in spiritual continuation emerging.

This sequence of ideas derives from studies of Western schoolchildren in the mid-twentieth century who have not experienced the death of a close relative. They are thus limited to a particular historico-cultural experience, or, rather, lack of experience. There are four reasons for caution about drawing from these results any strong conclusions about children's ability to understand death. The first I have mentioned already: there is variation even in these studies of comparatively similar samples in what is understood about death – at what age, for example, its finality is understood. The second is that death is an emotive subject, where even for adults a mature understanding can co-exist with feelings and ideas that deny the irreversibility and the universality of death. For example a bereaved person may find it impossible to accept that someone loved is dead and cannot be retrieved, or a healthy adult may be unwilling to consider what should happen to his or her possessions and responsibilities in the event of his or her death, and may therefore not make a will or other such plans. The third reason is that emotion, and anxiety in particular, may distort the account people give of what death is. An interesting study by Orbach *et al.* (1985) showed that anxiety impeded young children's expression of their ideas about death.

The fourth reason for caution, which needs rather more discussion, is that most child respondents in the research literature have little or no experience of death except in emotionally distant contexts. They may have seen real human deaths reported on the television news, or experienced the death of pet animals, but the loss of a close family member or close friend is unlikely to be within their experience. This would not have been the case for such children in the nineteenth century or earlier, when infant and child mortality was much higher, and when far more people died in their own homes rather than away in hospitals, hospices and so forth; nor would it be the case today for many children in the Third World. It appears that children who have suffered a death in the family may express far more adult feelings and ideas about this loss than children with no such experience, that the age of the child need not limit their understanding so severely as the literature on 'inexperienced' children would suggest. Eiser (1985) describes studies of children's reactions to the death of a sibling, and Mandell *et al.* (1983) and Burns *et al.* (1986) describe the responses of children who had lost a baby brother or sister through Sudden Infant Death Syndrome. Children who had suffered such a sudden and traumatic change in their family showed grief similar to adults' in its content and duration, even when they themselves were as young as 2. A therapeutic group described by Krasner and Beinart (1989) showed an understanding of death far in advance of the children's ages (4–7), and expressions of anger, sadness and resolution of feelings echoing those described in adults, for example by Parkes (1972). The expression of their ideas and feelings in their group meetings seemed to ameliorate the behaviour problems which had followed the death of their baby sibling, problems which seem typically to increase following a death in the family (Burns *et al.* 1986, Eiser 1985, Mandell *et al.* 1983). Experience thus seems to advance understanding, and discussion of death with young children is possible and may be helpful.

## Children's understanding of emotions

Understanding emotions is an important part of our understanding of ourselves and other persons. As 'natural psychologists' we use concepts of internal emotions to explain many actions: 'he kissed his mother because he loved her', 'he ran away because he was frightened, not because he wanted to play chase', and so forth. We not only explain actions, we seek to predict, control and use them. We thus need to have at least a pragmatic grasp of what emotions are commonly associated with what situations, and of how emotions are typically expressed in postures, movements, facial expressions and tones of voice. We may, as Darwin proposed, have both an innate repertoire of emotional expressions – ways of looking pleased or unhappy which are extremely similar not just in different cultures but in different species – and an innate ability to recognise these expressions (Darwin 1872), but we are also expected to learn cultural rules about what emotional expression is acceptable or admirable, to turn the evolutionarily universal quivering lip of distress to the stiff upper lip of English manhood at its traditional public school finest. Understanding emotions is thus an important part of children's 'theory of mind' (see final section of this chapter), part of their socialisation, part of their moral development (Meadows 1986, Nunner-Winkler and Sodian 1988) and part of their mental health. This is particularly the case if we presume that it is better to be aware of one's emotions and able to modulate them to some degree than to lack insight and control. We also have reason to believe that emotion and cognition intertwine in development (Attili 1989, Harris 1990); the effects of emotion on cognitive development are briefly discussed in Chapter 6.

There is a rapid increase in understanding of emotions over the period of infancy (Campos *et al.* 1983). By the end of the first year babies are well able to recognise whether a familiar adult is showing a positive or negative emotion and to begin to identify what has caused the emotion. Dunn (1988) convincingly demonstrates that early in the second year children move from reacting passively to another person's emotions to actively seeking to change them, providing comfort to someone who is distressed or distressing someone who has annoyed them. In doing this they show that they know it is possible to change emotional states, and that often they appreciate what has caused and what can change an emotion. Some may have quite a large repertoire of emotion-altering techniques which they can apply to others, for example trying several different ways to comfort an unhappy younger sibling. Parental handling of emotions is one of the variables behind individual differences in this. It seems that some parents, who demonstrate concern and who comfort, explaining what distress has occurred and why it is appropriate to comfort, tend to have children who as toddlers show more understanding of other people's views and feelings and respond more helpfully to someone else's distress (Light 1979, Zahn-Waxler *et al.* 1979).

Pre-school children who are abused by their parents, however, are more likely to react to another child's distress with hostility or with distress and fear of their own, and less likely to show active concern (Main and George 1985). This is not because they do not understand that distressing another child or acting aggressively are serious offences, as they distinguish them quite clearly from minor breaches of convention (Smetana, Kelly and Twentyman 1984). It may perhaps be that abused children have learned less well to inhibit their own aggression, or perhaps they become so disturbed by the other person's distress that they are no longer able to act in a comforting way and even act aggressively in order to get rid of the person whose distress is disturbing them; or perhaps, having seen their parents react to their own distress in non-comforting ways, they have learned to act in the same way themselves, though not yet to assert that causing distress is in the victim's good, or that 'it hurts me more than it hurts you'. The psychoanalyst Alice Miller (Miller 1985, 1987, 1990) argues that denial of the truth of one's own emotions and of other people's is one of the components of abusive parenting and one of the main causes of social psychopathology.

As children grow older, they become increasingly able to show a diversity of emotions and to react to them in others. Harris (1989, 1990; see also Gnepp and Klayman 1992) argues that they may show complex emotional reactions, for example ambivalence, as toddlers, long before they are aware that emotions may be mixed. Typically, children under about 6 will assert that only one emotion can be felt at one time. Harris (1983c) for example presented 6-year-olds and 10-year-olds with stories in which the protagonist might be expected to feel conflicting emotions, for example when a lost pet dog is eventually found, injured. The younger children typically said that the child who owned the dog would feel entirely happy, because the dog was found, or entirely sad, because it was injured, but not both happy and sad. Ten-year-olds acknowledged that the protagonists in such stories would experience both feelings at the same time. Similar age differences were found when children were questioned about their own experiences. Eight-year-olds who had just started at boarding school admitted to mixed feelings about the whole experience, but attributed their feelings of pleasure and excitement to the new opportunities of school and their negative feelings to their separation from home and their parents, that is, to two different aspects of being at boarding school. Thirteen-year-olds said they had mixed feelings about one single aspect of school which they could appraise from two different viewpoints, being simultaneously excited about their new lessons and worried about whether they would be able to cope with them (Harris and Lipian 1989). Harris (1990) suggests that this developmental shift occurs because there are two ways of appraising situations which arouse emotion. The first develops early, and translates fairly automatically into behaviour. A situation which has been associated with pleasure in the past evokes pleasure the next time it is encountered, a situation which has been associated with lack of pleasure evokes distress. A situation associated with both pleasure and lack of pleasure evokes ambivalent reactions, as in the 'ambivalently attached' infant (Ainsworth *et al.* 1975, Bretherton 1985) who seeks reunion with the mother but immediately rejects contact with her. This would seem to be a fairly simple conditioning process, which does not involve awareness of the emotions aroused, just an automatic reaction to the situation.

The second type of appraisal of emotions develops much more slowly. It involves appraisal not just of the situation that evokes emotion but of the emotion evoked. This makes it possible for a child to identify his or her own emotional reaction to a situation, to predict what emotion a particular situation would arouse, and to think of situations that would elicit a particular emotion. This appraisal can be more exhaustive or less so. The child examines the situation for aspects that are known to be associated with emotion. Typically, young children end this examination when one such aspect is found and the emotion identified (Gnepp *et al.*1987). Thus, in a situation such as receiving a present which is not what you hoped for, a young child might find 'I'm pleased when I get a present' and report pleasure, not going on to 'I'm disappointed that it isn't what I wanted' and the sadness that would result, and so denying that any negative emotion would be felt. Older children are more likely to examine the situation and its possible emotional consequences more exhaustively, and so acknowledge the possibility of ambivalent emotions. Some adults, acknowledging the ambiguity of everything, may be able to emphasise some emotions more than others and so use them to enhance their own self-esteem or effectiveness.

Harris is suggesting that early emotional responses are pretty well automatic and not monitored by the child, but that children monitor their emotional responses to an increasing degree as they grow up. They also become increasingly subject to the display rules which their culture prescribes for the expression of emotion: 'big boys don't cry', 'say "thank you" to Granny for the nice present (even though it's not what you want)'. A study by Cole (1986) found girls as young as 4 obeying these social display rules, in that they smiled when the experimenter presented them with a disappointing gift, though not when they examined their gift and experienced their disappointment alone. (Boys at this age did not attempt this masking strategy at all; girls were visibly disappointed or disgusted but smiled bravely.) Questioned by another experimenter, the little girls admitted they had been disappointed (and eagerly swapped the disappointing gift for a more attractive one); when asked whether the first experimenter would know what they felt they focused on what they had *told* the experimenter, not on their own facial expressions, nor did they mention having deliberately controlled their own expression of their emotion. These children said that someone else in the same situation would show the real emotion, even if they had a good reason to dissemble. Older children (see Harris 1990, Harris and Gross 1988, Harris *et al.* 1986) realise that real and apparent emotion may not coincide and that an observer may be deceived by the displayed emotion, taking it as real. Six-year-olds understood this if they understood *why* the protagonist was concerned to hide real emotion; 10-year-olds did not seem to need so much explicit information about motives.

This development in understanding that real and displayed emotions can be discrepant, and that observers and experiencers of emotions may differ in their understanding of the experiencer's emotional state if there is a discrepancy, Harris (1990) attributes to the child's awareness of two conflicting sorts of information. The child is aware of his or her own real emotions; but under social pressure to display a more acceptable emotion may do so and mislead observers, who attribute to the child an emotion different from the real one. The child may feel, for example, disappointment at an unattractive gift, but smile so convincingly that the donor says 'I'm so glad you really like it!' This could alert the child to the possibility of misleading others by displaying a more positive emotion than is really felt, and as we said earlier children will have been exhorted to do this. Gnepp and Hess (1986) report children's understanding of display rules in this sort of pro-social situation was more sophisticated than their understanding of how to falsify emotional displays for self-serving ends such as concealing one's guilt or embarrassment. However Harris (1990) mentions a study of emotionally disturbed children where egocentric and self-serving displays were better understood than pro-social ones.

Harris (1990: 209–10) sketches a very interesting and important picture of how the changes in children's understanding of emotion come about, drawing parallels with several other areas of development. He suggests that the task facing the child is to develop a representation of his or her behaviour which acknowledges how it is differentiated, in the case of emotions differentiated across socially-constructed situations. His preferred metaphor is one of 'amplification'. Children spontaneously produce behaviour which varies (with some appropriateness) from situation to situation, but this variation goes unnoticed unless it is amplified by some environmental correlate. For emotional displays one major correlate would be the social consequences of the emotion; these include other people's reactions and, perhaps especially, their comments on the emotion (see also Dunn 1988). If the child shows ambivalence, for example, the mixed emotional display makes other people respond to both its components, thus encouraging the child to recognise that more than one emotion is involved. Similarly, the feedback following emotional behaviour that successfully follows a display rule alerts children to the discrepancy between the emotion they are expressing and the one they feel. Thus children who are subjected, as Miller (1987) describes, to a regime in which they are only allowed to display socially prescribed emotions, even in situations which evoke negative ones, and where the displayed emotions are said to be the true ones and the real ones are denied, would be likely to grow up with a distorted understanding of emotion, and indeed distorted emotions. Other strategies for controlling emotion (Harris 1989) may be healthier.

## Children's concepts of persons

Research on the development of children's understanding of people is one of the largest bodies of work in the area of social cognition. Children and adults have to operate with other people in co-operation and competition; social isolates may suffer an impaired development (Curtiss 1977, Rutter 1985a, 1985b, Skuse 1984) and knowledge of persons may be a critical deficit in autism (Hobson 1990, Leslie and Frith 1990, Tager-Flusberg 1992) and as cognition itself has been argued to have evolved to serve social functions (Humphrey 1983) it is obviously an important topic. Nevertheless there are some puzzling paradoxes emerging from the relevant research.

One stream of research stems from a neo-Piagetian tradition. It has been

heavily influenced by his model of cognitive structures that limit understanding and functioning and succeed each other as discrete and coherent
stages (see Chapter 4 this volume). It also incorporates much that derives
from his assertion that children are egocentric, that is, that they are unable
to appreciate that other people have knowledge, feelings or views different
from their own. Often a neo-Piagetian interview technique is used in this
tradition of research. Such studies generally point a rather negative picture
of children's understanding of people (for reviews see Rogers 1978, Shantz
1983). One of the best-known and most cited studies is work by Livesley and
Bromley (1973). They asked their 7- to 15-year-old subjects to write free
descriptions of eight persons they knew, including themselves. They found
that the younger children's descriptions were predominantly in 'peripheral'
and 'external' terms, such as appearance, age and surroundings. Children
mentioned observable concrete characteristics and global evaluations such
as 'she's nice' rather than inferred or explanatory psychological characteristics. They used interests, abilities, likes and dislikes frequently in describing themselves but rarely in describing other people. By adolescence,
descriptions were becoming more abstract, more qualified with
acknowledgement of variation in different settings or at different times, and
more in terms of psychological dispositions, though such psychological
subtlety seemed to occur more in descriptions of themselves than in
descriptions of other people, where global verdicts and behaviour-based
descriptions remained common.

Similar results emerge from research on children's understanding of the
'self' (e.g. Broughton 1978, Selman 1980; see Damon and Hart 1988 for a
review of some other studies). Broughton describes successive stages in
accounts of the 'self'. Initially it is a 'body part' like the mind or the brain
and is described in physical terms: only at about the age of 8 did his subjects
define the self in internal psychological terms. (This account has since of
course been cast into doubt by recent work on children's theory of mind
which suggests the beginnings of a mind-body distinction before the age of 4
(see final section of this chapter).) Selman (1980) agrees that the first
distinction is between psychological experience and physical experience, but
in addition a distinction comes to be drawn between inner experience and
outer appearance and it is realised that the self can monitor its own thoughts
and feelings more directly than others can, or than self can monitor other
people's feelings and thoughts.

Damon and Hart (1988) discuss work by Aboud and Skerry in which
child and adult subjects first named characteristics that described the 'self'
and then said whether or not the self would still be 'the same person' if a
particular characteristic were changed. There was an increase with age in
naming psychological characteristics of the self and in saying that one would
not be the same person if a psychological characteristic was changed.
Chandler and his colleagues asked similar questions about the degree to

which fictional characters continued to be the same person despite a dramatic life event which changed their behaviour; a case in point was the miser Ebenezer Scrooge from Dickens's *A Christmas Carol*. Chandler's youngest subjects said he was still the same person on Christmas Day after his visions because he still had the same face, hair and house. Older children attributed personal continuity to central characteristics of self which remained unchanged, for example self-centredness.

These and other similar studies have been taken as showing that young children have a poor understanding of other people and older children a better one, in particular that young children cannot go beyond specific and concrete descriptions of persons, and that there is what John Flavell summed up in his 1977 textbook *Cognitive Development* as a development from 'surface' to 'depth'. It must be pointed out that it is still a debatable issue in the psychology of personality whether abstract descriptions based on generalised psychological dispositions are indeed 'better' than more concrete descriptions (see for example Hampson 1982). For the moment the critical point to be made is that it may be useful to examine separable facets of 'understanding persons' rather than going for a one-dimensional development.

The recent work by Damon and Hart (1988) does this with reference to the development of self-understanding. They use a model of the 'self' derived from the ideas of William James. This incorporates the 'me', the relatively objective material, social and spiritual or psychological characteristics that identify each self as a unique entity, and the 'I', the subjective experiential features such as awareness of oneself as an agent with a unique life history and experience, and continuing over time, distinct from others and capable of awareness of one's own awareness, that is, of self-reflection. This differentiated model seems to me far more useful than aggregating the various aspects of self-understanding, the more so since the interview evidence which Damon and Hart present suggests that developmental change is very far from general and uniform. They present a model of self-understanding in which seven 'schemes' each progress through four levels. The first level, characteristic of early childhood, involves categorical identifications; the second (middle to late childhood), comparative assessments involving consideration of the self as measured against others; the third (early adolescence), interpersonal implications of the self; the fourth (late adolescence) systematic beliefs, principles and plans. The seven 'schemes' are the physical, active, social and psychological selves, and the continuity, distinctness and agency of the self. They believe that earlier theorists were wrong to say that some aspects are not found in the young and others are given up as children develop; rather they say that at all ages children have some understanding of their physical, active, social, and psychological selves. Although one may be more conspicuous than another at a particular time (as in the earlier work's account of young children's physical descriptions of the self and older children's psychological ones), this does not mean that one is transformed into the other. Nor do children move neatly from one level to the next on all fronts at once: they are likely to make statements characteristic of several developmental levels at any given time.

Damon and Hart's data derive from 'clinical interviews' of Massachusetts schoolchildren: 82 between 1st and 10th grades at the testing that was the main source of data. (An earlier occasion was used to construct the levels-by-schemes model and 52 subjects took part in a later testing for longitudinal purposes.) There was a further replication sample, and smaller studies with children from a fishing village in Puerto Rico, a sample of anorexic girls and another of boys with conduct disorders. Inter-rater reliabilities, internal consistency of the interview questions and test-retest reliabilities over a period of a month were reasonably satisfactory. The *validity* of the method is not directly addressed, save by a defence of the clinical interview technique, and by the two smaller studies with adolescents who showed anorexia or conduct disorders: however Damon and Hart's work probably represents *valid interview accounts* of self-understanding.

Some of their examples of material may give a flavour of the work. The following snippets from interviews seem typical (Damon and Hart 1988: 59–69):

*What kind of person are you ?*
I have blue eyes.
*Why is that important?*
It just is.

(Level 1, physical self-scheme)

*How are you different from your mother?*
'Cause I play a lot and I read a lot.
*Is that what makes you different from your mom?*
Sure, my Mommy just watches television, cooks or cleans.
*And you read.*
And I write, and I play with my toys.

(Level 1, active self-scheme)

*What are you like?*
I'm bigger than most kids.
*Why is that important?*
I can run faster than everybody.

(Level 2, physical self-scheme)

*How will you be different in five years?*
I'll get more mature.
*When you say you'll get more mature, what do you mean when you say that?*

Like when you're getting older, like when you're little you don't know
stuff, a lot of stuff, and you say the wrong things. When you're getting
older, you know what to say. Like if you have a child, like they
wouldn't know what to do so you could tell them.

*(Level 2, psychological self-scheme)*

*What kind of person are you?*
Pretty rich.
*What difference does that make?*
Well, my family has a lot of money, so we can belong to the country club.

*(Level 3, physical self-scheme)*

*What kind of person are you?*
I'm a nice person.
*What's nice about you?*
I'm not selfish. Like if somebody says, they go to the teacher and say, 'I
don't have any ice-cream, and I don't have any lunch either, and I can't
have any money to buy any fruit. I need that lunch, and the lunch guys
won't give me any lunch.' I would say, 'Here, have my money.' I did
that to Shannon.

*(Level 4, physical self-scheme)*

*What are you especially proud of about yourself?*
I'm always learning and growing.
*How are you always learning and growing?*
I try to find out as much as I can about things, all different things, and
put it all together so I can really know what's going on. And I'm always
getting better and better at it.
*Why is that important?*
That's what's going to make me become the kind of person I want to be, a
person on top of things.

*(Level 4, psychological self-scheme)*

The successive 'levels' of the three remaining aspects of the self in Damon
and Hart's model do not fall into the comparatively generalisable pattern in
which first categorical identifications, then comparative assessments, then
interpersonal implications and finally systematic beliefs and plans become
possible. The 'agency' component of the self-as-subject is elicited by
questions such as 'How did you get to be the way you are? How could you
have turned out different?'. The first level of answers involve external
biological, supernatural or social forces: 'I just grew'. At the second level,
the person's own wishes or activities have an influence: 'I tried really hard to
be like I am now', 'Because I used to do all my homework'. At the third
level, communication with others is important: 'I learned from my parents. I
even learned from my friends, just listening to 'em and talking to 'em.' At the
fourth level, personal or moral evaluations of life possibilities influence a

person's actions. The next component of the self-as-subject is its continuity 'from year to year': at Level 1 this is said to rest on stable preferences, behaviour, or characteristics such as name, and at Level 2 on reference to immutable personality characteristics:

*How do you know it's always you?*
'Cause I still like science, and I still like swimming. And I'd still be doing science.
*So you still like the same things, so you know it's always you?*
Yeah.

(Level 1 example)

*How do you know it's always you?*
I've always been good at baseball.
*You've always been good at baseball?*
Yeah, and I always will be.

(Level 2 example)

Level 3 ideas about self-continuity involve the recognition of self by others, and at Level 4 the self's characteristics are seen as evolving from earlier ones, not as being simply identical with them: 'Well, nothing about me always stays the same, but I am always kind of like I was a while ago, and there is always some connection.' The final aspect of the self-as-subject is its distinctness, expressed in terms of it being different from every other self. This progresses from differences in characteristics such as fingerprints or having shoes with laces, via one-dimensional characteristics such as friendliness to one's unique combination of psychological and physical characteristics at Level 3 and one's unique subjective experiences at Level 4: 'Nobody else sees things or feels the same way about things as I do' (Damon and Hart 1988: 72–3, 76).

Damon and Hart's research provides some fascinating glimpses of children's ideas about themselves and various other matters, including the child as developmental psychologist, perhaps, in their accounts of how they got to be the way they are or might have turned out different! However, even the representative examples I have presented here suggest some problems with the work. First, are the questions and the prompts used fully appropriate? Questioning in the Piagetian *méthode clinique* is supposed to follow what the child says: in many examples the reader of Damon and Hart's book may have a sense of leading questions shaping the child's answers. Second, how coherently does the elicited material fit into the levels and the separate schemes? The physical, active, social and psychological schemes are not always separable in the data, though they do reflect distinctions drawn by William James and implicated in the more unidimensional models constructed by, for example, Broughton and Selman. Later levels incorporate earlier ones and a child is likely to make statements representative of several different levels: thus the analysis has had to use the modal levels 'to represent a subject's typical performance': 'on average, 61% of the chunks (separable statement plus explanation, clarification or explicit failure to provide one when given an opportunity) were at the modal level' (p. 89). Information on how subjects' statements were spread across levels is not given. Again, it is not entirely clear to an outsider why some of the examples given were classified at different levels: the 'Level 1' child quoted earlier who explains that she or he is the same from year to year ' 'cause I still like science, and I still like swimming' might be seen as differing from the 'Level 2' child (I've always been good at baseball') merely in using 'still' rather than 'always', for example. This sort of problem has long been endemic with the complex material elicited in *méthode clinique* interviews, and, to be fair, Damon and Hart do recognise the problem's existence. The dust-jacket claim that their interview methods and their analysis methods are new is not, perhaps, their responsibility.

I have laboured the methodological point somewhat because of the major paradoxical finding in this field, which I mentioned in the introductory paragraph of this section. Interview studies represent children as immature understanders of persons, dominated by notions which they have to grow out of but which might meanwhile be expected to impair their ability to get along with other people. Some stage or level theorists have seen immature concepts as reflected in inadequate social behaviour (such as 'egocentricity'); this view is undermined (as I will shortly describe) by the growing body of evidence that children are very skilled at many sorts of social interaction and may casually express a considerable and conscious understanding of persons. Other stage theorists (for example Damon and Hart) do not commit themselves to adverse judgements on young children's social understanding. Neither, however, do they explain why children change from one perfectly adequate level of understanding to another, a change which would be easier to explain if the later levels of understanding were in some way more useful than the earlier ones. The existence of differences between mature philosophers about what 'the self' might be could perhaps be seen as sufficient evidence that one of Damon and Hart's different levels is not self-evidently intrinsically better than another; so why should there be a developmental change from thinking somewhat like B. F. Skinner to thinking somewhat like Jean-Paul Sartre? No explanation exists; a little potential evidence does. Damon and Hart see comparison between self and others as predominant ('modal') in middle childhood, and see interpersonal relations in early adolescence as modal. Might this reflect the social predicaments of children at these ages, as they are embroiled in first school and getting good grades and then in all the early stages of mating behaviour, the getting dates and going steady which loom large in so many accounts of American adolescence? Damon and Hart's Puerto Rican subjects, growing up in a different culture, show a somewhat different pattern (chs. 8–9). The development of self-understanding seems likely to be one of the areas of social cognition where social factors go a long way toward determining developmental change.

This view could be further justified by the important work being done at present which investigates children's understanding of persons in a completely different way. Instead of neo-Piagetian studies of the 'cold' cognitions of children interviewed about themselves and other persons, we have detailed and systematic observations of children taking part in the normal daily interactions of their families and other social groups. An excellent account of some of the best of this work is provided by Judy Dunn in *The Beginnings of Social Understanding* (1988). She initially raises the discrepancy between the remarkably good ability that infants and very young children show in distinguishing and using people's actions and characteristics and the neo-Piagetian interview evidence that understanding other people develops extremely slowly, in spite of so many aspects of their development requiring social experience.

> Children develop their powers of communication, understanding and thought, their emotional security and their sense of themselves, within a complex social framework: do they nevertheless fail to grasp the nature of the moods, interests and relationships of others who share that world, or the ground rules of that world, until they are five or seven years old?
>
> (Dunn 1988: 3)

She then examines the 'social intelligence' of children as they grow up with siblings and parents. She emphasises the relationships between understanding on the one hand and the children's emotions, relationships and self-interest on the other, considering the children's behaviour and speech in 'the daily dramas of family life in which their powers of social intelligence are revealed and fostered' (p. 11).

She has systematically studied children of 3 and under in ordinary working-class and middle-class families in and around Cambridge, in their disagreements and confrontations with their mother and their siblings as well as in their co-operation, their comforting and their jokes. Some examples (which Dunn insists are representative of systematically gathered data, not anecdotal) give a flavour of the children's social understanding as revealed in their practice.

> John (21 months) and his older sister Annie have pushed stools up to the kitchen counter next to oven, to investigate cooking materials.
> *Mother to John*: Ah ah! Don't touch please. Hot! [removes child].
> *John*: [protest noise]
> *Mother*: Oh I know!
> *John* [angrily]: Annie going there!

*Mother to Annie*: Annie come right away. Right away.

(1988:53)

Sally (24 months) bouncing actively round the room sees chocolate cake on the table.

*Sally*: Bibby on.

*Mother*: You don't want your bibby on. You're not eating.

*Sally*: Chocolate cake. Chocolate cake.

*Mother*: You're not having any chocolate cake either.

*Sally*: Why? [whines] Tired.

*Mother*: You tired? Ooh!

*Sally*: Chocolate cake.

*Mother*: No chance.

(1988: 21)

Jay (30 months) is concerned about his older brother Len, who is crying because his mother scolded him and refused to comfort him after he had bitten Jay.

*Jay to Len*: Len. Don't – stop crying, mate. Stop it crying.

*Jay to Mother*: Len crying, Mummy! Len crying. Look. Me show you. Len crying.

*Jay to Len*: Look, Len. No go on crying (pats Len) . . . [Len still sobs.] Ah Len [Helps Len with Lego bag.] I put it back for Lennie, Hey? . . . [Shows Len a car.] There's this man in here. What's this, Len? What's this, Len? [Len sobs.]

*Mother to Len*: Do you want me to smack you?

*Len to Mother*: No.

*Mother*: Then just stop it, please.

*Len to Mother*: I'm trying to [sobs].

*Jay to Len* [still crying]: Stop crying, Len. Smack your bottom.

(1988: 94–5)

Polly (28 months) intervenes in her older sister's conversation with their mother about the sister's pretend game of shopping at Sainsbury's.

*Polly to Sib*: Better get your cheque book.

*Sib*: Yes . . .

[Later in pretend game]

*Sib to Mother*: Did I leave my bag there?

*Mother to Sib*: You didn't leave your bag at Sainsbury's, did you?

*Sib to Mother*: What I want?

*Polly to Sib* [Points out mislaid bag]: No at home!

*Mother to Sib*: You left it at home! . . .

*Sib to Mother* [confused about having lost her list and her bag]: Umm – what did I want then?

*Mother to Sib*: What did you want?

*Polly* [triumphantly]: I got all my shopping list in. I's got my shopping list in my bag.

(1988: 114–15)

And, finally, John (now aged 36 months) collaborates with his older sister in a fantasy game about what he is going to do with a bonfire.

*John*: I'm going to burn everyone. I'm going to burn Jimmy I am. To burn Jimmy Green. To burn Jimmy Green . . .

*Mother* to *John*: Well, I think you're horrid. Making fires to burn people.

*Annie* to *Mother*: Anyway he needs to burn Jimmy Green. Because he keeps biting him.

*Mother* to *Annie*: He doesn't keep biting him, Annie.

*Annie*: Yes he does. [to John] Doesn't he John?

*John*: Yes he does! He does bite me! You know he does. He does he does he does!

*Mother*: I think the boot's on the other foot!

*John*: No! [laughs]

*Mother*: Jimmy Green's a nice quiet little boy.

*John*: No! [laughs].

(1988: 164–5)

Her observations show children with an excellent practical grasp of others' feelings and intentions, and of general social rules, for example of how relationships within the family can be used:

by two years old, children are using maternal authority for support in their fights with siblings: they draw their mother's attention to the siblings' misdemeanours, while pointing out that they themselves have not acted in the same way.

(1988: 67)

Similarly, siblings share the amusement and excitement when one or both have done something which has been forbidden, egging each other on in delightful joint wickedness. Dunn sees children as developing social knowledge as family members, whose feelings of attachment, rivalry and affection motivate them to understand people's emotions, intentions and motivations and the social rules which govern their interaction. She further points out how the mother's behaviour carries both implicit and explicit messages about the social rules of the world in which the child is growing up, with many conversations about what was acceptable and what unacceptable behaviour: messages which differ in content in different cultures but are universally learned early in ordinary domestic discourse (Heath 1983, Shweder *et al.* 1990). The children had a considerable motivation to learn to cope with their social worlds, and their self-interest drove their understanding on. Cognitive development undoubtedly contributes to their sense of self and their emotions (Parke 1989, Sroufe 1979), but emotional experiences also fire cognitive development; in Dunn's data, it was in those contexts where children had experienced anger and distress that they later came to reason rather than merely protest, as if their emotion had heightened their attention to and intensified their reflection on their experiences. (Research on children's understanding of emotion may be mentioned here: see e.g. Gnepp and Klayman 1992, Gnepp *et al.* 1987, Harter and Buddin 1987, Harris 1989 and 1990, Nunner-Winkler and Sodian 1988, later sections of this chapter.)

> All these features suggest a model of the growth of social understanding in which development starts from the child's interest in and responsiveness to the behaviour and feelings of others. In the subsequent development of social understanding, contributions are made, first, by the intensity of the child's self-concern in the context of family relationships and, second, by the child's participation in the moral discourse of the family. In other words, the model gives weight both to the cognitive changes that lead to the child's developing sense of self and ability to participate in argument, and to the affective significance of the tension between this self-concern and the child's relationships with other family members. In discourse about the social world, both the affective and the cognitive messages are significant.
>
> (Dunn 1988: 186)

In her next sentence, Dunn points out that this model raises more questions than it answers. I will not address these questions here (though see Chapters 4 and 5 for discussion of related issues), but merely point out the discrepancy between the sophisticated social skills of Dunn's toddlers and the apparently scrappy ability in understanding of older children in interviews. Obviously children may act appropriately but still be unable to explain the principles behind their actions, just as adults may. There are a number of different senses in which one can be said to 'understand' something, as I have pointed out earlier in this chapter. My present point is that if children fail to display an adult understanding in that epitome of a non-practical situation, the clinical interview, their failure is not explained by attributing to them a global inability to understand arising from pervasive and ineradicable characteristics such as egocentricity or an overly behaviouristic outlook. Rather, what the child understands where must be mapped, and more specific explanations sought for both failures and successes. Again, this is a message applicable in areas of developmental psychology other than the child's understanding of persons.

## Children's understanding of socio-economic systems

Children's development, including their social cognition, has mainly been studied in terms of microsystems such as home or school, or mesosystems such as the relationships of agreement or discrepancy between home and school (Bronfenbrenner 1979). Home and school are of course the settings most immediately relevant to children, but they live also, as we all do, within wider socio-economic worlds. Their part in the economic and political system is less prominent than their part in the life of the family, and we may overlook it in ways that disadvantage children (Leach 1979 argues this strongly), but it is nevertheless of potential interest to developmental psychologists. Turiel (1983) argues that it is reflected in the three general categories of children's social cognition: their concepts of persons or psychological systems, their concepts of systems of social relations, organisation and institutions, and their moral judgements of justice, rights and welfare.

It may be helpful to consider, briefly, the relationships between children and the economic and political worlds. In our industrialised society children have a comparatively limited amount of economic activity. They are not normally economically productive, as child labour is forbidden by law, though some do work in the home or the family business or illegally in the so-called 'black' economy, and older children may have part-time jobs as baby-sitters, newspaper deliverers, shop assistants and so forth. While low on economic productivity, children may be substantial consumers. Their own direct purchasing power may not be large but they exert a significant influence on the purchases of others. Adults' patterns of expenditure are substantially altered by becoming a parent. As children become able to change adult expenditure by their direct requests as well as by their mere existence, they as well as their parents increasingly become the target of advertisement, and their reaction to advertising has been studied by social scientists as well as by advertisers and market researchers (Lea *et al.* 1987, Ward *et al.* 1977). Children can learn to be sophisticated and critical observers of advertising (Ward *et al.* 1977) but its role in their understanding of the economic world has not been fully examined.

Besides studies of children as consumers and producers there have been a number of studies of their understanding of socio-economic institutions such as shops, banks and money. These are concerned to document the succession of ideas which children hold as they develop towards the ideas and attitudes which adults commonly have about the economic systems of society, but also to explain how these changes occur. The social institutions concerned are mostly thought of as social systems which children can observe other people playing roles in, inferring economic laws from their observations of economic activity just as they might infer the laws of physics from watching the physical world. Studies of children rarely consider economic institutions and laws as being socially constructed, the result of ideologies inculcated in the course of socialisation, though a few writers do address this possibility (Dickinson 1990, Emler and Dickinson 1985). This anti-sociological approach may be linked with the dominance in this field of neo-Piagetian studies which emphasise children as rationally constructing models of economic activity on the basis of what they observe and of their limited practical involvement, a construction which is seen as analogous to dispassionately inferring the laws of nature.

Walkerdine and Lucey (1989) argue very strongly that this failure to consider the socio-political issues surrounding children's cognitive develop-ment is both intellectually inadequate and politically malign. They believe that psychologists studying cognitive development have overlooked the ways in which children are confronted with socio-political inequalities and constraints, in part because of their naïve assumption that children's experience is of a protected and privileged idyll in which all is economically, socially and interpersonally rosy. Such an assumption leads, they say, to failure to ask the right questions about how children come to grips with problematic issues such as class, sexism and power, and to the stigmatising of parenting which differs from an ideal (Meadows 1986: 185) accessible only to some privileged middle-class parents some of the time. As feminists and socialists, and as women of working-class origin transferred by educational sponsorship into the middle-class as professional intellectuals, they have insights here which have to be taken seriously even if they would leave much of developmental psychology in ruins!

Most of the studies of children's understanding of socio-economic systems involve questioning children, perhaps inevitably, since children do not normally vote, have bank accounts, or play many of the roles of economic or political persons directly, but do so through adults. This poses two problems. First, children's answers to questions such as 'What things, jobs, people are important in a town?' (Furth 1980) are often full of charm but hard to analyse. Many investigators have classified answers into neo-Piagetian stage analyses, although data about the uniformity of 'stage' across contexts or the separation of 'stages' are not usually conclusive, and are often simply not presented. Second, children's verbal accounts may or may not reflect their practical understanding. Piaget himself moved from eliciting verbal accounts of 'reality' as observed by the child to examining aspects of reality which lie within the grasp of the child's action. Studies of children as economic actors, perhaps via script elicitation or even role play, may provide information which complements what is gathered from interview questions.

Although economic roles, institutions and laws form an interlocking system, and how children see their interrelations is perhaps the most interesting aspect of their thinking, I will deal with the elements of children's construction of the economic world separately, beginning with children's understanding of shopping. Children get many opportunities to observe shopping, and so might be expected to understand it comparatively well. The central transaction in a shop might appear to be a simple exchange, between customer and shopkeeper, of goods and their value in cash. The shopkeeper has, and the customer wants, a bar of chocolate costing 30p; the customer gives the shopkeeper 30p and receives the chocolate in return. This is certainly the most visible part of shopping but it is far from the whole. The retail shopkeeper is himself or herself a customer to the wholesaler who supplies the shop with goods; the shop has assistants who exchange their labour for wages, and there are also various running costs such as rent, cleaning, lighting, etc. These components of the shop are less salient to the shopper, but they have significant effects on the cost of the items in the shop. Typically such costs are not visible to children, who seem to have some difficulty in grasping the existence of these components and their effects, let alone their scale. A further source of complexity and confusion is that the passage of money between the customer and shopkeeper may be two-way: the customer gives 50p and receives the chocolate bar and 20p in change. To a small child with little grasp of the monetary values involved, this may look like a ritual, or a profit to the customer who ends up with goods *and* money, rather than the exchange it is.

The broad outline of the development of children's understanding of shopping seems to be fairly well agreed, although there is disagreement in the literature about details such as the typical age of achievement of each level of understanding (e.g. Berti and Bombi 1988, Jahoda 1979, 1984). Under the age of about 6, children are said to understand that money has to do with buying, but they seem to see customer–shopkeeper transactions as rituals rather than as exchanges, not as payment but as something you have to do, perhaps analogous to saying 'thank you' for a present. Shopkeepers give money to customers as well as the reverse; indeed for Berti and Bombi's youngest subjects one of the ways of getting money was to go to a shop and be given it. At this age children believe that goods were given to the shop (by another shop), not bought by it, and they seem not to be aware of any 'overheads', for example not distinguishing between the shopkeeper and the shop assistants. Even when these last two misconceptions begin to weaken, at around 7 to 8, the idea that the price the shop charges the customer is the same as the price the wholesaler charges the shop remains strong. The shopkeeper merely passes on goods at the same price as their original cost: the overheads of the shop, if recognised at all, are met from some external source such as the Mint, social security or the government. It is felt to be unfair, theft or fraud, for the shopkeepers to charge a higher price than they have paid themselves; only at the age of about 11 do children realise that a 'mark up' between wholesale and retail price is necessary if the shopkeeper is to cover expenses and make a living (or a profit). The scale of 'mark ups', the extent of the profit made, probably isn't grasped by children; it is often enough a surprise to adults!

A similar development occurs in children's understanding of banks (Berti and Bombi 1988, Furth 1980, Jahoda 1979, 1984), though with some delay compared with their understanding of shops. Jahoda (1984), for example, presents data from Scottish working-class children aged between 11 and 16. The youngest, who might have shown a little understanding of profit in the context of shops, showed no idea of it in banks. They viewed banks as being much like money-boxes and borrowing from friends: you get out exactly what you put in; to get more or to pay for a loan would not be fair. Even if they knew about interest they had little idea where it came from, and still thought of the bank in interpersonal terms. In Berti and Bombi's study, of children from working-class and white-collar families, first there were ideas of banks as 'for giving money'; so people who only have a little money go to a bank and

> they give them a little, then they give them a bit more, and they get to have a lot of money . . . then he gets to have lots of money and he buys lots of furniture, or a house and then other things, like that.
>
> (Berti and Bombi 1988: 19)

and the bank is a place where money can be deposited to be safe from thieves and an equal amount can be withdrawn later if needed. Then came a recognition that banks use the money deposited with them to make loans, and, eventually, that lenders receive interest paid by borrowers. As children move through adolescence they show more appreciation of interest and the bank's use of the money deposited with it. Not all, however, understand the reciprocity of interest in the bank's lending and borrowing, and few appreciate that the bank must charge a higher interest on its loans than it pays on its deposits if it is to pay its own workers, cover its costs and realise a profit. Again, appreciation of what scale banks' profits are on, and what is done with them, is quite possibly unusual in adults.

Why is children's understanding of banks less mature than their understanding of shops? One obvious possibility is that they have far more contact with shops than with banks, many more opportunities to observe and think about shopping activities. Berti and Bombi (1988) suggest that an understanding of banks involves construing money as a type of merchandise, to be bought and sold like other goods. As they discuss, the problem of the circulation of goods and money is a complex one, and children have difficulty in understanding it. Banks' activity in making loans may be misconstrued (Jahoda 1984) if loans are understood in terms of loans between friends which are regulated by ideas of fairness and strict reciprocity, not by calculated profit. The 'bank loan' script and the 'borrowing from friends' script have some crucial differences, which it is all the more important to recognise in the days of inflation and freely available 'free' credit . . .

Berti and Bombi present fascinating data on children's ideas about the source of money. Even the youngest children knew there was an association between 'work' and 'money', though they might also entertain the idea that you get it from transactions in shops or that it somehow spontaneously generates itself in pockets or wallets (an idea to be found in numerous fairytales). They may also have an idea that one must pay to go to work, for example train drivers have had to buy the train they drive and may also go to work in an office to raise the money to purchase the train. Later, children insist that to get money it is necessary to work, and that the amount of money received is proportionate to the amount of work done. This notion runs up against the realities of social stratification and the existence of rich and poor people (see also Dickinson 1990, Emler and Dickinson 1985). Young children believe that almost everybody is rich, partly because money is freely given away by banks or shops and also because being 'rich' is defined as having enough money to cover basic needs. As working comes to be seen as the only way to make money, working is also seen as the way to become rich: the poor are poor 'because they don't work' and the rich are those who work the most. The idea becomes differentiated somewhat:

*Is every job good for getting rich?*
No, there are some where you get a little money and some where they give you lots.
*Which are the best ones for getting rich?*
The heaviest ones.
*If a man has a heavy job is he sure to get rich?*
No, sometimes they start wheezing and they can't go on any longer, because when you work you can't stop for a minute, it's not like school where you can stop and finish things at home.
*Can you also get very rich doing a heavy job?*
Yes, it depends on the boss, how much money he gives you, and you can't squabble about it, you have to take the money they give you.

(Berti and Bombi 1988: 72)

Later still children described riches as being associated not with hard work but with qualifications, or with highly responsible jobs, or with inheritance, crime, or political corruption. These children saw becoming rich as much more difficult, and hard work as having a much less powerful influence on riches. They also differentiated income levels much more, no longer regarding an adequate income as being 'riches'. Differentiation may proceed differently for children from different social classes, as Emler and Dickinson (1985) demonstrated. They asked children aged between 7 and 12 to estimate the weekly incomes of doctors, teachers, bus drivers and road sweepers, to explain why the incomes differed, and to say whether equality of income would 'be better'. The average estimates given by middle-class children for each job were higher than those of working-class children: doctors were seen as having the highest incomes, followed by teachers, bus drivers and, finally, road sweepers. Middle-class children gave much more differential in the estimates of income than working-class children did, as well as judging incomes to be higher overall.

The children were asked about the 'fairness' of the different amounts they had estimated for each job and of a hypothetical equality of remuneration. There were no significant differences in judgement of fairness by age or by social class, though it was less common for the oldest children or for middle-class ones to say that equality of income would be better. Most of the children justified inequality of income by reference to some form of equity consideration, such as differences in the work or the responsibility involved in the job or the amount of training required for it. Middle-class children were more sophisticated in their justification of inequality, producing more (and more varied) reasons. In Berti and Bombi's study, similarly, middle-class children more often mentioned criteria other than physical fatigue, such as the greater or less utility of the job, or the level of intellectual activity which it demands.

Thus, although most children believed that income differences were justified, middle-class children estimated that the inequalities were larger (though even they underestimated their scale). The absence of age differences argues against this class difference being caused by the fact that middle-class children might develop faster than working-class children, more quickly reaching a complex understanding of social systems. The different estimate levels seem more likely to be due to different information about incomes. Emler and Dickinson argue that social representation of economic inequalities are more detailed, extensive and salient in the middle class, and hence middle-class children have had more opportunity to assimilate their community's shared knowledge and belief about income inequality. Exactly what economic knowledge is to be found in what parts of the community, and where it comes from, remains to be investigated. This sort of information may not be readily accessible to young children (Berti 1991).

If there is, as researchers suggest, a sequence of development of understanding socio-economic systems, the question arises of what causes it. The field seems to have been dominated by neo-Piagetian stage descriptions (e.g. Berti and Bombi 1988, Furth 1980, Jahoda 1979, 1984) and, no doubt consequently, there are neo-Piagetian processes of change in the explanations offered for development. Both Furth (1980) and Jahoda (1979) describe children who are apparently constructing a more advanced response in the course of the interview, and see this as occurring because the intensive questioning of the interview creates a conflict between two elements of knowledge which were previously co-existing in isolation.

Constructing a more advanced response re-establishes the equilibrium which the conflict endangered. Conflict and equilibration require the prior possession of some items of correct knowledge, a level of cognitive development that allows awareness of contradictions, and the cognitive processes necessary for integrating previously separate pieces of information. Children who hold strong preconceptions that prevent them from asking themselves questions will not be able to make cognitive progress.

The equilibration model of cognitive development focuses mainly on the role of *intrapersonal* conflict, between different items of knowledge possessed by children. The interview evidence of Furth, Jahoda and others illustrates how it proceeds, but not how frequent it is as compared with other routes to development, or how durable the results of intrapersonal conflict are. Another Piagetian possibility is *interpersonal* conflict (Doise and Mugny (1984)). Berti and Bombi (1988: 206-8) describe a doctoral dissertation study by Gerardo Echeita concerned with Spanish children's acquisition of the understanding of shopkeepers' profits. Echeita's 6- to 9-year-old subjects played at being shopkeepers or customers. The two shopkeepers had to buy goods from the suppliers (the experimenter) and decide what price to sell them at. In each case one shopkeeper was known from a pre-test to believe that the shop price should be exactly the same as what the supplier had charged. In the first condition the other shopkeeper also believed this, so there was no conflict between them in deciding the retail price. In the second conditions the second shopkeeper believed the shop price was fixed arbitrarily; in the third condition he or she clearly understood that the retail price was higher than the wholesale price because of the need to make a profit. These two conditions were intended to lead to conflict over the right price and hence to developments in the understanding of 'profit'. Finally the 'customers' witnessed the shopkeepers' discussion but did not themselves participate directly.

The condition which produced the most dramatic conflict of ideas, between the 'same price' and the 'profit' shopkeepers, produced the most improvement between pre-test and a post-test 4 to 6 weeks later, especially amongst the 8-9-year-old children. The condition with no interpersonal conflict led to minimal changes in understanding profit: the 'customers' and the condition 2 shopkeepers, who had had a less intense experience of conflict of ideas, made some progress but less than those in condition 3 who had engaged in debate with a partner who understood why there had to be an increase in price. It is thus clear that interpersonal conflict can stimulate development, though the greater improvement in condition 3 children would reflect their having been confronted by a recognisably correct understanding irrespective of their having undergone any conflict. Echeita's study, like those in other contexts of socio-cognitive conflict (e.g. Doise and Mugny 1984, Light 1983, Perret-Clermont and Brossard 1985), does not establish whether children's progress is due to the interpersonal conflict between children with more and less advanced views, or to children simply seeing a better model than their own. This possibility clearly opens the prospect of there being efficacy in tutorial interventions. Berti and Bombi (1988: 208–15) describe a study of their own in which children's understanding of profit seemed to advance approximately equal amounts whether an adult gave them correct information (a much less Piagetian intervention) or whether they reorganised their ideas themselves after discovering an internal contradiction. More important than conflict or tutoring was whether the children had sufficient understanding to enable them to recognise the significance of the information they were given or discovered. This suggests that it may be more important to identify crucial pieces of information or ways of organising information within a domain than to 'explain' development by appealing to a notion as general, as abstract and as hard to exemplify in terms of behaviour as equilibration.

## Children's concepts of mind

One area of children's concepts and skills which has been considered in some depth recently is their beliefs about the mental world, their understanding of the processes which variously underlie perception, cognition, intention, emotion, belief and other mental states and activities. Such knowledge must surely have cognitive consequences, and play a role in the development of metacognition; it has also been argued (e.g. Dennett 1979, Humphrey 1983) that it is a critical contributor to successful social interaction, where understanding other people's mental states may enhance the possibility of making sense of their behaviour (and of manipulating it). The study of mind has also of course been an important part of philosophy. Many of the questions studied in relation to children, for example the distinction between 'appearance' and 'reality', have a long philosophical history. I cannot discuss all that has recently been done concerning children's 'philosophy of mind' here; among useful reviews and collections are Astington et al. 1988, Butterworth et al. 1991, Estes et al. 1989, Perner 1991a, Pillow 1988a, Wellman 1990, and a special issue of the *British Journal of Developmental Psychology* (1991(1)).

As in many other areas of the psychology of cognitive development, one source of ideas has been work done by Piaget, in this case ideas put forward in two early books, *The Child's Conception of the World* (1929) and *The Child's Conception of Physical Causality* (1930). He suggested that young children were egocentric and animistic and had difficulty discriminating between the physical and the psychological; for example they claimed that their own view was what other people could see, that dreams were external images which could be seen by people other than the dreamer, and that the sun, the wind and other natural objects were alive and conscious and followed them around. Some of the recent work on children's understanding of mental states and processes has been concerned to investigate these Piagetian findings. Wellman and Estes (1986), for example, investigated whether young children distinguished between mental events or objects, such as a dreamed of or imagined dog, and real ones, such as a real dog. They found that even 3-year-olds could make a better than chance judgement of which of the 'real' and 'mental' pair could be touched, seen by others, and which existed consistently over time, thus showing they appreciated three of the main criteria necessary for distinguishing between the real and the mental. They also knew that you could dream about or imagine but not really see or touch an object which is physically impossible or non-existent, such as a dog with fiery eyes as big as windmills. Thus the pre-school children in this study were not Piagetian 'realists', claiming that dreams and thoughts have a concrete and public existence. They were also making more adult ontological judgements than the children interviewed by Frank Keil (Keil 1981a), perhaps because Keil's subjects were asked about thought contents in general not about a specific thought-of dog. Older children made more mature distinctions between real and mental events, but the rudiments of the distinction were apparent in 3-year-olds. Wellman (1985a) suggests that some of the earlier findings of children attributing concrete existence to mental events may have been due to methodological differences, that young children's knowledge may be less accessible and stable than adults' and easily obscured by the difficulty of giving an adequate verbal explanation. Alternatively a child might use mentalistic language without it being based on an adult-like understanding of mental events. Methodological caution is needed.

John Flavell and his colleagues have perhaps been foremost in investigating an analogous distinction, between what an object 'looks like' and what it 'really and truly' is. In a typical study children are shown (by sight then by feel) a sponge that looks like a rock (or a candle shaped like an apple or a white shape behind a coloured cellophane filter) (Flavell 1986, Flavell et al. 1986). At various points in the procedure they are asked questions like 'When you look at this with your eyes right now, does it *look like* a rock or does it *look like* a sponge?' (the appearance question), or 'What is this really and truly – is it *really* and *truly* a sponge or is it *really* and *truly* a rock?' (the reality question). Adults and older children reply that it *looks like* a rock but it really and truly *is* a sponge. They also know that someone who has only *seen* the sponge would say it was a rock, being deceived by its misleading appearance; thus they appear to have two different 'mental representations' of the object, one of what it 'looks like' and another of what it 'really is'. Children under 4 tend to give the same answer to questions about appearance and about reality, so that they answer 'rock' or 'sponge' to both questions. Flavell (1988) interprets this as an inability to realise that the same object can be represented in different, seemingly contradictory, ways. Astington and Gopnik (1988) show that this refusal to manage different representations can be retrospective. Their 3-year-old subjects saw the sponge 'rock' and said it was 'a rock'; after feeling it, what they said was 'it is a sponge', 'it looks like a sponge' (a 'realist' error) and 'I thought it was a sponge when I first saw it'. They therefore deny the change in their own mental state, even though they may say that another person who hasn't felt the sponge may believe it to be a rock. The error occurs over different objects and pairings of modalities, for example a candle shaped like an apple or a white cardboard shape shown with a coloured cellophane filter, and has been resistant (so far) to training (Flavell 1988).

These findings on the appearance–reality distinction seem to be related to children's judgements of other people's mental states (Butterworth *et al.* 1991, Gopnik and Astington 1988, Moore, Pure and Furrow 1990, Perner 1991a, Wellman 1990). Piaget's suggestion that young children were 'egocentric' in such judgements (Piaget and Inhelder 1956) has spawned much research. Piaget and Inhelder asked what view could be seen from various points around a three-dimensional array of mountains. Their youngest subjects tended to choose a picture showing their own view irrespective of whether the viewpoint currently in question was their own or not. More recent studies, however, have shown the 'egocentric' error to be less common than Piaget described it and to be attributable in some degree to the difficulty of his task.

If simpler materials are used (or 'meaningful' ones (Donaldson 1978)) children have little difficulty in distinguishing someone else's view from their own (see Flavell 1985 for a review). By the age of 2½ to 3 years children seem to understand a great deal about what a person can see. They know that in order to see an object at least one of the observer's eyes must be open, and aimed in the direction of the object, while no other large opaque object comes between the observed and the observer. They understand about hiding objects (Pratt and Bryant 1990). They also know that what they themselves see is irrelevant to what another person sees. They can use this knowledge to enable an observer to see something, or to prevent this, as well as for diagnostic purposes. They are thus *not* egocentric in at least some of their assessment and use of other people's vision, though it is not clear whether under-4s are fully aware that lack of vision may mean lack of information (Pillow 1989, Taylor *et al.* 1991, Wimmer *et al.* 1988).

Wimmer *et al.* questioned children about their own and others' knowledge about a picture in a box. Three-year-olds were able to say whether they knew what the picture in the box was, but couldn't say how they knew (because they had seen it) or why they didn't know (because they hadn't seen it). Seven out of ten 4-year-olds could identify the reason for their knowledge or ignorance correctly, showing some understanding of the importance of access to information as a crucial source of knowledge. The researchers argue that even for the youngest children seeing the picture leads to a mental representation of what's in the box, which can be accessed in order to give the correct answer to whether you do or don't know what is in the box. From 4 years old onwards it also leads to registering the causal connection between having access to information (or not) and having knowledge (or not), for oneself and for other people; that is, understanding access to knowledge develops earlier than understanding what that access causes for one's cognition (Flavell *et al.* 1990, Mitchell and Robinson 1992, Pillow 1989, Ruffman and Olson 1989, Taylor *et al.* 1991). This is not surprising, given that young children must see things (in the sense of 'have them come within sight') without 'seeing' them in the epistemic sense of 'see' ('recognise', identify', 'know the significance of') even more than older people do. (The Australian Aborigines encountered by Captain Cook in 1770 took no notice of the 106-foot-long *Endeavour*, too large to be registered as a ship, appearing not to see it until Cook and his sailors disembarked into a smaller rowing boat (Hughes 1987). Children similarly lack experience of artefacts, and indeed of much else.)

In a study by Chandler and Helm (1984) children were shown a picture almost entirely obscured by a cardboard cover. A few ambiguous lines could be seen through a hole in the cover, and children, when asked what they were, would typically say they didn't know, or the lines were meaningless scribble. When the cover was removed, the ambiguous lines turned out to be part of the trunk of an elephant. The children were then asked what a naïve observer would see in the lines when the cover was replaced; they said that the lines would be correctly identified as the elephant's trunk. Similar results have been found by Taylor (1988) and Ruffman, Olson and Astington (1991). Children's understanding that the present perceptual experience will yield different information to people whose prior perceptual experience differences shows a major improvement between 3 and 5. What an informed observer knows about an object is assumed to enter the mind of the ignorant observer automatically, an assumption all too often made by adults also!

It has also been suggested that children under school age cannot simultaneously attend to the whole of a picture and to its parts at the same time (e.g. Elkind 1978, Vurpillot 1976). Thus, if shown a 'person' made up of fruits 4–5-year-olds typically mention the parts rather than the whole, as if the 'person' representation was not available to them. However in a more recent study (Prather and Bacon 1986) even 2–3-year-olds could identify both part and whole in a simpler picture (such as a triangle with sides defined by carrots) and 14 per cent spontaneously produced an 'integrated' description, for example, 'It's a triangle made of carrots'. It would seem that both materials and questioning techniques are important, but that multiple representations may be possible even for very young children.

A similar distinction can be made in the development of the understanding of 'know'. Children under 3 may understand 'know' as meaning 'have a true idea about', but it is a later achievement to add to this definition the requirement that the true idea should come from a certain and reliable source or inference, rather than from a guess which luckily turned out to be correct. Distinction between empirical certainties and logical certainties also develops later (e.g. Mitchell and Robinson 1992, Moore *et al.* 1989, Moshman and Franks 1986, Ruffman and Olson 1989).

Children may also have problems understanding that another person may have a false belief (as opposed to no belief at all as a result of having had no access to information, which as we have seen they seem to be able to recognise quite early). Investigation of children's understanding of false belief has been an especially lively and productive area of research. Such understanding is of particular interest because it elucidates whether the child appreciates that other people may have beliefs that are different from his or her own, and can allow diagnosis of what the child believes are the causes of beliefs. If the child's own beliefs about the situation are true, but the other's would be false, and the child can recognise that the other, acting on false beliefs, would do something different from the child, then we can be sure that the child imputes mental stages of belief to the other person, and predicts the other's behaviour on the basis of the imputed mental stages.

A substantial body of work has now been done using paradigms of various sorts. In one of the earliest studies (Wimmer and Perner 1983) the child was told a story in which a little boy put some chocolate in place *A* and then went away. During his absence, the chocolate was moved to place *B*. The boy then came back, hungry and wanting his chocolate. The child was asked where the little boy would look for his chocolate. Most 3-year-olds, and a substantial proportion of 4-year-olds, said that the boy would look in place *B* (where they knew the chocolate now was) not in place *A* (where the boy last saw it), thus showing that they did not understand where the boy would believe the chocolate to be (but see Siegal 1991).

Hogrefe *et al.* (1986) found a developmental lag in children's attribution of ignorance and false belief. Children were told stories where another person was excluded from information which was available to the child, for example that a box labelled 'Smarties' actually contained a pencil. Half of 3-year-olds and 80 per cent of 4-year-olds could say that the other person would not know what was in the Smarties box, but at this stage the children would not say that the other person would probably have the (false) belief that there were Smarties in the box. They would attribute to the other person their own mental representation of the box's contents; thus although the other person would not *know* what was in the box they would be thought to have a mental picture of the box containing a pencil. Just as in the retrospective judgement change in the study by Gopnik and Astington (1988) discussed above, there seems to be a difficulty in admitting alternative mental representations. This difficulty may lead to children's repudiation of their own earlier claim of belief. Typically, 3-year-olds would say when first seeing the Smarties box 'it has Smarties in'; but after seeing that the contents were in fact pencils, they would say that they had said on first seeing it that it had pencils in, even if reminded of the statement to the opposite effect they had made only a minute or two before (Gopnik and Astington 1988, Gopnik and Slaughter 1991, Schauble 1990, Wimmer and Hart 1991). Three-year-olds seem to have a real conceptual gap here (Astington and Gopnik 1991, Perner 1991, Wellman 1990): they have a problem in understanding that beliefs involve representations, and how their representations relate to reality.

Perner and his colleagues (e.g. Perner 1991b, Hogrefe *et al.* 1986) believe that there is a similar developmental lag for 'second-order' beliefs ('He thinks that I think that there is a pencil in the box'), success here developing during the early primary school years (but possibly beginning somewhat earlier (Chandler, Fritz and Hala 1989, Hala, Chandler and Fritz 1991, Sodian 1991)). Understanding of this sort makes bluff (and double bluff and all sorts of higher order games of deception) possible. They suggest that there is a repeated cycle of three stages of recognising and using alternative mental representations, first in visual perspective taking, then in knowing about other people's knowledge, then in higher order knowledge attribution ('John kicks Mary because John knows that Mary does not know that the teacher has arrived, and he wants her to know about it so he gives her a kick'). In the first stage the child is totally ignorant of others' beliefs: all other people see what I see or know what I know and so forth. In the second, transitional, stage, the child knows that different views or beliefs exist but has difficulty specifying them for another person and may inappropriately attribute his or her own mental representation to the other. In the third stage the child recognises the need to infer the other's mental representation, can do so and can apply the inference. This sort of achievement is invaluable for the development of interpersonal understanding. Autistic children seem to have particular problems with this (Baron-Cohen and Frith 1992, Frith 1990, Gillberg 1992, Hobson 1991, Klin *et al.* 1992, Perner *et al.* 1989, Tager-Flusberg 1992).

It would seem, then, that very young children can distinguish between their own knowledge and another person's when what is in question is inferences about what the other can or cannot see (or hear or know). But they run into difficulties in understanding that the same object may appear different from different positions or on different occasions to different observers. Pillow (1988a) suggests that young children may begin with a passive view of the origin of mental states, believing that the outside world produces an objective and unvarying copy of itself in the mind by being seen (or heard or whatever), and not understanding that the mind acts on this information to interpret it in ways influenced by each person's idiosyncratic knowledge and subjective states, so that individuals will pick up different information from the same sensory experience and construct different mental representations. A similar account is proposed by Flavell (1988). He brings together a considerable amount of evidence that children under 3 have learned a great deal about how people (themselves and others) can be 'cognitively connected' to the external world. They have learned, for example, that cognitive connections (such as seeing something) can change over time, are largely independent of other cognitive connections, are independent of other people's cognitive connections, and can entail other, subjective, experiences. However, young children do not understand that these 'connections' are made up of mental representations rather than being objective automatic links; in particular they do not understand that there can be a multiplicity of mental representations and interpretations that are seemingly contradictory.

This sort of understanding develops rapidly in the pre-school years. Accepting multiple representations seems to be easiest in the 'pretend' domain, which flourishes from the second year onwards (e.g. Leslie 1987, 1988a), or when 'desires' are the focus (Wellman and Woolley 1990), or when prediction or guessing is explicitly involved, or when the representation is clearly subjective (for example 3-year-olds are said to understand that cats think cat food tastes 'yummy' even though they themselves think it tastes 'yukky'), or when deceit is focused on (Butterworth *et al.* 1991, Chandler *et al.* 1989, Perner 1991a, Peskin 1992). Complete understanding that there may be different mental representations of the same object or event and that these may be equally 'valid' is undoubtedly a very sophisticated achievement indeed (and probably a fragile one, given how often we may fail to appreciate someone else's point of view). It involves a great deal of knowledge about mental events, including one's own cognitive processes (and hence it may be metacognitive), and also of the language and social context of cognition (Wellman 1985a, 1990). It has been said to be an essential component of the skills needed for living with other people (Humphrey 1983). Thus children's understanding of mind is perhaps a central issue in their cognitive and social development, as Wellman 1990 argues.

Theorists here, as elsewhere in the psychology of cognitive development, differ in their explanations of the causes of the development of children's 'theory of mind'. Some (e.g. Ferguson and Gopnik 1988, Perner 1991, Wellman 1985a, 1990) use 'theory' in the strong sense of 'quasi-scientific theory'; that is, they emphasise the coherence, the abstractness, the lawfulness of children's ideas about minds, and point out that like truly scientific theories they allow generalisation, explanation and prediction, and use evidence to support their ideas, even to the point of denying counter-evidence. They also stress the size and pervasiveness of the shift in ideas about minds which children go through between the ages of 2 and 5, and suggest that this shift shows that a general structural change and reorganisation is happening, not just the accumulation of new knowledge in essentially unrelated areas. They point out that it is people in the grip of a theory who are most likely to ignore or distort counter-evidence; they compare the children who denied they had a moment ago predicted that there would be Smarties in a Smarties box rather than the pencils they saw there immediately after their prediction (Gopnik and Astington 1988, Hogrefe *et al.* 1986, Wimmer and Hart 1991) with the children who had such difficulty in abandoning their theory about balancing blocks (Karmiloff-Smith 1988, Karmiloff-Smith and Inhelder 1974/5) and the scientists who may go to even greater lengths to protect their theories (Gosse 1907, Kuhn 1962). It would be the theory-like nature of the understanding which is to a considerable degree responsible for the rapidity of development on so many related concepts over a comparatively short period of time. Like Piagetian schemas, theories have built-in tendencies to self-improvement in the form of increasing coherence, inclusiveness, and flexibility, and the interaction between theory and the evidence available for testing is seen as driving the development of children's understanding, much as it drives the development of knowledge in science. Wellman (1990) summarises this position; Perner (1991a) provides a notably elegant argument of it from basic principles.

Other researchers in the area (e.g. Hobson 1991) believe that calling children's understanding of minds a 'theory' leads to insufficient recognition of the role of perception and knowledge (as opposed to theory-led inference) in the child's understanding. For example, there are observable regularities in the expression of some mental states, such as surprise or sadness, and these are used by infants, by pre-schoolers and by adults in not dissimilar ways. The early behaviourist way of understanding minds is certainly added to, but it is not superseded. The theory that a 'theory of mind' develops between the ages of 2 and 5 may introduce too great a discontinuity into our account of development, so that we both underestimate the competence of the very young and overestimate the coherence and abstractness of adults' thinking. Hobson (1991) prefers to emphasise the role of emotionally charged interactions and relationships with other people. We are biologically programmed to engage in such interactions and relationships, to the extent that we may have direct perceptual experience of other people's emotions just as we do of their physical experience or our own. Experience with other people who model the expressive behaviour of mental states, and who react to and comment on one's own, is the source of awareness of other people's mental states, of reflective self-awareness of one's own, and of one's 'folk-psychology' 'theory' of minds. This experience is something young children seize on with great interest, seeking to discuss other people's actions and motivations with their mothers, for example (Dunn 1988, Dunn *et al.* 1987). Hobson (1991: 47–8) argues:

> Once a child has acquired a grasp of body-anchored and 'outer-directed' subjectively experienced mental states on a largely if not exclusively non-inferential basis, then the child *can* employ inferences or other intellectual strategies to learn more about its own and others' minds . . . .

Theorizing is not the primary source of children's knowledge about minds, nor are minds first understood by children as especially private, 'theorizing' minds – they are the minds of people who are perceived and felt to act and feel, as well as turning out to be the minds of people who think and believe . . . .

The developmental progression is from an infant's perception and growing understanding of the public, psychologically expressive behaviour and attitudes of persons, to a young child's more sophisticated knowledge of the nature of persons and their potentially but only partially undisclosed minds.

Before we leave children's concepts of mind, a caveat is necessary. There continues to be controversy amongst professional philosophers and psychologists about what sort of 'philosophy of mind' is correct (or, better, appropriate). Fodor (1990) provides a 'guide' to a number of different positions on this question, and so, more soberly, does Lycan (1989). One central issue is the psychological status of 'beliefs', 'desires', 'intentions', and so forth, in explaining behaviour. Philosophers such as Ryle (1949) and psychologists such as Skinner (1953) have argued, forcefully and influentially, that mental representations and mental states in general do not really exist and so have no role in psychological explanation. They are 'the ghost in the machine', and what is of interest is the machine itself, the behaviour it emits, and the patterning of stimulation and reinforcement in the world which surrounds it. These theorists see it as at best useless and as at worst misleading to talk of the thinking machine having mental representations such as 'theories of mind'. They restrict their investigations to contingencies between measurable conditions and behaviours and do not attribute 'intentional states' such as beliefs, expectations and desires to the 'thinker'.

A more accepting position acknowledges that our language and our 'commonsense' or 'folk' psychology uses concepts of mental states and intentional descriptions. We may however use terms such as 'think' or 'believe' or 'intend' as convenient descriptions of how someone's behaviour makes sense to us, without having any idea about whether the description is correct or whether the mental state exists and causes behaviour. The descriptions have developed over the millennia of human social existence because their use facilitates social interaction, not because they were the product of systematic dispassionate study of people's minds. Folk psychology is no more a scientific theory than folk meteorology was, but it enables good enough 'getting on' with other people just as 'red sky in the morning, shepherd's warning' gave a good enough advice on what to do to shelter the sheep (or oneself). There may be dangers of reifying beliefs, desires, etc. in inappropriate ways, and of crediting people with 'theories of mind' which are too coherent and systematic, if there is a flexible *ad hoc* behaviourist reality.

Another caveat is one which has applied in other areas of the study of cognitive development. Siegal (1991) suggests (as have other researchers, see e.g. Donaldson 1978) that a great deal of the wrongness of young children's answers to adults' questions about such matters as conservation and theory of mind is caused by the adults' breach of normal conversational rules and children's reaction to an anomalous situation. In a number of experiments he has found, for example, that repetition of questions worsens performance on conservation tasks and on the appearance–reality distinction; that there are order effects on these and on gender constancy tasks; and that children would often explain that a wrong answer was given 'just pretending' or to tease or please the adult questioners. He points out that in the interviews used to test children's cognition the child is dealing with an interrogator who is much larger, more powerful and more knowledgeable, and who is in charge, however much gentleness and friendliness is shown. In such an unequal social interaction, correct answers may be fairly unproblematic, but incorrect answers may be associated with uncertainty about the situation, misinterpretation of what is going on under repeated questioning, attention-seeking or a desire to escape from the interview.

This criticism has to be taken seriously, not least because if it is correct an enormous amount of what is taken as 'fact' in children's cognitive development would turn out to be at best suspect, at worst a set of false negatives. Where researchers have been aware of these problems, and have used complementary methods to get at the child's understanding, I think we can continue to trust their data; but there are uncomfortably many papers in the literature where even the most elementary precautions were not taken, and children were asked silly questions and compared with a non-comparable sample of adults – the local undergraduate population being the normal source of 'adults'. Let readers beware, and researchers think very very carefully about what they are doing!

# Chapter 3

# Individual differences in cognitive development

Most of the literature on cognitive development focuses on the description of a generalised, universal, normal progress from the cognition of infancy to the cognition of adulthood, with little attention to variation in the rate or detailed patterning of this development, and less to the possibility of different developmental paths. Most of the literature on individual differences in cognition takes a non-developmental view, even when looking for the factors that, throughout the years of childhood, might be affecting the quantity and quality of cognition. There is an excuse for this separation, in the pragmatic need to limit researchers' focus and concentrate their efforts, and it has recently been argued that individual variation and cognitive development in any case have different causes (Anderson 1992). Nevertheless, my own feeling is that there should be some attempt to consider the work on individual differences *within* cognitive development, as this is likely to improve our understanding of both (see also Richardson 1991, Scarr 1992). Chapter 5 of this volume therefore looks at causes of differences in cognitive development.

The concern of this chapter is the way we understand differences between individuals in how they think, and in how their thinking develops: what are these differences, how have they come about, are they so great as to override similarities or are they merely differences in minor details? I am going to restrict myself to the normal range of cognitive abilities, though some allusions to the extremes may creep in. I will consider three of the main 'dimensions' of individual differences in cognition: intelligence, cognitive style and creativity.

## INTELLIGENCE

Conceptions of individuals as differing in 'intelligence' are by far the best known and most thoroughly worked-out accounts of 'individual differences'. In general terms, there is some degree of agreement (e.g. Chen *et al.* 1988, Nicholls *et al.* 1986, Sternberg and Detterman 1986, Sternberg and Powell 1983) about what 'intelligent behaviour' is: both laity and psychologist experts believe that intelligent persons will have good vocabularies, read with good comprehension, talk fluently and sensibly, make good decisions, plan well, be able to apply their knowledge to problems, determine how best to achieve goals, be interested in things around them, etc., while less intelligent persons will show fewer of these characteristics. Given a relevant sample of behaviour, most adults within a culture can assess how close an individual is to this sort of prototype, though they may have more difficulty if the individual is from a culture different from their own.

The list of things 'intelligent' people do in the last paragraph is a fairly general and heterogeneous one. Psychologists have been greatly concerned with how to make the items more specific and how to understand the relationships between them. Basic concepts about the precise nature of 'intelligence' have influenced this work very profoundly. Francis Galton, pioneering mental testing at the end of the last century, believed firmly that intelligence was a fixed and inherited capacity underlying all cognitive activity and all educational achievement and social eminence (and largely based on, or measurable via, sensitivity to physical stimuli (Sternberg and Powell 1983)). Those who, like Spearman, Burt and Eysenck, followed this line defined it as 'innate, general cognitive ability', and looked for simple tests which measured general intelligence or $g$ without contamination from different experience, knowledge or education. They developed sophisticated techniques for finding the communality between scores on measures of different sorts of 'intelligent' behaviour, notably factor analysis, though their analysis tended to be pragmatic rather than to contribute to cognitive theory. They did not develop a sophisticated developmental theory, perhaps because of their focus on *innate* general intelligence and their emphasis on rather simple measures such as digit span, although some attempts have been made to describe how different pictures of the structure of intelligence emerge from factor analytic studies at different ages. I will discuss this briefly later.

Another strand in attempts to define and measure intelligence has been heavily influenced by educational needs. At the turn of the century, Alfred Binet was asked by the educational authorities of Paris to devise tests which would pick out those children who were not capable of succeeding in the normal school regime so that they could be given special education rather than be left to fail. He developed a comparatively sophisticated theory of intelligence (Binet and Simon 1916, Sternberg and Powell 1983), but test items were chosen because they also represented the typical performance of children at successive ages, so that individuals could be assessed in terms of how well their performance came up to that of children of the same age, and where it was weaker, more like that of younger children. Most of the items comprised fairly complex tasks similar to those of everyday mental life, involving understanding language and reasoning, with verbal, spatial or numerical materials. Binet saw that the 'normal' children and the 'mentally retarded' children were not two clearly separate groups. 'Intelligence' as measured by his tests varied continuously along a scale, and his score was essentially a measure of average rate of growth of various mental functions from birth to the time of testing, that is, it measured present performance relative to the population norm, as the result of the cumulative performance and achievement to date. Binet's approach did not imply that 'intelligence' was fixed: given favourable opportunities retarded children might make up their deficit, and if things went wrong for the advanced group their rate of development might fall. However, since a test score is the result of the accumulation of earlier growth of mental functions, some degree of constancy in performance is inevitable.

Attempts to devise tests which would make predictions that could be useful to schools more often than not used the tests' agreement with measures of school achievement as a measure of test validity. On the whole, test items which involved using knowledge of the sort required in school show higher correlations with school achievement than do test items with little or no school-relevant content. While this is hardly surprising, it does illustrate how difficult it is to separate experience and potential, how we cannot determine from a measure taken after a particular history of experience what the score would have been after other, different, histories. The problem is obvious when the test used involves knowledge or skills which are clearly acquired to different degrees as a result of different experiences (hence the need to revise vocabulary tests to take out words like 'antimacassar' or 'haberdashery' which are in much less frequent use than previously), but it remains a problem in less obvious ways even when the test does not have such culturally specific content. Individuals may differ, for example, in how far they have learned to concentrate on psychophysical tasks or to answer questions co-operatively in the unusual social situation of being required to display one's knowledge despite its not being otherwise useable at the moment. Cognitive skills such as these are necessary for good performance in school and in doing intelligence tests; it seems likely, as I discuss in Chapter 5, that they develop as a result of the practice with which other people, parents and teachers especially, surround the child.

Thus there has been a tension between different meanings of 'intelligence' both in the specialised work of psychologists and in the way the term is understood by the general public. Eysenck provides a clear exposition of the three different meanings which have become familiar to psychologists as Intelligence A, Intelligence B and Intelligence C. Intelligence A is

> the biological fundament of cognitive processing, genetically based (perhaps entirely so), and responsible for individual differences in intellectual competence. Intelligence B, on the other hand, denotes the application of Intelligence A to ordinary life affairs and problems,

modified as this inevitably will be by personality differences, socio-
economic status, and educational, cultural and other environmental
factors . . . Intelligence C refers to the measurement of intelligence
(whether A or B) by means of specially constructed tests.

(Eysenck 1986: 1)

Which of these is the most important level of intelligence is something
theorists differ about. There is a great deal of very specialised literature on
the relationship between different tests of intelligence which is sometimes
purely about Intelligence C, as one intelligence test is used to validate or to
criticise another. Eysenck's own recent work focuses very much on Intelligence A, as I will describe later. The new accounts of intelligence deriving
from information-processing theory are linked to all three meanings, (e.g.
Anderson 1992, Carpenter and Just 1986, Sternberg 1985). Whichever
meaning is focused on, two issues have arisen: what items of behaviour are
both representative of intelligence and measureable, and how do possible
different components of intelligence fit together. What behaviour is to be
chosen and measured often reflects the original Galton–Binet differences as
well as whether Intelligence A is preferred to Intelligence B, or vice versa,
and we will discuss this more fully later; the organisation of components of
intelligence has received different sorts of solutions. The approach in the
psychometric literature has been largely centred on techniques such as
factor analysis, which have been used in attempts to see how far different
test performances can be explained in terms of a general underlying
cognitive capacity ($g$) rather than in terms of more specific abilities not
perhaps called on by more than one test. A great many structural models
have appeared in the psychometric literature (see e.g. Carroll 1982 and
Sternberg and Powell 1983). Many of these result from different applications of factor analytic techniques to a heterogeneous collection of test
items. Since, mathematically, there is an infinite number of ways in which
factors can be fitted to a set of scores on tests, and since there is no widely
accepted criterion for deciding which factor analysis-derived structure is
most acceptable, there are no obvious grounds for claiming one structural
model as more 'correct' than others. This approach has involved theory
mainly as a way to justify factor structure, rather than the reverse.
Information-processing approaches to intelligence have more often moved
from theory to accounts of the structure of intelligence (see Sternberg 1985)
but do not involve much consideration of Intelligence A.

Neither approach has given as much attention as one might wish to the
*development* of intelligence, which is our main concern here. The nearest
psychometric approximation to a developmental concept is probably R. B.
Cattell's distinction (Cattell 1971) between 'fluid' and 'crystallised' intelligence subfactors of $g$. Fluid intelligence is relatively independent of
systematic educational and cultural influences and is best measured by tests

which require mental manipulation of given abstract information, for example classification problems using squiggle shapes, inductive reasoning where content is irrelevant to the validity of the argument, figural analogies and series completion like Raven's Matrices tasks. Crystallised intelligence represents the person's accumulation of schooling, acculturation and other learning experiences, and is best measured via tests of vocabulary, general knowledge and comprehension, which require more knowledge of the cultural milieu. Both fluid and crystallised intelligence are said to increase through childhood to adolescence, but thereafter fluid intelligence is constant, or, in extreme old age, declines, while crystallised intelligence continues to increase for as long as people continue to accumulate knowledge and experience (Cattell 1971, Horn 1968, 1970).

While these models do usefully note the *range* of influences – from 'brain maturation' to 'educational experience' – which could affect 'intelligence', each of these needs far more specification as to what has an impact, and how, and when, and why, and on what aspect of 'intelligence'. A review of some current attempts to come to grips with parts of this formidable research schedule may be found elsewhere in this book. It also leaves open the question of what pattern of cognitive activities constitutes 'intelligence' at different ages, and there is less developmental evidence, and much less developmental theory, on this than one would like. A recent advance is some new evidence on the prediction of childhood intelligence from infancy, which had previously been problematic; recent studies (Bornstein and Sigman 1986, Rose *et al.* 1986) suggest that infant 'alertness' as shown in habituation and attention tasks predicts much of the variation in intelligence test score in early childhood. Thus there is some continuity in this rather fundamental aspect of cognition from infancy to childhood, just as there is some continuity in rankings on more composite intelligence test scores over the years of childhood. (It should be remembered, however, that a substantial proportion of individuals show marked changes in their IQ scores, some merely fluctuating wildly but some moving systematically up or down (Hindley 1965, Hindley and Owen 1978).)

The interesting findings about alertness in intelligence may usefully be related to recent attempts to identify and study a fundamental substratum of 'intelligence'. A number of researchers have been seeking to find simple measures of brain functioning or basic cognitive processing, which some of them see as the true core of intelligence (e.g. Eysenck 1982, 1986, Jensen 1982), though not all of them are overtly reductionistic, recognising that the simple measure is part of the complex structure of intelligent behaviour (Anderson 1989a, 1992). I will give a simple description of these approaches but it is not as yet clear how far they are coherent and reconcilable.

I will describe all but one of the measures used very briefly. All could be linked to a Galtonian concept, 'mental speed', and the researchers involved do, I think, tend towards the non-developmental model of intelligence as '*innate* general cognitive ability'. Although early research showed little relationship between 'mental speed' and 'intelligence', recent work (Jensen 1982) has found quite strong correlations between them. A subject's reaction time (RT) to, for example, a light going on, increases as the number of lights which might possibly go on increases. The rate of increase as well as the actual length of RT is greater for low IQ subjects than for high IQ ones: brighter subjects have faster RTs than duller ones, and the difference is greater the more possible lights there are. In a similar paradigm, Inspection Time (IT) is measured. The subject gets very brief exposures to two clearly different stimuli (such as two vertical lines, 3 : 2 in length) and then has an unlimited amount of time to report which is, for example, longer. The individual's IT score is the duration of exposure time at which the subject's judgement is 90–95 per cent correct. There seems to be a moderate negative correlation between IT and non-verbal IQ test scores (Anderson 1992, Brand 1982): lower IQ subjects need to see the stimuli for a longer time in order to be able to compare them correctly. IT is thought to measure how quickly subjects can encode incoming information into short-term memory. However, there has been some variability in the size and significance of the correlations between IT and IQ, with high correlations only being found if the IQ range is large and there are mentally retarded subjects in the group (Vernon 1985). Again, consistency and IQ are positively correlated. IT has been studied developmentally. There is debate about whether it remains the same over age. Anderson (1986, 1988, 1992) argues that it does, though other researchers, notably Nettelbeck and his colleagues, find that IT decreases throughout childhood and adolescence, which suggests an increase in the speed of basic information-processing (Nettelbeck 1986, Nettelbeck and Wilson 1985, Nettelbeck and Vita 1992, Wilson *et al.* 1992).

Similar replication problems and over-narrow interpretations of what the test requires seem to be occurring in the somewhat more cognitive tasks reviewed by Cooper and Regan (1982). Hunt *et al.* (1975) looked at correlations between verbal IQ scores and performance on tasks where the subjects had to say 'same' or 'different' in response to pairs of letters which were identical physically (A,A) or in name only (A,a). Their analysis of these tasks suggests that in the name identical (NI) task the subject has the extra job of retrieving the name associated with each visual pattern as compared with the physically identical (PI) task, so the NI–PI time difference represents the amount of time needed to access the names in memory. Subjects with high verbal IQs need less time to do this than subjects with low verbal IQs, so perhaps they have faster access to overlearned verbal material in memory. However they are also faster on both NI and PI trials, so the results may be picking up a general speed factor rather than differences in how efficiently verbal memory is accessed. A rather similar implication seems to come from studies of the components of reading in good and poor readers: good readers seem to have faster access to the names

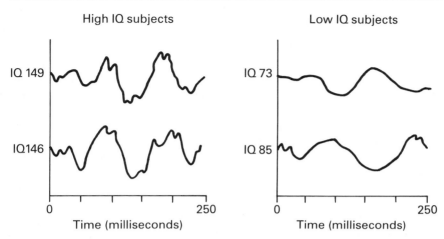

*Figure 3.1* Averaged evoked potentials for high IQ and low IQ subjects. The high IQ subjects have 'spikier' waveforms.
*Source:* Anderson 1992:52

of meaningful visual patterns and to have more appropriate language comprehension skills in general (Cooper and Regan 1982: 132–8; see also Chapter 2). In the case of reading, unusually sophisticated analyses of the cognitive processes involved are putting us within sight of quite a good account of reading and of individual differences in reading, though we are not yet very close to an account of the relationship between reading and other aspects of intelligence.

The last approach to be mentioned measures the electrical activity produced by the brain in response to a brief visual or auditory stimulation. Shortly after stimulation, for example, after the subject has heard a brief tone, there is a peak or 'evoked potential' in central nervous system activity. See Figure 3.1.

The size, latency and frequency of such evoked potentials can be measured, and averaged over a large number of trials to give the 'average evoked potential' or AEP; this measure is then correlated with IQ score. It is suggested that the AEP is a 'picture' of the individual's response to incoming information (A. E. Hendrickson 1982). The Hendrickson model describes how incoming information sets up electrical activity in nerve fibres and biochemical changes in the synapses between successive fibres and cells in the transmission of activity within the brain (for a simple introductory account of brain functioning see Chapter 5). The correct transmission of information is seen as requiring accurate recognition memory at a basic neuronal level, and it is assumed that individuals differ in their accuracy and hence in how long and complex a message they can transmit before an error leads to breakdown. The AEP provides an estimate of this accuracy, in that individuals whose recognition and transmission of information are inaccurate will tend to have varying reactions to the incoming stimulation, sometimes showing a large reaction but tending towards smaller and slower ones which fade quickly. Averaged over a lot of trials, an inaccurate-transmission individual, someone with a lot of erroneous 'noise' in the system, will have a flat unclear AEP, while a more accurate information processor will have a large quick sharp AEP. AEP differences will be paralleled by differences in 'real-life' learning and memory: an individual with a slow and 'crackly' central nervous system will be slow to process information, to create a memory store, to carry out simple and, more notably, complex cognitive processing, and to acquire and organise a knowledge base. Such an individual may thus be expected to do badly on intelligence tests, and on cognitive tasks in general.

The evidence on the association between AEP and IQ has to be said to be inconsistent. There seem to be reliability problems and replication problems, and Jensen has characterised the area as

> a thicket of seemingly inconsistent and confusing findings, confounded variables, methodological differences, statistically questionable conclusions, unbridled theoretical speculation, and, not surprisingly, considerable controversy.

(Jensen 1980: 709)

More recent reviews (Eysenck 1986, and Vernon 1985) are more positive about AEPs than this; Vernon sees the experimental research as insufficient and suggests that speed of processing, rather than a complex model of accuracy, might account for the results. Schafer (1982) relates evoked potentials to 'neural adaptability', comparing responses to inputs whose timing and nature are known or unpredictable. Unexpected input evokes a larger response than input which is expected, with a bigger difference for intelligent subjects than for mentally retarded ones. This might be seen as higher IQ people being quicker to habituate to completely predictable overlearned stimulation and better at reorienting attention to focus on novel stimulation, thus using limited neural energy and cognitive space more efficiently. There seems to be a high correlation (about 0.8) between neural adaptability, as seen in small AEPs to familiar expected stimulation plus large AEPs to unexpected novel stimulation, and IQ. Vernon (1985) suggests that the Hendricksons' work could be subsumed with Schafer's, though the former has the more elaborate biochemical model.

There is a certain plausibility in the idea that the speed and efficiency of the brain is an important component in the speed and efficiency with which a person deals with a cognitive task and hence his or her performance on IQ tests, particularly those where only a limited amount of time is available. I have more to say about this in Chapter 5, where I relate research on the brain to questions of the organisation and development of cognition.

However I see three problems with the accounts of the 'biological determinants of behavioural intelligence' described above. The first is a methodological one. The measurement of 'brain speed' is not unproblematic. Typically, getting an individual's AEP or reaction time means that he or she must tolerate the placement of electrodes (itself not a simple procedure) and the adjustment of measuring devices, and then must sit and listen to many repetitions of a brief tone or watch for flashes of a light. It cannot be assumed that everyone who undergoes this procedure will be consistent over its duration in motivation or affect, and in so far as these influence cortical activity they may produce variation in AEP or RT. As Mackintosh (1986) points out, the AEP will only show a complex pattern if the patterns it averages are themselves both complex and constant; if there is variability between trials with peaks of different sizes or at different points in time they will cancel each other out and the average trace will be flatter and shorter than the consituent ones. It does seem to be the case that lower IQ subjects vary more between trials, that is, that their score is less stable and less uniform, and hence their AEP is lower. This could indeed be due to the cognitive difference that Eysenck (1982, 1986) and the Hendricksons are suggesting (A. E. Hendrickson 1982, D. E. Hendrickson 1982); but somewhat less cognitive possibilities, such as ability to maintain a consistent level of attention to a boring task or willingness to co-operate with an experimenter, do suggest themselves. Even the recording of brain activity is to some extent a social activity and we might be unwise to assume that our measures are totally independent of the subject's motivation and ideas about what is going on. This may be particularly important when studying development. Eysenck (1986), without documenting them in detail, reports studies which relate AEP to age. He says that with increasing age the evoked potential is larger and arises faster, and the AEP is less variable. This might suggest that children's brains work faster and more efficiently, even on the level of very simple neural responses to simple stimulation, as they get older, a notion which bears an interesting relation to the accounts of information-processing development discussed in Chapter 4, but which may not be congruent with the idea of intelligence as a *fixed innate* cognitive characteristic. Nor, as I shall describe later, is it a notion that fits in with a very recent account of cognitive development put forward by Mike Anderson.

The second problem is whether evoked potentials are a simple and accurate measure of nervous system information-processing. Even if there are no motivational or attentional problems, the evoked potential is a somewhat indeterminate peak in more general electrical activity, which will be influenced in size and shape by all the other cortical activity going on, and distorted by the indirectness of our measurement. Until we understand how evoked potentials relate to neurone activity on the one hand and to cognitive processes on the other, we can only take them as an indirect measure of the efficiency of information-processing.

The third problem with models like the Hendricksons is the discrepancy in complexity between the understanding of the brain used in the model, and that emerging from current studies by neuropsychologists (see Chapter 5). 'Neural adaptability', 'neural efficiency' and so forth are crude concepts compared with the delicate analysis of neuroscientists. I will give two examples. The first is the Hendrickson assumption (A. E. Hendrickson 1982) that each synapse within an individual's brain will have the same probability of recognising a piece of information correctly, an assumption which greatly simplifies the complexity of brain structure and function. It seems to me undesirable, even at an early stage of research, to assume that the brain can be understood as a simple input-throughput-output system with nothing much in the way of interesting internal organisation and differentiation. Brain research on parallel and alternative pathways, multiple spread of information, links between psychologically different systems such as affect and cognition, and so forth, argues against such simplification. My second example is the comparatively non-developmental nature of these models. They show a poor fit with the recent evidence on how brain cells and connections continue to change and develop well into adult life, very much under the influence of experience (see Chapter 5). While individual differences in 'neural efficiency' might well lead to individual differences in ability to profit from experience and in what 'experience' is experienced – I find myself not doubting this in the least – individual differences in experience are just as likely to have repercussions for 'neural efficiency', and the models take little account of this possibility. There can be in this a whiff of reductionism, as when Eysenck (e.g. 1986) resolves the debate between Galton's and Binet's approaches so very much in favour of Galton, 'Intelligence A' and the psychophysiological measurement of intelligence, coming near to dismissing the study of Intelligence B as hopelessly unscientific.

### Anderson's new ideas in intelligence

Mike Anderson (1989a, 1992) offers some interesting speculations about the nature of intelligence and its development, which I integrate here with some points from elsewhere. He starts by stating three regularities in the data about intelligence. First, measurements of different cognitive abilities tend to be correlated, for example AEP is correlated with digit span which is correlated with vocabulary which is correlated with spatial analogy scores. Second, cognitive abilities increase with age at a similar rate and for a similar portion of the developmental curve. Third, individual differences in test scores are relatively stable over development: the alert baby becomes the bright schoolchild and the competent adult, although adult and child have a great deal of knowledge and many skills which the baby does not. Theories which centre intelligence on the general speed and efficiency of the individual's neurophysiology explain these regularities in terms of the neural processing which underlies all cognitive activity. These theories look more problematic however in dealing with irregularities, with why different abilities are not more strongly correlated, with why some individuals develop much faster in one area than others or have difficulties in one area while doing well in others, with why some individuals develop at a steady rate but others seem to fluctuate in their development. Some theorists have coped with such irregularities by suggesting that there are multiple separate intelligences (e.g. Gardner 1983, Howe 1989a), but such theories, emphasising different cognitive processes applied to different areas and acquired relatively independently of each other, have problems in coping with the regularities that we started by asserting. Only a theory which deals with intelligence and individual differences within a theory of thinking which specifies how basic neurophysiology relates to different kinds of information-processing, can explain both regularities and irregularities.

Anderson, in his model of the 'minimal cognitive architecture' of intelligence, suggests that there is a basic processing mechanism describable at the neurophysiological level. This is used by many different kinds of knowledge system and accounts for the general co-variation of different abilities. Individuals differ in the speed of their basic processing mechanism. People who can process information faster can cram more processing and more information into their limited capacity working memory before it becomes overloaded. Less information will be lost from working memory unprocessed, more will be usefully processed to solve the current problem or stored conveniently in long-term memory for use in the future. More information can be acquired, and more complex processing can be carried out. People with faster and more efficient basic processing mechanisms will learn more and reason better, getting more out of the same amount of experience, ending up with more and better organised knowledge and more practised processing.

The basic processing mechanism is not used in the acquisition of *all* the knowledge and skills we typically develop. Some knowledge and skills are developed largely through the operation of processing modules which are common to all, or virtually all, members of the human species, even those who are cognitively abnormal. These modules are the result of millennia of evolutionary usefulness. Anderson uses as example our ability to translate the two-dimensional stimulation on our retinas to a perception of a three-dimensional world. The vast majority of human beings can do this, whatever else is lacking because of immaturity or mental retardation, but such perception is far too complex for any presently-existing computer to cope with. Other examples might be drawn from the skills being discovered in very young infants, for example their co-ordination of vocalisation and gesture and their discrimination between people and objects, familiar and unfamiliar people, and between television pictures of Mother behaving normally in live conversation with them and of a recording of Mother conversing with them, played back to them with a 30-second delay (Trevarthen 1978, 1980). Other possible modules include the phonological encoding and syntactic analysis of language, and a 'theory of mind', or ability to think of other people as having mental states. Modules like these have evolved to fulfil universal processing functions in our species: brain research (Chapter 5) is discovering a great deal about them. Some are virtually 'wired in', others are 'experience-expectant' in that they utilise the sort of environmental information which has been ubiquitous throughout the evolution of the species and can be relied on to occur in any individual's experience. These depend on experience for their 'fine-tuning', often on experience during a particular 'sensitive period' of development, and if this experience is abnormal or missing the experience-expectant module comes to work abnormally or not at all. The perceptual deficits of kittens without normal visual experience in the first period after their eyes open are an obvious example, paralleled by the recently discovered acuity problems of human children whose shortsightedness is not corrected early enough.

As well as the experience that can reasonably be expected to occur regularly at a particular point in virtually everybody's life, so that 'experience-expectant' or 'wired-in' processing modules will serve us well, there are many environmental events which are less consistent in their occurrence or timing. The information-processing system has to be able to handle these too, and here another major source of individual differences lies. You can only acquire this somewhat more idiosyncratic knowledge (for example methods of counting, how to read, the rules of croquet, the skills of microbiology or art history) if it comes within your experience, and you then have to be able to process it appropriately. Anderson suggests that the basic processor is involved here, so that the faster processor will do better at seeing what distinguishes Picasso's paintings from Matisse's, or at counting by fives as well as by units, but that there are also 'specific processors' which may be more efficient in some areas than others, for example good verbal processing and less good spatial processing. The degree to which people develop cognitive abilities will depend on their general basic processing mechanism and on any relevant specific processor, and individual differences in speed and efficiency will apply to both general and specific mechanisms. 'Ability' will also depend on experience in two ways. If an information-processing module is involved, this must have 'come on-line' normally as a result of maturation within an at least minimally facilitating environment. If the environment has been grossly abnormal, or if the child is too young for the module to be operative, then the module will not operate properly and processing will not be possible. However most modules need only experience which everyone has, or even no experience of the outside world at all, so there will be little in the way of individual differences in modular functioning. More importantly for individual differences, experience will affect specific processors to a very significant extent: it provides them with the information they process, and without relevant information they will be of little use. They are, not 'experience-expectant', but 'experience-dependent'; however the basic processing mechanism is still important because it limits the efficiency with which use can be made of experience. Anderson believes that the basic processing mechanism is not itself affected by experience: it is this which is 'innate general cognitive ability'.

Intelligence, then, according to this theory, is made up of a basic processing mechanism, processing modules and a number of specific processors. These interact. There is little or nothing in the way of individual differences in modules, which are either there and processing universally available information in a universal way, or are not there and not processing, either because the individual is so immature that they have not 'come on-line', or because the environment has been so grossly abnormal that the module has been permanently impaired, or because of damage to the central or peripheral nervous systems. Every cat can see a normal three-dimensional world despite a two-dimensional image on the retina, unless it is a kitten whose eyes have not opened, or one who was brought up with very restricted visual displays in a research laboratory, or unless it has suffered blinding from damage to the visual cortex or to its eyes. The main source of individual differences for Anderson is variation in the speed of the basic processing mechanism, where faster processors can acquire more information in a given period of time and can do more complex processing without running into the limits of working memory. He believes that there is probably no developmental change in the speed of the basic processing mechanism, on the basis of his evidence that Inspection Time, which is a relatively 'pure' measure of processing speed not much affected by the subject's knowledge and strategies, is only weakly correlated with age (Anderson 1988). This evidence comes from children old enough to understand the IT task, however, so developmental changes earlier in life remain conceivable: babies may process some information more slowly and less efficiently than older people because of the comparative immaturity of the CNS (see Chapter 5) as well as because of their failure to understand what the task is.

Specific processors, like the basic processing mechanism, vary in their speed from person to person, and one particular person may have faster specific processors of one sort than of another, for example, fast verbal processing and slower spatial processing. The speed of the basic processing mechanism constrains all the specific processors, however, and if it is very slow differences between specific processors may be masked. (This suggestion may seem hard to reconcile with some of the cases of 'idiots savants', who, although severely retarded and presumably the possessors of an impaired basic processing mechanism, may show an outstanding ability to, for example, calculate calendar dates, or do mental arithmetic, or produce elaborate drawings (Hermelin and O'Connor 1990, Howe 1989c, Howe and Smith 1988, O'Connor and Hermelin 1990, Radford 1990). One answer to the dilemma might be to attribute these 'islands of excellence' to the functioning of processing modules: not modules which calculate dates but modules which focus attention and accumulate information in one particular narrow area. There is still controversy over how 'idiots savants' perform their feats (see e.g. Howe 1989c). A slow basic processing mechanism constrains the complexity of the cognitive processing that can be carried out by a specific processor and also constrains the complexity of knowledge that can be acquired in a specific domain. If basic processing is at a consistent speed throughout development, the baby who processes information slowly and inefficiently in an infant habituation experiment will be the child who is slow to acquire and accumulate knowledge and to use it in later cognitive processing, and so has a low IQ and poor educational achievement compared with children whose faster basic processing mechanisms allow them to get more out of the same experience. Basic processing speed may constrain what can be gained from any particular environment, but of course environments also differ in their usefulness for processing: a slow basic processor with a helpful environment may do very well compared with a fast basic processor whose environment is very unhelpful. Both processors and environments are indispensable for the development of cognition, both contribute to measured individual differences in cognition.

Anderson's ideas are stimulating and could develop into a helpful way to think of 'intelligence'. They have been criticised on the grounds that motivation and emotion, which will affect even estimates of Inspection Time, have not been sufficiently considered (Howe 1989b). Anderson (1989b, 1992) rebuts this on the grounds that a theory of such effects should not be constructed in an *ad hoc* fashion but should be principled, which postpones rather than negates Howe's point. His account of 'intelligence' as basic processing speed is also vulnerable to the points I raised earlier about the simplicity of psychologists' models of the brain, on the one hand, and the complexity of its structure and function as described by neuroscientists, on the other. Finally, for most assessment purposes, measurements of the 'intelligence' which incorporates a history of experience and involves using knowledge will be more relevant than purer measures. Just as in diagnosing the causes of reading failure or predicting the course of arithmetical development it has proved more useful to examine the child's use of the component skills of reading or arithmetic than to scrutinise or seek to improve more remote and abstract cognitive skills (see Chapter 2, sections on reading and arithmetic, Chapter 5, section on teaching thinking), in most educational settings variation in intelligent academic behaviour will be better understood by examining the child's performance of school-like tasks – perhaps using the Zone of Proximal Development (Chapter 4) as a diagnostic area – than by looking at Inspection Time. Sternberg's recent model of intelligence (Sternberg 1985), less innovative than Anderson's, may be more helpful at this level.

## The triarchic theory of intelligence

Robert Sternberg has recently proposed a model of intelligence which goes 'Beyond IQ' (Sternberg 1984, 1985). This 'triarchic' theory of intelligence has three subtheories: a subtheory of the components or internal mental mechanisms which underpin an individual's intelligent behaviour; an experiential subtheory of how intelligence is applied differentially to more novel or more familiar situations; and a contextual subtheory of how intelligence serves adaptation to one's environment.

Of these the componential subtheory is the most elaborately worked out, not surprisingly, given that Sternberg's earlier work stemmed from the field of information-processing. He suggests that there are three basic kinds of components of intelligence: metacomponents, performance components and knowledge-acquisition components. Metacomponents are clearly the constituents of metacognitive activity; they are involved in, for example, defining what a task is and how to tackle it (this task concerns reading and as I need to understand and pass an examination on the text I must read carefully); selecting appropriate cognitive processes to accomplish the task and combining them strategically (I will concentrate hard, read through first for main ideas and then again more slowly for details, I will make notes on the second and subsequent readings); allocating mental resources, monitoring their operation and evaluating performance (this bit is OK, I can go through it faster, but that earlier bit was really hard, I don't think I understood it, I'd better go back over it again when I can get somewhere away from distractions).

Performance components are lower-order processes which are called up to execute the plans which the metacomponents put together. They are processes such as inferring relations between stimuli, applying known relations and rules to new stimuli, comparing stimuli, choosing responses, working through chains of logical reasoning, etc. While metacomponents operate on cognitive components, performance components operate on data. Knowledge acquisition components are processes used in gaining new knowledge. The three main ones, necessary for nearing and for achieving insights, are selective encoding, selective combination and selective comparison. Relevant information has to be sifted out from what is irrelevant, coded into an integrated plausible useful whole and related to information which has been acquired previously.

Components vary in their specificity: some apply to only one task, some to a larger set, some are required for almost all cognition. They also vary in how closely they are interrelated. In some cases activating one component always activates another, and feedback from one also affects another, but in the present model it is metacomponents which have these sort of strong links and which also mediate between other components. Sternberg (1985: 110–11) uses the example of solving an anagram to illustrate this. The metacomponents define the task and decide on a certain tentative strategy for unscrambling the letters into another word; immediately the performance component responsible for the first step of the strategy takes over, and successive performance components are called on in turn. This activation produces action which produces feedback as to the operation and success of each performance component. Metacomponents monitor this feedback: if it is unsuccessful, the metacomponent which decides on changes in strategy may take over, and an alternative strategy or alternative solution be tried in the same way. As well as the specific information about the success of this strategy in this case, more general information is being acquired by the metacomponents about how to solve anagrams in general. Knowledge acquisition components sort this out and relate it to previous information stored in long-term memory. Next time the metacomponents define a task as being one of anagram solution, they can call on this accumulation of acquired knowledge about anagrams in general.

Cognitive development occurs in several ways in the subtheory of components. First, the knowledge acquisition components provide the means to a steadily developing store of relevant information. The increasing size of the knowledge base leads to better later acquisition and more subtle and flexible organisation of what is known; there is more to relate new information to, more to guide encoding, combination and comparison, and hence more effective use of knowledge. Second, the metacomponents can monitor, evaluate and modify themselves. Early in development they are largely ineffective but they have an enormous capacity for self-improvement (see Chapter 4). Self-monitoring by the metacomponents leads to better definition of tasks, better choice of performance components, better allocation of mental resources, and so forth. In principle there is here an unending feedback loop with the metacomponents transforming themselves from a jalopy to a Rolls-Royce. In practice, as we saw from the developmental literature, we probably settle, unless there is much external pressure for improvement or unusually few limitations of cost, for less perfection, for 'good enough' motoring.

Sternberg is suggesting that everyone uses components of these sorts when tackling cognitive tasks, irrespective of their culture and their experience. Experience is however one of the important dimensions of the triarchic theory of intelligence. The components which the componential subtheory describes involve intelligence to the extent that they are applied to relatively novel tasks or situations or become automatic and highly efficient quickly. What is being emphasised in the experiential subtheory is the ability to adapt previous understanding to new demands effectively, as opposed to the routine carrying-out of well-worn strategies and processes in isolation from each other. The ideal test is one which is novel enough to present some challenge, unique enough that routine cognition will not solve it, either because it has a new conceptual structure or because actually doing it requires new processes or a new combination of old processes. It should not however be too novel if it is to be useful for diagnostic purposes: if the person has no previously acquired knowledge at all to bring to bear on the task, then it will be impossible for him or her to do *anything*, intelligent or not, with it. Since the speed with which you give up on a task is affected by many other things other than intelligence, a too novel task will provoke little behaviour that is of any use for diagnosing intelligence.

The other important part of the experiential subtheory is its emphasis on automatisation. Sternberg argues (1985: 71) that complex information-processing tasks can only be executed because many of the operations required have become automatic. Arithmetic provides a good example. As I mentioned in Chapter 2, many arithmetical tasks require considerable knowledge, great accuracy, severe demands on memory and, preferably, an ability to check the plausibility of the answer (for example by estimating before actually calculating a sum). People who are not practised at long division or square roots or whatever do such tasks slowly and painfully (if they know how to at all) and make many mistakes. Computers, completely automated, do the constituent processes fast and accurately; they do so without knowledge, however, hence the gas bills for millions of pounds which are occasionally sent out after a decimal point has somehow been misplaced. Expert human calculators (Smith 1983) appear to have stocked their memories with immense quantities of relevant knowledge, to have devised unusual and ingenious methods for simplifying the calculations and using their results, and to have developed a sense of numbers having idiosyncratic 'personalities' which presumably both distinguishes the numbers and motivates the calculator (they sometimes do better when numbers they like rather than ones they dislike appear in the calculations).

It will be obvious that experience plays an important part in the development of human intelligence. The experiential subtheory points out two ways in which both individual differences and developmental changes can be explained. First, individuals with a superior ability to deal with novelty will show more rapid learning and consolidation of smooth controlled information-processing, so that automatisation will begin earlier in dealing with the task and will proceed faster. Second, the more processing has become automatic, the fewer cognitive resources it will require, and hence more resources will be available for dealing with the novel aspects of the task. Highly intelligent and more knowledgeable people, and children as their cognitive development progresses, will show better transfer of old learning to new tasks, see better analogies, use their intelligence components more effectively, and 'get the hang of' problems and skills more quickly.

The final component of the triarchic theory of intelligence is a subtheory on the context of intelligence. Sternberg is concerned here to link information-processing to the demands of the real world as reflected in definitions of intelligence (by Piaget and others) as 'adaptation'. People are not 'intelligent' in a vacuum, even when taking intelligence tests, and the contextual subtheory outlines different ways in which everyday intelligence is applied. The three 'basic' ways Sternberg describes are 'adaptation', or self-modification to fit one's environment better, to resolve the discrepancy between how one thinks or acts and how one believes one *ought* to think or act; 'shaping', or modifying the environment, a more risky strategy which often follows the failure of attempts at adaptation and which requires great knowledge of the environment if it is to succeed; and 'selection', or opting out of the unsatisfactory environment and finding a better one. Since the profitability of each of these strategies will depend on the context as well as on the individual, what is 'intelligent' will differ for different individuals in different predicaments and at different times. A British socialist in the late 1980s, for example, might find the state of politics unsatisfactory. In accordance with the contextual subtheory, he or she might equally intelligently try a 'shaping' strategy by working for the coming of a more socialist government, or 'selection', by living as completely as possible within a small group of the British population which was relatively socialist, or both; or he or she might try to adapt to Thatcherism by shifting to a belief in a nominally mixed but actually capitalist economy in which the poor receive charity at the whim of the well-off rather than having a right to share in the prosperity of the community. A Jewish socialist in Germany in 1933 would have a different range of options. The odds would be overwhelmingly against adapting to National Socialism or shaping it to be more favourable to Jews or left-wingers; 'selection', via emigration or resistance or concealment would be the only possible long-term choices. Intellectual development in the contextual subtheory occurs through a mixture of these sorts of process, applied to the new environments that children meet as they get older and venture out from the immediate family. The environments of home and school, for example, may make different demands on the child who must therefore act differently in the two settings: it may be easier to shape home to one's predilections than it is to shape school, and easier to select a context within school than it is to select a niche at home.

The reader may have gathered from my account of it that I find the contextual subtheory the least satisfactory part of Sternberg's triarchic model. It is distinctly less well worked out than the other two parts. While it does usefully correct the tendency to see real-life intelligence as reducible to scores on IQ tests it is not yet a scientific theory. It is impossible at present to specify much of it, for example to specify the range of ways in which people 'adapt to', 'shape' and 'select' their environments (while their environments are certainly shaping them, and no doubt also 'adapting to' and even 'selecting' them); thus, as with Piaget's Assimilation and Accommodation model (Chapter 4) it is hard to see how the theory can be falsified. Sternberg and Suben (1986) use Shirley Brice Heath's ethnographic accounts of three communities in the south-eastern United States (Heath 1983) to produce a lively description of how their different environments influence the intelligence that children bring to school, but their account ultimately adds little to Heath's beyond a plea for greater respect for societies whose socialisation processes and view of intelligence are not congruent with the values of schools and of conventional intelligence tests. 'Intelligence is largely the result of a socialisation process, and our understanding and assessment of intelligence must seriously take into account the nature of this process', they conclude (Sternberg and Suben 1986: 233). The earlier parts of this chapter dealt with models of intelligence which would dispute this assertion: in Chapter 5 I will return to studies of how environment and experience seem to affect cognition and examine the 'socialisation process'.

## Resumé: so what is 'intelligence' anyway?

Despite the progress made by new models of 'intelligence' such as Anderson's and Sternberg's, it could be argued that we should never have slid (as I deliberately did at the beginning of this section) from talking about 'intelligent behaviour' to talking about 'intelligence', that an erroneous and misleading reification has led us astray for nearly a century. This is the position incisively argued by Howe (1989a, 1989b, 1989c). He lists ten criteria that would justify the use of 'intelligence' as an explanatory concept not just as a descriptive measure, and argues that none of them can be met by our existing research-based knowledge. His central point is that all the claims for the existence in an individual of a stable quantity of a thing called 'intelligence' rest on the positive correlations between measures of performance on cognitive tasks which are presumed to require or involve the use of 'intelligence'. He does not deny that these correlations do exist: but he points out that they are not necessarily due to any particular underlying quality of the individual. Task performance may be related because both tasks require the same knowledge, the same learned skills, the same degree of perseverance or willingness to go 'beyond the information given', not only because they both require 'intelligence'. If the tasks being used for measuring 'intelligence' are of even moderate complexity, they will be highly likely to involve previously learned knowledge, skills and strategies, and it will probably be virtually impossible to specify what these are for any given task, let alone say what their developmental history has been for individuals. Calling the common ground of different tasks 'intelligence' merely provides it with a rather unspecific description.

Howe agrees that this objection applies much less strongly if the tasks used for measuring intelligence are very simple ones, tests of processes not contaminated by prior knowledge. Unfortunately the correlations between such tests have been inconsistent, and in the case of replicable studies have been low (0.3 or less). Howe cites Nettelbeck (1986) as pointing out that in any case even simple measures like IT can be influenced by variables other than 'intelligence'. Thus he states that 'intelligence', whether measured by simple psychophysiological tasks, somewhat more complex tasks involving learning, problem-solving or reasoning, or by traditional 'intelligence tests', remains an unspecified composite of knowledge, skills, strategies, and personality qualities, not necessarily the same from one individual to another or from one test occasion to another, and certainly not an 'innate general cognitive ability'. Anderson's view of course would be that Howe is underestimating the importance of basic speed of information-processing, which is seen relatively 'purely' in comparatively simple tests such as Inspection Time but also contributes in two ways to more complex tasks. First it allows more demanding information-processing to be carried out within the restrictions of working memory while the current task is actually being done, and second it has allowed the accumulation of more and better organised information and the perfecting of more sophisticated cognitive routines earlier in the individual's life (or, in the case of a slow processing speed, allowing less to be done in the present with a smaller and less well-processed store of acquired skill and knowledge).

Whether Howe is right or not, it is clearly desirable that our attempts to measure 'intelligence' should be scrutinized so that the reasons why a particular individual functions at a particular level may be more fully understood than a bald IQ figure can indicate. This is of course what responsible users of traditional intelligence tests do, and many would wish also to investigate individuals' performance under other circumstances too, looking at classroom behaviour or at the 'zone of proximal development' (see discussion of Vygotsky, in Chapter 4). Such an approach recognises that, to pick up a rather unpleasing metaphor used by a headmaster of my acquaintance, some people have brains like Minis while others have brains like Porsches, but (to extend the metaphor) the skills of the serviceman and the driver, not to speak of the fuel, the load and the demands of the terrain, are crucial to the way in which the engine runs, and thus to not only the speed at which the car travels but also its safety, the comfort of its occupants and the degree to which it pollutes its environment, to name only three other variables which are at least as important in deciding how 'good' the car's functioning is.

## The heritability of intelligence

One major area of the literature on 'intelligence' has not yet been discussed. The definition of intelligence as 'innate general cognitive ability', particularly in those definitions which emphasise intelligence as a consequence of fairly simple differences in the physical working of the brain, implies that intelligence will be heavily influenced by the individual's genes. We know (see Chapter 5) that several genetic abnormalities lead to severe mental retardation, and we are beginning to understand the causal chain between the gene defect or having an abnormal amount of chromosomal material, and the behavioural differences of individuals with conditions such as phenylketonuria or Down's Syndrome. It is quite clear that the development of the brain is under the control of a complex genetic programme (while also influenced by environmental events) and that, as Scarr and Kidd (1983) elegantly put it, 'the wrong amount of genetic material evidently messes up the program for brain development' (p. 380).

If the 'wrong' genetic material messes up brain development and hence brain performance and hence IQ when it is 'wrong' to a severe degree, might differences in IQ within the normal range have their source in more subtle degrees of genetic wrongness or rightness? It would, paradoxically, be easier to answer this question if there had been *fewer* attempts to establish a genetic basis for IQ. Investigations of its heritability have occupied much time and energy in the last seventy or eighty years with little profit, much bitter controversy, and some indefensible intervention in the lives of the powerless. Gould (1984) provides a powerful account of some of the atrocities which were a direct result of the belief that intelligence was easily measured, very largely inherited, and not to be improved by education or other environmental interventions. Before I review the evidence that this belief is seriously erroneous, there is some conceptual ground to cover.

In the sense in which geneticists use it, 'heritability' means something more precise than the 'capable of being inherited', which is the ordinary dictionary definition. Within a population, a trait varies over a certain range. This variance can be partitioned into a component due to relevant genetic differences within the population, a component due to environmental differences, and a component due to the interaction of genetic and environmental differences. If the trait in question were observed hair colour, for example, some variation would be due to genetic differences of blackness, brownness, blondeness and so forth, some to environmental differences such as nutrition or exposure to sunlight or artificial bleaches and colourings, and some to a gene-environment interaction, as when the girl with naturally mousy hair realises that her skin colour 'goes' naturally with a restricted range of light to mid-brown and russet, and gives up fantasies of being an ash-blonde or a Titian-haired beauty in favour of less extreme though still artificially-aided shades. Heritability is, at its broadest, the proportion of variation within the population which is due to genetic differences; it is sometimes taken to be that part of the entire genetic component which is due to additive genetic differences between individuals. It may be seen that what proportion of the variation is heritable is affected by how much environmental variation there is: if the environment does not allow the opportunity of changing the colour of your hair, then variation in hair colour will be much more closely associated with genetic variation than if bleaches and dyes are readily available and socially sanctioned. This means that an estimate of heritability of a trait derived from one population with a particular range of environments might not be an appropriate estimate for a population with different environments, or indeed for a genetically different population. The heritability of hair colour would be higher among pupils in the first year or two of secondary schooling than amongst their seniors in school, because the former do not so often show environmentally caused variance as the latter, where fashion, self-assertion, nascent aesthetic choice, more control over their own finances and a spirit of *il faut épater les bourgeois* (especially parents) have all increased and may make artificial colouring of hair much more likely. There might be another trough in the heritability of hair colour in the ageing population, where a number of individuals resort to artificial aids to conceal their greying, although this might be most marked in certain subgroups, such as actors, over-leisured ladies and politicians. Clearly we could not generalize heritability of observed hair colour from one population to another: a heritability estimate is always of heritability in the particular population studied, within the particular range of environments it experiences. It cannot predict heritability in novel environments; if the new range of environments has more relevant variation, then the proportion of trait variance due to environment will be greater and that due to heredity will be less, and if the new environments vary less, heritability will be greater.

It should be unnecessary to point out that even if a trait is strongly heritable, there can still be environmental influences on how the genetic program proceeds. Phenylketonuria is due to a single defective gene which causes a failure to produce the particular enzyme, phenylalanine hydroxylase, required to metabolise phenylalanine, got from protein in most ordinary human diets. This metabolic problem causes an accumulation of phenylalanine which swamps the developing nervous system of the baby and hence mental retardation develops. Since the genetic defect can be identified at birth and a diet which does not contain phenylalanine can be provided, it is possible to get round the metabolic deficiency, prevent the nervous system from being damaged and reduce the mental retardation to a minimal amount. The gene which causes phenylketonuria remains strongly heritable, but provided people with that gene have an environment free of phenylalanine while their brains are developing (and while, if they are pregnant women, their babies' brains are developing), the gene will not affect the trait of intelligence. Even a high heritability for normal intelligence would not mean that the nature of the environment was irrelevant to its level or its range.

Nor does a heritability estimate tell us *how* the genes actually affect the trait. In the case of phenylketonuria and some of the other genetic defects which have been studied (but *not* all those that are known) we have a good idea of what genes are involved and what sort of pathway there is between gene-protein-enzyme activity and physiology and brain functioning, and some (less) idea of how underlying physiology and brain functioning cause differences in intelligence and IQ score. We have this understanding, however, from studies of genes and brains, not from studies of IQ scores and pedigrees. These latter inform us about what sources are relevant to individual differences in intelligence in a population studied at a particular time under particular conditions; they do not tell us how the relevant sources contribute to the trait, nor which would still be relevant under different conditions, nor even in any very exact way which source is more important. While intuitively we may feel that a heritability of 80 per cent must determine one's score at least four times as much as a heritability of 20 per cent, or that if heritability is 80 per cent and 'environmentality' is 20 per cent the latter is negligible, it is a feeling that has to be resisted. We cannot argue from a population variance estimate to the exact position of an individual, nor ignore the fact that even a relatively strong hereditary influence is still dependent on and influenced by the environment it meets. Without some environment to grow up in, the gene cannot find expression, and even if it has the same effect in every environment in which it is found, somewhere there may be an environment which will change its expression.

Having made these warning remarks about heritability estimates, I can turn to the psychological literature. I shall deal with it extremely briefly as there is a great deal of work on the heritability of intelligence and much of it has far too high a ratio of prejudice to considered judgement. Biased accounts which are nevertheless worth some attention include Kamin (1974) on the anti-heredity side and Jensen (1980) on the hereditarian: I have made more use of a scholarly and dispassionate review by Scarr and Carter-Saltzman (1982); Scarr and Kidd (1983) contains some of the same material.

If a trait has a high heritability, that is, if its variation in a population is associated to a high degree with genetic variation, we would expect individuals to be similar on the trait in proportion to the extent which they shared the same relevant genes (I say 'relevant' since most of our genetic material seems to be virtually identical with our conspecifics, and some is shared with other primates and even mice). Thus genetically identical individuals such as monozygotic twins should be very similar indeed; parents and children, and brothers and sisters, who share an average of half their genes, fairly similar; and differences should increase as degree of relatedness decreases. This argument of course underlies the many twin studies and family studies which make up so much of the literature on intelligence. They have indeed found genetic relatedness to be associated with similarity of IQ scores.

Studies of members of the same families, however, have the intrinsic problem that genetically related parents and children and genetically related siblings normally live together, that is, they share each other's environments to a considerable if undefined extent. Further, parents not only pass on genetic material to their children and share their environment, they also do things because of their own genes, including those which they share with the child, which may affect the child; and the child's own genes and behaviour may affect the child's behaviour. Say the father has, and passes on to his daughter, a gene for enjoying reading. (Needless to say, this is an entirely fictional example. One does not have genes 'for enjoying reading', nor for being intelligent, nor for having a long nose. One has genes which lead to the building of particular proteins at particular times and so, in a long and complex chain of interactions with other genes and with non-genetic influences from the environment, eventually to having a physical or psychological characteristic. Not much is as yet known about this chain, but we do know for sure that it will *never* be possible to point to a gene and say 'that's what made the Bachs musical' or 'that's what makes Vanessa Redgrave a great actress'. However, it is worth following the argument as the fictional 'gene for enjoying reading' is a simplification sympathetic to the hereditarian case, which nevertheless fails to stand up even with this advantage.) Having this gene, the father will presumably seek opportunities of reading himself and will model 'enjoying reading' to the child, while not modelling those other activities whose time is taken up by the preferred activity of reading. The child with her genetic predilection for reading will also be given lots of experience of reading by her father, and will enjoy it; their observation of each other's enjoyment is surely likely to reinforce their activity and their similarity. The child's enthusiasm for books might rekindle an interest in the father that had found little expression while he was too busy with work for many enjoyments; the father's enthusiasm for reading is likely to be expressed in special educational efforts on his daughter's behalf. Even if the daughter does not inherit the 'loving reading' gene, she will still experience her father's enthusiasm for reading, certainly by observing him and probably also by being read to. The father may make special efforts to make reading attractive to this child in a wish to have her share his pleasures and because he knows that there are major educational advantages in liking to read. Parent and child behaviour may be very similar, but the similarity will be due to environmental similarity as well as shared genes. We might expect behavioural similarity to be greatest when there is likely to be parental shaping of young children towards a high level of a trait universally agreed to be desirable (such as reading well or, indeed, being intelligent), and similarity may decrease, particularly when there is less consensus on what level of a trait is best, as children become older and more independent, and leave the environmental pressures of their parents. There is some evidence for this argument (Luster and Dubow 1992, Scarr and Weinberg 1983). Gene-environment interactions on these lines may be very common, and they will greatly complicate heritability estimates based on genetically related people who live together.

The obvious strategy for getting round this problem is studies of genetically related people reared separately and unrelated people reared together. Earlier work in this area concentrated on studies of twins who had been brought up separately, hence Stephen Jay Gould's remark that the easiest way he knew of to make a living was to be an identical twin whose co-twin had been adopted at birth into another family, and to hire himself out to psychologists trying to estimate the heritability of IQ (and other personality traits). While this early work suggests that identical twins reared separately were still very similar indeed in IQ (i.e. that IQ is highly heritable) there are serious problems with the studies. The numbers of twins are small and they are very possibly not representative of the wider population. Further, the degree to which their environments differed, indeed even the degree to which their environments were separate, is very unclear. Many 'reared apart' twins were adopted by an aunt and brought up near their sibling, which suggests some communality of environment. Where the environment clearly differed, IQ scores tended to differ too (Bouchard et al. 1990). On the whole, not enough has been done to identify environmental differences which are relevant to intelligence (as we shall see in Chapter 5), and I do rather regret that the resources that went into chasing 'reared apart' twins didn't go into examining environments.

Adoption studies on the other hand provide very useful evidence on the heritability of intelligence. Adopted children are not genetically related to the family which rears them, so genetic differences and environmental differences are not confounded except in so far as the adoption agency tries to provide adoptive parents who resemble the biological ones. When there is more demand for babies to adopt than there are babies given up for adoption, agencies tend to select parents who are above average on such measures of 'suitability' as socio-economic status, educational level, intelligence and character (so far as they can gauge them). Adoptive parents are probably also unusually determined people, since becoming an adoptive parent requires you to convince so many other people of your deservingness and merits; they are probably not altogether representative of the population as a whole. While this does limit the generalisability of the studies somewhat, the fact that adoptive parents tend to provide better than average environments for their children has actually illuminated questions about the variability of IQ, as we shall see.

An ideal adoption study design has information on the IQs of all four parents for each child and compares adopted and biological siblings. While as yet no study provides this, there are two major conclusions from several recent studies (Horn 1983, Scarr and Weinberg 1983, Schiff and Lewontin 1986). The first is that the correlation between natural parent and child is higher than that between adoptive or rearing parent and child, which supports a stronger role for genes than for environment in intellectual resemblance between parent and child. The second is that children reared in adoptive families, with their social and economic advantages and with family members of above average intelligence, show a higher level of IQ score than would be expected from their biological parents' scores, if the biological parents come from disadvantaged social classes. This finding supports a strong role for environment in the intellectual level of children. The genes you inherit from your parents may determine the potential you have for intelligence, but the environment in which you are reared determines how nearly you reach that potential.

Two important points arise from the adoption studies of intelligence. The first concerns IQ differences between groups which differ genetically and environmentally. The Minnesota Transracial Adoption Study (Scarr and Weinberg 1983) looked at black, mixed-race and white children adopted into white families. It tested the hypothesis that these children would perform equally well on IQ tests, that is, that 'racial' differences in IQ are due to cultural factors not to genetic differences, and its results supported the hypothesis. Both black and mixed-race adopted children scored above the average for Minnesota's white population, considerably above the average for children reared in the black community, though about 6 IQ points below the natural children of the adoptive parents. This result, similar as it is to Eyferth's study of the illegitimate children of black and white American soldiers who occupied Germany after World War II and fathered children on local women (Flynn 1980), suggest that there is no convincing argument for a genetic cause for the lower average IQ score of American blacks.

The second point I want to make arises from the important French study by Michel Schiff and his colleagues (Duyme 1988, 1990, Schiff and Lewontin 1986, Schiff, Duyme, Dumaret and Tomkiewicz 1982). This study traced a sample of 32 children adopted within the first month of life into upper-middle-class families. Their biological mothers and the putative fathers were all unskilled workers. The children's IQ scores and school careers were compared with schoolchildren of the general population and of their original social class, and also with biological half-siblings. The children in this comparison group had the same biological mothers as the adopted children, though mostly a different father, and were near them in age. They had not been adopted into upper-middle-class families however; instead they were being reared in unskilled workers' families, mostly with their biological mother, though some were with grandparents or a foster mother. The results of some of the comparisons made are shown in Table 3.1.

It is quite clear from this that the adopted and non-adopted sibling samples were different from each other (despite sharing the same mother) and closely resembled their social class of rearing. The social class contrast was particularly marked in their school histories: upper-middle-class chil-

Table 3.1 School careers and IQ scores of French children adopted into middle-class families: comparisons with social class of origin and general population.

| Children's social class | Sample | School history | | | IQ | | | |
|---|---|---|---|---|---|---|---|---|
| | | | | | Group IQ Test | | WISC IQ | |
| | | No. of failures among 32 children of age of adopted and sibling sample | Failure rate (%) remedial class | Serious failure rate (%) (permanent special education) | Average | % below 85 IQ | Average | % below 85 IQ |
| Unskilled workers | Half-siblings of adopted children | 16.1 | 66 | 33 | 95.1 | 21 | 94.2 | 25 |
| | National surveys | 16.5 | 67 | 34 | 95.0 | 21 | – | |
| Upper middle class | Adopted children | 4 | 17 | 3 | 106.8 | 5 | 110.6 | 3 |
| | National surveys | 4 | 17 | 3 | 110 | 3 | – | |
| National norms | | 11.2 | 46 | 18 | 99.2 | 16 | 100 | 16 |

Source: Adapted from Schiff and Lewontin 1986: 90.

dren were much more likely to make uninterrupted progress through school. We will return to social class differences in educational performance in Chapter 5.

I have talked about heritability of intelligence so far without putting a figure to it. There are several reasons for this.

My main reason is that I am much more interested in what environments do to the development of the skills of intelligence than in the genetic differences which underpin differences in unanalysed IQ. This is not to diminish the interest and importance of studies of the brain and what makes brains differ in their production of intelligent behaviour; we are fortunate in working at a time when rapid advances are being made in understanding the way the brain works. I look forward to knowing more about it, but it seems to me unlikely that this knowledge will make environmental effects look unimportant, or establish a definition of intelligence as 'innate general cognitive ability' as being useful for psychological or educational purposes.

My second reason is that experts producing heritability estimates have varied considerably and violently in the figure they settled on. There is a rather strong relationship between the apparent political philosophy of the expert and his or her estimate of heritability. This, plus the lack of explicit and testable models of the genes behind the heritability, makes me disinclined to regard most estimates as scientifically unimpeachable. The 'best guess' of reputable scholars appears to be that the heritability of IQ scores in the white North American and British populations studied is between 40 per cent and 70 per cent. We know little or nothing about other populations, nor is it entirely clear what range of social classes is included even in the white British and North American samples. These are of course populations with relatively uniform environments and universal education, characteristics which will reduce the environmental variance and thus tend to inflate heritability. The only sensible position to take, it seems to me, is that intelligence is affected by one's genes both directly as they work to produce a more or less adequately functioning brain and indirectly through one's kin's behaviour and the environment one seeks out and elicits oneself; but that it is also malleable, affected by the environments to which one becomes adapted. Environments may be easier to manipulate than genes, but they certainly have not been studied in sufficient detail. We will examine environmental influences on cognitive development in Chapter 5.

## COGNITIVE STYLE: FIELD INDEPENDENCE AND REFLECTION–IMPULSIVITY

I will discuss two further dimensions of individual differences in cognition, field dependence–independence and reflection–impulsivity, briefly, as both seem to me to be too global and imprecise to be useful. Field dependence–independence (FDI) originated in Witkin's work (Witkin 1977, Witkin and

Goodenough 1981) on basic perceptual processes: it was a bipolar construct such that field dependent perceivers had difficulty in perceiving the constituent parts of a figure in the visual field as separate from the whole, while field independent perceivers were skilled at analysing the field into separate parts. It was usually measured using the Embedded Figures Test, in which the task was to pick out a simple figure which made part of the contours of a more complex one, or the Rod and Frame Test in which the rod typically had to be adjusted to a true vertical within a frame that was tilted out of alignment with the vertical. These tasks were seen as good indicators of a much more general cognitive style and personality dimension. Field independent (FI) people were good at the Embedded Figures Test and other tasks requiring perceptual restructuring because they were autonomous impersonal task-oriented people. Field dependent (FD) people, with a stronger interpersonal orientation and a greater sensitivity to social stimulation, were worse on restructuring tasks because of their reliance on other people and a less task-oriented approach. Early versions of the theory saw FI as clearly superior to FD; more recently the two have been seen as more equally valid alternatives, for example, field dependent people might be better at interpersonal and holistic tasks.

Developmentally, FDI could have two sorts of importance. The first concerns what causes it, the second how differences of cognitive style affect other aspects of development. Witkin and his colleagues suggested that different styles of childrearing had a strong influence on the development of field dependence or independence.

> Child-rearing practices that encourage separate autonomous functioning foster the development of differentiation in general, and, more particularly, of a field-independent cognitive style. In contrast, child-rearing practices that encourage continued reliance on parental authority are likely to make for less differentiation and a more field-dependent cognitive style.
>
> (Witkin and Goodenough 1981: 81–2)

Evidence from interviews with mothers supported this hypothesis but were not free of methodological flaws such as biased ratings of the interview material (Kagan and Kogan 1970, Kogan and Saarni 1989). More recent observational studies of mother–child interaction are summarised by Kogan (1983: 668) as 'disappointing': neither the within-culture nor the cross-cultural comparisons made have produced consistent and unproblematic results (Kogan 1983: 666–8, 670–2). The obvious alternative cause, biological differences, has also been studied, particularly in the context of the tendency of male subjects to show more field independence on the traditional tests, though not in studies of pre-school children doing versions which involved picking out a simple geometric form embedded in a meaningful picture of a person or object. Differences in hemispheric lateralisation may be involved, but what these are and why they happen are still controversial questions (for a review, see Waber 1977).

As to how being field dependent or field independent would affect other aspects of development, FDI impinges on a wide range of cognitive processes – not just spatial cognition but memory, learning and problem-solving – and has, as I said earlier, social implications also, through its association with different sorts of social competence. It is not clear whether FDI is independent of intelligence: there do seem to be fairly substantial correlations between the Embedded Figures Test and both $g$ and spatial intelligence (Satterly 1976, Vernon 1972), not surprisingly, given test content. Work by Nakamura and his colleagues (Nakamura and Finck 1980, Ruble and Nakamura 1972) suggested that FD children showed more task orientation and FI children more sensitivity to social cues. Children who had a low social orientation and high task effectiveness were all high on field independence: children who had a high social orientation tended to be more field dependent whether or not they were task oriented or had a sense of self-effectiveness. However, while FDI remains conceptually unclear and its measurement is fraught with problems, its use as a dimension of cognitive development is uncertain.

'Reflection–impulsivity' as a cognitive style refers to the extent to which a child can delay his or her response when searching for the correct answer to best choice in a context where what response to make is initially uncertain. The standard test here is the Matching Familiar Figures Test, which requires the subject to find the only picture in a set which is exactly the same as a standard figure. Children who make a choice quickly but also make many errors are called 'impulsive'; those who respond slowly but make few errors are called 'reflective'. It is assumed that impulsivity is a general trait and a disadvantage in most settings, particularly in education; hence the encouragement teachers give children to 'think, don't just guess'.

While there are some doubts about the psychometric adequacy of the Matching Familiar Figures Test (MFFT) just as there are about the Rod and Frame and Embedded Figures Tests (Block *et al.* 1986, Kagan 1987, Kogan 1983), the underlying issue of the relative importance placed on speed and on accuracy is one of great importance for cognitive psychology and for education. Children who are faced with a difficult detailed task may estimate the payoffs of strategies which emphasise speed or accuracy – or economy of effort; they may wish to please the tester or to get out of being tested. There is some evidence that there are indeed complexities in this: teachers rate children who are 'impulsive' as judged by their performance on the MFFT *not* as behaviourally impulsive but as anxious, cautious, vulnerable and self-doubting (Block *et al.* 1974, Block *et al.* 1986, Victor *et al.* 1985, Wapner and Connor 1986). Their MFFT style of fast-inaccurate responding presumably reflects their wish to escape from being tested and failing. It is not a successful strategy but neither is it a sign of general impulsivity. The evidence for reflection–impulsivity as correlated with ability to delay gratification and resist temptation is not strong (Kogan 1976, 1983).

An alternative account of reflection–impulsivity has been put forward by Zelniker and Jeffrey (1976, 1979). They suggest that more reflective children are dealing with the MFFT and other similar tasks in terms of more analysis of detail, while impulsive children do more global holistic processing. The more focused attention of reflective children may be more advantageous in many educational tasks, particularly perhaps if they can adjust the way they distribute their attention to the demands of the task. (It is possible that more focused parental language is associated with rapid language development and superior cognitive performance in young children (Lock *et al.* 1989, Meadows and Mills 1987, and see Chapter 5).) However, attention deployment and distribution of effort are not likely to be independent: it is certainly possible to increase children's reflectiveness by training them, using a variety of procedures (Kogan 1983: 682). It is not clear, however, how long such improvement lasts, how far it generalises, or whether what changes is the nature of the processing done, the resources devoted to it, or some combination of the two. Nor is it clear what caused individual differences in reflection–impulsivity in the first place.

Baron, Badgio and Gaskins (1986) pick up some of these issues in their discussion of 'cognitive style' as departure from optimally efficient behaviour on cognitive tasks rather than as a halfway house between ability and personality. They centre on 'impulsivity', seeing it as a tendency to stop too soon when trying to discover the solution to a cognitive task. An 'impulsive' child answers with the first possible response that comes to mind, thus risking errors which someone who persisted with thinking about the problem might not make, or gives up too readily when persistence might have produced an answer. This could be seen as underestimating the utility of making further cognitive effort. There will be a number of motivational and metacognitive reasons for such underestimating. A person may not value the payoff of further work, for example preferring the short-term reward of going to a party now to the more distant reward of high achievement, high income and high status which might result from studying but might not from partying (at least at the school pupil stage of the life cycle – things may be different when 'certification' comes from social contacts rather than from academic record). The varying approaches to study which I outline later differ in this sort of way. There may be differences also in the cost of further cognitive effort: cognition which is very painful or effortful may not seem to be worth it. An ideal, non-impulsive, thinker would balance the utility and the cost of thinking, and neither spend too much time polishing a 'good-enough' performance, nor carelessly throw in an underfinished not-quite-good-enough one. Both over-confidence and under-confidence may be involved in impulsiveness, the former suggesting that further thought is superfluous and the latter that it may not bring about any improvement. A person's characteristic explanations or 'attributions' of success or failure may also lead to giving up too soon (for an introduction see Dweck and Elliott 1983, Meadows 1986: 149–50, 193–5).

The complexity of reasons for impulsive premature answering of a question suggests that it might vary across tasks which differ in the attributions they evoke, the thinking they demand or the payoff they attract. Perhaps 'impulsivity' only applies to *some* tasks, where the person sees the task as involving intellectual competence, has a standard for what good performance would be on tasks in general and on this task in particular, and has to decide between several possible answers, none of which is immediately known to be right (Kagan *et al.* 1987). Siegler (1986, 1988) uses an information-processing model of associative strengths of different answers and individual differences in the 'strength' level which is acceptable as an answer; he sees these reflected in the strategy choices of good students, not-so-good students, and perfectionists. J. R. Anderson's work is an obvious influence on this sort of model (Anderson 1983, 1987).

'FDI' and 'reflection–impulsivity' are two examples of how individual differences in cognition have been conceptualised. Schmeck (1988) presents a number of conceptualisations and suggests that they can all be encompassed by 'one broad inclusive dimension of individual difference' of learning style, which he labels 'global versus analytic'. An extreme 'global' style involves field dependence, intuitive and emotional thinking, simultaneous processing of many aspects of experience, a tendency to impulsivity, and the formation of global impressions rather than precisely articulated analyses. Its pathological extreme could be called 'globetrotting' (Entwistle 1988, Pask 1988), an incomplete understanding based on overreadiness to see relationships between ideas or to come to conclusions without examining the evidence. At the other end of the stylistic dimension is an extreme 'analytic' style, involving field independence, sequential organised thinking, dispassionate noting of detailed objective 'facts', critical and logical thinking and a focus on learning step-by-step operations rather than a comprehensive overview. Here the pathological form is 'improvidence', an incomplete understanding based on detailed knowledge of many relevant facts which, however, fail to be integrated with broad principles, a 'can't see the wood for the trees' sort of cognition. Neither extreme is truly functional: an integration of the two, a balance of simultaneous and successive processing, of holism and analysis, will be more useful. Schmeck suggests that these cognitive styles develop as a result of the very young child's emotional reaction to failures of parental support and sensitivity. He uses ideas from psychoanalytic theorists such as Winnicott, suggesting that the child's self-awareness leads to pathological cognitive styles if the self-concept is emotionally negative, while self-acceptance is necessary for an integrated flexible cognitive style. There is little evidence on this sequence of causation, and Schmeck does not seem to be aware of the cultural limitations of the model of parent–child relations he uses. I discuss the complexities of parental influences on children's cognitive development in Chapter 5.

Some of the most interesting accounts of cognitive learning styles link them not with infant emotions but with current motivations. These studies often focus on examination of performance on particular well-defined tasks rather than assuming that 'cognitive style' is consistent over all occasions for learning or problem-solving. The differences they pinpoint cut across the global–analytic dimension: they are associated with different *motives* for cognitive activity which result in different *approaches* to it. Three main 'approaches' are suggested (Biggs 1984, 1988, Entwistle 1988, Entwistle *et al.* 1979, Marton 1983, 1988, Riding 1991, Volet and Chalmers 1992), 'surface', 'deep' and 'achieving'. Biggs in particular describes these approaches in students in secondary and tertiary education, but the same motives could no doubt apply earlier in development. 'Surface' students are concerned to obtain success (in terms of getting a qualification or a satisfactory grade) with minimal effort. They wish to avoid failure, and hence worry about tasks taking too long or, alternatively, having been worked on for too short a time for adequate performance. They tend to focus on 'essentials' – usually the factual data given in their textbooks and lectures which they judge to be important to their assessors – and work to reproduce them as accurately as possible. They are much less concerned with deeper levels of understanding, and they happily forget what was learned once they succeed in getting the qualification they sought. 'Deep' learners start from an intrinsic interest in the subject-matter and an intention to develop and use a personal under-standing of it. Self-actualisation, and enjoyment of learning for its own sake, combine with interest to focus them on the meaning of what they study. They are much less likely than 'surface' students to reproduce facts without amendment or criticism and without reference to underlying principles. 'Achieving' students are primarily interested in doing better than anyone else, getting the highest grades being a concrete demonstration of this. They may use 'deep' or 'surface' strategies, depending on the course requirements and the methods of assessment they face.

Of these three approaches, the theorists see the 'surface' learning style as least worthy of respect. They associate it with weak and anxious students, though acknowledging that curriculum and assessment in a considerable part of the education system may demand rote reproduction, not deep understanding and insight, let alone originality. This point about the interaction between task demands and student learning styles is an import-ant one. Some theorists assume (as I have pointed out earlier in this chapter) that a single sample of behaviour is sufficient for the diagnosis of cognitive style as this is seen as consistent over different tasks and situations and even developmentally, but fail to provide data which substantiate this view. Even if individuals are consistent in cognitive style, as does seem to be the case in a domain such as academic learning (Pask 1988, Siegler 1988) this consistency may be ascribed in part to institutional constraints such as examination techniques and other 'official' definitions of what is 'proper' learning. Primary school children may be exhorted to 'work it out' or to guess, science students may be expected to learn many highly specific facts and rules rather than go for global comprehension. Pask presents evidence that individuals can adopt the learning style appropriate to a particular task, though this versatility or sensitivity to context is itself differentially evident in different individuals! Siegler (1988) sees it in terms of individual differences in strategy choices, these choices being based on the amount of knowledge and the amount of certainty required for stating an item of knowledge as an answer.

It seems to me, then, that the accumulated work on 'cognitive style' has not as yet led to any clear conclusion on its place in the study of the development and acquisition of cognition in childhood. The view that 'cognitive style' is a general and stable trait seems to be losing ground to a view that styles are highly susceptible to task and situational influences, a shift that may be paralleled elsewhere in the psychology of cognitive development where domain-specific models are receiving more attention than very high level general ones. Similarly there is more recognition now that the demands of a particular task will be a major determinant of whether a cognitive style such as field independence or impulsivity is an advantage or a disadvantage. A more complex developmental progress is implied in this, as to assessment and causal explanations. A great deal needs to be clarified about who does what when, and with what degree of success, and what the antecedents and consequents are. Motivation factors, not much considered by the cognitive style approach, will be at work here. As I said apropos of intelligence it's not just the mental engine which determines performances, it's how you use it and on what.

## CREATIVITY

I shall deal very briefly with work on 'creativity' as an aspect of individual differences in cognition and cognitive development, and shall be critical of much that has been done. The root of my criticism of the area is the failure of theoreticians to be consistent and exact in their concept of what creativity is and how it works. The term is used to refer to the genius of Leonardo da Vinci and to the innovations of young children (or language-trained apes) in coining words to fill a gap in their vocabularies, via the novels of Jane Austen and the school compositions of an 8-year-old, without, I think, sufficient analysis of what these products and behaviours have in common and what differentiates them. Agreeing as I do with Edison's aphorism that 'Genius is one per cent inspiration and ninety-nine per cent perspiration', I want some theoretical differentiation between Leonardo and Washoe. I shall first review the literature on creativity in children, and then, via a return to earlier and out-of-fashion work on the intuitions of creative adults, indicate what may be involved in 'real', serious, creativity.

Commonly in the developmental literature, 'creativity' has been measured by and seen as largely synonymous with performance on divergent thinking tests (Guilford 1967) and even more narrowly with such tests' measure of 'ideational fluency': that is, how many uses can the subject think of for an object such as a brick. Even if measures with wider implications (but perhaps less objectivity and consensus) such as teacher ratings or excellence of artistic expression are taken, ideational fluency has been seen as the core of the concept of 'creativity'. The sheer number of responses produced has the considerable merit of being easy to count, hence it is a quick measure reliable between judges, who are less likely to agree on originality and appropriateness. Producing original uses for a brick is usually a consequence of producing many uses: bricks as building materials have to be got out of the way before bricks as doorstops or sources of reddish-brown powder are thought of, in other words it does appear that fluency is needed to generate originality (Kogan 1983). Similarly the evidence that creative people are more likely to think of 'remote associates' not just obvious associates, for example to see that the word 'party' is associated with each of the otherwise heterogeneous set 'line', 'Conservative' and 'stag', is 'unpersuasive' (Perkins 1988).

The identification of ideational fluency with creativity rests on the case that both require a broad deployment of attention, a wider consciousness of possibilities and implications, a freedom and spontaneity of personality which allows ideas to bubble forth. However Wallach (1971) puts forward a less attractive interpretation: the person who puts on a highly fluent and productive performance on a divergent thinking test may be showing obsessive tendencies, in an unwillingness to give up generating barely different answers, or an anxiety to please the tester, making a large number of responses in order to make a good impression. Here the need to distinguish between quantity and quality is particularly evident (see also Harrington, Block and Block 1983). And if we move out of the developmental literature to consider the 'creativity' of writers like Barbara Cartland (prolific but rather possibly not 'creative') and James Joyce (creative, but not particularly prolific), its importance is reinforced. It appears that it is quality not quantity of divergent thinking performance which predicts creativity recognised as such by teachers. Quantity is important, perhaps, if it stems from a willingness to postpone self-censorship, and provides material for further development, not because it is an end in itself.

The question of how to gauge the 'creativity' of a product is a complex one, and the various indices that might be proposed have all run into two difficulties: first, the lack of unanimities between judges, and second, the lack of correlation between different indices. 'Unusualness' is an obvious criterion, but although it can be assessed on the basis of statistical rarity (brick as building material makes up a higher proportion of 'uses for a brick' than does brick as a source of reddish powder, so the latter is more unusual and more 'creative'), some unusual 'uses' might be so bizarre that we might see them as pathological not as creative (bricks as radio receivers for the messages that little green men on Mars are sending out in an attempt to control my thought waves and make me assassinate William Shakespeare because Martians don't like his plays). 'Appropriateness' has been suggested as a further criterion and as a corrective to this problem, but this is a quality which raters agree on less well: a brick as a pillow seems definitively inappropriate to an American textbook writer (Rebok 1987: 322) but plausible, if dubiously comfortable, to someone who has admired the beautiful ceramic pillows of ancient China. There are historical as well as cultural problems here: some of Mozart's music, Mendel's theory and the mini-skirt all seemed inappropriate when they were first produced – 'too many notes' is supposed to have been one reaction to the first case – but have seemed more or less admirably creative, unusual and appropriate at a later date. Conversely later thinkers may repudiate earlier 'creativity': the theory that 'ontogeny recapitulates phylogeny', that the development of the individual from conception to maturity recapitulates the evolutionary development of the species, seemed unusual and appropriate to late-nineteenth-century philosophers, biologists and sociologists, including Herbert Spencer, G. Stanley Hall, Freud and, I suspect, Piaget (Gould 1977, Meadows 1986). Despite the fact that it displayed two higher level indices of creativity in that it helped to transform what was thought about development and about Man's place in the Universe and gave rise to qualitative shifts and to increases in theorising, and in that it provided a simple framework which contained and 'explained' phenomena of a complex diversity, it is now seen as false, hence inappropriate, and not perhaps so very original in the intellectual climate of the nineteenth century. Historians of science and of the arts can often find a precursor theory or product whose existence may be taken to lessen the 'originality', if not the excellence, of what had previously been taken as stunningly creative.

Some writers (e.g. Perkins 1988) are not deterred by these problems, saying that creativity is a 'fuzzy' concept and that we all agree on core instances so need not be too concerned about disagreement about more marginal ones. Unfortunately for developmentalists, our definition problem is particularly acute. Children are continually doing things (e.g. early words, early games) which are novel for them and appropriate, but have been done by millions of people before. Or they do things (e.g. invent a name) which are altogether novel and provide an appropriate solution to a problem, but later develop the normal consensual form and give up their earlier 'creative' solution.

It is not known whether 'creativity' as measured by divergent thinking tests or by teacher ratings is stable over the course of development, partly because it is not clear what 'creativity' consists of at different ages. It seems that many adult writers wrote also as children, but we do not know how many people write as children or as adults but not both, nor in what ways their writing was 'creative'. Nor is it known what conditions facilitate ideational fluency, let alone 'creativity': the research which suggested play or 'open' classroom environments fostered such behaviour is seriously flawed (Bennet *et al.* 1976, Kogan 1983, Smith and Sutton 1984). Torrance (1962, 1988) has had some notable success in identifying creative adolescents and also in training and support activities for students who were underperforming in school, but finer analyses are needed of both input and output.

A considerable amount of research has been done on the relationship between intelligence and creativity (e.g. Freeman *et al.* 1971, Getzels and Jackson 1962, Hudson 1970, Wallach and Kogan 1965). Much of this work is compromised by the two cognitive characteristics being defined in terms of intelligence test scores and creativity test scores, or by the use of ratings of one or the other which are even more approximate (such as school achievement tests as an index of the intelligence of more or less 'creative' professional adults). Not surprisingly the results are unclear. However it seems that intelligence and creativity are positively correlated in the general population, so that few persons with low IQ scores are recognised as 'creative' on tests or as professional artists or scientists (but see the research on 'creativity' in so-called 'idiots-savants', e.g. Howe 1989c, O'Connor and Hermelin 1990, Radford 1990). IQ does not predict creativity so well at an above average level: there may be a threshold level of intelligence necessary for creative achievement, but extra IQ points above that level (about 110–20) do not predict extra creativity. There obviously are highly intelligent people who do not produce creative work. Intelligence could therefore be seen as enabling rather than causing creativity. Perkins (1988) floats the idea that highly creative professionals are almost all highly intelligent because they needed high intelligence earlier in their careers in order to get the academic credentials and qualifications necessary for entry to their profession and the opportunity to be creative within it. Their high intelligence might have no further relevance to their present creativity. Whether this argument is persuasive no doubt depends on one's view of education and one's definitions of intelligence and creativity. Whether the cognitive processes which constitute 'intelligence' enable or promote 'creativity' is perhaps better considered by looking at them in more detail.

It is quite clear that for many creative people their creativity is very task specific, and built on a long period of gaining expertise on one particular area. The creativity of Chopin and Liszt, for example, was expressed almost entirely in piano music, that of Jane Austen in novels of exquisite social comedy, that of Mendel exclusively in genetics.

The cognitive processes involved operate on the basis of very specific content and mastery of form and subject-matter. The psychometric literature on creativity has been very general about processes; 'generate and select' is perhaps the core description, though tests like the Uses of Objects, even less specifically, require only generation of ideas. It is necessary to find an intermediate level of specificity and precision. A number of relevant activities appear in the reports of creative people about their own cognition (e.g. Getzels and Csikszentmihalyi 1976, Ghiselin 1954, Koestler 1964, Ochse 1990, Roe 1970).

Getzels and Csikszentmihalyi (1976), for example, investigated art students who were rated by their teachers as being creative. They spent more time on initial exploratory approaches to their work, were more able to change directions if new ideas or possibilities came up later, did not view their work as fixed and were more independent of precedent and prior thought. All in all they excelled in 'fending off closure', which enabled them to progress beyond the obvious to more novel solutions to problems. Elsewhere, creative people are described as having a preference for looking at problems from contradictory positions, and making particular fertile use of negations. Koestler (1964) emphasised the finding and use of analogies: both creativity and humour result, he said, from the intersection of two formerly distinct frames of reference. The problem-solving technique of 'brainstorming' also stresses banning criticism, deferring closure, encouraging fluent production of novel ideas, encouraging add-ons and analogies, and so forth. Those computer programs which have been set to make mathematical discoveries, such as D. B. Lenat's 'Automatic Mathematician' (AM) (Boden 1988, Lenat and Brown 1984) are provided with basic concepts and a set of generative rules for transforming them. New concepts and hypotheses are generated and then evaluated, guided by programmed-in criteria for what ideas are promising. AM has discovered some mathematical ideas which were not programmed in initially, and at least one minor idea which no other mathematician, automatic or not, had previously thought of, but many of its 'creations' were trivial, and of course its basic knowledge and its criteria were both provided by Lenat. AM may not be totally convincing as evidence that computers can be creative (see Boden 1987, 1990) but it does provide an interesting example of the profitability of 'explore, generalise and evaluate' cognitive programmes.

To be able to proceed like this requires certain cognitive attitudes, which do indeed turn up in reports on the personalities of creative persons. It involves choosing challenges rather than avoiding them, which is linked with autonomy, independence and ambition. It involves valuing appropriateness, which is defined (in perhaps somewhat transcendental terms) as (in the sciences) the consistency, parsimony, generalness and predictive power of theories, or (in the arts) as moral or emotional profundity in the representation of the meaning of life, human nature and so forth. It involves tolerance of risk, the ability to confront uncertainty, to enjoy complexity, to toy with and resolve ambiguity, etc. Such people as creative artists, scientists and architects (Ochse 1990) do seem to have these characteristics more than their less creative peers. The creative person also has, however, an exhaustive knowledge of his or her field, a sizeable basic repertoire of strategies and skills and information, acquired through a long and effortful involvement in the area. Radford (1990) reviews the literature on exceptional early achievement in a number of different fields: commonly, high achievers are not predictable from early excellence so much as from their investment of time and energy. Whether the creative attitude is applied even outside one's own area of expertise is not clear: some creative persons do seem to have been able to turn their skills to unrelated areas (I believe Rossini was a creative cook as well as a composer), and some of course are expert and even creative in more than one field, Leonardo da Vinci, Freud and Piaget being obvious examples.

The introspections of creative people (Ghiselin 1954, Ochse 1990, Wallas 1926) also provide an interesting summary of the stages of the creative process. The first is the long slog of familiarising oneself with the problem, gathering together and organising what might be the relevant information, acquiring the necessary expertise, investigating each avenue of solution. No solution, no satisfactory action, can be found, despite intensive work trying every possibility that suggests itself. Commonly in those cases where a creative solution is eventually found, the first stage of working hard on a problem is succeeded by a second stage of not working on the problem at all but letting it 'lie fallow': going on holiday (or merely to sleep) or working on something else. This is then followed by a third stage, an 'insight', a 'Eureka' reaction, which suggests the answer. Various dramatic instances of this are reported: Archimedes realising that the volume of an intricate object could be measured by measuring how much water it displaced in a full container, just as his own body displaced water in his overflowing bath, or Kekulé dreaming of how the atoms of carbon and hydrogen fitted together in molecules of benzene in a ring like a snake biting its own tail. The essential fourth stage is the working out and testing of the solution, which obviously resembles the first stage, and may lead to further cycles of hard work and discovery.

This cyclic pattern of the creative act seems plausible, but of course we do not have systematic data on whether it is indeed significantly associated with creative products, or whether there are many cycles like this which never get past stage 2 or cycles where a solution emerges as a result of stages 1 and 4, without any experience identifiable as 'lying fallow' or 'insight'. Nor do we know what quantity of stage 1 activity or stage 2 inactivity can lead to what profundity of stage 3 insight. Nevertheless this model of the creative cycle has at least two merits: it reminds us that by no means all cognitive activity is conscious, accessible and controllable, and it is deeply consoling to those of us who find ourselves rather frequently staring into space with an apparently empty mind: 'I'm not daydreaming, I'm letting an insight emerge.' The relevant *developmental* literature might thus be on play, exploration, 'pretend' and insight rather than on 'creativity' *per se* (Haight and Miller 1992, Harter and Chao 1992, P. Smith and Simon 1984, Smith *et al.* 1985), but also on motivation, effort, and tutoring (Radford 1990).

# Chapter 4

# Models of cognition in childho
## Metaphors, achievements and prob

I will begin my discussion of models of cognition in childhood by picking out two themes which have run through most of our discussion of children's thinking. One is the general question of how far children's thinking is different from adults' thinking. Here we can see a wide range of beliefs, from St Paul's eloquent assumption that children's thought is different from and inferior to adults' thought –

> But when that which is perfect is come, then that which is in part shall be done away.
> When I was a child, I spake as a child, I understood as a child, I thought as a child: but when I became a man, I put away childish things.
> For now we see through a glass, darkly; but then face to face: now I know in part; but then shall I know even as also I am known.
>
> (1 Corinthians 13: 10–12)

– to the contemporary emphasis on the structure and process of children's thought being similar to adults' from the very earliest years of schooling onwards, and the differences being due to children's ignorance of relevant material and their lesser practice at meditating on and describing their own thinking. I have discussed some of the research investigating what develops in children's thinking in Chapter 2, but the general question of degree of difference and of development is also very much a theme in the wider models of cognition surveyed in this chapter. The second theme is in many ways an even more fundamental one. It is the question of what models are appropriate for cognition: is it more helpful to think of ourselves as 'in essence limited capacity manipulators of symbols' (Siegler 1983: 129) very similar to slow and inaccurate computers; or as biological organisms with a long evolutionary history which has led to us having a brain which functions in particular ways and leads to particular cognitive activities just as we have evolved lungs, livers and a thumb articulated with fingers so that fine grasping is possible; or as members of social groups taking part in relationships and cultures, and using and developing our cognition within them and inseparable from them? Different models of human nature make erent assumptions about the relative importance of the social and the biological, of cognitive processes and physiological structures and problem context. Which metaphors seem appropriate arises from these assumptions and also constrains what questions will be asked and what answers will be seen as possible. I will argue that though we may learn a great deal about cognition by thinking of it as computation, as adaptation or as acculturation, we must be clear and explicit about our basic assumptions and remain aware of how our chosen metaphor may obscure important points which another model would have clarified. The discussion of several models of cognitive development which follows will include some assessment of how adequately the models match up to these demands.

## PIAGET'S MODEL OF COGNITIVE DEVELOPMENT

We begin with a model which set out its basic assumptions far more elaborately than any other and which took into account a uniquely wide range of biological and philosophical considerations. Piagetian theory was a tremendous intellectual achievement, and for all its faults, and despite all the idiocies committed on data by people who misunderstood what was important about it, has shaped the field in quite remarkable ways. It gives an account of cognitive processes which is still influential and is in certain respects probably basically correct, and needing mainly testing and specification; and an account of cognitive structure which has been more popular (because less abstract), but is clearly too rigid and does not deal adequately with the influence of cognitive material or cognitive context.

It would take several volumes larger than this to describe and evaluate Piagetian theory fully; here I will focus on a few of his most important ideas. For fuller accounts of Piaget's work, I would suggest 'beginner readers' begin with Donaldson 1978, Flavell 1985, and Brainerd 1978 (in ascending order of difficulty), and those who already have some acquaintance with his work might address themselves to his own classic account (Piaget 1983) and to important discussions of his last work by Gelman and Baillargeon (1983), Beilin (1992) and Vuyk (1981).

At the core of Piaget's model is the idea that cognition is one form of the adaptation between organism and environment which is seen through all the living world. The child, or indeed the adult, is all its life actively trying to make sense of the world, just as any organism must try to adapt to its environment. I have discussed the implications of evolutionary theory and brain research for cognitive development theory elsewhere (Meadows 1983, and Chapter 5 this volume; see also Young 1987); Piaget's main work on this, *Biology and Knowledge* (1971) is still an important book. He said that 'adaptation' in cognition proceeded by means of 'assimilation', or relating new information to pre-existing structures of knowledge and understanding, and 'accommodation', or by developing the old structures into new ones under pressure from new externally-given information or problems or from the pressure of internal contradictions by incompatible structures. These two cognitive processes or twin 'functional invariants' work together throughout the whole of cognitive life (the assimilation of new information must lead to some degree of accommodation in the old system of knowledge, if only to the minor degree of 'ah, here's another $X$: I've seen at least a hundred of those in my time, so now I've seen at least a hundred and one'), and together with the equally innate tendency to organise knowledge into coherent systems and smooth routines they give rise to a series of 'structures' of cognition, that is, ordered rules, categories, procedures and so forth which eventually amount to unified organisations of logical operations.

An example may help to clarify what 'assimilation', 'accommodation' and 'organisation' might look like at the level of observable behaviour. I devised it originally to make a number of points in a criticism of Piagetian theory, but I do not think it is in any way unfair to Piaget's intentions. The protagonist is an experienced cook. He or she has successfully cooked carrots and potatoes, carrots by boiling them, grating them raw for salads, and making carrot soup, potatoes by boiling, roasting, frying, mashing and making chips. The initial state of knowledge of ways of cooking carrots and potatoes could be represented as in the first matrix.

| Method | Carrots | Potatoes |
|---|---|---|
| Boiling | ✓ | ✓ |
| Chipping | not tried | ✓ |
| Frying | not tried | ✓ |
| Grating, for salad | ✓ | not tried |
| Mashing | not tried | ✓ |
| Roasting | not tried | ✓ |
| Soup | ✓ | not tried |

The cook now meets parsnips for the first time. The new vegetable is *assimilated* to the carrot repertory, perhaps on the basis of similarity of shape and texture. Parsnips boil very well, make a rather bland soup (Grigson (1980) recommends adding curry powder), and although they taste quite pleasant raw are not a visually attractive ingredient in salad. The cook also assimilates parsnips to the potato repertoire; parsnips need careful chipping or frying, mash well and are delicious roasted. The knowledge matrix after assimilation of parsnips would have one further column, as shown in the second matrix.

| Method | Parsnips |
|---|---|
| Boiling | ✓ |
| Chipping | possible |
| Frying | possible |

| | |
|---|---|
| Grating, for salad | maybe |
| Mashing | ✓ |
| Roasting | ✓ |
| Soup | maybe |

Assimilation is always accompanied by accommodation, however. The schema 'vegetables you can mash' is augmented with parsnips, for example, and the importance of butter is emphasised. The cook may accommodate further by extending the mashing schema to carrots, and hence to the full range of vegetable purées. Since roast potatoes and roast parsnips are successful, the schema 'roasting' may be tried out on carrots, with success. A fully developed knowledge system for cooking carrots, potatoes and parsnips might look something like the final matrix.

| Method | Carrots | Potatoes | Parsnips |
|---|---|---|---|
| Boiling | ✓ | ✓ | ✓ |
| Chipping | no | ✓ | possible |
| Frying | no | ✓ | possible |
| Grating, for salad | ✓ | no | maybe |
| Mashing | ✓ | ✓ | ✓ |
| Roasting | ✓ | ✓ | ✓ |
| Soup | ✓ | maybe | maybe |

This sort of procedure is obviously infinitely extendable. The same basic principles of assimilation, accommodation and organisation leading to a thoroughly developed knowledge structure will apply whatever new vegetable the cook encounters: turnips, celeriac, Jerusalem artichokes, and so forth.

Assimilation and accommodation are fundamental but abstract concepts which are at one and the same time immensely plausible and hard to tie down to specific behaviour, let alone specific brain activity or specific educational practice. They are almost certainly essential basic components of a good model of cognitive development, though they need considerably more specification (Beilin 1992, Gelman and Baillargeon 1983, Meadows 1983, 1986). Piaget's own main account was given in two books published in English in 1978, where he distinguishes between different sorts of assimilation. He postulated that there is a sort of natural instinct to assimilate: 'any scheme of assimilation tends to feed itself, that is, to incorporate outside elements compatible with its nature into itself' (Piaget 1978a), thus driving development on. This happens at three levels. The first is assimilating objects to schemes, as the infant does when grasping a new object, or as scientists had to when a new planet's existence was discovered. The second is assimilation between different schemes, for example eye–hand co-ordination or the sort of alternation between writing and critically reading one's own writing which is achieved by the secondary school pupil (see Chapter 2 this volume). The third and highest level is assimilation between subschemes and the totality which integrates them into a coherent whole; the concept of 'gravity', for example, is at the core of physicists' accounts of many quite different localised events, from the motion of the planets round the sun to the falling of Newton's apple. These assimilations are said to involve the scheme 'finding' or 'distinguishing' characteristics which match the scheme or are near neighbours to it, as opposed to others which negate or contradict it, though these too must in the end be co-ordinated into the total scheme. Thus both affirmations and negations are important. A balance between affirmations and negations is necessary for development, just as a balance between assimilation and accommodation is.

While this account of assimilation and accommodation is of great interest, a number of problems arise. Some cluster around the 'drive to assimilate'. It is not clear to me at what point this drive would be satisfied: the model appears to imply that there could always be further assimilation and accommodation, that the 'natural' state of cognitive development is progress towards a highly developed, subtle, sophisticated, intricately integrated, perfectly balanced cognitive system. Is this an empirical account of what is really done, or a rational reconstruction of ideal cognition? There is room for real doubt about whether most people really do go in for this sort of thorough thinking-out of everything (Boden 1982, Mischel 1971); perhaps here Piaget was using himself as a prototype and forgetting that the rest of us are, probably, sloppier thinkers, content with localised understanding, not pushing its limits outwards, and quite capable of believing contradictory things?

There are problems also over the question of what is or can be assimilated to a scheme, and how this is done. What degree of match, on what dimensions, means that a new object or event affirms a pre-existing scheme? What mismatch negates it? For example, suppose that I initially believed that every word of the Bible was literally true, and that, therefore, we knew the world was created in exactly seven days (in late October of 4004 BC, if I also believed Archbishop Ussher's biblical commentary). What would then be my adaptation to the theory of evolution and the evidence of geology and the fossil record? I could refuse to assimilate science and stick to creationism, or accommodate to science and reject the literal truth of the Bible; or, like some unhappy nineteenth-century scientists, suggest that God during his seven days' work created new rocks and animals containing evidence of an evolutionary history which had never actually happened. Of these three adaptations, the last is inherently unstable, leading for example to a pretty odd sort of God; the first is adaptation by restriction, like the amoeba who successfully protects itself against the drying up of its pond by retreating into a shell-like skin; only the second is likely to lead to further cognitive development and better understanding of the world. Whether it also leads to better adaptation in a wider sense depends on the socio-cultural context; for someone living amongst fundamentalists it might well lead to blasphemy trials and outright persecution.

This is an extreme example (though one which has occurred quite frequently – and violently – in both this century and the last), but it is a real problem (see also Chapter 2, this volume, on conceptual thought). Piaget's examples tend to be *post hoc*, and no one else has yet done better. We may also doubt whether affirmations and negations are equally readily dealt with by the thinker, as negations in logic, and in scientific theory building, seem to be so difficult to manage (see Kuhn 1962, Wason 1977). Further, in many areas it is extremely hard to see whether a new event affirms or negates a scheme; the concept is hard to apply in questions of moral or political judgement, for example, or in the visual arts. Russell (1978) argues that one of the important things we have to learn is, precisely, which kinds of knowledge have to be consistent and which do not.

Assimilation, accommodation and organisation, functioning together, were held together by an even more important (and mysterious) process called 'equilibration', Piaget believed. He saw equilibration as central to evolution, to all biological functioning and to cognition in particular. It was a central theoretical concept from the beginning to the end of his career, but it is hard to define it precisely, not least because Piaget's own account of it developed over the years. Essentially, perhaps, it marks his belief that although assimilation, accommodation and organisation functioned incessantly to deal with the information and the problems that continually impose themselves on the organism's attention, there was none the less stability in cognition to a considerable degree, not the constant shifting of cognitive structures which constant change – the maturation of the organism, its second-by-second experience of the environment, the pressures of the social world – might seem to force during development. 'Equilibration' is clearly a force for stability, via a self-regulation that balances external and internal changes. In some cases it works by restoring the previous stable state; in the cases which are more interesting for development, successful adaptation calls for a more radical and pervasive shift if balance is to be regained, an 'equilibration majorante' (Piaget 1978a).

Why did Piaget believe that cognition was an equilibrated system? He clearly believed that organisms *need* to maintain a stable internal equilibrium within the changes and uncertainties of the outside world, a belief which one can sympathise with. There are a number of biological systems of self-regulation which serve precisely this sort of need: the regulation of body temperature in warm-blooded animals is one example. If our blood temperature varies too far, our bodies automatically work to correct this, and if necessary set up conscious actions which change the temperature of our surroundings. Receptor cells in the hypothalamus, pre-set at a level of about 38.4°C by our genes, are activated when the blood temperature rises or falls beyond narrow limits, and signals from these receptors initiate sweating, shivering, panting, increased metabolism of fat from the liver and so forth. Sensory cells in the skin provide conscious sensations of heat or chilliness. These cells generate signals which activate the cerebral cortex and initiate programmes of activity such as taking off clothes or lighting the fire, which prevent further rise or fall in body temperature before it has changed substantially. The receptors in the hypothalamus innately and precisely signal deviation from the pre-set temperature level, and innately set in train effective responses, but are not conscious: the receptors in the skin, reporting to the cortex, inform it whether the skin is getting hotter or colder rather than indicating absolute temperature, and while we may or may not be conscious of our need and what to do about it, we have learned the appropriate conscious actions and can choose amongst them (see e.g. Young 1987). If something goes wrong with either the automatic or the behavioural self-regulation of body temperature, we lose our physiological equilibrium and may become quite seriously, even fatally, damaged, as in cases of heat stroke or hypothermia. 'Durable disequilibria constitute pathological organic or mental states' (Piaget 1968: 102).

The other root of Piaget's belief in cognitive equilibria must surely be related to the coherence, closure and self-structuring properties of logico-mathematical systems. The number system, for example, or the rules of formal logic, structure reasoning so as to lead on every occasion to true and non-contradictory answers. It is always true that '2 + 2 = 4', for example, and excludes the possibility that '2 + 2 = 5' or '2 + 1 = 4'; if 'every dog will have his day' then there can be no dog anywhere who has neither already had his day nor cannot legitimately look forward to it today or sometime in the future. The main question here, which we will return to elsewhere in this book, is whether such perfectly clear and consistent systems of knowledge are representative of knowledge as a whole and whether we use them easily; Piaget seems to have seen them as at least pre-eminently important and desirable.

Equilibration relies extremely heavily on the assumption of invariant regularities and consistencies in thought. It explains *how* cognitive develop-ment occurs in terms of 'need' for a coherently organised and consistent way of thinking. The changes and demands of the outside world produce in the thinker small 'perturbations' or 'conflicts' which lead the cognitive system to small automatic adjustments (of assimilation and accommodation) to cope with the conflicts and return either to the original cognitive equilibrium or to a new and better one. It is the momentary non-functioning of a cognitive scheme which both signals the presence of a 'perturbation' and is the sole motivator of efforts to seek a new equilibrium, but the non-functioning does not of itself indicate what the conflict is or how to solve it. Even in his most detailed account (1978a) Piaget did not succeed in specifying what con-tradictions are noticed or resolved or exactly which lead to cognitive progress. He warned that not all contradictions are fruitful, and speculated that structural contradictions are more relevant to cognitive development than are momentary contradictions due to perception or historical accident. A theory of effective spurs to cognitive change would be very useful, but is not available at present. In order to resolve disequilibrium in the direction of cognitive growth, you must be able to recognise (not necessarily consciously) that there is a disequilibrium, and as Rotman (1977) points out this is not unproblematic; you must similarly recognise at least approximately what has caused it; you must *want* to resolve it, rather than deciding to live with the contradiction (like the White Queen in *Through the Looking Glass* who deliberately practised believing impossible things before breakfast). There may also be, in many cases, alternative equally valid resolutions of the contradiction, and in other cases no resolution may be possible (as in various logical and mathematical paradoxes (Hofstadter 1979)). Bryant (1982a) argues that confirmation by two schemes leading to the same conclusion may lead to development more effectively than conflict.

Piaget did discuss (1978: 30–8) what makes one state of cognitive equilibrium 'better' than another; better equilibria can cope with more elements or dimensions, they are both more differentiated and more integrated, they co-ordinate and complete earlier equilibria, they are more flexible, and they provide more possibilities for interacting with a wider environment. This is a plausible description of a cognitive system but hard to translate into behavioural terms, and there are some problems in founding 'betterness' on increased complexity or width of application. It *is* obvious that adults do interact in more varied ways with their environment than infants do, and with more different aspects of it, and similarly that human–environment interactions are wider and more differentiated than amoeba–environment interactions. It should not be taken as obvious however that this makes humans or adults 'better' or 'better equilibrated' or 'better adapted to their environment' than amoebae or infants are (Midgley 1985, Ruse 1986). Nor does this account explain why 'lower' forms of life (such as amoebae) or of cognition are prevalent and apparently well adapted to the world. Would we have tabloid newspapers, for example, if equilibration really pushed cognition ever on?

Piaget somewhat compounded this problem by his insistence that cognitive development formed a single invariant sequence of stages. He insisted that these were a result of individual equilibratory construction, not due to an innate teleology of development, though he was clearly sympathetic to the work of biologists such as Waddington who demonstrated how much of embryological development and physical growth was pre-programmed while still under the influence of the organism's experience of the environment. 'Preformationism' has been a non-respectable position in much thinking about cognition (Mischel 1971), but in far more subtle, specific and limited forms is now appearing to be more viable as a basis to theories of cognition (see Chapter 5 this volume). We need to understand a great deal more than we do at present about the nature and mechanisms of genetic programming and central nervous system functioning (and about the nature and mechanisms of the effects of life experiences, which are if anything less well understood and no less complex), but modern biology, as Piaget was perhaps the earliest to see, has a great deal to offer to those concerned with cognition (see e.g. Young 1987). Nevertheless, the claim that the Piagetian sequence of stages is invariant and universal is not unproblematic. Significant problems remain in the diagnosis of stages whose internal consistency is not clear (see Gelman and Baillargeon 1983, Meadows 1975, Klausmeier and Sipple 1982), but the cross-cultural evidence suggests that besides these there are a number of significant variations not just in rate of development, which would have only marginal relevance to the validity of Piaget's theory, but in whether the later stages develop in the sort of form Piaget described. The sort of schooling the culture provides and the sorts of concepts it values seem to be the main determining factors (Dasen 1977, Laboratory for Comparative Human Cognition 1983). The evolutionary analogy would itself suggest that a single invariant sequence is less likely than a branching tree-like pattern: certain cognitive adaptations are developed but other possible adaptations remain potential rather than actualised, or are even given up. The time and resources required to develop mathematical or musical ability to the full, for example, might preclude even the normal development of other areas of cognition, let alone developing them too to their full potential. Post-Piagetian researchers, particularly in the United States, seem to be more concerned with domain-specific developments at present, and with emphasising the crucial role of acquired information, than with the general universal and relatively content-independent sorts of structures which make up the Piagetian stage sequence.

Piaget's use of 'structures' has been very influential, both at the basic conceptual level, where, as we will see, there are problems, and even more at the level of descriptions of behaviour, where his stage descriptions have caught many psychologists' imaginations. I think that much of this influence is now declining, and Piaget's own interest shifted towards an emphasis on 'procedures' towards the end of his life. (To some extent, this is a shift in level of description. 'Structures' are the timeless, abstract, universal laws of transformations and relations between objects or concepts, such as the mathematical system of real numbers; 'procedures' are the goal-directed behaviours which, occasion by occasion, we use. For example, commutativity ($8 + 2 + 7 = 7 + 2 + 8 = 2 + 7 + 8$, etc.) is part of the structure which underlies our successful procedures for adding up our bills, top to bottom or bottom to top, pence and pounds together or separately.) Nevertheless, some discussion of 'structures' and 'stages' is appropriate here.

It would be hard to deny that human thought, at least after infancy, is in some senses structured. It has rules, legitimate procedures and hierarchies of concepts. We are not completely bound by these structures, we may not be aware of them, and we do not, on the whole, have adequate descriptions of them, but generally we work within their system. So far, this is commonplace, a very vague description applicable to language, Piaget's formulations, number systems and even the extreme behaviourists' associative networks (Feldman and Toulmin, 1976). As we become more detailed, problems start to arise, and I want to discuss the forms some of these take in Piaget's work (see particularly Piaget 1970, 1971b).

The first problem is that of the ontological nature of 'structures', what sort of existence they have. The slightest sort of existence would be that of theoretical construct; thus we make no claims about whether there are such structures in the child but we describe his thinking in terms of organisations and properties which exist only in our theoretical analysis. If we keep to it, this is a fairly safe position, though it may look trivial – but it is all too easy to forget that the 'structures' are in our description not in the child's thought, and be carried away by our metaphor. Locating the structures in the child reifies them a degree beyond descriptive constructs, and serious problems arise. One is the question of *where* they are in the child, thinking, mind or brain all being possibilities. There are too many controversies about the relationship between these three to go into here (see also Chapter 5, section on idealism, dualism and materialism); Piaget's position was ultimately reductionist, that thinking is firmly centred in a neurophysiological base, but also that it must have an abstract description, the two levels being isomorphic. His description of the earliest stage of thought was primarily biological, that of the later stages primarily abstract and in terms of formal logic. This general position is a reasonable avoidance of the dilemma, though what the isomorphisms are remains as yet unknown.

A second problem is that we do not directly observe thinking or other cognitive processes, we infer them from observable behaviour. Inhelder and Piaget (1979), discussing the relationship between procedures and structures, reiterate that the best evidence for the existence of structures in the child's mind is what the child considers possible, impossible, or necessary, and some very interesting and ingenious research is being done in this area (see e.g. Russell 1981, 1982). However, unless we are extremely careful, clever and scrupulous, we may make the wrong inferences, and this is particularly likely when we are studying people different from ourselves or comparing groups different in age, class, or culture. Cole and Means (1981) discuss this question very thoroughly. Their strictures apply to much of Piaget's account of the inadequacies of young children's thought, which we will come back to. Piaget's formulation, which slides (often almost within a chapter) between structures which are in the theorist's description and identical or virtually identical structures which are in the child, was inadequate.

There is one further possible sort of existence for structures of thought, not incompatible with those already described. This is that they exist in some sense outside the individual, as in what Popper calls 'World 3' (Popper 1967, Popper and Eccles 1977). I know of no comment by Piaget on this idea, but it would not seem to be a part of his formulation of cognitive development. This sort of existence, though not entirely easy to understand, might be more easily related to Vygotsky's theory than to Piaget's (see later in this chapter).

Piaget was, then, not so precise as one could wish about the ontological status of structures, and his position was fraught with similar difficulties over his treatment of the relation he believed there to be between 'structures' and observable behaviour. It is often problematic to go from performance (which is comparatively observable) to competence (which has to be inferred from a sample of performance and from a theory of what competence is like). I have found myself in difficulties over the validity of the transition in much of the work on cognitive development discussed in this book; but Piaget's treatment of the problem has seemed to many psychologists to be peculiarly unsatisfactory. Behaviour is an important source of data for the theory, but it has to be *interpreted* before its degree of support for his theoretical claims can be assessed. This was clearly his procedure in most of his published 'experiments': a deliberately artificial situation is presented to the child and his thinking about it is probed and then interpreted by the experimenter, this 'thinking' being manifested primarily in the child's talk about the situation and secondarily in his manipulations of the material. The theory arises from the interpretations, not from the overt behaviour; and the behaviour is reported, selectively, as supporting illustration of the theory. Thus it can be for the reader a matter of considerable doubt and difficulty to relate what the child can be observed to do or, very often, say, and the abstract formal mental structures that are said to explain the child's activities, and this I will come back to when I discuss some questions of the empirical validity of Piagetian structures. It was, presumably, not a problem for Piaget, but then he was neither a psychologist nor an empiricist. The elucidation of thought by the examination of language does not seem to have struck him as particularly problematic. He believed that language was unable to convey what was not already established in thought. This would seem to imply that language is, at least slightly, retarded compared with thinking. Unless the lag is very small, this would mean that there would be occasions when the child's language was too underdeveloped to express the greater sophistication of his thinking. Using language to diagnose thought would in these cases give rise to false diagnoses of immature thinking; and there are indeed many demonstrations of 'failure of thinking' which appear to be due primarily to language difficulties (e.g. Donaldson 1978). Nor is the interpretation of children's language necessarily unproblematic.

There is one further central problem in Piaget's use of structures, which we must deal with before discussing the empirical validity of his work. This is two characteristics of structures which appeared very early in his work on them (Piaget 1952) and which relate to both his biologism and his description of structures in formal and abstract terms. Cognitive structures tend to form structured wholes (*structures-d'ensemble*), and this is what, once they are fully established, the concrete operational stage, the formal operational stage and other logico-mathematical systems consist of. 'Stages' are periods of relative equilibrium in the development of the child's thought, which is said to resemble the development of thought in the human species (this resemblance being one reason for Piaget's interest in children's thought, it being impossible to investigate the thought of, say, Australopithecus or Neanderthal Man). There are a number of points here which need a brief comment on a theoretical level; some we will return to, as they raise empirically answerable questions.

Both *structure-d'ensemble* and 'stage' imply the existence of a fairly tight relationship amongst a set of cognitive structures. On the whole, we would expect the structures which form a *structure-d'ensemble* to develop and appear together, and to react one upon the other. Piaget's theory also suggests that they form at each stage qualitatively different structures, being not just bigger but better (in terms of coherence, complexity and field of application, as we said earlier). Again, at a very general level this would appear really rather likely, but the detail of Piaget's models of *structures-d'ensemble* turns out to be unsatisfactory. Both concrete operations and formal operations are described in terms of logical systems which logicians regard as of poor quality (see e.g. Boden 1979: 80–6, Ennis 1978), and which are inferred from behavioural (largely verbal) data in ways that turn out, at least in the case of formal operations, to be quite simply wrong (Bynum *et al.* 1972).

In addition to these difficulties Piaget's model of stages has changed with development. The earlier model implied a stage sequence where transitions from stage to stage are the disequilibrated periods and are relatively brief, so that there are fairly abrupt changes from stage to stage. It is this model of clearly contrasted stages that dominated most popular accounts of Piagetian theory. In the later model there is a considerably less step-like development, and the preparation, achievement, consolidation and superseding of, say, concrete operations flow into one another smoothly and cover a period of several years. If this is the better picture (and, as I describe below, the empirical evidence is for the later more complex model not for the earlier one) the descriptive value of stage and *structure-d'ensemble* concepts begins to look very slight indeed. There are indications that psychologists studying cognitive development are moving away from their use (e.g. Beilin 1992, Flavell 1963, 1977, 1985).

In Piagetian theory the structures of thought are applicable to virtually any area of knowledge; they are seen as abstract content-free ways of reasoning. Piaget described them as fitting together into a succession of coherent and qualitatively different stages; the major ones are the sensori-motor, pre-operational, concrete operational and formal operational stages, and there are sequences of substages within the sensori-motor stage and within areas of operational thought, such as conservation of quantity. The structure of each stage is such that thought at any given moment is relatively consistent in its level across different content areas; consistency is especially to be expected at the times when concrete operations and, later, formal operations are fully developed, as both these stages are based on logical models. While logical systems are being constructed, temporary inconsistencies and fluctuations are to be expected, but an emphasis on differences between stages and similarities within them remains. In a child behaving according to the Piagetian model, performance on one test of, say, conservation predicts performance on other conservation tests and on other tests of concrete operations. Furthermore, the stage structure limits the possibilities of improving performance by instruction. The child cannot assimilate or accommodate to events which are too incompatible with his or her whole coherent system of understanding, and instruction can at best produce only a limited and possible temporary advance, isolated in the area being trained.

The sensori-motor stage develops over the first two years or so of the child's life and is therefore not relevant to a book focusing on the school-age child (but for an interesting review of it see Harris 1983a). The school years begin late in the 'pre-operational' period, cover 'concrete operations', and end during 'formal operations'. It is therefore appropriate to provide a very brief account of each stage. The pre-operational stage is described (1) as the period when children begin to use semiotic systems such as language and imagery, and (2) as a time when they lack operational thought, that is, flexible reversible reasoning which allows them to conserve, classify, seriate, co-ordinate perspectives, overcome misleading perceptual impressions, etc. Concrete operational children have these abilities: they can think much more systematically and quantitatively and their thinking is described in terms of formalised logical structures (the 'groupings') relating to classifications and relations in quantity and in space. The final formal operations stage is a more integrated and more abstract development from concrete operations, less tied to content and more capable of dealing with hypothetical material. Formal operations receive a more abstract holistic and rigorous description from Piaget. Logicians as well as psychologists have queried the models given for both the concrete operations and the formal operations stages (Vuyk 1981), and they remain controversial.

With this account of stages, Piagetian theory puts up a challenge which has attracted a good deal of research response. As I have said, direct evidence on the reality of assimilation, accommodation and equilibration has been hard to get: testing the stage model has been somewhat easier, though not altogether unproblematic. Sequences of stages are fairly well confirmed, though there have been some suggestions that their order is logically necessary (e.g. Smedslund 1980) and so of no empirical interest. Rate of progress through the sequence seems to vary somewhat between individuals, but this is far from crucial to Piagetian theory, which is concerned with the idealised 'normal' epistemic subject, not with individual differences. Rate also varies between cultures, degree of schooling and less formal educational experience being one of the main relevant variables; in some cultures there is little sign of formal operations. This finding is mildly embarrassing for a model which has been taken as claiming that formal operations is a universal high point of human cognition, but in fact Piaget's main account does not explicitly make such a claim (Inhelder and Piaget 1958). The role of social and environmental experience in cognitive development is an important issue which needs more investigation than the main stream of Piagetian thought provided. I discuss it elsewhere in this book (e.g. Chapter 5).

The behaviours typical of different stages appear in a fairly constant order, then, if not at a constant rate. Their appearance can certainly be accelerated by training (Brainerd 1983). Contrary to the predictions of the Piagetian account, training does produce improvement in performance which can be considerable, long-lasting and pervasive (see also Chapter 5). A variety of training methods have been seen to succeed, and it is not the case that 'neo-Piagetian' models, which conjure up equilibratory mechanisms or provoke discovery, are any more successful than methods involving imitation, didactic interaction, or the following of verbal rules. Initial stage level does not seem to predict the possibility of training or limit how effective it will be. Pre-schoolers have successfully been trained on the concrete operations tasks which they would not be expected to get right for another three or four years, and their performance after training appears as competent as that of untrained 8-year-olds (Brainerd 1983, Gelman and Baillargeon 1983). This has been interpreted as showing that there are minimal differences between the cognitive structures of pre-school children and those of primary school children. It does seem to be clear that Piaget painted far too negative a picture of children's thinking in the pre-operational stage (Beilin 1992, Vuyk 1981), and we might prefer a model of cognitive development which described more pre-school competence and (perhaps) a less complete later stage competence, with a gradual consolidatory transition rather than a qualitative shift during the school years (Braine and Rumain 1983, Donaldson 1978). However, there seems at present to be some danger of arguing away a developmental change in cognition rather than carefully analysing the extent and nature of the change.

One of the differences between younger and older children is in the degree and type of within-stage consistency they show, or how many *décalages*, that is, slips in level of performance, there are. The question here is how the different areas fit together as structured stages. The usual research design has been the obvious one of seeing how children's performances correlate across a number of tasks which each involve the same logical principles (e.g. conservation) or belong to the same stage (e.g. measure of class inclusion, weight conservation and perspective-taking, which all belong to the concrete operations stage). It is not always altogether clear how large a correlation is required to support the theory of within-stage consistency, and the statistical complexities are considerable. If, accidentally, one test is slightly more difficult than another, for example, this may lead to misleading patterns of synchrony (Brainerd 1978). On the whole, research studies have found less consistency between different areas of concrete operations than a simple model of logical structures which are constructed quickly and underlie all tasks would suggest (Gelman and Baillargeon 1983, Klausmeier and Sipple 1982, Meadows 1975). There have also been numerous inconsistencies between different measures of ostensibly the same operation, for example, conservation tests using materials which seem obviously equivalent to the adult but produce obstinately different responses from children (e.g. Beard 1963, Miller 1982, Uzgiris 1964). Some of these *décalages* are due to the 'figurative aspect' of the test situation; for example, if the transformed material in a conservation test looks very different from the original, then children will be less likely to give a conserving response than if the change in appearance is slight. Similarly, various changes in the social situation or in the language used help young children to conserve or manage class inclusion (e.g. Light *et al.* 1979, Siegel *et al.* 1978). Some *décalages* receive only a last resort explanation: that the objects involved offer more 'resistance' to the thinker. Piaget never dealt with the problem of *décalages* thoroughly. He was less interested in them than in how children managed the general principles underlying operational thought, for example how they had a feeling of certainty despite appearances which suggested otherwise. He thus had little to say about *décalages* except where they were common to all children, hence characteristic of his 'epistemic subject'. Recent work by Longeot (1978, Shayer *et al.* forthcoming) starts to deal with this omission, and with some of the problems of low correlations within stages, with a model which predicts when consistencies and *décalages* will occur. Longeot points again to the possibility that there may be discrepancies between the logico-mathematical structures of the epistemic subject and the natural thinking of children solving adaptive problems in real life: the distinctions between 'knowing' and 'doing' and between various degrees of 'having a concept' that I mentioned earlier. This work has also shown that there may be alternative paths to the same outcome, and such individual differences need to be accounted for. One possibility raised relates Piagetian concepts to psychometric ones: the suggestion is that there are different and partially independent sorts of intelligence (cf. Gardner 1983). There is interest also in the possibility that cognitive development is domain-specific rather than, as in Piagetian theory, general across domains. Investigation here obviously requires detailed descriptions by domain and comparison between them; this is very much what Piaget and Inhelder did in the series of studies which are still acknowledged as brilliant investigative observation.

## INFORMATION-PROCESSING MODELS OF COGNITIVE DEVELOPMENT

### Introduction

Psychologists using the information-processing approach to the study of cognition and cognitive development describe cognition as largely a matter of handling information in order to solve problems. They are primarily concerned with how information is selected, represented, stored, retrieved, transformed, and so forth. The focus is on what mental processes are used to deal with information, with how they are organised, and with how they change during learning or development. Computation is seen as the basis for human cognition, and sometimes computers are used to test hypothetical accounts of the information-processing that goes into solving a problem. Even if they are not, some attempt is made to specify the hypothetical cognitive processes sufficiently precisely for them to be tenable by experiments with people if not by computer simulation. The cognitive tasks investigated tend to be fairly tightly defined also, and they quite often have a Piagetian or psychometric pedigree. Siegler (1978, 1983, 1984, 1989b), for example, has done extensive analyses of a balance task, as I describe below, and Klahr (Klahr and Wallace 1976, Klahr 1984) of conservation and class inclusion. More recently, Anderson (1992) combines psychometrics and information-processing in an interesting model of cognitive development and intelligence. The basic assumption is that 'people are in essence limited capacity manipulators of symbols' (Siegler 1983: 129) and that analogies with the ways in which computers process information will be helpful. Just as computers operate by combining a number of microlevel distinct operations in an appropriate sequence, so humans are seen as using a fairly small number of elementary cognitive processes in a structured way over a period of time. Mental processes which mediate in varying ways between stimulus and response are emphasised, and in many aspects human cognition is seen as active and constructive, unlike the passive S-R models of classical behaviourism, or indeed the run-of-the-mill computer.

   Like Piagetian models, information-processing approaches to cognitive development seek to describe children's cognitive capabilities and limitations at successive points in their development, and to explain how a later and more advanced understanding emerges from an earlier less adequate one, that is, these models too are concerned with 'what develops' and with 'how does this development occur'. They deal with these questions by trying to specify what cognitive processes the child applies to what information, which processes in which order for how long, and what information, how represented, and when in the processing sequence. They also seek to specify how development occurs, what components of processes and representations are self-modifying, or can be modified by outside influences, or are resistant to change. They assume that knowing about adult information-processing (or computer information-processing) can lead to illuminating comparisons with children's information-processing (and vice versa).

In order to clarify issues which will arise in my later discussion of information-processing models of cognitive development, I will outline some concepts which have proved important in models of adults' information-processing. The first is derived from the work of Atkinson and Shiffrin (1968) whose account of the memory system has proved useful (see Chapter 2). They distinguish between memory structure and the control of memory; the former is analogous to computer hardware and constrains speed of operation and memory capacity, the latter is like the computer's software, specifying what processes should be carried out when for this particular task. They propose that memory includes several different stores; the details are not universally agreed but it seems to be helpful to think in terms of there being a sensory register, a short-term memory store and a long-term memory store, each of which could be divided up according to whether the incoming information is visual, auditory, olfactory or whatever. These memory stores are linked as shown in Figure 2.3. Each uses certain basic processes (which can only run at up to a certain maximum speed), and the sensory register and short-term memory stores are also limited in the amount of information they can take in and how long it lasts for. Atkinson and Shiffrin suggest that these memory structures are universal: all adults have them, and all children, and they may perhaps be 'wired-in' to the brain (see Chapter 5).

Memory control, however, can be changed by development or by learning. Control processes, such as rehearsal, operate on information within memory stores, and allow people to overcome the structural limitations of the system. Information is processed in the sensory register, which can only hold it for a fraction of a second, and then moves to the short-term memory store or 'working memory', which is analogous to the central processor of a computer. It is here that conscious and strategic processes operate. We can be conscious of what is in our working memory even though we are not conscious of what is in our sensory register or our long-term memory. Memory strategies mediate the transfer of information between working memory and the other memory stores. Using verbal rehearsal, for example, keeps information in working memory longer than its normal time limit of less than a minute and also makes it more likely that the information will be transferred to the permanent store of long-term memory; organising information into larger meaningful chunks overcomes the normal limited capacity of working memory. A case-study by Ericsson, Chase and Faloon (1980) illustrates this. The normal quantity of unrelated bits of information which can be held in working memory is about seven items, seven randomly ordered digits, for example. However given a few hours' daily practice for a year or so the student who was the subject of the case study could remember strings of 75 digits! He was able to do this because he organised groups of the random numbers into meaningful items. He happened to be an experienced cross-country runner who could encode numbers as race times; '3492' for example was encoded as a speed for the mile, as '3 minutes 49.2 seconds, near world record time'. With practice he could group such meaningful chunks into larger 'super groups'. His knowledge provided him with a strategy, which practice perfected, so that he could transcend the structural limitations of memory, at least for strings of numbers which could be grouped into patterns which resembled race times.

This study illustrates a point about information-processing which has been made by other theorists, for example Herbert Simon (1981). It is important to analyse the demands of the task if we are to understand the performance of people working on it. What they do is constrained by their own cognitive limitations, but it is also directed by what they think the task requires. A strategy may be used because it is adaptive for them on that task, not because it is the best strategy available. This is important developmentally for a number of reasons. What strategy of processing information is used will depend on what the task is seen to require, hence its familiarity will affect performance. It will also depend on what relevant information is available, and again children may lack information which older problem-solvers would have. The 'costs' of the strategies which could be brought to bear on a task may also be different for children: less easily assessed, in the first place, and less easily leading to a cost-benefit analysis. We may perhaps be, unlike computers, problem-solvers who are willing to settle for a 'good enough' near-solution to a problem if it would be very laborious to give up our not-quite-adequate strategy and replace it with a more efficient but more expensive one. We saw a number of examples of this 'get by by bodging it' in Chapter 2, for example the balancing strategies used by the subjects of the study by Karmiloff-Smith and Inhelder (1974/5), and the 'knowledge-telling' strategy in writing (Bereiter and Scardamalia 1987).

Information-processing models, then, are concerned with the encoding and transformation of information in the solving of cognitive problems. The core constructs are that there must be internal representations of information which cognitive processes act upon, generating, manipulating or transforming the initial representation. Representations and processes together make up the knowledge base, and it is assumed that this is large and rich in interconnecting links, so a particular piece of information can be accessed in many different ways from strong association to indirect inference. Although the knowledge base is to all intents and purposes infinitely large, some of its content may be difficult or impossible to reach on occasion, and only a very small subset of knowledge can be acted on at any one time, as there is only a limited quantity of attentional resources available to bring knowledge and processes into an active state and maintain them there. Some activation is automatic and requires little or no attention; other processes needing more immediate control make heavy demands on attentional resources. Automatic processing tends to be fast and to make minimal demands on resources, but it is not under voluntary control so it cannot easily be modified. Controlled processing is slower and uses up many more attentional resources, and may be less efficient, but it is easier to modify and fit flexibly to task demands and other varying aspects of each situation.

There is considerable and often heated debate about the ways in which people are able to represent knowledge (Block 1981, 1983, Boden 1988, Cooper and Shepard 1984, Pylyshyn 1980). The issues under debate include whether we have visual image representations of knowledge or solely verbal propositional ones, whether knowledge is declarative or procedural, explicit or inferred, and so on. Most of the debate is at the level of the formal and abstract description of the structure of knowledge, and it is not often linked with our increasing understanding of how the brain works (see Chapter 5). Siegler (1983, 1986) discusses a number of different ways of representing knowledge and information-processing, and makes the point that these models will be useful for analysing different tasks. Semantic networks, for example, seem to be most useful for pinning down a set of linked meanings, and thus for modelling a person's store of facts about the world or part of it, say facts about the music of Tchaikovsky. Production systems are more like knowledge about procedures, set up as smoothly executable routines for the performance of tasks such as addition, speaking, skiing, playing the violin and so forth. They may be harder to access and discuss than the semantic network of declarative knowledge, and seem to be organised for effective action rather than for self-awareness. Scripts represent generalised events: they are accounts of situations where both procedural and declarative knowledge are involved (Nelson 1986, and Chapter 2 this volume), such as playing in an orchestral concert.

These different ways of representing knowledge are more likely to be useful simplifications, which make it easier to analyse the information-processing demands of a task, than to be true reflections of genuinely separate ways of representing knowledge. In order to play the violin in an orchestra, for example, one certainly needs to have procedural knowledge, to get fingers and bow to the right places in a staggeringly rapid succession. But one also presumably follows a script of co-operating with other players and the conductor, and one may have available declarative knowledge about the style of the piece, its composer, other interpretations by other musicians, and which critics or talent-spotters are in the audience. These different sorts of knowledge are not independent, and even on a simplified task, such as would be used in a laboratory investigation, may be strong influences on behaviour. Where the subject's 'irrelevant' representations are not what the experimenter would expect, as may often be the case when the subject comes from a different culture (Cole and Means 1981) or different age group, performance may be adversely affected and the wrong cause for this failure inferred.

## Issues in information-processing

Information-processing models of cognition could be seen as tending towards the same two separate categories as other accounts of children's cognition, the first category being those which focus on the cognitive system *per se* and describe the very basic structures and processes which underlie all cognitive functioning, a largely syntactic approach, and the second category taking much more account of how the general system is applied to particular tasks.

This sort of polarisation can be seen in the AI literature, where some models are of General Problem Solvers and some are of more limited Expert Systems, as well as in the developmental literature reviewed here. On the whole the current trend seems to be towards working on the details of cognition in particular limited fields, on how the content of a task affects the ways in which a person (or a computer) adapts general processes in order to get the task done, and researchers have discovered a great deal of flexibility in how processes common to several tasks are used in each case. This has led to description of cognitive strategies and a recognition of the complexities of the interaction between cognitive activities, the skills, knowledge and attitudes of the learner or problem-solver, and the task demands. Strategic descriptions tend to be set out at a different level from the syntactic processes descriptions, as a comparison between, for example, the models of class inclusion proposed by Klahr and Wallace (1976) and by Case (1985) suggests. The former looks closer to a computer program, the latter to a common-sense account such as might be usefully taught to and understood by a child. As they stand, neither accounts for the 'horizontal *décalages*' documented in the literature. For example, in Siegel *et al.* (1978) class inclusion of different sorts of sweets was facilitated by a particular form of question ('Would you rather eat the sweets or the toffees?') and no doubt also by the motivation of gastronomic interest and understanding of the social setting of food distribution.

John Searle has argued very strongly that a computer that only used syntactic rules could not be said to have a mind. His argument (Searle 1984: 39–41, 1990) is as follows. Minds are entirely caused by processes going on inside the brain: 'brains cause minds'. 'Syntax is not sufficient for semantics', that is, form alone is conceptually different from meaning. 'Computer programs are entirely defined by their formal, or syntactical, structure' and 'Minds have mental contents; specifically, they have semantic contents'; mental activities refer to or concern things in the world. The conclusion which follows from these four premises is that 'No computer program by itself is sufficient to give a system a mind. Programs, in short, are not minds, and they are not by themselves sufficient for having minds.' Further, 'the way that brain functions cause minds cannot be solely in virtue of running a computer program': the computational properties of the brain are not enough to explain its functioning to produce mental states. As Searle asserts, brains are biological engines, their biology matters. An artificial brain, if it were to be able to do all the human brain can do, must have powers equivalent to those of the human brain, not just the power to implement computer programs.

AI specialists, and indeed other philosophers interested in AI (e.g. Boden 1988, 1989, Churchland and Churchland 1990, Gregory 1987, Haugeland 1985), do of course dispute these conclusions. Searle himself would not deny that computational descriptions may be interesting, though he is strongly sceptical about their long-term usefulness: 'The computer is probably no better and no worse as a metaphor for the brain than earlier mechanical metaphors. We learn as much about the brain by saying it's a computer as we do by saying it's a telephone switchboard, a telegraph system, a water pump, or a steam engine' (Searle 1984: 55–6). For my purposes in this book, I want merely to underline his point that there are two levels of description of cognition which are quite incontrovertibly important: the neurophysiological workings of brains, and the psychological level of behaviours like recognising faces, understanding language, social cognition and so forth. Adequate neurophysiological and behavioural descriptions and theories may make computational information-processing ones redundant. Since the information-processing metaphor still, for good and bad reasons, dominates the field, I will discuss it further here, but readers may wish to take my discussion in the light of the fact that I am much more impressed with the exciting findings that are coming out of recent brain research (see Chapter 5), and feel that the future lies there and in studies of cognitive behaviour in the real world rather than in abstract computational models of cognition. To see people as 'in essence limited capacity manipulators of symbols' (Siegler 1983: 129) is one possible view, but perhaps a misleadingly narrow one.

Boden discusses current computer models of learning and cognitive development, and the difficult conceptual questions involved. How are 'learning' and 'development' to be distinguished for example? What are the prerequisites for learning? Are there distinctions to be drawn between types of learning, and how relevant is the content and structure of what is learned?

Can the human learner be modelled by a computer system? These questions do not have simple obvious answers, and Boden believes that so far computer models of learning have been only partially successful (1988: 190–201). One model she discusses is a system designed by J. R. Anderson (for a full account see Anderson 1983). This system, ACT*, can perform a variety of tasks, using a repertory of cognitive skills, and it can gradually incorporate its items of declarative knowledge into procedures for solving problems. It is also capable of 'transfer' to new problems (Singley and Anderson 1989). The successful use of rules leads to their being strengthened, and being more likely to be used in future; their failure has the opposite effect. New rules are created in three main ways. In 'proceduralisation' an item of declarative knowledge which has been used in the same procedure several times comes to be represented as an integral part of the procedure as well as being part of the semantic network. In 'composition' a well-used sequence of operations is collapsed into one cohering package which gradually comes to be utilised in the place of its separate constituents. In 'tuning' successful and unsuccessful procedures are adjusted to work better. Analogies with rules which worked on similar problems are made; generalisation combines the rules which worked on two similar problem-solutions and derives a more general rule; discrimination introduces differentiations into a rule which has been applied to different problems; and, again, composition tidies procedures into smooth-running combinations. The computer instantiation of these rules provides a good analogue of human learners in Anderson's experiments. Boden however criticises it as being somewhat 'ad hoc', lacking sufficient task-analysis and a full underlying theory of what learning is. These problems amount to a 'vagueness' such that, Boden says, 'it is highly doubtful whether Anderson has a clear understanding of *just what his system can and cannot do*, and *why*' (Boden 1988: 207, her emphasis). As the ways in which ACT* learns seem very similar to those which developmentalists have suggested (see the next section), Boden's criticisms would seem to apply there too, with perhaps added force as the developmental models are even less closely tied to a systematic instantiation.

While constructs about representation, processes, knowledge base, attentional resources and executive control are to be found in most of the many information-processing models of cognition, these vary in detail and particularly in their attention to cognitive development. I will provide here an outline of the changes models try to account for, some description of typical information-processing models of cognitive development, and some discussion of possible developmental mechanisms. These should be read as the comments of someone outside the information-processing camp who has reservations about the metaphor of 'man-as-computer' and feels that the approach would benefit from detailed attention to the instantiation of minds as brains. Information-processing *aficionados* would no doubt take a different line (see e.g. Boden 1987, 1988 for a clear and fair account).

### Information-processing accounts of 'what develops'

Like other approaches to cognitive development, information-processing accounts seek to establish *what* develops, and *how* the development takes place. As to what develops, the candidates are basic capacities, strategies, metacognition, the knowledge base, or combinations of these.

By 'basic capacities' is meant processes such as recognition, scanning for information, categorisation, associating correlated events, learning, co-ordinating different modalities and integrating information. There is a vast literature on these processes (for useful reviews see Haith and Campos 1983, and for a brief introduction see Meadows 1986, chapter 2). Summarising it ruthlessly, it would appear that the rudiments of recognition, scanning, categorical perception, and various associations between different modalities, events and pieces of information can be observed even in very young children; but that each of these shows experience-related and age-related changes in speed, exhaustiveness and flexibility (e.g. Kail 1991a, 1991b). For example, even new-born infants show habituation to some stimuli, which requires some retention and recognition of the stimuli (Harris 1983a reviews the literature), but there are developmental improvements in how well stimuli are encoded, how much time is necessary for recognition and how much time recognition lasts for, what the effects of distractors are and what errors of inference are made, and so on. One controversial aspect of these developmental improvements is whether they relate to increases in the size of the information-processing capacity (see my discussion of Case's model, elsewhere in this chapter) or to changes in the strategic use of capacity whose size changes little (Kail 1986, 1988, Stigler *et al.* 1988). The two are not easily distinguished; evidence on how brains work will perhaps help to solve this question as well as clarifying how different inputs are integrated (see Chapter 5). Meanwhile it is now clear that extreme empiricism, the belief that the infant mind is a completely clean slate on which anything could be written, is not an acceptable position. Evidence from infants' behaviour (Haith and Campos 1983), from neuroscience (Young 1978, 1987) and from computational psychology (Boden 1988) shows that there is much inbuilt psychological structure from birth (for some recent discussion see Anderson 1992, Carey and Gelman 1991, and a special issue of *Cognitive Science* (vol. 14, 1990)). Unstructured learning systems can learn little of any interest, indeed Fodor (1976) argues that to learn a new concept one must already have a conceptual system capable of representing the 'new' item, and this pre-existing system must have been, ultimately, innate. This degree of nativism probably is too much (see e.g. Boden 1988, Haugeland 1985, Johnson-Laird 1983), both because its view of concept learning does not include all the processes by which concepts develop and because it omits full consideration of conceptual development as a process influenced by others who have already developed the concepts in question. However, learning and development – whether of skills or concepts – do clearly depend on cognitive structures which are complex from the start. They may also be constrained by the structure of the domain of knowledge involved, including the language used to talk about it (e.g. number systems, Longuet-Higgins 1987). Task analysis, as I've already said, may be crucial.

There are clearly developmental changes in cognitive strategies, the second candidate for an important role in cognitive development. Some of these are reviewed in my discussion of memory and the skills of reading, writing, arithmetic and general study skills (Chapter 2). In particular, it is clear that young children show less evidence of using deliberate strategic approaches to problems (at least of an academic rather than social or practical sort), and have smaller and less flexible repertoires of strategies than older children. To give a well-documented example, pre-school children rarely show deliberate efforts to remember information, may not allocate their resources efficiently to a memory task, and do not seem to notice that their non-strategic attempts to remember have led to poorer performance than they can achieve when they are taught to use a mnemonic technique (see e.g. Brown *et al.* 1983, Kail 1984). There are considerable improvements in memorising strategies, particularly over the primary school years. Changes in life's task demands, such as the requirements of the school curriculum and the need to co-ordinate home and school worlds, may contribute to this change. Awareness of one's own achievements and activities in remembering seem important also.

Such awareness, knowledge about and use of cognition are the concern of the field known as 'metacognition', or cognition whose own subject-matter is cognition. There is some debate over whether metacognition is separate from cognition that is about other aspects of the world, and about the role of conscious awareness; but it seems to be fairly clear that there are changes in children's knowledge about and control of their cognition as they get older. These are discussed in Chapter 2.

There is even less doubt that the knowledge base available to children increases as they get older. Theories which concentrated on universal cognitive processes set this sort of developmental change aside as uninteresting, just as studies of learning in adults tried to rule out knowledge as a contaminating variable. Recently there has been more interest in cognitive development within specific domains of knowledge, and these studies have suggested that the amount of knowledge available and the ways in which it is organised may have important effects even on universal cognitive processes, and may be one of the major components of cognitive development (e.g. Chi and Ceci 1987, Keil 1989). Just as we do not yet understand how metacognition and cognition interact, we do not really understand how content knowledge affects cognitive processes or how knowledge systems should be modelled. I describe some of the relevant work in Chapters 2 and 6: this seems likely to be a busy area for some time, as researchers seek to picture knowledge and cognition in an increasing number of domains. Studies which investigate the sources of knowledge and how it is organised and used will no doubt make more contribution to psychological theory than those which merely describe age difference in content.

As I said earlier, there have been a number of developmental models of general information-processing as well as the specific and detailed accounts of the information-processing which is involved in various levels of success or failure on a particular task, such as predicting the movement of a balance or answering a class inclusion test. The next section briefly describes the models proposed by Case (1974, 1978, 1984, 1985), Kail and Bisanz (1982), Keil (1984), Klahr (1984), Klahr and Wallace (1976), Siegler (1983, 1984, 1986, 1989b) and Sternberg (1984, 1985); Sternberg's model is also discussed in the section in intelligence (Chapter 3).

*Case's theory*

The first model I will outline is that proposed by Robbie Case (Case 1974, 1978, 1984, 1985). Case's work has roots in Piagetian theory and is similarly an attempt at a general theory of intellectual development. He tries to describe the complexity of infants' and children's cognition while differentiating them from adults'; to integrate cognitive, linguistic and social development while also allowing for (and accounting for) developments which are specific to different domains; and to use recent more sophisticated modelling techniques derived from cognitive psychology and computer science. The theory deals with the structure of children's thinking, with its successive stages, and with how transitions from stage to stage are made.

Case's central metaphor is of the child as a problem-solver,

> an organism that is endowed with certain natural desires, and that encounters certain natural barriers to their realization, but which also has the capability for overcoming these barriers by refining and re-combining the inborn procedures with which it comes equipped.
>
> (1985: 59)

Despite the use of the words 'organism' and 'natural' there is far less biological reference and discussion here than in Piagetian theory: Case's account of cognition is more mechanistic than organismic. The basic level of the model is of mental schemes, either *figurative* schemes which represent patterns of stimulation that the child has encountered several times and recognises, or *operative* schemes, which represent rules which can be used to transform the figurative schemes in various ways. For example, a child might recognise a picture, assimilating it to a figurative scheme, and be able to use an operative scheme representing relative size to say which object in the picture is biggest. The model also has, very importantly, *executive* schemes, which are representations of how to use figurative and operative schemes over a period of time to solve a particular problem or reach a particular goal. It is the executive schemes which determine what temporal sequence of figurative and operative schemes is called up. If, for example, the task is to say how many windows there are in the back of your house, you may need to call on a figurative representation of how the house looks and then an operative scheme to count the windows; if the task is to say whether or not the house is burglar-proof, the figurative and operative schemes called on will be rather different. Because of its problem-solving character, cognition has an affective character: from infancy onwards people are motivated to solve problems, to be pleased at their success and unhappy at their failure. Active problem-solving is an innate human characteristic, and even infants are capable of some control over both its cognitive and its affective aspects, though it is perhaps the nature of such control that changes most as development proceeds.

Case suggests that even neonates have figurative and operative cognitive schemes, and executive schemes have very early roots. Schemes are co-ordinated and form four major structured stages, each of which develops over a number of years into a stable system which then, differentiated and co-ordinated, serves as the building blocks for the next stage. These stages are recognisably Piagetian. In the first 'sensorimotor operations' stage, the child uses sensory representations (e.g. seeing a frightening face) and motor responses (e.g. leaving the room, hiding the eyes). In the second, 'representational operations', stage,' the child's representations include durable concrete internal images and their responses can produce additional representations (for example using a mental image of a scary face to draw a monster). In the stage of 'logical operations' representations are more abstract and more open to transformation though still on a simple level. The fourth, 'formal operations', stage involves complex representations and complex transformations of abstract information.

The stages differ in terms of the sort of executive schemes or control structures which are available. Minor shifts occur within a stage as executive schemes which are similar in complexity, form and function are co-ordinated; major between-stage shifts occur when schemes whose form and function differ are co-ordinated into overall structures with new emergent properties. There is a sequence of types of control structures within each stage, creating the sort of 'vertical *décalage*' or repetitions at new levels which Piaget described. The sequence within each stage shows an increasing number of simple schemes being put together: first the various schemes are consolidated separately, then two are co-ordinated, then these are elaborated as additional elements are incorporated. Case (1985, chapters 7–11) analyses behaviour on a variety of tasks achieved from infancy to adulthood in these terms, and in terms of the sort of operations involved, and uses his analysis to justify his claim of strong vertical *décalage* or repetition. It is not entirely clear to me (nor to Flavell 1984), however, that the analysis is really justified by the data rather than necessary for the claim. There is not always a completely obvious reason why a particular response to a task is analysed as made up of exactly this particular number of unitary schemes, nor whether schemes are all equal in the demands they make. Case's characterisation of substages emphasises similarity but does not dispel suspicions that development may show more differences than he allows, both in the sequence of development within different stages and in the levels of thought about different areas within the same stage ('horizontal *décalage*'). A precise measure of 'scheme demands' and a firm distinction between schemes which are truly indivisible units and those which are composites might be useful, but it is hard to see how they could be arrived at. Computer simulation might tell us what they were for computers, but it is not altogether clear how we can extrapolate from computers to people. And if information-processing ideas about developmental processes are correct, the demands which schemes make, and how separable they are, will change as they become more practised.

For all that his structural account seems at present less than perfectly justified (though an improvement in many ways on earlier structural models), Case has some interesting suggestions to make about developmental *processes*. He postulates innate capabilities for setting goals, formulating strategies to meet these goals, and for integrating different strategies into more complex and effective ones. He begins (1985, chapter 12) by pointing out that children have four general regulatory processes which orchestrate their mental activity. These are a tendency to problem-solving, a tendency to exploration, a tendency to imitation, and a capacity for mutual regulation with other people. Problem-solving involves searching for an operation which bridges the gap between the state of affairs which is to be found now, and a more desirable goal state. The child, faced with a less than optimum present situation (such as not being able to reach the toy on the floor from his or her seat in the high chair) and able to envisage a more desirable situation (having the toy to hand), searches for a strategy which will transform the former into the latter, and calls for help (or leaps out of the chair, or pulls the string that ties the dropped toy to the chair's arm, or whatever is possible). The first step in problem-solving is to search for operations which will transform the less pleasant, less desired state of affairs into the more pleasant, more desired, perhaps by matching the particular features of the problem and the goal ('distant toy', 'I can't move to get it') with features of schemes in the repertoire ('Mummy gets things for me', 'pulling strings moves distant things') and computing some sort of best fit. Next the proposed sequence of operations ('Get Mummy's attention, point out toy, show I want it back, accept toy') is evaluated for its effectiveness, either after actually being enacted or after an imagined 'dry run'. This can then lead to 'retagging' of the sequence so that it can be more easily accessed if it has succeeded ('when I said "Dolly please" Mummy gave me Dolly *and* a biscuit' or avoided if it has led to a negative outcome ('jumping out of the high chair really hurts'). Finally the schemes used become consolidated, or hierarchically integrated, as essential components run more automatically and inessential ones are dropped, and as separate components come together to form larger invariant units. Our child in the high chair might give up leaning over to stretch out an arm for the toy which is beyond arm's length, but begin to incorporate automatic 'please' and 'thank you' as parents demand an explicit acknowledgement of their services.

Case's second natural developmental process is exploration. Here the child does not have an explicit goal but does have a situation to which several possible schemes could apply. What happens here is a sort of 'suck it and see' procedure: the child tries out various schemes and notes their results. Schemes are chosen because they have features applicable to the starting situation, not because they are relevant to any particular goal, and typically several schemes will be applied in succession. As in problem-solving, the results are evaluated and the schemes retagged, and because several schemes have been tried out freely and in rapid succession they can be consolidated, their components varied, automated, integrated and so forth. Exploration is a 'bottom-up' process, while problem-solving is a 'top-down' one; it is also, in Piagetian terms, heavily assimilatory.

The third natural general developmental process is imitation. Often young children do not know what to do or what results could possibly be obtained, but more experienced people do have this knowledge and may act on it in the child's presence. Children can observe what those around them do and seem to have a strong natural tendency to imitate the actions of others, to get the same result, or for the sake of being like another person, or just for fun. The adult, or more skilled person, models both possible strategies for dealing with the situation and the goals that these strategies can achieve in this case. The child may focus on the action or on the goal; as in the cases of problem-solving and exploration which do not involve modelling themselves on other people, the schemes the child uses are evaluated, retagged and consolidated.

Case's final process is 'mutual regulation', or the adaptation of the child and another person to each other's feelings, cognitions and behaviour. This may be done to serve emotional or social ends, as in attempts to comfort or please, or to achieve dominance through assertion or aggression, or it may be task-oriented as when children and adults co-operate to solve a problem or instruct each other. The same common subprocesses of accessing schemes and experimenting with novel sequences, evaluating the consequences, retagging the schemes and consolidating them, apply. Case's main example here (1985: 270–1) is of what happens during deliberate instruction of a less skilled person by a more skilled one, and he does not elaborate on his brief nomination of affective mutual self-regulation as a means to intellectual development. Nevertheless, it seems to me to be a helpful advance for an information-processing model to make an explicit recognition of social facilitation of development and of cognition's affective roots. Both mutual regulation and imitation are Vygotskian learning processes.

All these four general learning processes are seen as arising early in infancy, and as occupying a considerable proportion of young children's time. Both their early emergence and their high frequency suggest that they are quite strong candidates for important developmental processes. Case believes they would give rise to the sort of stage transitions described earlier because they would produce a hierarchical integration of what were previously separate control structures. The subprocesses of activation, evaluation, retagging and consolidation are invariant and resemble Piaget's functional invariants of assimilation, accommodation and equilibration, but in the cases of imitation and mutual regulation are put to use in ways more reminiscent of Bruner and Vygotsky: the child inherits the cultural tools used by adults and, first by mutual regulation then in more and more internalised ways, can use them as his or her own independent strategies and skills. Case has said that the child has a more or less innate and invariant set of capacities – for setting goals, for activating existing schemes in novel sequences in pursuit of these goals, for evaluating the results, and for reworking or 'retagging' sequences that have been evaluated positively so that they can be generated intentionally in future, and for recalling such reworked structures and consolidating them so that they form smoothly functioning executive structures (Case 1984: 27–8). It is not clear how strongly he means these to be seen as literally invariant over the course of development; as Flavell (1984) points out it may be misleading rather than helpful to suppose that, for example, the 'goal-setting' of the neonate is very like the 'goal-setting' of the adolescent. Some sort of 'goal-setting' process is indeed likely to be useful both as a means to development and as a means to minute-by-minute survival, but we need more details of what 'goal-setting' is available at different points in development – and in different ecological settings and for individuals with different histories – than Case's reliance on functional invariants provides.

Consideration of this sort of issue might be very relevant to some of the problems that Case sees for his theory (1985: 282–8). One of these is that cognitive development takes such a long time. If it were solely a matter of the integration of subprocesses and substages, it should surely proceed faster than it does. Laboratory training studies suggest to Case that it should be possible to progress from the early sensori-motor structures to adolescent structures in about 250 half-days, or about a year, allowing for weekends off! Since the ordinary time-span required is about fifteen years, despite the claim Case made earlier that pre-school children are spending at least half their waking hours exploring, solving problems, imitating and so forth, the slowness of children's development is puzzling.

Further, if children have differing amounts of experience in different domains, as they presumably do, it is not clear why there seem to be (in Case's judgement) developments which are general and cross domains (Case 1984). Theorists who de-emphasise such shifts would not find them the problem that Case does, of course. He acknowledges that he cannot account for this. His two main suggestions are, essentially, that he has under-estimated the complexity of interdependences between different content domains (and he certainly has not dealt thoroughly with the acquisition and organisation of content as opposed to process) or that there may be maturational limits to the rate of cognitive change (which was of course Piaget's position), though quite why training can often transcend these, while normal development does not, remains unclear. It is however a maturational-limit model that he goes on to elaborate, though as a default option rather than as the basis for a research programme that could expand our understanding of cognitive development.

The main maturational constraint which Case discusses is the size of the short-term storage space (STSS) which a child has available for infor-mation-processing. He is picking up the idea (which appeared in neo-Piagetian theory and is commonplace in information-processing work) that human beings have limited attentional resources, which have to be divided between the current execution of operations, 'operating space', and storing or retrieving the results of operations which have just been carried out. There is a trade-off between these two: if a great deal of mental space or resources must be used for difficult operations, then less is available for storage, and vice versa. Short-term storage is seen as active, not just as dumping the results of operations in boxes, incidentally. A new cognitive acquisition can only be made if it demands no more working memory capacity than the child has available; if the child's working memory is too full for the new cognition, it will not be acquired. (This is the sort of model we used in our examination of learning to read, Chapter 2.) Case proposes that the capacity of STSS increases with development, but at a slow speed which restricts the overall rate of cognitive development. STSS increases because with the greater operating efficiency that comes with practice, the requirements of operating space decrease, and more of the total attentional resources are available for use as the STSS. Total resources do not change during development, but their distribution between operating and storage does: operating needs fewer resources as operations become more practised, more consolidated and more integrated, so that more space is available for holding their results ready for operation. Operations continue to develop and to become more and more slick for as long as they are practised. This implies that the major cognitive difference between adults and children is the amount of practice they have had on basic cognitive operations, and also on cognitive operations specific to a particular domain. Adults will almost always have had more practice on the general basic operations, but there may be some domains where the child has had more practice than the adult (new topics in the maths curriculum, for example, or childhood crazes such as puns and other word play) and may be the quicker and better thinker.

As I have discussed elsewhere (Meadows 1986), it is not going to be easy to distinguish whether there are changes in the totality of attentional resources available or merely, as Case (1984, 1985) suggests, in how they are distributed between operation and storage, because these two necessarily interact both in observable behaviour and within the model. Performance on a task will be a function of the strategy sequence used, the demands which that sequence makes on operating space and short-term storage space, and the size of the available attentional resources. We know that for many tasks there are developmental changes in strategies and in their demandingness, and in the existence and accessibility of relevant knowledge. Attempts to measure total resources or total available cognitive space have to hold these developmental changes constant if they are to distinguish between changes in the size of total space and changes in the way a space of unchanging size is used. A very precise analysis of tasks, of learner activities, of how tasks and learners change with practice, and of the interdependences between knowledge, strategies and processing, is required; and this is not going to be easy to achieve. Meanwhile the 'best guess' seems to be that developmental changes in absolute amount of processing space, if they exist at all, are less important than changes in how they are used. Changes in what information is stored and how it is accessed, and a wider range of more sophisticated processing possibilities which can gather and act on information, seem to be more important. Case does maintain, however, that these changes, which could obviously be very domain-specific, are held together so that cognitive development is homogeneous across domains, the 'homogenising' factor being maturational limits such as the degree of myelinisation of the central nervous system. I will look at what we are beginning to know about how the brain works in cognitive activities in Chapter 5.

## Kail and Bisanz's theory

Kail and Bisanz (1982) provide another account of the mechanisms of cognitive development. They see development as being generally in the direction of increasingly having rules and processes which are *sufficient*, in that they allow a wider scope of proficient problem-solving, as in the case of Siegler's balance scale task or Karmiloff-Smith and Inhelder's balancing objects task (e.g. Siegler 1978, Karmiloff-Smith and Inhelder 1974/5), where young children have only one strategy, which works excellently but only over a very limited range of situations, and older children have developed more complex and conditional rules, which lead to success in most predictions of balancing. They suggest that development also leads to a shift towards more *efficient* information-processing, to using procedures which are more powerful and require less slow and error-prone rote repetition. Using such procedures frees attentional resources for other cognitive activities. There is also development in the knowledge base, which incorporates more elements and organises them into larger and more meaningful units, which are increasingly linked on the basis of conceptual relationships not just perceptual similarities.

These developments are supported by increases in attentional resources, in total capacity or in use of the same capacity, or in increasingly effective and flexible use of a capacity which is itself increasing, and through processes which modify both declarative and procedural knowledge. These include processes which add or delete 'nodes' in the associative network (for example adding 'mammal' in between 'dog' and 'cat' on the one hand and 'animal' on the other) and processes which strengthen or weaken links (a visit to the slums of India, or to a kennel full of pit bull terriers, might weaken the association between 'dog' and 'pet'). There are also processes which compare procedures with other procedures or with goals or other external events, detecting either inconsistencies or regularities. Inconsistencies, as in Piagetian theory, need to be resolved by changes in the cognitive system; regularities which recur and demand resources lead to packaging and streamlining of procedures and to chunking of knowledge elements. They also contribute to the possibility of higher level organisation of knowledge and processes, and perhaps to one's confidence in the correctness and adequacy of one's processing (cf. Bryant 1982a). While these monitoring processes play an important part in cognitive development, they make heavy demands on attentional resources, and if these are not available to a sufficient extent the processes of consistency and inconsistency detection and consequent reorganisation cannot reach fruition. Resources become available through increased automatisation of cognitive processes, or through growth in the total information-processing capacity (if such growth occurs), or through changes in the knowledge base which alter the ways in which the cognitive system investigates and interprets its environment, hence altering the feedback which is monitored by the detector processes. That is, changes in the declarative and procedural knowledge base can enable the identification of regularities and inconsistencies which were previously undetectable. The modifications consequent on the detection of inconsistencies tend to generate more *sufficient* representations and processes, allowing cognition to apply to a wider range of phenomena without giving rise to too many exceptions and anomalies; modifications following the detection of regularities tend to generate more *efficient* representations and processes as links between elements and processes become smooth and automatic. Altogether there is a fairly steady development towards more complex and more hierarchically integrated cognition.

*Other accounts*

A certain similarity will already have emerged from my accounts of the models proposed by Case and by Kail and Bisanz. Some of it is no doubt due to my interpretation; but it deters me from providing equally long accounts of other available information-processing models. In brief, Sternberg's model (Sternberg 1984, 1985) is an information-processing analysis of intelligence with developmental implications. I discuss it more fully in the section on intelligence (Chapter 3). The main developmental mechanism is strategy construction based on the use of knowledge-acquisition components, performance components (which are processes such as encoding, drawing inferences, mapping relations between similar contents) and metacomponents which select and monitor performance, these last being 'the major basis for the development of intelligence' (Sternberg 1984: 172). Klahr and Wallace (1976, Klahr 1984) have 'generalisation' at the core of their developmental model. They focus on regularity detection and redundancy elimination, like Kail and Bisanz, and on the 'time-line' record of cognitive processing. The time-line contains the data on which generalisation is based. It is a record of how the cognitive system encountered and dealt with problem-solving situations. For example, a time-line concerned with the balance scale problem would have a record of what previous balances had looked like, what the child had therefore predicted and which side had in fact gone down. If these are retained in detail generalisations useful to the setting up of an effective production system may subsequently be made, by detecting regularities and eliminating redundancies. It is thus important that all the relevant information should be accurately encoded, otherwise the self-modifying cognitive system could not work. Siegler's model (Siegler 1983, 1984, 1986) stresses that much of children's knowledge is rule-governed, using 'if . . . then' question–answer patterns. Some aspects of these rules are quite broadly applicable, for example there may be fall-back rules which are resorted to in several different situations when information-processing demands overwhelm the cognitive system. He sees encoding as central to cognitive development, since if the crucial features are not adequately represented automatisation, generalisation and strategy construction cannot proceed fruitfully. A comparison of the accounts I have described is set out in Table 4.1. A longer account of Sternberg's work may be found in Chapter 3, and Sternberg (1984) includes essays on the mechanisms of cognitive development and further references. Anderson (1989, 1992, and see also Chapter 3) provides a recent and interesting model.

*Table 4.1* Information-processing accounts of cognitive development: some comparisons between models.

| Source | Change in knowledge base? | Change in attentional resources? | Knowledge modification processes | Domain-specific or general cognition? | Other features |
|---|---|---|---|---|---|
| Case 1984, 1985 | Not emphasised. | In use, not in total capacity; Short Term Storage System increases. | Differentiation and hierarchical integration, executive control structures become more complex. Goal setting, search, evaluation, retagging and consolidation. | Emphasis very much on general parallels across wide range of domains; processes universal, even evolution-based. | Stages: natural processes of problem-solving, exploration, imitation and mutual regulation, including instruction. Affective motives for cognition. |
| Kail and Bisanz 1982 | Number of elements increases; so does amount in chunks. More conceptual links, perceptual less salient. | Increase, possibly in total capacity, possibly in effective use related to knowledge. | Addition or deletion of knowledge nodes, strengthening and weakening of links. Inconsistency and regularity detectors. Chunking, automatisation and speed increases. | Model applies across domains but need not be uniform development. | |
| Keil 1979, 1984 | Main source of cognitive change. Structure of knowledge determines processes. | Not emphasised. | Increasing differentiation of knowledge and awareness of links. Higher order relations, coherence and juxtaposition in semantic field. Current knowledge and structural knowledge constrains on processing and learning. Processes cannot be independent of structure of knowledge involved. | Specific to domain. Expect experience to affect level. | Emphasis that there is less evidence for complex processing than for complex representation or structure from which processing is derived. Instruction may be important. |

| Reference | | | | | |
|---|---|---|---|---|---|
| Klahr 1984, Klahr and Wallace 1976 | Knowledge includes time-line record of own cognitive processing. | Better chunking, representation, production. | Self-modifying production systems (equivalent to Piagetian 'reflective abstraction'). Includes conflict resolution rules, selection of better strategies, elimination of redundancies, discrimination, generalisation etc. | Global structural reorganisations from local incremental modifications. | Development mainly internally system-driven, spontaneous not externally taught. Stages, at least in rules. |
| Siegler 1983, 1984, 1986, 1989b, Klahr and Siegler 1978 | Constitutes rules for specific and general problem-solving. Adequate encoding essential. | | Encoding, combination processes, monitoring. Synthesis becomes more accurate and efficient. Negative feedback in evaluation and selection of features. | Some processes biologically given, some learned. Experience is important. Analogies with evolution. | This is a process model at an early stage of generalisation from its origins in fine analysis of a limited range of tasks. |
| Sternberg 1984, 1985 | Knowledge acquisition central; selective encoding, and combination comparison. Increase in knowledge and changes in efficiency of its use lead also to more sophisticated later acquisition and easier performance. | Limited capacity, especially metacomponents. | Feedback from performance and acquisition components to metacomponents, which are self-monitoring and deal with feedback. Automatisation, repeated activation leading to detection and use of regularities and inconsistencies. Metacognition important. | Development of local subsystems of knowledge, general global system used in default of good local system. | Includes novice-expert and gifted-retarded descriptions. |

It seems to me that there are very similar models under discussion in these papers. Learning proceeds by association of new information with old information, either through the two occurring together in a regular way (contingency) or through the two being similar on some dimension (with infants perhaps having an innate preference for similarity on some dimensions, where similarity on others will be ignored); this is of course the assumption that has dominated information-processing work (and its predecessors in Learning Theory). The various theorists' proposed processes for change, for example, seem to form at least overlapping sets, with a frequent emphasis on self-monitoring and processes for automatisation and the detection of consistencies and inconsistencies. They take different positions on the role of the knowledge base; Case, for example, assumes it is minimally relevant to processing and Keil sees it as the main arena for cognitive change, and there seem to be parallel assertions about whether development is general across all domains and uniform in rate between them, or whether it varies very much from one domain to another. Similarly there is a degree of disagreement about how far development is influenced by the outside world, particularly by interaction with other people; Keil and Case specify instruction as a means to cognitive development, Klahr's model is primarily internally motivated, system-driven, not taught. Finally, the models centre on a similar range of tasks, problems derived from the cognitive psychology literature, though Case tries to extend his discussion in social and affective areas and Keil's focus is on knowledge systems which seem closer to semantic network studies. Indeed, the same data serve more than one model as evidence: Siegler's documentation of the balance task is used by other theorists for their own purposes.

Flavell (1984), reviewing the models described in Sternberg (1984), finds all of them interesting but none, as yet, convincing. His final comment is that 'there is more variety in *what* gets developed and also more variety in *how* these varied developments get accomplished' (p. 206) than the models, as yet, allow. The more interesting part of this comment refers to the possibility that different sorts of learners have different sorts of cognitive processes available to them, for example, that the developmentally early ways of processing information give rise to new mechanisms for processing information so that cognitive development proceeds in new ways. Becoming able to process language for discrepancies and agreements between literal meaning and the message that the speaker intends to convey, or to analyse words into phonemes, to give two examples, changes current understanding of discourse and of spelling respectively *and* gives tools for further developments. Flavell likens this to technological development: things are possible now that we have satellites or laser beams or non-stick cake tins which were impossible or very difficult before. Changes in information-processing mechanisms may be one of the sources of differences between novices and experts, or between the gifted and the ungifted; however, like

Keil, I think we should not forget the probability of different knowledge bases here.

One further point to be made about these models is that they do not use biological evidence. Though several theorists stress that they see their subjects as organisms produced by evolution, the models are mechanistic rather than organismic, even if the machine is an active, constructive and self-modifying one. What is being discussed is also, on the whole, 'cold' cognition rather than 'hot'; the sort of dispassionate, detached, cognition which is brought to bear on formal well-defined 'academic' tasks of not much immediate relevance to the desires of the problem-solver, let alone his or her survival. The cognitive processes described here are not closely linked to affect (except in Case's model, where goals are set by unrealised desires). This may reflect the models' origins in 'cognitive science', where computers and affect are incompatible, and affect is very hard for artificial intelligence to cope with. In view of the increasing amount of evidence that in the human brain there are strongly structural links between cognition and affect (Chapters 5 and 6), the disassociation may be unfortunate.

## New models of information-processing and cognitive development

It may be that some of these difficulties with information-processing models centred on analogy with the serially-operating digital computer will be reduced or even eliminated by new accounts of cognition, which put forward a rather different account of the architecture of cognition. The work on information-processing which I have discussed so far conceives of the mind as a system which represents information as syntactic symbols, operates on these symbols according to logical rules, and stores the resultant symbols in specified localities in a long-term memory store: just like a digital computer which takes in symbolic information into particular locations in its memory, retrieves them to be operated on by a central processing unit, and stores them again in appropriate places in memory. This metaphor for cognition has worked well for tasks which require conscious effort and strategic thought when human beings do them, such as playing chess or doing complex arithmetic to predict whether a beam will balance; it has not succeeded anything like so well with cognitive tasks which human beings perform without conscious or strategic effort, such as building a tower out of blocks or recognising an object in the environment. New models of information-processing which stay closer to the way we know brain neurones work may provide a better account of this sort of cognition.

These new approaches to cognition are creating a great deal of excitement. They are referred to in different ways, as 'parallel distributed processing', 'neural networks', or 'connectionism'. The work of James McClelland and David Rumelhart and their colleagues (McClelland and Rumelhart 1986, Rumelhart and McClelland 1986) is perhaps the best known example. For discussion of the approach see Bechtel and Abrahamsen 1991, Clark 1989, Minsky 1988. What is proposed varies from model to model, but the basic hypothesis is that information-processing involves a large number of units working contemporaneously in parallel, with units, like neurones, stimulating or inhibiting each other through networks of connections. These units process very small pieces of information, smaller than a meaningful symbol and so often called 'subsymbols'. Information is not stored in a localisable place but exists as a pattern of excitation and inhibition between units; thus instead of there being a slot in memory in which information about Piaget is stored, the system has information about Piaget only when particular sets of units are active and stimulating or inhibiting each other in particular connection patterns.

Units that are active together have their excitatory connections strengthened and their inhibitory connections weakened; for units that are not active together the reverse happens. This means that over time a network that repeatedly receives the same input will develop a strong set of excitatory connections and inhibitory connections; the units that have repeatedly been active together will come to excite each other more reliably and strongly than ever. Even if only some of the units are activated, the whole configuration will come into play; no single subsymbol of information is crucial and the configuration will be activated even if a few incorrect or irrelevant pieces of information are included in the generally correct package of incoming stimulation. There is no information store, no knowledge of rules, no metacognition, independent of the activated connections.

Connectionist models appear to have a number of very positive advantages. They seem to be in principle compatible with what we know about the nervous system (see Chapter 5), where neurones activate and inhibit each other in complex networks, carrying out basic processing so incredibly rapidly that parallel processing must be involved. The connectionist networks are not strongly deterministic in their functioning, so they can deal with conflicting information and find the best or most probable possible outcome. Thus they can use connections developed over old experiences to deal with new ones, or handle cases which are an exception to the usual rule. When their limits are reached, they do not crash suddenly and completely, but begin to perform less well; just like human brains they show gradually failing performance or 'graceful degradation'. They show 'content addressable memory', where a variety of different cues which are linked to the memory may summon it up: if enough of the units of a particular network are properly activated, the whole circuit comes to function. There is feedback, or 'back propagation', from later stages of processing back to earlier ones. Finally, connectionist networks can learn from experience by changing the weights of connections, the strength of the excitatory or inhibitory links between units; this would be the sort of gradual learning over many trials which is probably what we do when developing our coherent knowledge of language or arithmetic.

These characteristics suggest that connectionist network models may be very useful for some of the most crucial and problematic areas of cognitive development. They might provide a basis for the conceptually and practically difficult distinction between maturation and learning, between the development and the acquisition of cognition. Maturation changes in development might change characteristics of the network such as the maximum number of units that could be involved and the general and threshold activation levels, that is, they would involve the architectural structure of the system. Learning would change the fine-tuned detail of weights of connections between units and of connections between networks. Connectionist models might provide a mathematically based account of the phases of neurological development where there is a rapid proliferation of synapses followed by a period of weeding many of them out (see Chapter 5). They may provide a much more specific account of assimilation and accommodation than Piagetian theory has done. They may clarify whether development is sensibly described as 'stage-like', whether development is from one distinct, well-integrated and general across domains to another separate one, or whether there is continuity across a succession of small and gradual changes. Models of a normally functioning system may be tampered with to model impaired development or the effects of damage, and to suggest how problems might be remedied. It seems likely that current enthusiasm for connectionist models may lead to notable advances in our understanding of these and related issues.

## VYGOTSKY

The third major model of cognitive development to be discussed is that associated with the name of L. S. Vygotsky. I say 'associated with' for three reasons. First, Vygotsky died prematurely in 1934, his work unfinished, and his successors have developed his ideas, a development which has included disagreement (Kozulin 1986, 1990, Zinchenko 1985). Second, similar points were made contemporaneously by other theorists, notably Pierre Janet, G. H. Mead and J. M. Baldwin, and had appeared a century earlier in Hegel's philosophy (Markova 1982), and the developmental theory which is currently being used perhaps incorporates some of their insights too (Broughton and Freeman-Moir 1981, Van der Veer and Valsiner 1988). The third reason is a practical one. Vygotsky wrote in Russian and it is only comparatively recently that his writings have been translated into English. I am not one of the small minority of students of cognitive development who read Russian, so in order to approach Vygotsky's work I have to use it in translation into English. Sutton (1983) has shown that there are severe and pervasive problems in Vygotskian translation and that readers of translations must proceed with caution. However free from linguistic errors a translation may be, the labours of translator and editor, working perhaps thirty or more years after Vygotsky, mediate between the reader and what he wrote; how each of us understands his text is affected by our knowledge of current, post-Vygotskian, developmental psychology. (I remember seeing a performance of an early play by Chekhov in which he seemed to anticipate twentieth-century psychology with extraordinary specificity, forty or fifty years before these ideas occurred to psychologists. While literature (especially in the hands of Chekhov) may indeed be far more advanced in conveying understanding of human behaviour than psychology is, it has to be said that in this instance Chekhov's play had been newly translated into English by a woman who was very well read in twentieth-century psychology). Thus my access to Vygotsky is less immediate and less direct than my access to Piagetian psychology or to information-processing psychology, which I can read in the original with only occasional doubts about whether my mental translation into English has really captured the meaning. So far as presenting 'Vygotsky's theory' here is concerned, I have tried to focus on those ideas which are regarded as central by several English language commentators. To do so means that my description will be an introduction to current English language neo-Vygotskian writing rather than to the original work, whose exact extent and content is unknown to me, as to most developmental psychologists. However it is clear that a number of important themes emerge, which both point a significant contrast between the Vygotskian approach and the other models described in this chapter, and suggest important issues for the development of cognitive skills, which are most fully discussed in other parts of this book. A useful introduction is provided by the Laboratory of Comparative Human Cognition (1983), and Tharp and Gallimore (1988) and Wood (1988) use Vygotskian ideas in suggesting educational programmes.

Both the Piagetian model and the information-processing approach are based on one key idea: there are psychological structures (formal operations, concepts, working memory, intelligence, for example) in people's minds which explain their behaviour, which are invariant across cultures, settings and tasks, and which are essentially independent of the individual's relations to other individuals, to social practices, and to the cultural environment. Psychology is thus the study of the individual mind's inner workings, which are seen as developing through individual maturation or learning, or individual construction of an internal model of outside reality, or some combination of such factors in the individual mind. At the centre of Vygotskian theory is a radical challenge to this key idea: far from being internal and individualistic, cognitive abilities and capacities are formed and built up in part by social phenomena, they are public and intersubjective, created through interaction with the social environment. Any description of cognition which isolates it from the social interaction that constitutes it is seriously incomplete and may provide a distorted and misleading picture. In particular, it is essential to study the development of cognition if its mature forms are to be properly understood. Thus Vygotskian theory rests on quite different philosophical bases from other theories of cognitive development.

For our present purposes, the central idea in Vygotsky's theory of cognitive development is summed up in this frequently cited passage:

> in the process of development, children begin to use the same forms of behaviour in relation to themselves that others initially used in relation to them. Children master the social forms of behaviour and transfer these forms to themselves. . . . Logical argumentation first appears among children and only later is united within the individual and internalized. Child logic develops only along with the growth of the child's social speech and whole experience. . . . it is through others that we develop into ourselves and . . . this is true not only with regard to the individual but with regard to the history of every function. . . . Any higher mental function was external because it was social at some point before becoming an internal, truly mental functioning.
>
> . . . Any function in the child's cultural development appears twice, or on two planes. First it appears on the social plane, and then on the psychological plane. First it appears between people as an interpsychological category, and then within the child as an intra psychological category.
>
> (Vygotsky 1981, in translation by Wertsch 1981)

This emphasis on the primacy of the social world in cognitive development is very different from the emphases of the Piagetian and the information-processing approaches. Piaget, as we have seen, gave comparatively little attention to social interaction other than social disagreement on judgements, mainly between peers; and this he saw as only a minor source of the internal disequilibrium which may lead the individual to reflection and cognitive advance. The Piagetian thinker creates his or her own individual new ways of thinking and new concepts, and what these new thoughts are like stems from the individual's own experience of the logico-mathematical and physical worlds and perhaps from maturation, not from the social world or the language the thinker uses. This account left Piaget at something of a loss as to why individual constructivism should give rise to cognitive structures which were so highly similar across individuals (Meadows 1983, Rotman 1977). His explanation was based in the logical necessity of operational thought, not in the social or physical common ground of individuals' experience. Information-processing models, with the partial exception of Case's, say even less about anything except the individual thinker and his or her intellectual problem; they provide a distinctly non-social body of work, though this omission is remedied to some extent in some of the work on their practical application (e.g. Brown *et al.* 1983).

Vygotsky's assertion that cognitive development involves the internalisation, transformation and use of routines, ideas and skills which are learned *socially*, from more competent partners, thus forms a unique contrast to the individualistic cognitivist approach.

His account also solves, perhaps almost too completely, what has been called (Williams 1989) the 'bootstrapping problem' of explaining how more sophisticated cognitive competences can arise from less sophisticated ones. It is to all intents and purposes impossible to lift yourself up using the straps of the boots you are wearing; similarly it has been hard to see how a child might solve everyday cognitive problems such as realising that a word picks out a particular aspect of an object, without previously having a whole complex of concepts about that object and what can be done with it. 'Red' is intended by the knowledgeable speaker to refer to an object's colour: but how are naïve listeners to know that colour is what is meant, not location, size, function, ownership or name, or any combination of these, unless they have a prior notion of colour as a characteristic which can be separated out and commented on? A word can become a name, or a label, for an object only against a background of beliefs about which is being picked out by the word.

Both the origins of these beliefs, and their mapping on to language, will be problematic for those who assume that cognitive development is by individual construction. One solution is to say that cognitive processes and concepts are, ultimately, innate (e.g. Fodor 1981); a second is to seek precursors of the problematic skills in the hope that a full enough sequence will have small enough steps between successive levels of skill that the transition from one to the next will look easy to explain. Vygotsky's solution makes the innate ideas solution unnecessary, and moves the other to the realm of description not of explanation. It is that children develop more sophisticated cognitive competences despite only having simpler ones in their own repertoire, because adults (that is, older, more skilled persons available as teachers or models) have the more sophisticated competence and guide the child repeatedly through the relevant behaviour. The child as an individual does not have the resources necessary for the higher level of cognitive functioning, but the teaching adult does. Adult and child interact, the adult providing the structured context within which the child can act as though he or she was competent to solve the problem, and by so acting in such a context, the child can indeed reach the solution successfully. To begin with, the adult has to provide almost all the cognition necessary for the task, but as the child becomes more and more familiar with it the adult can leave more and more for the child to do, until at last the child can undertake the entire task successfully. Repetition of this 'scaffolding' of learning on related tasks extends the child's competence and eventually leaves him or her able to take on new examples with minimal adult support, or alone. The child's independent cognitive behaviour has developed from less sophistication and expertise to more, and the medium of development has been social interaction, apprenticeship to another, more skilled, person. Cognitive development is to be understood in terms of the child being trained to behave in ways which the culture has developed as cognitively useful. By so behaving, and by practising and reflecting on what is done, the child internalises the cognitive skills of the culture and can develop them and pass them on to the next generation.

Thus, for the neo-Vygotskian, there is no bootstrapping problem; rather the child is helped by the adult in the 'guided reinvention' of the accumulation of knowledge and ways of thinking which preceding generations have constructed. The skills required of the child are of observation and imitation, and of generalisation and decontextualisation, but even these fundamental skills develop under the fostering support of social interaction. Some of the skills learned from adults are what Bruner has called 'cultural amplifiers', cognitive tools which make thinking jobs easier. The Arabic number system which we now use has, I would imagine, made mathematical computation easier than it was for the Romans, with their more cumbersome way of writing numbers, while later inventions such as logarithms and electronic calculating machines have made computation easier still. Other cultural habits of thinking may impede cognitive development, although they are highly serviceable within their particular cultural domain. To give one ideologically delicate example, belief in the literal truth of the Book of Genesis precludes understanding evolutionary theory, which has proved a most useful cognitive amplifier in its organisation and explanation of biological phenomena; and to give one less delicate but less clearly documented example, some educational policy-makers have argued that the use of calculators impedes children's understanding of numbers in ways which reliance on traditional computation methods would facilitate. Whether helpful or not, the culture's ways of thinking surround children, are modelled to them by other users and discussed with them, and they may structure their language, their play, their schooling and their social interaction. The developing thinker does not have to create cognition out of an unpeopled vacuum, but may adopt and eventually internalise some of the cognitive content and processes provided by others.

Vygotsky suggested that in the course of development the child's own activities are shaped by the culture, or, more immediately, by the reactions of other people, and thus they move beyond what he admitted was to some extent a biological origin. Pointing, for example, is initially an unsuccessful reach for a too-distant object, which is responded to by the baby's mother as a sign that the baby wants the object. The child's movements are interpreted by the mother as an indicatory gesture. As she comes to the child's aid, the movement that was a gesture 'in-itself' becomes a gesture 'for-others'. The child, with some awareness of the communicative power of the movement, comes to use it as a deliberate gesture: the 'reaching' becomes reduced to movements which signal need but could not themselves achieve the desired object even if it were within reach, and other signals (such as cries, looks at the mother, and eventually words) are added. The child now addresses the gesture to adults who might bring about the desired result of grasping the object, rather than to the object itself which was the focus of interest in the first place. It also becomes possible to use the gesture for oneself: to point out, or touch, an object as part of directing one's own attention to it, as in counting a set of objects or as in the memory tasks described in Chapter 2. A similar sequence appears in the development of the 'higher mental functions', both processes such as selective attention, logical memory and concept formation, and language, writing, counting, drawing and other 'external' cultural skills (Vygotsky 1978a, and see Lock 1978).

At the heart of this development is one of the most important concepts in Vygotskian theory: 'internalisation'. It has been one of the returning difficulties of *Internalisation* understand the relationship between the *Selfconcious* her these are contrasted as completely di *self-concept* , or one reduced to the other, or some other relationship between the two postulated, as we see in, for example, the various solutions to the mind–body problem (see Chapter 5 this volume). Vygotsky gives an unusually precise answer to how external and internal relate, emphasising above all that it is a developmental relation where cognitive processes external to an individual are transformed to create a plane of internal processes. Uniquely, he stresses that internalisation is primarily seen in the context of social interactions, and he analyses it in terms of the systems of meaning (semiotic systems) which mediate social functioning, of which language is the most familiar. Internalisation is part of the construction of consciousness through human social interaction: the child takes on self-consciousness and self concept through social experiences (cf. Lewis and Brooks-Gunn 1979, Mead 1934), and cognitive consciousness and competence also arise socially.

> All higher mental functions are internalised social relationships. . . . Their composition, genetic structure, and means of action – in a word, their whole nature – is social. Even when we turn to mental processes, their nature remains quasi-social. In their own private sphere, human beings retain the functions of social interaction.
>
> (Vygotsky 1981: 164; see also Wertsch and Stone 1985: 166)

Thus Vygotsky is stressing a close and complex relationship between external social processes and internal psychological ones. The example of memory may help to illuminate this relationship. Cultures have developed their own mnemonic techniques, and these are normally made available to the members of the culture. The very young and the uneducated, who have not yet learned to use the culture's technique, may have ways of remembering which combine a biological basis with the effects of early learning; Vygotsky called these 'mneme' (Kozulin 1990). These ways of remembering may be very effective for the informal and repetitive experiences of the young child; as I described in Chapter 2 we are discovering more and more cognitive effectiveness in young children working on 'ecologically natural' tasks. As the individual is taught the culturally-mediated ways of remembering that the culture has developed ('mnemo-techniques'), these may displace the 'natural' processes so that they play a subordinate role in memory, and the memory skills of an acculturated adult represent a complex functional system which will be used more deliberately, more flexibly and with more self-awareness than the child's. To begin with, the child's biologically based memory is the centre of his or her own skill, and the culture's memory skills are an external world; as the cultural skills are learned they become internalised, take over much of the child's memorising and recall, and become integrated with skills of inference, concept use, and story-telling. Non-cultural memory processes remain essential for remembering, as the memory disorders found in patients with various sorts of brain damage show (Mayes 1988), but culturally learned skills may enhance these processes or make up for their deficiencies.

Internalisation changes the complexity of what is done, ultimately for the better but initially, perhaps, for the worse. Culturally provided skills are generally more sophisticated than the skills which they replace, and so the learner cannot usually manage them easily and well. The learner's version of a culturally provided skill will be cruder than the expert's; and it may indeed be cruder than the learner's own pre-existing skills. The small girl trying hard to learn to be 'a ballerina' may move more awkwardly in her ballet lesson than she does normally; the adult writer may resist learning word-processing because text compiles itself more smoothly with pen and paper than with keyboard and screen. 'Functional regression' may be part of the internalisation of any complex skill: it may be one of the reasons why cognitive development can seem slow and effortful (cf. Karmiloff-Smith and Inhelder 1974/5).

Internalisation, however, transforms the social process into the psychological, and thereby changes its structure and functions. This inevitably happens because the central process in internalisation is the gradual emergence of control over external processes, including control over external signs and systems of communication. Children perform actions, or use words and signals, without having a full understanding of their significance. They may know from their past successful usage that a particular action is a necessary part of getting the desired result (for example they may always wash their hands and display their cleanness before meals) without understanding *why* the action is important (because washing hands decreases the possibility of infection from dirt, a goal highly valued by their hygienic mothers). Similarly a child may know that a word refers to a particular object but not appreciate the full range of meaning it connotes. Social interaction necessarily involves the use of sign forms, including words, which have acquired a rich meaning over the generations of their use. Initial use, which may only involve a fragment of this meaning, progresses through generalisation to include more and more connotations. Vygotsky states that the

> basic distinguishing characteristic of the word is the generalised reflection of reality

and that

> in order to transmit some experience or content of consciousness to another person, there is no other path than to ascribe the content to a known class, to a known group of phenomena, and as we know this necessarily requires generalisation.
>
> Thus it turns out that social interaction necessarily presupposes generalisation and the development of word meaning i.e. generalisation becomes possible with the development of social interaction. Thus higher, uniquely human forms of psychological social interaction are possible only because human thinking reflects reality in a generalized way.
>
> (Wertsch and Stone 1985: 168)

It is not entirely clear to me whether this passage is asserting that generalisation is an intrinsic part of human thinking irrespective of generalisation being a necessary part of learning from other people's experience, or whether practice in generalising about what other people teach you leads to habitual generalisation. Of course the two interpretations are by no means incompatible, as Vygotsky is stressing a complex developmental pattern of relationships between internally-arising and externally-given generalisation. So far as developmental psychologists' concern with diagnosing children's competence is concerned, two important points arise. The first is that agreement between child and adult as to meaning at one point must not be taken as showing that they have the same full range of generalised meaning. Child and adult may agree on the referent of a word but not on the full meaning, or the child may know that an object is a member of a particular category by virtue of its possessing a particular attribute but not understand whether that attribute is merely characteristic or a defining property (Keil 1981b, Vygotsky 1986). Nor will the child initially use word or concept in an adult way. While the child or novice's understanding of words may be based on relatively simple and context-bound relationships between word and object, adults will understand them in terms of a complex system of meaning that involves relationships between words. 'Interested', 'curious', inquisitive', 'nosey', 'enthralled', absorbed', for example, carry subtly varied social and linguistic connotations. Children's difficulties with figurative language provide other examples (see Chapter 2).

The second point, which has implications which I will deal with more thoroughly later (Chapter 5), is that individuals may differ in their ability to provide generalisations for themselves or for others, and to profit from them. Some individuals may set up for others fertile situations of 'mediated learning' (Feuerstein *et al.* 1980), giving them experiences which an expert has framed, selected, highlighted and scaffolded in such a way that appropriate learning and transfer are facilitated. Some individuals, lacking such cognitive functioning, may fail to generalise even when to do so would prevent them from having to learn to solve each problem from the very beginning. Internalisation itself can presumably be more specific or more general, depending on the characteristics of child, adult, their interaction and the cultural content.

As well as an emphasis on the role of inter-psychological experience in intra-psychological cognitive development, on the importance of learning with and from other people, Vygotsky's theory has at its core the notion of 'mediation', the use of psychological 'tools' or 'signs', which allows a qualitative change in mental (or socio-historical) life. Language, for example, changes the relations of human beings to each other and to the non-human world from what those relations are in those who cannot use language. Mediation, or the use of communicable systems for representing reality as well as acting on it, is at the foundation of cognitive processes, which therefore cannot be reduced to automatic links between stimulus and response (as the Behaviourist psychology dominant in the West during Vygotsky's lifetime, and important also in Russia, would have argued). Signs, like artefact-type tools, are a product of the history of the culture. (Vygotsky's historical interests are, unfortunately, beyond the scope of this chapter, but see Kozulin 1986, 1990, Scribner 1985.) We have developed and grown up with a whole collection of symbols and of ways of problem-solving which shape our thinking. If we want to remember something, we can use writing as an *aide-mémoire*, or knots tied in a piece of string such as the Incas used, or rote learning of phrases and rules of rhyme and rhythm which together allow the near-verbatim recall of material such as long traditional stories (Lord 1960) or nursery rhymes. Signs can be used for communication between people or for communication with oneself, in thinking. They are embedded in activity, constructed through the subject's interactions with the world (and particularly, perhaps, with the other people in the world). And the sign systems one has available have a marked effect on the sort of consciousness and degree of cognitive organisation one has. Young children might operate on a practical level of intelligence and on a symbol system level independently, but adults would in most of their experience integrate the enactive and the symbolic levels. Language, the 'psychological tool' *par excellence*, is perhaps the most potent means of integrating practical (or procedural?) and symbolic (or declarative?) knowledge.

> [The child] plans how to solve the problem through speech and then carries out the prepared solution through overt activity. Direct manipulation is replaced by a complex psychological process through which inner motivations and intentions, postponed in time, stimulate their own development and realisation.
>
> (Vygotsky 1978a: 26)

Activity is mediated by the use of language for planning (and for monitoring and evaluating and other metacognitive activities), using (because language has social roots) a socially created and socially determined system of symbols and rules. The interweaving of thought and language, and their use within social interactions with more skilled partners who wish the child to learn, allow the child to move from fragmentary use without understanding to a coherent and flexible mastery of representational systems and cognitive skills. There is an increasingly profitable dialectic between the child's actions and the child's representations, and also between the child's understanding and other people's (Vygotsky 1986).

Here Vygotsky is placing far more emphasis on the origins and characteristics of representational systems than Piagetian or information-processing approaches do, though both of course are very much concerned with how problems are represented. His discussion of these semiotic issues is no more complete than the rest of his work could be, but it includes some points which have emerged as important from our earlier discussion of cognitive skills. Among them are the developmental course of language (and other forms of representation and of thinking) from social roots to a mature form which also incorporates internal communication; the dialectic interaction between the use of procedural knowledge, or 'activity', and declarative knowledge, which become increasingly interdependent as development proceeds; the role of metacognition and symbolic control of behaviour; and the effects on cognition of different cultural tools.

Much of Vygotsky's account of cognitive development focuses on the role of language. He saw it as one of the most important of 'psychological tools', culturally developed ways of behaving towards objects which allow high level cognitive functioning. Other psychological tools include counting systems, mnemonic techniques, writing and diagrams and maps. Integrating any of these into a psychological function such as memory or spatial perception transforms the mental functioning, in Vygotsky's view. The psychological tools are not merely facilitators or auxiliaries: their use allows (or even requires) qualitatively different functioning, 'revolutions' in thinking associated with changes in psychological tools. Kozulin (1990: 134–5) uses as an example different ways of measuring the passing of time. Early devices for measuring time used natural processes occurring steadily over time to record the passing of time intervals: for example, the shadow moving across the sundial, sand falling from top to bottom of an egg-timer, or water running to a marked height in a water-clock. Clockwork clocks provide a less immediate representation of passing time: the movements of the cogs, weights, pendulum, springs and so forth are too complex to show us the amount of time that has passed, even if they are visible, and we have to use the 'symbolic time' of the position of the hands on the dial; this means we have to learn to read the clock-face. Electronic digital watches provide a purely symbolic measure of time, and require us to use arithmetical knowledge to judge whether more time has elapsed between one pair of times than between another, as no physical analogue at all remains for the time.

Individuals 'appropriate' psychological tools from their social and cultural milieu. They do not inherit them as instincts or reflexes, they do not normally reinvent them from scratch, they do not discover them in their independent interactions with the natural world. In particular they learn to use tools through face to face communication and social interaction with other people who are also using psychological tools. Thus the tools have communication among their functions. Development involves, as we have said, initially interpersonal use of psychological tools, which increasingly become available for intrapersonal use.

> Social life creates the necessity of subordinating the individual's behaviour to social demands and in addition creates complex signalisation systems – the means of connection that direct and regulate the formation of conditional connections in the brains of individual humans.
>
> (Vygotsky 1960, translated by Wertsch (1985a))

Language is of course pre-eminent amongst the 'complex signalisation systems' which Vygotsky considered, and the relationship between language and thought was perhaps his central interest (Kozulin 1990, Vygotsky 1962, 1986). He proposed a distinction between pre-intellectual speech and pre-verbal thought. Children under 2 use vocal activity as a means of social contact and emotional expression, and are capable of systematic and goal-directed activity which does not require verbal operations. This first 'primitive' stage is followed by a stage of 'practical intelligence' in which the child's language uses syntactic and logical forms which have parallels in the child's practical problem-solving activity but are not linked to them in any systematic or useful way. In the third stage the child starts to use external symbolic means, such as language or other cultural tools, to help with internal problem-solving. It is at this stage that children can be heard to talk themselves through problems or to count by using their fingers as aids. Finally, such aids are internalised and problem-solving thought uses internal dialogue, while language can be used more to reflect on and develop thought than as a prop to support problem-solving.

Thus Vygotsky saw speech as beginning to have social functions very early in the child's life, developing amongst the child's 'complex and rich social contacts' into an increasingly powerful tool. Expression of emotions and maintenance of social contacts are followed by the use of language to communicate, to make reference, to represent ideas, to regulate one's own actions, initially within a context of social interaction and shared knowledge but increasingly independently of social partner and of supportive context. The child who talks to himself or herself is regulating and planning mental activities, not, as Piaget suggested, failing to communicate with others because of an overwhelming egocentricity (Vygotsky 1986). The child's private monologue is a precursor of the completely 'in the head' talking oneself through a problem (such as composing a sentence or working out the consequences of a particular chess move) which may facilitate solution for adults. Regulation of and by others using language, self-regulation by language; communication with others using language, communication with oneself using language: these merge within the developing individual, as he or she takes part in social interactions within the culture, into mature verbal thought. Language becomes more and more useful as a tool for abstract reflection. It also changes immediate perception and action, which become more and more integrated into a cognitive system which is to a large extent represented through language and expressed in language. The internalisation of perception leads to language mediation, which leads to greater cognitive freedom and flexibility (Lee 1985); cultural development fuses with organic development as the culture's higher mental functions are extended to and internalised by individuals. Internalisation brings about the socio-cultural determination of the human mind as the culture's 'psychological tools' become involved in controlling one's own mental processes (Davydov and Radzikhovskii 1985).

Vygotsky's emphasis on social interaction entails two important consequences which his own interest in education and in mental handicap (defectology) developed (Kozulin 1986, Sutton 1983, Vygotsky 1978a). The first is that more complex cognitive functioning will be possible in a dialogue between two individuals than is possible for those individuals alone, or at least for the less skilled individual, though at a late stage in development an individual may be able to provide his or her own interlocutor. The other consequence is that instruction could be a facilitator of cognitive development, not, as Piaget would have it, at best irrelevant and at worst a distortion (see, especially, Vygotsky 1986, chapter 6). 'Learning by transaction' is at the heart of cognitive development.

As by no means all the evidence which is relevant to these issues comes from Vygotskian researches I will review it in the final chapter of this book, which seeks to examine the contribution of social experiences to cognitive development. It will suffice here to mention a few observational studies in which children have been set to solve a problem with and without an interlocutor. David Wood (Wood 1980, 1988, Wood *et al.* 1978) observed mothers and 4-year-olds working together to construct a wooden pyramid. James Wertsch (1978, 1979, 1985a 1985b, Wertsch *et al.* 1980) recorded children working with their mothers on constructing a copy of a 'model' puzzle. Ellice Forman (Forman and Cazden 1985) made a longitudinal study of pairs of children solving problems such as chemistry experiments. On a rather larger scale, Vygotskian theory underpins the Kamehameha Elementary Education Project (Tharp and Gallimore 1988, Tharp *et al.* 1984). The data from these studies, and from others which are, for example, Piagetian in origin (e.g. Doise and Mugny 1984, Perret-Clermont and Brossard 1985), show that internalisation can be observed in children's use of tutorial interchanges, social interaction may facilitate performance on a task, and the improvement may transfer to similar tasks done alone later. If the limited quantity of focused interaction typically provided in these studies can produce such effects, how much more might day-in, day-out learning from mother? We lack naturalistic data on cognitively-productive social interaction in children's daily lives, though I review some in Chapter 5, but I will mention here that Ernst Moerk recently argued (Moerk 1989) that the LAD which Chomsky (1976) postulated to explain language development is most probably a LADY, the unfairly undervalued mother whose chatter and listening seems to him to be excellently fitted to producing an expert speaker. Given the Soviet (and indeed Marxist) context of this section, I will not restrain the exhortation 'Mothers of the world unite, you have nothing to lose but your deprecators!'

One important Vygotskian concept which has not yet been mentioned is the 'zone of proximal development' or ZPD. He presents it as part of a discussion of the interaction between 'learning' and 'development' (Vygotsky 1978a: 79–91). Here he argues that if we are to provide learning opportunities which will enable the child to develop we must determine at least two developmental levels. The lower of these is the sort of thing which the usual psychological and educational test measures, what the child can do independently; the higher is what the child can do with such assistance as demonstrations, prompts or leading questions.

> The zone of proximal development . . . is the distance between the actual developmental level as determined by independent problem solving and the level of potential development as determined through problem solving under adult guidance or in collaboration with more capable peers.
>
> (Vygotsky 1978a: 86)

Independent unaided problem-solving indicates what cognitive functioning the child has already mastered; problems which the child can only solve with assistance suggest what functions are not yet mature but are in the process of maturation. 'What a child can do with assistance today she will be able to do by herself tomorrow' (Vygotsky 1978a: 87). Diagnosis of the ZPD is necessary both for a full assessment of the child's abilities and for the optimum targeting of instruction. There is little profit from teaching aimed below the bottom of the ZPD because the child's functioning here is already mature, or from teaching aimed above the top of the ZPD, because the difference from the child's actual present functioning may be too great: 'the only "good learning" is that which is [slightly] in advance of development' (Vygotsky 1978a: 89); teaching is good only when it 'awakens and rouses to life those functions which are in a stage of maturing, which lie in the zone of proximal development' (Wertsch and Stone 1985: 165).

How does progress through the ZPD come about? In particular, how can 'good learning' be in advance of development? In one sense, we are back at the 'boot-strapping problem' here, and Bruner offers the 'teacher lifts the boot straps' answer. The teacher (adult or more competent peer)

> serves the learner as a vicarious form of consciousness until such a time as the learner is able to master his own action through his own consciousness and control. When the child achieves that conscious control over a new function or conceptual system, it is then that he is able to use it as a tool. Up to that point, the tutor in effect performs the critical function of 'scaffolding' the learning task to make it possible for the child, in Vygotsky's word, to internalise external knowledge and convert it into a tool for conscious control.
>
> (Bruner 1985: 25)

During the earliest periods of learning in the ZPD a child may have a very limited degree of understanding of what the task involves; the teacher offers a model or successive precise and simple directions, and the child merely observes or imitates. Gradually, as the child becomes able to cope with more components of an activity, and has more understanding of how they fit together, an understanding which will include more appreciation of what the goal is and how the means to it work, the adult reduces the assistance given and changes from very directive help to suggestion and encouragement. The adult needs to take less and less responsibility for the successful performance of the activity as the increasingly competent learner takes it on. The developmental task is to move from other-regulation to self-regulation (Brown et al. 1983); eventually the child provides his or her own scaffolding.

Here Vygotsky's observations on 'egocentric' speech are relevant (Vygotsky 1962, 1986). As is well known, he criticised Piaget's notion of egocentric speech as being a product of the child's inability to understand the world without solipsism (absolute egoism, exclusion of all knowledge except of oneself). Piaget believed that children's immature use of language was due to their lack of understanding of how to communicate with others who did not share their own knowledge, and that it disappeared as they became socialised. Vygotsky argued that 'egocentric' speech was speech used for overt self-regulation but produced in potentially communicative settings. Initially, the child's speech is purely social and communicates to others; gradually, adults' communicative and regulatory speech is internalised and as the child comes to be a cognitive self-regulator 'egocentric' speech is produced, which functions as part of the child's self-regulation but can also be seen (by listeners and by the child) as communicating to others, though in fact, being self-directed in origin, it does so inefficiently. Children at this age of course have difficulties in telling whether the speaker or the listener is responsible for a communication breakdown (Robinson and Robinson 1977, 1980, 1981). With further development 'egocentric' speech becomes 'inner speech', and the self-regulator's problem-solving dialogue with self is no longer observable. It may only become examinable when the task is difficult, or when an outsider asks for explicit 'talking-through' the problem. Self-regulation is overt during the early stages of achieving mastery of a task; once the task can be executed smoothly and independently, once it is 'automatised', self-consciousness may be disruptive and self-regulation will only be noticeable when task difficulty is great. Very great task difficulty may force recourse to other regulation; finding another helpful text, or seeking out an expert to answer one's questions or provide further training, for example.

If there is, as this account implies, a gradual transition from other-regulation to self-regulation as the child moves towards the upper part of the ZPD and becomes able to do independently what previously could only be done with assistance, it follows that there will be changes in the best form for assistance and other-regulation to take. Early in the learning cycle, assistance will be elaborate, explicit and frequent, as when the child is instructed through a close sequence of small steps. Later, assistance will be more abbreviated, less explicit and less frequent, with hints such as 'OK, what else could you look for?' rather than instructions such as 'Get the big yellow one that's over there'. Optimum assistance adapts itself to the learner's successes and failures (Bruner 1983, Tharp and Gallimore 1988, Wertsch 1978, 1979, 1985a, Wood 1980, 1988). The validity, and the educational implications, of this model of fostering cognitive development, will be discussed in Chapter 5.

Finally, I must make some reference to the fact that Vygotsky saw his work as a 'socio-cultural' theory of psychological processes. He emphasised that children pick up the socially constructed psychological tools that are available to them, and that these, superimposed on organic development, 'form a single line of socio-biological formation of the child's personality' (in Lee 1985: 74). Thus there will be both cultural and historical patterns in cognition. He used the ethnographic material on cultures which was available to him to investigate these issues, but also used parallels between development in the child and socio-historical development. His colleague A. R. Luria, for example, went in the early 1930s to remote parts of central

Asia where the mechanisation and collectivisation of agriculture were transforming the traditional peasant economy and way of life (Luria 1976). His intention was to compare the cognitive processes used by nonliterate 'unreformed' peasants and those who were participating in more modern ways of life. He did find some of the differences predicted by Vygotsky, for example illiterate and uneducated peasants sorted objects by their appearance and use (as young children do) while schooled respondents preferred more taxonomic sortings, but considerable controversy arose over the extent of the differences (see e.g. Cole and Griffin 1980), and even more over their interpretation (it was politically unacceptable to 'denigrate' the peasants by saying their thought was 'childlike'). Part of the problem was the lack of a detailed theory of the cognitive structure and processes provided by and required by the traditional peasant culture. A functional sorting of local artefacts is not self-evidently less useful than a taxonomic one. The sufficiently successful basis for the arrangement of objects in my kitchen cupboards, for example, is largely based on functional attributes such as 'vulnerable to mice', 'not to be got at by my small daughter', 'used here together', and taxonomic classifications (except those isomorphic with the perceptual characteristics of size and weight) are secondary. It seems quite likely that many of the cognitive processes which we take for granted as part of the normal repertoire of skills have become so as a result of us having been schooled in them, and using them in our everyday activities (see e.g. Cole and Means 1981 for discussion of this).

The concept of 'activity', which appears in Vygotsky's writings but has been developed since by Soviet psychologists, is of importance here (Davydov and Radzikhovskii 1985, Kozulin 1986, Wertsch 1981, Zinchenko 1985). Socially meaningful activity must be an explanatory principle and a basic unit of analysis in psychology. It is also seen to be a generator of consciousness, and activity mediated by psychological tools and interpersonal communication produces the higher mental functions. The analysis of activities must include consideration of their goals, and their embedding in the social context, for as social structures and processes influence what practical activities are engaged in, and these activities determine cognitive development, ultimately social consciousness and the modes of production (Vygotsky's was an explicitly Marxist theory) determine psychological development. Different cultures (and subcultures) have different activities and different goals; an individual's cognitive activity operates within both cultural constraints and cultural amplifiers, including cultural differences in the way the ZPD operates (see Cole 1985, Rogoff 1990, Stigler, Schweder and Herdt 1990, Valsiner 1988a, 1988b, Winegar 1989).

As Hundeide (1985), Mellin-Olsen (1987) and other educators have pointed out, the pupil's definition of an activity may differ radically from the teacher's, with resultant difficulties in their learning. As Tharp and Gallimore (1988) argue, the who, where, what, why and when of activity settings need to be considered. It may be more important to examine patterns of differences in cognition than the generalised and abstract models of Piaget and the information-processing theorists have supposed.

Thus Vygotsky's work contrasts with the approaches of Piaget and the 'information-processors' in its insistence on the relevance of the social, cultural and historical milieu to the individual's cognitive development. It also makes a far more incisive analysis of the learning process, and so is of great importance to educators, both in and out of school. There will be some further discussion of what families and schools do to help children learn and develop cognitive skills in Chapter 5, but I will just mention here an apparent paradox. If neo-Vygotskian 'scaffolding' of socially meaningful activity is the best way of helping learning, and schools do rather little of it (not least because it requires a teacher–pupil ratio of approximately one to one, a pretty detailed diagnosis of what skills exist, which are potential, and how to teach each one, and a very sensitively implemented teaching programme over an extended period of time – not the conditions that the ordinary school provides), how is it that schools are at all successful?

One obvious way out of the paradox is to say that schools are in fact *not* at all successful, and certain reviewers of the educational process do indeed take this position, though their proposed remedies range from de-schooling (e.g. the argument associated with Ivan Illich) to a far more authoritarian and didactic use of school time (e.g. various pronouncements by MPs), via an increase in neo-Vygotskian schooling (e.g. Tharp and Gallimore 1988). I have no sympathy with this position: schools seem to me to be remarkably successful under difficult conditions, though they might indeed be more successful if they could be more Vygotskian. Another solution of the paradox is to assert that there are ways of learning which involve less scaffolding by a teacher, and indeed there obviously are, in the various 'conditions of learning' described in so many classic educational textbooks (e.g. Gagné 1985). The 'Piagetian' model used in early childhood education (see Meadows and Cashdan 1988 for a critical discussion) and the traditional rote learning which Tharp and Gallimore 1988 attack so intensely are, in their contrasting ways, methods of learning, and even of facilitating cognitive development. What is interesting here is the relationship between different ways of learning. Might it possibly be the case, for example, that an early history of good scaffolding so to speak 'sets up' learners to become their own scaffolders, so that they can both take their own rote learning and mechanical information-processing 'beyond the information given', and act in a Piagetian mode as never-ceasing equilibrators, continually seeking a deeper and broader and more flexible understanding of their worlds? The few scraps of evidence relevant to this interesting and developmentally important possibility are discussed elsewhere in this book, notably in Chapter 5.

# Causes of change and variation in cognitive development

## INTRODUCTION

This chapter is concerned with causes of change and variation in cognitive development. It focuses on biological, environmental and social processes and events which might be thought to produce cognitive development. It asks the 'how' questions: how is cognition assembled during childhood? What internal and external factors influence the way in which cognitive behaviour develops and how do the developmental processes work? How do an individual's genes and experience interact during cognitive development? It is not a satisfactory answer to such questions, though it may provide a very early sketch map of what sort of terrain will have to be covered. It is not satisfactory for several reasons: in the first place there are my own inadequacies, but beyond that there is the two-strand problem of incomplete description and inadequate theory which characterised even the material on 'what' children's cognition is, which I discussed earlier in this book. 'How' questions, questions of cause, are notoriously harder to answer than descriptive 'what' ones. 'Cause' itself is an elusive and difficult concept; the sort of thing we are concerned with here is those events or processes on which cognitive development is conditional, which are *sufficient* causes (all that is required for it to proceed), or *necessary* causes (essential but perhaps not the only thing required) or *contributory* causes (useful, but neither necessary nor sufficient). Distinctions may also have to be made between predisposing factors, precipitating factors, and factors which, once development is on its way, sustain, reverse, limit, amplify, diminish or otherwise modify it. There may be overdetermination, belt and braces and safety pins all, co-operatively or independently, holding up the developmental trousers. We must also recognise that for something as complex as cognition there will perhaps be multiple causation, many factors involved in ways which may vary from person to person and time to time, so that the 'life histories' of cognitive development in different people may be completely different in what event or process was significant and when. There will be chains of causes: $X$ causes $Y$, but is itself caused by $W$ which is caused by $V$ which is caused by etc. How far we trace these chains back to the First Cause will depend on many factors: time, persistence, how good the data are, what we consider to be 'real' causes, how many unknown processes we can tolerate between 'cause' and 'effect'; and throughout we will achieve a much more satisfactory account, and have an infinitely better potential for therapeutic or educational intervention, if we consider *how* these causes work.

Much of the work on cognitive development to be found in the literature is of little use in tackling the 'how' questions. A somewhat decreasing proportion of it is concerned only with a 'what' question: what differences are associated with age differences. The 'differences' themselves may be suspect if they come from cross-sectional comparison of samples which are not really equivalent; all too many comparisons of children with 'adults' draw their 'adults' from the population of undergraduate students without considering if they represent the total population of all adults in the same way as children drawn from ordinary, that is non-selective, schools represent the total population of all children. Age difference data do not in themselves tell us anything much about why there are these differences, let alone how the younger children develop to become like the older ones. At best such data map out what has to be explained; good descriptions of what is the same and what has changed in each successive level provide what has to be explained and thus indicate what the 'how' answer must be. (To take one extreme, if there are *no* age differences, the 'how' will either identify an early completion of development or processes which maintain a stable state, or both.) Age difference data may also serve a useful function by showing that a cognitive process we take for granted in adults is problematic in young children, and thus needs to have its development examined. Piaget's demonstration that young children had difficulty with conservation is an example of this, though his ideas about developmental processes have perhaps stood up better to later work than his age differences description; so many 'age differences' have subsequently been whittled away by demonstrations of very early competence.

Although a case can be made that the causes of 'development' are different from the causes of 'individual differences' (e.g. Anderson 1992), I think that part of the problem here is a discussion of development in terms of universally applicable patterns and processes. If there is a cause which applies in the same way at the same point in every individual case, it will be hard to spot precisely because it is so all-pervasive. Suppose that I hypothesise – and quite possibly no one has done so before – that the tying of the severed umbilical cord is a necessary condition for learning to read. I would be prepared to bet that everyone who did not have their umbilical cord tied (or otherwise prevented from bleeding) did not learn to read, because there was blood loss which killed them; and that everyone who survived to learn to read had been saved from this fatal haemorrhage by having had their umbilical cord tied. My hypothesis is almost certainly true, there are biological notions of blood loss and death or brain damage behind it, and it could lead to other hypotheses about the effects of other haemorrhages on learning to read via associated brain damage or debility; but these other hypotheses might be much more interesting than my original one because it is so unlikely that there will be an exception to my rule that all readers once had their umbilical cords tied and cut. What we need as well as universals, I think, is an account of variation in development, so that we can illuminate how development generally happens by examining development in exceptional cases (as is being done in genetics, where anomalies causing pathological development have proved much easier to identify and understand than the genes associated with more subtle variations which are all within the 'normal' range of behaviour or structure). Age difference data tend to be weak on this sort of examination too; they may set up 'the (normal) 5-year-old' and 'the (normal) 10-year old' without much interest in (or even much acknowledgement of) those children who do not fit into the neat age-related patterns. This is understandable, given the difficulty of distinguishing between real individual differences and measurement error, but this sort of 'tidying-up' of data cuts out cases which by being exceptional provide good opportunities for investigating the processes which account for deviations from normal development. Radke-Yarrow (1991) makes a powerful argument for a disciplined use of case-studies of small samples: such a method would allow investigation of how development proceeds in context and in relation to other aspects of development, and how it is patterned over time.

Correlational data will be helpful in understanding development but do not of themselves answer causal questions. A correlation between $A$ and $B$ does not establish that $A$ causes $B$, or that $B$ causes $A$: $A$ and $B$ might be independently related to a third variable, $C$. For example, in the school age population there will be a positive correlation between height and reading ability; but clearly reading well does not make you grow taller, nor does being tall cause you to read better, rather both height and reading ability are associated with age, the latter via the accumulation of learning and experience for which age stands as an indicator. If $A$ invariably precedes $B$, that does not establish that $A$ causes $B$, nor does a lack of $A$ invariably preceding a lack of $B$ establish a causal relation, though this may tell us more than a correlation would. If we have both, plus a finding that supplying the missing $A$ (by training or other intervention) leads to the development of the $B$ which would (we suppose) otherwise have been missing, we begin to have a strong case for $A$ causing $B$. But we still need an account of *how* the causal chain worked. It will be clear by the end of this chapter that we are not very well provided with either good data or good theory on the 'causes' of cognitive development. Though strong cases have been made in certain areas (for example the role of phonological awareness in learning to read, of the failure of development of a cognitive coherence mechanism in autism, of mother's use of child-contingent language in language development), it is not yet clear whether these separate islands of causal explanation can be brought together, just as there is uncertainty at the descriptive level over whether there is cognition in general or whether there are more or less autonomous cognitive skills developing separately.

This chapter does not impose a false unity on this heterogeneous literature. It readdresses some of the material used descriptively in the earlier parts of this book to look for explanations of how and why cognitive development proceeds as it does. The amount and quality of the relevant material vary enormously. Many different disciplines are potential sources, but there are few interdisciplinary investigations to help bring coherence to a vast, patchy and ambiguous array of evidence. The chapter necessarily reflects the nature of the literature: it is heterogeneous and uncertain and its efforts at integration are tentative. It begins with an introductory account of recent work on brains and cognitive development. Although some theorists interested in cognition argue that its 'hardware' level is irrelevant to its 'software' (Anderson 1992, McShane 1991, Marr 1982), like some others interested in cognition (Churchland and Churchland 1990, Piaget 1971b), I believe that what *can* be said about cognition is that it is strongly associated with what the physical nature of the brain is, and so the more we seek to understand what current neuropsychology implies for cognitive development, the better. Discussion of brain development is followed by a brief look at genetic influences on cognitive development, and at the ways in which factors in the physical environment such as diet and lead pollution can be seen to influence children's cognition. These comparatively physiological sections are followed by a move to the social side of the 'nature–nurture' controversy, with discussion of some aspects of people's social experience. The last major concern of the chapter is the impact on children's cognitive development of the educational efforts of adults, especially their parents.

## BRAINS AND COGNITIVE DEVELOPMENT

### Introduction

As neuroscientists continue to make exciting discoveries about the structure, biochemistry and neurophysiology of how the brain develops and how it works, I think it becomes more and more necessary for psychologists to consider what the impact of discoveries at this level should be on psychological models of cognition and of cognitive development. Some discussion of these issues is the business of this section; I shall leave aside for the moment what ideas should be transmitted in the reverse direction. I feel some hesitation in undertaking this task, given millennia of disagreement about mind–brain relationships, the complexity of the neuroscience evidence and the speed with which it is being refined, revised and elaborated, and our distinctly partial accounts of cognitive behaviour, let alone the problems of linking different areas of research which have extremely different methodologies. However it does seem essential to try to convey the excitement and importance of understanding brain, cognition and cognitive development together and better. I will not, for reasons of lack of expertise and space, go into much detail on the physiology or anatomy of brains, preferring to refer readers to other sources. Those whose formal education in biology ended early, and indeed anyone who would profit from a thoughtful overview of a vast amount of knowledge, should begin by reading and thinking about J. Z. Young's *Philosophy and the Brain* (1987); another useful introduction to some fairly recent work is provided by the 1982 Wolfson College lectures (Coen 1985). Detailed reviews of more limited issues, mostly without much discussion of wider issues, may be found in volume 2 of the *Handbook of Child Psychology* (Haith and Campos 1983), and in a special issue of *Child Development* (volume 58, 1987, edited by Crnic and Pennington). Changeux (1987) gives a clear and elegant account of 'neuronal man' and proposes an interesting model of the neuroscience–cognition interface. P. S. Churchland (1986) writes elegantly on what a 'unified science of the mind–brain' should consider, and P. M. Churchland (1989) also comments on cognitive neurobiology. The volume edited by Gregory (1988) is of great interest to the general reader, and offers several brief articles on relevant topics, notably a very clear account of 'brain development' by Colwyn Trevarthen.

## 'Mind' and brain

There has been debate for hundreds of years about the nature of 'mind' and its relation to the brain (for a useful book of readings see Lycan 1989). The advances made in the physical sciences have led to the success of a model of the world as explainable in terms of physical systems of mindless particles and forces, mechanically interacting and without individual meaning. The workings of our own bodies are somewhat successfully described in these mechanical and material terms; just as we do not need any longer to explain thunder in terms of the gods' anger or heat in terms of the immaterial spirit 'phlogiston', so we do not need to postulate the existence of an *élan vital* to explain the properties of living organisms. However we experience ourselves (and normally other people and sometimes other animals (Byrne and Whiten 1988, Griffin 1976)) as capable of being conscious, free, morally responsible, rational agents, not just 'meaningless' physically ordered collections of atoms. At the core of the 'mind–body problem' is how to reconcile these two views of the world, to cope with the anomaly of our consciousness, our subjectivity, our capacity to have mental states which refer to something in the world other than themselves, and our sense that 'mind' can cause physical events (as when for example we decide to stop writing and prepare lunch, or to ignore our hunger for a little longer in order to get the mind–body problem out of the way) as well as physical events causing mental ones (seeing, hearing, feeling euphoric because of a drink, and so on), in an otherwise material and mechanical world.

## Idealism, dualism and materialism

One solution to this anomaly verges on denying the material nature of the world, viewing it all as a mental construct existing only in one's mind. In this 'idealist' stance, the only thing I can be sure exists is my own collection of mental states, which includes, presumably, an impressive degree of imagination ranging from a sense of having a body which is getting hungry to a recollection of Dr Johnson's comment on Bishop Berkeley's idealism *and* of where to look it up – or imagine I am looking it up, perhaps. (In Boswell's account, he and Johnson talk of this 'ingenious sophistry to prove the non-existence of matter, and that every thing in the universe is merely ideal. I [Boswell] observed, that though we are satisfied his [Berkeley's] doctrine is not true, it is impossible to refute it. I never shall forget the alacrity with which Johnson answered, striking his foot with mighty force against a large stone, till he rebounded from it, "I refute it *thus*" ' (Boswell [1791] 1979:122)). An extreme idealist theory does cope with the mental–physical problem (by denying the independent existence of the physical world), with the world-reference problem (since there is no world outside our imagination) and with subjectivity (since that is all there is). I think it might be hard to give an account in these terms of our different degrees of consciousness, including both its changes and its stability. It also gives rise to some interesting moral problems: could I justifiably feel complacent at the range and detail of my imagination, and what responsibility would I bear for having imagined the genocidal activities of the Nazis and other political persecutions, for example. But ultimately it fails because of its implausibility and, as Johnson points out, the stubborn evidence of our senses that our mental states have to do with material objects. Idealism, in this sense, and science are probably not capable of co-existence.

Thus there are two main alternatives: 'dualism', that there are two distinct kinds of entity in the world, the material and the mental, and a form of 'monism', 'materialism', that mental and physical processes are of the same kind, and that ultimately mental processes are physical. Dualism is not so easily dismissed as idealism, though the problem of how mental and physical, being completely different entities, can interact at all, let alone effectively, is an enormous one. Dualists assert that there is a distinctive *mental* aspect to the mind which is not reducible to physical terms. Some dualists deny that the mind is identical with the brain and think of the mind as a sort of non-physical substance, independent of the body in that it survives it after death, though mind and brain interact causally while the brain is intact. The laws of neuroscience, which describe how the brain works, have little or nothing to say about how the mind works, because mind and brain are different substances. The very distinguished neurophysiologist, John Eccles, for example, asserts dualistically that there is a self-conscious mind, operating under the higher-order rules of the mental world, monitoring and directing the material and mechanical brain. The non-material mind has the ideas, the emotions and the spirituality, while the brain is a rigidly operating machine doing nothing particularly glorious and certainly explainable in much the same sort of terms as a complex mechanism (Eccles 1989, Popper and Eccles 1977). In effect what he (like those dualists to be found in the general field of artificial intelligence) is doing is ignoring or trivialising the complexity of the structures and mechanisms which neuroscience is finding in the brain. AI specialists may conceivably be justified in concentrating on cognitive functioning rather than on the physical objects which allow or produce such functioning. However, I feel myself (and see also Churchland and Churchland 1990) that they would be wise to keep an eye on what better accounts of the physical substratum might have to say about limitations or facilitations of particular ways of functioning (why there seem to be quantity and time constraints in short-term memory but not in long-term memory, for example). Eccles's insistence on dualism is surprising, however, and it has been linked to his religious beliefs (see Wall 1985). Neither he nor anyone else gives a good account of the non-material mind and its interactions with the physical. Yet even the subtlest mental events – reasoning, moral feelings, political and aesthetic judgements – can be affected if the brain is affected by drugs or lesions. In addition, it is non-parsimonious to postulate two sorts of entities when one kind might do. For these reasons, and because it is becoming clearer and clearer that the brain, although mechanical in the sense of being describable in terms of physical structures and material processes and subject to scientific investigation, is enormously complex and beautifully organised, 'substance dualism' looks as though it is not viable, or at least not necessary.

Similar problems arise for another version of dualism, 'property dualism'. Property dualism is more viable, however, or at least is still being more vigorously asserted. The argument is that there are properties of mental functioning which cannot, in principle as well as in current fact, be reduced to physical functioning. Subjective experiences, for example, are produced by the brain and can in turn affect the brain but are not themselves identifiable with any physical properties of the brain: feeling happy, or believing that Napoleon was Emperor of France, are *mental* phenomena which cannot be adequately described and explained in terms of brain states. While this is true of many 'mental states' and 'mental processes' at present, an increasing amount of evidence links specific 'mental' activities to specific physical events in the brain. The debate may perhaps be taken to be about what is the 'best', that is, best documented, most fertile, most intelligible level of description; to do this implies recognising both that changes in our knowledge may lead to changes in which description is 'best', and that there are interesting questions to be asked about the relationships between levels. Neuroscience is showing us, in fact, more and more reasons to assert a monism that goes as far as saying that mentality is not separable from the brain. *All* observed mental activities are associated in time with some corresponding cerebral activity. In simple cases, for example when the finger is pricked by a pin, we can describe the physical processes that ensue in the nerves of the spinal cord and the brain and the 'mental' feeling of pain (see Wall 1985). In more complex cases, we cannot yet specify what these physical processes are, but the rapid advances of neuroscience give reason to hope that we may some time do so. Indeed, Wall's interesting account of 'pain and no pain' provides an argument against dualism by showing that there are variations in the relations between 'input' of stimulation at the periphery of the nervous system and 'output' accounts of what sort and amount of pain is being felt where, which cannot be explained in the dualist terms of a clever interpretive mind monitoring the mechanical proceedings of a simple material brain. The findings of recent neuroscience investigations are showing us more and more about the cerebral events which occur with mental events. For example when we recognise a face and name its owner there is a fairly constant succession of activation in particular parts of the cortex, first in cells which seem to specialise in face recognition and then in 'naming' cells (see Perrett *et al.* 1985, Young 1987: 125–8).

It seems sensible to refuse to separate mind (and consciousness) from the brain because consciousness incontrovertibly requires a functioning brain. If the brain is not functioning at all, the individual has no mental events at all; if the brain's functioning is disturbed (for example by damage in particular areas, or by abnormalities in neurotransmitters, or, temporarily, by drugs or alcohol), consciousness and mental functioning are also disturbed. These disturbances tell us, in fact, a lot about both brain functioning and mental events (see below). We do not have any evidence of disembodied minds which, independent of brains, control bodies (or indeed anything else, despite the claims made for 'psychic' or paranormal phenomena). There can be brain functioning without consciousness, if not, perhaps, without any mental events at all. Our brains are ceaselessly active, functioning, for example, while we are asleep, and even when we are awake, they are doing all sorts of things which we are not conscious of at the time, which we may indeed find insuperably hard to become conscious of. For example, we have great difficulty in becoming aware of many of our cognitive processes (see elsewhere in this chapter and in Chapter 2), and much of the information which we know is only called up when required, or only appears when a particular part of the brain is stimulated. Penfield's famous studies show that it must have been somewhere in the mind–brain system though we were not conscious of it until it was required, or that it was quickly reconstituted from stored elements (Squire 1987; see also the literature on parallel distributed processing (Bechtel and Abrahamsen 1991, Clark 1989, Minsky 1987)).

Research on the organisation and functioning of the brain and the nervous system is suggesting a degree of complexity and interrelationship between different parts which rules out very simple models. The sort of reductionism that dualists object to – claims that mental functioning can be entirely explained in terms of a few simple synaptic connections or waves of electrical activity or changes in the amount of a particular brain transmitter or stimulation and response within a single cell – now looks unsatisfactory from the basis of the neurosciences evidence as well as from the basis of asserting the complexity of mind. Brains just are not simple straight-in/straight-out machines where one thing leads rigidly to another. Rather, they have a number of elaborate 'programs' (Young 1978, 1987) for action which interact and which develop over the life-span, and which come into play on the basis of more-or-less internally modulated rhythms or as demanded by the needs of the moment in ways which assist in keeping the individual alive, and preferably, prospering. All living involves selection and choice, and thus, to be at all efficient, learning, that is, the remembering of experience and its organisation into whatever degree of coherence is possible and useful. Living things which react to a variety of stimuli in various ways may need to have mental activity, and in some cases consciousness or even self-awareness, to be able to use their programs for surviving and reproducing (particularly perhaps if they are social beings (Humphrey 1983)). Conscious experience and cognition are closely associated with brain activity; they are not things, even 'mental things', which can exist apart from it. They are characteristic properties of some but not all brain activities, and vary in character according to which parts of the brain are most active; they are not reducible to microlevel processes in a preparation of brain cells. The evidence is more and more of integrating links and interconnections between brain parts which had been thought to function separately. Searle (1984) draws the analogy between mind and brain, on the one hand, and the liquidity of water, the transparency of glass, or the solidity of wood on the other. The surface features of liquidity, solidity and transparency are *caused by* the behaviour of microlevel elements (the interactions between water molecules, the structural relationships of wood or glass molecules); they also *just are* features of those sorts of microlevel elements in those sorts of systems. We can usefully have scientific definitions in terms of the surface features (e.g. liquidity) as well as scientific descriptions of the microlevel elements (e.g. a water molecule). In fact we need both because their descriptive ranges are different; we cannot, for example, reach into a glass of water, pull out one molecule and say 'This one's wet' or 'This one's at 10°C', though such things can be said of the larger system, the water in the glass. The microlevel explanation is neither better nor worse than the macrolevel one. An account at any level of description can be an adequate explanation unless information in terms of other levels of description is needed to clarify the account, to remove ambiguity or prevent misunderstanding (cf. Wittgenstein 1976).

Searle's argument about the 'emergent' quality of mind brings us back to the possible usefulness of our present descriptions of minds. One focus of debate here has been the validity or falsity of 'folk psychology', the common-sense view which most ordinary adults hold about what human cognitive activity is and how it relates us to the world. As folk psychologists, we believe that we each have a mind,

> a unitary, integrated 'control centre' which receives, evaluates, intelligently manipulates, and stores information from the environment, sets goals in the light of the information, designs means for achieving them, and directs the bodily actions by which these means are executed. Our minds, we believe, perform these many different functions, encompassing many different volitional, affective, and cognitive states and processes. An ingredient of this concept is a distinction between an inner subjective realm of sensations, emotions, desires, intentions, plans, beliefs, fantasies, dreams, hypotheses, and other mental states, processes, and events on the one hand, and outer, objective, merely physical existence on the other.
>
> (Forguson 1989: 4)

This characterisation of 'minds' has served us quite well over millennia of social life; but currently debate centres on whether the categories of folk psychology, particularly its emphasis on logical processes and intentional states, are correct characterisations of mental states, and on whether they can be reduced to categories at the neurobiological level of description. One important stream in this complex and often heated debate is 'functionalism'. Much influenced by the computer metaphor for thought, functionalism focuses on cognition as symbol manipulation, and on the syntactic rules which are used to transform one abstract symbol into another. A strong contrast is made between the logical operations on symbols, which are seen as interesting, and the causal relations among the physical states of the computer (machine or brain) which is implementing the logical operations, which are seen as irrelevant, since it is assumed that any mechanism could do the job: human neurone, silicon chips, or old beer cans, if suitably put together, would be functionally equivalent (and equally uninteresting to the functionalists). The core idea of functionalism is that mental states are characterised in terms of the abstract causal relations to environmental input, to other internal states, and to output. Being 'in love', for example, is a mental state which has characteristic causal relations to one's own behaviour, such as giving especial care to one's appearance, writing more poems than usual, rushing to the ringing telephone if there is any possibility that the Beloved is on the other end; to other, internal, states, such as one's beliefs about the Beloved, desire for the Beloved's presence, indifference to others who are normally of some interest; and to external input, for example a heightened attention to all Beloved-relevant stimulation (and a tendency to see all stimulation of whatever sort as evocative of him or her). How these patterns or characteristic causal relations are realised – in male or female matter, or in nonhuman matter of some sort – is unimportant to the functionalist, whose interest is in the cognitive system in its own right. This stance, of course, is necessary for those who hope to use computers and other machines to model human cognition (see Chapter 4). It is also justified by the true assertion that there may be something important in common if not in the 'being in love' at least in the 'mate seeking' of a human, a chimpanzee, a stickleback and a spider, though there might be different neural events and processes in each species; or indeed that there might be different neural events underlying the 'being in love' of two different humans or of one human on different occasions (King Henry VIII in his successive liaisons and marriages, for example). The argument of multiple realisability, of the same mental relations being instantiated or realised in many differentiable ways, with human central nervous systems being only one sort, reduces the importance of knowing about how human brains work. Neuroscience can only tell us about engineering details – chemical, structural, electrical or molecular – for one particular embodiment of the functional relations which make up brain states, and is therefore seen by the philosophical functionalists as a less useful level of description than cognitive psychology, which focuses directly on the functional organisation of cognition (Pylyshyn 1980).

I feel, for obvious reasons, sympathetic to the view that we continue to need investigations of mental life at the psychological level, that psychology cannot be reduced to neuroscience. However, the functionalist position that neuroscience is *irrelevant* to understanding cognitive functions seems to me to be rash in the extreme. In part, this is because our main alternative access to what functional mental states and processes we have is through folk psychology, the 'common-sense' assumptions listed by Forguson (1989: 4) and vigorously debated by a number of philosophers (e.g. Churchland 1989, Churchland 1986, Dennett 1987, Fodor 1983, Forguson 1989, Stich 1983).

Folk psychology has worked quite well for millennia, but its 'homey generalisations' (Churchland 1986), however rich and complicated, are not necessarily so perfect as to need no revision. A person's 'folk psychology' changes in the course of his or her development (see Chapter 2 this volume); there have also been historical changes in folk psychology, for example a decline in its use of explanations involving possession by demons to account for unacceptable or inexplicable behaviour, and an increase in materialist explanations in terms of physiological structures: 'it's me nerves, doctor'. Further, folk psychology runs into both philosophical problems and problems of discrepancy with the evidence of scientific psychology. For example, folk psychology assumes that we have more or less direct and correct access to our mental states, that we have 'awareness'. But we have not managed to produce a clear account of what 'awareness' is, and introspection has many times led people to pronouncements about their mental activities which other external evidence suggests cannot be correct (e.g. Churchland 1989, Nisbett and Wilson 1977). Nor is it impossible that even such complex states as 'awareness' may (in the future) be elucidated by neuroscience, which could help clarify the phenomena that folk psychology is unclear about by reformulating them in more scientific terms. Folk psychology may continue to be what we use in our everyday dealings with other people – it has been used for these purposes for many many more years than scientific psychology or neuroscience have, so its comparatively greater success here is not surprising – but it may be misleading when we are seeking a scientific understanding of mind or brain or cognitive development.

I have sketched some issues in the mind–brain controversy. There remains considerable and often heated debate about the nature of 'mind' and its relation to brain. Being neither a philosopher nor a neuroscientist I can do no more than alert readers to this problem, refer them to other discussions (e.g. Blakemore and Greenfield 1987, Bunge 1980, Churchland 1986) and proceed to questions about how the brain system works in cognition and cognitive development. These are dealt with from a pragmatic view on the mind–brain relation: that it makes sense to talk of ideas, beliefs, memories and so forth but that these are associated with, perhaps attributable to, physical events and structures in the brain.

## How the brain works: fragments of a minimal sketch

J. Z. Young (1985, 1987) emphasises that the brain contains in some form of record all the information that makes possible the actions of our everyday life, including our cognition – all our capacity for conscious life. He points out that all living things have the fundamental purpose of continuing their lives (or the lives of their genes) and do this by using 'programs', instructions for complex sequences of physical changes which deal with information from past and present, from the body and its environment, in order to keep things going or developing. At all sorts of levels in the brain there are programs for functions such as breathing, sleeping and waking, producing coherent language, perceiving particular shapes and orientations (including faces and the direction they are looking), remembering, evaluating and so on. The brain sometimes seems to have one particular locale which is crucial to running a particular function, for example the reticular formation deep in the core of the brain is crucially involved in sleep–wake cycles, but input from and output to other parts of the brain are also involved in the minute-by-minute running of the program. Increasingly, neuroscience is identifying both the individual parts which are crucially involved in serving a particular brain function *and* the 'democratic' way in which they operate together with other parts. This is an immensely difficult enterprise as most of the investigative techniques known at present test for the activity and effect of small numbers of nerve cells, perhaps single cells, but enough is known for us to feel that probably most brain function is localised in some degree, that is, that different areas of the mature brain are *not* equally capable of doing the same job, but also that the millions of nerve cells in the brain are connected in extraordinarily complex networks not necessarily confined to adjacent areas of the brain. The brain is always active, though individual cells may show no activity at a particular moment, and somehow the *pattern* of activity, of connections between nerve cells and impulses circulating in time between them, signals to us how to decide which alternative version of a program will keep us functioning optimally at the moment.

This sort of system for dealing with information has some important characteristics worth noticing, some of which differentiate it from at least the present generation of computers. It is ceaselessly active; much of its activity is endogenous; it has the capacity of keeping itself alive and well-functioning; it uses parallel processing; it selects its input; it has an enormous ability to learn; its learning and functioning are related to its evaluation of what is best for its genotype. It is the composer of its own music, the conductor, the orchestra, and even much of the audience. It is also dependent for its actions on receiving signals from both the outside world and endogenous changes in hormonal state. There is probably little point in asking *why* brain functioning is like this, as answers can only range from 'it just is' to *post hoc* discussions of, for example, the greater evolutionary usefulness of such a system. But there are all sorts of interesting questions about exactly how the system works (which I must leave to neuroscientists, for example Changeux (1987), to deal with) and what the system's workings imply for behaviour and development. It is some of these that I want to address now, by looking a little more closely at some examples of relatively well-documented structure and functioning.

## An introductory description of the brain

It is outside the scope of this book to go into much detail about the anatomy, physiology and biochemistry of the brain, but it seems appropriate to provide a brief introductory structural account here. Readers who are confident in this area should skip to the next section. Changeux (1987) provides an introduction to the excitement of the field, or see Gregory (1988), particularly the section on the nervous system.

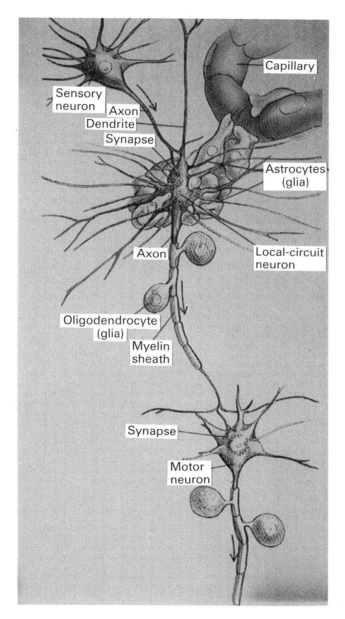

*Figure 5.1* The basic structure of nerve cells: schematic drawing of neurone showing axon, dendrites, synapses and glial cells.
*Source*: Bloom, Lazerson and Hofstadter 1985

Brains, and the more peripheral parts of the nervous system, are made up of cells (as is all animal tissue). For our purposes the essential cells are the nerve cells or neurones. Figure 5.1 shows their basic structure. These are large as body cells go, with a cell body which has many filamentary prolongations of cytoplasmic tissue protruding from it, the dendrites. One protrusion is far longer than the others, and this is called the axon; it may be as much as one metre in length. Nerve fibres from one cell link it to many other cells, the fibres running between each other in a complex network such that each cell is covered with nerve endings from many other cells, and each cell sends out fibres which join up with other cells' central cell bodies. There are connections between the sensory receptors (such as eyes, ears, receptor cells in the skin and joints), via the cells of the peripheral nervous system, to the central nervous system (the brain and spinal cord), and outwards from the brain to muscles to allow control of posture and movement. Not all the stimulation that a sensory receptor receives is passed on to the central nervous system's highest levels. It is first processed in the receptors and again at various levels of its progress through the central nervous system. The receptors in the eye, for example, convert light signals on the retina into electrical ones which pass up the optic nerve and through a succession of 'relay stations' to the visual cortex at the back of the brain. If an unchanging light falls on exactly the same cells of the retina for long enough they eventually cease to be activated by it and no further signals are sent to the visual cortex until the light changes. Nor does all the information coming from the receptors to the brain and resulting in output signals back to peripheral parts of the body become conscious; much information about body posture, for example, comes in and is automatically acted on so that we remain upright without having to 'think' about it. To give another example, it may be that the brightness of the daylight around us affects our activity levels and emotional states, as it certainly affects the behaviour of hibernating animals. Maintaining bright artificial light stimulation on dull days has been suggested as a preventative for some cases of depression.

The central nervous system works by integrating signals from one set of nerve cells with another. Signals consist of a group of electrical impulses which pass from the cell body out to the end of the nerve fibres. A neurone becomes active under the influence of many factors, such as the chemical state of its local environment, the pattern of excitation and inhibition it is receiving (and has just received), and its characteristic threshold of excitability. There are both excitatory neurones which send off signals saying 'Do something' and inhibitory neurones which say 'Keep quiet'. The latter are necessary in part because the neurones of the central nervous system may spontaneously generate their own messages: they do not, like telephone lines, lie quiet until there is activity at the periphery. Any given neurone, therefore, may be receiving both excitatory and inhibitory messages from thousands of other neurones, and would send signals on to many others. This involves complex patterns of organisation of what I called 'sets' of nerve cells at the beginning of this paragraph. There is convergence of nerve endings from many other neurones on to one neurone; there is divergence of nerve fibres from one neurone on to many other neurones. There is lateral inhibition, where if one group of neurones is strongly excited those neurones immediately surrounding it will be strongly inhibited and those a little further away more weakly inhibited, thus emphasising complexity and contrast.

Once signals have started in a nerve fibre the electrical impulses continue to its end. Here they reach the synapse, a minute gap between the nerve ending and the cell body or dendrites of the next cell. If the message passes over the synapse to the next cell, impulses are generated which continue on to further synapses and thus to further parts of the network. This transmission across the synapse depends on whether the signals from the neurone before the synapse can excite the post-synaptic nerve cell, but transmission can also be prevented by inhibitory signals which weaken or block the signals from the first cell on the incoming side of the synapse. Fibres from different nerve cells which lie close together can affect each other.

When the electrical impulses of nerve cells reach their endings a chemical substance is put out into the synaptic gap, and these substances, 'neurotransmitters', react with receptor sites on the outgoing side of the synapse, on the post-synaptic neurone, to change the excitability of the neurone and perhaps transmit a further electrical signal on to further synapses and further cells. There are many different neurotransmitters, among them acetylcholine, noradrenaline, dopamine and various hormones and peptides. In some cases a particular neurone employs a particular neurotransmitter, so, for example, cholinergic neurones synthesise and emit acetylcholine, but the various neurones in a chain of nerve fibres may emit and be acted on by different transmitters. Some functions are carried out by parts of the nervous system working together using the same neurotransmitter throughout, for example dopamine is secreted by the neurones concerned with waking the brain from sleep. Other functions are carried out with many neurotransmitters, for example the muscles of the alimentary canal are made to contract by acetylcholine, noradrenaline and many peptides.

As there are about $10^{12}$ nerve cells in the brain, as these can be saying either 'Go' or 'Stop' at various levels of intensity from total inactivity to a rapid propagation of large bursts of activity, as they each have very many connections to other nerve cells, as they use a number of different chemical neurotransmitters, and as their firing is organised in time as well as in space, the total pattern of nervous activity in the brain can be seen to be, potentially, very complicated. Only with recent advances in the technology of the neurosciences is much headway being made into discovering how this 'total pattern' is set up. The scale of the problem becomes more obvious if two facts are juxtaposed. The $10^{12}$ neurones consist of comparatively few different types, and synapses look even more alike; thus it will be hard to tell one from another in the branching, interlacing tangles of fibres. It would take between 3,000 and 30,000 years to count all the synpases in the human cortex, even at the improbable rate of 1,000 per second, even if they could be teased apart. The information-processing system of the human brain is 'wired up' in a way which can justly be called formidably complex. Further, not only is one individual brain slightly different from another,

> at any given time an unknown number of these [neurones in the brain] are probably altering their connections, and may be altering their basic characteristics, our attempts to obtain any sort of complete determination of neural connectivity are fraught with practical and also theoretical difficulties. The numbers being dealt with are so large and so uncertain that . . . no statement of the complete structure of the nervous system can ever be correct; by the time the statement is made, it will be out of date.
>
> (Gregory 1988: 542)

However, the possibility of understanding the structure and functioning of the brain is perhaps not quite so remote and improbable as this summation would imply. Researchers have reached a fairly advanced understanding of how comparatively simple neural circuits work in invertebrate animals such as the sea slug, *Aplysia californica*. They have also made great advances in studying the connection patterns which underlie some of the simpler reflex actions of vertebrates, and in the arrangement of brain cells into maps of the sensory information received from the eyes, the ears and the skin. The functioning of the brain is known to be dependent on its structure; switching nerve pathways leads to predictable changes in reflexes, stimulation of particular parts of the brain leads to particular specific sensations or hallucinations, and surgical lesions to the brain or damage to it, as from accidents or strokes, lead to changes in functioning which vary according to the area damaged. Structure is also dependent on functioning, as my later discussion of brain development in the next section emphasises. There are closely similar and very orderly patterns of neural connections from one part of the nervous system to another, so that even if individual neurones differ a little they are of the same class overall. The details of the circuits are, as we will see, the result of normal stimulation and functioning of the growing system during development. Abnormal stimulation will produce major changes in the connection pattern and consequently in how it functions.

So far we have talked about neurones and patterns of neurones without considering the anatomy of the brain. Figures 5.2 and 5.3 show its structure. It is essentially an enlargement of the head end of the spinal cord. Moving

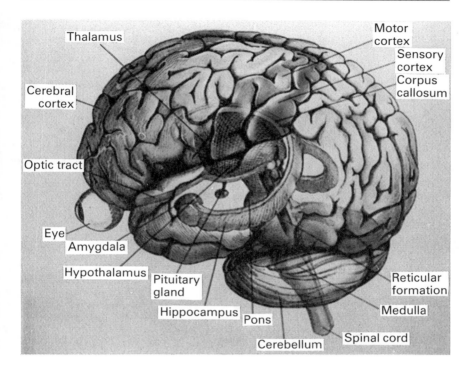

*Figure 5.2* The anatomy of the brain (1): schematic drawing showing the left cerebral hemisphere and the limbic system.
*Source*: Bloom, Lazerson and Hofstadter 1985

up from the spinal cord we find the hindbrain, the medulla oblongata and the pons. The cerebellum develops outwards and backwards from the hindbrain, the midbrain lies immediately above and in front of it, and the cerebral hemispheres lie around and above all the rest. The left and right cerebral hemispheres are the familar grey convoluted structures which we all think of as 'brains'; they are divided into the frontal lobes, which lie behind the forehead, the temporal lobes (behind the temples), the parietal lobes (top back of the head), and the occipital lobes (back of the head). They are basically a sheet of nerve cells crumpled up so that a large area fits into the comparatively small volume of the skull. The nerve cells over much of this area are arranged in columns with six layers; vast numbers of nerve fibres run into and out of them and there are millions of connecting 'interneurons'. There are comparatively few types of cells; the cerebral cortex is built up of very many instances of a small number of basic elements. Connections run into the cerebral cortex from the sensory receptors and the lower parts of the brain, and between the two hemispheres, and between different areas of each hemisphere, and to the midbrain, cerebellum and brain stem.

*Figure 5.3* The anatomy of the brain (2): schematic drawing showing the internal structures of the brain.
*Source:* Bloom, Lazerson and Hofstadter 1985

Normally the left cerebral hemisphere is the leading partner in many cognitive activities. It dominates in speech, in language comprehension and in right hand learned skills such as writing and sewing; it controls the right hand side of the body. The right hemisphere, associated with the left hand side of the body, is better at shape perception and hearing non-verbal sounds. However, normally the two hemispheres work together, and neither monopolises any cognitive activity. They are linked by a thick bundle of nerve fibres known as the corpus callosum, and through the brain stem lower in the central nervous system. The two hemispheres can be induced to show evidence of their different 'preferred' capacities in patients where the corpus callosum has been cut (as a treatment for severe and persistent epilepsy), but normally information about the world is constantly reflected to all parts of the brain.

The world provides us with a massive amount of stimulation. The brain can select amongst this input, emphasising one sort and playing down another. Some of these selective biases are 'wired in' prior to any experience, for example the human infant's selective attention to human voices, faces and smells, but we also learn to attend to or to ignore particular sorts of information. Stimulation of any sort which could become conscious goes to the thalamus, in the midbrain, and from there to the appropriate area of the cortex, where each sense has its own primary sensory area. Each primary sensory area in the cortex is surrounded by its secondary sensory area, and is connected to it by its nerve fibres. Each secondary sensory area is connectioned with the corresponding secondary sensory area of the other cerebral hemisphere, with all the other secondary sensory areas in its own cerebral hemisphere, and with the association areas, where various kinds of sensory information are elaborated and integrated into a meaningful whole. The different association areas are interconnected and connected to the motor areas, which themselves have connections from the thalamus and from other parts of the cerebral cortex.

Thus there are areas of the cortex specialised for vision (in the occipital lobe), for hearing and for smelling (in the temporal lobe and pyriform cortex), for touch (in the convolution or postcentral gyrus which runs, roughly, from ear to ear), and so forth. In these areas there are orderly 'maps' of incoming stimulation, for example several maps of the retina in the visual cortex. These preserve information about the spatial pattern of visual stimulation. The different maps tend to be concerned with different aspects of the stimulation, for example one may deal with its orientation, another with its colour or movement. Activity in these maps has to be precisely co-ordinated, but organising perception into separate units allows comparatively economical neural networks to function efficiently. Localised processing of a simple characteristic of stimulation such as size or colour is co-ordinated with other processing as required by the task at hand, so that it is widespread cortical activity which makes up complex cognition, even if simple cognition could be said to be localised.

The hypothalamus is a small area in the midbrain under the thalamus. It organises body metabolism and controls body temperature, the states of being awake or asleep and of being aggressive, afraid, and sexually aroused. But the cerebral hemispheres may also be involved in these feelings, assessing their meaning and deciding on a programme of behaviour which may involve modification of stereotyped automatic responses organised in the hypothalamus. Body temperature may be kept constant, for example, by responses such as sweating in which the hypothalamus is the crucial organiser, or by a cerebrally-mediated response such as getting up to turn the air conditioner on. Areas of the temporal lobes and a number of other areas including the hypothalamus seem to be involved in emotional states and behaviour, with hormones in the local blood supply being particularly important. The whole of the brain is supplied with blood, which provides it with oxygen, glucose, hormones and other necessary substances. The brain controls the secretion of hormones by the endocrine glands, and is itself subject to the action of these hormones. What we usually think of as 'emotion' and what we usually think of as 'cognition' are not completely separate brain functions.

Although I have been emphasising the interco-nnectedness of brain structure and of brain functioning, it is probably helpful to an initial understanding of the brain to indicate a few of the localised functions of the brain. The various kinds of cognitive activity discussed in this book are centred in the cerebral hemispheres. Spatial thinking depends on an area in the right hemisphere between the temporal, parietal and occipital lobes; mathematical thinking on approximately the same area in the left hemisphere. Articulating speech and hearing speech depend on areas in and around the left temporal lobe, and language comprehension and verbal memory on the left parietal lobe. The visual cortex is in the occipital lobe at the back of the head. Social behaviour and mood involve the frontal lobes and the regions around the thalamus and hypothalamus. Damage in one of these areas is likely to impair the relevant type of functioning, but so many areas are involved in cognitive tasks of any complexity – doing arithmetic, for example, involves seeing or hearing numbers, memory, reasoning, verbal comprehension, computation, eye movements, either articulation for a verbal answer or the hand arm, etc., movements of writing, and quite conceivably emotions of anxiety, complacency, triumph or despair – that any brain damage may have some effect on many tasks, and it will take very widespread brain damage to wipe out any function completely. We learn a great deal from studying brain damage, but inferences to normal functioning are not unproblematic (Mayes 1988, Shallice 1989; for an introduction see Eysenck and Keane 1990).

## Brain development and cognitive development

Knowledge of how the brain develops has developed at an accelerating pace over the last century (for reviews of more recent research see Greenough and Juraska 1986, Gregory 1988, Gunnar and Nelson 1992). Until quite recently it was supposed that the brain had a set of innately wired pathways, which were modified to a relatively small extent by experience, probably by the history of use and disuse of nerve cell connections. Learning, through the establishment of simple conditions reflexes, added all the elaboration of cognition to the pre-set biology of the brain. This passive associative model fails because it both underestimates the interco-ordinations between nerve cells and fails to account for what is now known about their developmental history.

The neurones which integrate nerve impulses from different parts of the nervous system develop patterns of connections and of activity even in the earliest months, before birth. They transmit substances which play a key role in the regulation of nerve cell growth and differentiation throughout the developing brain (and can play something of the same role if implanted into adult brains which have been damaged). By the time the embryo is 8 weeks old, and the cells which will develop into the neocortex appear, the lower parts of the brain have already developed an elaborate structure on which further growth is based. The embryo nerve cells interact with each other's genetically controlled messages, with the hormones and growth substances produced by cells, with nerve impulses conducted through the network of nerve connections, and with input from the wider environment provided by the mother's body. Though to begin with nerve cell interactions are generated by activity intrinsic to the brain, it is the timing and patterning of external stimulation which determines the precise detail of neural networks, editing, sorting and pruning connections. After birth, babies can be seen to be eagerly attentive to visual stimulation, contrasts of light against dark, for example, holding their gaze as they scan repeatedly over the contrast contour (Aslin and Smith 1988, Banks and Salapatek 1983, Tees 1986). New stimulation gives the unfinished neuronal circuits further grounds for the selection of functional nerve connections, and rapid changes in the structure of the brain occur in the first six months of life. For example (Trevarthen 1988a), the corpus callosum which connects the two cerebral hemispheres has about $10^{10}$ nerve fibres in it at birth, but a large proportion is eliminated in early infancy so that connections within each hemisphere are separated from between-hemisphere connections, and within-hemisphere connections are made more precise and effective (Kinsbourne and Hiscock 1983). This creates the basis for detailed perception, elaborated representation and refined cognitive programmes which enable mastery of experience. Development such as this goes on throughout childhood (and perhaps throughout life), with continuity between the early mechanisms of brain growth and the later mechanisms of learning from experience, with brain tissue continuing to be self-organising. Different areas of the brain reach maturity at different ages, so that a particular task may be associated with one area of the brain early in life, and later in development other areas may be implicated in its exercise (Goldman-Rakic 1987, Greenough and Black 1992).

Prenatal development leads to a brain at birth which has as many nerve cells as the adult's and all the typical adult parts. What it does not have is all the immensely intricate network of intercellular connections, the $10^{15}$ synapses between dendrites and nerve cells which allow for the complexity of adult cognition. Some of these connections form prenatally under developmental programmes more or less independent of external stimuli (though of course the foetus does receive some stimulation when *in utero*), but increasingly the connections between nerve cells are set up in association with stimulation which is actively sought and used. Throughout development there is either a selection amongst existing connections or an overproduction followed by selective elimination (during infancy, for example, the density of synapses is *greater* than later in development). Both genetic coding of biochemical processes and the experience of different patterns of electrical and chemical activity contribute to the formation of differentiated networks. Increasingly stimulation from outside the brain shapes these networks, and is necessary for sorting out precise sensory (and no doubt cognitive) systems. Connections not only proliferate, a large proportion of them die, so what is left is more specific and effective. Lack of patterned visual stimulation, for example, or a distorted pattern such as experience restricted to vertical lines only, leads to permanent deficits in the visual system if suffered at the time when the interconnections of nerve cells are developed (Banks and Salapatek 1983, Singer 1986, Tees 1986). Binocular stereoptic perception of depth, for example, requires both coincidence of stimulus patterns received from the two eyes and inputs from the reticular formation in the brain stem, thus controlled movements of the eyes in precise union are necessary. Both maturation and experience are necessary for such developments.

Some parts of the brain mature more rapidly than others. The cerebral cortex is a comparatively late developer. Its nerve cells are not distributed in the fully adult pattern until six months after birth, and dendritie connections not fully mature until adolescence. Many of its features, including a degree of left–right asymmetry and possible lateralisation from this, have developed before birth (Molfese and Segalowitz 1988), but some psychological functions have to be carried out in 'stop gap' ways prior to the maturation of the brain part which serves this function in the adult brain. There are however many 'pre-adaptations', where brain structures seem to be in readiness for action before they are needed (for example, specialisation of left hemisphere areas involved in language four months before birth). Another important area of postnatal brain development is the growth of an insulating sheath of myelin around nerve fibres, a process which continues throughout infancy and childhood. Myelinisation leads to faster and more efficient conduction of nerve impulses, and this may contribute to more precise and streamlined cognition.

## How the brain learns and remembers

All stimulation of the intact nervous system goes to the cerebellum, the brain stem and the limbic centres, the parts of the brain which organise balance, arousal, emotion and other vital functions. The cerebral cortex receives input via the thalamus. As I said earlier, each primary sensory area of the cortex is connected to its surrounding secondary sensory area. Each secondary area is connected with the corresponding area in the other hemisphere, with all the other secondary sensory areas in the same hemisphere, and with the association areas, which as their name implies are concerned with connecting the various kinds of input to make a coherent system. The various association areas are interconnected and connected to the motor areas. These multiple connections are laid down during development and elaborated by endogenous changes in the brain and by experience. A brain system does not work in isolation, even before the developing brain has fine-tuned its interconnections by its experience.

It is worth noting that some parts of the brain are specialised for social behaviour. Parts of the frontal lobes, again comparatively late in their maturation, are involved in attention to the feelings and behaviour of other people. They are linked to areas of the brain concerned with emotion, and are the areas which were lesioned in radical leucotomies and were lost in the famous case of Phineas Gage who had a crowbar accidentally blown through his frontal lobes. He lost what the doctors called 'the balance, or equilibrium, so to speak, between his intellectual faculties and animal propensities', becoming obstinate and capricious, not deferring to other people's needs or advice. Leucotomised patients similarly were insensible of the effects of their behaviour on other people, as if the effects of social conditioning had been lost. The nervous system develops in a social context and under the influence of a genetic endowment which allows individuals to function as members of a social group. As Trevarthen (1988a: 108) neatly says:

> the state of morphogenetic regulators in an immature organism depends upon the affections and interests of more mature conscious beings, and upon the way the brains of these beings from the preceding generation have been programmed with cultural rituals and beliefs in an earlier childhood. Growing human brains require cultivation by intimate communication with older human brains.

A total understanding of the brain and its cognition must allow for this fact: models such as are used in artificial intelligence are deficient insofar as they do not do so.

*Memory*

In Chapters 2 and 4 of this book I discussed some of the psychological models of learning and remembering and their development. These models were, on the whole, descriptions of people's behaviour, not of the 'mechanics' of memory. Here I am concerned with some recent neuroscience studies of what happens in an individual nerve cell or a system of such cells when an organism learns, remembers and forgets.

All animals contain a complex memory record in their DNA, a memory which guides their development within the environments they encounter without, so far as we know, being itself modified by those encounters. This DNA-based memory has the content it does because it has enabled the animal's ancestors to behave in ways which allowed their reproductive survival, ways which are therefore likely to be adequate in future environments not too drastically different from the ancestral ones. Virtually all animals are also capable of at least elementary forms of learning, of a behavioural plasticity which means they can react more effectively to the details of the situation that arise, adapting their remembered programme of action to what is demanded of them on each occasion. This learning probably involves changes in the connections between nerve cells such that useful pathways are selected from the earlier multiplicity of pathways. It is likely that there are short-lived changes in the electrical properties of the neurones which correspond with the changes in behaviour known as the short-term memory-system (STM) or working memory. Long-term memory probably involves much more permanent modifications in synapses and nerve cell circuits, including changes in how many synapses there are and in the biochemistry of the neurotransmitters involved in the network. Obviously it is hard to study exactly what is happening in human brains, but similar forms of elementary learning and memory are found across a wide span of the phylogenetic scale. Many recent investigations of the basic cellular changes during learning have therefore used invertebrate animals which have simple nervous systems and, often, large nerve cells, and are consequently easy to study.

Eric Kandel and his colleagues have worked on learning in *Aplysia californica*, a marine mollusc also known as the sea slug, sea snail or sea hare. This animal would not be beautiful to those of us who are repelled by the idea of a slug up to one metre long and one kilogram in weight, even if found in distant seas and laboratories, not in our own back gardens; but it is capable of habituation, sensitisation and even classical conditioning, and as it has only a few neurones and these are of enormous size researchers have found it possible to map connections between cells and establish what electrical and chemical changes are occurring during learning. It appears (Bailey and Kandel 1985, Teyler and Fountain 1987) that habituation and sensitisation, and probably classical conditioning, result from alterations in how excitable nerve cells are and in connections between synapses, particularly through alterations in the strength of already existing connections by modulations in how much chemical neurotransmitter is released. In the case of habituation and sensitisation of *Aplysia*'s gill-withdrawal reflex, these changes happen at the presynaptic connection of the sensory neurone on to the motor neurones. Development determines the presence of contacts between sensory and motor neurones, but not the strength of the connections. Short-term memory in habituation involves a transient depression in synaptic efficiency, long-term memory (lasting for days and week) a functional inactivation of previously existing connections, so that habituated animals have fewer active zones with less transmitter released at each. Similarly, sensitised and conditioned animals have enhanced synaptic transmission between sensory neurone and motor neurone, with more zones active, each of which is bigger and emits more neurotransmitter. The chemistry of learning in *Aplysia* involves a complex sequence of six or so chemicals, including the amount of calcium ions available, resulting in more neurotransmitter flowing in the case of sensitisation and less in the case of habituation. As a long-term change this may possibly include an alteration in how the genetic material can express itself and the subsequent synthesis of chemicals. Similar changes involving selective changes in the efficacy of synaptic connections (long-term potentiation or LTP) seem to occur during the learning processes of other animals, such as the fruit fly, *Drosophila*, the octopus, and the rat, and to last for long periods relative to the length of the life of the animal; it seems at least possible that they occur in the much more complex brains of humans and other mammals.

The success of neuroscience studies in demonstrating synaptic changes has been considerable. There has not so far been as much progress in the extremely complex task of specifying how changes in different neural pathways become related, as they must do if we can call up the same piece of information to different questions, or if we integrate information from different sources, or if we generalise from one piece of learning to a more universal principle. There is no one particular area in the brain which is the memory store. Although parts of the neocortex are probably involved in the storage of the results of complex learning, and the hippocampus may be involved in memory integration, it may be that memories are stored in the parts of the brain which mediate the perceptions on which these memories are based. There might be multiple memory systems in both working memory and long term memory, cf. Rumelhart's Parallel Distributed Processing (Rumelhart and McClelland 1986). Such a multiple system might well show the little unevennesses that we may be aware of in ourselves, our good memory for faces and our poor memory for names for example. Similarly declarative memory and procedural memory may operate and be stored somewhat differently. Amnesia (Mayes 1988, Shallice 1989) varies in its effects (as the site of the brain damage causing it also varies) but if the lesions are in the medial temporal region, particularly in the hippocampus, the patients are likely to have a normal short-term memory and to be able to recall a normal amount of information learned long ago, but to have difficulty when required to learn new information or to recall events which occurred at the time just before the amnesia began. Declarative memory is much more affected than procedural memory. Squire (1987) suggests that the crucial areas are necessary for the acquisition and consolidation of declarative memories, in interaction with the cortical association areas where these memory representations are finally stored. Developmentally, declarative memory seems to be a later accomplishment than procedural memory (Bachevalier 1992, Bachevalier and Mishkin 1984, Squire 1987), which might account for infantile amnesia, the unavailability of memories dating from the first year or two of infancy to the older child or adult (Morton 1990, and see Chapter 2, section on infantile amnesia).

*Learning from experience*

There may be interesting analogies to be drawn between learning and the natural selection which occurs during, for example, evolution, and in the working of the body's immune system. If the nervous system does learn and remember by the selection of nerve connections and responses which are useful, and the elimination of those which are not, under the influence of experience, we would expect it to have certain features. Those parts of it concerned in learning should contain a very large number of cells and interconnections, all slightly different; and this is indeed the case. The parts of the human brain most associated with learning, such as the cortex, the hippocampus and the cerebellum have millions of cells, each of which may receive thousands of synapses; regions such as the hypothalamus, which regulates all sorts of basic physical functions according to innate pro- grammes which work so well normally that they do not need to be modified by learning (though they may be supplemented by a learned system in the cortex, as in the case of body temperature, mentioned elsewhere in this chapter), have relatively few cells. Cortical cells vary a great deal, too, in what they respond to. In the visual cortex, for example, the young kitten or monkey has cells which innately are most responsive to a particular contour or orientation but which also respond, to begin with, to other similar stimulation. With visual experience these cells become more sharply tuned and reliable; if the animal's experience is artificially limited, for example by it only being allowed to see an environment of vertical stripes, only those cells which are innately programmed to respond to vertical and near-vertical contours will mature, and those with other orientations will cease to be excitable (Banks and Salapatek 1983, Changeux 1987, Greenough and Black 1992). There seems to be selection by competition, as in this case, and by co-operation, as when simultaneous input from both eyes is necessary for the development of binocular vision cells in the kitten. Young (1987) calls this 'associative synaptogenesis'; it is important because it allows for the development of patterns of cells which record the regular combinations of events that occur in the world, and hence better representations of its regularities, and perhaps its 'affordances' (Gibson 1979).

Greenough, Black and Wallace (1987) suggest that this learning by selection occurs as an 'experience-expectant' developmental process. The process utilises the sort of environmental information which has been ubiquitous throughout the evolution of the species (Gottlieb 1991, Greenough 1991), and can be relied upon to occur in any individual's experience (unless that individual, like the laboratory kittens mentioned above, has encountered a most unusual seriously distorted environment). Neural mechanisms have evolved which, expecting this normal environmental information, use the input to shape the specifics of neural development. One important mechanism is the innate generation of an enormous number of synaptic connections between neurones, with selection based on experience determining which connections are strengthened and which, so to speak, wither away. The timing of the experience may be crucial. There is much evidence of 'sensitive periods', for example in the visual system (Banks and Salapatek 1983, Greenough and Black 1992, Movshon and Van Sluyters 1981), during which experience has a profound and permanent effect on the development of the system; the same experience or deficit in experience at a different time may have little or no effect. The 'effects' of abnormal experience such as sensory restriction can include impaired behaviour, abnormal neurophysiological development, and less complex morphological development: the degree to which recovery is possible is almost certainly slight at best, though animals such as humans may devise other means of coping with their handicap.

It may seem odd that the evolutionary process has left development dependent on receiving the right sorts of experience at the crucial moment, rather than 'wiring it in'. However, having the genes programme a general outline of what the system should be like, and then taking advantage of expectable experience to get the system finely tuned to environmental details which actually occur, allows for a highly ordered and appropriate pattern to emerge from a much less organised one. Sensory systems seem to start with a strong predisposition to function in a particular way, and if experience is near enough to normal they will do so; while if experience is too far from normal the system will function in an unusual way, usually less effectively, but there may be some compensatory changes in other systems. Myopic children, for example, with less good distance vision, may not find it easy to be expert bird spotters or squash players but are often extremely good at nearsighted or tactile tasks such as reading or needlework (Tees 1986).

Individuals may perhaps differ in various ways, for example the amount of relevant experience they 'expect' or need for adequate functioning, their resistance to adverse experience and their compensation for it, or their ability to produce suitable experience, perhaps through social interaction. We do not yet have much in the way of neuroscience investigations of individual differences, apart from some very interesting clinical studies; but behavioural studies of, for example, temperament and stress and the child's ecology are suggesting differential vulnerability and strength which may have a biological base (e.g. Garmezy and Rutter 1985, Rutter, 1988, 1992).

As well as the experience that can be reasonably expected to occur regularly at a particular period in virtually everybody's life, so that 'experience-expectant' learning processes can be set to use it in 'fine-tuning' nerve systems, there are many environmental events which are less consistent in their occurrence or timing, perhaps even being unique to only one individual. Brains need to be able to respond to these sorts of experience too. Animals who interact with a miscellany of objects in a complex environment have been shown to do better at a range of cognitive tasks than those reared in the dull, indeed sensorily deprived, cages of the typical laboratory animal (Greenough and Black 1992, Greenough, Black and Wallace 1987); comparisons of the brains of rats reared in standard and more complex environments show that the latter probably have more synaptic connections, particularly in the visual cortex but probably also in other cortical and sub-cortical regions. Active interaction with an interesting environment can increase synapse numbers in adult rats (including 'middle-aged' ones) as well as in the developing young, and the experience of being trained on tasks such as maze-running probably also brings about specific morphological changes in the brain. It seems to be possible for experience to give rise to synapse development even at quite late ages, perhaps by synapses being formed quite rapidly as a result of neuronal activity and surviving in so far as they fit the appropriate pattern of connections (Greenough 1984): a case perhaps of exercise acting on the brain just as it would on the rest of the body. We do not know yet whether these late-formed synapses are the same or are formed in the same way as those which appear early in development. Early development seems to produce a surplus of synapses which are then pruned back by experience to a useful subset. Later in life synapses seem to be generated in response to experience which provides important information, probably in a more localised way but again involving selective preservation of part of a relatively unpatterned growth. Here it is not at all clear that there are 'sensitive periods' during which learning is easier, and while there are spurts in the generation of nerve cells and connections between them in particular areas, Greenough and his colleagues think it improbable that such spurts are synchronous over the brain as a whole (Greenough, Black and Wallace 1987: 552–3). Understanding how brain growth proceeds is important as a corrective to simplistic models of cognitive growth. Epstein (1974a, 1974b, 1990), for example, proposed that there were periods of sudden overall increase in brain size, which were associated with the 'sudden' changes between Piagetian stages. His data showed spurts in head circumference at particular ages, and he inferred from these changes in head size that there were spurts in brain size which matched Piagetian spurts in cognition. His 'phrenoblysis' hypothesis looks weak however, because it is unlikely that the brain grows in spurts, because it is unlikely that there are sudden and general transitions between cognitive stages, because it is unlikely that head circumference is a good measure of brain size or brain size of cognitive power, and finally because other researchers have failed to find Epstein's pattern of size changes anyhow (e.g. Hudspeth and Pribram 1990, McCall 1990, McCall *et al.* 1983). 'Phrenoblysis' has had its brief and inglorious day, but other theories of the same type continue to emerge. For example Lynn (1989) argues away the 20 point rise in average IQ over the last thirty years by invoking increase in height and head size over the same period (dubious in Western Europe and North America) and the correlation of 0.21 between head size and IQ scores (such a correlation would account for 5 per cent of the variance). Attempts to explain away the IQ rise as due to fewer forceps deliveries would seem to be equally dubious.

An asynchronous relationship of brain areas, that is, a staggering of the developmental schedule for different functions, would allow one system to act as a foundation for another, for example early visual and motor skills could act as the foundations for later understanding of spatial relations, the activity of the organism in acquiring and organising experience being of the greatest importance. It could also allow for some 'catch-up' growth rectifying earlier disadvantage. This sort of development would involve subtle variations between individuals who had slightly varying experience; it is what Gottlieb (1983, 1991) calls 'probabilistic epigenesis' rather than completely predetermined genetic blueprinting.

Psychologists studying people's remembering behaviour have found it useful to distinguish between different sorts of memory, for example 'episodic' and 'semantic' memory, or 'long-term memory' and 'working memory' (see Chapter 2 this volume, and Squire (1987)). Teyler and Fountain (1987) survey some of the evidence on whether different sorts of memory have different locales in the brain or depend on different neurophysiological processes. The hippocampus seems to be crucial for response timing and working memory. The famous patient H. M., whose hippocampus was removed with the rest of his temporal lobes in an attempt to cure his epileptic fits, lost his ability to remember what had happened only a few minutes before and thus much of his ability to retain newly learned information (Mayes, 1988, Shallice 1989). It is also thought to be important in the remembering of temporal and spatial relations between events and objects, needed in building up a 'cognitive map' of the environment (O'Keefe and Nadel 1978, Teyler and Fountain 1987, Young 1987). Exactly how this is done is not clear at present. Young (1987) emphasises how relations in time and space between thousands of individual nerve cells form complex representations of useful information in time and space, organised both in terms of associated facts and in terms of useful programmes for action. Some patients suffering from amnesia have impaired memory for facts ('declarative' information) while their procedural memory for skills using those same facts is, relatively, preserved. Remembering how to act through a sequence of behaviour but not how to describe or reflect on or to vary it significantly has been seen as the sort of capacity for representation young infants have (Bachevalier 1992, cf. Bruner's 'enactive' representation, Bruner 1966). It may mean that it is possible to operate within a limited familiar world but not to retrieve information voluntarily into consciousness, nor to maintain a consciously accessible personal memory (Goodman and Haith 1987). Similar discrepancies can be induced in rats by disruption of hippocampal function (Teyler and Fountain 1987), procedural memory being very much harder to disrupt. Exposure to lead pollution seems to have an adverse effect on hippocampal development which might partially account for the impairments of learning and memory found in children with high blood lead levels (see below, section on lead pollution and cognitive development). Exposure to carbon monoxide (for example from parents who smoke heavily) and to other pollutants (Jacobson *et al.* 1984, 1992) may have similar adverse effects.

If we summarise what recent neuroscience studies are suggesting to us about how the brain learns and remembers, it seems to be emerging that such processes depend on the possibility of alterations of the connections between neurones, alterations in their sensitivity, efficacy, number, mapping of interconnections, etc.; and that such alterations, both temporary and permanent, occur throughout life. A number of brain centres operate together as a complex system, so that signals from the outside world and signals from other parts of the body indicate whether (and in what way) an action has been rewarding, and so should be learned and repeated, or not. Advantageous programmes are more likely to be repeatedly used and smoothly learned and remembered; less rewarding ones tend to fall out of use. The patterns of connections which are set up by a combination of inheritance of general structures and tendencies and fine-tuning of specifics through environmental experience represent the organism's knowledge of the environment, to some degree as a topographical and time-based map, but more generally as a representation which produces the behaviour appropriate to the environmental situation and the organism's evolutionary goals. Memory and learning can be facilitated or upset by stimulation, lesions, drugs, or toxins. Normally they operate as a united system comprising the knowledge and life patterns of the individual. In these brain workings lies the subjective unity of his or her mind and personality.

# GENES AND THE PHYSICAL ENVIRONMENT IN COGNITIVE DEVELOPMENT

My discussion of brain development focused on the complex and inescapable interaction of intrinsic and extrinsic factors in cognitive development, on genetic and environmental effects. We know with certainty that development in general is dependent on both genes and environment; we are beginning to know about how differences in either lead to differences in development. I will present here, briefly, a few comparatively well-studied areas of work on the role of genes and the physical environment in cognitive development. Discussion of the social environment follows this section.

## Genetic anomalies and cognitive development

I discussed the literature on the heritability of intelligence earlier in this book (Chapter 3). There I described models of what psychological differences constitute differences in the intelligence of genetically normal people, and what pattern of resemblance there appears to be between family members, biological or adopted. My concern here is first to note what sort of *genetic* model is likely to be useful in describing cognitive behaviour, and second to look briefly at some genetic anomalies and their effects on cognitive development.

As McHugh and McKusick (1991), Plomin (1986, 1991) and Scarr and Kidd (1983) describe, most human behavioural traits show multifactorial inheritance, that is, their transmission depends on more than one of a number of genetic and environmental factors. The expression of a gene depends on the environment of development: the effect of environmental factors may differ for genetically different individuals, so that there is gene–environment interaction. Environmental factors may be correlated with genotypic ones; a single gene locus (or environmental incident) may be critical for a trait, but its effect may be modified by other gene loci (or environmental factors) which interact with the critical gene (or event); many genes (or many environmental factors) may combine in an additive way to produce a trait. Sophisticated techniques will be necessary to sort out which of these complex patterns of inheritance best describes the relationship between genotype and phenotype for a particular trait. The task is given a further dimension of difficulty by the extensive time that development takes. The individual's genes code for functioning over time, indeed over the whole life-span to the extremes of old age, including regulation of development, maturing and ageing; 'genetic timing' and 'environmental timing' will fit together in very complicated ways which have profound effects on behaviour, with the influence of genes possibly *increasing* over time (McCartney et al. 1990, Plomin and Rende 1991). The literature on sensitive periods in perceptual development, for example, shows that the same environmental deficit will have a marked effect at one period in an animal's life and little or no noticeable effect at earlier or later periods (e.g. Aslin *et al.* 1983, Aslin and Smith 1988, Gottlieb 1992, Greenough 1991). There may be similar developmental differences in emotional development (for example in attachment, Rutter 1981) and, conceivably, in cognition. In other words, it is inappropriate to say that someone is intelligent or has a good memory or a particularly high degree of artistic ability because he or she has 'the right gene'. Variation within the normal range of cognitive traits may begin with variation in genes, but several genes will be involved and they will have operated in a delicate and intricate pattern of interaction with other genes and environmental factors over a long pathway of development, with the environment and the whole life history contributing to the eventual cognitive ability, just as the genes do (Aldhous 1992, Cardon *et al.* 1992, Rutter 1992).

It may be helpful here to point out that recent advances in medical genetics are revealing more complex patterns of inheritance than Mendelian genetics allows. Mendel's brilliant work was done on an organism, the garden pea, which behaves genetically as he insightfully described: it has two sets of chromosomes with paired instructions for development (it is 'diploid'), which lead to various 'all-or-none' traits (or 'phenotypes') such as pod shape or pea colour, whichever parent the particular gene comes from, with little or no variability between individuals. Things are not quite so simple as this in human beings. For example, the same gene may lead to different phenotypes in different individuals. The condition known as Von Recklinghausen NF 1 involves an abnormal gene on chromosome 17 (17q11.2) (Pyeritz 1991) and most people affected by it have abnormal pigmentation and benign tumours, some but not all have other tumours, skeletal defects, and mental retardation and learning disabilities; it is not yet clear how these effects are produced and why they vary so much between individuals. It has recently also become known (Hoffman 1991, Pyeritz 1991) that genetic information inherited from the mother may be expressed differently from the same information inherited from the father, which violates one of Mendel's laws. This phenomenon is known as 'genetic imprinting'. For example, deletion of part of chromosome 15 (the fairly large segment 15q11–13) leads on to two different syndromes of mental retardation, Prader-Willi Syndrome (which includes being obese and slow-moving) and Angelman Syndrome (which includes hyperactivity). People who inherited the defective chromosome from their mothers show Angelman Syndrome; people with Prader-Willi Syndrome seem mostly to have inherited the defective chromosome from their fathers. In another sort of genetic imprinting, people who inherit Huntington's Disease from their fathers tend to develop it earlier in life than people who inherit it from their mothers. It is not yet clear how genetic imprinting works, though the processes of gene regulation in development seem to be involved.

Finally, the traditional picture of all or none inheritance and 'dominant' and 'recessive' genes needs to be modified. In Mendel's peas, plants which had a +/– combination were the same as those with a –/– pair at the given locus: the – gene determined a trait identically in the heterozygote +/– and the homozygote –/–. In humans, the same 'dominance' sometimes occurs; but more often careful examination shows that there are intermediate levels of change in phenotype. Sickle cell anaemia appears in people homozygous for the HbS gene; those with one HbS and one HbA gene were thought to be unaffected, indistinguishable from people who had HbA/HbA, so sickle cell anaemia was seen as a 'recessive' trait. More recently, people with HbS/HbA, though not anaemic, have been found to have an abnormal phenotype. Two HbS have different effects from one HbS, which differs in its effects from no HbS. It is now also known that the genetic material in the nucleus of the egg and the nucleus of the sperm is not the only genetic material which affects development. The cytoplasm around the nucleus of each cell contains DNA too, and this too is inherited by the developing foetus. Most of this material comes from the egg, as the sperm is too small to have much cytoplasm. Thus there is a possibility of 'maternal' or 'cytoplasmic' inheritance. Some rare cases of pathological development of the optic nerves arise in this way.

Even those genetic anomalies which are simple enough for us to have achieved an understanding of their effect on cognition show how behaviour is dependent on both the genotype and the environment. Phenylketonuria (PKU) is a well-known disease associated with an identified abnormal gene on chromosome 12 (Woo 1991). The defective gene leads to the absence of a particular enzyme, phenylalanine hydroxylase, which is needed to convert the phenylalanine from protein in the diet into tyrosine. In the absence of the enzyme, phenylalanine cannot be metabolised and used in the body, and cannot be got rid of. High concentrations of phenylalanine result in an excess of chemicals which are normally only present in minute quantities, but in the person with PKU they are present at toxic levels. They interfere with the development and growth of the central nervous system; the brain develops normally to birth, but once the baby starts a diet which contains phenylalanine in protein the developing nerve cells are vulnerable, and the connections between nerve cells begin to be damaged and broken down. Reduced brain development and irreversible mental retardation (with severe emotional and behavioural disturbance) result. Thus the genetic anomaly leads to marked anomalies in cognitive development.

However, it only does so in the normal environment, specifically if the PKU baby receives a normal diet. If a special dietary environment is provided during the period of brain development, if the infant is fed on a diet which does not contain phenylalanine, no such excess of deleterious chemicals is built up and the central nervous system can develop more or less normally. The genetic defect is still there, but it has no effect in the special environment where there is little or no phenylalanine. PKU individuals still cannot produce phenylalanine hydroxylase, but if they do not need it to deal with phenylalanine because their diet contains none, they avoid the most serious consequences of their abnormality. Diets which contain even small amounts of phenylalanine may produce brain damage and some cognitive impairment even in late childhood (Smith *et al.* 1990, 1991).

Once brain development is complete, the individual with PKU is not harmed by a normal diet, as the mature nervous system appears to be resistant to the high levels of toxic chemicals which accumulate. However, if a woman with PKU, whose own retardation has been prevented by a restricted diet during her infancy and childhood, takes an unrestricted diet containing phenylalanine during her pregnancy, the baby may be born with severe mental retardation resulting from excess phenylalanine, even though it has inherited the normal gene for phenylalanine hydroxylase from its father. The build-up of phenylalanine in the pregnant woman does not affect her own brain because her mature nervous system is relatively resistant to it, but it swamps the circulation of the developing foetus and causes abnormal neurological development *in utero*. The child's prenatal environment gives it PKU mental retardation, even though it does not itself have the genetic abnormality that leads to PKU (Konner 1982, Scarr and Kidd 1983).

Many other rare genetic defects are associated with mental retardation, through, for example, the errors of metabolism which they cause. Some commoner abnormalities also need to be mentioned here. There has been a very large amount of research (Yang-Feng 1991) on individuals who have inherited not 46 chromosomes but a greater or smaller amount of chromosomal material. Most surviving individuals with more or less than 46 chromosomes have either anomalous combinations of Xs and Ys, or an extra member for chromosome pair 21. One extra X or Y chromosome does not seem to have a marked consistent effect on cognitive development, and may go unnoticed. Having only one sex chromosome, an X (Turner's Syndrome), probably does lead to cognitive anomalies (McCauley *et al.* 1987, Rovet and Netley 1982). Turner's Syndrome women tend to do exceptionally poorly on tests of spatial thinking such as mental rotation tasks, and they may also do worse on tests such as the Wechsler items Arithmetic, Digit Span, Picture Completion and Object Assembly. Their verbal intelligence is normal. They appear fairly normal physically during childhood, though of short stature, but they do not produce hormones at the normal levels of adolescence and adulthood and are sterile. There could be a number of possible explanations for their poorer spatial ability. Rovet and Netley, and McCauley *et al.* suggest that their missing X chromosome leads to an acceleration in cell division rates, hence faster brain maturation with less lateralisation and less right hemisphere involvement in nonverbal cognitive abilities. Another possibility is a lack of androgenisation in childhood. S. M. Resnick *et al.* (1986) found that girls who had had elevated levels of androgens prenatally showed enhanced spatial ability when tested in their teens; they also engaged in more activities involving spatial manipulation, though this seemed to be a consequence of their high level of spatial ability, not a cause of it. Hines and Shipley (1984) found evidence of greater cerebral lateralisation in such girls.

Another X chromosome anomaly which leads to abnormal cognitive development, in this case mental retardation, has attracted a great deal of interest recently because advances in techniques for examining genetic material have led to identifying exactly what part of the chromosome is abnormal. Abnormality on band Xq27 leads to a distinctive phenotype: a degree of 'physical overgrowth' so that the males who suffer from this 'Fragile X Syndrome' are tall, have large heads, foreheads, noses and protruding ears, and, particularly, large testes. They are moderately mentally retarded, especially in their delayed speech development; there is some association with hyperactivity and autism, with repetitive behaviours such as handflapping and an aversion to eye contact with parents (Cohen *et al.* 1989, Loehlin *et al.* 1988, Turner and Jacobs 1983). 'Fragile X Syndrome' may be a comparatively common cause of mental retardation, and one reason why there is an excess of males who are mentally retarded (Plomin 1991).

The commonest genetic anomaly leading to mental retardation, indeed one of the commonest causes of moderate to profound mental retardation, is Down's Syndrome. Down's Syndrome (DS) individuals mostly have a third version of chromosome 21 because of an incorrect division of parental chromosomes during the formation of the egg. Occasionally the error occurs during the formation of the sperm or during the early development of the embryo. In the latter case, mosaicism, not all the cells may carry the defect, and the impairment of the individual will be dependent on the proportion of cells which have the extra chromosome (Coyle *et al.* 1991). Down's Syndrome is associated with maternal age, perhaps because the egg of an older mother having existed longer has had more time to be exposed to damaging environmental factors, or perhaps because of age-linked differences in her hormonal status, but it is becoming commoner in younger mothers, where it may be associated with use of oral contraceptives (Zaremba 1985). The chromosomal anomaly leads to a number of physical anomalies: the characteristic facial features, heart defects, increased susceptibility to infections, and other physical traits. There is also a high incidence of neurological disorders, for example brains which are smaller and lighter and have abnormal convolutions in several areas, a reduction in the total number and density of neurones, and abnormal patterns of dendrites connecting neurones. The central nervous system of Down's individuals who survive into mid-adulthood invariably develops the pathology characteristic of Alzheimer's Disease (Coyle *et al.* 1991, Loehlin *et al.* 1988), and there may be genetic links between the two syndromes (Zaremba 1985).

The cognitive abilities and educational achievements of Down's children vary considerably. Carr (1985) ventures the following points as a tentative summary, although there are considerable individual differences: virtually all Down's Syndrome individuals are handicapped to some degree, the majority being severely handicapped. There is progressive decline in IQ scores from near normal in the early months to lower scores in the school years (see also Carr 1988); the Down's Syndrome child seems to have particular difficulty in making progress from sensori-motor intelligence to verbal and conceptual intelligence, with perhaps less consistent test performance than a normal child. There are particular problems in auditory processing, memory and metacognition. The overall pattern of development proceeds through the same sequence as in cognitively normal children but there is less coherence between achievement in different domains and overall achievement falls further and further behind the normal level, particularly if the child is brought up in an institution. Morss (1985) sees this pattern of 'developmental delay' as reflecting poor learning style. Down's children seem to need more exposures to material before they learn spontaneously, and to lack cognitive strategies and transfer.

Down's Syndrome children often show marked language delay. This is associated with hearing difficulties (Davies 1985) and preceded by impairments in vocalisation, referential looking and intersubjective communication between infant and mother in the first year of life (Gunn 1985, Jones 1979). Mothers may have a harder time communicating with the Down's child because of the reduced eye contact, less synchronicity of action and less alternation of conversational turns that they achieve; mothers' input becomes correspondingly more directive and restricted. The Down's child's lesser linguistic competence provokes less stimulating language from the mother, and may thus contribute to further retardation of language and cognition. Their syntactic production tends to be simpler than normal, though semantic and pragmatic aspects of language may be more nearly normal for their chronological age.

Some recent studies of reading skills in Down's Syndrome children are summarised by Buckley (1985). Informal case studies and small surveys show a substantial number of Down's children learning to read independently and for pleasure (see also Carr 1988). Three intervention studies produced reading skills in advance of the children's mental ages, in some cases up to their chronological ages. Some children appeared to develop spoken language from reading, rather than the reverse, finding learning to deal with written language easier than dealing with spoken language. This reversal of the usual developmental order may be associated with some of Down's children's specific deficits: they commonly have hearing defects which would make hearing speech sounds difficult; they have short-term memory deficits for auditory information; they have articulatory difficulties; and they have difficulties linking auditory and vocal inputs and outputs. These deficits would cumulatively make learning spoken language difficult, in so far as phonological processes are involved; possibly Down's children are learning to read outside the phonological route from written word to meaning (see Chapter 2, section on reading). Buckley's own research (1985) shows them making semantic errors, such as 'closed' for 'shut', 'go to bed' for 'sleep', which would support this interpretation of their learning. However non-intervention-study measures of reading skills show less impressive achievements (Carr 1988).

I have only been able to give a brief summary of work on cognition in Down's Syndrome, and so have risked simplifying the picture of their deficits and achievements. I must stress that Down's individuals vary just as normal individuals do in their cognitive and personality characteristics: some are profoundly handicapped, some can cope with normal schooling and live comparatively independent lives as adults. However recent research (O'Connor 1987, Stern 1987) has begun to specify precisely the difficulties and deficits which are associated with the syndrome. The chromosomal abnormality causes sensory deficits (and probably central nervous system differences) which affect cognitive processes, but the effects of these on achievement involve interaction with environmental factors. Carr (1988) reports a longitudinal study of Down's children from 6 weeks to 21 years. Along with the usual profile of a decline in scores from infancy, she finds some consistent sub-group differences: girls score better than boys on both IQ tests and educational tests; home-raised children do better than those reared away from home, on verbal ability, reading-level and arithmetic tests, but not on IQ tests; and non-manual socio-economic status (SES) children do very significantly better than manual SES children on language and arithmetic tests, reading accuracy and reading level scores, and non-significantly better on reading comprehension despite their lack of superiority in IQ. Thus more advantaged backgrounds were producing more skilled children, skilled in advance of their level of general ability and to a degree which could be a source of real pride and pleasure to the children themselves. The 'resilience and courage' of parents was helping these children to satisfactory lives (Carr 1988: 429). It was also demonstrating again the complex intertwining of genetic and environmental influences in cognitive development: the wonderful devotion of these parents was making an enormous positive contribution to children whose genetic endowment was unpromising.

## Lead pollution and cognitive development

The physical development of the brain is subject to environmental influences as well as genetic ones. High dosages of certain substances, for example mercury and lead, are known to poison the nervous system. Some of the substances are, at a low level, common environmental pollutants. It may be the case that they cause brain damage even at low levels, particularly to the rapidly developing brains of children. Lead is one of the best known of these pollutants, and so there has been public concern about its effects, and steps have been taken to reduce environmental lead levels. It is used less in paints, cosmetics and the canning process than in earlier years, unleaded petrol is now available more freely and used by an increasing number of car drivers, and lead water pipes are no longer installed in domestic water systems, though many remain in older housing. However, lead remains a common potential danger to the developing brain, and children may ingest a considerable amount of lead from the air near roads with heavy traffic, from soft water supplied by lead pipes, from plants grown in contaminated soil, from painted objects which they lick or chew, and from dust licked off dirty fingers, dropped sweets and so forth. (An epidemiological study by Wilson *et al.* (1986) examined children's blood lead levels in the lead smelting town of Port Pirie, South Australia. There was a fairly high degree of pollution throughout the town, but the risk of having a high blood lead level was increased fourfold by having a household member working with lead at the smelter, sixfold by having flaking paint outside the house, threefold by being a nailbiter, fourfold by having dirty hands and fivefold by having dirty clothes, both these as rated by the child's teachers. Ambient lead dust ingested orally would seem to be the source here.) Which source is most important will obviously vary; there has been some, somewhat circumstantial, evidence that lead from petrol has been a major contributor (Rutter 1983b).

High levels of lead in the body (measured in the blood or the teeth) are associated with intellectual impairment, behaviour problems such as hyperactivity, and, at the highest levels, gross neuropathology. This is why infants who compulsively pick at and chew painted furnishings or other objects ('pica') are doing themselves no good at all. The severity of these effects is greatest at highest lead levels, and decreases as they decrease. The timing of lead ingestion may influence the behavioural effects, through different stages of neuromaturation perhaps (Shaheen 1984). It used to be thought that lead levels below 40 micrograms (mg) per 100 ml in the blood had no adverse effects. Different studies, and hence different reviews, came to different conclusions: Rutter (1983a) interpreted research to that date as showing a consistent small effect of low levels of lead on psychological functioning, Harvey (1984) preferred a verdict of 'not proven' as did Smith (1985). The inconsistent research results may be due to methodological differences, for example in the measurement of lead levels, in demographic characteristics of samples, in the definition of 'high' and 'low' lead levels used, and in statistical analyses. One important complication is that lead level and social disadvantage are correlated, so the associations between raised lead levels and cognitive deficits in children might be due to confounding social and environmental variables. The latter are hard to control and can only be partialled out in studies of large samples using sophisticated statistical techniques. Small samples and simple analyses could not reveal a small but real effect.

Three recent studies of school children have made considerable progress towards clarifying what effects lead at low levels may have on cognition. Silva et al. (1988) studied 579 11-year-olds in Dunedin, New Zealand, as part of the longitudinal Dunedin Multidisciplinary Health and Development Study. As well as giving blood samples, the children were assessed for IQ and reading, behaviour problems as seen by teachers and parents, and various background variables such as frequent changes of residence or of school, poor family relations or mental health and some characteristics of the mother. These variables made it possible to take social, environmental and background factors into account. The study showed that raised blood lead level was associated with a very small but statistically significant increase in children's behaviour problems, inattention and hyperactivity; though there was no effect on IQ scores, reading showed a small effect of blood lead level. Fulton et al. (1987), Thomson et al. (1989) and Raab et al. (1990) studied 501 children aged 6–9 living in central Edinburgh. Here there was a relationship between blood lead level and ability which was still significant after various social and environmental variables had been controlled for, with even comparatively low levels of blood lead having an effect. Again the Rutter scales were used to assess behaviour disorders in the children, and an interviewer collected data on the home background (these data included an ability test for one of the parents). Blood lead levels were significantly correlated with behaviour and hyperactivity even when confounding variables were taken into account. Again, the size of the correlation was not large; blood lead appeared to be having a small but statistically significant bad effect on ability, achievement and behaviour.

The third study I will mention (Fergusson et al. 1988a, 1988b, 1988c) measured lead level in teeth and measures of intelligence, cognitive ability and attention/activity level in a birth cohort of New Zealand children. Ninety-five per cent of the children born in the Christchurch region of New Zealand in 1977 gave one of their shed first 'milk' teeth to 'the Christchurch Child Development Study "Tooth Fairy" ', who sent them each a thank-you letter and 50 cents and assayed the lead level in each tooth. Dentine lead levels were highest for children from socially disadvantaged families, those who lived in old wooden houses (which might have been painted with paint containing lead), those who had lived for a protracted period on streets with high traffic density, and those who had engaged in pica. Children who were high on more than one of these variables tended to have proportionately higher lead levels. Socially disadvantaged children tended to have higher lead levels even if all these variables were taken into account. The authors speculate that these children may have had greater exposure to industrial lead through living in homes with manual workers, or that there may be systematic differences in diet and exposure to dirt (Fergusson *et al.* 1988a, and the study by Wilson *et al.* 1986 referred to earlier).

The Christchurch researchers then correlated dentine lead levels with cognitive and school achievements made when the children were 8 and 9, that is, shortly after they had shed and given up the assessed tooth. It was assumed that both tooth and cognitive scores reflected their accumulated exposure to environmental lead. Measures of parents' education, the family's socio-economic conditions, the child's perinatal and educational history, and of aspects of the home environment (including for how long the child was breastfed, the mother's smoking habits, and measures of mother–child interaction using the HOME Inventory) were correlated with test scores as co-variates for dentine lead levels, thus controlling for variation on these factors. As in other studies, lead level was associated with intelligence test scores but the association was reduced to statistical non-significance if the confounding social disadvantage measures were taken into account. Scores on school achievement tests remained significantly correlated with dentine lead. The lead-test correlations remained stable over the period of a year from age 8 to age 9. The researchers suggest that this poorer school performance comes about because even the comparatively low levels of exposures to lead in their sample may cause nervous system damage which leads to deficits in attention, which in turn impair long-term school achievement. Their third paper (Fergusson *et al.* 1988c) shows that dentine lead level is significantly associated with teachers' and mothers' ratings of inattentive and restless behaviour (using items from the Rutter scales). The correlations remained statistically significant when confounding variables were allowed for. It is, however, small. In all three papers, Fergusson *et al.* provide an exemplary tabulation and discussion of the strengths and weaknesses of their evidence; they thus provide conviction for their 'opinion that the weight of the evidence suggests the presence of a very small causal association by which increases in lead values are associated with increases in rates of inattentive/restless behaviour' (Fergusson *et al.* 1988c: 822). However, they point out that their data cannot rule out the possibility that the causation is in the opposite direction, that children who are for other reasons restless and inattentive may act in certain ways which increase the lead in their bodies: they might spend less time in the comparatively clean air of home with a good book and more time out on the streets and scrabbling in the dirt, for example. A study of neonatal blood lead levels (Bellinger 1987) suggests that this reverse causal path, though possible, does not destroy the case for lead causing damage. Samples of blood were taken from the umbilical cords of newborn babies, and lead levels from those samples were correlated with later scores on baby intelligence tests; the correlations were small but significant even when confounding variables were taken into account. The 'overactivity causing lead level' sequence presumably would not apply *in utero*. It has to be noted, however, both that some other studies (e.g. Ernhart *et al.* 1986) have found only non-significant results in neonatal assessment, and that other pollutants may have similar effects. For example Jacobson *et al.* (1984, 1992) found that children who had been exposed prenatally to a high level of polychlorinated biphenyls (PCBs) (because their mothers had eaten fish contaminated with PCBs during pregnancy) had worse scores on the Brazelton Neonatal Scales as neonates and more errors in short-term memory at the age of 4. Any period of neurological development may be vulnerable.

Thus it seems to be probable that even low level exposure to lead in the environment (and conceivably to other pollutants) is associated with a tendency to attention deficits, emotional reactivity and hyperactivity and to worse performance in school. The effects of lead interact with the effects of other socio-economic variables, probably being more severe for socially disadvantaged children than for middle class ones (Shaffer 1985). However the association is not strong: it only shows up in large samples which are carefully measured. Lead does not all by itself cause inattentiveness or educational retardation or delinquency or hyperactivity, but it does contribute to some such problems. Preventing lead poisoning, provided the substitutes for lead have fewer adverse effects, will have small but not insignificant benefits.

## Nutrition and cognitive development

It has been clear for at least a century that children who are underfed to a serious degree may grow up (if they survive) to do comparatively poorly in school and on more formal tests of cognitive development. This was obvious to reformers at the turn of the century such as Margaret McMillan, whose pioneering work in nursery education provided for the feeding (and washing) of the children's bodies as well as for the stimulation of their minds (Bradburn 1989). It was obvious to the officials of Boards of Education and Local Education Authorities, such as Sir Cyril Burt (Burt 1955). It is still obvious in the Third World, where half or more of the children in many countries suffer from some degree of malnutrition and around one child in twenty is severely malnourished (World Health Organisation statistics, Lozoff 1989). What is less obvious is precisely how this poorer performance comes about, and what interventions might reduce the disadvantage. A considerable amount of work has been done on the links between differences in nutrition and differences in cognitive development, but considerable controversy remains (Dobbing 1987). I will review here some of the research on the effects of severe malnutrition on intellectual performance, and, more briefly, some of the research on dietary effects within a population which is in general well or at least adequately fed. It will be seen that both areas involve complex questions and that many investigations have serious methodological difficulties.

*Malnutrition and cognitive development*

The classic hypothesis was that undernutrition during the vulnerability of a 'critical period' early in life would seriously distort the development of the brain, and, because the brain determines the character and intelligence of the person, would seriously distort his or her cognitive performance (Bedi 1987). The brains of children who die of starvation are lighter in weight, contain fewer cells and less total protein than normal (Smart 1987). The more detailed studies possible on laboratory animals show a wide range of effects of malnutrition, including smaller brain size, decreased numbers of neurones, glial cells, dendrites and synaptic connections, slower peripheral nerve conduction, slower electroencephalograph frequencies in sleep and waking states, and changes in the pattern of neurotransmitters and other brain chemicals (Bedi 1987, Lozoff 1989). Normal brain development involves the proliferation of brain cells and then a reduction in their number. Undernutrition while cells are being formed leads to a particularly reduced final number; later undernutrition affects the growth and myelinisation of nerve fibres, while the growth and development of the body in general is also retarded. These changes in brain structure should not be interpreted simply (Bedi 1987, Smart 1987) but it is probably not too misleading for the non-expert to think of these malnourished animals as having a deficit in brain development, a reduction in the interconnections of nerve cells and a slowing of the transmission of neural impulses among them. It has been inferred from this that early malnourishment also causes permanent behavioural deficits which cannot be rectified because the underlying brain is damaged.

This pessimistic inference however must be resisted. Research has not so far established exactly how the various changes in the brain associated with malnutrition might lead to it functioning less efficiently. Starved animals have smaller brains, for example; but they also have smaller bodies, such as would normally only need smaller brains running them. Structural changes have been found to be particularly marked in the cerebellum; but Levitsky and Strupp comment that there are few reports of deficits in fine motor co-ordination, which the cerebellum controls, in either humans or laboratory animals (Dobbing 1987: 47). Nor is it clear how far deficits in brain development can be compensated for by later development. Environmental enrichment has beneficial effects on brain and behaviour in previously malnourished animals (see Katz and Davies 1983), but probably does not completely eliminate the physical effects of malnutrition. In fact it is perhaps as difficult to alter a laboratory animal's nutrition without affecting other aspects of its environmment as it is to alter a human child's. A common way of providing infant rats with good or poor nutrition is to alter the size of the litter the mother has to feed; members of a very large litter each get less milk than members of a small one. However they also have a different sort of social experience: more siblings to interact with, and different mothering, as small, immobile, growth-retarded rat pups elicit more maternal contact than large active pups do (Smart 1987), just as mothers of undernourished human children spend more time in contact with the children, allowing them more time suckling (Galler 1987). This increased maternal contact time has important implications, which I will pick up later. For the moment, the point is that even in laboratory studies of animals it is unlikely that nutritional status is the only difference between 'well-nourished' and 'poorly-nourished' animals (Winick 1976). Nutritional status has direct effects on brain development, but it also has direct effects on health and mortality, emotionality, energy level and exploration, which could bring about further effects on cognitive development as the malnourished, inactive, timid animal fails to explore the stimulation the environment offers. These more or less motivational effects might or might not be reversed when a better diet or different living conditons are introduced, though growth retardation itself will decrease exploratory opportunities, since it leads to mobility developing later and so to restrictions in interaction with the environment. Environments which provide impoverished sensory input are known to affect the development of the brain, decreasing the proliferation of dendrites and synaptic connections: effects which it may be hard to distinguish from the effects of malnutrition. Thus there are several vital gaps in the research data which need filling before it could be validly inferred that malnutrition (aside from the associated deficits in stimulation and experience) causes physical changes in the brain (and that these are permanent and irreversible) which lead (by what pathways?) to deficits in cognitive development (and that these too are permanent and irreversible). There is evidence for changes in the brain; we do not know what these imply for the mind.

The realisation of the interaction between nutrition and the environment even in the laboratory is important for studies of human malnutrition, where nutritional and environmental disadvantage co-exist inextricably. Most malnourished children live in conditions of poverty, environmental deprivation and social disadvantage, and recent research suggests that the effects of malnutrition and the effects of familial and social-environmental disadvantage exacerbate each other (Barrett 1987). World Health Organisation statistics show that a horrifyingly high percentage of children in the developing world (and some even in the United States and Europe) are malnourished, their potential development perhaps thereby impaired, even if not curtailed by early death. A number of research studies 'in the field' have looked for the effects of early nutrition on later achievement (e.g. Grantham-McGregor 1987). Typically, children who have been diagnosed as having marasmus (severe deficiency of protein and calories, particularly in the first year of life) or kwashiorkor (protein deficiency) are later compared with adequately fed children. There are enormous difficulties in making a valid comparison, as Rumsey and Rapoport (1983) and Richardson (1984) discuss. Comparison children are often 'matched' on convenient (but fairly gross) socio-economic measures such as being in the same class at school; sometimes siblings who were not malnourished are selected. Neither of these provides a really satisfactory control. Richardson's work in Jamaica examined (by interviews and home observations) a range of environmental variables in hospitalised malnourished boys and in classmates without a history of malnourishment (Richardson 1976, 1984, see also Dobbing 1987: 193–6). It was found that the malnourished boys were significantly less well off on such variables as caretaker's upbringing, reproductive history and level of capability, housing conditions and crowding, intellectual stimulation at home, amount of schooling and mortality of siblings. These findings cast doubt on any conclusion that the lower IQ and worse school performance of the malnourished boys could be attributed solely to their period of malnutrition rather than to their horribly extensive experience of disadvantage. In a multiple regression analysis, boys from the least disadvantaged settings seemed to suffer less from malnutrition than those from the most disadvantaged settings, being 2 IQ points behind their comparison classmates, while the most disadvantaged boys showed a 9 IQ point deficit. Thus the effects of malnutrition are embedded in a very complex social and biological context, and vary with it. Sibling comparisons reduce the variation to that found within a family, but this has recently been argued to be extremely significant developmentally (Plomin and Daniels 1987, Scarr 1985), and may be especially marked in these studies: if one member of a pair of siblings has been severely malnourished and the other has not, surely they must differ in other aspects of their experience – temperament, parental affection, 'historical' differences such as changes in family income – or why should one sibling have had a more favourable diet than the other? The other siblings may also have been malnourished, but less noticeably.

However difficult the proper control of variables between comparison and malnourished groups may be (Grantham-McGregor 1987), it seems to be a fairly consistent finding that undernutrition is associated with long-term and deleterious effects on development (Barrett 1987, Galler 1987, Lozoff 1989). Galler and her colleagues have done a longitudinal study of a sample of 129 children in Barbados who had suffered severe marasmus (protein-energy undernutrition) in infancy, comparing them with 129 children of similar social class who had no history of malnutrition. The children who had suffered a period of undernutrition eventually caught up on physical growth, but continued to have lower cognitive performance and school achievement, with an increase in attention problems and poorer social skills (Galler 1987). Although the environment throughout childhood was somewhat more disadvantaged for the malnourished children than for the controls, Galler concludes that the early period of malnutrition was the major contributor to their impaired development. Richardson, discussing the disparity between Galler's findings in Barbados and his own in Jamaica, suggests that this is too strong a conclusion (Dobbing 1987: 193–7). Both studies indicate that the complexities of how variables in the environment interact in development must be addressed, if we are to understand the mechanisms by which a period of undernutrition early in life brings about its effects.

Barrett (1987) criticises the research into malnutrition and cognitive development which used intelligence, conceptualised as 'innate general cognitive ability' and measured with IQ tests, as the main outcome variable. Measuring IQ is justified if the researcher has a theory of a causal relationship between malnutrition and general level of intellectual development, not if IQ is chosen merely because IQ tests are comparatively easily administered. I agree with Barrett that it is regrettable that other variables are not considered: Barrett's own research in Guatemala found that early supplementary feeding of chronically malnourished children did not predict performance on cognitive tests but did have long-term effects on attention, emotional expression, social involvement and persistence (Barrett 1987, Barrett et al. 1982). These more fine-grained variables were examined because the researchers hypothesised that malnutrition would disrupt caregiver–child interaction, affecting attention, responsiveness to social stimulation and the ability to elicit responses from others; that the child would learn to withdraw from new situations, would have difficulty in coping with routine stressful situations, would lack persistence, and would be withdrawn and lethargic. Such a pattern of behaviour conserves the energy which is in short supply when calories are lacking, but also tends to isolate the developing child from stimulation and opportunities to learn. Undernourished children demand and receive less stimulating interchange with their caretakers, spend more time in close bodily contact (often suckling for long periods which maximises the amount of milk taken in, but not the amount of information taken in about the wider outside world), and spend less time in exploring the social and physical environment (Lozoff 1989). If, as may be the case, the child's mother or other caregivers are themselves chronically undernourished, anaemic or depressed, the stimulation offered to the child and the caretakers' responsiveness to the child's initiatives may also be reduced (Cravioto and Arrieta 1979, Salt, Galler and Ramsey 1988). Child and environment, both undernourished and mutually understimulated, form a huddled bundle of helplessness and hopelessness, all their energy needed for bare survival, and the idea of doing well on an IQ test becomes a sick joke. Even sicker and no joke at all is the idea that only the demonstration of long-lasting IQ deficits would justify taking malnutrition seriously and trying to eradicate it.

In contrast to the pervasive chronic malnutrition endemic in the developing world, a few children who are not growing up in poverty suffer periods of starvation early in life because of conditions such as pyoric stenosis (a malformation of the digestive tract which leads to projectile vomiting of food) or cystic fibrosis (a genetically caused condition where food is not digested normally). The period of malnourishment is usually short. Research on the later development of these children, although it cannot separate the effect of the period of undernutrition from other effects of the child's illness such as hospitalisation and stress on the family, does allow some separation of malnutrition and wider social disadvantage. Research findings are inconsistent; there seems to be little effect on IQ scores except when the children are very young, but there may be some deficits in attention and memory (Ellis and Hill 1975, Lloyd-Still et al. 1974, Richardson 1 '84). There are occasional 'natural experiments' when famine strikes a population which is normally well-nourished, so that people whose brains were developing fast at the time of the famine can be compared with those undergoing such development at another time, under normal conditions. One such brief atypical famine occurred during the winter of 1944–5 when the occupying forces cut off food supplies to the civilian population of part of Holland and there were severe general nutritional difficulties for about six months. Boys who were foetuses or newborns at the time were tested when they began military service at the age of 18, in the early 1960s. No effects of their or their mother's period of acute malnourishment could be found (Stein et al. 1975). There are no details of the women's diets in pregnancy, so it is possible that they may have been protected against the general famine in some way, and no details of the boys' condition at birth or through the first year. Nevertheless this was a famine probably comparable with the experimental deprivation which has led to persistently poorer functioning in rats (Dobbing 1987). It did not have effects discernible in testing for army recruitment after nearly twenty years of normal good Dutch feeding. Whether this lack of effect indicates a true absence of deficit due to famine, or initial deficits which were recovered from as these babies grew up, or insufficiently sensitive testing methods obscuring real deficits, it is impossible to tell.

If malnutrition is hypothesised to cause deficits in brain development and consequently in cognition, then preventing malnutrition by providing adequate food should allow normal brain growth and cognitive development. A research study which provided food supplements for an 'experimental' group drawn from a population at risk from malnutrition and compared them with an unsupplemented matched control group could test the hypothesis. However, as well as the ethical problem of helping only some of those at risk (which implies allowing those not helped to suffer in order to have a cleaner research design) and the wider ethical issues due to the fact that providing food aid changes the ecology of food supplies in the community so that recipients may become dependent on the supplementary feeding and be put at a disadvantage when this form of aid comes to an end (Galbraith 1980), there are problems of comparability between the 'experimental' and 'control' groups and of monitoring the invervention. The nominally 'supplementary' food may replace the child's normal diet, or may be consumed in whole or in part by other members of the family; or if the whole family is fed (to eliminate this latter difficulty), there may be changes in the behaviour of other members of the family which affect their interaction with the child. Supplementing the diet of women during pregnancy and lactation, for example, is likely to enhance their interaction with their babies as well as the babies' brain development. There seems to be fairly consistent evidence, once these methodological difficulties are taken into account, that supplementation of the food supply of nutritionally deprived populations does have benefits for cognition, particularly if it continues from the child's prenatal life well into early childhood. In several studies children have done better in school readiness tests or made more progress in the first few years of school (Grantham-McGregor 1987, Grantham-McGregor *et al.* 1987), an achievement which might well affect their parents' and teachers' judgement of their potential and thus their later achievement (see elsewhere in this chapter). Intervention which combines nutritional supplementation with rehabilitation through social and educational intervention does seem to be more effective, however, and it is worth feeding the mother as well as the child (e.g. Cravioto and Arrieta 1979, Sinisterra 1987).

'Failure to thrive' is the term applied to children in industrialised societies who do not grow as expected but whose impaired growth has no identifiable organic cause (Skuse 1984). The classic explanation for these children's difficulties was psychological deprivation, the lack of a warm and responsive relationship with the mother: not being loved enough took away the child's ability to make use of his or her food, not enough psychological nourishment led to not enough physical nourishment. A classic study by Widdowson (1951) documented this happening in orphanage children in the care of two different nurses, one of whom quite incontrovertibly put her charges off their food. But the classic explanation is not now seen as being adequate to explain failure to thrive.

Children with failure to thrive tend to come from disadvantaged low-income families, with problems such as unemployment, overcrowding, marital difficulties, social isolation and adverse environmental conditions. Their mothers report more negative feelings about their own childhoods and more life stresses for themselves and their partners when interviewed during their pregnancy. They have more difficulty feeding their newborn infant; the process of inadequate feeding and nurture seems to start early and to have roots far back in the mother's life and in the wider family environment. Difficulties occur before the infant's growth failure begins, but the growth failure itself and its associated developmental deficits of cognitive delays and behaviour problems are likely to perpetuate the difficulties. Intervention which supports the family as well as feeding the child is necessary (Skuse 1985, Super *et al.* 1990), just as in the case of undernutrition in the non-industrialised world.

As well as undernutrition, children may lack a particular component in the diet, for example having a diet which does not provide them with enough iron, calcium or vitamins. Some of these specific dietary deficiencies appear to have adverse consequences for cognitive development, though there is considerable (and heated) controversy about this. Lozoff (1988) reviews research on iron deficiency. Deficiency is quite common in infants and children, particularly between 6 and 24 months: iron deficient infants tend to be tired, fearful, irritable, apathetic and distractible. Anaemia is associated with lower developmental quotients on mental test scores, and with lower motor development, though lesser degrees of iron deficiency have not been shown to lead to poorer scores. Anaemic infants have been said to improve rapidly when given iron supplements, but recent controlled research (see Lozoff 1988 for a review) suggests that these improvements on tests were probably largely due to practice effects, as anaemic infants treated with placebos and non-anaemic untreated infants improve to a similar degree. Better controlled studies have failed to find improvement in infants' test scores after two or three months of iron therapy, sufficient to correct their anaemia, though there was some sign of improvement in motor scores. Pollitt's work (Lozoff 1988) suggests that iron therapy for anaemic older children might reduce their cognitive impairment, also improving their attention and their energy levels. Anaemia in adults limits work capacity and activity: an anaemic mother might have a hard time providing developmental stimulation for her children. In view of the evidence on the importance of interaction with the mother both for malnourished children (Salt *et al.* 1988) and well fed ones (which I reviewed elsewhere in this chapter), both parental and child anaemia should be prevented.

Benton (1990) reviews research on vitamin and mineral intake and psychological functioning. Many members of the medical profession and nutritionists argue that if the diet supplies sufficient protein and calories all the necessary micronutrients come associated with them, and there are unlikely to be deficiencies. Benton examines the alternative argument that there may be deficiences, either because some individuals need an especially high intake of particular micronutrients, or because the diet may give rise to a sub-clinical deficiency even in the average individual. The existing research suggests that this hypothesis needs to be taken seriously. The evidence is not conclusive, because there are inconsistencies in findings and not all those studies which support the hypothesis are well designed, using double-blind techniques to rule out positive effects of supplementary diets due to consumer belief, for example. It is also not clear whether supplying micronutrients benefits those who are already taking in the normally recommended quantity as well as those whose diet was clearly very deficient. Finally, we do not know how micronutrients affect cognitive performance and development: whether their effects should be looked for in changes in the chemistry of neurotransmitters in the brain, or in better behaviour such as increased attention to the boring tests used to assess cognition, or in a decrease in ill health.

### Dietary substances and cognitive behaviour

We have discussed the effects on cognitive development of diets which are *deficient*, in calories or vitamins and trace metals. Recently there has been interest in the effects of Western diets of highly processed fatty and sugary food, and suggestions that some food additives and some deficiencies in more 'natural' foods might exert an adverse influence on children's behaviour and hence on their cognition. In part because of the high level of public interest, this has proved to be a difficult area to research: parents' desire to see a positive result from the new diet they are giving their child has led to dramatic improvements in problematic behaviour, which are greatly reduced if the dietary changes are introduced in a properly controlled double-blind fashion. More positive change is seen on parent report of mood and behaviour than on laboratory tests or standard psychometric assessments, a discrepancy which might be due to parental optimism (and an ineffective treatment) or to insensitive formal tests (and a more effective treatment), and is hard to interpret.

Rumsey and Rapoport (1983) assess the behavioural and cognitive effects of certain constituents of diet in children. One substance which children in the United States consume in large quantities is caffeine, which is found in coffee, tea, cocoa, chocolate and cola beverages. Caffeine is known to affect the central nervous system, enhancing arousal and facilitating automatic responding on well-learned tasks. People who normally abstain from caffeine find its side-effects aversive, while high users report positive effects, and withdrawal symptoms if they do not consume caffeine. It has been suggested that caffeine calms down hyperactive children, but placebo effects seem to be involved. It may stimulate anxiety symptoms in some children. Consumption of sugar and refined carbohydrates as a high proportion of the diet may be correlated with more aggressive and destructive behaviour in hyperactive children and with more activity in normally active control children. Food additives have received much publicity as hypothesised

,es of hyperactivity in genetically vulnerable or allergic individuals. Here
ontrolled studies have supported the hypothesis but their lack of
methodological rigour means that their results are uninterpretable. Properly
conducted research shows inconsistencies in results. Rumsey and Rapoport
(1983) suggest that possibly some children's behaviour does improve when
additives are eliminated from their diet though it is not clear that it worsens
again when the additives are secretly reintroduced as a 'challenge'. Very
careful research is needed to overcome methodological problems in the
selection of cases, the double-blind administration of restrictions and
challenges, control for placebo effects and sensitive but objective assessment
of behaviour. Meanwhile, the safest diet seems to be a healthily mixed and
not over-refined one, that, to put it a little crudely, what's good for one's
bowels is what's good for one's behaviour. . .

## THE SOCIAL WORLD AND COGNITIVE DEVELOPMENT

In the earlier part of this chapter I looked at non-social causes of cognitive
development; now I move to the social side of development. A great deal of
the literature on the role of other people in children's cognitive development
can be placed in three groups. The first points out more or less permanent
characteristics of adults, such as their social class or intelligence or family
structure, which are associated with different cognitive outcomes for the
child. The second looks at activities (and beliefs) of parents which make
them, moment by moment, more or less effective supporters or inducers of
their children's learning. The third looks at interaction between the child
and teachers (or fellow pupils) in a similar way. In discussing this work, I
will be seeking for elucidation of *how* adults' characteristics or activities or
beliefs might affect children's cognition.

I must first refer (see also Rutter 1992) to the methodological difficulty
which complicates discussion of the effects of parent–child interaction just
as it bedevils the study of the heritability of intelligence. Parents may be seen
to have a significant impact on their children's cognition just as they have
been seen to be significantly similar in IQ; but what part of this similarity or
this impact is due to shared genes and what part to shared environment?
Genes and environment interact and have their effect in complex ways (e.g.
Cardon *et al.* 1992, Plomin 1990a, Rutter 1988, 1992, Scarr 1992). The
association between parent input and child output may come about through
one or more of several different routes. First, parent and child might share
the same crucial genetic material, which finds expression in a particular
cognitive characteristic (for example, particularly quick and efficient
memory) irrespective of environmental influence. Or, second, there might be
specifiable gene–environment interaction: possessors of the crucial gene
may tend to create or to be offered, and then to benefit from, a particular
environment which would have a different effect on someone without the

crucial gene (an environment with much confident reliance on spontaneous remembering and lack of sympathy for forgetfulness, say). Or, third, the parent's behaviour might affect the child directly even though the child does not share the same gene (by modelling good memory and deploring forgetfulness, or by omitting training in mnemonics which the parent has never had to use). Or, fourth, the parent's behaviour (or the child's) may lead to changes in the structure and functioning of their lives which in turn affect the development of the child (too good a memory, an inability to forget as well as to forgive, might lead to a high level of reminding a difficult spouse of past faults and thus via recrimination to discord and divorce, which in turn affect the children's emotional states and thus their cognition). Or, fifth, environmental factors independent of parent or child character-istics but experienced by both generations might cause similarities in their development (schooling which requires the repetition on demand of memor-ised facts, for example). Or, finally!, the same result might come about through different experiences in the different generations (high achievement and upward social mobility in the parent through hard work despite an unprivileged and even unsupportive environment, followed by high achieve-ment and further social mobility in the child through the parent's purchase of good education and social opportunities; perhaps followed, if we believe the 'clogs to clogs in three generations' of nineteenth-century folklore, by fecklessness in the well-educated grandchild).

I have used baroque (and totally imaginary) examples to make my point about the complexity of causes of both the similarities and the differences between parents and children. Plomin (1991) and Scarr and McCartney (1983) make similar points about how different types of genotype–environ-ment effects must be considered within developmental theory. First, genetically related people may provide the child with an environment correlated with the child's genotypes, so, for example, through this 'passive' correlation the child who has inherited a genetic tendency to high intelli-gence may be surrounded by the possessions and activities of highly intelligent parents and siblings. Second, the child's own genetic character-istics may evoke responses from other people which are related to the child's genotype: particular encouragement of the child's interest in books, for example, or alternatively a pressure to 'get your nose out of that book and get some fresh air and exercise'. (Sex stereotyped provision of toys, or indeed anti-sexist provision of the toys traditionally associated with the opposite sex, would be examples of this 'reactive' correlation between genotype and environment, picking up a comparatively obvious part of the child's genotype.) Third, the child may actively seek or create an environ-ment to the full development of its genetic propensities – 'ecological niche picking' which maximises the impact of congenial aspects of the environ-ment and minimises the less genotypically suitable bits. (These might be compared with Sternberg's ideas about the cultural context of intelligence

(Chapter 4).) Scarr and McCartney propose that although 'passive', 'reactive' and 'active' genotype–environment correlations all occur in the course of development, their relative importance changes with age. The influence of passive effects is greatest in infancy, and declines as the child's individuality becomes more recognisable and its opportunities for selecting experiences increase. Reactive effects continue through life, while active effects increase from infancy to adolescence as the child encounters successively wider environments with more variation to select from. This proposal implies that siblings will be more similar as young children, when passive genotype–environment effects dominate and they share the same family environment, than they are as adolescents, when their experience varies more and more and they may even be seeking to be as different from each other as possible (Schachter 1982). There does seem to be some evidence for such a change (see e.g. Bouchard *et al.* 1990, Dumaret and Stewart 1985, Dunn 1991b, Plomin 1986, 1990a, 1990b, Scarr and Weinberg 1983), for example the higher correlation between the IQs of adoptive parents and young adopted children than between those of adoptive parents and adopted children grown up to adolescence.

Thus studies of the effects of parents on children's cognitive development have to cope with the problem of sorting out these causal chains. It will be necessary to take into account the possibility that what seems to be an effect of experiencing a particular type of interaction or other social factor is not in fact largely genetically determined, or, indeed, vice versa. There clearly is a great deal of genetic programming in development, but we cannot neglect the effect of the environment; as we have seen, the physical environment has significant effects on the brain, and adoption into an advantaged social environment raises IQ. Our concern here is how.

## Family background and children's cognitive development

There has been evidence for at least the last century that cognition or, more specifically, educational achievement, is associated with family background. From at least Galton's 'hereditary genius' onwards, children with more middle-class backgrounds or more educated parents do better throughout their educational careers, staying in education longer and having higher achievement at most stages. They also tend to do somewhat better on IQ tests, in particular contributing relatively few cases to the population of marginally subnormal scorers, and to a lesser degree on Piagetian tests. The socio-economic status (SES) of the family is still a fairly good predictor of children's academic achievement (Blake 1989, Jencks 1975, Rutter 1985b, 1992, Schaffer 1992a, White 1982).

This 'social address' research (Bronfenbrenner 1979, 1986) focuses on comparing people from different categories (with different 'social addresses') rather than on the intervening structures or processes which might explain how the address label comes to be associated with different developmental outcomes. Thus its results are often open to several inter- pretations. Further, the correlations between SES measures and cognitive outcomes are not enormously high; for example the extensive and complex analyses of Marjoribanks (1979) found measured 'family environment' correlated 0.45 with achievement in English and Mathematics and 0.29 to 0.34 with intelligence. Thus 'family environment' accounted for between 9 per cent and 20 per cent of the variance in cognitive achievement scores. Very importantly, social address studies do not adequately rule out genetic factors: studies which try to control for inherited differences in intelligence by partialling out the mother's IQ or the parents' educational level typically find the correlations between family background and children's performance in school or on IQ tests are reduced (Gottfried 1984), sometimes to a very insignificant level.

It is not entirely clear how a variable like socio-economic status affects children's cognitive achievement, what sort of explanatory model is appro- priate. The correlation between SES and intelligence or educational achievement might reflect class differences in innate 'intelligence' (Eysenck 1971), though the adoption studies suggest it does not. There might be differences in the behaviour which facilitates good performance on IQ tests and in school (the possibility which I discuss here); there might be different reactions by schools and other tests to children differing in SES (a possibility dismissed by Jensen (1980) so far as his intelligence research is concerned, but not entirely to be ruled out). There might be different opportunities avialable to the different social classes (for example better- funded schools in wealthier areas), even in a social system which believes it is meritocratic and open to all those who are talented. These possibilities are by no means mutually exclusive. Whichever may apply, we surely need to look closely at the moment by moment way the effect is brought about. 'Socio-economic status' is merely a convenient index which stands for but does not specify an assortment of correlated causes – variations in health as well as wealth, privilege as well as potential. It must surely be some of these underlying factors which 'cause' variation in cognition, not SES of itself. Work which looks at more specific variables may be more useful, and it is these variables which I want to discuss more fully. This strategy will make it easier to address the question of why there is variation *within* classes and other overtly similar backgrounds, and to elucidate causal chains. We cannot however entirely dismiss class itself as a significant factor in development in so far as it reflects inequalities of health, education and opportunity. Class-based indices may continue to be the most economical predictors of achievement.

The Collaborative Perinatal Project (Broman *et al.* 1987) followed a very large sample in the United States from before birth into the early school years to look for the causes of cognitive deficit. Their findings suggest different causal patterns for mild retardation (IQ between 50 and 69) and severe retardation (IQ less than 50). Severe retardation was likely to be linked to overt central nervous system disorder, mainly Down's Syndrome or the after-effects of rubella before birth or meningitis after it. Seventy-two per cent of the severely retarded white children and 14 per cent of the mildly retarded whites had CNS damage. More black children were retarded without definite CNS disorder, but it was again four or five times as common in the severely retarded black children. Children who were later severely retarded were more likely to have had problems in the perinatal period; they were more likely to have poor AGPAR scores, that is, to be in poor condition immediately after birth, and to be small in size, have low head circumferences and so forth. That is, the severely retarded children commonly showed symptoms of being at risk of abnormal development at or shortly after birth, and their retardation was caused to a significant degree by problems they were born with, or by later overt physical damage.

Different factors seem to be at work for the mildly retarded children. First, it was linked to socio-economic status, being very rare in high SES groups, and commoner in blacks (4.6 per cent) than whites (1.15 per cent). It was associated with lower SES at birth, with lower levels of maternal education, with lower age of the mother at the child's birth, with less maternal care, and with worse housing. There was some association with poor placental functioning, breech deliveries and poorer perinatal condition, factors which predicted severe mental retardation, but these were all less effective than social factors in discriminating between the mildly mentally retarded children and the borderline normal children. White children who were mildly mentally retarded at 7 had tended to show poorer early cognitive skills; for example, 42 per cent of them had abnormal expressive language at the age of 3. This earlier indication of problems was less clear in black children, where 77 per cent of mildly retarded 7-year-olds had had normal language expression at 3. Broman et al. (1987) conclude that the causes of mild mental retardation are not primarily medical, but that social and environmental factors predominate. Their data, to their regret, do not clarify such factors.

I must note, briefly, that in considering family background we have to recognise that it may impinge differently on different individuals within the same family; in effect, they each have their own unique environment despite living together. McCall (1983), Scarr (1985), Plomin (1989, 1991) and Plomin and Daniels (1987), for example, claim that there is as much variance within families as between them, that siblings differ as much as unrelated people. As the commentaries on the Plomin and Daniels paper show, this remains a matter of debate (for example, their analysis may not have distinguished adequately between variance within the family and general error variance). However, it may be as well to look at the contribution of non-shared environment to cognitive development. There is little evidence, indeed little idea of what 'non-shared environment' might be, to show whether it is not impossibly idiosyncratic. However, one way in which children's experience in the family may differ is in their ordinal position in the sequence of siblings. It seems that first-born and only children may tend to have earlier and better language development (including higher verbal IQs) and slightly higher scholastic achievement than later born children, especially those in large families with small age gaps between sibs (e.g. Blake 1989, Gottfried and Gottfried 1984, Rutter 1985b, Zajonc 1983). First-born children are known to get more interaction and talk with their parents. They may be more likely to be the leaders than the followers in their play with their younger siblings, particularly having the advantage of more advanced skills to teach their sibs and so consolidate them in themselves, and are more subject to pressure from their parents to achieve developmental milestones and good educational results. Their relatively good performance could therefore be taken as evidence for the effect of parent–child interaction on development. It cannot easily be explained in non-interactional terms. There is no obvious genetic reason why first-born children should be more intelligent, and though some late-born children may suffer through the association between higher parental age and Down's Syndrome there are reproductive problems also for very young mothers. If the ordinal effect exists (and there is some controversy about it, see e.g. Blake 1989, Galbraith 1982, Plomin 1986), it is an example of systematic environmental influences on cognitive development which differ for individuals within families.

A recent American study (Blake 1989) provides a rigorous scrutiny of several large sets of data to examine the links between family size and achievement. Blake finds a consistent difference in total educational attainment between the offspring of small and large families. Those from large families are less likely to complete high school, to get through the earlier stage of grade school without being kept down to repeat a grade, to have high verbal IQ scores, or to have high educational goals. Their achievement is more closely constrained by their social origins, they have less confidence in their abilities than those abilities would justify, and they are more likely to underperform in school relative to their ability scores. These differences between small and large families are found throughout the range of social groups, though they are mitigated by such other social forces as high parental socio-economic status, a cultural emphasis on educational attainment or an exceptionally cohesive kin network.

Blake argues that the cause of this difference between sibsize groups in their cognitive attainment is that parents' efforts to support their children's cognition are a crucial factor in its development, and that these parental efforts are 'diluted' if they have to be spread over many children. She cites various pieces of evidence for this explanation: the advantage in verbal IQ but not in non-verbal IQ for children from small families, which suggests parental attention and interaction as a cause; the increased amount of time that such children spend at home engaged in intellectual and cultural pursuits and in playing alone, and the greater frequency of being read to that they report they enjoyed as pre-schoolers; the decrease in sibsize effect in families from social groups which foster educational achievement.

The analysis provided by Blake is primarily concerned with differences between families, but it does examine the effect of birth order within families. Blake's analysis suggests that there is little effect on cognitive ability, but that the middle children in large families do particularly badly, because they have older siblings who will beat them in the competition for resources, and they will experience a long period while younger siblings are being born and using up parental attention. Again, family interaction patterns are seen as crucial, with interaction with parents being more supportive for cognitive development and educational attainment than interaction with siblings can be.

Another within-family variation which might be associated with cognitive development is the child's gender. As IQ tests have traditionally been composed in such a way as to minimise sex differences, and theorists like Piaget have not shown a strong interest in individual differences let alone sex-linked ones, the largest body of relevant evidence is on educational achievement. Girls tend to do better than boys on most measures until some time in adolescence, when their performance on mathematical objects declines relative to that of boys (Anastasi 1985, Eccles 1985). The reasons for this poorer performance are still a matter of controversy (Walkerdine 1989) but as girls who do persevere with mathematics in school do about as well as boys it probably involves a failure to engage with a difficult subject with a 'masculine' image (and indeed curriculum, Walkerdine 1989): in other words a social and motivational difference rather than a cognitive one. On the whole, although I would quite like to uphold a super-feminist case for the innate merits and talents of my own sex, it seems more probable that similar causes lie behind the early superiority of girls. Explanations in terms of girls' 'faster rate of maturation' are possible, but not unproblematic; it is fairly clear on the other hand that small girls seek to co-operate with and talk with their mothers and teachers, and spend less time in rough and tumble play with peers and similar activities of low direct relevance to educational achievement (see Hutt *et al.* 1989, Meadows and Cashdan 1983, Tizard *et al.* 1976). Again, boys and girls may have systematically different environments even within the same school or family, more different later in life than earlier.

It is worth noting that it would appear from intensive observational studies of mothers with their children that mothers treat their children very similarly. A videotape study (Dunn, Plomin and Nettles 1985) looked at mothers interacting with each of two of their children at the age of 12 months. The amount of affection, verbal attention and control shown to each child was extremely like that shown to its sibling at the same age. Mothers' behaviour changed as the children grew older, that is, they were sensitive to their children's developmental advances, so that when the younger child was 12 months old it was receiving the same maternal behaviour as the older child had at the same age, and maternal behaviour to the older child had changed, being now appropriate to its greater age (in this study, nearly 4). Studies of older children's views of how they and their siblings were treated by their parent find that they report they are treated differently however (Daniels and Plomin 1985, Plomin 1986), though parents believed they treated their children similarly. We do not as yet know whether this discrepancy is due to differences between observation and interview measures, or whether children are treated more similarly when very young and less so as they get older and have more varied experiences outside the home. Nor is it clear whether subjective differences in how children feel they are treated might have as much effect on development as objectively observable differences.

## Family language and children's cognition

As much of the way that culture is transmitted both in the home and at school is verbal, it seems appropriate to look briefly at the way in which language in the family affects children's cognitive development. Many studies have picked up aspects of language use as potentially relevant to how children acquire language, the style of their ultimate language use, and the ease with which later skills of cognition and literacy are developed (e.g. Crain-Thoreson and Dale 1992, Hess et al. 1984, Lieven, Pine and Dresner Barnes 1992, Meadows 1986, Rice 1989, Snow et al. 1991, Wells 1985). The causal issues are complex, but much research suggests that children whose parents provide 'child-contingent' language develop language fast and do well cognitively. In this sort of language as used to young children there are various syntactic, semantic and pragmatic modifications which cumulatively provide the young child with a good model to learn from, perhaps such a good model that no Chomskian innate knowledge of language is required (Moerk 1989). Among the many adjustments are attention getters and holders, such as a frequent use of the child's name, a high pitch or exaggerated intonation, and many gestures and touches; restriction of semantic content, for example by talking more than usual about the 'here and now', or by running commentary on the child's activity; selection of vocabulary, using 'baby names' such as 'tummy' and choosing from several possible labels the one best known to the child, 'dog' rather than 'Pekinese'; syntactic restriction to comparatively brief and simple sentences without, for example, passives or subordinate clauses, but with lots of repetitions; a specialised strategy of discourse, high on expansions and extensions of the child's own utterances, high on contemporaneous comment on ongoing activities, and high on questions, directions, prompts and modelling of discourse, and produced more slowly than language to adults. This sort of language has been called 'baby-talk' or 'motherese'; it is a relatively consistent, organised, simplified and redundant set of utterances.

Western middle-class parents are quite likely to use 'motherese' to their young children, and to do so often in the context of books and stories. Their language is closely contingent on the child's stage of cognitive and linguistic development, and it directs the child's attention on the development of a structured linguistic representation of reality. Two points have to be made about why 'motherese' is used. It is evoked by the child as well as provided by the parent. As Wells says,

> for most of the time the relatively finely tuned modelling of meanings and forms that the frequency data reveal occurs incidentally, as adults carry on conversations with their children for quite other purposes – to control the child's behaviour in the interests of his safety and their joint well-being, to share in and extend his interests, to maintain and enrich their interpersonal relationship and so on. Success in achieving these aims requires that the majority of the adults' contributions be pitched at a level of complexity that is not too far beyond the child's linguistic ability. However, this is achieved quite spontaneously by most adults under the control of feedback from the child's comprehension and production and does not require deliberate attention. The tuning that occurs is thus as much a response to, as a determinant of, the sequence in the child's learning. . . . It appears, therefore, that the influence of the input on the child's learning is enabling rather than determining. Once the child has the prerequisite cognitive understanding of the distinction which is encoded by a particular linguistic category, frequent appropriately contextualized occurrences of the category in the speech that is addressed to the child provide opportunities for him to make the connection between linguistic category and non-linguistic experience.
>
> (Wells 1985: 380–1)

Further, 'motherese' or any other use of language is presented to the child because of the rules and beliefs that the culture and the language impose. Parental interaction with children is based on beliefs about what children are like, how they should learn, and for what purposes and by what methods they should be socialised. These beliefs reflect the culture and the status of the family within it. Ervin-Tripp and Strage describe four styles of interaction with children found in different cultural environments. These are:

> 1) ignoring them conversationally until they are older, 2) challenging them to participate, modelling what to say, and praising success, 3)

accommodating to them by simplification and a special style of speech, and 4) helping them speak by prompts and questions.

(Ervin-Tripp and Strage 1985: 75)

Child-contingent language, as it stars in the language development literature, is characterised by (3) and (4): (2) is what the working-class black children of Trackton (Heath 1983) grow up with; (1) seems mainly to occur in certain small-scale traditional societies (Ochs and Schieffelin 1983), though it is an extreme of the prescription traditional in Europe that 'children should be seen and not heard'. Children grow up into normally competent language users apropos their culture even in groups which rarely or never use 'motherese', so it clearly is not *necessary* for language development. Children are able and willing to learn from whatever language they encounter, to seek out meaning and knowledge actively as well as to imitate the parent's behaviour. They may have other interactional and conversational partners, such as siblings or older children who are their caretakers, and are likely to have developed language which differentiates between partners of different skills and status (Dunn 1988, Dunn and Kendrick 1982, Heath 1983, Shatz and Gelman 1973, 1977).

There are different 'routes into language'. These appear in various forms in the literature. Moerk (1989) lists three major processes in the early acquisition of language, processes applicable also in cognitive development. The first is 'rote learning' which includes overt and covert repetitions and simple imitations. The second is 'pattern abstraction', involving the perception of rhythmic and melodic patterns, semantic and cognitive patterns, and syntactic structures. The third is rule learning. Moerk suggests that young children rarely or never have rules as part of their declarative knowledge, that though they could be inferred from the procedures which produce acceptable language they rarely are. Heath (1983, 1986) describes the language learning of Trackton children, growing up in a rich language environment which goes on regardless of them, as involving first rote repetition, then repetition with variations, then participation. The Trackton child must select for himself or herself what to practise from the 'noisy' 'multiple-channelled stream of stimuli' that is the linguistic and social context (Heath 1986), while in 'motherese' the more skilled adult partner focuses the child's attention. Lock *et al.* (1989) suggest that imitation and analysis are dual processes in language acquisition: each might be enhanced or hindered by the communication strategies for assimilating, analysing, evaluating and using both the language and its related cognitive skills. Some children may prefer, some adults facilitate imitation (Bates *et al.* 1988); others may focus on analysis (Bijou 1989, Lieven 1982).

Katherine Nelson (1973, 1981, 1985) and other researchers (see Lock *et al.* 1989 but also Lieven *et al.* 1992, Pine 1992) have reported apparent differences in children's strategy for using language as they learn to talk. Some children are 'referential', using language to talk about things in an analytic way, while others are 'expressive', using many more unanalysed social formulas in language meant mainly for social interaction. Whether these are two ends of a continuum or two separate categories is not clear; nor is it clear whether these styles originate in a preference of the children or in the behaviour and language use of their culture and their interlocutors. Lock *et al.* (1989) suggest the latter:

> it is not that infants develop differently by the exercise and practice of their individual skills; those skills, and the infants themselves, are constructed differently via socially-constitutive interaction.

In the end, it would seem that any combination of these 'routes into language' results in a broadly similar sequence of language development (Wells 1985) and broadly similar levels of language competence. But the emphasis is on 'broadly': there may well be differences which seem small in themselves but have far-reaching effects. Differences in orientation to literacy (see Chapter 2) are one example. The meeting of home language and the school is another. Teachers and children undoubtedly react to each other's language (see e.g. Cazden 1988, Edwards 1986, Meadows 1986, Weinstein 1991), affecting the teacher's view of the child's skills and probable achievement and the child's view of whether school is a compatible extension of home. Differences in use of language will also result in differences in cognition about language, and in different shades of expertise in particular uses of language, for example answering display questions, telling stories, realising that what was meant is not literally the same as what was said, that a comment has the function of a command, and so forth (e.g. Heath 1983, King 1978, Robinson 1983). Children whose family experience of language includes school-like language tend to settle into school more easily and to do better there than children whose family language is different from the school's. Some of these children may reject (or be rejected by) the school because of the difference, and their cognitive skills will thus not incorporate those of the school's curriculum; others may become users of two dialects, one for home and one for school. Having two dialects or languages may be experienced as potentially or actually alienating (Heath 1983, Rodriguez 1980), particularly if one of them is subject to negative attitudes and discrimination, and if there is no active support for the bilingual child to learn and use both. In more favourable circumstances being bilingual or bidialectical probably facilitates cognition about language (Diaz 1985, Hyltenstam and Obler 1989, McLaughlin 1984, Paradis and Lebrun 1984), bringing greater cognitive flexibility and a more advanced conceptualisation of language itself.

Children in school who are using the school's dialect as their own second language, not as native speakers, face a number of disadvantages. Their own language may not have given them so much practice on specialised skills important in the school's language, for example answering display questions, telling or discussing stories, or analysing objects or events; thus they will be less expert in these skills. Their own language may be socially judged as the mark of a stigmatised social group, and stereotypes of that group's behaviour and potential achievement may interfere with recognition of individual children's behaviour and potential. Because teacher and pupil have different languages they may meet communication problems, and at best they may have to translate each other's utterances as well as acting on them. The effort of doing this may divert cognitive resources away from the focus of the interaction, the question the child is to answer or the problem that is to be solved. It may be harder for the teacher to provide help at the appropriate level and for the pupil to internalise the ideas presented in a 'foreign' language. Children from minority groups and from the working class may have to do more w)rk than middle-class children to get the same results. They may be more likely to be labelled as 'stupid' or 'mildly retarded' (cf. Broman *et al.* 1987), just as we would all be less likely to shine on a demanding task if we were simultaneously having to translate it from a less familiar language.

### Family 'teaching styles' and children's cognition

Recent studies place family differences in language use in the context of how parents facilitate their children's development and acquisition of cognitive skills. Various researchers have looked at how mothers teach their children, by observing mother and child working together on a task such as drawing a pattern (e.g. Hess and Shipman 1965), assembling a puzzle (e.g. McNaughton and Leyland 1990), constructing a model object (Wertsch 1979, Wertsch *et al.* 1980, Wood and Middleton 1975, Wood *et al.* 1978), reading a book (Pellegrini *et al.* 1990), number tasks (Saxe *et al.* 1987) or various other games and problems (Freund 1990, Heckhausen 1987, Hodapp *et al.* 1984, Kontos 1983). Schaffer (1992b) discusses these 'joint involvement episodes' as context for development. Wood and his colleagues, for example (Wood and Middleton 1975, Wood, Wood and Middleton 1978), carefully observed 4-year-olds as they assembled a wooden pyramid. The mothers were asked to teach the child how to put the pyramid together and the children were finally assessed on their independent performance. The complexity of the construction was such that a child of 4 could not complete it alone, but could succeed if given supportive instruction.

Mothers varied in how well they provided such instruction. Wood describes several different ways in which the mother controlled the child's next activity. The least controlling was a general verbal prompt such as 'now you make something'; a more specific verbal instruction, such as 'get four big blocks', would tell the child more about what he or she must do in the next stage of the task. Non-verbal help, such as pointing out the relevant material, preparing material so that the child only has to assemble it, or even doing the work as a demonstration which the child only has to watch, might also be provided. These levels of instruction vary in how much they leave to the child's initiative and how much they take over responsibility for the task.

Wood finds that the mother's style of teaching, her use of these different levels, affects how well the child learns to do the task, how far the pyramid is completed when at last the child is asked to assemble it alone. The mothers who teach most effectively seem to use two 'rules' to guide their choice of levels. The first is that if the child fails to succeed at a given level of help, then the level of help or control should be increased and a little less left to the child's unaided activity. The second rule is that if the child succeeds at a given level, the next instruction may offer a little less help. The child's failure is followed by making things a bit easier, his or her success by allowing them to be a bit more challenging.

This looks like the sort of effective instruction which has been described in language development studies and in Vygotskian theory as 'scaffolding'. Bruner encapsulates it thus:

> If the 'teacher' in such a system were to have a motto, it would surely be 'where before there was a spectator, let there now be a participant'. One sets the game, provides a scaffold to assure that the child's ineptitudes can be rescued by appropriate intervention, and then removes the scaffold part by part as the reciprocal structure can stand on its own.
>
> (Bruner 1983: 60)

This scaffolding is seen as an effective Language Acquisition Support System (just as important as the Chomskian Language Acquisition Device which was internal to the child), and an analogous procedure seems to be an effective means of facilitating the cognitive development of young children. (And, to digress for a moment, the social and emotional development; see Eisenberg and Mussen 1989, Heath 1983, Kaye 1984). The learner is inducted into a predictable format of interaction: his or her role in it is orchestrated and supplemented by actions which highlight critical features and information, buffer the learner's attention against distractions, channel the learner's activities so that there is freedom to succeed and not too much freedom to go wrong. Errors are turned into opportunities to learn, procedures are commented on and explained, efforts are praised, and responsibility for doing the task is gradually transferred to the learner, contingent on his or her having demonstrated an ability to succeed.

Wood's pyramid construction studies and other research using the same approach (e.g. Wertsch 1979, Wertsch et al. 1980) showed an association over the short time period of the study between the mother's teaching style and the child's success in learning a new task. Subsequent work has examined mothers' use of scaffolding styles in their normal play with their children, and has allowed investigation of variables such as the role of the family's social class, the task's difficulty, and the child's ability in determining how scaffolding occurs and works. Pellegrini *et al.* (1990), for example, looked at how the mothers of black children on Head Start pre-school programmes interacted with their children over books, and found that mothers' level of teaching was adjusted to their children's competence, thus contradicting suggestions that scaffolding is an exclusively middle-class activity (cf. also Tizard and Hughes 1984).

Saxe *et al.* (1987) provide interesting documentation of a wide range of aspects of children's early number development. They interviewed and tested 78 children aged 2½ and 4½, interviewed their mothers about the children's everyday number activities, and recorded mother–child interaction on a set of number-based tasks. The tests given to the child, for example, included reciting counting words to as high a figure as possible, telling a puppet which of two named numbers (e.g. 'three, two' or 'six, eleven') was bigger, reading written numbers, counting items in a set, judging the effect of adding or subtracting one, and counting out items to match the number in a given set. Saxe *et al.* were interested in the mathematical contexts actively negotiated by the child and others, in how the child's own generation of a goal in accord with his or her current conception of numerical activities lead to new understandings and in how parental facilitation occurred, via parents' provision of more complex goals, activities or contexts. They were concerned to provide a developmental analysis of the child's understandings, an analysis of the cultural goals the child's activities were directed towards, and an analysis of the way in which the child's goals emerge and shift within an adult-supported activity. They compared working-class and middle-class white Brooklyn children at 2½–3 or 4–6 years of age.

They expected and found a developmental shift over this age range, and social class differences, with a small superiority for middle-class children at 2 but a large one at 4, particularly on tasks involving cardinal number, numerical reproduction and arithmetic which had high level goals. Children would often use a strategy from a low level of numerical functioning for what was really a higher level task, for example the task of counting a model set and then counting out units to match it was often done by trial and error moving of objects without any overt attempts at numerical representation. Children who scored highly tended to have parents who had high aspirations for them, and delivered a high level of stimulation via maternal language and the play materials provided, and via a flexible teaching style coupled with a belief that learning can be influenced.

Mothers and children were observed interacting on two tasks, one where the child had to count a single array and one where the child had to put out as many pennies as there were Cookie Monsters. In both cases there was considerable evidence of successful maternal scaffolding. Mothers matched the type of instruction they gave to how difficult the child was finding each subgoal, giving more specific instructions on harder tasks and more complex instructions to older and more accurate children, and making instructions more specific after the child made an error. Many children succeeded in the tasks when working with the mother but not alone, and were able to adjust their behaviour in correspondence with their mother's instructions, thus achieving more complex goals in interaction. An effective problem-solving environment emerged by negotiation, where the mother adjusted the task's organisation to the child's efforts, and the child's efforts were adapted to the mother's instruction.

Asked about their normal use of numerical activities, more than 70 per cent of mothers said their child showed a marked interest in them and at least three times a week counted something, looked in number books, or used numbers in play. Older children's activities were more complex than younger children's, and middle-class children's than working-class ones', with the range of complexity increasing with age as higher level goals were increasingly added to lower level ones. Mothers reported changing tasks as the same level of numerical reasoning was applied to harder tasks, for example counting more numerous sets of objects, or as the child reached the same goal with less assistance. Usually the mothers had several activities serving similar goals in play at the same time. Children regularly participated in number activities at varying levels of complexity, often activities which were the dyad's own inventions.

The data of Saxe et al. (1987) thus suggest there is maternal scaffolding of young children's numerical activities, and that this functions rather effectively. The child's ability to generate numerical goals enables and constrains his or her participation in social number activities; mothers scaffold this participation so that the child achieves more in partnership than alone and so comes to understand goals more advanced than his or her own; this facilitated understanding enables participation in more complex goals and interactions, and so on.

An alternative strategy of research used to examine the effects of parental teaching style of children's cognitive development is to use questionnaires, with or without observations, to describe features of the family's 'cognitive ecology'. Several American investigators have used the Home Observation for Measurement of the Environment (or HOME Inventory) as a measure of the quality of the environment available to the child at home (e.g. Bee et al. 1982, Bradley and Caldwell 1980, 1984, Bradley et al. 1989, Gottfried 1984, Luster and Dubow 1992). The HOME Inventory for newborn to 3-year-old children gathers data on mothers' responsivity, avoidance of restriction and punishment, organisation of the environment, play materials, maternal involvement in the child and opportunities for variety in daily stimulation, through a combination of mother's statements and the interviewer's observation, during interview, of her behaviour and the home. Its 45 items are somewhat heterogeneous and atheoretical, sometimes subjective, and have been criticised as biased towards middle-class values, for example, 'Mother's speech is distinct, clear and audible', 'At least 10 books are present and visible', 'Mother structures child's play periods'. HOME scores do however show moderate correlations with IQ assessments, over quite a number of years, particularly the subscales of maternal involvement and responsivity and play materials. Correlations using HOME scores from infants are lower than scores from assessments of 2-year-olds or older children, a result similar to that of other studies. This might suggest that cognition during infancy may be heavily genetically programmed, so that environmental variation influences cognitive development less than it may at later ages, though differences in item content may also be relevant.

The dimensions of the inanimate environment which are picked up by HOME and similar instruments as predictors of cognitive development are the availability of age-appropriate play materials, the possibility of free visual and physical exploration of the environment, and lack of over-crowding and unstructured stimulation. McPhee, Ramey and Yeates (1984) and Schaffer (1992a) suggest the core principle of development uniting these is that there should be a reasonable match between the amount of stimulation available and the child's ability to use it. Stimulation which is contingent on the child's need, attractive, predictable and allowing him or her control and independence, that is, stimulation which is like scaffolding, is optimal for development. Other people may be important mediators of the stimulation of the home, as interpreters or simply as providers. Parent activities which 'encourage development', in joint play or through providing appropriate and varied materials and experiences, are relevant to cognitive achievement. The core is warm participation in socially and intellectually stimulating interactions, with adults showing reciprocity with children, being responsive to them, but also providing some structured, directed experiences with encouragement and praise. Possibly the child participant in such interaction derives an enhanced sense of being competent and effective as well as receiving good cognitive opportunities and helpful interpretations and support from the adult. There are quite consistent positive correlations between the amount of adult–child interaction of this sort and the child's cognitive development, which remain even when maternal IQ and educational level are partialled out in an attempt to control for passive genotype–environment interaction effects (Gottfried 1984, Luster and Dubow 1992).

Early verbal interactions have been of particular interest to developmentalists. I discussed these in the previous section. Wells's work on individual differences in language development and later cognitive achievements such as reading and other aspects of school performance suggests that, within mainstream British culture, child-contingent language, quite strongly resembling Wood's 'scaffolding', facilitates but is not essential for the development of the full range of syntactic, semantic and pragmatic features of language (Wells 1985). Tizard and Hughes (1984) see this sort of behaviour as likely to promote the cognitive activities of the working-class pre-school girls they observed with their mothers. Sigel and his colleagues describe 'distancing strategies', with which parents encourage children to reflect upon their experience via requiring its representation – 're-presentation' – and so its 'de-contextualisation' (Sigel 1982b, Sigel et al. 1991, cf. Donaldson 1978). They believe that differential use of these strategies on the tasks they have set up influence children's behaviour. The pattern of results is complex, with variation between tasks and with differences between the effects of mothers' and fathers' behaviour; but, for example, children were more likely to create 'rational descriptions' in a story task if the mother made 'high-level mental demands'. Distancing strategies were important in association with other factors, including the parents' beliefs about appropriate strategies and the nature of child development (Goodnow 1984, McGillicuddy-Delisi 1982, Miller 1986). The context in which the parents' behaviour is measured is important; Sigel's subjects behaved differently on his two tasks while the language used by Wells's subjects, both children and adults, varied significantly according to the activity being engaged in (Wells 1985). Thus different amounts of engaging in particular activities will give differing opportunities for language and interaction that might facilitate cognitive development. For example reading and 'looking at books' lead to high levels of 'representational speech', particularly, for pre-schoolers, naming and labelling objects in context, while caretaking and eating lead to relatively high amounts of controlling speech (Davie et al. 1984, Wells 1985, ch. 8).

It may be seen that although there is a fair degree of agreement on the general nature of parent–child interaction which correlates with children's cognitive development, interpretive questions, and many questions of detail, remain. The validity of findings is heavily dependent on using the right sort of measurement, in the first place. The HOME Inventory studies, for example, which find a moderate positive correlation between their scales and child outcomes, use a set of items which summarise and may amalgamate behaviour which might usefully be differentiated further. A more microlevel 'ethological' approach might elucidate patterns which are more amenable to theoretical interpretation and more helpful for intervention or training than global 'responsivity' or 'involvement'. Studies such as David Wood's show the advantages of using a finer-grained level of behaviour (and of having a coherent developmental model) but data from ordinary interaction in the home are desirable if an ecologically representative picture is to be drawn. Studies which focus exclusively on one aspect of parent–child interaction, for example language or even more narrowly 'distancing strategies', may elucidate variation in cognitive development associated with this factor but are obliged to consign all other factors, not studied, to the status of sources of error variance. Worse than this, they may not even realise the importance of their focal factor if it is a necessary cause but not powerful except in combination with another unstudied factor. A study which compares groups which have and which lack the behaviour pattern of interest over a long period of time is to be desired, as there may be long-term effects of interaction as well as short-term ones, and, as David Wood implies in the 'scaffolding' model, what is facilitative behaviour may well change as the child grows older (or the learner becomes more expert). Finally, we need an explicit theory of *how* interaction affects development so that causal chains can be analysed; it should also be sensitive to the problems of distinguishing between psycho-social and genetic effects.

## Children whose cognition is not 'scaffolded'

I have described a pattern of social interaction between adult and child which may be an important support of good cognitive development. The case for it rests at present on a variety of pieces of evidence which are suggestive rather than conclusive. One component which we have not yet examined is what happens to children who miss out on this sort of social interaction. If it is crucial for normal development, children who have not had it should show abnormalities – specifically, deficits and difficulties – in their cognitive development. If they show no such abnormalities, such support cannot be necessary for development, though it might facilitate it in the normal run of things. I propose to touch on three sorts of case: studies of children who have suffered extreme social deprivation and grossly inadequate (or malevolent) caretaking; studies of social groups which do not normally use 'scaffolding' and 'motherese' as the populations usually studied by psychologists typically do; and studies which make fine-grained analyses of variation in interaction between depressed mothers and their children.

### Children who have suffered extreme deprivation in early childhood

A few children have been discovered in and rescued from conditions of extreme deprivation of social interaction. There are a few famous cases where it has been claimed that the child may have completely lacked any human contact, living with non-human animals and surviving only because they provided substitute parental care, and these children resemble 'beasts', 'savages' or 'idiots' (Gesell 1942, Maclean 1979, Zingg 1940). However these cases are typically badly documented, and both the description of the state of the children when first found and the treatment they receive in an effort to rehabilitate them may owe more to the rescuers' preconceptions about what is morally correct than to detailed objective observation, systematic assessment or principled pedagogy. The 'feral' child who is an exception to this, being both well-documented and the recipient of a rehabilitation programme inspired by well-thought-out educational principles, is the boy known as 'Victor' (Lane 1976). Victor was captured in the forests of Aveyron in southern France in 1800, when he was aged about 13. He had certainly been living wild there for at least three years, and probably his isolation had begun in his early childhood. After his capture he was taken to Paris and put into the care of Jean-Marc Itard and his housekeeper, Madame Guerin. Itard was a remarkable man, a pioneer in the education of the handicapped and the deaf, and he kept a very detailed record of Victor's development. He devised a system of patient and careful training procedures which remarkably anticipate twentieth-century behaviour modification techniques. Victor, when first rescued, functioned at a level of sensori-motor intelligence, sometimes showing remarkable sensory acuity and sometimes no reaction at all; he had no language and no social skills, and little emotional display. Under Madame Guerin's tutelage, and with the supervision and training of Itard, he progressed to some conceptual thought and moral feelings, especially of empathy, but his language development was disappointing, his social skills rudimentary, and his emerging sexuality and emotions disturbing to both the adults responsible for him and the boy himself. Poor Victor showed so little recovery towards a normal developmental course that it has remained a matter of controversy from his own time to ours whether his defective development might not have had physical roots, not just social ones. Here the question which applies to all children neglected to such a degree has to be faced: is it possible that they were so badly treated because those responsible for them believed that they were in some way abnormal, even before they were abandoned? Consideration of Victor's symptoms and achievements has led some psychologists to suggest that he was probably autistic (Bettelheim 1967, Frith 1990), though Lane (1976) maintains that this diagnosis rests on a selective use of the evidence.

Victor's isolation from human contact is unique. It has been more common for children to suffer deprivation of social interaction, perceptual stimulation, sensori-motor experience, emotional support or adequate nutrition while still in the care of adults. Not long after Victor was found in post-Revolutionary France, Kaspar Hauser turned up in post-Napoleonic Bavaria (Frith 1990, Lang n.d., Phillips 1980). He was about 16; he had a minute vocabulary, much of it used parrot-fashion, but could read and write a little; could barely walk, would eat only bread and water, could not bear strong light but could see in the dark. It appeared that he had always lived in a dark room with a low ceiling, where he sat on straw on the ground. There he never heard a sound or saw a bright light, was supplied with bread and water by a man who stood behind him to do so, and had only a couple of wooden horses for playthings. He made rapid progress with first a foster family and then a tutor; he was an appealing young man with an air of innocence about him, and rumours developed that he was of noble birth. It was thought that perhaps he was an illegitimate son of Napoleon, or the rightful Crown Prince of Baden, kidnapped from his cradle and cruelly imprisoned by his usurper. He became one of the local celebrities, and indeed he was of interest to a wide circle of aristocrats and politicians including an English nobleman who paid for his keep and education. His cognitive progress slowed down and he was accused of being lazy and inattentive, though whether this was ineradicable deficit or the reaction of a socially-petted adolescent to an unsympathetic, even hostile, teacher is unclear. Five years after he first appeared in Nuremberg, he suffered a mysterious knife wound, from which he died. Who he was, where he came from and who killed him cannot be known; people's myths about foundlings and the intrigues of courts obscure the case. But it does seem that Kaspar Hauser was made to suffer many years of social and physical deprivation, and that he made a notable recovery when returned to normal life in his late teens.

Some modern cases of social deprivation are documented in a fashion which makes inferences about how deprivation affects cognitive development rather easier to draw. Skuse (1984) reviews four well-known cases of extreme deprivation. Three are American. Anna, the illegitimate daughter of a mother whose Stanford-Binet IQ was 50, was kept from infancy until after her fifth birthday wedged into a chair in a storage room, her arms tied above her head. Isabelle, illegitimate daughter of a deaf-mute mother, was kept shut away with her in a dark room until she was nearly 7. Genie was confined to one small bare room by her psychotic father until she was nearly 14, beaten and barked at rather than talked to, tied to a potty-chair or confined in a sleeping bag made like a straitjacket in a crib covered with wire mesh (see also Curtiss 1977). Skuse's next case is the monozygotic Czech twins P. M. and J. M., who spent their first year more or less normally in a children's home and the next six months with an aunt, but for the next 5½ years were in the care of a weak-minded father and a stepmother straight out of Grimms' Fairy Tales, who brought up the two little boys in almost total isolation, beating them, locking them up for long periods in the cellar, and never allowing them out of the house (see also Koluchova 1976). Fujinaga et al. (1990) report on two Japanese children similarly brought up, kept in a shed near their parents' house and allowed to crawl in the yard, but beaten, never talked to or played with or treated with affection. For all these children, and for four other children, Mary, Alice, Beth and Louise, who were less cruelly treated and less socially and perceptually deprived (Skuse 1984), fairly detailed information is available on the state they were in when first rescued from their horrible conditions, and on at least some aspects of their later development.

The children are not identical in the deficits they showed initially, nor in how these problems persisted. Some of those who had had very restricted perceptual environments were initially suspected of sensory impairments because their hearing or vision did not fit the usual pattern. For example Genie, who had been kept in a room where she could not see anything further than ten feet away, was short-sighted to exactly this degree. On the whole there was a very rapid development of normal vision and hearing. All the children initially had severely limited spoken language and gesture and their language comprehension was poor. Once they were rescued, and received normal or enhanced language experience, Isabelle, the Czech twins and three of Skuse's less deprived girls rapidly developed virtually normal language skills, and the Japanese siblings made slower but substantial progress. Anna, Genie and the last of Skuse's cases, Mary, remained severely retarded in their language; Anna and Genie also remained far below age-appropriate levels on non-verbal intelligence tests, though in the other cases non-verbal IQs were superior to verbal IQ scores. All of the children developed good or adequate motor skills; the Japanese boy became a successful marathon runner. The Czech twins, Isabelle, the Japanese siblings, and Skuse's cases Alice, Beth and Louise were able to cope with normal school, and the Czech and Japanese children are known to have held down ordinary jobs.

Skuse suggests that the victims of extreme sensory and social deprivation whom he describes shared a number of characteristic cognitive deficits: 'motor retardation, absent or very rudimentary vocal and symbolic language, grossly retarded perceptuomotor skills' (1984: 563). They also lacked emotional and social expression and (understandably) social skills. Of these, the language deficit and the social-emotional problems seemed to be most profound, and the rate of improvement in motor and perceptual skills was much faster. Anna, Genie and Mary, who showed some non-verbal abilities but a complete absence of language, had the worst cognitive outcomes; speech therapy and life in a good environment with fostering adults enabled rapid development of language and cognitive abilities in the other children. If anything, cognition recovered rather better than social and emotional skills, though problems with complex language or with attention remained in some cases, and verbal IQ was depressed relative to performance IQ.

These distressing cases suggest that growing up under conditions of extreme deprivation will prevent the development of normal cognition and language; but that if there is no overt genetic anomaly (as there was in Mary's case) and no gross malnutrition (as in Anna's and Genie's) there may be a rapid improvement in ability, to within the normal range, given stimulating loving care in a small group. The 'scaffolding' metaphor suggests the provision of a supportive framework within which to construct the cognitive edifice. These severely deprived children had no scaffolding, little sight of other people's buildings, and a restricted supply of bricks, and anything cognitive they might manage to construct was at best ignored and at worst beaten out of them. It is not surprising that they had managed to construct very little. It is heartening that they were able to do so on rescue. There is very little evidence here for a 'critical period' during which the child must have 'scaffolding' and after which it is too late, apart from the failures of Victor and Genie to develop useful language after having none to adolescence. We might use these data, with data on IQ and ageing and on brain development late in life (see earlier parts of this chapter), to justify maintaining the working hypothesis that deprivation leads to deficit at any date; but that there can be a good prognosis if stimulation and support are provided after the period of deprivation.

## Cultural similarities and differences in parent–child interaction

Two assumptions have to be avoided: that all cultures are 'really' the same in the way they handle parent–child interaction, and that cultures which differ from one's own are worse, unnatural, or inefficient. Blatantly wrong though they are, such ethnocentric biases all too easily creep into one's thinking. I therefore approach discussion of how cultures differ and are similar in parental facilitation of children's cognitive development with some caution, and with an instruction to the reader to proceed similarly. My discussion is also very brief.

In general terms, all cultures make arrangements for children's activities and responsibilities which change as the children's competence develops and extends to new situations. Children everywhere participate in cultural activities that socialise them into the skilled roles and behaviour of their culture. Often, perhaps most often, this is done through structuring the child's activities within the family, providing appropriate instruction within joint activities and allowing children to be active participants in their own socialisation. Ethnographic studies of many cultures provide examples: girls learning to weave in Guatemala (Rogoff 1986), becoming a tailor in Liberia (Greenfield and Lave 1982, Lave 1990), learning about 'clean' and 'unclean' behaviours in India (Shweder et al. 1990). Rogoff (1990) suggests that the structuring of activities for novices to work in close involvement with others is ubiquitous, though cultures differ in the content that the novice has to learn and in how communication and participation are arranged.

Differences between cultures in the knowledge which the learner has to acquire are easy to acknowledge, harder to identify, harder still to place a value on. Raven (1980) provides a salutary example of the problems that may arise if the skills and knowledge valued by one culture are pushed insensitively on to another: inner-city working-class mothers taught to play with their young children in middle-class ways did so and believed that it would have a good effect on the children's learning behaviour in school, but that it would be at the cost of unfitting the child for the tougher street-wise activities of the neighbourhood. Another example of a cultural difference, this time in the manner of using cognitive skills, comes in the contrast between the individualistic competitive ethos of schooling in much of the West and the self-effacing, co-operative style of non-Western groups such as Native Americans and the Japanese, a stylistic difference which may constitute part of a different sense of self (Markus and Kitayama 1991) and certainly is part of the difficulty such children have in American classrooms (e.g. Tharp and Gallimore 1988, Weinstein 1991). As I discussed earlier, black and white groups differ in their attitudes to stories both as consumers and producers (Cazden 1988, Heath 1983, Weinstein 1991), with consequences for the children's cognitive development directly, through the information, skills and attitudes they learn, and indirectly, through other people's evaluations of their storying.

Children grow up with a particular culture and so are presented with (and protected from) problems which differ from culture to culture, and indeed which change in culturally imposed ways as the child gets older. The sorts of children that researchers are most familiar with, Western and middle class, have to become experts in literacy, and so have to learn in early childhood to attend to and use differences in the little two-dimensional squiggles that are letters (see the section on reading, Chapter 2). Being literate at a high level has its own rewards, but children have to engage with literacy and numeracy because they are among the core skills of the school curriculum, and are seen as national priorities – compulsory parts of the National Curriculum, for example – because they are seen as essential for the economic health and development of the nation. Other groups may have different goals, in which universal literacy is low down the priorities; and these goals may be quite as good for the present functioning and the future survival of the group as Western ones are. Understanding development involves studying children's behaviour (and their interaction with other people in particular) in the context of the goals that are locally valued, without imposing our own goals or our assumptions about what goals are worthwhile. It also involves the recognition that all goals have costs attached, that we cannot achieve all possible positive outcomes simultaneously and without any cost, and the recognition that the same ultimate outcome may be achieved in different ways – learning to read is an example of a development which can take several different routes, none of which is clearly 'better' than the others in the long term.

Different cultures prescribe different things to be learned, and also vary how they communicate with children. I have discussed some of the literature on adult–child talk earlier in this chapter, and will now only make the point that some of the variation in adult–child talk is associated with other differences in adult–child interaction. For example the other modes of communication available differ if one pair are in skin-to-skin contact and facing the same way and one pair are physically more distant and cannot easily look at the same object (Rogoff 1990, Trevarthen 1988b). Cultures differ also in the question of whose place it is to initiate talk: in some, adult and child are equals in taking turn in conversation, in others adult initiates and child deferentially responds, in others there is child–older child talk rather than child talk with adults (Ochs 1988, 1990). It must be stressed that parent–child interaction takes place within a context of other people, other potential social partners. Older children or grandparents or other members of the extended family may play with the child more than parents do. These non-parent caregivers may determine children's activities and responsibilities, working with the child in guided participation in the skills of the culture. Being the child's parent in the sense of 'biological parent' is certainly not necessary for such interaction. Western children are, ethnographic studies show, unusually segregated from adult occupational and recreational activities, and learn about the skills of such activities in the separate and specialised context of school much more than non-Western children do. Learning by observation and by eavesdropping will occur less frequently when children are thus excluded from the adult world. Children will have less responsibility for their own learning, and adults will make more formal and explicit attempts to teach them.

## Cognitive development in the children of depressed mothers

The argument of the earlier parts of this section has been that children need, or at least benefit from, sensitive, child-contingent 'scaffolding' of their attention, thinking and concentration during the early stages of their cognitive development and their education. I move now to recent work on the development of the children of depressed mothers because it seems possible that depressed mothers are often not able to scaffold their preschoolers' activities, and that this shortage of scaffolding and concomitant emotional difficulties have their effect on the child's cognitive behaviour.

Depression is alarmingly common amongst the mothers of young children. Population studies (e.g. Brown and Harris 1978, Richman, Stevenson and Graham 1982) find noticeable depression in up to 40 per cent of women; low socio-economic status, lack of a confiding relationship, several preschool children (perhaps especially if they include twins) and no satisfying job increases the risk of depression. It is also becoming apparent that the children of depressed parents are probably at increased risk of psychiatric disorder. The evidence is not yet sufficiently clear to quantify this risk and there are still numerous debates and disagreements: see reviews by Coyne and Downey (1991), Dix (1991), Downey and Coyne (1990), and a special issue of *Developmental Psychology* (1990, 26(1): 1–67). A number of conceptual and methodological problems contribute to this lack of clarity. One is that 'depression' varies from case to case, and there is still controversy about diagnostic criteria (see e.g. Barker 1988, Rutter *et al.* 1986). It used to be thought of as involving a single episode which usually

resolved without lasting impairment, but it may actually more character-
istically involve recurring episodes of severe depression with residual
difficulties even during more positive periods. Thus the child may be
exposed to 'depression' of varying severity for a longer time than any one
officially diagnosed episode. Depression is also associated with anxiety and
'personality disorders' such as aggression and undue dependence, and often
occurs as a reaction to difficulties in people's lives such as economic
adversity, poor interpersonal relationships, marital conflict and breakup,
lack of social support and housing problems, all of which might be expected
to impinge on children directly and independently of their parents'
depression. It may be associated with factors which are entirely or largely
'in' the child, such as prematurity, multiple births, serious handicap, difficult
'temperament'; or depression may accompany the stresses and emotional
demands of parenting, when one's offspring is simultaneously the best and
brightest thing in the universe and the source of one's sleep deprivation,
one's anxieties about feeding and health, yet another sticky and indelible
stain on the carpet, and some singularly aversive highpitched noises.

It will not be easy to tease out what psychological difficulty is leading to
what, given the variation in mothers' depression, in the degree to which their
parenting is supplemented by other people's, and in the age of the child
during the period(s) of depression. This last is a particularly important
point: what is appropriate parenting changes with age, this being one of the
things that good parenting recognises, and the skills needed at one age may
be affected by depression more or less than the skills appropriate at another
age. Further, children's own reactions to their mother's depression are likely
to be age-dependent; children of different ages will probably have had
different lengths of time exposed to a mother suffering from episodes of
depression or less severe negative feelings. It is hard to compare research
samples which are not always completely documented on variables such as
these and are often also small enough to show results due to idiosyncrasies
of individuals.

Despite these methodological and conceptual problems, some tentative
conclusions seem to be emerging (Downey and Coyne 1990, Rutter 1990).
School-aged children of depressed parents tend to have more adjustment
problems than children of non-depressed parents, including poorer ratings
on behaviour and emotion checklists, higher levels of psychiatric treatment,
poorer physical health, academic deficits and lack of social competence. In
particular, they may be especially liable to becoming depressed themselves.

It is quite possible that parent and child are both distressed and depressed
because they share genes or because they share the same unsupportive and
stressful environment. However studies which include detailed observations
of parent–child interaction suggest that the link between parental depression
and child adjustment, especially the child's cognitive adjustment, may lie
centrally in features of the interaction of depressed mothers and their

children. I will use as example a recent study, the SLUFP project which I became involved in (Cox *et al.* 1987, Meadows and Mills 1987, Mills and Funnell 1983, Mills *et al.* 1985, Pound *et al.* 1982). The first stage of this study involved detailed observations of depressed and 'control' mothers (the latter demographically very similar but without psychiatric symptoms) at home with their 2-year-old children, observations which focused on their joint activity and on episodes of control or distress. The children were observed again in any pre-school setting they attended, and during their second term in infant school (at age 6), when teacher ratings and scores on a computer vigilance task were added to the intelligence tests taken at 2½ and 6. The mothers were extensively interviewed about their lives, marriages and other circumstances at the 2½-year-old stage, but, regrettably, not at the 6-year-old stage. All were white, working class, British born, inner London families, in two-parent families with the father in employment at the outset of the study.

It must be said at the outset that some of the depressed mothers were parenting sensitively and sensibly, and their children were problem-free at all ages. But the larger part of the depressed group reported that their children had extensive behaviour problems, and here the mother–child interaction tended to show a less promising pattern, particularly if there was marital discord in the family. These mothers were less likely to respond to their 2-year-olds' overtures, to extend their children's behaviour in 'scaffolding' ways, to facilitate social interaction, and to pre-empt conflict by managing the interaction so that problems did not reach overt conflict. They were more likely to be very withdrawn and despairing in mood, or to be intrusive, critical and hostile, reacting to the child's episodes of distress with anger and controllingness. There was less overt positive enjoyment of mother–child interaction, less joint play and less imaginative co-operation, and though there was no decrease in physical warmth and cuddles some of this seemed to be the mother using the child as a comfort object. Some of these children seemed to be carrying the responsibility for looking after their mothers, glancing up from their intelligence test continually to ask 'You all right Mum?', fetching ashtray after ashtray after being asked to get one, in at least one case making the comforting cup of tea.

When the children were seen in school at the age of rising 6, it was the children who had had depressed mothers *and* behaviour problems at 2 who differed from the rest. They were significantly less good at concentrating on school tasks and at developing their activity beyond a very simple repetitive level; they received more poor ratings from teachers on social and academic problem checklists; they had much more difficulty with the formal tests when these involved sustained attention. As I observed them throughout the school day, the metaphor that they built up in my mind was 'anxious puddings': inert, unresponsive, heavily defended children whose first reaction was 'I can't do it' and whose second was to shut themselves off from all occasions when they might have to try. In short, they looked like depressed, underachieving children who were not engaging themselves with the opportunities which the school offered and were somewhat distressed by its cognitive and social challenges. Given the limited resources of the school system it seemed likely that they might never be enticed out of this into a higher level of engagement, achievement and enjoyment. The continuity of problems from 2½ to 6, which was statistically significant at better than the 0.01 level, looked likely to be maintained to later ages.

Other studies have also shown various of the effects we found in our sample, for example: negative self concept and attributions (Hammen *et al.* 1987, 1990), guilt and anxiety (Radke-Yarrow 1991, Zahn-Waxler and Kochanska 1990), being withdrawn with peers (Zahn-Waxler *et al.* 1984) and with demanding tasks (Kochanska 1991), insecure attachment (Radke-Yarrow and Sherman 1985), attention problems (Cogill *et al.* 1986, Cohler *et al.* 1977, Jacobvitz and Sroufe 1987, Wahler and Dumas 1989), and less parental facilitation of children's activity (Estrada *et al.* 1987, Radke-Yarrow and Kuczynski 1983, Rutter 1990).

There may be the beginnings of a case here for some more specific links between parenting and child behaviour than we have seen before. These may act directly on and through cognition and via the participants' emotional states. It seems possible, firstly, that depressed mothers, with sadder, slower and flatter ways of speaking and acting (Bettes 1988, Breznitz and Sherman 1987, Mills *et al.* 1985, Pound *et al.* 1982, Radke-Yarrow *et al.* 1990), with less empathy and involvement in other people's activities (Dix 1991, Slade 1987), and with little or no positive emotion, are much less likely to be able to produce the positive and child-contingent parenting which supports and extends the development of young children's cognition and language. This may be particularly important for young children, who need the scaffolding and emotional support for cognitive effort which they cannot yet sustain for themselves:

> Parenting is a particularly complex form of social interaction. The sustained effortful behaviour that it involves is likely to prove difficult for depressed parents, especially when their children are young and exaggerated affective tone and a high tolerance for aversive behaviour are required.
>
> (Downey and Coyne 1990: 61)

As in the SLUFP sample, this experience of parenting which lacks responsiveness to the child, is non-contingent and non-facilitating, and does not extend the child's activity imaginatively may be associated with slower and more limited development of cognition and language, with a depressed verbal IQ, with less symbolic play and with impaired concentration and engagement in school. Second, parenting which deals with control issues by imposing obedience unilaterally or by abdicating control totally in the face of even minimal child resistance misses the opportunities for teaching children to reason, understand and negotiate which less distressed mothers may provide; its consequences at school age might include difficulties with classroom routine and co-operation with other children, as well as, perhaps, less empathy and understanding. Third, parenting which is sad and helpless seems to be associated with child behaviour which is anxious, guilt-ridden and helpless (Zahn-Waxler and Kochanska 1990); it is one of the clearer and more noteworthy findings emerging from the research literature that the psychiatric problems of the children of depressed parents tend to involve depressive symptoms. The depressed mothers in the SLUFP study often reported that their own mothers had suffered from depression, an apparent stability of symptom over three successive generations. This continuity gets to look nastily inescapable when a further point is added: because depression is unattractive and associated with lack of energy, it may be that the depressed mother suffers from inadequate social support networks outside the family (Brown and Harris 1978, Coyne and Downey 1991), and because depressed mothers tend to have depressed partners and unsupportive marriages (Downey and Coyne 1990), the young child may not have a non-depressed person available either within the family or outside it to provide happier parenting.

I will end this section by stressing three things. First, this is all very much 'work in progress' and this pattern of effects of maternal depression on children's cognitive development is a matter of intelligent speculation rather than of firm fact. Second, it would be wrong, it would be wicked to blame the mothers, who are usually doing as well as anyone could in horribly unhelpful circumstances; rather blame us all for our lack of concern for the support of the psychological health of young children and their caregivers. Third, to return to the wider subject matter of this book, this area provides important intimations of how the development and acquisition of cognition in childhood is bound up inextricably with emotion, a topic I return to in the final chapter.

## THE SCHOOL AS A SETTING FOR THE DEVELOPMENT AND ACQUISITION OF COGNITION

A chapter on social influences on the development and acquisition of cognition in childhood has to recognise that children are involved in social institutions other than the family. Of these many have received little attention. I do not know of much research on children's induction into religious ideas in church settings, for example, nor on the cognitive skills they acquire through youth organisations. The major social institution which is relevant to our present concerns is, however, the school, and the problem here is too much research rather than too little. I shall not seek to summarise the literature on how schools affect children's cognitive development (for American reviews see Brophy 1986, Brophy and Good 1986, Snow *et al.* 1991, Weinstein 1991, and the 1989 volume of the *International Journal of Educational Research*, and for British studies, Mortimore *et al.* 1988, 1989, Rutter 1985b, Rutter *et al.* 1979, Tizard *et al.* 1988). Instead, I will focus on whether effective schooling involves the sort of scaffolding which seems to be associated with effective cognitive functioning in the family.

An enormous quantity of research has been done on why some schools or teachers seem to foster pupils' achievement better than others. This is not a simple problem: it is complicated by differences in the level of skills and knowledge that the pupils start from, by differences in their abilities, by differences in their cognition-related activities outside school, by problems in measuring achievement, by problems in identifying and measuring relevant school or teacher characteristics, and by other complexities. Researchers have not always succeeded in coping with these problems, and 'findings' do not always stand up to further scrutiny. However a number of points relevant to school 'scaffolding' can be made. Students learn best when they are engaged in academic tasks which are clearly introduced to them and which they can proceed through steadily, making consistent progress with few failures (ideally almost none when they have to work independently, and not many when the teacher is there to provide feedback and guidance); when the teacher has established a classroom orientation towards conscientious academic work, and supervises and instructs actively within the classroom; and when the teacher's behaviour supports students' efforts through behaviour such as question sequences which establish easy facts which have to be combined to answer a harder problem, allowing an appropriate time for a student to produce an answer, providing regular and extensive feedback, praising specifically rather than generally, and acknowledging achievements in a positive but non-intrusive way (Brophy 1986, Fraser 1989, Mortimore *et al.* 1989). This package of behaviours looks like scaffolding, as it might be manifested under the notably difficult circumstance of having to do it for twenty or thirty learners at once.

'Scaffolding in the classroom' has to be differentiated to fit the characteristics of the learners. Very young pupils need more instruction in the routines and procedures of the classroom and of learning, and being involved in the development of basic skills they should have frequent opportunities to practise them and receive feedback on them. Older pupils who have internalised how to be a pupil and are now applying well-learned basic skills may not need to participate in the activity so overtly, and may learn with more impersonal instruction: they can provide a greater degree of scaffolding for themselves. Similarly, low achievers need more structuring of their learning by their teachers: more active instruction, more feedback, higher success rates and smaller steps in cognitive demands, more practice, more support and more encouragement. Thus 'scaffolding' may have to be adjusted to the individual's current competence and permanent or temporary idiosyncrasies; no wonder that teaching is such a demanding and highly skilled activity!

The research on 'effective teaching' focuses on increases in cognitive achievement, often measured as performance on tests or in examinations. Some educationalists (Scheerens and Creemers 1989) would argue that the measures used overemphasise the acquisition of knowledge which is only used in tests, and which does not become an accessible and applicable part of the learner's knowledge base. This sort of 'knowledge-transforming' learning may require particular sorts of social input; one approach which seems particularly promising is 'co-operative learning' (Brown and Palincsar 1989). This is an alternative to the individualist learning that is required in most classrooms, and which may be inappropriate for many learners (Heath 1983, Tharp and Gallimore 1988).

Brown and Palincsar focus their discussion of co-operative learning on 'reciprocal teaching', which provides a simple introduction to group discussion techniques aimed at understanding and remembering text content. It takes place in a co-operative learning group in which an adult teacher and a group of students take turns leading a discussion on the content of a section of text that they are jointly attempting to understand. Four strategic activities are given guided practice: questioning, clarifying, summarising and predicting. The group member whose turn it is to be leader begins the discussion by asking a question on the main content and ends by summarising it. In between, disagreements are resolved by rereading and discussion of questions and answers; after the summary, the group leader asks for predictions about future content. The adult teacher is the model for these strategic activities initially, and provides feedback and guidance appropriate to the needs of the current discussion leader and the other group members. The group members have joint responsibility for understanding and discussing the text; the leader is responsible for orchestrating the dialogue and the listeners for being supportive critics in the elucidation of content and the resolution.

Why does reciprocal teaching work well? First, it highlights *explanation*. These participants in the discussion have to offer explanations, interpretations, justifications and resolutions to problems. The listeners in the group call on the discussion leaders to back up their arguments with relevant data and so elaborate and extend them, increasing the coherence of the knowledge structure. This involves both support for what is said and arguments which are in conflict with it. The *support* activities of the group include shared responsibility for thinking, which shares out the effort and reduces anxiety because no one contribution need be a complete solution or able to stand independently of others; modelling cognitive processes, because group members share roles such as summariser, recorder, 'yes-butter', and corrector and can both see how other members perform these roles and use other people's enactments to complement their own performance; and sharing expertise, as individuals' knowledge and skills can be combined and responsibility for covering the ground shared out. The *conflict* activities of the group include insistence on clarification, justification and elaboration, which can result in fundamental cognitive restructuring (Doise and Mugny 1984). Individuals can come to perform these group activities for themselves, as they internalise all the thinking roles, insist on clarifying and justifying themselves and try out their own counter-examples and summaries.

Lave (1990) provides an interesting discussion of the underlying principles of 'understanding-in-practice' and of 'understanding-via-schooling'. He argues that the former is the more powerful source of enculturation:

> knowledge-in-practice, constituted in the settings of practice, based on rich expectations generated over time about its shape, is the site of the most powerful knowledgeability of people in the lived-in world. The encompassing, synthesizing intentions reflected in a theory of under-standing-in-practice make it difficult to argue for the separation of cognition and the social world, the form and content of learning, or of learning and its 'applications'. Internalization is a less important vehicle for transmission of the experience the world has to offer, in this view, than activity in relation with the world.
>
> (Lave 1990: 323)

Thus, learning in school may be deeply problematic. School is part of 'real life' – a major part of it for children, fifteen thousand hours or so of it in the West – but it differs from children's non-schooled life in at least two cognitively relevant ways. First, it concentrates to a considerable extent on procedures which are divorced from real world procedures by being more algorithmic, more closed, and more specific. Second, learning focuses on problems prescribed by the curriculum rather than problems the learners spontaneously want to solve. This may lead to the learners learning procedures and applying them correctly to classroom examples but incorrectly or not at all to analogous problems encountered outside school, as seems to be all too common in everyday mathematics (Chapter 2, section on mathematics). The goals of learning have not been clear, the procedure has been overspecified, and the practice has not come to be flexible or to be 'owned', as would have happened in the 'understanding-in-practice' of apprenticeship. At the root of this there may be different metaphors of learning. The dominant one in Western education and psychology makes the subject-matter the environment in which the child moves: the problem-solver moves through the successive steps of the problem as if contained by it. 'Understanding-in-practice' makes the learners constitute the problem for themselves: the child's understanding and goals define the problem, give meaning and value to the subject-matter and the process of learning it, and integrate it into the learner's life and activity.

Given that the development of an understanding about learning and about what is being learned inevitably accompanies learning, in the more conventional sense, it seems probable that learners whose understanding is deeply circumscribed and diminished through processes of explicit and intense 'knowledge transmission' are likely to arrive at an understanding of themselves as 'not understanding' or as 'bad at what they are doing' even when they are not bad at it (such seems the fate of the vast majority of the alumni of school math classes). On the other hand, learners who understand what they are learning in terms that increasingly approach the breadth and depth of understanding of a master practitioner are likely to understand themselves to be active agents in the appropriation of knowledge, and hence may act as active agents on their own behalf.

(Lave 1990: 325)

## TEACHING THINKING

Enhancing cognitive development, or facilitating cognitive acquisition, are central concerns of education. It is clear that people who have developed or acquired a good repertoire of strategies, both high level general ones and narrower highly specialised ones, and can apply them to a wide range of learning and problem-solving situations, are likely to be highly effective in their cognition. They are likely to be better learners, reasoners, readers, writers, memorisers, scientists, mathematicians, intelligence test takers and so forth than people who have smaller or more rigid repertoires of strategies, will be more likely to be 'Universal Expert' or 'Renaissance Man'. As well as having a good repertoire of strategies, they will know a lot about how, when and why to operate these strategies, that is, they will have a high degree of metacognitive knowledge and reflective awareness. This knowledge makes them able to operate strategies effectively on familiar tasks, and to see how they can be applied to new tasks, perhaps in a slightly modified form. They will also need an extensive base of declarative knowledge, the facts on which their cognitive strategies can work, or which can make strategic thought simpler or even unnecessary (if you have learned the definition and pronunciation of 'flaccid' you won't have to employ any strategic effort to discovering them; if you haven't see p. 7 this volume or any good dictionary!). Strategy, metacognition and basic knowledge are well co-ordinated in the cognitively competent person: they can operate in the appropriate sequence, often more or less automatically, and flexibly according to how the task's demands are being met. Finally, good thinkers will have a confident attitude to cognitive tasks; they will be willing to extrapolate from the familiar to the unfamiliar, to take risks and to go 'beyond the information given', to make mistakes and learn from them, to succeed and not take their success for granted but be able soberly to identify its sources. In short they will be people who enjoy thinking.

Human cultures do, on the whole, value such activities, and many invest a great deal of their resources in efforts to equip their young members with cognitive strategies, knowledge and an aptitude for transfer. Cultures differ, of course, in what knowledge and what cognitive skills they emphasise, and in the form the education system takes; but generally a good ability to learn cognitive skills and apply them appropriately to any situation that is met is a universal cultural goal. School systems are commonly held to be responsible for teaching their students to think effectively and are also commonly accused of failing to do so. Evaluating the truth of this accusation is beyond the scope of this book, though a brief overview of some of the research on the differential effectiveness of schools may be found in the preceding section. I will here provide a brief account of what psychology suggests are the features of good thinking, and of what might be suggested about how to teach it.

Resnick offers a list of 'key features of higher order thinking', which forms a useful starting-point for our discussion.

> Higher order thinking is *nonalgorithmic*. That is, the path of action is not fully specified in advance.
>
> Higher order thinking tends to be *complex*. The total path is not 'visible' (mentally speaking) from any single vantage point.
>
> Higher order thinking often yields *multiple solutions*, each with costs and benefits, rather than unique solutions.
>
> Higher order thinking involves *nuanced judgment* and interpretation.
>
> Higher order thinking involves the application of *multiple criteria*, which sometimes conflict with one another.
>
> Higher order thinking often involves *uncertainty*. Not everything that bears on the task at hand is known.
>
> Higher order thinking involves *self-regulation* of the thinking process. We do not recognize higher order thinking in an individual when someone else 'calls the plays' at every step.
>
> Higher order thinking involves *imposing meaning*, finding structure in apparent disorder.
>
> Higher order thinking is *effortful*. There is considerable mental work involved in the kinds of elaborations and judgments required.
>
> (Resnick 1987b: 3)

The cognitive skills involved here, although called 'higher order', in fact pervade even 'basic skills' such as reading, simple arithmetic, and knowing whether it will soon be tea-time. Recent research on what happens when people read a passage of text, for example (see Chapter 2), show that the reader uses a combination of recognising or decoding words, calling on relevant linguistic knowledge, topic knowledge and genre knowledge already stored in memory, and 'high level' general cognitive processes such as making inferences, noting connections, checking and organising text information and additional external information, deleting irrelevant material and so forth, in order to construct a mental representation not of the literal extant text itself but of the mental representation the writer hoped to induce in the reader. Knowledge and skills like these are generally agreed to be the main components of what we do when we comprehend text. Successful readers are better at them than unsuccessful readers; to a considerable extent they have become so skilled that text comprehension processes proceed automatically, that is, without conscious effort or deliberate attention, and some of them (for example phonological decoding) may even no longer be used unless automatic processing breaks down. Deliberate conscious efforts to comprehend what is read are made when the topic is unfamiliar so that prior knowledge cannot aid interpretation; when the language is unusual or anomalous; when the argument or genre or inferences presented are unusual or complicated, particularly dense, for example; or when the reader intends to study and remember the text rather than just get the gist of it. Skilled readers can both skim and understand text automatically and use deliberate effortful comprehension processes when appropriate. Unskilled readers, including children learning to read, need to be able to apply them too: even beginning reading is not just word recognition or letter-to-sound decoding (Oakhill and Gainham 1988). Worryingly, it seems that children who are having difficulty learning to read may get less opportunity to practise these skills than more successful children because their learning is focused on decoding skills (see Francis 1982).

Resnick argues that children's difficulties with school mathematics centre on their failure to link their own independently developed mathematical concepts and procedures with the formal rules and algorithms taught in school. Again, dealing with a mathematical problem involves recognising the numerical (or algebraic or geometric or whatever) symbols, calling on relevant knowledge which may be either entirely mathematical, that is, formal, or may be real world general knowledge, and producing the appropriate computations. Many mathematical difficulties arise because symbols are manipulated and computations carried out without any reference to their meaning, although consideration of what they mean would allow a check on the accuracy and appropriateness of the manipulations. Conversely, if appropriate algorithms are lacking, even a well-understood practical situation may only be dealt with approximately and by trial and error; only someone who can compute and measure angles accurately will be able to divide a circular cake into seven equal slices, the rest of us have to divide by eight and distribute the extra slice by deservingness or favouritism rather than by the equal shares principle.

As with reading, skilled mathematical problem-solving seems to involve much metacognitive behaviour – checking, monitoring, relating to other instances, evaluating alternative strategies, defining a sequence of subgoals –

and good mathematics learners get more practice at these activities than do poor ones. Much the same is true throughout the rest of the curriculum, as various papers in Dillon and Sternberg (1986) argue. Successful thinkers elaborate problems and rearrange them into new forms which are easier to deal with; they evaluate proposed solutions for their consistencies and inconsistencies, and examine their implications; they seek and use analogies with other similar situations. Such processes have long been seen as the defining properties of intelligent behaviour (see Sternberg 1982, 1985, and Chapter 3 this volume) and have recently been argued to be among the 'mechanisms of cognitive development' (Siegler 1989b). Recent research in artificial intelligence has found that a number of such basic and general processes are used in many complex tasks. Simulation programmes in several different domains use means–end analysis, subgoal formation, generate-and-test routines, 'executive' or 'metacognitive' procedures and so forth; for each particular problem these processes are applied to an organised body of domain-specific knowledge.

A variety of instructional procedures has been applied in the attempt to transmit knowledge and induce understanding. These can be reviewed in terms of how well they serve the goal of producing people with a rich and flexible repertoire of strategies.

One educational approach eschews instruction, advocating that children should discover or invent strategies themselves, either through their own unaided exploration of the world or with an adult as background provider of fertile learning opportunities. This approach, which has been much used in early childhood education, drew much support from Piagetian theory though it has earlier roots, for example in Rousseau's *Émile*. Its guiding principle is encapsulated in Piaget's own summary of his theory:

> Remember also that each time one prematurely teaches a child something he could have discovered for himself, that child is kept from inventing it and consequently from understanding it completely.
>
> (Piaget 1983: 175)

This is a strong position to take, implying as it does that instruction is virtually always a bad thing. Children undoubtedly do invent their own cognitive strategies, for example in early arithmetic there are many cases of children inventing addition and subtraction strategies (see Hughes 1986, Siegler 1986, and Chapter 2 this volume). However, these strategies often contain mistakes, or 'bugs' (Brown and Burton 1978). Some may in any case be imperfect versions of strategies observed in other people or informally taught by them, not 'inventions de novo' (Saxe *et al.* 1987). And the discovery or invention of a complex strategy is likely to depend on prior mastery of simpler ones and of a great deal of knowledge, although it can be taught to someone who has not done this prior learning and then used by them. The number of people who 'spontaneously' discovered logarithms, for example, is considerably smaller than the number of people who have been taught to use them. There are important limits to the potential usefulness of discovery learning (e.g. Brainerd 1978, 1983, Desforges 1989, Meadows and Cashdan 1988), though its respect for the child's spontaneous activity is important.

The provision of appropriate models to be observed is another comparatively *laissez-faire* form of education. Clearly we are all able to learn from our observations of other people and our imitations of them: early language learning and early socialisation provide many examples. No one taught an under-2-year old who had better remain anonymous to protest at adults' unwanted intervention in her affairs by shouting 'Shut up' and 'You're really sick, you're really really sick', but a small amount of observation of older children (in the first case) and television soap opera (in the second) provided sufficient models. Observing and imitating a model's overt behaviour can be a good way to learn; but in practice, if complex behaviour is involved it requires a comparatively clear model, sufficient time to observe it, and perhaps the prior development of many skills which are components of the model's behaviour. The novice often cannot see what the expert is doing, let alone imitate it, let alone appreciate why it is done. An educationally helpful model will do more than merely model: there will be acts which are demonstrations and instructions and comments on the learner's imitations, not simply parts of the normal execution of the skilled behaviour. Such 'educational modelling' behaviour will be especially necessary for learners who only have an immature repertoire of cognitive and metacognitive skills. It is obviously a component of Vygotskian ways of teaching thinking.

Discovery learning and the observation and imitation of models both presume more activity on the part of the learner than the teacher. Obviously this balance of action and initiative can be reversed. There is a long educational tradition of active teacher intervention in the learning of pupils, so that teachers tell learners things, lead them over and over again through the activity they have to learn, correcting their errors as they take each small step and generally shaping their behaviour. This sort of instruction can be very effective: if the learner goes through the exercises enough times the cognitive processing becomes habitual – practice makes perfect. The danger is that practice may make you set in your ways, prevent you, as Piaget pointed out, from understanding how a strategy works and how it may be modified and applied to new tasks, or from inventing a new strategy which might be better than the taught one. Abstracting such understanding from the use of the strategy will probably require both extensive practice and using it on a gradually widening range of examples (see section on transfer). Alternatively, instruction can include explanations of how the strategy works, as well as instruction on how to do it. It seems to be most useful to provide the learner with information about how the strategy enhances performance: demonstrating that it is 'cost-effective' is an important component of ensuring the strategy continues to be used. The more that a learner knows about a strategy the more likely it is to be transferred appropriately to other tasks (Brown *et al.* 1983).

'Instruction' is of course a composite involving modelling, examples, practice and explanation: the teacher presents knowledge (procedural, declarative and metacognitive), samples the learner's understanding of it, and provides further explanation as required, prior to involving the students in practice and discussion of their achievements. Explicit and well-structured instruction can teach children to execute many cognitive strategies; generalising this learning to new tasks requires learning about how, when and where the strategies can be used. Although the main direction of transmission of knowledge is from teacher to learner, the teacher needs to be sensitive to the learner's skills and reactions, particularly perhaps if the learner is very young or very much a novice. The neo-Vygotskian account of cognitive development (Chapter 4 this volume) of course emphasises that thought develops through social interaction. Adults 'scaffold' the child through the task to be carried out, doing the parts the child cannot do and arranging the situation so that the child can take his or her part. They direct attention to currently relevant features of the task; they suggest what might be considered, remembered or done; they model appropriate actions and strategies; they supervise and provide feedback on the child's actions. Adult and child take turns to carry out the steps of the task, with responsibility for its execution gradually shifting from adult to child; the strategies needed for the task are modelled, overtly, again and again, and the child practises them again and again; the adult gives the child a little more independence after a successful action, and a little more support if there has been a failure or difficulty. The child is helped to progress through the 'zone of proximal development' (Vygotsky 1981, Wood 1988).

Ann Brown and her colleagues have shown that this is a very effective method of instruction (see Brown and Campione 1986, Brown and Ferrara 1985, Brown and Reeve 1987, Palincsar and Brown 1984), as well as a direct means for studying cognitive development (Siegler and Crowley 1991), and there is an increasing number of observational studies showing that adults do indeed often engage in this sort of interaction with children (see Ellis and Rogoff 1982, Lieven 1978, Rogoff and Gardner 1984, Wells 1982a, 1986, Wertsch 1985a, Wood 1988). It is not clear whether the amount of such interaction a child takes part in is related to the rapidity or quality of cognitive development (but see sections on family 'teaching styles', and 'social deprivation and cognitive development' on pp. 319–29) or how the components of 'scaffolded learning and teaching' need to be balanced. One important point about really good scaffolding is that it teaches the learner not just knowledge or strategies but how to be a self-scaffolder, what I have called elsewhere a 'self-running problem-solver' (Meadows and Cashdan

1988). The amount of adult time, sensitivity and commitment required is formidable, so children need to learn to be their own cognitive supports, to be both the trellis and the upward-growing vine, to change the metaphor somewhat. To quote Brown *et al.* (1983: 124):

> Mature thinkers are those who provide conflict trials for themselves, practise through experiments, question their own basic assumptions, provide counter examples to their own rules, and so on. Although a great deal of thinking and learning may remain a social activity, mature reasoners become capable of providing the supportive-other role for themselves through the process of internalisation. Under these systems of tutelage, the child learns not only how to get a particular task done independently but also learns how to set about learning new problems. In other words, the child learns how to learn.

The desired result of learning to think includes, then, at least four major components: many problem-solving strategies, many metacognitive skills, an enormous knowledge base with which these can operate, and a commitment to thinking well and both independently and socially. The different approaches to teaching which I have outlined can be commented on in terms of how they facilitate each of these components. It does seem that learning to execute complex cognitive strategies is easier if the cognitive processes involved are presented with extensive and explicit detail (Bereiter and Bird 1985, Brown *et al.* 1984, Pressley *et al.* 1987). Other less explicit teaching methods can lead to strategy discovery (see Bjorklund and Jacobs 1985, Ornstein and Naus 1985, Ornstein *et al.* 1988), but it is not clear how to make discovery highly probable, nor that discovered strategies are better in either cognitive or motivational ways than learned strategies. More didactic teaching methods such as guided practice can be useful in increasing the efficiency with which a strategy is used, and if they include discussion of the importance of the strategy over a range of contexts, may avoid the danger that the strategy will be learned passively and applied by rote only in a very limited range of situations. Knowing when and where to apply a strategy, and knowing which of one's repertoire of strategies will fit a particular task, are related parts of learning to think. The former is probably facilitated by learning about a range of tasks similar to the ones on which the strategy has already been applied, the latter by extensive practice on using the strategy on the task, plus, perhaps, analysis of the structural features of the task (e.g. Chi *et al.* 1980).

'Metacognitive' and skills attitudes, for example that effort is necessary, that it may be more useful to 'get the feel of the problem' generally before attempting to find a solution than to generate a possible solution quickly, that you are a person who can have confidence in your ability to solve problems, probably develop best from teaching which provides a great deal of sensitive individualised interaction between teacher and learner. An attentive teacher can intervene to make sure that the learner's successes are recognised and failures are overcome, can model or instruct helpful strategies which keep motivation at a useful level, and can help the learner to make helpful attributions for success and failure rather than unhelpful ones ('I got that one wrong because I didn't notice $X$' not 'I got that one wrong because I'm stupid', 'I got that right because I did $Y$' not 'I got that right because it was my lucky day'). Discovery learning may have positive effects on motivation because of its encouragement of the learner's autonomy – the 'I did it all myself' boast will come more easily here – but may not encourage metacognitive analysis. Regimented instruction may serve neither motivation nor metacognition well if it bores the learner and omits space for reflection and generalisation. Neither rote learning nor self-centred discovery are immediately compatible with socially co-operative learning, though they could alternate with it.

Finally, many strategies need an extensive and well-organised base of factual knowledge on which to operate. Some are specific to particular domains of knowledge. I have touched on the role of knowledge acquisition in cognitive development elsewhere in this volume (Chapter 2). It may thus be educationally effective to teach strategies and domain-relevant information at the same time, to seek to link procedural and declarative knowledge. It seems likely that having efficient cognitive strategies for use in a particular domain will enhance both the acquisition and the organisation of factual knowledge in that domain (e.g. Chi and Ceci 1987), so that strategies and knowledge basis improve together. Traditional didactic educational methods emphasise the acquisition of knowledge without considering how knowledge structures and cognitive processes interact, and thus risk the production of knowledge which is applied only in a restricted subset of the situations to which it is relevant, and is not easily examined, criticised and revised. Knowledge acquired through dialogue and subjected to metacognitive examination may be both more flexible and more fruitful.

A large number of courses and programmes for improving thinking skills have been composed (for reviews see Coles and Robinson 1989, Resnick 1987b, Segal et al. 1985, Vye et al. 1988). Not all these programmes have been formally evaluated, and indeed there should perhaps be some debate about what measure of students' improvement should be taken. One of the commonest measures is students' performance on exercises very similar to those which have been taught, which is an appropriate measure but a limited one in so far as the programmes are supposed to teach skills which can be applied over a wider range of the curriculum. Such transfer is desirable but may be difficult to achieve or maintain (see section on transfer, Chapter 2). Intelligence test scores or general school achievement measures may also be used, but these are not necessarily sensitive to improvements in specific thinking skills: a standardised reading test score might be a somewhat indirect measure of students' ability to elaborate or summarise text.

Conversely, although in normal educational conditions there is a positive correlation between thinking skills and educational achievement, this does not establish a causal relationship between them such that improving thinking skills will also improve educational achievement. Measures of specific thinking skills as applied to problems which vary in their resemblance to those on which the student was trained are needed.

A striking example of positive results on such assessments come from studies by Ann Brown and her colleagues (Brown and Reeve 1987, Brown *et al.* 1984, Ferrara *et al.* 1986, Palincsar and Brown 1984). They achieved improvement in reading comprehension via a more deliberate and interpretive approach to text, and this transferred to classroom and private reading and was maintained over a period of months. It is not yet clear exactly what was learned; it may have been that the overt self-conscious strategies which were taught continued to be used overtly and self-consciously throughout, or that they became automated to be used consciously only when comprehension broke down; or that practice on these skills activated other aspects of reading, and improvement on these was more important than the taught strategies themselves; or that the programme cured the emotional difficulties associated with the students' earlier history of being poor at reading and so removed obstacles to reading better. Fine-grained assessment might tease apart these various possibilities, but it could be argued that there is probably an extensive interaction between cognitive, affective and motivational processes.

Resnick (1987b) argues that 'prudent educational practice' should teach cognitive skills explicitly but embedded in the traditional school disciplines. A discipline-embedded approach provides a natural knowledge base and environment of instances on which to practise cognitive skills. As she says, 'one cannot reason in the abstract; one must reason about something', even if that 'something' is part of a formal and abstract system such as logic or mathematics. Disciplines also provide traditional criteria for what is good thinking: mathematics has formal proofs, the physical sciences combinations of inductive and deductive thinking and a respect for objective empirical evidence, the arts and humanities somewhat different rules for constructing arguments, weighing alternatives and evaluating evidence. The criteria for 'higher order cognitive skills' listed on p. 334 (Resnick 1987b: 3) enter into disciplines to varying degrees, but practising any discipline using such skills will enhance learning of that discipline and may encourage the use of the skills in others too. Educationally, transfer may be produced most widely if 'higher order' reading, writing, mathematics and reasoning skills, potentially 'enabling disciplines', are focused on (e.g. Lehman *et al.* 1988).

Resnick advocates cultivating a 'disposition' to think in a skilled way. This she sees as facilitated by social interaction, first because it provides models, second because it allows scaffolding, third because social support and social validation may help convince students that they have the ability, the permission and even the obligation to engage in a kind of critical analysis that does not always accept problem formulations as presented or that may challenge an accepted position.

(Resnick 1987b: 41)

Here motivational research (Connell and Wellborn 1991, Dweck and Elliot 1983, Lepper 1981, Nicholls 1978, and elsewhere in this volume) is clearly relevant.

## SOCIAL INFLUENCES ON CHILDREN'S COGNITIVE DEVELOPMENT: RECAPITULATION AND THEORETICAL DISCUSSION

In order to make sense of what the existing evidence tells us about social and interactional influences on children's cognition, and to integrate this chapter with the earlier parts of this book, it may be useful to reconsider, briefly, what the major theories of cognitive development say about social factors in cognitive development. Of the three 'models' of cognitive development discussed in Chapter 4, Vygotsky's says most about social facilitation, Piaget's less, and the information-processing approach least (with the exception of Case's account of the child's innate predilection for observation, imitation and emotionally motivated learning). It is essentially the Vygotskian approach which is most relevant here, though I will first recapitulate and discuss some of Piaget's ideas, and the idea of observation and imitation as the major route to socially based learning.

Piaget (1932, 1983) listed social influences as one of the four major factors behind cognitive development (the others being equilibration, maturation, and the child's individual experience of the physical and logical-mathematical world), but insisted that children must already have the relevant cognitive structures in order to profit from social influences, that social interaction could only complete their development, not create it. Thus social interaction would only affect cognitive development at times when the child's individually constructed cognitive structures are nearing completion, when the child is a 'transitional' conserver, for example, beginning to give up non-conserving answers in favour of conservation. Further, young children were said to be too egocentric to recognise that there might be a discrepancy between their own ideas and someone else's, and therefore would be less able than older children to use such discrepancies and undergo the cognitive conflict which Piaget saw as essential to cognitive development. Finally, Piaget believed that 'symmetrical' interactions between peers would facilitate cognitive development in ways which 'asymmetrical' interactions between adult and child could not, because adult and child are too unlike in cognitive skills and social status for the child to be able to be an active participant in resolving cognitive disagreement. The Piagetian account of social influences on cognitive development therefore limits them quite severely, and focuses centrally on the symmetrical and active negotiation of cognitive conflict between equals.

The long-running debate over whether this Piagetian account is satisfactory continues (see e.g. Bearison *et al.* 1986, Brainerd 1983, Bryant 1982a, 1985, Doise 1985, Emler and Valiant 1982, Perret-Clermont 1980, Perret-Clermont and Brossard 1985, Russell 1981, Russell *et al.* 1990). There is disagreement, for example, about the relative efficiency of intra-individual conflict, inter-individual conflict, and inter-individual co-operation and confirmation and of active and passive engagement, and over whether symmetrical or asymmetrical relationships are more effective facilitators of learning. The role of age in this is also unclear, but if younger children and older children do, as Piaget suggested, differ in their openness to social facilitation of learning, this difference may be contributing to the inconsistency in the findings of different research studies. There are also difficulties about how cognitive changes are assessed: often the criterion is advance to a successful performance of a task, to becoming a conserver, for example, and smaller advances, such as a longer period of working on the task even though the right solution is not found, or understanding the solution when someone else gives it, are not looked for, though they might be more likely consequences if the amount of exposure to learning opportunities is small.

Thus, although the Piagetian model has given rise to a considerable body of work on the social facilitation of cognitive development, it does not yet provide specific answers about when and how such facilitation occurs, nor about how socially induced learning is incorporated into what remains a mainly individually generated developmental course. Socio-cognitive conflict provokes disequilibrium which the child then equilibrates; thus all the problems with what equilibration is and how it works which I raised in Chapter 4 arise. Finally, the Piagetian model sees other people as a part of the child's total environment not so very different from its other parts, facilitating cognitive development because they hold views of the outside world differing from the child's own, more than because they have social goals and intentions. In view of the increasing evidence of children's tendency to treat persons and inanimate objects as different in kind from babyhood onwards (see Kaye 1984, Trevarthen 1982), we might do well to look at theories which take a more social-centred approach to cognition.

Social learning theory (Bandura 1977b) proposes that children learn by observing and imitating others. It is argued that children do naturally imitate (cf. Case 1985), that social reinforcement motivates this, that models to be imitated are usually socially desirable (for example in being more competent cognitively than the learner), and that thus children will often learn through observation and imitation of more skilled cognition than their own. In this account of learning, the person who is imitated may not be deliberately modelling behaviour, so the 'social' component of the learning process is in the social reward outcomes of imitation and the social desirability of the model, rather than in the process of learning or in social interaction between imitator and imitated. I think it is helpful to be reminded that children do learn by imitation of 'accidental' models, models who are not seeking to teach them, but questions of what 'imitation' is, how it works, remain. What conditions are necessary for imitation to be possible? How near must the learner's initial skills be to what is imitated? Does behaviour first learned through imitation undergo further change; for example if it is, as Piaget suggested, very much accommodation, is it followed by assimilation, and would that alter the imitated behaviour? Does the way the model presents the behaviour which is imitated affect how easy it is to imitate it, or how durable and well-learned the imitation is? Social learning theory as such has not provided answers to these questions. They are however taken seriously in the most influential of current social-centred theories of cognition, that originating in Vygotsky's work.

For Vygotsky (as for G. H. Mead), cognition originates in social interaction and centres on children's appropriation of cultural tools, goals and activities, which they internalise in their coming to be fully functioning members of their cultures. Interaction with other people, especially more skilled people who take the responsibility for keeping the interaction within the learner's Zone of Proximal Development, and who use language and non-verbal teaching strategies to facilitate the child's learning, is a central part of this. The more competent partner structures the interaction so that the child is able to participate in increasingly complex ways, eventually managing all the actions necessary for a successful completion of the task. There is a transition from other-regulation to self-regulation so that eventually no support from another person is necessary, though recognition and praise from a skilled other may remain welcome, as the Nobel Prize system shows! Ultimately this 'scaffolding' technique of teaching has been so well internalised by the learners that they can provide it for themselves in new learning situations; the learning child internalises the teacher's actions and reflections, transforming them into his or her own way of solving that particular problem or doing that particular task, but also internalising and developing more general tools – how to observe, how to imitate, how to analyse, how to scaffold one's own cognitive activity or another person's. These powerful 'metacognitive' activities contribute to making the learner into a 'self-running problem-solver' (Meadows and Cashdan 1988). The neo-Vygotskian model of teaching centres on scaffolding: the model of learning involves a wide range of processes ranging from mindless imitation to reflective abstraction of general principles of metacognition. It could thus be seen as the best current candidate for understanding social influences on cognitive development. Whether it is sensible to determine a 'best' model at present is a question in need of further discussion, however; it is given some in Chapter 6.

# Chapter 6

# Questions, problems – and possibilities

The final chapter of the ideal book on the development and acquisition of cognition in childhood might contain one or more of the following components: a recapitulation of the most important points made earlier; an overview of the field which provides a clear and comprehensive synthesis of work to date; an exciting new theory indicating where future research should be done; an inspired and practicable pedagogy and curriculum. This chapter contains none of these components. I would like to be able to provide them, but I cannot. There is little to be gained from summarising earlier chapters when they are themselves all too summary accounts of much more material. The field is too heterogeneous and in parts uncertain to allow a synthesis (indeed one of the disagreeable surprises of working on this book was the degree to which the same phenomena could be subjected to incompatible models, not all of them even mutually intelligible, and another was how much research still focused on 'getting age differences' with only minimal appeal to explanation and theory, thus having little linkage to any model). I do have theoretical ideas about cognitive development, but not an exciting new theory, indeed I have learned from examining the theories of cognitive development which I discuss in this book that theoretical progress is more likely to be made at a level where behaviour is carefully specified (as in the analysis of what 'phonological awareness' is and how it relates to reading) than at the level of behaviour so general and all-pervasive that it is abstract and untestable (as, for example, assimilation and accommodation). I have tried to present material on cognitive development which is relevant to the concerns of teachers, but again the research literature suggests there is no universally appropriate curriculum and pedagogy (and there remains a substantial discrepancy between the practices which the developmental psychologist who has studied children's cognitive development might suggest, and the practices which an under-resourced and over-stressed school system can implement).

So I find I can't end with a solution, or even a set of solutions, that I really believe to be correct. Further, although I believe that what I have said in earlier chapters is, largely, true and may even cohere, and in my life as a parent and teacher I act on it, I do not want it to pass unquestioned. Instead, I am going to highlight some problems and omissions, in the hope that if we can produce some good thinking on these we will make further progress towards understanding the development and acquisition of cognition in childhood.

## PROBLEMS OF DIAGNOSIS

Diagnosing cognitive development involves a troublesome tangle of assessment and conceptualisation problems. It is necessary to know what cognition is involved in a particular task, for example reading or making a logical inference or conserving number. 'Is involved in' could mean 'what cognition is necessary', 'what cognition is sufficient' and 'what cognition people actually do'; developmentalists necessarily take on this last meaning particularly acutely as 'people' may well do different things if they differ in age, experience or understanding. Finding out what cognititive processes are necessary or sufficient for a task might be done by armchair analysis or by computer simulation; finding out what people do involves getting out there and assessing them. Any such assessment will have to involve a finely tuned test procedure. False positives may arise if the task allows guessing, hints at the right answer, or could be 'solved' by processes other than the ones thought to be necessary: a child might 'read' a text correctly because it is so familiar it has been memorised, for example. Conversely, there is the problem of false negatives: the child might not understand the task instructions, might not attend to essential information or might forget it part way through, might have misleading ideas about what is being asked for, might not be motivated to address the task properly, might have emotional problems such as anxiety about being tested, might be unable to verbalise an answer even though it has been correctly worked out, might be put off an answer because the experimenter seems to be expecting something else. All the problems of work with people from a different 'culture' from the tester's (Cole and Means 1981) apply to work with children and may be all the more intractable because we expect them to approach the task with assumptions and expectations very much like our own. The recent history of work on cognitive development is full of demonstrations that earlier assessments showing children failing on tasks had produced false negatives, and that in other tests of 'the same task' children could succeed (e.g. Light and Perret-Clermont 1989).

A diagnosis of a child's cognition might be more secure if it rests on the child's response to a range of assessments rather than relying on one test situation. However this of course raises the problem of inconsistency between test results from different versions of the task. If the different versions have been constructed in a principled way so that the ways in which they differ are clear, then test–test variability may reveal a great deal about the demands of the tasks and what cognition is crucial, what optional. It may also reveal things about the cognition of the individual, because one of the conceptual problems linked to the diagnosis of cognition is what we mean when we say someone 'has' or 'understands' a particular cognitive process or structure, even more perhaps when we say someone 'does not have' it. There may be a good match between 'competence' and 'performance', or disastrous lapses on the one hand and flashes of over-achievement on the other. It may be worth thinking how 'understanding' might vary in systematic ways: it might vary in its accessibility, in how well it can be used, in its links to other cognitive contents, in its range of application, in its certainty. Thinking of cognition as being developed in social contexts, even of it as constituted by social contexts, will be one important dimension of this. Vygotsky's ideas about the Zone of Proximal Development and Ann Brown's about microgenetic testing suggest that assessment of the child as a collaborator with a more expert person, or of the child during training on the concept, may be a most illuminating part of diagnosing cognitive development. More radically, this view might under-mine the idea that cognition is a matter of internal understanding and that we can attribute competence or the possession of a cognitive rule, process or structure to an individual, in favour of the idea that such rules, processes or structures are only our ways of describing behaviour which was learned in and cannot ever be independent of social practices (Gellatly 1989). The behaviour provides instances of cognitive principles: it is not controlled, let alone explained, by them. What we need is good descriptions of behaviour which we link with good models of rules and processes without reifying the latter; and the behaviour will be studied in its social contexts, which must also be well described. Getting such descriptions and models is a goal worth aiming for, but achieving it is not going to be easy.

## PATTERNS OF COGNITIVE DEVELOPMENT

There are marked changes in cognitive behaviour over the years of childhood; new concepts, skills and strategies emerge. Do they do so in a consistent pattern? How are the various aspects of cognitive development related? Are there consistent sequences or co-occurrences of development? Are changes qualitatitive or quantitative? Are there 'stages'? Are there individual differences between children in their cognitive development? Are any such individual differences quantitative or qualitative, consistent or unpatterned? These are questions which have been controversial for thirty or forty years, and could be traced further back. They are also questions whose answers are unclear, even in principle. Among the issues involved are, again, questions of diagnosis and conceptualisation.

When I discussed concepts of what 'cognitive development' is, in Chapter 4, I outlined Piaget's model, which describes it as largely an organism-generated sequence of universal stages, each characterised by a stable and coherent structure of principles or operations; the information-processing model, which focuses on more local sequences of skills within domains and describes sequences in behaviour which are logically necessary rather than broad general stages; and the Vygotskian model, which sees cognition as socially constituted and again places little emphasis on separate stages (though some of Vygotsky's work, for example the development of concepts, might be a partial exception to this). These models differ in their basic conceptual assumptions: Piaget's could be called organismic, information-processing's mechanistic, Vygotsky's social-constructivist. Interest in 'stages' is more common in theories which use an organismic metaphor, and most of the work on cognitive stages centres on the Piagetian model. The degree to which Piagetian stages can be seen in children's cognitive behaviour has been a matter for fierce debate and considerable uncertainty, such that John Flavell, one of the best-informed people in the field, published two incompatible decisions in the same year and called himself 'undecided to the point of public self-contradiction' (Flavell 1985, commenting on Flavell 1982a and 1982b). It is an intractable problem. Diagnosing a 'stage' is going to involve all the difficulties of assessment and conceptualisation which arise in diagnosing even a single cognitive operation, increasing exponentially as the number of tests and operations increases. If a number of tasks require the same basic cognitive operations and these operations form a coherent stage, then success on these tasks (given tests of equivalent sensitivity or difficulty) should be achieved at much the same time. There is remarkably little evidence of this happening. Rather a lot of claims of 'stages', including Piaget's and, I suspect, the 'theory of mind' research more recently, relies on the change from $A_1$ to $A_2$ occurring over the same age range as the change from $B_1$ to $B_2$, $C_1$ to $C_2$, and so forth; but the children (and even the researchers) who provided data on A are not the same individuals as those who provided data on B: sometimes the design is completely cross-sectional so that the children who showed behaviour $A_1$ are a different (younger) sample from those who behaved in an $A_2$ way. I felt twenty years ago, as I began my PhD, that claims of stages would be more firmly grounded if they had evidence on tests of several of the operations that together constituted a stage for all subjects, gathered longitudinally so that the co-occurrence of change could be examined. At that time there were no such studies. Mine (Meadows 1975) found no evidence of 'staginess' in children's performance on nine tests of 'concrete operations', and as these tests were well used in the Piagetian literature, and as the operations which they diagnosed were central to the stage, I emerged from the activity with little belief in the existence of clear-cut, coherent, rapidly achieved stages. Diehard Piagetians may continue to assert their stage model and point out the faults of the assessments that provide no evidence of stages, but while researchers find rather considerable unevenness and even regression in performance (Flavell

1982b, Gelman and Baillargeon 1983, Klausmeier and Sipple 1982, Meadows 1975, Vuyk 1981), the onus is on them to provide a fault-free demonstration of stages. The development of performance is age-related, but being stagelike in the sense of being clearly discontinuous, cohesive, synchronous or even across tasks requires stronger evidence than is available in most areas.

Stage models of cognitive development tend also to neglect the possibility of individual differences except those related to the individual's position in the stage sequence. Some are not even interested in differences in rate of progress through the stages. One uniform path through the stage sequence is assumed to be normal, natural and inevitable. This may not be a wise assumption. Models of cognitive development which see it as in large part socially constituted and culturally specific, and which link it to motivation and emotion and therefore to personality, would assume that, on the contrary, there would be several different – even many different – pathways from early to mature cognition. Perhaps a biologically based model of cognition, using parallels with evolution, and aware of how brain development proceeds by the proliferation and selective dying-off of nerve cell connections and experience-expectant and experience-dependent development, would similarly propose that there might be marked individual differences in cognitive development. Again, the problems of conceptualisation and diagnosis arise.

In short, there are enormous methodological problems in providing a good account of the 'what' of cognitive development. A number of different approaches are possible; each is, I suspect, necessary but not sufficient. Perhaps the most commonly used is laboratory equipment-type assessment of performance. This can provide data about performance and some of the factors that affect it, but it uses a social situation that is unfamiliar to young children and they may not show optimum performance for the reasons I discussed apropos of 'false negatives' earlier in this section. A *series* of careful experiments may clarify complex performance and even reveal abilities which have not been apparent in the world outside the laboratory. Laboratory studies can also assess the effects of changes in conditions or compare subjects, and they are very useful for training studies. However the effects shown in the laboratory can only be extrapolated to the outside world with great caution: it will be necessary to examine the 'real world' carefully to see whether the same factors are working in the same way.

Descriptions of what individuals do in the real social world complement laboratory assessments. They can provide evidence on cognitive behaviour and how it is affected by various factors, but real world conditions are less controlled (and more complex) than the laboratory, and causes and consequences will almost certainly be less clear. Real life interventions, such as educational programmes, can produce strong evidence for causal effects if they have adequate controls, but it may be difficult to tease out exactly what in the intervention brought about the effect. We have to have dialogue, indeed dialectics, between laboratory and real world studies.

## PROBLEMS OF EXPLANATION

As well as describing the phenomena of cognitive development, we might wish to explain them. As well as the question 'what are children's cognitive behaviours?' there are the questions 'why are they like that?' and 'why and how do they change?'. These look like even harder questions than the 'what' ones, and not separate from them. If, for example, we described some aspect of cognition as being unchanged from its earliest measurement to maturity, our 'change' question would concern *lack* of change: 'why is it stable and unmodified for so long?'. Uncertainties and errors about 'what' will lead to uncertainties and errors about 'why' and 'how'; uncertainties and errors about 'why' and 'how' will lead to problems about 'what'.

It may be helpful to begin my brief discussion of this problem with the four different sets of causal question which ethologists have found it useful to distinguish. These are the complementary cornerstones of the systematic study of behaviour (Hinde 1982, 1987). What is the proximal cause of behaviour, the immediate stimulus which triggered it? How does the behaviour develop, what is its ontogenetic course from infancy to maturity? What is its function, what is it for? How did this behaviour evolve, how did it change during evolution? These four sorts of 'cause' are distinguishable but also linked, and we are going to have to proceed in a way that allows comparison and cross-classification between attempts to explain behaviour at these different complementary levels.

The 'why' of cognitive development could profitably be looked at, I think, at most of these ethological levels. A complete examination in this way would be an enormous undertaking; here I will just draw together some relevant points, mainly at the evolutionary level. Human beings have, like all other animals, come to be as they are now through a long evolutionary history during which natural selection favoured individuals with particular characteristics and these characteristics were passed on to succeeding generations. One part of this selection process has worked in such a way that considerable cognitive development after birth is both necessary and possible. Human beings have large brains in large skulls and pelvises too narrow for a large skull to pass through without damage to both mother and baby: the foetus's skull must not get too large before birth and there will therefore be considerable brain growth after it. Human beings live in social groups and therefore need complex cognitive skills for their interaction with each other. Human beings amplify their limited sensori-motor powers with tools and therefore need complex cognitive skills for their interaction with the non-human world. Human beings produce small numbers of offspring, have minimally-sized litters of immature and completely helpless babies, who therefore need a long period of being taken care of by more adult human beings. Many infant characteristics persist in human beings for much longer than they do in other species (Gould 1977). This 'neoteny', or slowing down of maturation, allows us among other things a much longer period during which we can learn from experience and during which other people can teach us. Cognitive development as such can be seen as just one inevitable aspect of evolutionary destiny (Wohlwill 1973).

Development in the cognitive area (and in the affective, the motivational and the social areas) no doubt does have this evolutionary component to it. But two limiting points have to be taken into account. First, the degree to which evolution specifies what cognitive development may be is highly debatable. Given what we know about the openness of the developing brain to learning from experience (Chapter 5), and about the effect of experience on the development of behaviour, I doubt whether the evolutionary component dictates very much very strongly. Discussion continues about the possible 'innateness' of various cognitive capacities, for example language, face recognition, distinguishing between the animate and inanimate worlds, notions of causality, notions of number. Part of the problem is the complex set of meanings that 'innate' has:

> At least six meanings are attached to the term: present at birth; a behavioural difference caused by a genetic difference; adapted over the course of evolution; unchanging throughout development; shared by all members of a species; and not learned.
>
> (Bateson 1991b: 21)

Further than this, something which is innate in even several of these senses may nevertheless be modified subsequently by learning from experience. My ability to vocalise is innate, but my vocal behaviour is substantially modified from its beginnings in infancy by a complex history of learning from experience.

I must also point out that many cognitive skills have been invented too recently to be subject to evolutionary pressures. Evolution by natural selection takes several generations, and it is unlikely in the extreme that natural selection has provided us with the cognitive skills of computer use, understanding calculus, or even reading. So far as we know, human brains have not changed much in size or complexity over the last few thousand years (Gottlieb 1983), although over these years there has been an immense change in the use of cognitive skills, both in their spread across more and more of the population and in the invention of new skills and applications. Whatever evolution-given prerequisite skills we bring to reading, mathematics, science, the arts, or the humanities, we learn to use these skills in ways that go far beyond their evolutionarily specified foundations and are unlikely to be strictly limited by evolution. Cognitive development, like physical maturation, takes place within the normal expectable human environment. Variations in this environment will affect its fine-tuning, and may, if extreme, affect it more radically. Prodigious achievers (Radford 1990) and socially deprived children (Skuse 1984) demonstrate two extremes due very largely to exceptional environments. What sort of environmental experience affects a cognitive skill to a noticeable degree will vary according to what sort of cognitive skill is being considered; cognition such as Piaget's sensori-motor stage, which has presumably been characteristic of most human infancy for thousands and thousands of years, will be less affected by experience than recently invented cognitive skills such as computer use or memorising strategies. Enrichment studies, deprivation studies, and, perhaps most of all, training studies, will be useful in examining environmental effects; and as I discuss in the last section of this chapter, we badly need a good account of the environment in cognitive development.

Both the evolutionary and the functional level of questions about behaviour draw attention to the fact that behaviour requires resources and involves costs and benefits. This is not so often considered in the literature on cognitive development as it might be, and we have no highly developed description of the economics of cognition. I will venture a few preliminary remarks. Cognitive development will depend on the availability of resources within the individual, within other persons, and in the surrounding environment. Resources of working memory (see sections on information-processing models and on memory), of knowledge and skills available from earlier learning (see sections on concepts and on constraints in development), of motivation and energy, of a correctly working nervous system (see Chapters 3 and 5) will be necessary inside the individual; external resources will include caretakers' and teachers' structuring of the child's time and space and motivation, and the information, sustenance and rewards offered. Deficiencies in one sort of resource may be compensated for by riches in another, as when devoted parents manage to teach a handicapped child to reach average levels of performance in school (Chapter 5) or a very intelligent child can maintain his or her concentration despite poor parenting which has negatively scaffolded his abilities (Chapter 5). Resources may be concentrated on one area of development to the cost of other areas, as in 'hothouse' training of prodigies or the activities of 'idiot savants' (Chapters 3 and 5). External resources may be controlled initially by the parents, who also use their internal resources to supplement the child's immature capacities (as in scaffolding, see especially Chapter 5), and later more control may be exercised by the child.

Changing cognitive behaviour may require an input of time and energy higher than is available, so that there is a certain inertia and delay in achieving further growth (e.g. Karmiloff-Smith and Inhelder 1974/5). Cognitive processes may be a drain on resources until they are well practised and automatic (Chapter 4), when they may contribute positively to further development by providing basic skills or material for analogies or processes which get round difficulties. Environments may require particular sorts of cognition and support particular sorts of cognition; what is 'functional' in the evolutionary long term and the immediate short term will depend on the balance of internal and external needs and resources that the individual is faced with. Clearly, no 'explanation' of cognitive development is going to be able to rely on only one factor: a more or less Piagetian list of maturation, social experience, physical experience and assimilation or accommodation looks like the minimum which we must develop.

## CONSTRAINTS ON COGNITIVE DEVELOPMENT

I mentioned in earlier chapters the problem of how children can ever begin on the task of understanding phenomena which are highly complex and could have an infinite number of structures. One example was the problem of inferring the meaning of a word: how can one work out what a term such as 'red' refers to unless one already has the appropriate concept? Without a concept of 'colour', 'red' might refer to anything to do with the objects it labels: their colour, indeed, but equally that they are pointed out, or that they are visible, or that they exist. A number of psychologists suggest that we cannot learn without some a priori constraints on our learning, where by constraints is meant 'factors intrinsic to the learner which result in a non-random selection among the logically-possible characteristics of an informational pattern' (Keil 1990: 137). As learners, we have to have something which enables us to choose between the alternative models we could construct of any given occurrrence: a bias towards assuming that a word refers to a whole object not a part of it, unless that is specifically signalled (Markman 1990); a bias towards understanding events in causal terms, or needing a causal explanation of events (Brown 1990, Gelman 1990); a bias towards counting in a principled way (Gelman 1990, Gelman and Meck 1983, 1986), are among recent suggestions. Having biases of these sorts would reduce the complexity and the uncertainty of an array to a somewhat more manageable level. To put it in a Piagetian way, we cannot assimilate information unless there is something to assimilate it to; to put it in a mainstream American way, we need a reasonable degree of match between what we already know and what we have to learn.

Constraints on cognition could be of various sorts and have a range of different causes. Some very wide-ranging constraints would arise from the nature of the human nervous system. Our senses provide us with visual and auditory information which we rely on in our cognition; we make much less use of smell, though it may affect us more than we ordinarily suppose. We seem to learn by building up networks of associations which are constantly being reconstituted and modified. We have a limited attention span and short-term memory and cannot process too many different things at the same time. Characteristics such as these put some constraints on what we learn and how we learn it, and although they are weak constraints, modifiable by experience and training, they operate from birth to death over a wide range of cognitive domains. Some physical characteristics apply over a more limited area: our colour perception and our use of different speech sounds are based on physical sensitivities and have implications for such diverse areas as colour categorisation and learning to read. We may develop skills in these areas which transform them from their constrained beginnings, but a number of biases remain.

A special issue of *Cognitive Science* contains papers on such constraints in cognitive development. Newport (1990) argues that there are maturational changes in language learning. Processing constraints mean that children faced with complex stimuli such as language form a representation of *pieces* of those stimuli only, while adults make a more complex representation of the whole. Children, having only fragmentary representations, are in a better position for analysing them into components and hence learning from them than they would be if they had a complex representation without any idea of how to select an analysis. Computer simulations apparently suggest that it is easier to analyse and learn about fragments than about a very complex whole even if the fragments are random, and there might be biases in what aspects of the stimuli are represented such that the fragments are not random. Newport suggests that it is because they normally function on the basis of analysed scraps rather than on the basis of fully represented wholes that children are able to pick up language to communicate with so quickly, while taking a much longer time to perfect its details and represent it as a whole system to be reflected on; and to do well on component-based learning tasks while being worse than adults on tasks which require the integration of complex stimuli. Markman (1990) suggests further constraints in children's learning of language: they work on the assumption that new words apply to new objects as a whole, not to parts, that different words apply to different objects so that one object should not be referred to by different words, and that names apply taxonomically not thematically. Thus a child learning a new word, as in 'that's a goose', would constrain its meaning to the newly encountered fowl as an entity, not to its waddle or its feathers; would regard it as inappropriate to an object which already has a known label, such as a chicken; and would apply 'goose' to 'goose-like' objects such as swans and ducks, not to objects thematically linked to geese, such as eggs, ponds, nursery rhymes, lawnmowers and the nightwatchmen of ancient Rome.

Gelman (1990) extends the discussion to cognitive development. She suggests that it is directed by skeletal sets of domain-specific principles, with their rules of application and of which entities they apply to. These constitute the structured outline of the domain. An example is the 'how-to-count' principles (Gelman and Gallistel 1978, Gelman and Meck 1983, 1986), which are related to the wider principles of arithmetical reasoning.

These domain-specific principles may constrain learning even if they are not part of the learner's explicitly represented understanding of the domain, as in the counting activities of infants and very young children. Some may be implicit in the general information-processing mechanisms we use (particularly if they apply across domains, as short-term memory's organisation should do), and some might be wired-in to the brain. An example of this might be the way in which we map information across modalities, maintaining a single unitary spatial matrix, not allowing an entity mapped in two modalities to be placed at two different positions in our mental representation of where things are in space. Wired-in constraints like this may have a critical period during which their functioning becomes integrated and fixed (see Chapter 5). They might also reflect evolutionary internalisation of certain external, physical, constraints on objects (Gottlieb 1983, Keil 1990), perhaps what Gibson called their 'affordances' (Gibson 1979); presumably organisms which generally acted as if a seen object should be heard to be at the seen location and not elsewhere would be more likely to survive and reproduce than those which did not.

Domain-specific principles establish the boundaries of relevant stimulation (for example the colour of objects is irrelevant to counting them, except when the task is to count objects of a particular colour). They constrain both what information is taken in and how it is responded to. They provide a skeleton which the stimulation can be wrapped around. Thus they help the learner to solve problems of relevance and coherent storage at a time when he or she has not yet learned much: they give a 'leg-up' by providing a kind of mental apparatus which supports learning, structured tools for attending to information and storing it. These are, of course, the sorts of support which the scaffolding adult gives the learner (see Chapters 2, 4 and 5 this volume). *Cognitive Science*'s special issue does not focus on scaffolding as a supplier of constraints on cognitive development, though several of the contributors to the issue recognise its importance. Perhaps one of the constraints we bring to learning is an attention to other people's selection of information and their structuring of events.

Brown (1990) points out the importance of understanding the basic causal mechanism for learning about information, for transferring what is learned to other occasions, and for analogical reasoning. She argues that if they do understand causes, children learn relatively easily, are persistent and self-motivated and show goal-directed spontaneous error correction and rehearsal, insightful learning and rapid transfer (for other data see Brown 1989). Children have predispositions to learn about particular kinds of things, showing early sensitivity to critical cues and systematic exploratory learning of the relevant causal knowledge (das Gupta and Bryant 1989). By the age of 7 or 8 they have fairly efficient general-purpose learning processes, and further learning is a combination of the information they have to acquire, and the development of increasingly complex applications of that knowledge.

These domain-specific constraints on development are reminiscent of M. Anderson's suggestion of 'modules' in the development of intelligence (Anderson 1989a, 1992, and see Chapter 3 above). We have little hard evidence of their existence, and little that explains why they would exist and how they affect development. A third sort of 'constraint' is perhaps more obvious. What you have learned influences what you learn next, both in the process of learning and in what sort of representation you make of what is learned. Someone who is a novice in an area may learn a new piece of information as an isolated fact, with no close connection to the rest of the domain and no implications for it. The same piece of information will be linked into the domain for the expert, and may confirm, or supplement, or overturn the way the domain is understood. There may be quite strong domain-specific constraints on cognition within that domain, especially in the ways in which prior learning affects new learning. The model we have of a particular topic will affect how we deal with new material on that topic, and, through our use of analogies, may affect our cognition in other domains. Whether this is an advantage or not will depend on the adequacy of the model.

## COGNITION AND EMOTION IN DEVELOPMENT

One of the omissions of the earlier chapters of this book has been the omission of anything like an adequate discussion of the interplay of emotion and cognition in cognitive development. This reflects what has been until recently an almost complete failure to recognise any affective streak in cognitive development. Most of the literature on cognitive development pays no attention whatever to emotion. The information-processing model is affect-free as well as asocial, in theoretical principle as well as in practice. Piaget's work touched on emotion in the early stages but apart from mentioning it as a process which energised cognitive development said little about it; even Vygotsky's account of cognitive development in culturally based settings and interactions largely neglected the emotional side of people's experience. Studies of intelligence ignore emotion (Sternberg being the nearest to considering it), and it remains well below visibility even in work on cognitive style and creativity. Paul Harris's work on children's understanding of emotions fills a gap in the literature on the development of cognitive content (Harris 1989, and Chapter 2 this volume), and is one of the examples of how careful experiment and ecologically valid samples can help to clarify important issues; but elsewhere emotion is a Cinderella of cognitive development.

I won't pretend to be her fairy godmother, but I can begin to bring together some of the recent work which might be put together into the magic coach that will take her to the ball. There begins to be a case for regarding the interface of emotional well-being, cognitive models of the world, and social relationships as a prime area for an integrated understanding of development with applications both to 'normal' development and to developmental psychopathology.

In order to focus my discussion on what seems to me to be most exciting at this point of the book, I am going to deal very briefly indeed with some of the wide range of issues that could be raised. First, although I would have liked to extend my account of the brain and cognitive development with an account of the brain in cognitive-and-emotional development, there are debates here which are not easy to resolve (see e.g. Fisher *et al.* 1990, Gray 1990, Le Doux 1989, Panksepp 1990). The debate beginning with William James's analysis of emotion in the 1880s continues. While it seems to be agreed that 'emotion' involves perception, appraisal and reaction *vis-à-vis* a disturbing event, there is disagreement over the sequencing and the locality of brain processing information about emotion-producing stimulation and their cognitive appraisal. All sorts of complex issues are involved over the conceptual nature of emotion, the identification of the brain areas involved and their interconnections, how affective and cognitive information-processing compare and interact, the specificity or ambiguity of emotional arousal, the accessibility to conscious awareness of affective information-processing, the timing of events in the emotion sequence, how short-term changes in a neural network dealing with an emotional situation are reflected in longer-term ones, and so on. Campos *et al.* (1989) and Lazarus (1991) point out that changes in our conception of emotion are emerging. The traditional view was that emotion was a special subjective state, intrapsychic rather than relation-based. They believe that it involves, rather, processes of establishing, maintaining or disrupting relations between a person and the internal or external environment, when such relations are significant to the individual because they are relevant to goals, or involve emotional communication with other individuals, or have purely hedonic qualities of physical pain, discomfort or pleasure. Thus, among my potential emotions at the moment might be positive ones, from being near to reaching the goal of finishing writing this book, from the physical beauty of the summer day just outside the window, from the music coming from the radio behind me where the end of *The Marriage of Figaro* is speaking of forgiveness and reconciliation. There might also be negative ones, physical discomfort in an overworked right wrist, anxiety about whether what I am writing is appropriate, missing the small daughter who is at the moment away with her friends. None of these seem to be at the moment to be of great importance, so my conscious emotional state is merely mildly positive. A cognitive appraisal of the individual's relations with the environment establishes their significance and is a necessary component of emotion.

Campos *et al.* (1989) also emphasise that emotions have interpersonal consequences: they function to maintain, elicit or end other people's behaviour and to signal to others. For example, the individual's expressions of joy, of success in progressing towards a goal, function to maintain other people's positive interactions, while expressions of sadness, of relinquishing a relation with the environment, of individual helplessness when adaptive action is impossible, signal to elicit help and comfort from others. The actual reaction of the others is not of course guaranteed: the 3-year-old artist's joy at her beautiful felt pen drawing on the kitchen floor may elicit from her mother not joy at its aesthetic qualities but anger at its interference with the maternal goal of clean floors and drawings restricted to proper pieces of paper. However, well-meaning interactants are likely to acknowledge each other's emotions even if they cannot themselves share them: discussion of why emotions are or are not shared or acceptable seems to be an important part of the child's curriculum (Dunn 1988, Dunn *et al.* 1987). It is also possible to argue that human cognition evolved to a highly complex level because individuals living in large permanent social groups had to lead complex social lives, in which an ability to use emotional signals appropriately, and to attend particularly closely to emotion-arousing situations (as small children do) would be especially important (e.g. Byrne and Whiten 1988, Humphrey 1983).

This view of emotion as being concerned with the relationships of events to an individual's needs and goals links it to motivation, to social interaction and to cognition. It gives equal status to the person's appreciation of the significance of events, the person's feelings which are monitors of events, and the individual's coping strategies, the ways he or she deals with the environment. Such a model necessarily implies developmental change, notably in cognitive appraisal and in coping strategies. I will not attempt a full account of the issues and the data in this area here (see pp. 127–9 above, Harris 1989, Lazarus 1991, Thompson 1990a, for further discussion), but merely mention a few points concerning how this development seems to happen. I want to stress the centrality of emotional regulation, of having to compromise between the perhaps intense and egocentric emotional expression which might come spontaneously, and the perhaps more demure and restricted emotional expression which the culture's rules of etiquette prescribe. (Etiquette may of course prescribe an amplification and exag-geration of a naturally moderate emotional expression; the most familiar English middle-class example of this is probably making 'thank yous' for gifts which are not especially exciting.) It seems that learning emotional regulation fits very well into the apprentice–master model, as it proceeds by a combination of adults doing it for the infant or young child, adults scaffolding the child's attempts, adult and child discussing and reflecting on what is done, and responsibility passing gradually from the more skilled adult to the becoming-skilled child (Thompson 1990b). Similar processes may contribute to the learning of complex social emotions such as guilt (Zahn-Waxler and Kochanska 1990). What is perhaps of particular developmental interest is what range of individual differences arise from differences in parental handling of the child's emotions. The volume edited by Thompson (1990a) includes some interesting reviews of the development of children under abnormal parenting conditions.

My focus here is on the possibility that people may have 'emotional biases' which influence their cognitive development. Malatesta (1990) argues that individuals become predisposed to a characteristic mood state as a result of biologically based traits such as temperament which are operated on by repetitive social experiences. Certain emotional states are frequent and salient, and become part of feelings about the self, so that they can then influence a wide range of behaviours, such as perception, emotional expression, cognitive processing and social relations. On the whole, there may be considerable stability in this so that something like a strong and pervasive personality trait is built up over time to operate in a self-perpetuating way. La Frenière and Sroufe (1985), for example, found significant stability in measures of aggression, affiliativeness and affect in young children; Kagan (1984) found shyness and behavioural inhibition showing continuity from childhood to early adulthood (see also Kagan *et al.* 1987).

There is not a great deal of evidence on how emotional state affects cognition. Experimentally induced moods have been shown to produce short-term cognitive biases in perception, learning, judgement and memory (Anastasi 1985, Bower 1981, Williams *et al.* 1988); children who were habitually aggressive made different appraisals of people's intentions towards them from those of more peaceful children (Dodge *et al.* 1986), and maltreated children and control (non-maltreated) children processed aggressive and non-aggressive stimuli differently (Cicchetti 1990, Rieder and Cicchetti 1989). Mood probably biases attention and ability (and willingness) to concentrate, and may bias what could be considered more purely cognitive processes through its effects on the network of connotations of any stimulus. Particular cognitive activities may come to have emotional connotations themselves (maths anxiety, for example), and cognitive processes may become part of the regulation of emotion (Santostefano 1985).

There are likely to be developmental changes in the perception, appraisal and regulation of emotional states. Infants react to notable changes with emotion, negatively if their goals are interfered with, positively if goals are reached or confirmed. Emotional expressions are detectable from birth, and there seems to be individual stability in the expression of anger and sadness over the first two years. By 9 months of age or thereabouts other people's emotional expression may guide the baby's own expression of affect. In babies there is a fairly clear relationship between their emotion, its expression, and the circumstances which caused it: caretakers perceive, interpret, act on and comment on the child's mood, so sensitising the child to emotional cues and the linkages between expression, behaviour and causal stimulation. There are stable individual differences here (Dunn *et al.* 1987) which affect the rate of children's development of emotional discourse and understanding. Systematic shaping of children's emotional behaviour may be part of the way in which caretakers influence their development; the range and type of comments which caretakers make about emotional states may determine both the child's emotional expression and the sorts of emotional state that can be communicated to others and to oneself (Bretherton 1990, Lewis and Michalson 1983, Miller 1985), perhaps to a psychopathological degree. Interpretations of other people's emotions are also likely to be affected by our own emotional experience. Our 'working model' of people has a strong emotional component.

Perhaps because so much of the work which unites social, emotional and cognitive strands in development stems from a practical interest in developmental psychopathology, which often involved the examination of the mother–child relationship, it focuses on early repeated social interactions with familiar partners as the main source of emotional organisation and cognition. Interaction with caretakers leads to attachment which is secure, or anxious, or ambivalent, or disorganised (Ainsworth *et al.* 1978, Bretherton and Waters 1985, Radke-Yarrow and Sherman 1985), and so to 'working models' of relationships. In secure relationships, these models can become more complex and integrated as the child is confident, communicative, and well in tune with the adult partner. The insecurely attached child, whose signals are consistently ignored or misunderstood, whose efforts are not supported or respected, and who does not get useful feedback from the partner, is at risk of more negative emotional states and of building a cognitive model which is less coherent, less accurate and less modifiable (Bretherton 1990, Rutter 1991, Saarni 1990).

Children who are ill-treated or neglected by their caretakers are one population where the relationship between social, emotional and cognitive development is of particular interest. I have discussed such cases in Chapter 5, and will not extend that discussion here. That research supports the idea that different emotional biases arise, largely through social interactions which elicit, emphasise and allow some emotions more than others. Different 'working models' are built up and cognitive biases contribute to the maintenance of an organisation of cognition and affect and social behaviour through a subjective understanding of the world. This has ramifications for motivation, self concept, attributional style, metacognition and achievement (e.g. Carr *et al.* 1991, Dweck and Elliot 1983). The fine-tuning of cognitive development has an affective component, and researchers need to recognise this.

## IMAGINATION

The earlier chapters of this book discuss quite a wide range of ways of thinking, but they are primarily problem-solving, skill-based, and, to a large extent, literate. Even my discussion of creativity focused on the self-consciously applied skills, attitudes and knowledge which are necessary for significant creative achievement. This bias towards systematic, analytic, evaluative and deliberate cognitive effort reflects the bias of the literature and the preoccupations of educational policy makers; but it neglects 'imagination'. I am unhappy with this, as imaginative play is such a central characteristic of childhood and a source of such delight. I therefore make a few speculative points about 'imagination' here.

There is much philosophical debate about the nature of imagination, which I will not review here (but see Reddiford 1980, Ryle 1949, ch. 8, Sartre 1972, Warnock 1976). In psychology and education it carries a contradictory set of associated meanings; on the one hand irrational, merely fanciful, a pale shadow of reality, deceiving, trivial, useless, something which children do but should be educated out of; and on the other hand it is seen as free and poetic, as in the Romantic vision of the child born 'trailing clouds of glory' but all too soon subjected to the shades of the educational prison house. This debate is of course closely related to debate about the nature and worth of 'play', just as play activities are often used as evidence of imagination. However we clearly must not confuse imagination and play (Meadows 1986: 23–30, Meadows and Cashdan 1988); play involves at various times intelligent exploration, discovery, mastery, problem-solving and imitation, as well as imagination, and imagination can, as I shall discuss, be apparent in situations which are not playful.

The etymological root of 'imagination' is the Latin *imago*, meaning an image or representation, and thus at the core of the concept is the capacity to conceive of what is not actually happening here and now. Such a capacity may have pretty mundane results (as in much of the sex stereotyped role-play of pre-schoolers); or it may lead to more unusual results. Like creativity, imagination has to work with knowledge and skills even if it transforms them into the unreal and impossible, and so some domains may not offer many opportunities for imaginative thinking (Barrow 1988). The criteria of 'unusualness' and 'effectiveness' may apply to imagination as well as to creativity, though the same conceptual problems arise (see Chapter 3).

A further set of epithets applied to 'imagination' is made up of terms such as 'fantasy', 'storytelling', and 'egocentrism', 'mind-wandering'; varieties of indulgence in the imaginary dissociated from the real. These words are often used pejoratively, to justify the suppression of imagination, and may lie behind the way it has been pushed out of cognition into play (and, if the classification system of *Psychological Abstracts* represents the field, into investigations of sexual ideas). Such a pejorative use may be regrettable, not least because 'reasoning' and 'imagination' are not truly independent (Reddiford 1980, Dias and Harris 1988, 1990). Egan (1988a and 1988b) makes an interesting case for imagination in precisely this sense of fantasy and making stories as a valid component of cognition. He starts from John Dewey's definition of the imaginative as 'a warm and intimate taking-in of the full scope of a situation', a definition which highlights the importance of emotion in cognition. Egan suggests that young children's mental lives are full of imagination, not just because their ignorance makes it difficult for them to distinguish between the improbable but really real (earning a living by wittering on about developmental psychology) and the probable but not really real (Father Christmas, animals that talk, fairies, inter-stellar travel), but also because they are actively engaged in making unified sense of the world, and the freedom and exaggeration of fantasy are an important means to the end they are actively engaged in, making unified sense of the world. The 'mythic' thinking typical of non-literate groups serves the same goal. Fantasy and imagination involve the elaboration of impossibilities, a creative play on the abstractions which lie beneath the fantastic content: abstractions which the child is often emotionally involved in, such as the conflict between good and evil, and the powerlessness of the very young. These sorts of issues are the concern of the myths, fairy stories and folktales which were once a contributor to everyone's way of understanding the world and are now part of the province of childhood. Egan suggests that mythic understanding dominates the thinking of young children (and that their curriculum should therefore be centred on it) and remains a constituent of mature understanding. I think his account has a lot of faults – not a great deal of behavioural evidence, some unclear definitions, some value-laden judgements – but it does make the useful point that there are a variety of 'bonnes à penser' (Egan 1988b: 63), of 'good things to think with', and imaginative thinking is one collection of these, which has been comparatively neglected.

## FINAL SECTION

In this book I have examined our understanding of the child as thinker, dealing with material describing children's thinking, examining dimensions of individual differences, looking at theoretical models and causal influences. The work has been heterogeneous. I have had to piece together evidence from varying approaches in a number of different fields, a process which inevitably means some poorly-fitting assemblies and yawning gaps, because the research methods of many studies, while adequate for the work's immediate purposes, are not adequate for the big developmental questions.

Behavioural research on children, for the most part, is not geared to investigating transactions, encompassing a multiplicity of influences, measuring environment in non-static and developmental terms, addressing developmental questions developmentally, or accounting for individual differences in development . . . [The] discrepancy between conceptual sophistication, on the one hand, and paradigmatic and methodological insufficiencies, on the other, brings an unsettling disequilibrium to developmental research.

(Radke-Yarrow 1991: 391–2)

However, as Piaget claimed that being in 'an unsettling disequilibrium' was a major spur to cognitive development, I want to take this potentially depressing summary as a challenge not as a criticism. So, in this final section, I want to begin to suggest some shifts in research paradigm which may help us tackle the not yet answered questions of the field. The choice of 'questions' reflects my own priorities (on the psychology–education–parenting interface) and my own research experience (a shift from assessment within the Piagetian paradigm to direct and extended observation of behaviour in 'real-world' contexts). This is a summary restatement of themes that will have emerged from the earlier chapters of this book, and I hope that people reading this section will refer back to relevant material elsewhere.

Children's development occurs in, and has to be examined in, environments. This is so obvious as to be taken for granted, but we do not have anything like a good or thorough analysis and understanding of environments. They are too often ignored, or simplified, or dismissed as too variable and arbitrary to be studied scientifically. Or they are dealt with in terms of single variables such as structural features which are assumed to affect all individuals equally and so need no direct measurement. Examples such as studies of the effect of pre-school attendance which do not look at the variation in quality within each pre-school setting, or of the effects of 'social address' variables such as being part of a one-parent family, come to mind. These studies tell us something about differences between group averages but leave the causal variables underexposed. Further research looking at variables within groups, or using variables which are good candidates for bringing about causal change directly, will be necessary.

We have to take the study of environments seriously. They may be studied experimentally. Here it has to be assumed that behaviour in a laboratory simulation of the 'real world' bears a reasonably close resemblance to behaviour in the real world itself. At the extreme, it is assumed that children answering a stranger's questions in a strange laboratory (or in an unfrequented and presumably less strange corner of their school) will answer in a way representative of their ordinary thinking and talking. The problem here is whether this situation produces behaviour which does indeed occur elsewhere, or whether it does not on the contrary lead to a serious misrepresentation of the child. Even if it does not, it will be necessary to compare the artificial and the real environments carefully at some point. The same problem of representativeness applies of course to 'real life' environments; have they been sampled in a way that represents all the ways in which the environment is, day by day, or at least those parts of life in the environment thought to be important in principle? A sample of parental behaviour would show less child-contingent language for children between 3 and 10 than for babies if it was restricted to the small hours of the morning, for example. This would not necessarily show that babies got more child-contingent language than older children in toto!

Environments may be assessed by asking the people who live in them to describe or rate them, a procedure which can also produce interesting data but which is, necessarily, an indirect and possibly subjectively-biased measure. It may be the only possible method for large-scale studies (which also often use gross structural variables such as SES or family size), but it is no substitute for fine-grained, systematic and extended observation of interaction in the environment.

Such observation needs to be based on a sensible conceptualisation of the environment, and, because it is likely to be time-consuming, expensive, and demanding so far as the environments studied are concerned, it would be wise to embark on it informed by the relevant theoretical literature and by the insights as to variables worth study gained from the less conclusive methodologies which I have just criticised. Because of the 'economic' problems of systematic observation, samples are likely to be small, and the work may verge on case-study. Intensive studies of a small number of cases have been rare in recent work on cognitive development, though they made significant contributions earlier in the history of psychology, have made up a large part of research in language development and developmental psychopathology, and contribute much of the evidence on the effects of brain damage (see Shallice 1989 on this methodology in this last area). They will be especially useful for answering questions about children who are unusual, for example children whose early level of achievement is extraordinarily high, or who suffer appalling conditions as they grow up, or who do not respond as usual to training or testing. They may include investigation of several different aspects of behaviour, or several different conditions or life events, which have different effects in combination from their influences singly. Longitudinal case-studies can pick up irregularities in the pace of development, which are averaged out of view in large samples, but may provide important clues to the processes of developmental change (and checks on the validity of a developmental model, as in my study of Piagetian stages). In an ideal world, the subjects of case-studies would be in a known position relative to the population as a whole, for example being the intensively studied part of a population study. A recent account by Doria Pilling (1990) provides an example of the usefulness of such linkage between case-studies and a population studied with questionnaires. She writes about members of the 1958 National Child Development Study cohort, who, despite suffering severe social disadvantage in early childhood, were relatively successful as young adults, with relatively good educational achievement or well above average economic status in their twenties. These individuals' histories add to what we know about the importance of parental support for their children's cognitive development. Similarly studies such as Quinton and Rutter (1988) and current work on depression, mothering, and outcomes for the children (see Chapter 5 above), clarify what other research methods suggest, and document the complex histories which lead development down different pathways from childhood to adult life.

I think longitudinal studies are going to be another essential part of coming to understand cognitive development. Again, they are more expensive (and much slower) than cross-sectional studies, though they do not always need to extend over very long periods. They require a particularly clear conceptualisation of what are 'continuities' and what are 'changes' in behaviour, various precautions to separate the effects of increases in competence with development from increases in familiarity with and confidence in the test situation, and, inconveniently, a scrupulous and sophisticated understanding of the appropriate statistical techniques. The comparatively intense contact between researcher and subject also brings the ethics of research to the foreground as an issue: a one-off session of testing with a child in school may not require much more than the agreement of all interested parties and careful handling of the child's sensitivities by the tester, but getting data about ecologically real behaviour over a long period of time has to be recognised to be a big demand on subjects for, perhaps, little return. Researchers have to be concerned to minimise the costs and maximise the benefits to their subjects. They also have to recognise that their relationship with their subjects will not be a neutral one, and ethical problems may arise for them as researcher and as morally responsible person. What do you do if the child's answers to your questions suggest experience of sexual abuse from a family member, or if the parents ask for advice on the education of their child? Can you withhold advice which would lead to a change in the child's experience that you would rather exclude from your research design?

I am now almost at the end of this discussion of the child as thinker, or rather at the place where my discussion stops for the moment, as further discussion is not only possible but essential. I will end by recapitulating points made in various earlier sections.

1) Children do their thinking, as we all do, in a world which presents a particular set of physical, social and conceptual problems in a particular range of settings and experiences. What makes for successful thinking depends on the problem and its context. It is appropriate to read this book

with some care and a lot of critical thought, but not with the warm unreasoning engagement you might bring to a favourite light novelist, nor with the sort of attention to the sound of what is said that you might bring to poetry. 'Good' and 'poor' performance are, to a considerable extent, situation specific.

2) The point that there are different sorts of good performance makes untenable the idea of 'development' as a uni-dimensional progress from less advanced to more advanced functioning, for example more 'complex' cognition. Evolutionary theory makes a similar point. In general evolution has led to more complexity only if more complexity leads to a higher degree of reproductive success. Very simple organisms may persist without any change towards complexity for millions of years if they are successful in reproducing in their environments and there is no relevant environmental change to reduce this success. Even in human beings, the correlation between greater cognitive complexity and greater reproductive success is not self-evidently high and positive (the eugenicists at the turn of the century, and a sprinkling of mainly right-wing theorists to this day, advocated control of people's reproduction precisely because they believed the correlation was high and negative and that the stupid would out-breed the intelligent). Development may tend towards better success, but what 'success' is will depend on the environmental challenges that the organism meets.

3) As well as there being different sorts of good performance reached by different paths, different paths or different means may lead to the same end, more or less effectively or efficiently or happily. Almost all Western children learn to read, but they do so in a number of different ways. Their repertoire of reading processes is somewhat related to the path to reading that they have taken, but there seems to be little long-term developmental significance in what path you take except through the disadvantage suffered by children who are slow to read. Those children have extra problems with school subjects for which normal reading level is assumed, may suffer from being less skilled than their peers, and may miss out on the enjoyment and information which can be gained from reading.

4) Given this co-variation of context, performance and development, what may be important about cognitive 'complexity' is the availability of a range of alternative strategies and the ability to select between them as appropriate to the particular situation. People whose repertoire of strategies is very limited or inflexible may do very well if they only encounter familiar problems, but much less well if a problem demands a new or modified strategy. This implies that cognitive processes have to become somewhat independent from the contexts in which they were first developed, to become at least potentially autonomous tools. Moving from being scaffolded by a more expert person to being able to support one's own

cognition is an example of this. The process will never be complete, and cognition is always, I repeat, embedded in a context.

5) We badly need to understand 'contexts' better. Since my discussion of what this involves is only a few pages back, I will leave this assertion without further elaboration.

6) However, we have good reason to believe that the social and interpersonal context is particularly important in the development of complex cognitive skills. It has been argued that human language and cognition evolved to serve social purposes: primates who live in large permanent groups engage in long-term relationships, multi-party interactions and cooperative alliances, which require cognitive complexity and sophisticated social cognition. We have incontrovertible evidence that much of cognitive development in childhood involves the acquisition of culturally specific cognitive skills through culturally specified social interaction: being observer and apprentice to the work skills of your parent, or being taught to read or do calculus in formal schooling. Some cognition is less social than this, in that the individual child addresses the physical world directly in some area where the adult has no vested interest. Many of the topics Piaget himself addressed were of this sort, and parental interest in teaching conservation to their pre-school children is largely post-Piagetian. There may even be parental implying of non-conservation in suggestions that there is less of a disliked foodstuff on the plate if it is cut up into bits. But even in areas independent of adults there will be social components to the cognition as both the 'non-social' task and the 'individual' thinker are related to a wide range of social tasks and understandings. *Descriptions* of tasks and of thinking can, perhaps, leave aside this social dimension, but its omission from models will leave them incomplete as *explanations* of development.

7) The socialness of cognition implies a number of interesting possibilities. Conceivably, socially based cognition will be more advanced than cognition that is more separate from the social world. For example, we may be able to achieve more in co-operation with another person than we can alone; we may understand a point or carry through a process better in a task with social content than in one with non-social content (provided the social content fits our social experience); we may have a more complex and effective understanding of the social world than we have of the non-social world, being better folk psychologists than we are folk physicists.

8) Further, the socialness of cognition implies, as does the connectedness of the 'cognitive' and 'emotional' areas of the brain, that there will be an intimate interplay between cognition and emotion in both the short term and the long term. The person's self concept and understanding of other people will have to be considered here. So will his or her motivation to engage with a cognitive problem or with learning a cognitive skill.

Thus, having begun this book by widening conventional definitions of cognitive development somewhat to include culturally based cognitive skills such as reading and writing, using the traditional dividing-up of psychology into cognitive, affective, conative and social areas, I have ended it by arguing that these areas should not be separated in any strong sense, that much that is of interest in developmental psychology lies in the areas of overlap between the four. This makes things more complex, but also more exciting. I hope I have conveyed some of the excitement as well as some of the problems, and that this book will help further development of work on 'the child as thinker'.

# Bibliography

Aber, J. L. and Allen, J. P. (1987) 'The effects of maltreatment on young children's socio-emotional development: an attachment theory perspective', *Developmental Psychology* 23: 406–44.

Achenbach, T. M. and Edelbrock, C. S. (1981) 'Behavioral problems and competencies reported by parents of normal and disturbed children aged four through sixteen', *Monographs of the Society for Research in Child Development*: 46(1).

Ackerman, B. P. (1986) 'Children's sensitivity to comprehension failure in interpreting a nonliteral use of an utterance', *Child Development* 57: 485–97.

Ackerman, P. L., Sternberg, R. J. and Glaser, R. (1989) *Learning and Individual Differences: Advances in Theory and Research*, New York: Freeman.

Acredolo, C. and Horobin, K. (1987) 'Development of relational reasoning and avoidance of premature closure', *Developmental Psychology* 23: 13–21.

Acredolo, L. and Goodwyn, S. (1988) 'Symbolic gesturing in normal infants', *Child Development* 59: 450–66.

Ainsworth, M., Blehar, M. C., Waters, E. and Wall, S. (1978) *Patterns of Attachment: a Psychological Study of the Strange Situation*, Hillsdale, NJ: Erlbaum.

Aldhous, P. (1992) 'The promise and pitfalls of molecular genetics', research news article, *Science* 257: 164–5.

Alexander, T. M. and Enns, J. T. (1988) 'Age changes in the boundaries of fuzzy categories', *Child Development* 59: 1372–86.

Allen, G. L., Kirasic, K. C., Siegel, A. W. and Herman, J. F. (1979) 'Developmental issues in cognitive mapping: the selection and utilisation of environmental landmarks', *Child Development* 50: 1062–70.

Allport, D. A. (1980) 'Patterns and actions', in G. Claxton (ed.) *Cognitive Psychology: New Directions*, London: Routledge.

Ames, G. J. and Murray, F. B. (1982) 'When two wrongs make a right: promoting cognitive change by social conflict', *Developmental Psychology* 18: 894–7.

Anastasi, A. (1985) 'Reciprocal relations between cognitive and affective development – with implications for sex differences', *Nebraska Symposium on Motivation*, vol. 32, Lincoln, Nebr.: University of Nebraska Press.

Anderson, J. R. (1983) *The Architecture of Cognition*, Cambridge, Mass.: Harvard University Press.

Anderson, J. R. (1987) 'Skill acquisition: compilation of weak-method problem solution', *Psychological Review* 94: 192–210.

Anderson, J. R. and Thompson, R. (1989) 'Use of analogy in a production system architecture', in S. Vosniadou and A. Ortony (eds) *Similarity and Analogical Reasoning*, Cambridge: Cambridge University Press.

Anderson, M. (1986) 'Inspection time and IQ in young children', *Personality and Individual Differences* 5: 677–86.

Anderson, M. (1988) 'Inspection time, information processing and the development of intelligence', *British Journal of Experimental Psychology* 6: 43–57.

Anderson, M. (1989a) 'New ideas in intelligence', *The Psychologist* 2(3): 92–4.

Anderson, M. (1989b) Letter, *The Psychologist* 2(8): 331.

Anderson, M. (1992) *Intelligence and Cognitive Development*, Oxford: Blackwell.

Andersson, B. E. (1992) 'Effects of day-care on cognitive and socio-emotional competence of thirteen-year-old Swedish schoolchildren', *Child Development* 63: 20–36.

Angoff, W. H. (1988) 'The nature–nurture debate, aptitudes, and group differences', *American Psychologist* 43: 713–20.

Anooshian, L. J. and Young, D. (1981) 'Developmental changes in cognitive maps of a familiar neighbourhood', *Child Development* 52: 341–8.

Antell, S. E. and Keating, D. P. (1983) 'Perception of numerical invariance in neonates', *Child Development* 54: 695–701.

Applebee, A. (1978) *The Child's Conception of Story*, Chicago, University of Chicago Press.

Arnheim, R. (1956) *Art and Visual Perception: a Psychology of the Creative Eye*, London: Faber.

Ashcraft, M. H. and Fierman, B. A. (1982) 'Mental addition in third, fourth and sixth graders', *Journal of Experimental Child Psychology* 33: 216–34.

Aslin, R. N., Pisoni, D. B. and Jusczyk, P. W. (1983) 'Auditory development and speech perception in infancy', in M. M. Haith and J. J. Campos (eds) *Handbook of Child Psychology*, vol. 2, New York: Wiley.

Aslin, R. N. and Smith, L. B. (1988) 'Perceptual development', *Annual Review of Psychology* 39: 435–71.

Astington, J. W. and Gopnik, A. (1988) 'Knowing you've changed your mind: children's understanding of representational change', in J. W. Astington, P. L. Harris and D. R. Olson (eds) *Developing Theories of Mind*, Cambridge: Cambridge University Press.

Astington, J. W. and Gopnik, A. (1991) 'Theoretical explanations of children's understanding of the mind', *British Journal of Developmental Psychology* 9: 7–31.

Astington, J. W., Harris, P. L. and Olson, D. R. (eds) (1988) *Developing Theories of Mind*, Cambridge: Cambridge University Press.

Atkinson, R. C. and Shiffrin, R. M. (1968) 'Human memory: a proposed system and its control processes', in K. W. Spence and J. T. Spence (eds) *Advances in the Psychology of Learning and Motivation*, vol. 2, New York: Academic Press.

Attili, G. (1989) 'The case of ambivalence: the interface between emotional and cognitive development', in A. de Ribaupierre (ed.) *Transition Mechanisms in Child Development*, Cambridge: Cambridge University Press.

Avis, J. and Harris, P. L. (1991) 'Belief–desire reasoning among Baka children: evidence for a universal conception of mind', *Child Development* 62: 460–7.

Azmitia, M. (1988) 'Peer interaction and problem-solving: when are two heads better than one?', *Child Development* 59: 87–96.

Azmitia, M. and Perlmutter, M. (1989) 'Social influences on young children's cognition: state of the art and future directions', in H. W. Reese (ed.) *Advances in Child Development and Behaviour*, vol. 21, New York: Academic Press.

Bachevalier, J. (1992) 'Cortical versus limbic immaturity: relation to infantile amnesia', in M. Gunnar and C. A. Nelson (eds) *Developmental Behavioral*

*Neuroscience: Minnesota Symposium on Child Psychology*, vol. 24, Hillsdale, NJ: Erlbaum.

Bachevalier, J. and Mishkin, M. (1984) 'An early and a late developing system for learning and retention in infant monkeys', *Behavioral Neurosciences* 98: 770–8.

Baddeley, A. D. (1976) *The Psychology of Memory*, New York: Harper & Row.

Baddeley, A. D. (1990) *Human Memory*, London: Erlbaum.

Baddeley, A. D. and Lewis, V. J. (1981) 'Interactive processes in reading: the inner voice, the inner ear and the inner eye', in A. M. Lesgold and C. A. Perfetti (eds) *Interactive Processes in Reading*, Hillsdale, NJ: Erlbaum.

Bahrick, H. P., Bahrick, P. O. and Wittinlinger, R. P. (1975) 'Fifty years of memory for names and places: a cross-sectional approach', *Journal of Experimental Psychology: General* 104: 54–75.

Bailey, C. and Kandel, E. R. (1985) 'Molecular approaches to the study of short-term and long-term memory', in C. W. Coen (ed.) *Functions of the Brain*, Oxford: Clarendon Press.

Bakeman, R. and Brown, J. V. (1980) 'Early interaction: consequences for social and mental development at three years', *Child Development* 51: 437–47.

Baker, L. (1984) 'Spontaneous versus instructed use of multiple standards for evaluating comprehension: effects of age, reading proficiency and type of standard', *Journal of Experimental Child Psychology* 38: 289–311.

Baker, L. and Brown, A. L. (1984) 'Metacognitive skills of reading', in D. Pearson (ed.) *Handbook of Reading Research*, New York: Longmans, Green.

Bandura, A. (1977a) 'Self-efficacy: toward a unifying theory of behavioral change', *Psychological Review* 84: 191–215.

Bandura, A. (1977b) *Social Learning Theory*, Englewood Cliffs, NJ: Prentice Hall.

Bandura, A. (1981) 'Self referent thought: a developmental analysis of self-efficacy', in J. H . Flavell and L. Ross (eds) *Social Cognitive Development*, Cambridge: Cambridge University Press.

Banks, M. S. and Salapatek, P. (1983) 'Infant visual perception', in M. M. Haith and J. J. Campos (eds) *Handbook of Child Psychology* vol. 2, series ed. P. H. Mussen, New York: Wiley.

Baranes, R., Perry, M. and Stigler, J. W. (1989) 'Activation of real-world knowledge in the solution of word problems', *Cognition and Instruction* 6: 287–318.

Barker, P. (1988) *Basic Child Psychiatry*, Oxford: Blackwell Scientific.

Barnes, D. M. (1989) ' "Fragile X" syndrome and its puzzling genetics', *Science* 243: 171–2.

Barnes, S., Gutfreund, M., Satterly, D. J. and Wells, C. G. (1983) 'Characteristics of adult speech which predict children's language development', *Journal of Child Language* 10: 65–84.

Baron, J. (1978) 'Intelligence and general strategies', in G. Underwood (ed.) *Strategies in Information Processing*, New York: Academic Press.

Baron, J. (1985) *Rationality and Intelligence*, Cambridge: Cambridge University Press.

Baron, J. (1988) *Thinking and Deciding*, Cambridge: Cambridge University Press.

Baron, J. and Sternberg, R. (eds) (1987) *Teaching Thinking Skills*, New York: Freeman.

Baron, J., Badgio, P. C. and Gaskins, I. W. (1986) 'Cognitive style and its improvement: a normative approach', in R. J. Sternberg (ed.) *Advances in the Psychology of Human Intelligence*, Hillsdale, NJ: Erlbaum.

Baron-Cohen, S. (1992) 'Out of sight or out of mind? Another look at deception in autism', *Journal of Child Psychology and Psychiatry* 33: 1141–56.

Baron-Cohen, S. and Frith, U. (1992) 'Autism and misrepresentation', *The Psychologist* 5: 163.

Baron-Cohen, S., Leslie, A. M. and Frith, U. (1985) 'Does the autistic child have a "theory of mind"?' *Cognition* 21: 37–46.

Barrett, D. E. (1987) 'Undernutrition and child behaviour: what behaviours should we measure and how should we measure them?' in J. Dobbing (ed.) *Early Nutrition and Later Achievement*, London: Academic Press.

Barrett, D. E., Radke-Yarrow, M. and Klein, R. E. (1982) 'Chronic malnutrition and child behavior: effects of early caloric supplementation on social-emotional functioning at school age', *Development Psychology* 18: 541–66.

Barrett, M. D. and Light, P. H. (1976) 'Symbolism and intellectual realism in children's drawings', *British Journal of Educational Psychology* 46: 198–202.

Barrow, R. (1988) 'Some observations on the concept of imagination', in K. Egan and D. Nadaner (eds) *Imagination and Education*, Milton Keynes: Open University Press.

Barsalou, L. (1987) 'The instability of graded structure: implications for the nature of concepts', in U. Neisser (ed.) *Concepts and Conceptual Development: Ecological and Intellectual Factors in Categorisation*, Cambridge: Cambridge University Press.

Barsalou, L. (1989) 'Intra-concept similarity and its implications for inter-concept similarity', in S. Vosniadou and A. Ortony (eds) *Similarity and Analogy*, Cambridge: Cambridge University Press.

Bartlett, F. C. (1932) *Remembering*, Cambridge: Cambridge University Press.

Bartsch, K. and Wellman, H. M. (1988) 'Young children's conceptions of distance', *Developmental Psychology* 24(4): 532–41.

Barwick, J., Valentine, E., West, R. and Wilding, J. (1989) 'Relations between reading and musical abilities', *British Journal of Educational Psychology* 59: 253–7.

Bates, E. and MacWhinney, B. (1979) 'A functionalist approach to the acquisition of grammar', in E. Ochs and B. Schieffelin (eds) *Developmental Pragmatics*, New York: Academic Press.

Bates, E., Bretherton, I. and Snyder, L. (1988) *From First Words to Grammar: Individual Differences and Dissociable Mechanisms*, Cambridge: Cambridge University Press.

Bates, E., Bretherton, I., Beeghly-Smith, M. and McNew, S. (1982) 'Social bases of language development: a reassessment', in H. W. Reese and L. P. Lipsitt (eds) *Advances in Child Development and Behaviour*, vol. 16, New York: Academic Press.

Bateson, P. (ed.) (1991a) *The Development and Integration of Behaviour: Essays in Honour of Robert Hinde*, Cambridge: Cambridge University Press.

Bateson, P. (1991b) 'Levels and processes', in P. Bateson (ed.) *The Development and Integration of Behaviour: Essays in Honour of Robert Hinde*, Cambridge: Cambridge Univesity Press.

Beal, C. R. (1987) 'Repairing the message: children's monitoring and revision skills', *Child Development* 58: 401–8.

Beard, R. (1963) 'The order of concept development: studies in two fields', *Educational Review* 15: 105–17, 228–37.

Bearison, D. J., Magzamen, S. and Filardo, E. K. (1986) 'Socio-cognitive conflict and cognitive growth in young children', *Merrill-Palmer Quarterly*, 32: 51–72.

Bechtel, W. and Abrahamsen, A. (1991) *Connectionism and the Mind: an Introduction to Parallel Processing in Networks*, Oxford: Blackwell.

Bedi, K. S. (1987) 'Lasting neuroanatomical changes following under-nutrition during early life', in J. Dobbing (ed.) *Early Nutrition and Later Achievement*, London: Academic Press.

Bee, H. L., Barnard, K. E., Eyres, S. J., Gray, C. A., Hammond, M. A., Spietz, L. A., Snyder, C., and Clark, B. (1982) 'Prediction of IQ and language skills from perinatal status, child performance, family characteristics and mother–infant interaction', *Child Development* 53: 1334–56.

Beech, J. and Colley, A. (eds) (1987) *Cognitive Approaches to Reading*, Chichester: Wiley.

Beilin, H. (1980) 'Piaget's theory: refinement, revisionism or rejection?' in R. G. Kluwe and H. Spada (eds) *Developmental Models of Thinking*, New York: Academic Press.

Beilin, H. (1992) 'Piaget's enduring contribution to developmental psychology', *Developmental Psychology* 28: 191–204.

Bellinger, D. (1987) 'Longitudinal analyses of prenatal and postnatal lead exposure and early cognitive development', *New England Journal of Medicine* 316: 1037–43.

Bellugi, U., Bihrle, A., Neville, H., Doherty, S. and Jernigan, T. (1992) 'Language, cognition and brain organisation in a neurodevelopmental disorder', in M. Gunnar and C. A. Nelson (eds) (1992) *Developmental Behavioral Neuroscience: Minnesota Symposium on Child Psychology*, vol. 24, Hillsdale, NJ: Erlbaum.

Belsky, J. (1981) 'Early human experience: a family perspective', *Developmental Psychology* 17: 3–23.

Belsky, J., Rovine, M. and Taylor, D. G. (1984) 'The Pennsylvania Infant and Family Development Project, III: the origins of individual differences in infant–mother attachment: maternal and infant contributions', *Child Development* 55: 718–28.

Bennett, N. with Jordan, J., Long, G. and Wade, B. (1976) *Teaching Styles and Pupil Progress*, London: Open Books.

Bennett, W. J. (1987) 'The role of the family in the nurture and protection of the young', *American Psychologist*, 42: 246–50.

Benton, D. (1990) 'Vitamin/mineral supplementation and intelligence', *The Lancet* 336: 175–6.

Benton, D. (1992) 'The Benton and Roberts study', *The Psychologist* 5: 403–6.

Benton, D. and Cook, R. (1991) 'Vitamin and mineral supplements improve the intelligence scores and concentration of 6-year-old children', *Personality and Individual Differences* 12: 1151–8.

Benton, D. and Roberts, G. (1988) 'Effects of vitamin and mineral supplementation on intelligence of a sample of schoolchildren', *The Lancet* i: 140–3.

Bereiter, C. and Bird, M. (1985) 'Use of thinking aloud in identification and teaching of reading comprehension strategies', *Cognition and Instruction* 2: 91–130.

Bereiter, C. and Scardamalia, M. (1982) 'From conversation to composition: the role of instruction in a developmental process', in R. Glaser (ed.) *Advances in Instructional Psychology*, vol. 2, Hillsdale, NJ: Erlbaum.

Bereiter, C. and Scardamalia, M. (1987) *The Psychology of Written Composition*, Hillsdale, NJ: Erlbaum.

Bereiter, C. and Scardamalia, M. (1989) 'Intentional learning as a goal of instruction', in L. B. Resnick (ed.) *Knowing, Learning and Instruction*, Hillsdale, NJ: Erlbaum.

Berg, C. A. and Sternberg, R. J. (1985) 'Response to novelty: continuity versus discontinuity in the developmental course of intelligence', in H. Reese (ed.) *Advances in Child Development and Behaviour*, vol. 19, New York: Academic Press.

Bergeman, C. S. and Plomin, R. (1988) 'Parental mediators of the genetic relationship between home environment and infant mental development', *British Journal of Developmental Psychology* 6: 11–19.

Berlin, B. and Kay, P. (1969) *Basic Color Terms: Their Universality and Evolution*, Berkeley, Calif.: University of California Press.

Berndt, T. J. and Heller, K. A. (1985) 'Measuring children's personality attributions', in S. R. Yussen (ed.) *The Growth of Reflection in Children*, New York: Academic Press.

Berry, J. W., Irvine, S. H. and Hunt, E. B. (1988) *Indigenous Cognition: Functioning in Cultural Context*, Dordrecht: Martinus Nijhooff.

Bertenthal, B. I. and Fischer, K. W. (1978) 'Development of self-recognition in the infant', *Developmental Psychology* 14: 44–50.

Berti, A. E. (1991) 'Capitalism and Socialism: How 7th graders understand and misunderstand the information presented in their Geography textbooks', *European Journal of Psychology of Education* 6: 411–21.

Berti, A. E. and Bombi, A. S. (1988) *The Child's Construction of Economics*, Cambridge: Cambridge University Press.

Bettelheim, B. (1967) *The Empty Fortress: Infantile Autism and the Birth of the Self*, New York: Free Press.

Bettes, B. (1988) 'Maternal depression and motherese: temporal and intonational features', *Child Development* 59: 1089–96.

Beveridge, M. (ed.) (1982) *Children Thinking Through Language*, London: Edward Arnold.

Beveridge, M. and Brierly, C. (1982) 'Classroom constructs: an interpretive approach to young children's language', in M. Beveridge (ed.) *Children Thinking Through Language*, London: Edward Arnold.

Bialystock, E. (1986) 'Factors in the growth of linguistic awareness', *Child Development* 57: 498–510.

Bibace, R. and Walsh, M. E. (eds) (1981) 'Children's conceptions of illness', *New Directions for Child Development*, vol. 14, San Francisco: Jossey-Bass.

Biggs, J. B. (1984) 'The role of metalearning in study processes', Paper given at British Psychological Society Education Section Conference, Cambridge, September 1984.

Biggs, J. B. (1988) 'Approaches to essay writing', in R. R. Schmeck (ed.) *Learning Strategies and Learning Styles*, New York: Plenum Press.

Bijou, S. W. (1989) 'Psychological linguistics: implications for a theory of initial development and method of research', in H. W. Reese (ed.) *Advances in Child Development and Behaviour*, vol. 21, New York: Academic Press.

Bijstra, J., van Geert, P. and Jackson, S. (1989) 'Conversation and the appearance–reality distinction: what do children really know and what do they answer?' *British Journal of Developmental Psychology* 7: 43–53.

Billow, R. M. (1975) 'A cognitive developmental study of metaphor comprehension', *Developmental Psychology* 11: 415–23.

Billow, R. M. (1981) 'Observing spontaneous metaphor in children', *Journal of Experimental Child Psychology* 31: 430–45.

Binet, A. and Simon, T. (1916) *The Development of Intelligence in Children*, Baltimore, Md.: William & Wilkins.

Bjorklund, D. F. and Jacobs, J. W. III (1985) 'Associative and categorical processes in children's memory: the role of automaticity in the development of organisation in free recall', *Journal of Experimental Child Psychology* 39: 599–617.

Bjorklund, D. F. and Zeman, B. R. (1982) 'Children's organisation and metamemory awareness in their recall of familiar information', *Child Development* 53: 799–810.

Black, J. E. and Greenough, W. T. (1991) 'Developmental approaches to the memory process', in J. L. Martinez and R. P. Kesner (eds) *Learning and Memory: a Biological View*, New York: Academic Press.

Blake, J. (1989) *Family Size and Achievement*, Berkeley, Calif.: University of California Press.

Blakemore, C. and Greenfield, S. (1987) *Mindwaves: Thoughts on Intelligence, Identity and Consciousness*, Oxford: Blackwell.

Blinkhorn, S. and Hendrickson, D. E. (1982) 'Averaged evoked responses and psychometric intelligence', *Nature* 295: 596-7.

Block, J., Block, J. H. and Harrington, D. M. (1974) 'Some misgivings about the Matching Familiar Figures Test as a measure of reflection-impulsivity', *Developmental Psychology* 10: 611-32.

Block, J., Gjerde, P. F. and Block, J. H. (1986) 'More misgivings about the Matching Familiar Figures Test as a measure of reflection-impulsivity: absence of construct validity in preadolescence', *Developmental Psychology* 22: 820-31.

Block, N. (ed.) (1981) *Imagery*, Cambridge, Mass.: Bradford Books/MIT Press.

Block, N. (1983) 'Mental pictures and cognitive science', *Philosophical Review* 92: 499-541.

Bloom, F. E., Lazerson, A. and Hofstadter, L. (1985) *Brain, Mind and Behavior*, New York: W. H. Freeman.

Bobrow, D. and Collins, A. M. (eds) (1975) *Representation and Understanding*, New York: Academic Press.

Boden, M. (1979) *Piaget*, London: Fontana.

Boden, M. (1982) 'Is equilibration important? A view from artificial intelligence', *British Journal of Psychology* 73: 165-73.

Boden, M. (1987) *Artificial Intelligence and Natural Man*, Brighton: Harvester.

Boden, M. (1988) *Computer Models of Mind*, Cambridge: Cambridge Univesity Press.

Boden, M. (1989) *Artificial Intelligence in Psychology*, Boston, Mass.: MIT Press.

Boden, M. (1990) *The Creative Mind*, London: Weidenfeld & Nicolson.

Bolter, J. F. and Long, C. J. (1985) 'Methodological issues in research in developmental neuropsychology', in L. C. Hartlage and C. F. Telzrow (eds) *The Neuropsychology of Individual Differences*, New York: Plenum Press.

Borkowski, J. G. (1985) 'Signs of intelligence: strategy generalisation and metacognition', in S. R. Yussen, *The Growth of Reflection in Childhood*, New York: Academic Press.

Bornstein, M. H. and Sigman, M. D. (1986) 'Continuity in mental development from infancy', *Child Development* 57: 251-74.

Boswell, J. [1791] (1979) *The Life of Johnson*, Harmondsworth: Penguin Books.

Bouchard, T. *et al.* (1990) 'Sources of human psychological differences: the Minnesota study of twins reared apart', *Science* 250: 223-8.

Bower, G. H. (1981) 'Mood and memory', *American Psychologist* 36: 129-48.

Bower, G. H., Gilligan, S. G. and Monteiro, K. P. (1981) 'Selectivity of learning caused by affective states', *Journal of Experimental Psychology: General* 110(4): 451-73.

Bowerman, M. (1989) 'Learning a semantic system: what role do cognitive predispositions play?', in M. L. Rice and R. L. Schiefelbusch (eds) *The Teachability of Language*, Baltimore, Md.: Brookes.

Bradburn, E. (1989) *Margaret McMillan: Portrait of a Pioneer*, London: Routledge.

Bradley, L. and Bryant, P. E. (1983) 'Categorising sounds and learning to read: a causal connection', *Nature* 301: 419-21.

Bradley, R. H. and Caldwell, B. M. (1980) 'The relation of the home environment, cognitive competence, and IQ among males and females', *Child Development* 51: 1140–8.

Bradley, R. H. and Caldwell, B. M. (1984) '174 Children: a study of the relationship between home environment and cognitive development during the first five years', in A. W. Gottfried (ed.) *Home Environment and Early Cognitive Development*, New York: Academic Press.

Bradley, R. H., Caldwell, B. M. and Rock, S. L. (1988) 'Home environment and school performance: a ten-year follow-up and examination of three models of environmental action', *Child Development* 59: 852–67.

Bradley, R. H., Caldwell, B. M., Rock, S. L., Ramey, C. T., Barnard, K. E., Gray, C., Hammond, M. A., Mitchell, S., Gottfried, A. W., Siegel, L. and Johnson, D. L. (1989) 'Home environment and cognitive development in the first 3 years of life: a collaborative study involving six sites and three ethnic groups in North America', *Developmental Psychology* 25: 217–35.

Braine, M. D. S. and Rumain, B. (1983) 'Logical reasoning', in J. H. Flavell and E. M. Markman (eds) *Handbook of Child Psychology*, vol. 3, series ed. P. H. Mussen, New York: Wiley.

Brainerd, C. J. (1978) *Piaget's Theory of Intelligence*, Englewood Cliffs, NJ: Prentice Hall.

Brainerd, C. J. (1979) *The Origins of the Number Concept*, New York: Praeger.

Brainerd, C. J. (ed.) (1982) *Progress in Cognitive Development*, vol. 1, *Children's Logical and Mathematical Cognition*, New York: Springer-Verlag.

Brainerd, C. J. (1983) 'Modifiability of cognitive development', in S. Meadows (ed.) *Developing Thinking*, London: Methuen.

Brainerd, C. J., Kingma, J. and Howe, M. L. (1985) 'On the development of forgetting', *Child Development* 56: 1103–19.

Brand, C. and Deary, I. Z. (1982) 'Intelligence and "inspection time"', in H. J. Eysenck (ed.) *A Model for Intelligence*, Berlin: Springer-Verlag.

Bransford, J. D. (1979) *Human Cognition*, Belmont, Calif.: Wadsworth.

Bransford, J. D., Goldman, S. R. and Vye, N. J. (1991) 'Making a difference in people's ability to think', in L. Okagaki and R. J. Sternberg (eds) *Directors of Development: Influences on the Development of Children's Thinking*, Hillsdale, NJ.: Erlbaum.

Breitmayer, B. J. and Ramey, C. T. (1986) 'Biological nonoptimality and quality of postnatal environment as codeterminants of intellectual development', *Child Development* 57: 1151–65.

Bremner, J. G. (1980) 'The infant's understanding of space', in M. V. Cox (ed.) *Are Young Children Egocentric?* London: Batsford.

Breslow, L. (1981) 'Reevaluation of the literature on the development of transitive influences', *Psychological Bulletin* 89(2): 325–51.

Bretherton, I. (1985) 'Attachment theory', in I. Bretherton and E. Waters (eds) *Growing Points of Attachment Theory and Research: Monographs of the Society for Research in Child Development* 50: 3–35.

Bretherton, I. (1990) 'Open communication and internal working models: their role in the development of attachment relationships', in R. A. Thompson (ed.) *Socioemotional Development : Nebraska Symposium on Motivation, 1988*, vol. 36, Lincoln, Nebr.: University of Nebraska Press.

Bretherton, I. and Beeghly, M. (1982) 'Talking about internal states: the acquisition of an explicit theory of mind', *Developmental Psychology* 18: 906–21.

Bretherton, I. and Waters, E. (eds) (1985) *Growing Points of Attachment Theory and Research: Monographs of the Society for Research in Child Development* 50(1–2): 1–320.

Bretherton, I., Fritz, J., Zahn-Waxler, C. and Ridgeway, D. (1986) 'Learning to talk about emotions: a functionalist approach', *Child Development* 57: 529–48.

Bretherton, I., McNew, S. and Beeghly-Smith, M. (1981) 'Early person knowledge as expressed in gestural and verbal communication: when do infants acquire a "theory of mind"?', in M. E. Lamb and L. R. Sherrod (eds) *Infant Social Cognition*, Hillsdale, NJ: Erlbaum.

Brewin, C. (1985) 'Depression and causal attributions: what is their relation?', *Psychological Bulletin* 9: 297–309.

Brewster, A. B. (1982) 'Chronically ill hospitalised children's concepts of their illness', *Pediatrics* 69: 355–62.

Breznitz, Z. and Sherman, T. (1987) 'Speech patterning of natural discourse of well and depressed mothers and their young children', *Child Development* 58: 395–400.

Briars, D. J. and Siegler, R. S. (1984) 'A featural analysis of preschoolers' counting knowledge', *Developmental Psychology* 20: 607–18.

Brissenden, T. (1988) *Talking about Mathematics*, Oxford: Blackwell.

Broberg, A. G., Hwang, C. P., Lamb, M. E. and Bookstein, F. L. (1990) 'Factors related to verbal abilities in Swedish preschoolers', *British Journal of Developmental Psychology* 8: 335–49.

Brody, G. H., Pellegrini, A. D. and Sigel, I. E. (1986) 'Marital quality and mother–child and father–child interactions with school-aged children', *Developmental Psychology* 22: 291–6.

Brodzinsky, D. M. (1982) 'Relationship between cognitive style and cognitive development: a 2-year longitudinal study', *Developmental Psychology* 18: 617–26.

Broman, S., Nichols, P. L., Shaughnessy, P. and Kennedy, W. (1987) *Retardation in Young Children: a Developmental Study of Cognitive Deficit*, Hillsdale, NJ: Erlbaum.

Bromley, D. B. (1978) *Natural language and the development of the self: Nebraska Symposium on Motivation 1977*, Lincoln, Nebr.: University of Nebraska Press.

Bronfenbrenner, U. (1979) *The Ecology of Human Development*, Cambridge, Mass.: Harvard University Press.

Bronfenbrenner, U. (1986) 'Ecology of the family as a context for human development', *Developmental Psychology* 22: 723–42.

Brophy, J. (1986) 'Teacher influences on student achievement', *American Psychologist* 41: 1069–77.

Brophy, J. and Good, T. (1986) 'Teacher behaviour and student achievement', in M. Wittrock (ed.) *Third Handbook of Research on Teaching*, New York: Macmillan.

Broughton, J. M. B. (1978) 'Development of concepts of self, mind, reality and knowledge', in W. Damon (ed.) *New Directions for Child Development*, vol. 1, San Francisco: Jossey-Bass.

Broughton, J. M. B. (1982) 'Genetic logic and the developmental psychology of philosophical concepts', in J. M. B. Broughton and D. J. Freeman-Moir (eds) *The Cognitive-developmental Psychology of J. M. Baldwin*, Norwood, NJ: Ablex.

Broughton, J. M. B. and Freeman-Moir, D. J. (1981) *The Cognitive-developmental Psychology of James Mark Baldwin: Current Theory and Research in Genetic Epistemology*, Norwood, NJ: Ablex.

Brown, A. L. (1975) 'The development of memory: knowing, knowing about knowing, and knowing how to know', in H. W. Reese (ed.) *Advances in Child Development and Behaviour*, vol. 10, New York: Academic Press.

Brown, A. L. (1988) 'Motivation to learn and understand: on taking charge of one's own learning', *Cognition and Instruction* 5: 311–21.

Brown, A. L. (1989) 'Analogical learning and transfer: what develops?', in S.

Vosniadou and A. Ortony (eds) *Similarity and Analogical Reasoning*, Cambridge: Cambridge University Press.

Brown, A. L. (1990) 'Domain-specific principles affect learning and transfer in children', *Cognitive Science* 14: 107–33.

Brown, A. L. and Barclay, C. R. (1976) 'The effects of training specific mnemonics on the metamnemonic efficiency of retarded children', *Child Development* 47: 71–80.

Brown, A. L. and Campione, J. C. (1972) 'Recognition memory for perceptually similar pictures in preschool children', *Journal of Experimental Child Psychology* 95: 55–62.

Brown, A. L. and Campione, J. C. (1986) 'Psychological theory and the study of learning disabilities', *American Psychologist* 41: 1059–68.

Brown, A. L. and Campione, J. C. (1988) 'Communities of learning and thinking: or a context by any other name', *Contributions to Human Development* 21: 108–26.

Brown, A. L. and Day, J. D. (1983) 'Macrorules for summarising texts: the development of expertise', *Journal of Verbal Learning and Verbal Behaviour* 22: 1–14.

Brown, A. L. and De Loache, J. S. (1978) 'Skills, plans and self-regulation', in R. S. Siegler (ed.) *Children's Thinking : What Develops*? Hillsdale, NJ: Erlbaum.

Brown, A. L. and Ferrara, R. (1985) 'Diagnosing zones of proximal development', in J. V. Wertsch (ed.) *Culture, Communication and Cognition*, Cambridge: Cambridge University Press.

Brown, A. L. and Kane, M. J. (1988) 'Preschool children can learn to transfer: learning to learn and learning from example', *Cognitive Psychology* 20: 493–523.

Brown, A. L. and Palincsar, A. S. (1989) 'Guided, cooperative learning and individual knowledge acquisition', in L. B. Resnick (ed.) *Knowing, Learning and Instruction*, Hillsdale, NJ: Erlbaum.

Brown, A. L. and Reeve, R. A. (1987) 'Bandwidths of competence: the role of supportive contexts in learning and development', in L. S. Liben (ed.) *Development and Learning: Conflict or Congruence?*, Hillsdale, NJ: Erlbaum.

Brown, A. L. and Scott, M. S. (1971) 'Recognition memory for pictures in preschool children', *Journal of Experimental Child Psychology* 11: 401–12.

Brown, A. L., Palincsar, A. S. and Armbruster, B. B. (1984) 'Instructing comprehension: fostering activities in interactive learning situations', in H. Mandl, N. Stein and T. Trabasso (eds) *Learning and Comprehension of Texts*, Hillsdale, NJ: Erlbaum.

Brown, A. L., Bransford, J. D., Ferrara, R. A. and Campione, J. C. (1983) 'Learning, remembering and understanding', in J. H. Flavell and E. M. Markman (eds) *Handbook of Child Psychology*, vol. 3, *Cognitive Development*, series ed. P. H. Mussen, New York: Wiley.

Brown, G. and Harris, T. (1978) *Social Origins of Depression*, London: Tavistock.

Brown, J. S. and Burton, R. B. (1978) 'Diagnostic models for procedural bugs in basic mathematical skills', *Cognitive Science* 2: 155–92.

Brown, R. (1958) 'How shall a thing be called?' *Psychological Review* 65: 14–21.

Brozek, J. (1978) 'Nutrition, malnutrition and behavior', *Annual Review of Psychology* 29: 157–77.

Bruner, J. S. (1957) 'Going beyond the information given', in H. Gruber (ed.) *Contemporary Approaches to Cognition*, Cambridge, Mass.: Harvard University Press.

Bruner, J. S. (1966) 'On cognitive growth', in J. S. Bruner, R. R. Olver and P. M. Greenfield (eds) *Studies in Cognitive Growth*, New York: Wiley.

Bruner, J. S. (1968) *Toward a Theory of Instruction*, New York: Norton.

Bruner, J. S. (1973) 'Organisation of early skilled action', *Child Development* 44: 1–11.

Bruner, J. S. (1976) 'From communication to language – a psychological perspective', *Cognition* 3: 255–87.

Bruner, J. S. (1983) *Child's Talk*, New York: Norton.

Bruner, J. S. (1985) 'Vygotsky: a historical and conceptual perspective', in J. V. Wertsch (ed.) *Culture Communication and Cognition*, Cambridge: Cambridge University Pess.

Bruner, J. S., Goodnow, J. J. and Austin, G. A. (1956) *A Study of Thinking*, New York: Wiley.

Bruner, J. S., Olver, R. and Greenfield, P. M. (eds) (1966) *Studies in Cognitive Growth*, New York: Wiley.

Bryant, P. E. (1974) *Perception and Understanding in Young Children*, London: Methuen.

Bryant, P. E. (1982a) 'The role of conflict and of agreement between intellectual strategies in children's ideas about measurement', *British Journal of Psychology* 73: 243–52.

Bryant, P. E. (ed.) (1982b) 'Piaget: issues and experiments', special issue; *British Journal of Psychology* 73(2): 157–313.

Bryant, P. E. (1985) 'Parents, children and cognitive development', in R. A. Hinde, A.-N. Perret-Clermont and J. Stevenson-Hinde (eds) *Social Relationships and Cognitive Development*, Oxford: Clarendon Press.

Bryant, P. E. and Alegria, J. (1990) 'The transition from spoken to written language', in A. de Ribaupierre (ed.) *Transition Mechanisms in Child Development*, Cambridge: Cambridge University Press.

Bryant, P. E. and Bradley, L. (1980) 'Why children sometimes write words which they do not read', in U. Frith (ed.) *Cognitive Processes in Spelling*, London: Academic Press.

Bryant, P. E. and Bradley, L. (1983) 'Psychological strategies and the development of reading and writing', in M. Matthew (ed.) *The Psychology of Written Language*, Chichester: Wiley.

Bryant, P. E. and Bradley, L. (1985) *Children's Reading Problems*, Oxford: Blackwell.

Bryant, P. E., Bradley, L., Maclean, M. and Crossland, J. (1989) 'Nursery rhymes, phonological skills and reading', *Journal of Child Language* 16: 407–28.

Bryant, P. E. and Goswami, U. (1987) 'Phonological awareness and learning to read', in J. Beech and A. Colley (eds) *Cognitive Approaches to Reading*, Chichester: Wiley.

Bryant, P. E. and Impey, L. (1986) 'The similarities between normal children and dyslexic adults and children', *Cognition* 24: 121–37.

Bryant, P. E., Jones, P., Claxton, V. and Perkins, J. (1972) 'Recognition of shapes across modalities by infants', *Nature* 240: 303–4.

Bryant, P. E., Maclean, M., Bradley, L. L. and Crossland, J. (1990) 'Rhyme and alliteration, phoneme detection, and learning to read', *Developmental Psychology* 26: 429–38.

Bryant, P. E. and Trabasso, T. (1971) 'Transitive inferences and memory in young children', *Nature* 232: 456–8.

Bucci, W. (1978) 'The interpretation of universal affirmative propositions', *Cognition* 6: 55–77.

Buckley, S. (1985) 'Attaining basic educational skills: reading, writing and number', in D. Lane and B. Stratford (eds) *Current Approaches to Down's Syndrome*, London: Holt, Rinehart & Winston.

Bullinger, A. and Chatillon, J-F. (1983) 'Recent theory and research of the Genevan School', in J. H. Flavell and E. M. Markman (eds) *Handbook of Child Psychology*, vol. 3, New York: Wiley.

Bullock, M. (1985) 'Animism in childhood thinking: a new look at an old question', *Developmental Psychology* 21: 217–55.

Bunge, M. (1980) *The Mind–Body Problem*, Oxford: Pergamon.

Burden, R. L. (1987) 'Feuerstein's Instrumental Enrichment Programme: important issues in research and evaluation', *European Journal of Psychology of Education* 2(1): 3–16.

Burns, E. A., House, J. D. and Ankenbauer, M. R. (1986) 'Sibling grief reaction to Sudden Infant Death Syndrome', *Pediatrics* 78: 458–87.

Burt, C. (1937) *The Backward Child*, London: University of London Press.

Burt, C. (1955) *The Subnormal Mind*, Oxford: Oxford University Press.

Bus, A. G. and van Ijzendoorn, M. H. (1988) 'Mother–child interactions, attachment and emergent literacy: a cross-sectional study', *Child Development*, 59: 1262–72.

Butterworth, G. (1975) 'Object identity in infancy: the interaction of spatial location codes in determining search errors', *Child Development* 46: 866–70.

Butterworth, G. (1977) 'Object disappearance and error in Piaget's Stage IV task', *Journal of Experimental Child Psychology* 23: 391–401.

Butterworth, G. (1978) 'Thought and things: Piaget's theory', in A. Burton and J. Radford (eds) *Perspectives on Thinking*, London: Methuen.

Butterworth, G. and Hicks, L. (1977) 'Visual proprioception and postural stability in infancy', *Perception* 6: 255–62.

Butterworth, G. and Light, P. (eds) (1982) *Social Cognition: Studies of the Development of Understanding*, Brighton: Harvester.

Butterworth, G., Harris, P., Leslie, A. and Wellman, H. (1991) *Perspectives on the Child's Theory of Mind*, Oxford: Oxford University Press.

Bynum, T. W., Thomas, J. A. and Weitz, L. J. (1972) 'Truth-functional logic in formal operational thinking', *Developmental Psychology* 7: 129–32.

Byrne, R. W. and Whiten, A. (1988) *Machiavellian Intelligence: Social Expertise and the Evolution of Intellect in Monkeys, Apes and Humans*, Oxford: Clarendon Press.

Byrnes, J. (1988) 'Formal operations: a systematic reformulation', *Developmental Review* 8, 66–87.

Calkins, L. (1983) *Lessons from a Child: on the Teaching and Learning of Writing*, Exeter, NH: Heinemann.

Callanan, M. A. (1985) 'How parents label objects for young children: the role of input in the acquisition of category hierarchies', *Child Development*, 56: 508–23.

Camaioni, L. (1990) 'The role of social interaction in the transition from communication to language', in A. de Ribaupierre (ed.) *Transition Mechanisms in Child Development*, Cambridge: Cambridge University Press.

Campbell, R. and Butterworth, B. (1985) 'Phonological dyslexia and dysgraphia in a highly literate subject: a developmental case and associated deficits of phonemic awareness', *Quarterly Journal of Experimental Psychology* 37A: 435–75.

Campione, J. C., Brown, A. L. and Ferrara, R. A. (1982) 'Mental retardation and intelligence', in R. J. Sternberg (ed.) *Handbook of Human Intelligence*, Cambridge: Cambridge University Press.

Campione, J. C., Brown, A. L., Ferrara, R. A. and Bryant, N. R. (1984) 'The zone of proximal development: implications for individual differences and learning', in B. Rogoff and J. Wertsch (eds) *New Directions for Cognitive Development: the Zone of Proximal Development*, San Francisco: Jossey-Bass.

Campos, J. J., Campos, R. G. and Barrett, K. C. (1983) 'Emergent themes in the study of emotional development and emotional regulation', *Developmental Psychology* 25: 394–402.

Cantor, J. H. and Spiker, C. (1989) 'Children's learning revisited: the contemporary scope of the Modified Spence Discrimination Theory', in H. W. Reese (ed.) *Advances in Child Development and Behaviour*, vol. 21, New York: Academic Press.

Caplan, M. Z. and Hale, D. F. (1989) 'Preschoolers' responses to peers' distress and beliefs about bystander intervention', *Journal of Child Psychology and Psychiatry* 30(2): 231–42.

Capron, C. and Duyme, M. (1989) 'Assessment of effects of socio-economic status on IQ in a full cross-fostering study', *Nature* 340: 552–4.

Caramazza, A., McCloskey, M. and Green, B. (1981) 'Naive beliefs in "sophisticated" subjects: misconceptions about trajectories of objects', *Cognitia* 9: 117–23.

Cardon, L. R., Fulker, D. W., De Fries, J. C. and Plomin, R. (1992) 'Continuity and change in general cognitive ability from 1–7 years of age', *Developmental Psychology* 28: 64–73.

Carey, S. (1985) *Conceptual Change in Childhood*, Cambridge, Mass.: MIT Press.

Carey, S. (1986a) 'Cognitive science and science education', *American Psychologist* 41(10): 1123–30.

Carey, S. (1986b) 'Constraints on semantic development', in W. Demopoulos and A. Marras (eds) *Language Learning and Concept Acquisition*, Norwood, NJ: Ablex.

Carey, S. (1987) 'Theory change in childhood', in B. Inhelder, D. de Caprona, A. Cornu-Wells (eds) *Piaget Today*, Hillsdale, NJ: Erlbaum.

Carey, S. (1988) 'Conceptual differences between children and adults', *Mind and Language* 3(3): 167–81.

Carey, S. (1991) 'Knowledge acquisition: enrichment or conceptual change', in S. Carey and R. Gelman (eds) *The Epigenesis of Mind*, Hove: Erlbaum.

Carey, S. and Gelman R. (1991) (eds) *The Epigenesis of Mind*, Hove: Erlbaum.

Carpenter, P. A. and Just, M. A. (1986) 'Spatial ability: an information-processing approach to psychometrics', in R. J. Sternberg (ed.) *Advances in the Psychology of Human Intelligence*, Hillsdale, NJ: Erlbaum.

Carpenter, T. P. (1986) 'Conceptual knowledge as a foundation for procedural knowledge', in J. Hiebert (ed.) *Conceptual and Procedural Knowledge: the Case of Mathematics*, Hillsdale, NJ: Erlbaum.

Carpenter, T. P. and Moser, J. M. (1983) 'The acquisition of addition and subtraction concepts', in R. Lesh and M. Landau (eds) *Acquisition of Mathematics Concepts and Processes*, New York: Academic Press.

Carpenter, T. P., Moser, J. M. and Romberg, T. A. (eds) (1982) *Addition and Subtraction: a Cognitive Perspective*, Hillsdale, NJ: Erlbaum.

Carr, J. (1985) 'The development of intelligence', in D. Lane and B. Stratford (eds) *Current Approaches to Down's Syndrome*, London: Holt, Rinehart & Winston.

Carr, J. (1988) 'Six weeks to twenty-one years old: a longitudinal study of children with Down's Syndrome and their families', *Journal of Child Psychology* 29: 407–31.

Carr, M., Borkowski, J. G. and Maxwell, S. E. (1991) 'Motivational components of underachievement', *Developmental Psychology* 27: 108–18.

Carr, M., Kurtz, B. E., Schneider, W., Turner, L. A. and Borkowski, J. G. (1989) 'Strategy acquisition and transfer among American and German children: environmental influences on metacognitive development' *Developmental Psychology* 25(5): 765–71.

Carraher, T. N., Carraher, D. W. and Schiemann, A. D. (1985) 'Mathematics in the streets and in schools', *British Journal of Developmental Psychology* 3: 21–9.

Carrasquillo, A. (1987) 'Bilingualism, early language and cognitive development', in B. Fillion, C. N. Hedley and E. C. Di Martino (eds) *Home and School: Early Language and Reading*, Norwood, NJ: Ablex.

Carroll, J. B. (1982) 'The measurement of intelligence', in R. J. Sternberg (ed.) *Handbook of Human Intelligence*, Cambridge: Cambridge University Press.

Carruthers, P. (1992) *Human Knowledge and Human Nature*, Oxford: Oxford University Press.

Carter, P., Pazak, B. and Kail, R. (1983) 'Algorithms for processing spatial information', *Journal of Experimental Child Psychology* 36: 284–304.

Case, R. (1974) 'Structures and strictures, some functional limitations on the course of cognitive growth', *Cognitive Psychology*, 6: 544–73.

Case, R. (1984) 'The process of stage-transition: a neo-Piagetian view', in R. J. Sternberg (ed.) *Mechanisms of Cognitive Development*, New York: Freeman.

Case, R. (1985) *Intellectual Development: Birth to Adulthood*, New York: Academic Press.

Case, R., Hayward, S., Lewis, M. and Hurst, P. (1988). 'Towards a neo-Piagetian theory of cognitive and emotional development', *Developmental Review* 8: 1–51.

Case, R., Marini, Z., McKeough, A., Denis, S. and Goldberg, J. (1986) 'Horizontal structure in middle childhood: cross-domain parallels in the course of cognitive growth', in I. Levin (ed.) *Stage and Structure: Reopening the Debate*, Norwood, NJ: Ablex.

Caspi, A., Elder, G. H., Bem, D. J. (1987) 'Moving against the world: life-course patterns of explosive children', *Developmental Psychology* 23: 208–313.

Cassidy, J. (1988) 'Child–mother attachment and the self in six-year-olds', *Child Development* 59: 121–34.

Cataldo, S. and Ellis, N. (1988) 'Interactions in the development of spelling, reading and phonological skills', *Journal of Research in Reading* 11(2): 86–109.

Cattell, R. B. (1971) *Abilities: Their Structure, Growth and Action*, Boston: Houghton-Mifflin.

Cavanaugh, J. C. and Perlmutter, M. (1982) 'Metamemory: a critical examination', *Child Development* 53: 11–28.

Cazden, C. (1988) *Classroom Discourse: the Language of Teaching and Learning*, Portsmouth, NH: Heinemann.

Ceci, S. (1990) *On intelligence . . . more or less: a Bio-Ecological Theory of Intellectual Development*, New York: Prentice Hall.

Ceci, S. J. and Bronfenbrenner, U. (1985) 'Don't forget to take the cup cakes out of the oven: prospective memory, strategic time monitoring, and context', *Child Development* 56: 152–64.

Ceci, S. J. and Liker, J. (1986) 'A day at the races: the study of IQ, expertise and cognitive complexity', *Journal of Experimental Psychology: General* 115: 225–6.

Cellérier, G. (1987) 'Structures and functions', in B. Inhelder, D. de Caprona and A. Cornu-Wells (eds) *Piaget Today*, Hillsdale, NJ: Erlbaum.

Chall, S. J. (1967) *Learning to Read: the Great Debate*, New York: McGraw Hill.

Chall, S. J. (1983) *Stages of Reading Development*, New York, McGraw Hill.

Chall, S. J., Jacobs, V. and Baldwin, L. (1990) *The Reading Crisis: Why Poor Children Fall Behind*, Cambridge, Mass.: Harvard University Press.

Chandler, M. (1988) 'Doubt and developing theories of mind', in J. W. Astington, P. L. Harris and D. R. Olsen (eds) *Developing Theories of Mind*, Cambridge: Cambridge University Press.

Chandler, M. and Helm, D. (1984) 'Developmental changes in the contributions of shared experience to social role-taking competence', *International Journal of Behavioural Development* 7: 145–56.

Chandler, M., Fritz, A. S. and Hale, S. M. (1989) 'Small-scale deceit: deception as a marker of 2, 3 and 4 year olds' theory of mind', *Child Development* 60: 1263–77.

Changeux, J. P. (1987) *Neuronal Man*, Oxford: Oxford University Press.

Chapman, M. and Lindenberger, U. (1988) 'Functions, operations and decalage in the development of transitivity', *Developmental Psychology* 24: 542–51.

Chapman, M. and McBride, M. L. (1992) 'Beyond competence and performance: children's class inclusion strategies, superordinate class cues, and verbal justifications', *Developmental Psychology* 28: 319–27.

Chase, W. G. and Simon, H. (1973) 'Perception in chess', *Cognitive Psychology* 4: 55–8.

Chen, M. J., Holman, J., Francis-Jones, N. and Burmeister, L. (1988) 'Concepts of intelligence of primary school, high school and college students', *British Journal of Experimental Psychology* 6: 71–82.

Cheng, P. and Holyoak, K. (1985) 'Pragmatic reasoning schemas', *Cognitive Psychology* 17: 391–416.

Cherlin, A. J. *et al.* (1991) 'Longitudinal studies of effects of divorce on children in Great Britain and the United States', *Science* 252: 1386–9.

Chi, M. T. H. (1978) 'Knowledge structures and memory development', in R. S. Siegler (ed.) *Children's Thinking: What Develops?* Hillsdale, NJ: Erlbaum.

Chi, M. T. H. (ed.) (1983) *Trends in Memory Development Research*, Basle: Karger.

Chi, M. T. H. and Ceci, S. (1987) 'Content knowledge: its role, representation and restructuring in memory development', in *Advances in Child Development and Behavior*, vol. 20, New York: Academic Press.

Chi, M. T. H. and Koeske, R. D. (1983) 'Network representation of a child's dinosaur knowledge', *Developmental Psychology* 19(1): 29–39.

Chi, M. T. H., Feltovich, P. and Glaser, R. (1980) 'Categorisation and representation of physics problems by experts and novices', *Cognitive Science* 5: 121–52.

Chi, M. T. H., Hutchinson, J. E. and Robin, A. F. (1989) 'How inferences about novel domain-related concepts can be constrained by structured knowledge', *Merrill-Palmer Quarterly* 35(1): 27–62.

Chomsky, N. (1968) *Language and Mind*, New York: Harcourt Brace Jovanovich.

Chomsky, N. (1986) *Knowledge of Language: its Nature, Origin and Use*, New York: Praeger.

Chukovsky, K. (1976) 'The sense of nonsense verse', in J. S. Bruner, A. Jolly and K. Sylva (eds) *Play: its Role in Development and Evolution*, Harmondsworth: Penguin Books.

Churchland, P. M. (1989) *A Neurocomputational Perspective: the Nature of Mind and the Structure of Science*, Cambridge, Mass.: Bradford & MIT Press.

Churchland, P. M. and Churchland, P. S. (1990) 'Could a machine think?' *Scientific American*, January 1990: 26–31.

Churchland, P. S. (1986) *Neurophilosophy: Toward a Unified Understanding of the Mind/Brain*, Cambridge, Mass.: MIT Press.

Cicchetti, D. (1990) 'The organisation and coherence of socioemotional, cognitive, and representational development: illustrations through a developmental psychopathology perspective on Down's Syndrome and child maltreatment', in R. A. Thompson (ed.) *Socioemotional Development: Nebraska Symposium on Motivation, 1988*, vol. 36. Lincoln, Nebr.: University of Nebraska Press.

Clark, A. (1989) *Microcognition: Philosophy, Cognitive Science, and Parallel Distributed Processing*, Cambridge, Mass: MIT Press.

Clark, E. V. (1973) 'Non-linguistic strategies and the acquisiton of word meanings', *Cognition* 2: 161–82.

Clark, E. V. (1983) 'Meaning and concepts', in H. H. Flavell and E. M. Markman (eds) *Handbook of Child Psychology*, vol. 3, series ed. P. H. Mussen, New York: Wiley.

Clark, M. M. (1976) *Young Fluent Readers*, London: Heinemann.

Clay, M. (1979) *Reading: the Patterning of Complex Behaviour*, London: Heinemann.

Clay, M. (1983) 'Getting a theory of writing', in B. Kroll and G. Wells (eds) *Explorations in the Development of Writing*, Chichester: Wiley.

Cochran-Smith, M. (1984) *The Making of a Reader*, Norwood, NJ: Ablex.

Coe, R. N. (1984) *When the Grass was Taller: Autobiography and the Experience of Childhood*, New Haven, Conn.: Yale University Press.

Coen, C. W. (ed.) (1985) *Functions of the Brain*, Oxford: Clarendon Press.

Cogill, S. R., Caplan, H. L., Alexandra, H., Robson, K. M. and Kumar, R. (1986) 'Impact of maternal depression on cognitive development of young children', *British Medical Journal* 292: 1165–7.

Cohen, D. and Mackeith, S. A. (1991) *The Development of Imagination*, London: Routledge.

Cohen, G. (1983) *The Psychology of Cognition*, London: Academic Press.

Cohen, I. L., Vietze, P. M., Sudhalter, V., Jenkins, E. C. and Brown, W. T. (1989) 'Parent–child dyadic gaze patterns in fragile X males and in non-fragile X males with autistic disorder', *Journal of Child Psychology and Psychiatry* 30(6): 857–64.

Cohler, B. J., Grunebaum, H. U., Weiss, J. L., Gamer, E. and Gallant, D. H. (1977) 'Disturbance of attention among schizophrenic, depressed and well mothers and their young children', *Journal of Child Psychology and Psychiatry* 18: 115–35.

Cole, M. (1985) 'The zone of proximal development: where culture and cognition create each other', in J. V. Wertsch (ed.) *Culture, Communication and Cognition*, Cambridge: Cambridge University Press.

Cole, M. (1990) 'Cognitive development and formal schooling: the evidence from cross-cultural research', in L. C. Moll (ed.) *Vygotsky and Education*, New York: Cambridge University Press.

Cole, M. and Griffin, P. (1980) 'Cultural amplifiers reconsidered', in D. R. Olson (ed.) *The Social Foundations of Language and Thought*, New York and London: Norton.

Cole, M. and Means, B. (1981) *Comparative Studies of How People Think: an Introduction*, Cambridge, Mass.: Harvard University Press.

Cole, P. M. (1986) 'Children's spontaneous control of facial expression', *Child Development* 57: 1309–21.

Coleman, A. (1985) *Utopia on Trial: Vision and Reality in Planned Housing*, London: Hilary Shipman.

Coleman, M. (1982) 'Take one, leave one: young children's concepts of subtraction', Unpublished M.Ed. thesis, University of Bristol.

Coles, M. J. and Robinson, W. D. (1989) *Teaching Thinking: a Survey of Programmes in Education*, Bristol: The Bristol Press.

Collerson, J. (1983) 'One child and one genre: developments in letter writing', in B. Kroll and G. Wells (eds) *Explorations in the Development of Writing*, Chichester: Wiley.

Colley, A. M. (1987) 'Text comprehension', in J. R. Beech and A. M. Colley (eds) *Cognitive Approaches to Reading*, Chichester: Wiley.

Collins, A. and Smith, E. E. (1982) 'Teaching the process of reading comprehension', in D. K. Detterman and R. J. Sternberg (eds) *How and How Much Can Intelligence be Increased?*, Norwood, NJ: Ablex.

Collins, W. A. and Gunnar, M. R. (1990) 'Social and personality development', *Annual Review of Psychology* 42: 387–416.

Connell, J. P. and Wellborn, J. G. (1991) 'Competence, autonomy and relatedness: a motivational analysis of self-system processes', in *Minnesota Symposium on Child Psychology* vol. 23, Hillsdale, NJ: Erlbaum.

Conroy, J. S. (1984) 'Towards a framework for language functioning in learning mathematics', Paper given at the Fifth International Congress on Mathematics Education, Adelaide, Australia, August 1984.

Cook, M. (1984) *Levels of Personality*, London: Holt, Rinehart & Winston.

Coon, H., Fulker, D. W., De Fries, J. C. and Plomin, R. (1990) 'Home environment and cognitive ability of seven-year-old children in the Colorado Adoption Project: genetic and environmental etiologies', *Developmental Psychology* 26: 459–68.

Cooper, L. A. and Regan, D. T. (1982) 'Attention, perception and intelligence', in R. J. Sternberg (ed.) *Handbook of Human Intelligence*, Cambridge: Cambridge University Press.

Cooper, L. A. and Shepard, R. N. (1984) 'Turning something over in the mind', *Scientific American* 251(6) (December): 106–14.

Cormier, S. M. and Hagman, J. D. (1987), *Transfer of Learning: Contemporary Research and Applications*, San Diego, Calif.: Academic Press.

Cornell, E. H., Heth, C. D. and Broda, L. S. (1989) 'Children's wayfinding: response to instructions to use environmental landmarks', *Developmental Psychology* 25(5): 755–64.

Cousins, J. H., Siegel, A. W. and Maxwell, S. E. (1983) 'Wayfinding and cognitive mapping in large-scale environments: a test of a developmental model', *Journal of Experimental Child Psychology* 35: 1–20.

Covington, M. V. (1987) 'Instruction in problem-solving planning', in S. L. Friedman, E. K. Scholnick and R. R. Cocking (eds) *Blueprints for Thinking: the Role of Planning in Cognitive Development*, New York: Cambridge University Press.

Cowan, P. (1982) 'The relationship between emotions and cognitive development', in W. Damon (ed.) *New Directions for Child Development*, vol. 16, San Francisco: Jossey-Bass.

Cowie, H. (ed.) (1984) *The Development of Children's Imaginative Writing*, London: Croom Helm.

Cox, A. D., Puckering, C., Pound, A. and Mills, M. (1987) 'The impact of maternal depression in young children', *Journal of Child Psychology and Psychiatry* 28: 917–28.

Cox, M. V. (ed.) (1980) *Are Young Children Egocentric?*, London: Batsford.

Cox, M. V. (1986) *The Child's Point of View: the Development of Cognition and Language*, Brighton: Harvester.

Coyle, J. T., Oster-Granite, M. L., Reeves, R., Hohmann, C., Corsi, P. and Gearhart, J. (1991) 'Down's Syndrome and the Trisomy 16 Mouse: impact of gene imbalance on brain development and aging', in P. R. McHugh and V. A. McKusick (eds) *Genes, Brain and Behaviour*, New York: Raven Press.

Coyne, J. C. and Downey, G. (1991) 'Social factors and psychopathology: stress, social support, and coping processes', *Annual Review of Psychology* 42: 401–25.

Crain-Thoreson, C. and Dale, P. S. (1992) 'Do early talkers become early readers? Linguistic precocity, preschool language, and emergent literacy', *Developmental Psychology* 28: 421–9.

Cravioto, J. and Arrieta, R. (1979) 'Stimulation and mental development of malnourished infants', *The Lancet* 2: 899.

Crisafi, M. A. and Brown, A. L. (1986) 'Analogical transfer in very young children: combining two separately learned solutions to reach a goal', *Child Development* 57: 953–68.

Crnic, L. S. and Pennington, B. F. (eds) (1987) 'Developmental psychology and the neurosciences', *Child Development* 58: 533–717.

Cromer, R. (1987) 'Language acquisition, language disorder and cognitive development', in W. Yule and M. Rutter (eds) *Language Development and Disorders*, London: MacKeith Press and Oxford: Blackwell Scientific Publications.

Cromer, R. (1991) *Language and Thought in Normal and Handicapped Children*, Oxford: Blackwell.

Crook, C. H. (1984) 'Factors influencing the use of transparency in children's drawing', *British Journal of Developmental Psychology* 2: 213–21.

Crook, C. H. (1985) 'Knowledge and appearance', in N. H. Freeman and M. V. Cox (eds) *Visual Order*, Cambridge: Cambridge University Press.

Crook, T., Raskin, A. and Eliot, J. (1981) 'Parent–child relationships and adult depression', *Child Development* 52: 950–7.

Crowder, R. G. (1982) *The Psychology of Reading: an Introduction*, Oxford: Oxford University Press.

Cunningham, C. C., Glenn, S. M., Wilkinson, P. and Sloper, P. (1985) 'Mental ability, symbolic play and receptive and expressive language of young children with Down's Syndrome', *Journal of Child Psychology and Psychiatry* 26: 255–65.

Cunningham, J. G. and Weaver, S. L. (1989) 'Young children's knowledge of their memory span: effects of task and experience', *Journal of Experimental Child Psychology* 48: 32–44.

Curtiss, S. (1977) *Genie: a Psycholinguistic Study of a Modern-day 'Wild child'*, New York: Academic Press.

Czerniewska, P. (1992) *Learning about Writing*, Oxford: Blackwell.

Damon, W. and Hart, D. (1982) 'The development of self-understanding from infancy through adolescence', *Child Development* 53: 841–64.

Damon, W. and Hart, D. (1988) *Self-understanding in Childhood and Adolescence*, Cambridge: Cambridge University Press.

Daniels, D. and Plomin, R. (1985) 'Differential experiences of siblings in the same family', *Developmental Psychology* 21: 747–60.

Darlington, R. B. (1991) 'The long-term effects of model preschool programs', in L. Okagaki and R. J. Sternberg (eds) *Directors of Development: Influences on the Development of Children's Thinking*, Hillsdale, NJ: Erlbaum.

Darwin, C. (1872) *The Expression of the Emotions in Man and Animals*, London: Murray.

das Gupta, P. and Bryant, P. E. (1989) 'Young children's causal inferences', *Child Development* 60: 1138–46.

Dasen, P. (1977) 'Are cognitive processes universal? A contribution to cross-cultural Piagetian psychology', in N. Warren (ed.) *Studies in Cross-cultural Psychology*, London: Academic Press.

Davidson, P. M. (1987) 'Early function concepts: their development and relation to certain mathematical and logical abilities', *Child Development* 58: 1542–55.

Davie, C. E., Hurt, S. J., Vincent, E. and Mason, M. (1984) *The Young Child at Home*, Windsor: NFER-Nelson.

Davies, B. (1985) 'Hearing problems', in D. Lane and B. Stratford (eds) *Current Approaches to Down's Syndrome*, London: Holt, Rinehart & Winston.

Davis, P. J. (1987) 'Repression and the inaccessibility of affective memories', *Journal of Personality and Social Psychology* 53: 585–93.

Davis, R. B. (1986) 'Conceptual and procedural knowledge in mathematics: a summary analysis', in J. Hiebert (ed.) *Conceptual and Procedural Knowledge: the Case of Mathematics*, Hillsdale, NJ: Erlbaum.

Davydov, V. V. and Radzikhovskii, L. A. (1985) 'Vygotsky's theory and the activity-oriented approach in psychology', in J. V. Wertsch (ed.) *Culture, Communication and Cognition*, Cambridge: Cambridge University Press.

Day, J., French, L. A. and Hall, M. (1985) 'Social influences on cognitive development', in D. L. Forrest-Pressley, G. E. MacKinnon and G. T. Waller (eds) *Metacognition, Cognition and Human Performance*, Orlando, Fla.: Academic Press.

Dean, A., Malik, M., Richards, W. and Stringer, S. (1986) 'Effects of parental maltreatment on children's conceptions of interpersonal relationships', *Developmental Psychology* 22: 617–26.

Dean, R. S. (1985) 'Foundation and rationale for neuropsychological bases of individual differences', in L. C. Hartlage and C. F. Telzrow (eds) *The Neuropsychology of Individual Differences*, New York: Plenum Press.

De Fries, J. C., Plomin, R., and La Buda, M. C. (1987) 'Genetic stability of cognitive development from childhood to adulthood', *Developmental Psychology* 23: 4–12.

De Jong, G. (1989) 'The role of explanation in analogy: or, the curse of an alluring name', in S. Vosniadou and A. Ortony (eds) *Similarity and Analogical Reasoning*, Cambridge: Cambridge University Press.

De Loache, J. S. (1987) 'Rapid change in the symbolic functioning of young children', *Science* 238: 1556–7.

De Loache, J. S. (1989) 'The development of representation in young children', in W. H. Reese (ed.) *Advances in Child Development and Behaviour*, vol. 22, New York: Academic Press.

De Loache, J. S., Kolstad, V. and Anderson, K. N. (1991) 'Physical similarity and young children's understanding of scale models', *Child Development* 62: 111–26.

Dempster, F. N. (1981) 'Memory span: sources of individual and developmental differences', *Psychological Bulletin* 89: 63–100.

Denham, S. A., Renwick, S. M. and Holt, R. W. (1991) 'Working and playing together: prediction of preschool social-emotional competence from mother–child interaction', *Child Development* 62: 242–9.

Dennett, D. (1979) *Brainstorms*, Hassocks, Sussex: Harvester.

Dennett, D. (1987) *The Intentional Stance*, Cambridge, Mass.: MIT Press.

de Ribaupierre, A. (1990) *Transition Mechanisms in Child Development*, Cambridge: Cambridge University Press.

DES (1990) *English in the National Curriculum, No. 2*, London: HMSO.

Desforges, C. (ed.) (1989) *Early Childhood Education*, Edinburgh: Scottish Academic Press for the British Journal of Educational Psychology.

Desforges, C. and Cockburn, A. (1987) *Understanding the Mathematics Teacher*, Basingstoke: Falmer Press.

Deutsch, D. (1982) *The Psychology of Music*, New York: Academic Press.

DHSS (1980) *Inequalities in Health*, Report of a working group on inequalities in health, Chairman, Sir Douglas Black, London: Department of Health and Social Security.

Dias, M. G. and Harris, P. L. (1988) 'The effect of make-believe play on deductive reasoning', *British Journal of Developmental Psychology* 6: 207–21.

Dias, M. G. and Harris, P. L. (1990) 'The influence of the imagination on reasoning by young children', *British Journal of Developmental Psychology* 8: 305–18.

Diaz, R. M. (1985) 'Bilingual cognitive development: addressing three gaps in current research', *Child Development* 56: 1376–88.

Dickinson, J. (1990) 'Adolescent representations of socio-economic status', *British Journal of Developmental Psychology* 8: 351–71.

Dillon, R. F. and Sternberg, R. J. (1986) *Cognition and Instruction*, New York: Academic Press.

Di Martino, E. C. (1987) 'The language of social regulation in young children', in B. Fillion, C. N. Hedley and E. C. Di Martino (eds) *Home and School: Early Language and Reading*, Norwood, NJ: Ablex.

di Sessa, A. (1982) 'Unlearning Aristotelian physics: a study of knowledge-based learning', *Cognitive Science* 6: 37–76.

di Sessa, A. (1983) 'Phenomenology and the evolution of intuition', in D. Gentner and A. L. Stevens (eds) *Mental Models*, Hillsdale, NJ: Erlbaum.

Dix, T. (1991) 'The affective organisation of parenting: adaptive and maladaptive processes', *Psychological Bulletin* 110: 3–25.

Dobbing, J. (1981) 'The later development of the brain and its vulnerability', in J.A. Davis and J. Dobbing (eds) *Scientific Foundations of Pediatrics*, London: Heinemann Medical.

Dobbing, J. (ed.) (1987) *Early Nutrition and Later Achievement*, London: Academic Press.

Dodge, K. A., Pettit, G. S., McClaskey, C. L. and Brown, M. M. (1986) 'Social competence in children', *Monographs of the Soceity for Research in Child Development* 51: 1–80.

Doise, W. (1985) 'Social regulations in cognitive development', in R. A. Hinde, A.-N. Perret-Clermont and J. Stevenson-Hinde (eds) *Social Relationships and Cognitive Development*, Oxford: Clarendon Press.

Doise, W. and Mugny, G. (1984) *The Social Development of the Intellect*, Oxford: Pergamon.

Donaldson, M. (1978) *Children's Minds*, London: Fontana.

Donaldson, M. (1982) 'Conservation: what is the question?', *British Journal of Psychology* 73(2): 199–208.

Donaldson, M. and Balfour, G. (1981) 'Less is more: a study of language comprehension', *British Journal of Psychology* 59: 461–71.

Donaldson, M., Grieve, R. and Pratt, C. (eds) (1983) *Early Childhood Development and Education*, Oxford: Blackwell.

Dorval, B. and Eckerman, C. O. (1984) 'Developmental trends in the quality of conversation achieved by small groups of acquainted peers', *Monographs of the Society for Research in Child Development* 49(2), serial no. 206: 1–91.

Dowker, A. (1989) 'Rhymes and alliteration in poems elicited from young children', *Journal of Child Language* 16: 181–202.

Downey, G. and Coyne, J. C. (1990) 'Children of depressed parents: an integrative review', *Psychological Bulletin* 108: 50–76.

Downing, J. (1979) *Reading and Reasoning*, New York: Springer-Verlag.

Dumaret, A. and Stewart, J. (1985) 'IQ, scholastic performance and behaviour of sibs raised in contrasting environments', *Journal of Child Psychiatry and Psychology* 26: 553–80.

Dunn, J. (1987) 'Understanding feelings: the early stages', in J. Bruner and H. Haste (eds) *Making Sense: the Child's Construction of the World*, London: Methuen.

Dunn, J. (1988) *The Beginnings of Social Understanding*, Oxford: Blackwell.

Dunn, J. (1991a) 'Relationships and behaviour: the significance of Robert Hinde's work for developmental psychology', in P. Bateson (ed.) *The Development and Integration of Behaviour*, Cambridge: Cambridge University Press.

Dunn, J. (1991b) 'The developmental importance of differences in siblings' experiences within the family', in K. Pillemer and K. McCartney (eds) *Parent-child Relations Throughout Life*, Hillsdale, NJ: Erlbaum.

Dunn, J. (1992) 'Lessons from the study of children's conversations', *Merrill-Palmer Quarterly* 38: 139–49.

Dunn, J. and Kendrick, C. (1982) *Siblings: Love, Envy and Understanding*, London: Grant McIntyre.

Dunn, J., Bretherton, I. and Munn, P. (1987) 'Conversations about feeling states between mothers and their young children', *Developmental Psychology* 23: 132–9.

Dunn, J., Plomin, R. and Nettles, M. (1985) 'Consistency of mothers' behavior towards infant siblings', *Developmental Psychology* 21: 1188–95.

Duyme, M. (1988) 'School success and social class: an adoption study', *Developmental Psychology* 24: 203–9.

Duyme, M. (1990) 'Antisocial behaviour and post-natal environment: a French adoption study', *Journal of Child Psychology and Psychiatry*, 31(5): 699–710.

Dweck, G. S. and Elliott, E. S. (1983) 'Achievement motivation', in E. M. Hetherington (ed.) *Handbook of Child Psychology*, New York: Wiley.

Eccles, J. (1985) 'Sex differences in achievement patterns', in *Nebraska Symposium on Motivation*, vol. 32, Lincoln, Nebr.: University of Nebraska Press.

Eccles, J. (1989) *Evolution of the Brain: Creation of the Self*, London: Routledge.

Eckler, J. A. and Weininger, O. (1989) 'Structural parallels between pretend play and narratives', *Developmental Psychology* 25(5): 736–43.

Eckstein, S. G. and Shemesh, M. (1992) 'Mathematical models of cognitive development', *British Journal of Mathematical and Statistical Psychology* 45: 1–18.

Edwards, B. (1979) *Drawing on the Right Side of the Brain*, Los Angeles, Calif.: J. P. Tarcher.

Edwards, C. P. and Lewis, M (1979) 'Young children's concepts of social relations: social functions and social objects', in M. Lewis and L. A. Rosenblum (eds) *The Child and its Family: Genesis of Behaviour*, vol. 2, New York: Plenum Press.

Edwards, J. (1986) 'Language and educational disadvantage: the persistence of linguistic "deficit" theory', in K. Durkin (ed.) *Language Development in the School Years*, London: Croom Helm.

Egan, K. (1988a) 'The origins of imagination and the curriculum', in K. Egan and D. Nadaner (eds) *Imagination and Education*, Milton Keynes: Open University Press.

Egan, K. (1988b) *Primary Understanding: Education in Early Childhood*, New York: Routledge.

Egan, K. and Nadaner, D. (eds) (1988) *Imagination and Education*, Milton Keynes: Open University Press.

Egeland, B., Jacobvitz, D. and Sroufe, L. A. (1988) 'Breaking the cycle of abuse', *Child Development* 59: 1080–8.

Ehri, L. C., Wilce, L. S. and Taylor, B. B. (1987) 'Children's categorisation of short vowels in words and the influence of spellings', *Merrill-Palmer Quarterly* 33(3): 393–421.

Eisenberg, A. R. (1985) 'Learning to describe past experiences in conversation', *Discourse Processes* 8: 177–204.

Eisenberg, N. and Mussen, P. H. (1989) *The Roots of Prosocial Behaviour in Children*, Cambridge: Cambridge University Press.

Eisenberg, N. and Sayer, J. (1988) *Empathy and its Development*, Cambridge: Cambridge University Press.

Eiser, C. (1985) *The Psychology of Childhood Illness*, New York: Springer-Verlag.

Eiser, C. (1988) 'Explaining illness to children', *Communication and Cognition* 20: 277–90.

Eiser, C. and Eiser, J. R. (1987) 'Explaining illness to children', *Communication and Cognition* 20(2/3): 277–90.

Eiser, C. and Patterson, D. (1983) ' "Slugs and snails and puppy-dogs' tails": children's ideas about the insides of their bodies', *Child: Care, Health and Development* 9: 233–40.

Eiser, C., Eiser, J. R. and Lang, J. (1989) 'Scripts in children's reports of medical events', *European Journal of Psychology of Education* 4(3): 377–84.

Eiser, C., Patterson, D. and Eiser, J. R. (1983) 'Children's knowledge of health and illness: implications for health education', *Child: Care, Health and Development*, 9: 285–92.

Eiser, C., Town, C. and Tripp, J. H. (1988) 'Illness experience and related knowledge amongst children with asthma', *Child: Care, Health and Development* 14: 11–24.

Elkind, D. (1978) *The Child's Reality: Three Developmental Themes*, Hillsdale, NJ: Erlbaum.

Elley, W. B. (1989) 'Vocabulary acquisition from listening to stories', *Reading Research Quarterly* 24: 174–87.

Ellis, A. W. (1984) *Reading, Writing and Dyslexia in Cognitive Analysis*, London: Erlbaum.

Ellis, C. E. and Hill, D. E. (1975) 'Growth, intelligence and school performance in children with cystic fibrosis who have had an episode of malnutrition during infancy', *Journal of Pediatrics* 87: 565–8.

Ellis, H. D. (1990) 'Developmental trends in face recognition', *The Psychologist* 3: 114–19.

Ellis, N. (1988) 'The development of literacy and short-term memory', in M. M. Gruneberg, P. E. Morris and R. N. Sykes (eds) *Practical Aspects of Memory: II*, Chichester: Wiley.

Ellis, N. and Large, B. (1987) 'The development of reading: as you seek so shall you find', *British Journal of Psychology* 78: 1–28.

Ellis, N. and Large, B. (1988) 'The early stages of reading: a longitudinal study', *Applied Cognitive Psychology* 2: 47–76.

Ellis, S. and Rogoff, B. (1982) 'The strategies and efficacy of child versus adult teachers', *Child Development* 53: 730–5.

Emler, N. and Dickinson, J. (1985) 'Children's representations of social inequalities: the effects of social class', *British Journal of Developmental Psychology* 3: 191–8.

Emler, N. and Valiant, G. (1982) 'Social interaction and cognitive conflict in the development of spatial co-ordination skills', *British Journal of Psychology* 73: 295–304.

English, L. (1992) 'Children's use of domain-specific knowledge and domain-general strategies in novel problem solving', *British Journal of Educational Psychology* 62: 203–16.

Ennis, R. H. (1978) 'Conceptualization of children's logical competence: Piaget's propositional logic and an alternative proposal', in L. S. Siegel and C. J. Brainerd (eds) *Alternatives to Piaget*, New York: Academic Press.

Entwistle, D. R. and Stevenson, H. W. (1987) 'Schools and development', *Child Development* 58: 1149–50.

Entwistle, N. (1988) 'Motivational factors in approaches to learning', in R. R. Schmeck (ed.) *Learning Strategies and Learning Styles*, New York: Plenum Press.

Entwistle, N., Hanley, M. and Ratcliffe, G. (1979) 'Approaches to learning and levels of understanding', *British Educational Research Journal* 5: 99–114.

Epstein, H. T. (1974a) 'Phrenoblysis: special brain and mind growth periods: I. Human brain and skull development', *Developmental Psychobiology* 7: 207–216.

Epstein, H. T. (1974b) 'Phrenoblysis: special brain and mind growth periods: II. Human mental development', *Developmental Psychobiology* 7: 217–24.

Epstein, H. T. (1990) 'Stages in human mental growth', *Journal of Educational Psychology* 82: 876–80.

Ericsson, K. A., Chase, W. G. and Faloon, S. (1980) 'Acquisition of a memory skill', *Science* 208: 1181–2.

Ernhart, C. B., Wolf, A. W., Kennard, M. J., Erhard, P., Filipovich, H. F., Sokol, R. J. (1986) 'Intrauterine exposure to low levels of lead: the status of the neonate', *Archives of Environmental Medicine* 41(5): 287–91.

Ervin-Tripp, S. and Strage, A. (1985) 'Parent–child discourse', in T. A. Van Dijk (ed.) *Handbook of Discourse Analysis*, vol. 3, *Discourse and Dialogue*, London: Academic Press.

Estes, D., Wellman, H. and Woolley, J. D. (1989) 'Children's understanding of mental phenomena', in H. W. Reese (ed.) *Advances in Child Development and Behaviour*, vol. 22, New York: Academic Press.

Estrada, P., Arsenio, W. F., Hess, R. D. and Holloway, S. (1987) 'Affective quality of the mother–child relationship: longitudinal consequences for children's school-relevant cognitive functioning', *Developmental Psychology* 23: 210–15.

Eysenck, H. J. (1971) *Race, Intelligence and Education*, London: Temple Smith.

Eysenck, H. J. (ed.) (1982) *A Model for Intelligence*, Berlin: Springer-Verlag.

Eysenck, H. J. (1986) 'The theory of intelligence and the psychophysiology of cognition', in R. J. Sternberg (ed.) *Advances in the Psychology of Human Intelligence*, vol. 3, Hillsdale, NJ: Erlbaum.

Eysenck, M. W. (1988) 'Anxiety and attention', *Anxiety Research* 1: 9–16.

Eysenck, M. W. and Keane, M. T. (1990) *Cognitive Psychology: a Student's Handbook*, London: Erlbaum.

Fabricius, W. V., Sophian, C. and Wellman, H. M. (1987) 'Young children's sensitivity to logical necessity in their inferential search behavior', *Child Development* 58: 409–23,

Fagan, J. F. (1973) 'Infants' delayed recognition memory and forgetting', *Journal of Experimental Child Psychology* 16: 424–50.

Fagan, J. F. (1976) 'Infants' recognition of invariant features of faces', *Child Development* 45: 351–6.

Fagan, J. F. and Singer, L. T. (1983) 'Infant recognition memory as a measure of intelligence', in L. P. Lipsitt (ed.) *Advances in Infancy Research*, vol. 2, Norwood, NJ: Ablex.

Farr, M. (1985) *Advances in Writing Research*, vol. 1, *Children's Early Writing Development*, Norwood, NJ: Ablex.

Farrar, M. J. and Goodman, G. S. (1992) 'Developmental changes in event memory', *Child Development* 63: 173–87.

Farrar, M. J., Raney, G. E. and Boyer, M. E. (1992) 'Knowledge, concepts and inferences in childhood', *Child Development* 63: 673–91.

Fehr, L. A. (1978) 'Methodological inconsistencies in the measurement of spatial perspective taking ability: a cause for concern', *Human Development* 21: 302–15.

Feldman, C. F. (1988) 'Early forms of thought about thoughts: some simple linguistic expressions of mental state', in J. W. Astington, P. L. Harris and D. R. Olson (eds) *Developing Theories of Mind*, Cambridge: Cambridge University Press.

Feldman, C. F. and Toulmin, S. (1976) 'Logic and the theory of mind', in *Nebraska Symposium on Motivation*, Lincoln, Nebr.: University of Nebraska Press.

Fenson, L. (1985) 'The transition from construction to sketching in children's drawings', in N. H. Freeman and M. V. Cox (eds) *Visual Order*, Cambridge: Cambridge University Press.

Ferguson, C. A. and Slobin, D. A. (eds) (1973) *Studies of Child Language Development*, New York: Holt, Rinehart & Winston.

Fergusson, D. M., Fergusson, J. E., Horwood, L. J. and Kinzett, N. G. (1988a) 'A longitudinal study of dentine lead levels, intelligence, school performance and behaviour: Part 1, Dentine lead levels and exposure to environmental risk factors', *Journal of Child Psychology and Psychiatry* 29: 781–92.

Fergusson, D. M., Fergusson, J. E., Horwood, L. J. and Kinzett, N. G. (1988b) 'Part 2, Dentine lead and cognitive ability', *Journal of Child Psychology and Psychiatry* 29: 793–810.

Fergusson, D. M., Fergusson, J. E., Horwood, L. J. and Kinzett, N. G. (1988c) 'Part 3, Dentine lead levels and attention/activity', *Journal of Child Psychology and Psychiatry* 29: 811–24.

Ferrara, R. A., Brown, A. L. and Campione, J. C. (1986) 'Children's learning and transfer of inductive reasoning rules: studies of proximal development', *Child Development* 57: 1087–99.

Feuerstein, R., Rand, Y., Hoffman, M. and Miller, R. (1980) *Instrumental Enrichment*, Baltimore, Md.: University Park Press.

Field, T., Sandberg, D., Garcia, R., Vega-Lahr, N., Goldstein, S. and Guy, L. (1985) 'Pregnancy problems, post-partum depression and early mother–infant interactions', *Developmental Psychology* 21: 1152–6.

Fischer, K. W. (1987) 'Relations between brain and cognitive development', *Child Development* 58: 623–32.

Fischer, K. W. and Bidell, T. (1991) 'Constraining nativist inferences about cognitive capacities', in S. Carey and R. Gelman (eds) *The Epigenesis of Mind*, Hove: Erlbaum.

Fischer, K. W., Shaver, P. R. and Carnochan, P. (1990) 'How emotions develop and how they organise development', *Cognition and Emotion* 4: 81–127.

Fisher, R. (1990) *Teaching Children to Think*, Oxford: Blackwell.

Fivush, R. (1984) 'Learning about school: the development of kindergarteners' school scripts', *Child Development* 55: 1697–709.

Fivush, R. (1987) 'Scripts and categories: interrelationships in development', in U. Neisser (ed.) *Concepts and Conceptual Development*, Cambridge: Cambridge University Press.

Fivush, R. and Hamond, N. R. (1989) 'Time and again: effects of repetition and retention interval on 2 year olds' event recall', *Journal of Experimental Child Psychology* 47: 259–73.

Fivush, R., Gray, J. T. and Fromhoff, F. A. (1987) 'Two-year-olds talk about the past', *Cognitive Development* 2: 393–409.

Fivush, R., Kuebli, J. and Clubb, P. A. (1992) 'The structure of events and event representations: a developmental analysis', *Child Development* 63: 188–201.

Flavell, J. H. (1963) *The Developmental Psychology of Jean Piaget*, Princeton, NJ: Van Nostrand.

Flavell, J. H. (1971) 'First discussant's comments: what is memory development the development of?', *Human Development* 14: 272–8.

Flavell, J. H. (1977) *Cognitive Development*, Englewood Cliffs, NJ: Prentice Hall.

Flavell, J. H. (1978a) 'The development of knowledge about visual perception', in *Nebraska Symposium on Motivation, 1977*, Lincoln, Nebr.: University of Nebraska Press.

Flavell, J. H. (1978b) 'Comments on Brown and De Loache's paper', in R. S. Siegler (ed.) *Children's Thinking: What Develops?*, Hillsdale, NJ: Erlbaum.

Flavell, J. H. (1982a) 'On cognitive development', *Child Development* 53: 1–10.

Flavell, J. H. (1982b) 'Structures, stages and sequences in cognitive development', in *Minnesota Symposium on Child Psychology* vol. 15, Hillsdale, NJ: Erlbaum.

Flavell, J. H. (1984) 'Discussion', in R. J. Sternberg (ed.) *Mechanisms of Cognitive Development*, New York: W. H. Freeman.

Flavell, J. H. (1985) *Cognitive Development*, 2nd edn., Englewood Cliffs, NJ: Prentice Hall.

Flavell, J. H. (1986) 'The development of children's knowledge about the appearance–reality distinction', *American Psychologist* 41: 418–25.

Flavell, J. H. (1988) 'The development of children's knowledge about the mind: from cognitive connections to mental representations', in J. W. Astington, P. L. Harris and D. R. Olson (eds) *Developing Theories of Mind*, Cambridge: Cambridge University Press.

Flavell, J. H. and Markman, E. M. (eds) (1983) *Handbook of Child Psychology*, vol. 3, *Cognitive Development*, series ed. P. H. Mussen, New York: Wiley.

Flavell, J. H. and Ross, L. (eds.) (1981) *Social Cognitive Development: Frontiers and Possible Futures*, Cambridge: Cambridge University Press.

Flavell, J. H. and Wellman, H. M. (1977) 'Metamemory', in R. V. Kail and J. W. Hagen (eds) *Perspectives on the Development of Memory and Cognition*, Hillsdale, NJ: Erlbaum.

Flavell, J. H., Beach, D. R. and Chinsky, J. M. (1966) 'Spontaneous verbal rehearsal in a memory task as a function of age', *Child Development* 37: 283–99.

Flavell, J. H., Green, F. L. and Flavell, E. R. (1986) 'Development of knowledge about the appearance–reality distinction', *Monographs of the Society for Research in Child Development* 51(1), serial no. 212.

Flavell, J. H., Green, F. L. and Flavell, E. R. (1989) 'Young children's ability to differentiate appearance–reality and level 2 perspectives in the tactile modality', *Child Development* 60: 201–13.

Flavell, J. H., Flavell, E. R., Green, F. L. and Moses, L. J. (1990) 'Young children's understanding of fact beliefs versus value beliefs', *Child Development* 61: 915–28.

Flynn, J. R. (1980) *Race, IQ and Jensen*, London: Routledge & Kegan Paul.

Flynn, J. R. (1987) 'Massive IQ gains in 14 nations: what IQ tests really measure', *Psychological Bulletin* 101: 171–91.

Fodor, J. A. (1976) *The Language of Thought*, Hassocks, Sussex: Harvester.

Fodor, J. A. (1981) *Representations: Philosophical Essays on the Foundations of Cognitive Science*, Brighton: Harvester.

Fodor, J. A. (1990) 'Fodor's guide to mental representation: the intelligent Auntie's vade-mecum', in J. A. Fodor, *A Theory of Content and Other Essays*, Cambridge, Mass.: MIT Press.

Foorman, B. and Siegel, A. W. (1986) *Acquisition of Reading Skills: Cultural Constraints and Cognitive Universals*, Hillsdale, NJ: Erlbaum.

Forbes, D. D. S. (1988) 'A two-year-old's memory observed', *The Psychologist* 1: 27–31.

Ford, M. E. (1979) 'The construct validity of egocentrism', *Psychological Bulletin* 86: 1169–88.

Forgas, J. (ed.) (1981) *Social Cognition*, New York: Academic Press.

Forguson, L. (1989) *Common Sense*, London: Routledge.

Forguson, L. and Gopnik, A. (1988) 'The ontogeny of commonsense', in J. W. Astington, P. L. Harris and D. R. Olson (eds) *Developing Theories of Mind*, Cambridge: Cambridge University Press.

Forman, E. A. and Cazden, C. B. (1985) 'Exploring Vygotskian perspectives in education: the cognitive value of peer interaction', in J. V. Wertsch (ed.) *Culture, Communication and Cognition*, Cambridge: Cambridge University Press.

Forrest-Pressley, D., MacKinnon, G. and Waller, T. (1985) *Metacognition, Cognition and Human Performance*, vols 1 and 2, Orlando, Fl.: Academic Press.

Fowler, W. (ed.) (1986) *Early Experience and the Development of Competence*, San Francisco: Jossey-Bass.

Francis, H. (1992) 'Patterns of reading development in the first school', *British Journal of Educational Psychology* 62: 225–32.

Francis, J. (1982) *Learning to Read: Literate Behaviour and Orthographic Knowledge*, London: George Allen & Unwin.

Fraser, B. J. (1989) 'Research syntheses on school and instructional effectiveness', *International Journal of Educational Research* 13(7): 707–19.

Frederiksen, C. H. and Dominic, J. F. (1981) *Writing: the Nature, Development and Teaching of Written Communication*, vol. 2, *Writing: Process, Development and Communication*, Hillsdale, NJ: Erlbaum.

Freeman, J., Butcher, H. J. and Christie, T. (1971) *Creativity: a Selective Review of Research*, London: Society for Research into Higher Education.

Freeman, N. (1975) 'Do children draw men with arms coming out of their head?', *Nature* 254: 416–17.

Freeman, N. (1980) *Strategies of Representation in Young Children: Analysis of Spatial Skills and Drawing Processes*, London: Academic Press.

Freeman, N. (1987) 'Current problems in the development of representational picture-production', *Archives de Psychologie* 55: 127–52.

Freeman, N. (1988) 'Children's drawings of humans', in R. L. Gregory (ed.) *The Oxford Companion to the Mind*, Oxford: Oxford University Press.

Freeman N. and Cox, M. V. (eds) (1985) *Visual Order: the Nature and Development of Pictorial Representation*, Cambridge: Cambridge University Press.

Freeman, N., Lloyd, S. and Sinha, C. G. (1980) 'Infant search tasks reveal early concepts of containment and canonical usage of objects', *Cognition* 8: 243–62.

Freud, S. (1973) *Introductory Lectures on Psychoanalysis*, vol. 2 of the Pelican Freud Library, Harmondsworth: Penguin Books.

Freud, S. (1977) *Three Essays on the Theory of Sexuality*, vol. 7 of the Pelican Freud Library, Harmondsworth: Penguin Books.

Freund, L. S. (1990) 'Maternal regulation of children's problem-solving behaviour and its impact on children's performance', *Child Development* 61: 113–26.

Freund, L. S., Baker, L. and Sonnenschein, S. (1990) 'Developmental changes in strategic approaches to classification', *Journal of Experimental Child Psychology* 49: 343–62.

Friedman, S. L., Scholnick, E. K. and Cocking, R. R. (eds) (1987) *Blueprints for Thinking: the Role of Planning in Cognitive Development*, New York: Cambridge University Press.

Frith, U. (1980a) 'Reading and spelling skills', in M. Rutter (ed.) *Scientific Foundations of Developmental Psychiatry*, London: Heinemann.

Frith, U. (ed.) (1980b) *Cognitive Processes in Spelling*, London: Academic Press.

Frith, U. (1990) *Autism*, Oxford: Blackwell.

Frye, D. and Moore, C. (eds) (1991) *Children's Theories of Mind: Mental States and Social Understanding*, Hove: Erlbaum.

Fujinaga, T., Kasuga, T., Uchida, N. and Saiga, H. (1990) 'Long-term follow-up study of children developmentally retarded by early environmental deprivation', *Genetic, Social and General Psychology Monographs* 116: 1.

Fulton, M., Raab, G. M., Thomson, G. O. B., Laxen, D. P. H., Hunter, R. and

Hepburn, W. (1987) 'Influence of blood lead on the ability and attainment of children in Edinburgh', *The Lancet* i: 1221–6.

Furnham, A. (1992) 'Lay understanding of science: young people and adults' ideas of scientific concepts', *Studies in Science Education* 20: 29–64.

Furstenberg, F., Brooks-Gunn, J. and Morgan, S. P. (1969) *Adolescent Mothers in Later Life*, Cambridge: Cambridge University Press.

Furth, H. (1980) *The World of Grownups*, New York: Elsevier North Holland.

Fuson, K. C., Pergament, G. G., Lyons, B. G. and Hall, J. W. (1985) 'Children's conformity to the cardinality rule as a function of set size and counting accuracy', *Child Development* 56: 1429–36.

Fuson, K. C., Richards, J. and Briars, D. J. (1982) 'The acquisition and elaboration of the number word sequence', in C. J. Brainerd (ed.) *Progress in Cognitive Development*, vol. 1, *Children's Logical and Mathematical Cognition*, New York: Springer-Verlag.

Fuson, K. C. and Hall, J. W. (1983) 'The acquisition of early number word meanings: a conceptual analysis and review', in H. P. Ginsburg (ed.) *The Development of Mathematical Thinking*, New York: Academic Press.

Gagné, R. M. (1985) *The Conditions of Learning and Theory of Instruction*, New York: Holt, Rinehart & Winston.

Galbraith, J. K. (1980) *The Nature of Mass Poverty*, Harmondsworth: Penguin Books.

Galbraith, R. C. (1982) 'Sibling spacing and intellectual development: a closer look at the confluence models', *Developmental Psychology* 18: 151–73.

Galler, J. R. (1987) 'The interaction of nutrition and environment in behavioural development', in J. Dobbing (ed.) *Early Nutrition and Later Achievement*, London: Academic Press.

Galotti, K. M. (1989) 'Approaches to studying formal and everyday reasoning', *Psychological Bulletin*, 105(3): 331–51.

Gardner, H. (1973) *The Arts and Human Development*, New York: Wiley.

Gardner, H. (1974) 'Metaphors and modalities: how children project polar adjectives onto diverse domains', *Child Development* 45: 84–91.

Gardner, H. (1980) *Artful Scribblers*, New York: Basic Books.

Gardner, H. (1983) *Frames of Mind: the Theory of Multiple Intelligences*, London: Heinemann.

Gardner, W. and Rogoff, B. (1990) 'Children's deliberateness of planning according to task circumstances', *Developmental Psychology* 26: 480–7.

Garmezy, N. and Rutter, M. (1985) 'Acute reactions to stress', in M. Rutter and L. Hersov (eds) *Child and Adolescent Psychiatry: Modern Approaches*, Oxford: Blackwell.

Garner, R. (1987) *Metacognition and Reading Comprehension*, Norwood, NJ: Ablex.

Garnham, A. (1983) 'What's wrong with story grammars', *Cognition* 15: 145–54.

Garnham, A. (1985) *Psycholinguistics: Central Topics*, London: Methuen.

Gartley, W. and Bernasconi, M. (1967) 'The concept of death in children', *Journal of Genetic Psychology* 110: 71–85.

Gathercole, S. E. and Baddeley, A. D. (1989a) 'The role of phonological memory in normal and disordered language development', in C. Von Euler, I. Lundberg and G. Lennerstrand (eds) *Brain and Reading*, London: Macmillan.

Gathercole, S. E. and Baddeley, A. D. (1989b) 'Development of vocabulary in children and short-term phonological memory', *Journal of Memory and Language* 28: 200–13.

Gauvain, M. and Rogoff, B. (1986) 'The influence of the goal on children's expectations and memory of large-scale space' *Developmental Psychology* 22: 72–7.

Gauvain, M. and Rogoff, B. (1989) 'Collaborative problem-solving and children's planning skills', *Developmental Psychology* 25: 139–51.

Gelb, I. J. (1963) *A Study of Writing*, Chicago: University of Chicago Press.

Gellatly, A. (1989) 'The myth of cognitive diagnostics', in A. Gellatly, D. Rogers and J. A. Sloboda (eds) *Cognition and Social Worlds*, Oxford: Clarendon Press.

Gelman, R. (1990) 'First principles organise attention to and learning about relevant data: number and the animate–inanimate distinction as examples', *Cognitive Science* 14: 79–106.

Gelman, R. (1991) 'Epigenetic foundations of knowledge structures: initial and transcendent constructions', in S. Carey and R. Gelman (eds) *The Epigenesis of Mind*, Hove: Erlbaum.

Gelman, R. and Baillargeon, R. (1983) 'A review of some Piagetian concepts', in J. H. Flavell and E. Markman (eds) *Handbook of Child Psychology* vol. 3, *Cognitive Development*, series ed. P. H. Mussen, New York: Wiley.

Gelman, R. and Gallistel, C. R. (1978) *The Child's Understanding of Number*, Cambridge, Mass.: Harvard University Press.

Gelman, R. and Meck, E. (1983) 'Preschoolers' counting: principle before skill', *Cognition* 13: 343–59.

Gelman, R. and Meck, E. (1986) 'The notion of principle: the case of counting', in J. Hiebert (ed.) *Conceptual and Procedural Knowledge: the Case of Mathematics*, Hillsdale, NJ: Erlbaum.

Gelman, R. and Spelke, E. (1981) 'The development of thoughts about animate and inanimate objects: implications for research on social cognition', in J. H . Flavell and L. Ross (eds) *Social Cognitive Development*, Cambridge: Cambridge University Press.

Gelman, S. A. and Kremer, K. E. (1991) 'Understanding natural cause: children's explanations of how objects and their properties originate', *Child Development* 62: 396–414.

Gelman, S. A. and O'Reilly, A. W. (1988) 'Children's inductive inferences within superordinate categories: the role of language and category structure', *Child Development* 59: 876–87.

Gelman, S. A. and Wellman, H. M. (1991) 'Insides and essences: early understandings of the non-obvious', *Cognition* 38: 213–44.

Genesee, F. (1989) 'Early bilingual development: one language or two?' *Journal of Child Language* 16(1): 161–79.

Gentner, D. (1977) 'Children's performance on a spatial analogies task', *Child Development* 48: 1034–9.

Gentner, D. (1988) 'Metaphor as structure-mapping: the relational shift', *Child Development* 59: 47–59.

Gentner, D. (1989) 'The mechanisms of analogical learning', in S. Vosniadou and A. Ortony (eds) *Similarity and Analogical Reasoning*, Cambridge: Cambridge University Press.

Gentner, D. and Gentner, D. R. (1983) 'Flowing waters or teeming crowds: mental models of electricity', in D. Gentner and A. L. Stevens (eds) *Mental Models*, Hillsdale, NJ: Erlbaum.

Gentner, D. and Stevens, A. L. (eds) (1983) *Mental Models*, Hillsdale, NJ: Erlbaum.

Gentner, D. and Toupin, C. (1986) 'Systematicity and surface similarity in the development of analogy', *Cognitive Science* 10: 277–300.

Gesell, A. (1942) *Wolf Child and Human Child*, London: The Scientific Book Club.

Getzels, J. W. and Csikszentmihalyi, M. (1976) *The Creative Vision: a Longitudinal Study of Problem Finding*, New York: Wiley.

Getzels, J. W. and Jackson, P. W. (1962) *Creativity and Intelligence*, New York: Wiley.

Ghiselin, B. (ed.) (1954) *The Creative Process*, Berkeley, Calif.: University of California Press.

Gholson, B. and Beilin, H. (1979) 'A developmental model of human learning', in H. W. Reese and L. P. Lipsitt (eds) *Advances in Child Development and Behaviour*, vol. 13, New York: Academic Press.

Gibson, E. J. (1969) *Principles of Perceptual Learning and Development*, New York: Appleton-Century-Crofts.

Gibson, E. J. (1988) 'Exploratory behaviour in the development of perceiving, acting and the acquiring of knowledge', *Annual Review of Psychology* 39: 1–42.

Gibson, J. J. (1979) *The Ecological Approach to Visual Perception*, Boston: Houghton-Mifflin.

Gick, M. L. and Holyoak, K. J. (1987) 'The cognitive basis of knowledge transfer', in S. Cormier and J. D. Hagman (eds) *Transfer of Learning: Contemporary Research and Applications*, San Diego, Calif.: Academic Press.

Giles, H. and St Clair, R. N. (eds) (1985) *Recent Advances in Language, Communication and Social Psychology*, London: Erlbaum.

Gillberg, C. L. (1992) 'Autism and autistic-like conditions: subclasses among disorders of empathy', *Journal of Child Psychology and Psychiatry* 33: 813–42.

Ginsburg, H. P. (1977) *Children's Arithmetic: the Learning Process*, New York: Van Nostrand.

Ginsburg, H. P. (ed.) (1983) *The Development of Mathematical Thinking*, New York: Academic Press.

Girotto, V., Light, P. and Colborn, C. (1988) 'Pragmatic schemas and conditional reasoning in children', *Quarterly Journal of Experimental Psychology* 40A(3): 469–82.

Glaser, R. (1984) 'Education and thinking: the role of knowledge', *American Psychologist* 39: 93–104.

Gleason, J. B., Hay, D. and Cain, L. (1989) 'Social and affective determinants of language acquisition', in M. L. Rice and R. L. Schiefelbusch (eds) *The Teachability of Language*, Baltimore, Md.: Brooks.

Glucksberg, S. and Keysar, B. (1990) 'Understanding metaphorical comparisons: beyond similarity', *Psychological Review* 97(1): 3–18.

Gnepp, J. and Hess, D. L. R. (1986) 'Children's understanding of verbal and facial display rulers', *Development Psychology* 22: 103–8.

Gnepp, J. and Klayman, J. (1992) 'Recognition of uncertainty in emotional inferences: reasoning about emotionally equivocal situations', *Developmental Psychology* 28: 145–58.

Gnepp, J., McKee, E. and Domanic, J. A. (1987) 'Children's use of situational information to infer emotion: understanding emotionally equivocal situations', *Developmental Psychology* 23: 114–23.

Goldberg, W. A. and Easterbrooks, M. A. (1984) 'Role of marital quality in toddler development', *Developmental Psychology* 20: 504–14.

Goldman, A. I. (1986) *Epistemology and Cognition*, Harvard, Mass.: Harvard University Press.

Goldman, R. and Goldman, J. (1982) *Children's Sexual Thinking*, London: Routledge & Kegan Paul.

Goldman-Rakic, P. S. (1987) 'Development of cortical circuitry and cognitive function', *Child Development* 58: 601–22.

Goodman, G. S. and Goodman, Y. M. (1979) 'Learning to read is natural', in L. B. Resnick and P. A. Weaver (eds) *Theory and Practice of Early Reading*, vol. 1, Hillsdale, NJ: Erlbaum.

Goodman, G. S. and Haith, M. M. (1987) 'Memory development and neurophysiology: accomplishments and limitations', *Child Development* 58: 713–17.

Goodnow, J. J. (1973) 'Compensation arguments on conservation tasks', *Developmental Psychology* 8(1): 140.

Goodnow, J. J. (1977) *Children's Drawing*, London: Fontana.

Goodnow, J. J. (1984) 'On being judged "intelligent" ', *International Journal of Psychology* 19: 391–406.

Goodnow, J. J. (1990) 'The socialization of cognition', in J. W. Stigler, R. A. Shweder and G. H. Herdt (eds) *Cultural Psychology: Essays on Comparative Human Development*, Cambridge: Cambridge University Press.

Goody, J. (1977) *The Domestication of the Savage Mind*, Cambridge: Cambridge University Press.

Goody, J. and Watt, I. (1968) 'The consequences of literacy', in J. Goody (ed.) *Literacy in Traditional Societies*, Cambridge: Cambridge University Press.

Goodyer, I. M. (1990) *Life Experiences, Development and Childhood Psychopathology*, Chichester: Wiley.

Gopnik, A. (1988) 'Concepts and semantic development as theory change', *Mind and Language* 3(3): 197–216.

Gopnik, A. and Graf, P. (1988) 'Knowing how you know: young children's ability to identify and remember the sources of their beliefs', *Child Development* 59: 1366–71.

Gopnik, A. and Slaughter, V. (1991) 'Young children's understanding of changes in their mental states', *Child Development* 62: 98–110.

Gordon, E. W. and Armour-Thomas, E. (1991) 'Culture and cognitive development', in L. Okagaki and R. J. Sternberg (eds) *Directors of Development: Influences on the Development of Children's Thinking*, Hillsdale, NJ: Erlbaum.

Gosse, E. (1907) *Father and Son*, London: Heinemann.

Goswami, U. (1986) 'Children's use of analogy in learning to read: a developmental study', *Journal of Experimental Child Psychology* 42: 73–83.

Goswami, U. (1988a) 'Orthographic analogies and reading development', *Quarterly Journal of Experimental Psychology* 40A: 239–68.

Goswami, U. (1988b) 'Children's use of analogy in learning to spell', *British Journal of Developmental Psychology* 6: 21–33.

Goswami, U. (1989) 'Relational complexity and the development of analogical reasoning', *Cognitive Development* 4: 251–68.

Goswami, U. (1990a) 'A special link between rhyming skill and the use of orthographic analogies by beginning readers', *Journal of Child Psychology and Psychiatry*, 31(2): 301–11.

Goswami, U. (1990b) 'Phonological priming and orthographic analogies in reading', *Journal of Experimental Child Psychology* 49: 323–40.

Goswami, U. (1991a) 'Analogical reasoning: what develops? A review of research and theory', *Child Development* 62: 1–22.

Goswami, U. (1991b) 'Learning about spelling sequences: the role of onsets and rimes in analogies in reading', *Child Development* 62: 1110–23.

Goswami, U. and Brown, A. L. (1990b) 'Melting chocolate and melting snowmen: analogical reasoning and causal relations', *Cognition* 35: 69–96.

Goswami, U. and Brown, A. L. (1990a) 'Higher-order structure and relational reasoning: contrasting analogical and thematic relations', *Cognition* 36: 207–26.

Goswami, U. and Bryant, P. (1990) *Phonological Skills and Learning to Read*, Hove: Erlbaum.

Gottfried, A. W. (ed.) (1984) *Home Environment and Early Cognitive Development: Longitudinal Research*, New York: Academic Press.

Gottfried, A. W. and Gottfried, A. E. (1984) 'Home environment and cognitive development of young children of middle-socioeconomic-status families', in A. W. Gottfried (ed.) *Home Environment and Early Cognitive Development: Longitudinal Research*, New York: Academic Press.

Gottlieb, G. (1983) 'The psychobiological approach to developmental issues', in M. M. Haith and J. J. Campos (eds) *Handbook of Child Psychology*, vol. 2, New York: Wiley.

Gottlieb, G. (1991) 'Experimental canalization of behavioural development: theory', *Developmental Psychology* 27: 4–13.

Gould, S. J. (1977) *Ontogeny and Phylogeny*, Cambridge, Mass.: Harvard University Press.

Gould, S. J. (1984) *The Mismeasure of Man*, Harmondsworth: Penguin Books.

Gould, S. J. (1987) *Time's Arrow, Time's Cycle: Myth and Metaphor in the Discovery of Geological Time*, Cambridge, Mass.: Harvard University Press.

Goward, L. and Rabbitt, P. (1988) 'What intelligence tests don't measure', in M. M. Gruneberg, P. E. Morris and R. N. Sykes (eds) *Practical Aspects of Memory*, vol. 2, Chichester: Wiley.

Grantham-McGregor, S. (1987) 'Field studies in early nutrition and later achievement', in J. Dobbing (ed.) *Early Nutrition and Later Achievement*, London: Academic Press.

Grantham-McGregor, S., Schofield, W. and Powell, C. (1987) 'The development of severely malnourished children who received psychosocial stimulation: six year follow-up', *Pediatrics* 79: 247–54.

Gratch, G., Appel, K. J., Evans, W. F., Le Compte, G. K. and Wright, N. A. (1974) 'Piaget's Stage IV object concept error: evidence of forgetting or object conception?', *Child Development* 45: 71–7.

Graves, D. (1983) *Writing: Teachers and Children at Work*, Heinemann.

Gray, E. M. (1991) 'Analysis of diverging approaches to simple arithmetic', *Educational Studies in Mathematics* 22.

Gray, J. A. (1987) 'The mind–brain identity as a scientific hypothesis: a second look', in C. Blakemore and S. Greenfield (eds) *Mindwaves*, Oxford: Blackwell.

Gray, J. A. (1990) 'Brain systems that mediate both emotion and cognition', *Cognition and Emotion* 4: 269–88.

Greenfield, P. M. and Lave, J. (1982) 'Cognitive aspects of formal education', in D. Wagner and H. Stevenson (eds) *Cultural Perspectives on Child Development*, San Francisco: Freeman.

Greenough, W. T. (1984) 'Structural correlates of information storage in the mammalian brain: a review and hypothesis', *Trends in Neurosciences* 7: 229–33.

Greenough, W. T. (1986) 'What's special about development? Thoughts on the bases of experience-sensitive synaptic plasticity', in W. T. Greenough and J. M. Juraska (eds) *Developmental Neuropsychology*, New York: Academic Press.

Greenough, W. T. (1991) 'Experience as a component of normal development: evolutionary considerations', *Developmental Psychology* 27: 14–17.

Greenough, W. T. and Black, J. E. (1992) 'Induction of brain structure by experience: substrates for cognitive development', in M. Gunnar and C. A. Nelson (eds) *Developmental Behavioural Neuroscience: Minnesota Symposium on Child Psychology*, vol. 24, Hillsdale, NJ: Erlbaum.

Greenough, W. T. and Juraska, J. M. (eds) (1986) *Developmental Neuropsychology*, New York: Academic Press.

Greenough, W. T., Black, J. E., and Wallace, C. S. (1987) 'Experience and brain development', *Child Development* 58: 539–59.

Gregory, R. L. (1987) 'In defence of artificial intelligence – reply to John Searle', in C. Blakemore and S. Greenfield (eds) *Mindwaves*, Oxford: Blackwell.

Gregory, R. L. (ed.) (1988) *The Oxford Companion to the Mind*, Oxford: Oxford University University Press.

Grice, H. P. (1975) 'Logic and conversation', in P. Cole and J. L. Morgan (eds) *Syntax and Semantics*, vol. 3, *Speech Acts*, New York: Academic Press.

Griffin, D. R. (1976) *The Question of Animal Awareness*, New York: Rockefeller University Press.

Griffiths, M. and Wells, G. (1983) 'Who writes what, and why', in B. Kroll and G. Wells (eds) *Explorations in the Development of Writing*, Chichester: Wiley.

Grigson, J. (1980) *Jane Grigson's Vegetable Book*, Harmondsworth: Penguin Books.

Grize, J.-B. (1987) 'Operatory logic', in B. Inhelder, D. de Caprona and A. Cornu-Wells (eds) *Piaget Today*, Hillsdale, NJ: Erlbaum.

Groen, G. J. and Parkman, J. M. (1972) 'A chronometric analysis of simple addition', *Psychological Review*, 97: 329–43.

Grotevant, H. and Carlson, C. (1987) 'Family interaction coding systems: a descriptive review', *Family Process* 26: 49–74.

Guilford, J. P. (1967) *The Nature of Human Intelligence*, New York: McGraw Hill.

Gunn, P. (1985) 'Speech and language', in D. Lane and B. Stratford (eds) *Current Approaches to Down's Syndrome*, London: Holt, Rinehart & Winston.

Gunnar, M. and Maratsos, M. (eds) (1992) *Modularity and Constraints in Language and Cognition: Minnesota Symposium on Child Psychology*, vol. 25, Hillsdale, NJ: Erlbaum.

Gunnar, M. and Nelson, C. A. (eds) (1992) *Behavioral Developmental Neuroscience: Minnesota Symposium on Child Psychology*, vol. 24, Hillsdale, NJ: Erlbaum.

Gutfreund, M. (1989) *Bristol Language Development Scales*, Windsor: NFER-Nelson.

Hagen, J. W. and Hale, G. H. (1973) *The development of attention in children: Nebraska Symposium on Motivation, 1973*, Lincoln, Nebr.: University of Nebraska Press.

Hagen, J. W., Hargrove, S. and Ross, W. (1973) 'Prompting and rehearsal in short-term memory', *Child Development* 44: 201–4.

Hagerman, R. J. (1992) 'Fragile X syndrome: advances and controversy', *Journal of Child Psychology and Psychiatry* 33: 1127–40.

Haight, W. and Miller, P. J. (1992) 'The development of everyday pretend play: a longitudinal study of mothers' participation', *Merrill-Palmer Quarterly* 38: 331–49.

Haith, M. M. and Campos, J. (eds) (1983) *Handbook of Child Psychology*, vol. 2, *Infancy and Development Psychobiology*, series ed. P. H. Mussen, New York: Wiley.

Hala, S., Chandler, M. and Fritz, A. S. (1991) 'Fledgling theories of mind: deception as a marker of three-year-olds' understanding of false beliefs', *Child Development* 62: 83–97.

Hall, N. (1987) *The Emergence of Literacy*, London: Hodder & Stoughton.

Hall, W. S. (1989) 'Reading comprehension', *American Psychologist* 44: 157–61.

Halliday, M. A. K. (1975) *Learning How to Mean*, London: Edward Arnold.

Halverson, C. F. and Waldrop, M. F. (1976) 'Relations between preschool activity and aspects of intellectual and social behaviour at age 7½', *Developmental Psychology* 12: 107–12.

Hamlyn, D. W. (1978) *Experience and the Growth of Understanding*, London: Routledge & Kegan Paul.

Hamlyn, D. W. (1990) *In and Out of the Box: on the Philosophy of Cognition*, Oxford: Blackwell.

Hammen, C., Gordon, D., Burge, D., Adrian, C., Jaenicke, C. and Hiroto, D. (1987) 'Maternal affective disorders, illness and stress: risk for children's psychopathology', *American Journal of Psychiatry* 144: 736–41.

Hammen, C., Burge, D. and Stansbury, K. (1990) 'Relationship of mother and child variables to child outcomes in a high-risk sample: a causal modeling analysis', *Developmental Psychology*, 26: 24–30.

Hampson, S. E. (1982) *The Construction of Personality*, London: Routledge & Kegan Paul.

Hampton, J. A. (1990) *Concepts*, London: Erlbaum.

Hannon, P. (1989) 'How should parental involvement in the teaching of reading be evaluated?', *British Educational Research Journal* 15: 33–40.

Hansen, J. and Bowey, J. A. (1992) 'Orthographic rimes as functional units of reading in fourth grade children', *Australian Journal of Psychology* 44: 37–44.

Harbeck, C. and Peterson, L. (1992) 'Elephants dancing in my head: a developmental approach to children's concepts of specific pains', *Child Development* 63: 138–49.

Hargreaves D. J. (1986) *The Developmental Psychology of Music*, Cambridge: Cambridge University Press.

Harper, L. V. and Huie, K. S. (1987) 'Relations among preschool children's adult and peer contacts and later academic achievement', *Child Development* 58: 1051–65.

Harrington, D. M., Block, J. H. and Block, J. (1983) 'Predicting creativity in preadolescence from divergent thinking in early childhood', *Journal of Personality and Social Psychology*, 45: 609–23.

Harris, P. L. (1983a) 'Infant cognition', in M. M. Haith and J. J. Campos (eds) *Handbook of Child Psychology*, vol. 2, New York: Wiley.

Harris, P. L. (1983b) 'The child as psychologist', in M. Donaldson, R. Grieve and C. Pratt (eds) *Early Childhood Development and Education*, Oxford: Blackwell.

Harris, P. L. (1983c) 'Children's understanding of the link between situation and emotion', *Journal of Experimental Child Psychology* 36: 490–509.

Harris, P. L. (1989) *Child and Emotion: the Development of Psychological Understanding*, Oxford: Blackwell.

Harris, P. L. (1990) 'Children's understanding of mixed emotions', in A. de Ribaupierre (ed.) *Transition Mechanisms in Child Development: the Longitudinal Perspective*, Cambridge: Cambridge University Press.

Harris, P. L. and Gross, D. (1988) 'Children's understanding of real and apparent emotions', in J. W. Astington, P. L. Harris and D. R. Olson (eds) *Developing Theories of Mind*, Cambridge: Cambridge University Press.

Harris, P. L. and Lipian, M. S. (1989) 'Understanding emotion and experiencing emotion', in C. Saarni and P. L. Harris (eds.) *Children's Understanding of Emotion*, Cambridge: Cambridge University Press.

Harris, P. L., Donnelly, K., Guz, G. R. and Pitt-Watson, R. (1986) 'Children's understanding of the distinction between real and apparent emotion', *Child Development* 57: 895–909.

Hart, R. A. (1979) *Children's Experience of Place: a Developmental Study*, New York: Irvington Press.

Harter, S. and Buddin, B. J. (1987) 'Children's understanding of the simultaneity of two emotions: a five-stage developmental acquisition sequence', *Developmental Psychology* 23: 388–99.

Harter, S. and Chao, C. (1992) 'The role of competence in children's creation of imaginary friends', *Merrill-Palmer Quarterly* 38: 350–63.

Hartlage, L. C. and Telzrow, C. F. (eds) (1985) *The Neuropsychology of Individual Differences*, New York: Plenum Press.

Hartlage, P. L. (1985) 'A survey of developmental neurologic conditions: implications for individual neuropsychological differences', in L. C. Hartlage and C. F. Telzrow (eds) *The Neuropsychology of Individual Differences*, New York: Plenum Press.

Hartley, D. (1985) *Understanding the Primary School*, London: Croom Helm.

Harvey, P. G. (1984) 'Lead and children's health: recent research and future questions', *Journal of Child Psychology and Psychiatry* 25: 517–22.

Hasselhorn, M. (1992) 'Task dependency and the role of category typicality and metamemory in the development of an organisational strategy', *Child Development* 63: 202–14.

Haugeland, J. (1985) *Artificial Intelligence: the Very Idea*, Cambridge, Mass.: MIT Press.

Hawkins, T., Pea, R. D., Glick, J. and Scribner, S. (1984) ' "Merds that laugh don't like mushrooms": evidence for deductive reasoning by preschoolers', *Developmental Psychology* 20: 584–94.

Hayward, C. (1982) *Literary Theme Development in the Nursery Classroom*, unpublished M.Ed. thesis, University of Bristol.

Heath, S. B. (1983) *Ways with Words*, Cambridge: Cambridge University Press.

Heath, S. B. (1986) 'What no bedtime story means: narrative skills at home and at school', in B. Schieffelin and E. Ochs (eds) *Language-socialisation across Cultures*, Cambridge: Cambridge University Press (originally published 1982 in *Language in Society* 11: 49–76).

Heath, S. B. (1989) 'The learner as cultural member', in M. L. Rice and R. L. Schiefelbusch (eds) *Teachability of Language*, Baltimore, Md.: Brookes.

Heckhausen, J. (1987) 'Balancing for weaknesses and challenging developmental potential: a longitudinal study of mother–infant dyads in apprenticeship interactions', *Developmental Psychology* 23: 762–70.

Henderson, L. (1982) *Orthography and Word Recognition in Reading*, London: Academic Press.

Hendrickson, A. E. (1982) 'The biological basis of intelligence: theory', in H. J. Eysenck (ed.) *A Model for Intelligence*, Berlin: Springer-Verlag.

Hendrickson, D. E. (1982) 'The biological basis of intelligence: measurement', in H. J. Eysenck (ed.) *A Model for Intelligence*, Berlin: Springer-Verlag.

Hendrickson, D. E. and Hendrickson, A. E. (1980) 'The biological basis of individual differences in intelligence', *Personality and Individual Differences* 1: 3–33.

Henn, H. (1987) 'The National Writing Project in Manchester', *Greater Manchester Primary Contact* 4(3).

Hermelin, B. and O'Connor, N. (1990) 'Art and accuracy: the drawing ability of idiot-savants', *Journal of Child Psychology and Psychiatry* 31(2): 217–28.

Hess, R. D. and Shipman, V. C. (1965) 'Early experience and the socialisation of cognitive modes in children', *Child Development* 36: 869–86.

Hess, R. D., Holloway, S. D., Dickson, W. P. and Price, G. G. (1984) 'Maternal variables as predictors of children's school readiness and later achievement in vocabulary and mathematics in sixth grade', *Child Development* 55: 1902–12.

Hewstone, M. (1989) *Causal Attribution: from Cognitive Processes to Collective Beliefs*, Oxford: Blackwell.

Hiebert, J. (ed.) (1986) *Conceptual and Procedural Knowledge: the Case of Mathematics*, Hillsdale, NJ: Erlbaum.

Hiebert, J. (1988) 'A theory of developing competence with written mathematical symbols', *Educational Studies in Mathematics* 19(3): 333–55.

Hiebert, J. and Lefevre, P. (1986) 'Conceptual and procedural knowledge in mathematics: an introductory analysis', in J. Hiebert (ed.) *Conceptual and Procedural Knowledge: the Case of Mathematics*, Hillsdale, NJ: Erlbaum.

Hinde, R. A. (1982) *Ethology*, London: Fontana.

Hinde, R. A. (1987) *Individuals, Relationship and Culture: Links between Ethology and the Social Sciences*, Cambridge: Cambridge University Press.

Hinde, R. A., Perret-Clermont, A.-N. and Stevenson-Hinde, J. (eds) (1985) *Social Relationships and Cognitive Development*, Oxford: Clarendon Press.

Hindley, C. B. (1965) 'Stability and change in abilities up to five years: group trends', *Journal of Child Psychology and Psychiatry* 6: 85–100.

Hindley, C. B. and Owen, C. F. (1978) 'The extent of individual change in IQ for ages between 6 months to 17 years, in a British longitudinal sample', *Journal of Child Psychology and Psychiatry* 19: 329–50.

Hines, M. and Shipley, C. (1984) 'Prenatal exposure to Diethyl-stilbestrol (DES) and the development of sexually dimorphic cognitive abilities and cerebral lateralisation', *Developmental Psychology* 20: 81–94.

Hobson, R. P. (1990) 'On acquiring knowledge about people and the capacity to pretend: response to Leslie (1987)', *Psychological Review* 91(1): 114–21.

Hobson, R. P. (1991) 'Against the theory of "Theory of Mind" ', *British Journal of Developmental Psychology* 9: 33–51.

Hodapp, R. M., Goldfield, E. G. and Boyatzis, C. J. (1984) 'The use and effectiveness of maternal scaffolding in mother–infant games', *Child Development* 55: 772–81.

Hodges, R. M. and French, L. A. (1988) 'The effect of class and collection labels on cardinality, class-inclusion and number conservation tasks', *Child Development* 59: 1387–96.

Hofer, M. A. (1987) 'Early social relationships: a psychobiologist's view', *Child Development* 58: 633–47.

Hoff-Ginsberg, E. (1986) 'Function and structure in maternal speech: their relation to the child's development of syntax', *Developmental Psychology* 22: 155–63.

Hoffman, M. (1991) 'Unraveling the genetics of Fragile X syndrome', *Science* 252: 1070.

Hofstadter, D. R. (1979) *Godel, Escher, Bach: an Eternal Golden Braid*, Harmondsworth: Penguin Books.

Hogrefe, G.-J., Wimmer, H. and Perner, J. (1986) 'Ignorance vs. false belief: a developmental lag in attribution of epistemic states', *Child Development* 57: 567–82.

Holland, J., Holyoak, K. J., Nisbett, R. E. and Thagard, P. R. (1986) *Induction: Processes of Inference, Learning and Discovery*, Cambridge, Mass.: MIT Press.

Holyoak, K. J. and Nisbett, R. E. (1988) 'Induction', in R. J. Sternberg and E. E. Smith (eds) *The Psychology of Human Thought*, Cambridge: Cambridge University Press.

Honderich, T. (1987) 'Mind, brain and self-conscious mind', in C. Blakemore and S. Greenfield (eds) *Mindwaves*, Oxford: Blackwell.

Horn, J. L. (1968) 'Organisation of abilities and the development of intelligence', *Psychological Review* 75: 242–59.

Horn, J. L. (1970) 'Organisation of data on life-span development of human abilities', in L. R. Goulet and P. B. Baltes (eds) *Life-span Developmental Psychology: Research and Theory*, New York: Academic Press.

Horn, J. M. (1983) 'The Texas Adoption Project: adopted children and their intellectual resemblance to biological and adoptive parents', *Child Development* 54: 268–77.

Horn, W. F. and Packard, T. (1985) 'Early identification of learning problems: a meta-analysis', *Journal of Educational Psychology* 77: 597–607.

Hotopf, W. H. N. (1977) 'An examination of Piaget's theory of perception', in B. A. Geber (ed.) *Piaget and Knowing: Studies in Genetic Epistemology*, London: Routledge & Kegan Paul.

House, B. J. (1989) 'Some current issues on children's selective attention', in H. W. Reese (ed.) *Advances in Child Development and Behaviour*, vol. 21, New York: Academic Press.

Hoving, K. L., Spencer, T., Robb, K. Y. and Schulte, D. (1978) 'Developmental changes in visual information processing', in P. A. Ornstein (ed.) *Memory Developnment in Children*, Hillsdale, NJ: Erlbaum.

Howe, C., Tolmie, A. and Rodgers, C. (1992) 'The acquisition of conceptual knowledge in science by primary schoolchildren: group interaction and the understanding of motion down an incline', *British Journal of Developmental Psychology* 10: 113–30.

Howe, M. J. A. (1984) *A Teacher's Guide to the Psychology of Learning*, Oxford: Blackwell.

Howe, M. J. A. (1989a) 'Separate skills or general intelligence: the autonomy of human abilities', *British Journal of Educational Psychology* 59: 351–60.

Howe, M. J. A. (1989b) Letter, *The Psychologist* 2(6): 244.

Howe, M. J. A. (1989c) *Fragments of Genius: Idiots Savants and the Psychological Investigation of Remarkable Feats by Mentally Retarded Individuals*, London: Routledge.

Howe, M. J. A. and Smith, J. (1988) 'Calendar calculating in "idiots savants": how do they do it?' *British Journal of Psychology* 79: 371–86.

Howe, M. L., Brainerd, C. J. and Kingma, J. (1985) 'Storage-retrieval processes of normal and learning-disabled children: a stages-of-learning analysis of picture-word effects', *Child Development* 56: 1120–33.

Howe, M. L., O'Sullivan, J. T., Brainerd, C. J. and Kingma, J. (1989) 'Localizing the development of ability differences in organised memory', *Contemporary Educational Psychology* 14: 336–56.

Hudson, L. (1970) 'The question of creativity', in P. E. Vernon (ed.) *Creativity*, Harmondsworth: Penguin Books.

Hudspeth, W. J. and Pribram, K. H. (1990) 'Stages of brain and cognitive maturation', *Journal of Educational Psychology* 82: 881–4.

Hughes, M. (1983) 'What is difficult about learning arithmetic?', in M. Donaldson, R. Grieve and C. Pratt (eds) *Early Childhood Development and Education*, Oxford: Blackwell.

Hughes, M. (1986) *Children and Number: Difficulties in Learning Mathematics*, Oxford: Blackwell.

Hughes, M. and Donaldson, M. (1979) 'The use of hiding games for studying the coordination of viewpoints', *Educational Review* 31: 133–40.

Hughes, R. (1987) *The Fatal Shore*, London: Collins Harvill.

Hulme, C. (1987) 'Reading retardation', in J. R. Beech and A. M. Colley (eds) *Cognitive Approaches to Reading*, Chichester: Wiley.

Hulme, C., Thomson, N., Muir, C. and Lawrence, A. (1984) 'Speech rate and the development of short-term memory span', *Journal of Experimental Child Psychology* 38, 241–53.

Humphrey, N. (1976) 'The social function of intellect', in P. Bateson and R. Hinde (eds) *Growing Points in Ethology*, Cambridge: Cambridge University Press.

Humphrey, N. (1983) *Consciousness Regained: Chapters in the Development of the Mind*, Oxford: Oxford University Press.

Hundeide, K. (1985) 'The tacit background of children's judgements', in J. V. Wertsch (ed.) *Culture, Communication and Cognition*, Cambridge: Cambridge University Press.

Hunt, E. B. (1978) 'Mechanisms of verbal ability', *Psychological Review* 85: 109–30.

Hunt, E. B. (1983) 'On the nature of intelligence', *Science* 219: 141–6.

Hunt, E. B., Lunneborg, C. and Lewis, J. (1975) 'What does it mean to be high verbal?' *Cognitive Psychology* 7: 194–227.

Hutt, J., Tyler, S., Hutt, C. and Christopherson, H. *Play, Exploration and Learning: a Natural History of the Preschool*, London: Routledge.

Huttenlocher, J. and Burke, D. (1976) 'Why does memory span increase with age?' *Cognitive Psychology* 8: 1–31.

Hyltenstam, K. and Obler, L. K. (1989) *Bilingualism across the Lifespan*, Cambridge: Cambridge University Press.

Ingram, N. and Butterworth, G. (1989) 'The young child's representation of depth in drawing: process and product', *Journal of Experimental Child Psychology* 47: 356–69.

Inhelder, B. and Piaget, J. (1958) *The Growth of Logical Thinking from Childhood to Adolescence*, New York: Basic Books.

Inhelder, B. and Piaget, J. (1964) *The Early Growth of Logic in the Child*, London: Routledge.

Inhelder, B. and Piaget, J. (1973) *Memory and Intelligence*, London: Routledge & Kegan Paul.

Inhelder, B. and Piaget, J. (1979) 'Procédures et structures', *Archives de Psychologie* 47: 165–76.

Isbell, B. J. and McKee, L. (1980) 'Society's cradle: an anthropological perspective on the socialisation of cognition', in J. Sants (ed.) *Developmental Psychology and Society*, London: Macmillan.

Istomina, Z. M. (1975) 'The development of voluntary memory in preschool-age children', *Soviet Psychology* 13: 5–64.

Jacobson, J. L. and Wille, D. E. (1986) 'The influence of attachment pattern on developmental changes in peer interaction from the toddler to the preschool period', *Child Development* 57: 338–47.

Jacobson, J. L., Jacobson, S. W., Padgett, R. J., Brumitt, G. A. and Billings, R. L. (1992) 'Effects of prenatal PCB exposure on cognitive processing efficiency and sustained attention', *Developmental Psychology* 28: 297–307.

Jacobson, J. L., Jacobson, S. W., Schwartz, P. M., Fein, G. G. and Dowler, J. K. (1984) 'Prenatal exposure to an environmental toxin: a test of the multiple effects model', *Developmental Psychology* 20: 523–32.

Jacobvitz, D. and Sroufe, L. A. (1987) 'The early caregiver–child relationship and attention-deficit disorder with hyperactivity in kindergarten: a prospective study', *Child Development* 58: 1496–504.

Jahoda, G. (1979) 'The construction of economic reality by some Glaswegian children', *European Journal of Social Psychology* 9: 115–27.

Jahoda, G. (1984) 'The development of thinking about socio-economic systems', in H. Tajfel (ed.) *The Social Dimension*, vol. 1, Cambridge: Cambridge University Press.

James, W. (1890) *The Principles of Psychology*, New York: Dover.

Jarman, C. (1979) *The Development of Handwriting Skills*, London: Basil Blackwell.

Jencks, C. (1975) *Inequality: a Reassessment of the Effect of Family and Schooling in America*, Harmondsworth: Penguin Books.

Jennings, K. D., Harmon, R. J., Morgan, G. A., Gaiter, J. L. and Yarrow, L. J. (1979) 'Exploratory play as an index of mastery motivation: relationships to persistence, cognitive functining and environment measures', *Developmental Psychology* 215: 386–94.

Jensen, A. R. (1980) *Bias in Mental Testing*, New York: Free Press.

Jensen, A. R. (1982) 'Reaction time and psychometric *g*', in H. J. Eysenck (ed.) *A Model for Intelligence*, Berlin: Springer-Verlag.

Jensen, A. R. (1989) 'Review: Raising IQ without increasing "g"?', *Developmental Review* 9: 234–58.

Johnson, C. N. (1988) 'Theory of mind and the structure of conscious experience', in J. W. Astington, P. L. Harris and D. R. Olson (eds) *Developing Theories of Mind*, Cambridge: Cambridge University Press.

Johnson, C. N. and Wellman, H. M. (1982) 'Children's developing conceptions of the mind and brain', *Child Development* 53: 222–34.

Johnson, D. (1991) 'The effectiveness of a genre-based approach to the academic literacy of teacher-trainers and teacher-trainees in Zimbabwe', unpublished Ph.D. thesis, University of Bristol.

Johnson, J. and Pascual-Leone, J. (1989) 'Developmental levels of processing in metaphor interpretation', *Journal of Experimental Child Psychology* 48: 1–31.

Johnson, K. E., Mervis, C. B. and Boster, J. S. (1992) 'Developmental changes in the structure of the mammal domain', *Developmental Psychology* 28: 74–83.

Johnson-Laird, P. (1983) *Mental Models*, Cambridge: Cambridge University Press.

Johnson-Laird, P. N. (1988) *The Computer and the Mind: an Introduction to Cognitive Science*, Cambridge, Mass.: Harvard University Press.

Johnson-Laird, P. N. (1989) 'Analogy and the exercise of creativity', in S. Vosniadou and A. Ortony (eds) *Similarity and Analogical Reasoning*, Cambridge: Cambridge University Press.

Johnson-Laird, P. N. and Wason, P. C. (eds) (1977) *Thinking*, Cambridge: Cambridge University Press.

Johnson-Laird, P. N., Oakhill, J. and Bull, D. (1986) 'Children's syllogistic reasoning', *Quarterly Journal of Experimental Psychology* 38A: 35–8.

Jones, O. H. M. (1979) 'A comparative study of mother–child communication with Down's syndrome and normal infants', in D. Shaffer and J. Dunn (eds) *The First Year of Life*, Chichester: Wiley.

Jorm, A. F. (1983) 'Specific reading retardation and working memory: a review', *British Journal of Psychology* 74: 311–42.

Joyce, J. [1916] (1960) *A Portrait of the Artist as a Young Man*, Harmondsworth: Penguin Books.

Jussim, L. (1986) 'Self-fulfilling prophecies: a theoretical and integrative review', *Psychological Review* 93(4): 429–45.

Just, M. A. and Carpenter, P. A. (1987) *The Psychology of Reading and Language Comprehension*, Boston: Allyn & Bacon.

Kagan, J. (1964) 'Information processing in the child: the significance of analytic and reflective attitudes', *Psychological Monographs* 78: 578.

Kagan, J. (1984) *The Nature of the Child*, New York: Basic Books.

Kagan, J. (ed.) (1987) *The Emergence of Moral Concepts in Young Children*, Chicago: University of Chicago Press.

Kagan, J. (1987) 'Misgivings about the Matching Familiar Figures Test: a brief reply', *Developmental Psychology* 23: 739–40.

Kagan, J. and Kogan, N. (1970) 'Individual variation in cognitive processes', in P. H. Mussen (ed.) *Carmichael's Manual of Child Psychology*, vol. 1, 3rd edn, New York: Wiley.

Kagan J., Kearsley, R. B. and Zelazo, P. R. (1978) *Infancy: its Place in Human Development*, Cambridge, Mass.: Harvard University Press.

Kagan, J., Lapidus, D. R. and Moore, M. (1978) 'Infant antecedents of cognitive functioning: a longitudinal study', *Child Development* 49: 1005–23.

Kagan, J., Reznick, S. J. and Snidman, N. (1987) 'The physiology and psychology of behavioural inhibition in children', *Child Development* 55: 2212–25.

Kahneman, D., Slovic, P. and Tversky, A. (1982) *Judgment under Uncertainty: Heuristics and Biases*, New York: Cambridge University Press.

Kail, R. (1986) 'Sources of age differences in speed of processing', *Child Development* 57: 969–87.

Kail, R. (1988) 'Reply to Stigler, Nusbaum and Chalip', *Child Development* 59: 1154–7.

Kail, R. (1990) *The Development of Memory in Children*, 3rd edn (1st edn 1979, 2nd edn 1984), San Francisco: Freeman.

Kail, R. (1991a) 'Processing time declines exponentially during childhood and adolescence', *Developmental Psychology* 27: 259–66.

Kail, R. (1991b) 'Developmental change in speed of processing during childhood and adolescence', *Psychological Bulletin* 109: 490–501.

Kail, R. and Bisanz, J. (1982) 'Information processing and cognitive development', in *Advances in Child Development and Behaviour*, New York: Academic Press.

Kail, R. V. and Hagen, J. W. (eds.) (1977) *Perspectives on the Development of Memory and Cognition*, Hillsdale, NJ: Erlbaum.

Kamin, L. J. (1974) *The Science and Politics of I.Q.*, Potomac, Md.: Erlbaum.

Kamler, B. and Kilarr, G. (1983) 'Looking at what children can do', in B. Kroll and G. Wells (eds) *Explorations in the Development of Writing*, Chichester: Wiley.

Karmiloff-Smith, A., (1979) *A Functional Approach to Child Language: A Study of Determiners and Reference*, Cambridge: Cambridge University Press.

Karmiloff-Smith, A. (1981) 'Getting developmental differences or studying child development?', *Cognition* 10: 151–8.

Karmiloff-Smith, A. (1984) 'Children's problem solving', in M. Lamb, A. Brown and B. Rogoff (eds.) *Advances in Developmental Psychology*, vol. 3, Hillsdale, NJ: Erlbaum.

Karmiloff-Smith, A. (1986) 'From meta-processes to conscious access: evidence from children's metalinguistic and repair data', *Cognition* 23: 95–147.

Karmiloff-Smith, A. (1988) 'The child is a theoretician, not an inductivist', *Mind and Language* 3(3): 183–95.

Karmiloff-Smith, A. (1991) 'Beyond modularity: innate constraints and developmental change', in S. Carey and R. Gelman (eds) *The Epigenesis of Mind*, Hove: Erlbaum.

Karmiloff-Smith, A. and Inhelder, B. (1974/5). 'If you want to get ahead, get a theory', *Cognition* 3: 195–212.

Katz, H. B. and Davies, C. A. (1983) 'The separate and combined effects of early undernutrition and environmental complexity at different ages on cerebral measures in rats', *Developmental Psychobiology* 16: 47–58.

Kaye, K. (1984) *The Mental and Social Life of Babies*, London: Methuen.

Keasey, B. (ed.) (1977) *Social cognitive development: Nebraska Symposium on Motivation*, vol. 25, Lincoln, Nebr.: University of Nebraska Press.

Keeney, T. J., Cannizzo, S. R. and Flavell, J. H. (1967) 'Spontaneous and induced verbal rehearsal in a recall task', *Child Development* 38: 953–66.

Keil, F. C. (1979) *Semantic and Conceptual Development*, Cambridge, Mass.: Harvard University Press.

Keil, F. C. (1981a) 'Children's thinking: what never develops?', *Cognition* 10: 159–66.

Keil, F. C. (1981b) 'Constraints on knowledge and cognitive development', *Psychological Review* 88: 197–227.

Keil, F. C. (1984) 'Mechanisms in cognitive development and the structure of knowledge', in R. J. Sternberg (ed.) *Mechanisms of Cognitive Development*, New York: Freeman.

Keil, F. C. (1986) 'The acquisition of natural kind and artifact terms', in W. Demopoulos and A. Marras (eds) *Language Learning and Concept Acquisition*, Norwood, NJ: Ablex.

Keil, F. C. (1987) 'Conceptual development and category structure', in U. Neisser (ed.) *Concepts and Conceptual Development*, Cambridge: Cambridge University Press.

Keil, F. C. (1989) *Concepts, Kinds and Cognitive Development*, Boston: MIT Press.

Keil, F. C. (1990) 'Constraints on constraints: surveying the epigenetic landscape', *Cognitive Science* 14: 135–68.

Keil, F. (1991) 'The emergence of theoretical beliefs as constraints on concepts', in S. Carey and R. Gelman (eds) *The Epigenesis of Mind*, Hove: Erlbaum.

Keil, F. C. (1992) 'The origins of an autonomous biology', in M. Gunnar and M. Maratsos (eds) (1992) *Modularity and Constraints in Language and Cognition: Minnesota Symposium on Child Psychology*, vol. 25, Hillsdale, NJ: Erlbaum.

Keil, F. C. and Batterman, N. (1984) 'A characteristic-to-defining shift in the development of word meaning', *Journal of Verbal Learning and Verbal Behaviour* 23: 221–36.

Keil, F. C. and Kelly, M. H. (1986) 'Theories of constraints and constraints on theories', in W. Demopoulos and A. Marras (eds) *Language Learning and Concept Acquisition*, Norwood, NJ: Ablex.

Kihlstrom, J. F. and Harackiewicz, J. M. (1982) 'The earliest recollection: a new survey', *Journal of Personality* 50: 134–47.

Kimura, Y. and Bryant, P. E. (1983) 'Reading and writing in English and Japanese: a cross-cultural study of young children', *British Journal of Psychology* 1: 143–53.

King, R. (1978) *All Things Bright and Beautiful?*, London: Wiley.

Kinsbourne, M. (1980) 'Brain-based limitations on mind', in R. W. Rieber (ed.) *Mind and Body*, New York: Academic Press.

Kinsbourne, M. and Hiscock, M. (1983) 'The normal and deviant development of functional lateralisation of the brain', in M. M. Haith and J. J. Campos (eds) *Handbook of Child Psychology*, vol. 2, *Infancy and Developmental Psychobiology*, series ed. P. H . Mussen, New York: Wiley.

Kirtley, C., Bryant, P., Maclean, M. and Bradley, L. (1989) 'Rhyme, rime and the onset of reading', *Journal of Experimental Child Psychology* 48: 224–45.

Kister, M. C. and Patterson, C. J. (1980) 'Children's conceptions of the causes of illness: understanding of contagion and use of immanent justice', *Child Development*, 51: 839–46.

Kitchener, R. F. (1986) *Piaget's Theory of Knowledge: Genetic Epistemology or Scientific Reason*, New Haven, Conn.: Yale University Press.

Kitcher, P. (1988) 'The child as parent of the scientist', *Mind and Language* 3(3): 217–28.

Klahr, D. (1984) 'Transition processes in quantitative development', in R. J. Sternberg (ed.) *Mechanisms of Cognitive Development*, New York: Freeman.

Klahr, D. and Siegler, R. S. (1978) 'The representation of children's knowledge', in H. W. Reese and L. P. Lipsitt (eds) *Advances in Child Development*, New York: Academic Press.

Klahr, D. and Dunbar, K. (1988) 'Dual search space during scientific reasoning', *Cognitive Science* 12: 1–48.

Klahr, D. and Wallace, G. (1976) *Cognitive Development: an Information-processing View*, New York: Erlbaum.

Klausmeier, H. J. and Sipple, T. S. (1982) 'Factor structure of the Piagetian stage of concrete operations', *Contemporary Educational Psychology* 7: 161–80.

Klein, P. S., Forbes, G. B. and Nadar, P. R. (1975) 'Effects of starvation in infancy (pyloric stenosis) on subsequent learning abilities', *Journal of Pediatrics* 87: 8–15.

Klin, A., Volkmar, F. R. and Sparrow, S. S. (1992) 'Autistic social dysfunction: some limitations of the theory of mind hypothesis', *Journal of Child Psychology and Psychiatry* 33: 861–76.

Kobasigawa, A. (1977) 'Retrieval factors in the development of memory', in R. V. Kail and J. W. Hagen (eds) *Perspectives on the Development of Memory and Cognition*, Hillsdale, NJ: Erlbaum.

Kochanska, G. (1991) 'Patterns of inhibition to the unfamiliar in children of normal and affectively ill mothers', *Child Development* 62: 250–63.

Koestler, A. (1964) *The Act of Creation*, London: Hutchinson.

Kogan, N. (1976) *Cognitive Styles in Infancy and Early Childhood*, Hillsdale, NJ: Erlbaum.

Kogan, N. (1983) 'Stylistic variation in childhood and adolescence: creativity, metaphor and cognitive styles', in J. H. Flavell and E. M. Markman (eds) *Handbook of Child Psychology*, vol. 3, series ed. P. H. Mussen, New York: Wiley.

Kogan, N. and Saarni, C. (1989) 'Cognitive styles in children: some evolving trends', *Early Child Development and Care*, 43: 101–28.

Kohlmann, C.-W., Schumacher, A. and Streit, R. (1988) 'Trait anxiety and parental child-rearing behavior: support as a moderator variable?', *Anxiety Research* 1: 53–64.

Kohn, M. (1977) *Social Competence, Symptoms and Underachievement in Childhood: a Longitudinal Perspective*, New York: Wiley.

Koluchova, J. (1976) 'Severe deprivation in twins: a case study', in A. M. Clarke and A. D. B. Clarke (eds) *Early Experience: Myth and Reality*, London: Open Books.

Komatsu, L. K. and Galotti, K. M. (1986) 'Children's reasoning about social, physical and logical regularities: a look at two worlds', *Child Development* 57: 413–20.

Konner, M. (1982) *The Tangled Wing: Biological Constraints on the Human Spirit*, London: Heinemann.

Kontos, S. (1983) 'Adult–child interaction and the development of metacognition', *Journal of Educational Research* 77: 43–64.

Kozulin, A. (1986) 'Vygotsky in context', in L. S. Vygotsky, *Thought and Language*, A. Kozulin (ed.), Cambridge, Mass.: MIT Press.

Kozulin, A. (1990) *Vygotsky's Psychology*, Brighton: Harvester.

Krasner, S. M. and Beinart, H. (1989) ' "The Monday Group": a brief intervention with the siblings of infants who died from Sudden Infant Death Syndrome (SIDS)', *Newsletter of the Association for Child Psychology and Psychiatry* 11(4): 11–17.

Kreutzer, M., Leonard, C. and Flavell, J. (1975) 'An interview study of children's knowledge about memory', *Monographs of the Society for Research in Child Development* 40(1), serial no. 159.

Kristeva, J. (1986) *The Kristeva Reader*, Oxford: Blackwell.

Kroll, B. and Wells, G. (eds) (1983) *Explorations in the Development of Writing*, Chichester: Wiley.

Kuhn, D. (1989) 'Children and adults as intuitive scientists', *Psychological Review* 96(4): 674–89.

Kuhn, D. (1992) 'Thinking as argument', *Harvard Educational Review*, 62: 155–74.

Kuhn, D., Amsel, E. and O'Loughlin, M. (1988) *The Development of Scientific Thinking Skills*, San Diego, Calif.: Academic Press.

Kuhn, T. S. (1962) *The Structure of Scientific Revolutions*, Chicago: Chicago University Press.

Kulhavy, R. W., Lee, J. B. and Caterino, L. C. (1985) 'Conjoint retention of maps and related discourse', *Contemporary Educational Psychology* 10: 28–37.

Kurtz, B. E. and Weinert, F. E. (1989) 'Metamemory, memory performance and causal attributions in gifted and average children', *Journal of Experimental Child Psychology* 48: 45–61.

Kuzmak, S. D. and Gelman, R. (1986) 'Young children's understanding of random phenomena', *Child Development* 57: 559–66.

Laboratory of Comparative Human Cognition (1982) 'Culture and intelligence', in R. J. Sternberg (ed.) *Handbook of Human Intelligence*, Cambridge: Cambridge University Press.

Laboratory of Comparative Human Cognition (1983) 'Culture and cognitive development', in W. Kessen (ed.) *Handbook of Child Psychology*, vol. I, *History Theory and Method*, New York: Wiley.

La Buda, M. C., De Fries, J. C., Plomin, R. and Fulker, D. W. (1986) 'Longitudinal stability of cognitive ability from infancy to early childhood: genetic and environmental etiologies', *Child Development* 57: 1142–50.

La Frenière, P. J. and Sroufe, A. (1985) 'Profiles of peer competence in the preschool: interrelations between measures, influences of social ecology, and relation to attachment history', *Developmental Psychology* 21: 46–69.

Lakoff, G. (1987) *Women, Fire and Dangerous Things: What Categories Reveal About the Mind*, Chicago: Chicago University Press.

Landau, B., Smith, L. B. and Jones, S. S. (1988) 'The importance of shape in early lexical learning', *Cognitive Development* 3: 299–321.

Lane, D. and Stratford, B. (1985) *Current Approaches to Down's Syndrome*, London: Holt, Rinehart & Winston.

Lane, J. (1990) 'The culture of acquisition and the practice of understanding', in J. W. Stigler, R. A. Shweder and G. H. Herdt (eds) *Cultural Psychology: Essays on Comparative Human Development*, Cambridge: Cambridge University Press.

Lane, S. R. and Lane, S. A. (1986) 'Rationality, self-esteem and autonomy through collaborative enquiry', *Oxford Review of Education* 12(3): 263–73.

Lang, A. (ed.) (n.d.) *The True Story Book*, London: Longmans.

Lange, G. and Pierce, S. H. (1992) 'Memory-strategy learning and maintenance in preschool children', *Developmental Psychology* 28: 453–62.

Lange, G., Mackinnon, C. E. and Nida, R. E. (1989) 'Knowledge, strategy and motivational contributions to preschool children's object recall', *Developmental Psychology* 25(5): 772–9.

Lansdown, R. and Benjamin, G. (1985) 'The development of the concept of death in children aged 5–9 years', *Child Care, Health and Development*, 11: 13–20.

Larkin, J. (1983) 'The role of problem representation in physics', in D. Gentner and A. L. Stevens (eds) *Mental Models*, Hillsdale, NJ: Erlbaum.

Larkin, J., McDermott, J., Simon, D. P. and Simon, H. A. (1980) 'Expert and novice performance in solving physics problems', *Science* 208: 1335–42.

Laszlo, J. L. and Bairstow, P. J. (1985) *Perceptual–motor Development: Developmental Assessment and Therapy*, London: Holt, Rinehart & Winston.

Laurendeau, M. and Pinard, A. (1970) *The Development of the Concept of Space in the Child*, New York: International Universities Press.

Lane, H. (1976) *The Wild Boy of Aveyron*, London: George Allen & Unwin.

Lave, J. (1990) 'The culture of acquisition and the practice of understanding', in J. W. Stigler, R. A. Shweder and G. H. Herdt (eds) *Cultural Psychology: Essays on Comparative Human Development*, Cambridge: Cambridge University Press.

Lawler, R. W. (1981) 'The progressive construction of mind', *Cognitive Science*, 5: 1–30.

Lawson, A. E. (1985) 'A review of research on formal reasoning and science teaching', *Journal of Research in Science Teaching* 22: 569–617.

Lazar, A. and Torney-Purta, J. (1991) 'The development of the subconcepts of death in young children: a short-term longitudinal study', *Child Development* 62: 1321–33.

Lazarus, R. S. (1991) 'Progress on a cognitive motivational relational theory of emotion', *American Psychologist* 46: 819–34.

Lea, S. E. G., Tarpy, R. M. and Webley, P. (1987) *The Individual in the Economy*, Cambridge: Cambridge University Press.

Leach, P. (1979) *Who cares? A New Deal for Mothers and Their Small Children*, Harmondsworth: Penguin Books.

Leahy, R. L. (1981) 'Development of the conception of economic inequality, I: descriptions and comparisons of rich and poor people', *Child Development* 52: 523–32.

Leahy, R. L. (1983) 'Development of the conception of economic inequality, II: explanations, justifications and concepts of social mobility and change', *Developmental Psychology* 19: 111–25.

Le Doux, J. (1989) 'Cognitive–emotional interactions in the brain', *Cognition and Emotion* 3: 267–89.

Lee, B. (1985) 'Intellectual origins of Vygotsky's semiotic analysis', in J. V. Wertsch (ed.) *Culture Communication and Cognition*, Cambridge: Cambridge University Press.

Lee, S., Stigler, J. W. and Stevenson, H. W. (1986) 'Beginning reading in Chinese and English', in B. Foorman and A. Siegel (eds) *Acquisition of Reading Skills*, Hillsdale, NJ: Erlbaum.

Lee, V. E., Brooks-Gunn, J. and Schnur, E. (1988) 'Does Head Start work? A 1-year follow-up comparision of disadvantaged children attending Head Start, no preschool, and other preschool programs', *Developmental Psychology* 24: 210–22.

Lehman, D., Lempert, R. O. and Nisbett, R. E. (1988) 'The effects of graduate training on reasoning', *American Psychologist* 43: 431–42.

Lenat, D. B. and Brown, J. S. (1984) 'Why AM and Eurisko appear to work', *Artificial Intelligence* 23: 269–94.

Lepper, M. R. (1981) 'Intrinsic and extrinsic motivation in children: Detrimental effects of superfluous social controls', in *Minnesota Symposium on Child Psychology*, vol. 14: Hillsdale, NJ: Erlbaum.

Lesh, R. and Landau, M. (eds) (1983) *Acquisition of Mathematics Concepts and Processes*, New York: Academic Press.

Leslie, A. M. (1987) 'Pretense and representation: the origins of "Theory of Mind" ', *Psychological Review* 94: 412–26.

Leslie, A. M. (1988a) 'Some implications of pretense for mechanisms underlying the child's theory of mind', in J. W. Astington, P. L. Harris and D. R. Olson (eds) *Developing Theories of Mind*, Cambridge: Cambridge University Press.

Leslie, A. M. (1988b) 'The child's understanding of the mental world', in R. L. Gregory (ed.) *The Oxford Companion to the Mind*, Oxford: Oxford University Press.

Leslie, A. M. (1990) 'Pretence, autism and the basis of "Theory of Mind" ', *The Psychologist* 3: 120–3.

Leslie, A. M. and Frith, U. (1990) 'Prospects for a cognitive neuro-psychology of autism: Hobson's choice', *Psychological Review* 97(1): 122–31.

Levin, I. (1982) 'The nature and development of time concepts in children: the effects of interfering cues', in W. J. Friedman (ed.) *The Developmental Psychology of Time*, New York: Academic Press.

Levin, I. (ed.) (1986) *Stage and Structure: Reopening the Debate*, Norwood, NJ: Ablex.

Levine, S. C., Jordan, N. C. and Huttenlocher, J. (1992) 'Development of calculation abilities in young children', *Journal of Experimental Child Psychology* 53: 72–103.

Levinson, P. J. and Carpenter, R. L. (1974) 'An analysis of analogical reasoning in children', *Child Development* 45: 857–61.

Lewis, M. and Brooks-Gunn, J. (1979) *Social Cognition and the Acquisition of Self*, New York: Plenum Press.

Lewis, M. and Michalson, L. (1983) *Children's Emotions and Moods: Developmental Theory and Measurement*, New York: Plenum Press.

Lewis, V. (1987) *Development and Handicap*, Oxford: Blackwell.

Liben, L. S. (1981) 'Spatial representation and behavior: multiple perspectives', in L. S. Liben and N. Newcombe (eds) *Spatial Representation and Behavior Across the Life Span*, New York: Academic Press.

Liberman, I. Y. and Shankweiler, D. (1991) 'Phonology and beginning reading', in L. Rieben and C. A. Perfetti *Learning to Read*, Hove: Erlbaum.

Liberman, I. Y., Shankweiler, D., Liberman, A. and Fowler, C. (1977) 'Phonetic segmentation and reading in the beginning reader', in A. S. Reber and D. L. Scarborough (eds) *Toward a Psychology of Reading*, New York: Wiley.

Lieven, E. V. M. (1978) 'Conversations between mothers and young children: individual differences and their possible implication for the study of language learning', in N. Waterson and C. Snow (eds) *The Development of Communication*, Chichester: Wiley.

Lieven, E. V. M. (1982) 'Context process and progress in young children's speech', in M. Beveridge (ed.) *Children Thinking Through Language*, London: Edward Arnold.

Lieven, E. V. M., Pine, J. M. and Dresner Barnes, H. (1992) 'Individual differences in early vocabulary development: redefining the referential–expressive distinction', *Journal of Child Language* 19: 287–301.

Light, P. H. (1979) *The Development of Social Sensitivity*, Cambridge: Cambridge University Press.

Light, P. H. (1983) 'Social interaction and cognitive development: a review of post-Piagetian research', in S. Meadows (ed.) *Developing Thinking*, London: Methuen.

Light, P. H. (1986) 'Context, conservation and conversation', in M. Richards and P. H. Light (eds) *Child of Social Worlds*, Cambridge: Polity Press.

Light, P. H., Buckingham, N. and Robbins, A. H. (1979) 'The conservation task as an interactional setting', *British Journal of Educational Psychology* 49: 304–10.

Light, P. H. and Humphreys, J. (1981) 'Internal relationships in young children's drawings', *Journal of Experimental Child Psychology* 31: 521–30.

Light, P. H. and Perret-Clermont, A.-N. (1989) 'Social context effects in learning and testing', in A. Gellatly, D. Rogers and J. A. Sloboda (eds) *Cognition and Social Worlds*, Oxford: Clarendon Press.

Linn, M. C. (1986) 'Science', in R. F. Dillon and R. J. Sternberg (eds) *Cognition and Instruction*, New York: Academic Press.

Linn, M. C. and Peterson, A. C. (1985) 'Emergence and characterization of sex differences in spatial ability: a meta-analysis', *Child Development* 56: 1479–98.

Lipman, M., Sharp, A. M. and Oscanyan, F. S. (1980) *Philosophy in the Classroom*, Philadelphia, Pa.: Temple University Press.

Livesley, W. J. and Bromley, D. B. (1973) *Person Perception in Childhood and Adolescence*, London: Wiley.

Lloyd-Still, J. D., Hurwitz, I. and Shwachman, H. (1974) 'Intellectual development after severe malnutrition in infancy', *Pediatrics* 43: 306–11.

Lock, A. (ed.) (1978) *Action, Gesture and Symbol: the Emergence of Language*, London: Academic Press.

Lock, A., Service, V., Brito, A., Young, A. and Chandler, P. (1989) 'The social structuring of infant cognition', in A. Slater and G. Bremner (eds) *Infant Development*, London: Erlbaum.

Locurto, C. (1988) 'On the malleability of IQ', *The Psychologist* 11: 431–5.

Loehlin, J. C., Horn, J. M. and Willerman, L. (1989) 'Modelling IQ change: evidence from the Texas Adoption Project', *Child Development* 60: 993–1004.

Loehlin, J. C., Willerman, L. and Horn, J. M. (1988) 'Human behaviour genetics', *Annual Review of Psychology* 38: 101–33.

Loftus, E. F. (1979) *Eyewitness Testimony*, Cambridge, Mass.: Harvard University Press.

Lohman, D. F. (1989) 'Human intelligence: an introduction to advances in theory and research', *Review of Educational Research*, 59: 333–73.

Longeot, F. (1978) *Les Stades operatoires de Piaget et les facteurs de l'intelligence*, Grenoble: Presses Universitaires de Grenoble.

Longstreth, L. E., David, B., Carter, L., Flint, D., Owen, J., Rickert, M. and Taylor, E. (1981) 'Separation of home intellectual environment and material IQ as determinants of child IQ', *Developmental Psychology* 7: 532–41.

Longuet-Higgins, H. C. (1987) *Mental Processes: Studies in Cognitive Science*, Cambridge, Mass.: MIT Press.

Lorch, E. P., Bellack, D. R. and Augsbach, L. H. (1987) 'Young children's memory for televised stories: effects of importance', *Child Development* 58: 453–63.

Lord, A. B. (1960) *The Singer of Tales*, Cambridge, Mass.: Harvard University Press.

Lovett, M. W. (1987) 'A developmental approach to reading disability: accuracy and speed criteria of normal and deficient reading skill', *Child Development* 58: 234–60.

Lozoff, B. (1988) 'Behavioral alterations in iron deficiency', *Advances in Pediatrics* 35: 331–60.

Lozoff, B. (1989) 'Nutrition and behavior', *American Psychologist* 44: 231–6.

Luria, A. R. (1969) *The Mind of a Mnemonist*, London: Cape.

Luria, A. R. (1976) *Cognitive Development: its Cultural and Social Foundations*, Cambridge, Mass.: Harvard University Press.

Luster, T. and Dubow, E. (1992) 'Home environment and maternal intelligence as predictors of verbal intelligence: a comparison of preschool and school-age children', *Merrill-Palmer Quarterly* 38: 151–75.

Lycan, W. G. (1989) *Mind and Cognition*, Oxford: Blackwell.

Lynn, R. (1989) 'A nutrition theory of the secular increases in intelligence: positive correlations between height, head size and IQ', *British Journal of Educational Psychology* 59: 372–7.

Lytton, H. and Romney, D. M. (1991) 'Parents' differential socialization of boys and girls: a meta-analysis', *Psychological Bulletin* 109: 267–96.

McCabe, A. (1989) 'Differential language learning styles in young children: the importance of context', *Developmental Review* 9: 1–20.

McCall, R. B. (1983) 'Environmental effects on intelligence: the forgotten realm of discontinuous nonshared within-family factors', *Child Development* 54: 408–15.

McCall, R. B. (1990) 'The neuroscience of education: more research is needed before application', *Journal of Educational Psychology* 82: 885–8.

McCall, R. B., Meyers, E. D., Hartman, J. and Roche, A. F. (1983) 'Developmental changes in head-circumference and mental-performance growth rates: a test of Epstein's phrenoblysis hypothesis', *Developmental Psychobiology* 16: 457–68.

McCartney, K. (1984) 'The effect of quality of daycare environment on children's language development', *Developmental Psychology* 20: 244–60.

McCartney, K., Harris, M. J. and Bernieri, F. (1990) 'Growing up and growing apart: a developmental meta-analysis of twin studies', *Psychological Bulletin* 107: 226–37.

McCartney, K., Wagner Robeson, W., Jordan, E. and Mouradian, V. (1991) 'Mothers' language with first- and second-born children: a within-family study', in K. Pillemer and K. McCartney (eds) *Parent–child Relations Throughout Life*, Hillsdale, NJ: Erlbaum.

McCauley, E., Kay, T., Ho, J. and Treder, R. (1987) 'The Turner Syndrome: cognitive deficits, affective discrimination and behaviour problems', *Child Development* 58: 464–73.

McClelland, J. L., Rumelhart, D. E. and the PDP Research Group (1986) *Parallel Distributed Processing: Explorations in the Micro-structure of Cognition, vol. 2, Psychological and Biological Models*. Cambridge, Mass.: MIT Press.

McCloskey, M., Caramazza, A. and Green, B. (1980) 'Curvilinear motion in the absence of external forces: naive beliefs about the motion of objects', *Science* 210: 1139–41.

Maccoby, E. and Jacklin, C. (1974) *The Psychology of Sex Differences*, Stanford, Calif.: Stanford University Press.

McDevitt, T. M., Hess, R. D., Kashiwagi, K., Dickson, W. P., Miyake, N. and Azuma, H. (1987) 'Referential communication accuracy of mother–child pairs and children's later scholastic achievement: a follow-up study', *Merrill-Palmer Quarterly* 33: 171–85.

McGillicuddy-DeLisi, A. V. (1982) 'The relationship between parents' beliefs about development and family constellation, socioeconomic status, and parents' teaching strategies', in L. M. Laosa and I. E. Sigel (eds) *Families as Learning Environments for Children*, New York: Plenum Press.

McGilly, K. and Siegler, R. S. (1989) 'How children choose among serial recall strategies', *Child Development* 60: 172–82.

McGlaughlin, A., Empson, J., Morrissey, M. and Sever, J. (1980) 'Early child development and the home environment: consistencies at and between four pre-school stages', *International Journal of Behavioural Development* 3: 299–309.

McGue, M. (1989) 'Nature–nurture and intelligence', *Nature* 340: 507–8.

McHugh, P. R. and McKusick, V. A. (eds) (1991) *Genes, Brain and Behaviour*, New York: Raven Press.

Mackay, D., Thompson, B. and Schaub, P. (1970) *Breakthrough to Literacy*, London: Longman.

Mackintosh, N. J. (1986) 'The biology of intelligence', *British Journal of Psychology* 77: 1–18.

McKusick, V. A. (1991) 'Advances in medical genetics in the past 30 years', in P. R. McHugh and V. A. McKusick (eds) *Genes, Brain and Behaviour*, New York: Raven Press.

McLaughlin, B. (1984) *Second Language Acquisition in Childhood*, vol. 1, *Preschool Children*, Hillsdale, NJ: Erlbaum.

Maclean, C. (1979) *The Wolf Children*, Harmondsworth: Penguin Books.

Maclean, M., Bryant, P. and Bradley, L. (1987) 'Rhymes, nursery rhymes, and reading in early childhood', *Merrill-Palmer Quarterly* 33(3): 255–81.

McNally, S., Eisenberg, N. and Harris, J. D. (1991) 'Consistency and change in maternal child-rearing practices and values: a longitudinal study', *Child Development* 62: 190–8.

McNamara, T. P. (1986) 'Mental representations of spatial relations', *Cognitive Psychology* 18: 87–121.

McNaughton, S. (1987) *Being Skilled: the Socializations of Learning to Read*, London: Methuen.

McNaughton, S. and Leyland, J. (1990) 'The shifting focus of maternal tutoring across different difficulty levels on a problem-solving task', *British Journal of Developmental Psychology* 8: 147–55.

MacPhee, D., Ramey, C. T. and Yeates, K. O. (1984) 'Home environment and early cognitive development: implications for intervention', in A. W. Gottfried (ed.) *Home Environment and Early Cognitive Development: Longitudinal Research*, Orlando, Fla.: Academic Press.

McShane, J. (1991) *Cognitive Development: an Information-processing Approach*, Oxford: Blackwell.

Main, M. and George, C. (1985) 'Responses of abused and disadvantaged toddlers to distress in agemates: a study in the day care setting', *Developmental Psychology* 21: 407–12.

Malatesta, C. Z. (1990) 'The role of emotions in the development and organisation of personality', in R. A. Thompson (ed.) *Socioemotional Development: Nebraska Symposium on Motivation, 1988*, vol. 36, Lincoln, Nebr.: University of Nebraska Press.

Mandell, F., McAnulty, E. H. and Carlson, A. (1983) 'Unexpected death of an infant sibling', *Pediatrics*, 72(5): 652–7.

Mandler, J. M. (1983) 'Representation', in P. H. Mussen (ed.) *Handbook of Child Psychology*, vol. 3, New York: Wiley.

Mandler, J. M. and Johnson, N. S. (1977) 'Remembrance of things parsed: story structure and recall', *Cognitive Psychology* 9: 111–51.

Mann, V. A., Tobin, P. and Wilson, R. (1987) 'Measuring phonological awareness through the invented spellings of kindergarten children', *Merrill-Palmer Quarterly* 33(3): 365–91.

Mant, C. M. and Perner, J. (1988) 'The child's understanding of commitment', *Developmental Psychology* 24(3): 343–51.

Maratsos, M. (1983) 'Some current issues in the study of the acquisition of grammar', in P. H. Mussen (ed.), *Handbook of Child Psychology*, vol. 3, New York: Wiley.

Maratsos, M. (1989) 'Innateness and plasticity in language acquisition', in M. L. Rice and R. L. Schiefelbusch (eds) *The Teachability of Language*, Baltimore, Md.: Brookes.

Marean, G. C., Werner, L. A. and Kuhl, P. K. (1992) 'Vowel categorisation by very young infants', *Developmental Psychology* 28: 396–405.

Marjoribanks, K. (1979) *Families and their Learning Environments: an Empirical Analysis*, London: Routledge.

Markman, E. M. (1973) 'The facilitation of part–whole comparisons by use of the collective noun "family" ', *Child Development* 44: 837–40.

Markman, E. M. (1977) 'Realising that you don't understand: a preliminary investigation', *Child Development* 48: 986–92.

Markman, E. M. (1979) 'Realising that you don't understand: elementary school children's awareness of inconsistencies', *Child Development* 50: 643–55.

Markman, E. M. (1981) 'Comprehension monitoring', in W. P. Dickson (ed.) *Children's Oral Communication Skills*, New York: Academic Press.

Markman, E. M. (1987) 'How children constrain the possible meanings of words', in U. Neisser (ed.) *Concepts and Conceptual Development*, Cambridge: Cambridge University Press.

Markman, E. M. (1989) *Categorization and Naming in Children: the Problem of Induction*, Boston: MIT Press.

Markman, E. M. (1990) 'Constraints children place on word meaning', *Cognitive Science* 14: 57–77.

Markman, E. M. and Callahan, M. A. (1983) 'An analysis of hierarchical classification', in R. J. Sternberg (ed.) *Advances in the Psychology of Human Intelligence*, vol. 2, Hillsdale, NJ: Erlbaum.

Markman, E., Cox, B. and Machida, S. (1981) 'The standard sorting task as a measure of conceptual organisation', *Developmental Psychology* 17: 115–17.

Markova, I. (1982) *Paradigms, Thought and Language*, New York: Wiley.

Markova, I. (1987) *Human Awareness: its Social Development*, London: Hutchinson.

Marks, L. E., Hammeal, R. J. and Bornstein, M. H. (1987) 'Perceiving similarity and comprehending metaphor', *Monographs of the Society for Research in Child Development* 52(1), serial no. 215.

Markus, H. R. and Kitayama, S. (1991) 'Culture and the self: implications for cognition, emotion and motivation', *Psychological Review* 98: 224–53.

Marler, P. and Terrace, H. (1984) *The Biology of Learning*, Berlin: Springer-Verlag.

Marmurek, H. H. C. and Rinaldo, R. (1992) 'The development of letter and syllable effects in categorisation, reading aloud and naming', *Journal of Experimental Child Psychology* 53: 277–99.

Marr, D. (1982) *Vision: a Computational Investigation into the Human Representation and Processing of Visual Information*, San Francisco: Freeman.

Marsh, R. W. (1985) 'Phrenoblysis: real or chimera?', *Child Development* 56: 1059–61.

Marshall, J. C. (1987a) 'Routes and representations in the processing of written language', in E. Keller and M. Gopnik (eds) *Motor and Sensory Processes in Language*, Hillsdale, NJ: Erlbaum.

Marshall, J. C. (1987b) 'The cultural and biological context of written language', in J. Beech and A. Colley (eds) *Cognitive Approaches to Reading*, Chichester: Wiley.

Martlew, M. (1983) *The Psychology of Written Language: Development and Educational Perspectives*, Chichester: Wiley.

Marton, F. (1983) 'Beyond individual differences', *Educational Psychology* 3: 289–304.

Marton, F. (1988) 'Describing and improving learning', in R. R. Schmeck (ed.) *Learning Strategies and Learning Styles*, New York: Plenum Press.

Marton, F., Asplund Carlsson, M. and Halasz, L. (1992) 'Differences in understanding and the use of reflective variation in reading', *British Journal of Educational Psychology* 62: 1–16.

Massey, C. M. and Gelman, R. (1988) 'Preschoolers' ability to decide whether a photographed unfamiliar object can move itself', *Developmental Psychology* 24(3); 307–17.

Masterson, J., Laxon, V. and Stuart, M. (1992) 'Beginning reading with phonology', *British Journal of Psychology* 83: 1–12.

Matthews, G. (1980) *Philosophy and the Young Child*, Cambridge, Mass.: Harvard University Press.

Matthews, M. H. (1984) 'Cognitive mapping abilities of young boys and girls', *Geography* 69: 327–36.

Matthews, M. H. (1987) 'The influence of gender on the environmental cognition of young boys and girls', *Journal of Genetic Psychology* 147: 295–302.

Matthews, M. H. (1992) *Making Sense of Place: Children's Understanding of Large-scale Environments*, Hemel Hempstead: Harvester.

Mayer, R. (1982a) 'Different problem solving strategies for algebra word and equation problems', *Journal of Experimental Psychology: Learning, Memory and Cognition* 8: 448–62.

Mayer, R. (1982b) 'Memory for algebra story problems', *Journal of Educational Psychology* 74: 119–216.

Mayer, R. (1985) 'Mathematical ability', in R. J. Sternberg (ed.) *Human Abilities: an Information-processing Approach*, New York: Freeman.

Mayes, A. R. (1988) *Human Organic Memory Disorders*, Cambridge: Cambridge University Press.

Mead, G. H. (1934) *Mind, Self and Society*, Chicago: University of Chicago Press.

Meadows, S. (1975) 'The development of concrete operations: a short-term longitudinal study', Ph.D. thesis, University of London.

Meadows, S. (1977) 'An experimental investigation of Piaget's analysis of class inclusion', *British Journal of Psychology* 68(2): 229–37.

Meadows, S. (ed.) (1983) *Developing Thinking: Approaches to Children's Cognitive Development*, London: Methuen.

Meadows, S. (1986) *Understanding Child Development*, London: Hutchinson.

Meadows, S. and Cashdan, A. (1983) *Teaching Styles in Nursery Education: Final Report to SSRC*, Sheffield: Sheffield City Polytechnic.

Meadows, S. and Cashdan, A. (1988) *Helping Children Learn: Contributions to a Cognitive Curriculum*, London: David Fulton.

Meadows, S. and Mills, M. (1987) 'End of grant report to ESRC on project C00232101: "Preschool parenting style and children's cognition: follow-up on starting school" '.

Medin, D. L. and Wattenmaker, W. D. (1987) 'Category cohesiveness, theories and cognitive archeology', in U. Neisser (ed.) *Concepts and Conceptual Development*, Cambridge: Cambridge University Press.

Mehler, J., Bertoncini, J., Barrier, J. and Jassik-Gerschenfeld, D. (1978) 'Infant recognition of mother's voice', *Perception* 7: 491–7.

Meichenbaum, D., Burland, S., Gruson, L. and Cameron, R. (1985) 'Metacognitive assessment', in S. R. Yussen (ed.) *The Growth of Reflection in Children*, New York: Academic Press.

Mellin-Olsen, S. (1987) *The Politics of Mathematics Education*, Dordrecht: Reidel.

Mervis, C. B. (1987) 'Child-basic object categories and early lexical development', in U. Neisser (ed.) *Concepts and Conceptual Development*, Cambridge: Cambridge University Press.

Meyers, M. and Paris, S. (1978) 'Children's metacognitive knowledge about reading', *Journal of Educational Psychology* 70: 680–90.

Midgley, M. (1985) *Evolution as a Religion: Strange Hopes and Stranger Fears*, London: Methuen.

Miller, A. (1985) *Thou Shalt Not Be Aware: Society's Betrayal of the Child*, London: Pluto Press.

Miller, A. (1987) *For Your Own Good: Hidden Cruelty in Child-rearing and the Roots of Violence*, London: Virago.

Miller, A. (1990) *The Untouched Key: Tracing Childhood Trauma in Creativity and Destructiveness*, London: Virago.

Miller, K. F. and Paredes, D. R. (1990) 'Starting to add worse: effects of learning to multiply on children's addition', *Cognition* 37: 213–42.

Miller, P. H. and De Marie-Dreblow, D. (1990) 'Social-cognitive correlates of children's understanding of displaced aggression', *Journal of Experimental Child Psychology* 49: 488–504.

Miller, P. and Sperry, L. L. (1987) 'The socialization of anger and aggression', *Merrill-Palmer Quarterly* 33(1): 1–31.

Miller, P. H. and Zalenski, R. (1982) 'Preschoolers' knowledge about attention', *Developmental Psychology* 18(6): 871–5.

Miller, P. J., Mintz, J., Hoogstra, L., Fung, H. and Potts, R. (1992) 'The narrated self: young children's construction of self in relation to others in conversational stories of personal experience', *Merrill-Palmer Quarterly* 38: 45–68.

Miller, S. A. (1982) 'On the generalizability of conservation: a comparison of different kinds of transformation', *British Journal of Psychology* 73(2): 221–30.

Miller, S. A. (1986) 'Parents' beliefs about their children's cognitive abilities', *Developmental Psychology* 22: 276–84.

Miller, S. A. (1986) 'Certainty and necessity in the understanding of Piagetian concepts', *Developmental Psychology* 22(1): 3–18.

Mills, M. and Funnell, E. (1983) 'Experience and cognitive processing', in S. Meadows (ed.) *Developing Thinking*, London: Methuen.

Mills, M., Puckering, C., Pound, A. and Cox, A. (1985) 'What is it about depressed mothers that influences their children's functioning?', in J. Stevenson (ed.) *Recent Advances in Developmental Psychopathology*, Oxford: Pergamon.

Minsky, M. (1988) *The Society of Mind*, New York: Simon & Schuster.

Mischel, T. (ed.) (1971) *Cognitive Development and Epistemology*, New York and London: Academic Press.

Mitchell, P. and Robinson, E. J. (1992) 'Children's understanding of the evidential connotations of "know" in relation to overestimation of their own knowledge', *Journal of Child Language* 19: 167–82.

Moely, B. E. (1977) 'Organisational factors in the development of memory', in R. V. Kail and J. W. Hagen (eds) *Perspectives on the Development of Memory and Cognition*, Hillsdale, NJ: Erlbaum.

Moerk, E. L. (1989) 'The LAD was a lady and the tasks were ill-defined', *Developmental Review* 9(1): 21–57.

Molfese, D. and Segalowitz, S. J. (eds) (1988) *Brain Lateralisation in Children: Developmental Implications*, New York: Guilford Press.

Moll, L. C. (ed.) (1990) *Vygotsky and Education: Instructional Implications and Applications of Socio-historical Psychology*, Cambridge: Cambridge University Press.

Moog, H. [1968] (English translation 1976) *The Musical Experience of the Pre-school Child*, London: Schott Music.

Moore, C., Bryant, D. and Furrow, D. (1989) 'Mental terms and the development of certainty', *Child Development* 60: 167–71.

Moore, C., Pure, K. and Furrow, D. (1990) 'Children's understanding of the modal experience of speaker certainty and uncertainty and its relation to the development of a representational theory of mind', *Child Development* 61: 722–30.

Moore, E. G. J. (1986) 'Family socialization and the IQ test performance of traditionally and transracially adopted black children', *Developmental Psychology* 22: 317–26.

Moore, R. (1986) *Childhood's Domain*, London: Croom Helm.

Moravcsik, J. M. (1990) *Thought and Language*, London: Routledge.

Morgan, F. (1989) 'Writing in perspective', *Education* 174(14): 303.

Morrison, F. J., Holmes, D. L. and Haith, M. M. (1974) 'A developmental study of the effects of familiarity on short-term visual memory', *Journal of Experimental Child Psychology* 18: 412–25.

Morss, J. R. (1985) 'Early cognitive development: difference or delay?', in D. Lane and B. Stratford (eds) *Current Approaches to Down's Syndrome*, London: Holt, Rinehart & Winston.

Mortimore, P. and Mortimore, J. (1986) 'Education and social class', in R. Rogers (ed.) *Education and Social Class*, Lewes: Falmer Press.

Mortimore, P., Simmons, P., Stoll, L., Lewis, D. and Ecob, R. (1998) *School Matters: the Junior Years*, Wells: Open Books.

Mortimore, P., Sammons, P., Stoll, L., Lewis, D. and Ecob, R. (1989) 'A Study of effective junior schools', *International Journal of Educational Research* 13(7): 753–68.

Morton, J. (1980) 'The logogen model and orthographic structure', in U. Frith (ed.) *Cognitive Processes in Spelling*, London: Academic Press.

Morton, J. (1990) 'The development of event memory', *The Psychologist* 1: 3–10.

Morton, J., Hammersley, R. H. and Bekerian, D.A. (1992) 'Headed records: a model for memory and its failures', *Cognition* 20: 1–23.

Morton, J. and Patterson, K. (1980) 'A new attempt at an interpretation, or an attempt at a new interpretation', in M. Coltheart, K. Patterson and J. Marshall (eds) *Deep Dyslexia*, London: Routledge.

Moses L. J. and Flavell, J. (1990). 'Inferring false beliefs from actions and reactions', *Child Development* 61: 929–45.

Moshman, D. and Franks, B. A. (1986) 'Development of the concept of inferential validity', *Child Development* 57: 153–65.

Moshman, D. and Timmons, M. (1982) 'The construction of logical necessity', *Human Development* 25: 309–23.

Movshon, J. A. and Van Sluyters, R. C. (1981) 'Visual neuronal development', *Annual Review of Psychology* 32: 477–522.

Mumford, M. D. and Gustafson, S. B. (1988) 'Creativity syndrome: integration, application and innovation', *Psychological Bulletin* 103: 27–43.

Murphy, G. L. and Medin, D. L. (1985) 'The role of theories in conceptual coherence', *Psychological Review* 92: 289–316.

Myers, N.A. and Perlmutter, M. (1978) 'Memory in the years from two to five', in P. A. Ornstein (ed.) *Memory Development in Children*, Hillsdale, NJ: Erlbaum.

Myles-Worsley, M., Cromer, C. C. and Dodd, D. H. (1986). 'Children's preschool script reconstruction: reliance on general knowledge as memory fades', *Developmental Psychology* 22(2): 22–30.

Nakamura, C. Y. and Finck, D. N. (1980) 'Relative effectiveness of socially-oriented and task-oriented children and predictability of their behaviours', *Monographs of the Society for Research in Child Development* 45(3–4), serial no. 185.

Naslund, J. C. and Schneider, W. (1991) 'Longitudinal effects of verbal ability, memory capacity and phonological awareness on reading performance', *European Journal of Psychology of Education* 6: 375–92.

Naus, M. J., Ornstein, P. A. and Aivano, S. (1977) 'Developmental changes in memory: the effects of processing time and rehearsal instructions', *Journal of Experimental Psychology* 23: 237–51.

Needleman, H. L., Gunnoe, C., Leviton, A., Reed, M., Peresie, H., Maher, C. and Barrett, P. (1979) 'Deficits in psychologic and classroom performance of children with elevated dentine lead levels', *New England Journal of Medicine* 300: 689–95.

Neisser, U. (ed.) (1987) *Concepts and Conceptual Development: Ecological and Intellectual Factors in Categorisation*, Cambridge: Cambridge University Press.

Nelson, K. E. (1971) 'Memory development in children: evidence from non-verbal tasks', *Psychonomic Science* 25: 346–8.

Nelson, K. E. (1973) 'Structure and strategy in learning to talk', *Monographs of the Society for Research in Child Development*, 38(1–2) serial no. 149.

Nelson, K. E. (1978) 'How young children represent knowledge of their world in and out of language', in R. S. Siegler (ed.) *Children's Thinking: What Develops?*, Hillsdale, NJ: Erlbaum.

Nelson, K. E. (1981) 'Social cognition in a script framework', in J. H. Flavell and L. Ross (eds) *Social Cognitive Development: Frontiers and Possible Futures*, Cambridge: Cambridge University Press.

Nelson, K. E. (1985) *Making Sense: The Acquisition of Shared Meaning*, London: Academic Press.

Nelson, K. E. (1986) *Event Knowledge: Structure and Function in Development*, Hillsdale, NJ: Erlbaum.

Nelson, K. (ed.) (1989a) *Narratives from the Crib*, Cambridge, Mass.: Harvard University Press.

Nelson, K. E. (1989b) 'Strategies for first language teaching', in M. L. Rice and R. L. Schiefelbusch (eds) *The Teachability of Language*, Baltimore, Md.: Brookes.

Nelson, K. E. and Gruendel, J. (1979) 'At morning it's lunchtime: a scriptal view of children's dialogues', *Discourse Processes* 2: 73–94.

Nelson, K. E. and Gruendel, J. (1981) 'Generalised event representations, basic building blocks of cognitive development', *Advances in Developmental Psychology*, vol. 1, Hillsdale, NJ: Erlbaum.

Nelson, K. E. and Kosslyn, S. M. (1976) 'Recognition of previously labelled or unlabelled pictures by 5 year olds and adults', *Journal of Experimental Child Psychology* 21: 40–5.

Nesselroade, J. R. and Baltes, P. B. (1979) *Longitudinal Research in the Study of Behaviour and Development*, London: Academic Press.

Nettelbeck, T. (1986) 'Inspection time and intelligence', in P. A. Vernon (ed.) *Speed of Information Processing and Intelligence*, New York: Ablex.

Nettelbeck, T. and Vita, P. (1992) 'Inspection time in two childhood age cohorts: a constraint or a developmental function?', *British Journal of Developmental Psychology* 10: 180–97.

Nettelbeck, T. and Wilson, J. (1985) 'A cross-sequential analysis of developmental differences in speed of visual information processing', *Journal of Experimental Child Psychology* 40: 1–22.

Nettelbeck, T. and Young, R. (1989) 'Inspection time and intelligence in 6 year old children', *Personality and Individual Differences* 10: 605–14.

Newcombe, N. and Dubas, J. S. (1992) 'A longitudinal study of predictors of spatial ability in adolescent females', *Child Development* 63: 37–46.

Newcombe, N. E., Rogoff, B. and Kagan, J. (1977) 'Developmental changes in recognitive memory for pictures of objects and scenes', *Developmental Psychology* 13: 337–41.

Newell, A. and Simon, H. A. (1972) *Human Problem-solving*, Englewood Cliffs, NJ: Prentice Hall.

Newman, D., Griffin, P. and Cole, M. (1989) *The Construction Zone*, Cambridge: Cambridge University Press.

Newport, E. L. (1990) 'Maturational constraints on language learning', *Cognitive Science* 14: 11–28.

Nicholls, A. L. and Kennedy, J. M. (1992) 'Drawing development: from similarity of features to depiction', *Child Development* 63: 227–41.

Nicholls, J. G. (1978) 'The development of the concepts of effort and ability, perception of academic attainment, and the understanding that difficult tasks require more ability', *Child Development* 49: 800–14.

Nicholls, J. G., Patashnick, M. and Mettetal, G. (1986) 'Children's conceptions of ability and intelligence', *Child Development* 57: 636–45.

Nicolson, R. and Fawcett, A. (1990) 'Automaticity: a new framework for dyslexia research?', *Cognition* 35: 159–82.

Ninio, A. and Bruner, J. S. (1978) 'The achievement and antecedents of labelling', *Journal of Child Language* 5: 1–15.

Nisbett, R. and Ross, L. (1980) *Human Inference: Strategies and Shortcomings of Social Judgement*, Englewood Cliffs, NJ: Prentice Hall.

Nisbett, R. and Wilson, T. (1977) 'Telling more than we know: verbal reports on mental processes', *Psychological Review* 84: 231–59.

Nold, E. W. (1981) 'Revising', in C. H. Fredericksen and J. F. Dominic (eds) *Writing: the Nature, Development and Teaching of Written Communication*, vol. 2, Hillsdale, NJ: Erlbaum.

Novak, J. D. (1988) 'Learning science and the science of learning', *Studies in Science Education* 15: 77–101.

Nunner-Winkler, G. and Sodian, B. (1988) 'Children's understanding of moral emotions', *Child Development* 59: 1323–38.

Nuttall, D. L., Goldstein, H., Prosser, R. and Rasbash, J. (1989) 'Differential school effectiveness', *International Journal of Educational Research* 13(7): 769–76.

Oakhill, J. and Garnham, A. (1988) *Becoming a Skilled Reader*, Oxford: Blackwell.

O'Brien, D. (1987) 'The development of conditional reasoning: an iffy proposition', in H. W. Reese (ed.) *Advances in Child Development and Behaviour*, vol. 20, New York: Academic Press.

Ochs, E. (1988) *Culture and Language Development: Language Acquisition and Language Socialisation in a Samoan Village*, Cambridge: Cambridge University Press.

Ochs, E. (1990) 'Indexicality and socialization', in J. W. Stiger, R. A. Shweder and G. H. Herdt (eds) *Cultural Psychology*, Cambridge: Cambridge University Press.

Ochs, E. and Schieffelin, B. (eds) (1979) *Developmental Pragmatics*, New York: Academic Press.

Ochs, E. and Schieffelin, B. (1983) *Acquiring a Conversational Competence*, London: Routledge & Kegan Paul.

Ochse, R. (1990) *Before the Gates of Excellence: the Determinants of Creative Genius*, Cambridge: Cambridge University Press.

O'Connor, N. (1987) 'Cognitive psychology and mental handicap', *Journal of Mental Deficiency Research* 31: 329–36.

O'Connor, N. and Hermelin, B. (1984) 'Idiot savant calendrical calculators: maths or memory?', *Psychological Medicine* 14: 801–6.

O'Connor, N. and Hermelin, B. (1990) 'The recognition failure and graphic success of idiot-savant artists', *Journal of Child Psychology and Psychiatry* 31(2): 203–15.

Okagaki, L. and Sternberg, R. J. (eds) (1991) *Directors of Development: Influences on the Development of Children's Thinking*, Hillsdale, NJ: Erlbaum.

O'Keefe, J. and Nadel, L. (1978) *The Hippocampus as a Cognitive Map*, Oxford: Clarendon Press.

Olson, D. R. (1977) 'From utterance to text: the bias of language in speech and writing', *Harvard Educational Review* 47: 257–81.

Olson, D. R. (ed.) (1980a) *The Social Foundations of Language and Thought: Essays in Honor of Jerome S. Bruner*, New York: Norton.

Olson, D. R. (1980b) 'Some social aspects of mearning in oral and written language', in D. R. Olson (ed.) *The Social Foundations of Language and Thought: Essays in Honor of Jerome S. Bruner*, New York: Norton.

Olson, D. R. (1988) 'On the origins of beliefs and other intentional states in children', in J. W. Astington, P. L. Harris and D. R. Olson (eds) *Developing Theories of Mind*, Cambridge: Cambridge University Press.

Olson, D. R. and Astington, J. W. (1986) 'Children's acquisition of metalinguistic and metacognitive verbs', in W. Demopoulos and A. Marras (eds) *Language Learning and Concept Acquisition*, Norwood, NJ: Ablex.

Olson, D. R. and Torrance, N. G. (1983) 'Literacy and cognitive development', in S. Meadows (ed.) *Developing Thinking*, London: Methuen.

Olson, D. R. and Torrance, N. (eds) (1991) *Literacy and Orality*, Cambridge: Cambridge University Press.

Olson, S. L., Bates, J. E. and Bayles, K. (1985) 'Mother–infant interaction and the development of individual differences in children's cognitive competence', *Developmental Psychology* 20: 166–79.

Olson, S. L., Bates, J. E. and Kaskie, B. (1992) 'Caregiver–infant interaction antecedents of children's school-age cognitive ability', *Merrill-Palmer Quarterly* 38: 309–30.

Opie, I. and Opie, P. (1967) *The Lore and Language of Schoolchildren*, London: Oxford University Press.

Opie, I. and Opie, P. (1969) *Children's Games in Street and Playground*, Oxford: Clarendon Press.

Opie, I. and Opie, P. (1985) *The Singing Game*, Oxford: Oxford University Press.

Orbach, I., Gross, Y., Glaubman, H. and Berman, D. (1985) 'Children's perception of death in humans and animals as a function of age, anxiety and cognitive ability', *Journal of Child Psychology and Psychiatry* 26: 453–63.

Ornstein, P. A. and Naus, M. J. (1985) 'Effects of the knowledge base on children's memory knowledge', in H. W. Reese (ed.) *Advances in Child Development and Behaviour*, vol. 19, New York: Academic Press.

Ornstein, P. A., Baker-Ward, L. and Naus, M. J. (1988) 'The development of children's mnemonic skills', in F. Weinert and M. Perlmutter (eds) *Memory Development: Universal Changes and Individual Development*, Hillsdale, NJ: Erlbaum.

Orton, A. (1987) *Learning Mathematics: Issues, Theory and Classroom Practice*, London: Cassell.

Ortony, A. (1988) 'Metaphor', in R. L. Gregory (ed.) *The Oxford Companion to the Mind*, Oxford: Oxford University Press.

Palermo, D. S. (1989) 'Knowledge and the child's developing theory of the world', *Advances in Child Development and Behaviour* 21: 269–97.

Palincsar, A. and Brown, A. L. (1984) 'Reciprocal teaching of comprehension-fostering and monitoring activities', *Cognition and Instruction* 1: 117–75.

Palisin, H. (1986) 'Preschool temperament and performance on achievement tests', *Developmental Psychology* 22: 766–70.

Panksepp, J. (1990) 'Gray zones at the emotion/cognition interface: a commentary', *Cognition and Emotion* 4: 289–302.

Papousek, H. (1967) 'Experimental studies of appetitional behaviour in human newborns and infants', in H. W. Stevenson, E. H. Hess and H. L. Rheingold (eds) *Early Behaviour*, New York: Wiley.

Paradis, M. and Lebrun, Y. (1984) *Early Bilingualism and Child Development*, Lisse: Swets & Zeitlinger.

Paris, S. G. (1978) 'The development of inference and transformation as memory operations', in P. A. Ornstein (ed.) *Memory Development in Children*, Hillsdale, NJ: Erlbaum.

Paris, S. G. and Jacobs, J. E. (1984) 'The benefits of informed instruction for children's reading awareness and comprehension skills', *Child Development* 55: 2083–93.

Paris, S. G. and Lindauer, B.K. (1978) 'Constructive aspects of children's comprehension and memory', in R. V.Kail and J. W. Hagen (eds) *Perspectives on the Development of Memory and Cognition*, Hillsdale NJ: Erlbaum.

Parke, R. (1989) 'Social development in infancy: a 25-year perspective', in H. W. Reese (ed.) *Advances in Child Development and Behaviour*, vol. 21. New York: Academic Press.

Parkes, C. M. (1972) *Bereavement: Studies in Grief in Adult Life*, London: Tavistock.

Parkins, E. J. (1988) 'Equilibration and cognition: a review and elaboration of Piaget's genetic epistemology', *Genetic, Social and General Psychology Monographs*, 114(1): 77–96.

Pascual-Leone, J. (1970) 'A mathematical model for the transition rule in Piaget's developmental stages', *Acta Psychologica* 32: 301–45.

Pask, G. (1988) 'Learning strategies, teaching strategies and conceptual or learning style', in R. R. Schmeck (ed.) *Learning Strategies and Learning Styles*, New York: Plenum Press.

Patterson, C. J., Kupersmidt, J. B. and Vaden, N. A. (1990) 'Income level, gender, ethnicity and household composition as predictors of children's school-based competence', *Child Development* 61: 485–94.

Patterson, K. E. and Morton J. (1985) 'From orthography to phonology: an attempt at an old interpretation', in K. E. Patterson, J. C. Marshall and M. Coltheart (eds) *Surface Dyslexia: Neuropsychological and Cognitive Studies of Phonological Reading*, Hillsdale, NJ: Erlbaum.

Peery, J. C., Peery, I. W. and Draper, T. W. (1987) *Music and Child Development*, New York: Springer-Verlag.

Pellegrini, A. D., Perlmutter, J. C., Galda, L. and Brody, G. H. (1990) 'Joint reading between black Head Start children and their mothers', *Child Development* 61: 443–53.

Pellegrini, D. S., Masten, A. S., Garmezy, N. and Ferrarese, M. J. (1987) 'Correlates of social and academic competence in middle childhood', *Journal of Child Psychology and Psychiatry* 28: 699–714.

Pennington, B. F. (1990) 'The genetics of dyslexia', *Journal of Child Psychology and Psychiatry* 31(2): 193–201.

Perera, K. (1984) *Children's Writing and Reading: Analysing Classroom Language*, Oxford: Blackwell.

Perfetti, C. A., Beck, I., Bell, L. C. and Hughes, C. (1987) 'Phonemic knowledge and learning to read are reciprocal: a longitudinal study of first-grade children', *Merrill-Palmer Quarterly* 33(3): 283–319.

Perkins, D. N. (1981) *The Mind's Best Work*, Cambridge, Mass.: Harvard University Press.

Perkins, D. N. (1988) 'Creativity', in R. J. Sternberg and E. E. Smith (eds) *The Psychology of Human Thought*, Cambridge: Cambridge University Press.

Perlmutter, M. (ed.) (1980) *New Directions for Child Development*, vol. 10, *Children's Memory*, San Francisco: Jossey-Bass.

Perlmutter, M. (ed.) (1985) *Intellectual development: Minnesota Symposium on Child Psychology*, vol. 19, Hillsdale, NJ: Erlbaum.

Perner, J. (1988a) 'Developing semantics for theories of mind: from propositional attitudes to mental representation', in J. W. Astington, P. L. Harris and D. R. Olson (eds) *Developing Theories of Mind*, Cambridge: Cambridge University Press.

Perner, J. (1988b) 'Higher-order beliefs and intentions in children's understanding of social interaction', in J. W. Astington, P. L. Harris and D. R. Olson (eds) *Developing Theories of Mind*, Cambridge: Cambridge University Press.

Perner, J. (1991a) *Understanding the Representational Mind*, Cambridge, Mass.: MIT Press.

Perner, J. (1991b) 'On representing that: the asymmetry between belief and desire in children's theory of mind', in D. Frye and C. Moore (eds) *Children's Theories of mind: Mental States and Social Understanding*, Hove: Erlbaum.

Perner, J. and Davies, G. (1991) 'Understanding the mind as an active information processor: do young children have a "copy theory of mind"?', *Cognition* 39: 51–69.

Perner, J. and Ogden, J. E. (1988) 'Knowledge for hunger: children's problem with representation in imputing mental states', *Cognition* 29: 47–61.

Perner, J., Leekam, S. and Wimmer, H. (1987) 'Three-year olds' difficulty with false belief: the case for a conceptual deficit', *British Journal of Developmental Psychology* 5: 125–37.

Perner, J., Frith, U., Leslie, A. M. and Leekam, S. R. (1989) 'Exploration of the autistic child's theory of mind: knowledge, belief and communication', *Child Development* 60: 689–700.

Perrett, D. I. *et al.* (1985) 'Visual analysis of movements by neurones in the temporal cortex of the macaque monkey: a preliminary report', *Behavioural Brain Research* 16: 153–70.

Perret-Clermont, A.-N. (1980) *Social Interaction and Cognitive Development*, London: Academic Press.

Perret-Clermont, A.-N. and Brossard, A. (1985) 'On the interdigitation of social and cognitive processes', in R. A. Hinde, A.-N. Perret-Clermont and J. Stevenson-Hinde (eds) *Social Relationships and Cognitive Development*, Oxford: Clarendon Press.

Perret-Clermont, A.-N. and Schubauer-Leoni, M. L. (1981) 'Conflict and cooperation as opportunities for learning', in W. P. Robinson (ed.) *Communication in Development*, London: Academic Press.

Peskin, J. (1992) 'Ruse and representations: on children's ability to conceal information', *Developmental Psychology* 28: 84–9.

Peters, A. M. (1983) *The Units of Language Acquisition*, Cambridge: Cambridge University Press.

Peters, M. (1991) 'Sex differences in human brain size and the general meaning of differences in brain size', *Canadian Journal of Psychology* 45: 507–22.

Pettit, G. S., Dodge, K. A. and Brown, M. M. (1988) 'Early family experience, social problem solving patterns, and children's social competence', *Child Development* 59: 107–20.

Phillips, J. (1980) 'Kaspar Hauser', *The Times*, Saturday 16 August: 7.

Piaget, J. (1929) *The Child's Conception of the World*, London: Routledge & Kegan Paul.

Piaget, J. (1930) *The Child's Conception of Physical Causality*, London: Routledge & Kegan Paul.

Piaget, J. (1932) *The Moral Judgment of the Child*, Harmondsworth: Penguin Books.

Piaget, J. (1952) *The Child's Conception of Number*, New York: Basic Books.

Piaget, J. (1954) *The Construction of Reality in the Child*, New York: Basic Books.

Piaget, J. (1959) *The Language and Thought of the Child*, London: Routledge & Kegan Paul.

Piaget, J. (1962) *Play, Dreams and Imitation in Childhood*, New York: Norton.

Piaget, J. (1968) *Six Psychological Studies*, London: University of London Press.

Piaget, J. (1969) *The Child's Conception of Time*, London: Routledge & Kegan Paul.

Piaget, J. (1970) *Genetic Epistemology*, New York: Columbia University Press.

Piaget, J. (1971a) 'The theory of stages in cognitive development', in D. R. Green, M. P. Ford and G. B. Flanner (eds) *Measurement and Piaget*, New York: McGraw-Hill.

Piaget, J. (1971b) *Biology and Knowledge*, Edinburgh: Edinburgh University Press.

Piaget, J. (1971c) *Sructuralism*, London: Routledge & Kegan Paul.

Piaget, J. (1977) *The Grasp of Consciousness: Action and Concept in the Young Child*, London: Routledge & Kegan Paul.

Piaget, J. (1978a) *The Development of Thought: Equilibration of Cognitive Structures*, Oxford: Blackwell.

Piaget, J. (1978b) *Success and Understanding*, London: Routledge & Kegan Paul.

Piaget, J. (1983) 'Piaget's theory', in W. Kessen (ed.) *Handbook of Child Psychology*, vol. 1, series ed. P. H. Mussen (previously published 1970 in P. H. Mussen (ed.) *Carmichael's Manual of Child Psychology*, 3rd edn, vol. 1, New York: Wiley.

Piaget, J. and Inhelder, B. (1956) *The Child's Conception of Space*, London: Routledge & Kegan Paul.

Piaget, J. and Inhelder, B. (1969) *The Psychology of the Child*, London: Routledge & Kegan Paul.

Piaget, J., Inhelder, B. and Szeminska, A. (1960) *The Child's Conception of Geometry*, London: Routledge & Kegan Paul.

Piatelli-Palmarini, M. (1989) 'Evolution, selection and cognition: from "learning" to parameter setting in biology and in the study of language', *Cognition* 31: 1–44.

Pick, H. L. and Lockman, J. J. (1981) 'From frames of reference to spatial representations', in L. S. Liben, A. H. Patterson and N. Newcombe (eds) *Spatial Representation and Behaviour across the Life Span*, New York: Academic Press.

Pillemer, D. B. and White, S. H. (1989) 'Childhood events recalled by children and adults', in H. W. Reese (ed.) *Advances in Child Development and Behaviour*, vol. 21, New York: Academic Press.

Pillemer, D. B., Goldsmith, L. R., Panter, A. T. and White, S. H. (1988) 'Very long-term memories of the first year in college', *Journal of Experimental Psychology: Learning, Memory and Cognition* 14: 709–15.

Pillemer, K. and McCartney, K. (eds) (1991) *Parent–child Relations Throughout Life*, Hillsdale, NJ: Erlbaum.

Pilling, D. (1990) *Escape from Disadvantage*, London: Falmer Press.

Pilling, D. (1992) 'Escaping from a bad start', in B. Tizard and V. Varma (eds) *Vulnerability and Resilience in Human Development*, London: Jessica Kingsley.

Pillow, B. H. (1988a) 'The development of children's beliefs about the mental world', *Merrill-Palmer Quarterly* 34(1): 1–32.

Pillow, B. H. (1988b) 'Young children's understanding of attentional limits', *Child Development* 59: 38–46.

Pillow, B. H. (1989) 'Early understanding of perception as a source of knowledge', *Journal of Experimental Child Psychology* 47: 116–29.

Pine, J. M. (1992) 'How referential are "referential" children? Relationships between maternal-report and obervational measures of vocabulary composition and usage', *Journal of Child Language* 19: 75–86.

Plomin, R. (1986) *Development, Genetics and Psychology*, Hillsdale, NJ: Erlbaum.

Plomin, R. (1989) 'Environment and genes: determinants of behavior', *American Psychologist* 44: 105–11.

Plomin, R. (1990a) *Nature and Nurture*, Pacific Grove, Calif.: Brooks/Cole.

Plomin, R. (1990b) 'The role of inheritance in behaviour', *Science* 248: 183–8.

Plomin, R. (1991) 'Behavioural genetics', in P. R. McHugh and V. A. McKusick (eds) *Genes, Brain and Behavior*, New York: Raven Press.

Plomin, R. and Daniels, D. (1987) 'Why are children in the same family so different from one another?', *Behavioral and Brain Sciences* 10: 1–60.

Plomin, R. and Rende, R. (1991) 'Human behavioral genetics', *Annual Review of Psychology* 42: 161–90.

Pool, D. L., Shweder, R. A. and Much, N. C. (1983) 'Culture as a cognitive system: differentiated rule understandings in children and other savages', in E. T. Higgins, D. N. Ruble and W. W. Hartrup (eds) *Social Cognition and Social Development: a Socio-Cultural Perspective*, Cambridge: Cambridge University Press.

Poortinga, Y. P. and van de Vijver, F. J. R. (1988) 'Culturally invariant parameters of cognitive functioning', in J. W. Berry, S. H. Irvine and E. B. Hunt (eds) *Indigenous Cognition: Functioning in Cultural Contexts*, Dordrecht: Martinus Nijhoff.

Popper, K. R. (1967) *Objective Knowledge*, Oxford: Clarendon Press.

Popper, K. R. and Eccles, J. C. (1977) *The Self and its Brain*, Berlin: Springer-Verlag.

Poulsen, D., Kintsch, E., Kintsch, W. and Premack, D. (1979) 'Children's comprehension and memory for stories', *Journal of Experimental Child Psychology* 28: 379–403.

Pound, A., Mills, M., Puckering, C. and Cox, A. (1982) 'Maternal depression and family functioning', in C. M. Parkes and J. Stevenson-Hinde (eds) *The Place of Attachment in Human Behaviour*, London: Tavistock.

Prather, P. A. and Bacon, J. (1986) 'Developmental differences in part–whole identification', *Child Development* 57: 549–58.

Pratt, C. and Bryant, P. E. (1990) 'Young children understand that looking leads to knowing (so long as they are looking into a single barrel)', *Child Development* 61: 973–82.

Pressley, M. and Levin, J. R. (1980) 'The development of mental imagery retrieval', *Child Development* 51: 558–60.

Pressley, M., Borkowski, J. G. and O'Sullivan, J. (1985) 'Children's metamemory and the teaching of memory strategies', in D. L. Forrest-Pressley, G. E. Mackinnon and T. G. Waller (eds) *Metacognition, Cognition and Human Performance*, vol. 1, Orlando, Fla.: Academic Press.

Pressley, M., Forrest-Pressley, D. L., Elliott-Faust, D. and Miller, G. E. (1985) 'Children's use of cognitive strategies, how to teach strategies, and what to do if they can't be taught', in M. Pressley and C. J. Brainerd (eds) *Cognitive Learning and Memory in Children*, New York: Springer-Verlag.

Pressley, M., Snyder, B. L. and Cariglia-Bull, T. (1987) 'How can good strategy use be taught to children? Evaluation of six alternative approaches', in S. M. Cormier and D. J. Hagman (eds) *Transfer of Learning: Contemporary Research and Applications*, San Diego, Calif.: Academic Press.

Presson, C. C. (1982) 'The development of map reading skills', *Child Development* 53: 196–9.

Presson, C. C. (1987) 'The development of spatial cognition: secondary uses of spatial information', in N. Eisenberg (ed.) *Contemporary Topics in Developmental Psychology*, New York: Wiley.

Puckering, C. and Rutter, M. (1987) 'Environmental influences on language development', in W. Yule and M. Rutter (eds) *Language Development and Disorders*, London: MacKeith Press and Oxford: Blackwell Scientific Publications.

Pumphrey, P. and Elliot, C. (eds) (1990) *Children's Difficulties in Reading, Spelling and Writing*, London: Falmer Press.

Pyeritz, R. E. (1991) 'Formal genetics in humans: Mendelian and non-Mendelian inheritance', in P. R. McHugh and V. A. McKusick (eds) *Genes, Brain and Behaviour*, New York: Raven Press.

Pylyshyn, Z. W. (1978) 'When is attribution of beliefs justified?', *Behavioral and Brain Sciences* 1: 592–3.

Pylyshyn, Z. W. (1980) 'Computation and cognition: issues in the foundation of cognitive science', *Behavioral and Brain Sciences* 3: 111–34.

Pylyshyn, Z. W. (1981) 'The imagery debate: analogue media versus tacit knowledge', *Psychological Review* 88: 16–45.

Quinton, D. and Rutter M. (1988) *Parenting Breakdown: the Making and Breaking of Inter-generational Links*, Aldershot: Avebury.

Raab, G. M., Thomson, G. O. B., Boyd, L., Fulton, M. and Laxen, D. P. H. (1990) 'Blood lead levels, reaction time, inspection time and ability in Edinburgh children', *British Journal of Developmental Psychology* 8: 101–18.

Rabbitt, P. M. A. (1988) 'Human intelligence', *Quarterly Journal of Experimental Psychology* 40A: 167–85.

Rachlin, H. (1989) *Judgment, decision and choice*, San Francisco: Freeman.

Radford, J. (1990) *Child Prodigies and Exceptional Early Achievers*, Lewes: Harvester.

Radke-Yarrow, M. (1991) 'The individual and the environment in human behavioural development', in P. Bateson (ed.) *The Development and Integration of Behaviour*, Cambridge: Cambridge University Press.

Radke-Yarrow, M. and Kuczynski, L. (1983) 'Perspectives and strategies in child-rearing: studies of rearing by normal and depressed mothers', in D. Magnusson and V. Allen (eds) *Human Development: An Interactional Perspective*, New York: Academic Press.

Radke-Yarrow, M. and Sherman, T. (1985) 'Interaction of cognition and emotions in development', in R. A. Hinde, A.-N. Perret-Clermont and J. Stevenson-Hinde (eds) *Social Relationships and Cognitive Development*, Oxford: Clarendon Press.

Radke-Yarrow, M., Belmont, B., Nottelmann, E. and Bottomly, L. (1990) 'Young children's self-conceptions: origins in the natural discourse of depressed and normal mothers and their children', in D. Cichetti and M. Beeghly (eds) *The Self in Transition*, Chicago: University of Chicago Press.

Raven, J. (1980) *Parents, Teachers and Children: a Study of an Educational Home*

*Visiting Scheme*, London: Hodder & Stoughton, for the Scottish Council for Research in Education.

Raymond, C. L. and Benbow, C. P. (1986) 'Gender differences in mathematics: a function of parental support and student sex typing?', *Developmental Psychology* 22: 808–19.

Rebok, G. W. (1987) *Lifespan Cognitive Development*, New York: Holt, Rinehart & Winston.

Reddiford, G. (1980) 'Imagination, rationality and teaching', *Journal of Philosophy of Education* 14: 205–13.

Reese, H. W. (1989) 'Discrimination set learning in children', in H. W. Reese (ed.) *Advances in Child Development and Behaviour*, vol. 21, New York: Academic Press.

Resnick, L. B. (1983) 'A developmental theory of number understanding', in H. P. Ginsburg (ed.) *The Development of Mathematical Thinking*, New York: Academic Press.

Resnick, L. B. (1987a) 'Constructing knowledge in school', in L. S. Liben (ed.) *Development and Learning*, Hillsdale, NJ: Erlbaum.

Resnick, L. B. (1987b). *Education and Learning to Think*, Washington, DC: National Academy Press.

Resnick, L. B. (1987c) 'The development of mathematical intuition', in M. Perlmutter (ed.) *Minnesota Symposium on Child Psychology*, vol. 19, Hillsdale, NJ: Erlbaum.

Resnick, L. B. (1989a) 'Developing mathematical knowledge', *American Psychologist* 44: 162–9.

Resnick, L. B. (1989b) *Knowing, Learning and Instruction: Essays in Honor of Robert Glaser*, Hillsdale, NJ: Erlbaum.

Resnick, L. B. and Weaver, P. A. (1979) *Theory and Practice of Early Reading*, vols 1 and 2, Hillsdale, NJ: Erlbaum.

Resnick, L. B., Berenbaum, S. A., Gottesman, I. I. and Bouchard, T. J. (1986) 'Early hormonal influence on cognitive functioning in congenital adrenal hyperplasia', *Developmental Psychology* 22: 191–8.

Ricciuti, H. N. (1991) 'Malnutrition and cognitive development: research-policy linkages and current research directions', in L. Okagaki and R. J. Sternberg (eds) *Directors of Development: Influences on the Development of Children's Thinking*, Hillsdale, NJ: Erlbaum.

Rice, M. L. (1989) 'Children's language acquisition', *American Psychologist* 44: 149–56.

Rice, M. L. and Woodsmall, L. (1988) 'Lessons from television: children's word learning when viewing', *Child Development* 59: 420–9.

Richardson, K. (1991) *Understanding Intelligence*, Milton Keynes: Open University Press.

Richardson, S. A. (1976) 'The relation of severe malnutrition in infancy to the intelligence of school children with differing life histories', *Pediatric Research* 10: 57–61.

Richardson, S. A. (1984) 'The consequences of malnutrition for intellectual development', in J. Dobbing (ed.) *Scientific Studies in Mental Retardation*, London: Royal Society of Medicine, and Macmillan.

Richman, N., Stevenson, J. and Graham, P. (1982) *Pre-school to School: a Behavioural Study*, London: Academic Press.

Riding, R. J. (ed.) (1991) 'Learning styles', double issue of *Educational Psychology* 11(3 and 4): 193–393.

Riding, R. and Mathias, D. (1991) 'Cognitive styles and preferred learning mode, reading attainment and cognitive ability in 11 year old children', *Educational Psychology* 11: 383-93.

Rieben, L. and Perfetti, C. A. (1991) *Learning to Read*, Hove: Erlbaum.

Rieder, C. and Cicchetti, D. (1989) 'An organisational perspective on cognitive control functioning and cognitive-affective balance in maltreated children', *Developmental Psychology* 25: 482-93.

Riley, M. S., Greeno, J. G. and Heller, J. I. (1983) 'The development of children's problem-solving ability in arithmetic', in H. P. Ginsburg (ed.) *The Development of Mathematical Thinking*, New York: Academic Press.

Rizzo, T. A. and Corsaro, W. A. (1988) 'Toward a better understanding of Vygotsky's process of internalisation: its role in the development of the concept of friendship', *Developmental Review* 8: 219-37.

Roberts, G. C., Block, J. H. and Block, J. (1984) 'Continuity and change in parents' child-rearing practices', *Child Development* 55: 586-97.

Robins, L. and Rutter M. (1991) *Straight and Devious Pathways from Childhood to Adulthood*, Cambridge: Cambridge University Press.

Robinson, E. J. (1983) 'Metacognitive development', in S. Meadows (ed.) *Developing Thinking*, London: Methuen.

Robinson, E. J. and Mitchell, P. (1992) 'Children's interpretation of messages from a speaker with a false belief', *Child Development* 63: 639-52.

Robinson, E. J. and Robinson, W. P. (1977) 'Development in the understanding of the cause of success and failure in verbal communication', *Cognition* 5: 363-78.

Robinson, E. J. and Robinson, W. P. (1978) 'Development of understanding about communication: message inadequacy and its role in causing communication failure', *Genetic Psychology Monographs* 98: 233-79.

Robinson, E. J. and Robinson, W. P. (1980) 'Egocentrism in verbal referential communication', in M. V. Cox (ed.) *Are Young Children Egocentric?*, London: Batsford.

Robinson, E. J. and Robinson, W. P. (1981) 'Ways of reacting to communication failure in relation to the development of children's understanding about verbal communication', *European Journal of Social Psychology* 11: 189-208.

Robinson, E. J. and Robinson, W. P. (1982) 'The achievement of children's verbal referential communication skills: the role of metacognitive guidance', *International Journal of Behavioural Development* 5: 329-55.

Robinson, E. J. and Robinson, W. P. (1983) 'Communication and metacommunication: quality of children's instructions in relation to judgments about the adequacy of instructions and the locus of responsibility for communication failure', *Journal of Experimental Child Psychology* 36: 305-20.

Robinson, F. P. (1946) *Effective Study*, New York: Harper & Row.

Rodgers, B. (1983) 'The identification and prevalence of specific reading retardation', *British Journal of Educational Psychology* 53: 369-73.

Rodriguez, R. (1980) 'An education in language', in L. Michaels and C. Ricks (eds) *The State of the Language*, Berkeley, Calif.: University of California Press.

Roe, A. (1979) 'A psychologist examines sixty-four eminent scientists', in P. E. Vernon (ed.) *Creativity: Selected Readings*, Harmondsworth: Penguin Books.

Rogers, C. (1978) 'The child's perception of other people', in H. McGurk (ed.) *Issues in Childhood Social Development*, London: Methuen.

Rogoff, B. (1982) 'Integrating context or cognitive development', in M. E. Lamb and A. L. Brown (eds) *Advances in Developmental Psychology*, vol. 2, Hillsdale, NJ: Erlbaum.

Rogoff, B. (1986) 'Adult assistance of children's learning', in T. E. Raphael (ed.) *The Contexts of School Based Literacy*, New York: Random House.

Rogoff, B. (1990) *Apprenticeship in Thinking*, Oxford: Oxford University Press.

Rogoff, B. and Gardner, W. (1984) 'Adult guidance of cognitive development', in B. Rogoff and J. Lave (eds) *Everyday Cognition: its Development in Social Context*, Cambridge, Mass.: Harvard University Press.

Rogoff, B. and Lave, J. (eds) (1984) *Everyday Cognition: Its Development in Social Context*, Cambridge, Mass.: Harvard University Press.

Rondal, J. (1987) 'Language development and mental retardation', in W. Yule and M. Rutter (eds) *Language Development and Disorders*, London: MacKeith Press and Oxford: Blackwell Scientific Publications.

Rosa, A., Ochaita, E., Moreno, E., Fernandez, E., Carretero, M. and Pozo, J. (1984) 'Cognitive development in blind children: a challenge to Piagetian theory', *Quarterly Newsletter of the Laboratory of Comparative Human Cognition* 6: 75–81.

Rosch, E. H. (1978) 'Principles of categorization', in E. H. Rosch and B. B. Lloyd (eds) *Cognition and Categorization*, Hillsdale, NJ: Erlbaum.

Rosch, E. H. (1981) 'Prototype classification and logical classification: the two systems', in E. Scholnick (ed.) *New Trends in Cognitive Representation: Challenges to Piaget's Theory*, Hillsdale, NJ: Erlbaum.

Rosch, E. H. and Lloyd, B. B. (eds) (1978) *Cognition and Categorization*, Hillsdale, NJ: Erlbaum.

Rosch, E. H., Mervis, C. B., Gray, W. D., Johnson, D. M. and Boyes-Braem, P. (1976) 'Basic objects in natural categories', *Cognitive Psychology* 8: 382–439.

Rose, D. H., Slater, A. S. and Perry, J. (1986) 'Prediction of childhood intelligence from habituation in early infancy', *Intelligence* 10: 251–63.

Rose, K. (1983) *King George V*, London: Weidenfeld.

Rose, S. A. and Blank, M. (1974) 'The potency of context in children's cognition: an illustration through conservation', *Child Development* 45: 499–502.

Rose, S. A., Feldman, J. F. and Wallace, I. F. (1988) 'Individual differences in infants' information processing: reliability, stability and prediction', *Child Development* 59: 1177–97.

Rose, S. P. R. (1981) 'What should a biochemistry of learning and memory be about?', *Neuroscience* 6: 811–21.

Rose, S. P. R. (1988) 'Memory: biological bases', in R. L. Gregory (ed.) *The Oxford Companion to the Mind*, Oxford: Oxford University Press.

Rosengren, K. S., Gelman, S. A., Kalish, C. W. and McCormick, K. (1991) 'As time goes by: children's early understanding of growth in animals', *Child Development* 62: 1302–20.

Rosenshine, B. (1987) 'Direct instruction', in M. J. Durkin (ed.) *The International Encyclopedia of Teaching and Teacher Education*, 257–63, Oxford: Pergamon.

Ross, L. (1981) 'The "intuitive scientist" formulation and its developmental implications', in J. H. Flavell and L. Ross (eds) *Social Cognitive Development*, Cambridge: Cambridge University Press.

Rotman, B. (1977) *Jean Piaget: Psychologist of the Real*, Hassocks, Sussex: Harvester Press.

Rovee-Collier, C. and Hayne, H. (1987) 'Reactivation of infant memory: implications for cognitive development', in H. W. Reese (ed.) *Advances in Child Development and Behavior*, New York: Academic Press.

Rovet, J. and Netley, C. (1982) 'Processing deficits in Turner's syndrome', *Developmental Psychology*, 18(1): 77–94.

Ruble, D. N. and Nakamura, C. Y. (1972) 'Task orientation versus social orientation in young children and their attention to relevant social cues', *Child Development* 43: 471–80.

Ruffman, T. K. and Olson, D. R. (1989) 'Children's ascription of knowledge to others', *Developmental Psychology* 25: 601–6.

Ruffman, T., Olson, D. R. and Astington, J. W. (1991) 'Children's understanding of visual ambiguity', in G. Butterworth, P. L. Harris, A. M. Leslie, and H. M. Wellman (eds) *Perspectives on the Child's Theory of Mind*, Oxford: Oxford University Press.

Rumelhart, D. E. (1977) 'Toward an interactive model of reading', in S. Dornic (ed.) *Attention and Performance*, vol. 6, Hillsdale, NJ: Erlbaum.

Rumelhart, D. E. (1989) 'Toward a microstructural account of human reasoning', in S. Vosniadou and A. Ortony (eds) *Similarity and Analogical Reasoning*, Cambridge: Cambridge University Press.

Rumelhart, D. E. and McClelland, J. L. (eds) (1986) *Parallel Distributed Processing: Explorations in the Microstructure of Cognition*, Cambridge, Mass.: MIT Press.

Rumsey, J. M. and Rapoport, J. L. (1983) 'Assessing behavioral and cognitive effects of diet in pediatric populations', in R. J. Wurtman and J. J. Wurtman, *Nutrition and the Brain*, vol. 6, *Physiological and Behavioral Effects of Food Constituents*, New York: Raven Press.

Ruse, M. (1986) *Taking Darwin Seriously: A Naturalistic Approach to Philosophy*, Oxford: Blackwell.

Russell, J. (1978) *The Acquisition of Knowledge*, London: Macmillan.

Russell, J. (1981) 'Dyadic interaction in a logical reasoning problem requiring inclusion ability', *Child Development* 51: 1322–5.

Russell, J. (1981) 'Why "socio-cognitive conflict" may be impossible: the status of egocentric errors in the dyadic performance of a spatial task', *Educational Psychology* 1: 159–69.

Russell, J. (1982) 'Propositional attitudes', in M. Beveridge (ed.) *Children Thinking Through Language*, London: Edward Anold.

Russell, J. (1984) *Explaining Mental Life: Some Philosophical Issues in Psychology*, London: Macmillan.

Russell, J. (1988) 'Making judgments about thoughts and things', in J. W. Astington, P. L. Harris and D. R. Olson (eds) *Developing Theories of Mind*, Cambridge: Cambridge University Press.

Russell, J., Mills, I. and Reiff-Musgrove, P. (1990) 'The role of symmetrical and asymmetrical social conflict in cognitive change', *Journal of Experimental Child Psychology* 49: 58–78.

Rutter, M. (1978) 'Early sources of security and competence', in J. S. Bruner and A. Garton (eds) *Human Growth and Development*, Oxford: Oxford University Press.

Rutter, M. (1981) *Maternal Deprivation Reassessed*, Harmondsworth: Penguin Books.

Rutter, M. (1983a) 'Cognitive deficits in the pathogenesis of autism', *Journal of Child Psychology and Psychiatry* 24: 513–31.

Rutter, M. (1983b) 'Low level lead exposure: sources, effects and implications', in M. Rutter and R. R. Jones (eds) *Lead versus Health*, Chichester: Wiley.

Rutter, M. (1985a) 'Family and school influences on behavioural development', *Journal of Child Psychology and Psychiatry* 26: 349–68.

Rutter, M. (1985b) 'Family and school influences on cognitive development', *Journal of Child Psychology and Psychiatry* 26(5): 683–704.

Rutter, M. (ed.) (1988) *Studies of Psychosocial Risk: the Power of Longitudinal Data*, Cambridge: Cambridge University Press.

Rutter, M. (1990) 'Commentary: some focus and process considerations regarding effects of parental depression on children', *Developmental Psychology* 26: 60–7.

Rutter, M. (1991) 'A fresh look at "maternal deprivation" ', in P. Bateson (ed.) *The Development and Integration of Behaviour*, Cambridge: Cambridge University Press.

Rutter, M. (1992) 'Nature, nurture and psychopathology: a new look at an old topic', in B. Tizard and V. Varma (eds) *Vulnerability and Resilience in Human Development*, London: Jessica Kingsley.

Rutter, M. and Giller, H. (1983) *Juvenile Delinquency*, Harmondsworth: Penguin Books.

Rutter, M. and Jones, R. R. (eds) (1983) *Lead Versus Health: Sources and Effects of Low Level Lead Exposure*, Chichester: Wiley.

Rutter, M. and Madge, N. (1976) *Cycles of Disadvantage*, London: Heinemann.

Rutter, M. and Schopler, E. (eds) (1978) *Autism: a Reappraisal of Concepts and Treatment*, New York: Plenum Press.

Rutter, M. and Yule, W. (1976) 'Reading difficulties', in M. Rutter and L. Hersov (eds) *Child Psychiatry: Modern Approaches*, Oxford: Blackwell.

Rutter, M., Izard, C. E. and Read, P. B. (1986) *Depression in Young People: Developmental and Clinical Perspectives*, New York: Guilford Press.

Rutter, M., Maughan, B., Mortimore, P. and Ouston, J., with Smith, A. (1979) *Fifteen Thousand Hours: Secondary Schools and their Effects on Children*, London: Open Books.

Rutter, M., Tizard, J., Yule, W., Graham, P. and Whitmore, K. (1976) 'Research report: Isle of Wight studies 1964–1974', *Psychological Medicine* 6: 313–32.

Ryan, E. B., Ledger, G. W. and Weed, K. A. (1987) 'Acquisition and transfer of an integrative imagery strategy by young children', *Child Development* 58: 443–52.

Ryle, G. (1949) *The Concept of Mind*, London: Hutchinson.

Saarni, C. (1990) 'Emotional competence: how emotions and relationships become integrated', in R. A. Thompson (ed.) *Socioemotional development: Nebraska Symposium on Motivation, 1988*, vol. 36. Lincoln, Nebr.: University of Nebraska Press.

Sacks, O. (1985) *The Man Who Mistook his Wife for a Hat*, London: Duckworth.

Salt, P., Galler, J. R. and Ramsey, F. C. (1988) 'The influence of early malnutrition on subsequent behavioral development: VII, The effects of maternal depressive symptoms', *Developmental and Behavioral Pediatrics* 9: 1–5.

Santostefano, S. (1985) *Cognitive Control Therapy with Children and Adolescents*, Elmsford, NY: Pergamon Press.

Saracho, O. (1985) 'Young children's play behaviours and cognitive ages', *Early Child Development and Care* 22: 1–18.

Sartre, J.-P. (1972) *The Psychology of Imagination*, London: Methuen.

Satterly, D. J. (1976) 'Cognitive styles, spatial ability and school achievement', *Journal of Educational Psychology* 68: 36–42.

Saunders, G. (1988) *Bilingual Children*, Clevedon, Pa.: Multilingual Matters.

Saxe, G. B. (1988) 'The mathematics of child street vendors', *Child Development* 59: 1415–25.

Saxe, G. B., Guberman, S. R. and Gearhart, M. (1987) 'Social processes in early number development', *Monographs of the Society for Research in Child Development* 52(2): serial no. 216.

Scardamalia, M. (1977) 'Information processing capacity and the problem of horizontal *décalage*: a demonstration using combinatorial reasoning tasks', *Child Development* 48: 28–37.

Scardamalia, M. (1981) 'How children cope with the cognitive demands of writing', in C. H. Fredericksen and J. F. Dominic (eds) *Writing: the Nature, Development and Teaching of Written Communication*, vol. 2, Hillsdale, NJ: Erlbaum.

Scardamalia, M. and Bereiter, C. (1983) 'The development of evaluative, diagnostic and remedial capabilities in children's composing', in M. Martlew (ed.) *The Psychology of Written Language: Development and Educational Perspectives*, Chichester: Wiley.

Scardamalia, M. and Bereiter, C. (1986) 'Writing', in R. F. Dillon and R. J. Sternberg (eds) *Cognition and Instruction*, New York: Academic Press.

Scarr, S. (1985) 'Constructing psychology: making facts and fables for our times', *American Psychologist* 40: 499–512.

Scarr, S. (1992) 'Developmental theories for the 90s: development and individual differences', *Child Development* 63: 1–19.

Scarr, S. and Carter-Saltzman, L. (1982) 'Genetics and intelligence', in R. Sternberg (ed.) *Handbook of Human Intelligence*, Cambridge: Cambridge University Press.

Scarr, S. and Kidd, K. K. (1983) 'Developmental behaviour genetics', in P. H. Mussen (ed.) *Handbook of Child Psychology*, vol. 2, New York: Wiley.

Scarr, S. and McCartney, K. (1983) 'How people make their own environments: a theory of genotype → environment effects', *Child Development* 54: 424–35.

Scarr, S. and Weinberg, R. A. (1983) 'The Minnesota adoption studies: genetic differences and malleability', *Child Development* 54: 260–7.

Schachter, F. F. (1982) 'Sibling deidentification and split-parent identification: a family trend', in M. Lamb and B. Sutton-Smith (eds) *Sibling Relationships*, Hillsdale, NJ: Erlbaum.

Schafer, E. W. (1982) 'Neural adaptability: a biological determinant of behavioural intelligence', *International Journal of Neuroscience* 17: 183–91.

Schaffer, H. R. (1992a) 'Early experience and the parent–child relationship: genetic and environmental interactions as developmental determinants', in B. Tizard and V. Varma (eds) *Vulnerability and Resilience in Human Development*, London: Jessica Kingsley.

Schaffer, H. R. (1992b) 'Joint involvement episodes as context for development', in H. McGurk (ed.) *Childhood Social Development*, Hove: Erlbaum.

Schaffer, H. R. and Crook, C. K. (1980) 'Child compliance and maternal control techniques', *Developmental Psychology* 16: 54–61.

Schank, R. C. (1980) 'Language and memory', *Cognitive Science* 4: 243–84.

Schank, R. C. and Abelson, R. (1977) *Scripts, Plans, Goals and Understanding*, Hillsdale, NJ: Erlbaum.

Schauble, L. (1990) 'Belief and revision in children: the role of prior knowledge and strategies for generating evidence', *Journal of Experimental Child Psychology* 49: 31–57.

Scheerens, J. and Creemers, B. P. M. (1989) 'Conceptualizing school effectiveness', *International Journal of Educational Research* 13(7): 691–706.

Schieffelin, B. B. and Cochran-Smith, M. (1984) 'Learning to read culturally: literacy before schooling', in H. Goelman, A. Oberg and F. Smith (eds) *Awakening to Literacy*, London: Heinemann.

Schiff, M. and Lewontin, R. (1986) *Education and Class: the Irrelevance of I.Q. Genetic Studies*, Oxford: Clarendon Press.

Schiff, M., Duyme, M., Dumaret, A. and Tomkiewicz, S. (1982) 'How much *could* we boost scholastic achievement and I.Q. scores: a direct answer from a French adoption study', *Cognition* 12: 165–96.

Schmeck, R. R. (1988) *Learning Strategies and Learning Styles*, New York: Plenum Press.

Schneider, W. (1985) 'Developmental trends in the metamemory–memory behavior relationship', in D. L. Forrest-Pressley, G. E. MacKinnon and T. G. Waller (eds)

*Metacognition, Cognition and Human Performance*, vol. 1, Orlando, Fla.: Academic Press.

Schneider, W. and Körkel, J. (1989) 'The knowledge base and text recall: evidence from a short-term longitudinal study', *Contemporary Educational Psychology* 14: 382–93.

Schneider, W. and Pressley, M. (1989) *Memory Development between 2 and 20*, Berlin: Springer-Verlag.

Schneider, W. and Weinert, P. E. (1990) 'Universal trends and individual differences in memory development', in A. de Ribaupierre (ed.) *Transition Mechanisms in Child Development*, Cambridge: Cambridge University Press.

Scholnick, E. K. and Wing, C. S. (1992) 'Speaking deductively: using conversation to trace the origins of conditional thought in children', *Merrill-Palmer Quarterly* 38: 1–20.

Schwartzman, H. (1978) *Transformations: the Anthropology of Children's Play*, New York: Plenum Press.

Scribner, S. (1985) 'Vygotsky's uses of history', in J. V. Wertsch (ed.) *Culture, Communication and Cognition*, Cambridge: Cambridge University Press.

Scribner, S. and Cole, M. (1981) *The Psychology of Literacy*, Cambridge, Mass.: Harvard University Press.

Searle, J. R. (1984) *Minds, Brains and Science*, Harmondsworth: Penguin Books.

Searle, J. R. (1990) 'Is the brain's mind a computer program?', *Scientific American*, January: 20–5.

Segal, J. W., Chipman, S. F. and Glaser, R. (eds) (1985) *Thinking and Learning Skills*, 2 vols, Hillsdale, NJ: Erlbaum.

Seitz, V., Rosenbaum, L. K. and Apfel, N. H. (1985) 'Effects of family support intervention: a ten-year follow-up', *Child Development* 56: 376–91.

Selman, R. L. (1980) *The Growth of Interpersonal Understanding*, New York: Academic Press.

Selman, R. L. (1981) 'The child as a friendship philosopher', in S. R. Asher and J. M. Gottman (eds) *The Development of Children's Friendships*, Cambridge: Cambridge University Press.

Senner, W. (ed.) (1989) *The Origins of Writing*, Lincoln, Nebr.: University of Nebraska Press.

Serafine, M. L. (1988) *Music as Cognition: the Development of Thought in Sound*, New York: Columbia University Press.

Shaffer, D. (1985) 'Brain damage', in M. Rutter and L. Hersov (eds) *Child and Adolescent Psychiatry: Modern Approaches*, Oxford: Blackwell.

Shaheen, S. J. (1984) 'Neuromaturation and behaviour development: the case of childhood lead poisoning', *Developmental Psychology* 20: 542–50.

Shallice, T. (1989) *From Neuropsychology to Mental Structures*, Cambridge: Cambridge University Press.

Shantz, C. U. (1983) 'Social cognition', in J. H. Flavell and E. M. Markman (eds) *Handbook of Child Psychology*, vol. 3, New York: Wiley.

Shantz, C. U. (ed.) (1989). 'Children's cognitive and social-cognitive development: domain specificity and generality', *Merrill-Palmer Quarterly* (invitational issue), 35(1): 1–142.

Shatz, M. (1978) 'The relationship between cognitive processes and the development of communication skills', in *Nebraska Symposium on Motivation, 1977*, Lincoln, Nebr.: University of Nebraska Press.

Shatz, M. and Gelman, R. (1973) 'The development of communication skills', *Monographs of the Society for Research in Child Development* 38(5), serial no. 152.

Shatz, M. and Gelman, R. (1977) 'Beyond syntax: the influence of conversational constraints on speech modifications', in C. E. Snow and C. A. Ferguson (eds) *Talking to Children*, Cambridge: Cambridge University Press.

Shepard, R. N. (1967) 'Recognition memory for words, sentences and pictures', *Journal of Verbal Learning and Verbal Behaviour* 6: 156–63.

Shields, M. M. and Duveen, G. (1982) 'The young child's image of the personal and social world: some aspects of the child's representation of persons', Paper presented at the International Sociological Association Conference, Mexico City, August 1982.

Shultz, T. R. and Cloghesy, K. (1981) 'Development of recursive awareness of intention', *Developmental Psychology* 17: 465–71.

Shuter-Dyson, R. and Gabriel, C. [1968] (2nd edn, 1981) *The Psychology of Musical Ability*, London: Methuen.

Shweder, R. A., Mahapatra, M. and Miller, J. G. (1990) 'Culture and moral development', in J. W. Stigler, R. A. Shweder and G. H. Herdt (eds) *Cultural Psychology: Essays on Comparative Human Development*, Cambridge: Cambridge University Press.

Siegal, M. (1988) 'Children's knowledge of contagion and contamination as causes of illness', *Child Development* 59: 1353–9.

Siegal, M. (1991) *Knowing Children: Experiments in Conversation and Cognition*, Hove: Erlbaum.

Siegal, M. and Beattie, K. (1991) 'Where to look first for children's knowledge of false beliefs', *Cognition* 38: 1–12.

Siegal, M. and Robinson, J. (1987) 'Order effects in children's gender constancy responses', *Developmental Psychology* 23: 283–6.

Siegal, M. and Share, D. L. (1990) 'Contamination sensitivity in young children', *Developmental Psychology* 26: 455–8.

Siegal, M., Waters, L. J. and Dinwiddy, L. S. (1988) 'Misleading children: causal attributions for inconsistency under repeated questioning', *Journal of Experimental Child Psychology* 45: 438–56.

Siegel, J. (1988) *Educating Reason: Rationality, Critical Thinking and Education*, London: Routledge.

Siegel, L. S. (1972) 'Development of the concept of seriation', *Developmental Psychology* 6: 135–7.

Siegel, L. S. (1978) 'The relationship of language and thought in the preoperational child: a reconsideration of nonverbal alternatives to Piagetian tasks', in L. S. Siegel and C. J. Brainerd (eds) *Alternatives to Piaget*, New York: Academic Press.

Siegel, L. S. and Ryan, E. B. (1988) 'Development of grammatical-sensitivity, phonological, and short-term memory skills in normally achieving and learning disabled children', *Developmental Psychology* 24(1): 28–37.

Siegel, L. S., McCabe, A. E., Brand, J. and Matthews, L. (1978) 'Evidence for the understanding of class inclusion in preschool children: linguistic factors and training effects', *Child Development* 49: 688–93.

Siegler, R. S. (1976) 'Three aspects of cognitive development', *Cognitive Psychology* 8: 481–520.

Siegler, R. S. (ed.) (1978) *Children's Thinking: What Develops?*, Hillsdale, NJ: Erlbaum.

Siegler, R. S. (1981) 'Developmental sequences within and between concepts', *Monographs of the Society for Research in Child Development* 46: 1–74.

Siegler, R. S. (1983) 'Information processing approaches to development', in W. Kessen (ed.) *Handbook of Child Psychology*, vol. 1, series ed. P. H. Mussen, New York: Wiley.

Siegler, R. S. (1984) 'Mechanisms of cognitive growth: variation and selection', in R. J. Sternberg (ed.) *Mechanisms of Cognitive Development*, New York: Freeman.

Siegler, R. S. (1986) *Children's Thinking*, Englewood Cliffs, NJ: Prentice Hall.

Siegler, R. S. (1987) 'The perils of averaging data over strategies: an example from children's addition', *Journal of Experimental Psychology (General)* 116: 250–64.

Siegler, R. S. (1988) 'Individual differences in strategy choices', *Child Development* 59: 833–51.

Siegler, R. S. (1989a) 'How domain-general and domain-specific knowledge interact to produce strategy choices', *Merrill-Palmer Quarterly* 35(1): 1–26.

Siegler, R. S. (1989b) 'Mechanisms of cognitive development', *Annual Review of Psychology* 40: 353–79.

Siegler, R. S. and Crowley, K. (1991) 'The microgenetic method: a direct means for studying cognitive development', *American Psychologist* 46: 606–20.

Siegler, R. S. and Richards, D. D. (1982) 'The development of intelligence', in R. J. Sternberg (ed.) *Handbook of Human Intelligence*, Cambridge: Cambridge University Press.

Siegler, R. S. and Robinson, M. (1982) 'The development of numerical understandings', in H. W. Reese and L. P. Lipsitt (eds) *Advances in Child Development and Behaviour*, vol. 16, New York: Academic Press.

Siegler, R. S. and Shipley, C. (1987) 'The role of learning in children's strategy choices', in L. S. Liben (ed.) *Development and Learning*, Hillsdale, NJ: Erlbaum.

Sigel, I. (1982a) 'Reproductive, perinatal and environmental factors as predictors of the cognitive and language development of preterm and fullterm infants', *Child Development* 53: 963–73.

Sigel, I. (1982b) 'The relationship between parental distancing strategies and the child's cognitive behavior', in L. M. Laosa and I. E. Sigel (eds) *Families as Learning Environments for Children*, New York: Plenum Press.

Sigel, I., Stinson, E. T. and Flaugher, J. (1991) 'Socialisation of representational competence in the family: the distancing paradigm', in L. Okagaki and R. J. Sternberg (eds) *Directors of Development: Influences on the Development of Children's Thinking*, Hillsdale, NJ: Erlbaum.

Silk, A. M. J. and Thomas G. V. (1986) 'Development and differentiation in children's figure drawings', *British Journal of Psychology* 77: 399–410.

Silk, A. M. J. and Thomas, G. V. (1988) 'The development of size scaling in children's figure drawings', *British Journal of Developmental Psychology* 6: 285–99.

Silva, P. A., Hughes, P., Williams, S. and Faed, J. M. (1988) 'Blood lead, intelligence, reading attainment and behaviour in eleven-year-old children in Dunedin, New Zealand', *Journal of Child Psychology and Psychiatry* 29: 43–52.

Simon, H. (1981) *The Sciences of the Artificial*, Cambridge, Mass.: MIT Press.

Sinclair, A., Jarvella, R. J. and Levelt, W. J. M. (1978) *The Child's Conception of Language*, Berlin: Springer-Verlag.

Sinclair, H. (1987) 'Conflict and congruence in development and learning', in L. S. Liben (ed.) *Development and Learning*, Hillsdale, NJ: Erlbaum.

Sinclair, H. and Sinclair, A. (1986) 'Children's mastery of written numerals and the construction of basic number concepts', in J. Hiebert (ed.) *Conceptual and Procedural Knowledge: the Case of Mathematics*, Hillsdale, NJ: Erlbaum.

Singer, D. G. and Singer, J. L. (1990) *The House of Make-Believe: Play and the Developing Imagination*, Cambridge, Mass.: Harvard University Press.

Singer, J. L. (ed.) (1973) *The Child's World of Make-believe*, New York: Academic Press.

Singer, J. L. (1975) *Daydreaming and Fantasy*, London: Allen & Unwin.

Singer, W. (1986) 'Neuronal activity as a shaping factor in postnatal development of visual cortex', in W. T. Greenough and J. M. Juraska (eds) *Developmental Neuropsychology*, New York: Academic Press.

Singley, M. K. and Anderson, J. R. (1989) *The Transfer of Cognitive Skills*, Cambridge, Mass.: Harvard University Press.

Sinisterra, L. (1987) 'Studies on poverty, human growth and development: the Cali experience', in J. Dobbing (ed.) *Early Nutrition and Later Achievement*, London: Academic Press.

Skinner, B. F. (1957) *Verbal Behaviour* New York: Appleton Century Crofts.

Skuse, D. (1984) 'Extreme deprivation in early childhood, I: diverse outcomes for three children in an extraordinary family; II: theoretical issues and a comparative review', *Journal of Child Psychology and Psychiatry* 25: 523–42, 543–72.

Slade, A. (1987) 'A longitudinal study of material involvement and symbolic play during the toddler period', *Child Development* 58: 367–75.

Slobin, D. (1985) *The Cross-linguistic Study of Language Acquisition*, vols 1 and 2, Hillsdale, NJ: Erlbaum.

Sloboda, J. A. (1985) *The Musical Mind: the Cognitive Psychology of Music*, Oxford: Oxford University Press.

Sloboda, J. A. and Rogers, D. (1987) *Cognitive Processes in Mathematics*, Oxford: Oxford University Press.

Smart, J. L. (1987) 'The need for and the relevance of animal studies of early undernutrition', in J. Dobbing (ed.) *Early Nutrition and Later Achievement*, London: Academic Press.

Smedslund, J. (1980) 'Analyzing the primary code: from empricism to apriorism', in D. R. Olson (ed.) *The Social Foundations of Language and Thought*, New York and London: Norton.

Smetana, J. G., Kelly, M., and Twentyman, C. T. (1984) 'Abused, neglected and nonmaltreated children's conceptions of moral and socio-conventional transgressions', *Child Development* 55: 277–87.

Smith, B. S., Ratner, H. H. and Hobart, C. J. (1987) 'The role of cuing and organisation in children's memory for events', *Journal of Experimental Child Psychology* 44: 1–24.

Smith, E. E., Langston, C. and Nisbett, R. (1992) 'The case for rules in reasoning', *Cognitive Science* 16: 1–40.

Smith, F. (1973) *Psycholinguistics and Reading*, New York: Holt, Rinehart & Winston.

Smith, F. (1978) *Reading*, Cambridge: Cambridge University Press.

Smith, F. (1982) *Writing and the Writer*, London: Heinemann.

Smith, I., Beasley, M. G. and Ades, A. E. (1990) 'Intelligence and quality of dietary treatment in phenylketonuria', *Archives of Disease in Childhood* 65: 472–8.

Smith, I., Beasley, M. G. and Ades, A. E. (1991) 'Effect on intelligence of relaxing the low phenylalanine diet in PKU', *Archives of Disease in Childhood* 66: 311–16.

Smith, J. D. and Caplan, J. (1988) 'Cultural differences in cognitive style development', *Developmental Psychology* 24: 46–52.

Smith, L. B. (1989a) 'From global similarities to kinds of similarities: the construction of dimensions in development', in S. Vosniadou and A. Ortony (eds) *Similarity and Analogical Reasoning*, Cambridge: Cambridge University Press.

Smith, L. B. (1989b) 'A model of perceptual classification in children and adults', *Psychological Review* 96: 125–44.

Smith, L. B. and Sera, M. D. (1992) 'A developmental analysis of the polar structure of dimensions', *Cognitive Psychology* 24: 99–142.

Smith, M. (1985) 'Recent work on low-level lead exposure and its impact on behaviour, intelligence and learning', *Journal of the American Academy of Child Psychiatry* 24: 24–32.

Smith, P. K. and Simon, T. (1984) 'Object play, problem-solving and creativity in children', in P. K. Smith (ed.) *Play in Animals and Humans*, Oxford: Blackwell.

Smith, P. K., Simon, T. and Emberton, R. (1985) 'Play, problem-solving and experimenter effects', *British Journal of Developmental Psychology* 3: 105–7.

Smith, S. B. (1983) *The Great Mental Calculators*, New York: Columbia University Press.

Snow, C. E., Barnes, W. S., Chandler, J., Goodman, I. F. and Hemphill, L. (1991) *Unfulfilled Expectations: Home and School Influences on Literacy*, Cambridge, Mass.: Harvard University Press.

Snowling, M. J. (1987) *Dyslexia: a Cognitive Developmental Perspective*, Oxford: Blackwell.

Snowling, M. J. (1991) 'Developmental reading disorders', *Journal of Child Psychology and Psychiatry*, 32: 49–77.

Sodian, B. (1991) 'The development of deception in young children', *British Journal of Developmental Psychology* 9: 173–88.

Sodian, B., Taylor, C., Harris, P. L. and Perner, J. (1991) 'Early deception and the child's theory of mind: false trails and genuine markers', *Child Development* 62: 468–83.

Sodian, B. and Wimmer, H. (1987) 'Children's understanding of inference as a source of knowledge', *Child Development* 58: 424–33.

Solomon, Y. (1989) *The Practice of Mathematics*, London: Routledge.

Somerville, S. C. and Bryant, P. E. (1985) 'Young children's use of spatial coordinates', *Child Development* 56: 604–13.

Song, M.-J. and Ginsberg, H. P. (1987) 'The development of informal and formal mathematical thinking in Korean and U.S. children', *Child Development* 58: 1286–96.

Sophian, C. (1988) 'Early developments in children's understanding of number: inferences about numerosity and one-to-one correspondence', *Child Development* 59: 1397–414.

Speece, M. W. and Brent, S. B. (1984) 'Children's understanding of death', *Child Development* 55: 1671–86.

Spencer, C., Blades, M. and Morsley, K. (1989) *The Child in the Physical Environment: the Development of Spatial Knowledge and Cognition*, Chichester: Wiley.

Spiker, C. C. (1989) 'Cognitive psychology: mentalistic or behavioristic?', in H. W. Reese (ed.) *Advances in Child Development and Behaviour*, vol. 21, New York: Academic Press.

Spilich, G. J., Vesonder, G. T., Chiesi, H. L. and Voss, J. F. (1979) 'Text processing of domain-related information for individuals with high and low domain knowledge', *Journal of Verbal Learning and Verbal Behaviour* 18: 275–90.

Squire, L. R. (1987) *Memory and Brain*, Oxford: Oxford University Press.

Sroufe, L. A. (1979) 'Socioemotional development', in J. D. Osofsky (ed.) *Handbook of Infant Development*, New York: Wiley.

Sroufe, L. A. (1983) 'Infant–caregiver attachment and patterns of adaptation in preschool: the roots of maladaptation and competence', in *Minnesota Symposium on Child Development*, vol. 16, Hillsdale, NJ: Erlbaum.

Sroufe, L. A. and Fleeson, J. (1986) 'Attachment and the construction of relationships', in W. Hartup and Z. Rubin (eds) *Relationships and Development*, Hillsdale, NJ: Erlbaum.

Stage, S. A. and Wagner, R. K. (1992) 'Development of young children's phonological and orthographic knowledge as revealed by their spellings', *Developmental Psychology* 28: 287–96.

Stambrook, M. and Parker, K. C. H. (1987) 'The development of the concept of death in childhood', *Merrill-Palmer Quarterly* 33(2): 133–57.

Standing, L. (1973) 'Learning 10,000 pictures', *Quarterly Journal of Experimental Psychology* 25: 207–22.

Starkey, P. (1992) 'The early development of numerical reasoning', *Cognition* 43: 93–126.

Starkey, P. and Cooper, R. S. (1980) 'Perception of number by human infants', *Science* 100: 1033–5.

Starkey, P. and Gelman, R. (1982) 'The development of addition and subtraction abilities prior to formal schooling', in T. P. Carpenter, J. M. Moser, and T. A. Romberg (eds) *Addition and Subtraction: a Developmental Perspective*, Hillsdale, NJ: Erlbaum.

Starkey, P., Spelke, E. S. and Gelman, R. (1990) 'Numerical abstraction by human infants', *Cognition* 36: 97–127.

Steedman, C. (1982) *The Tidy House*, London: Virago.

Stein, Z., Susser, M., Saenger, G. and Marolla, F. (1975) *Famine and Human Development*, Oxford: Oxford University Press.

Stern, J. (1987) 'The biochemical approach to mental handicap', *Journal of Mental Deficiency Research* 31: 357–64.

Sternberg, R. J. (ed.) (1982) *Handbook of Human Intelligence*, Cambridge: Cambridge University Press.

Sternberg, R. J. (ed.) (1984) *Mechanisms of Cognitive Development*, New York: Freeman.

Sternberg, R. J. (1985) *Beyond IQ: a Triarchic Theory of Human Intelligence*, New York: Cambridge University Press.

Sternberg, R. J. (1988a) 'Explaining away intelligence: a reply to Howe', *British Journal of Psychology* 79: 527–33.

Sternberg, R. J. (1988b) *The Nature of Creativity: Contemporary Psychological Perspectives*, Cambridge: Cambridge University Press.

Sternberg, R. J. and Davidson, J. E. (eds) (1986) *Conceptions of Giftedness*, New York: Cambridge University Press.

Sternberg, R. J. and Detterman, D. K. (1986) *What is Intelligence?*, Norwood, NJ: Ablex.

Sternberg, R. J. and Gardner, M. K. (1982) 'A componential interpretation of the general factor in human intelligence', in H. J. Eysenck (ed.) *A Model for Intelligence*, Berlin: Springer-Verlag.

Sternberg, R. J. and Powell, J. (1983) 'The development of intelligence', in J. H. Flavell and E. M. Markman, *Handbook of Child Psychology*, vol. 3, series ed. P. H. Mussen, New York: Wiley.

Sternberg, R. J. and Smith E. E. (1988) *The Psychology of Human Thought*, Cambridge: Cambridge University Press.

Sternberg, R. and Suben, O. (1986) 'The socialization of intelligence', in M. Perlmutter (ed.) *Perspectives on Intellectual Development, Minnesota Symposium on Child Development* 19.

Stevens, J. H. and Bakeman, R. (1985) 'A factor analytic study of the HOME scale for infants', *Developmental Psychology* 21: 1196–203.

Stevenson, D. L. and Baker, D. P. (1987) 'The family–school relation and the child's school performance', *Child Development* 58: 1348–57.

Stevenson, H. W., Lee, S.-Y. and Stigler, J. W. (1986) 'Mathematics achievement of Chinese, Japanese and American children', *Science* 231: 693–9.

Stevenson, H. W., Chen, C., Lee, S.-Y. and Fuligni, A. J. (1991) 'Schooling, culture and cognitive development', in L. Okagaki and R. J. Sternberg (eds) *Directors of Development: Influences on the Development of Children's Thinking*, Hillsdale, NJ: Erlbaum.

Stevenson, H. W., Parker, T., Wilkinson, A., Hegion, A. and Fish, E. (1976) 'Longitudinal study of individual differences in cognitive development and scholastic achievement', *Journal of Educational Psychology* 68: 377–400.

Stewart, A. J. and Healy, J. M. (1989) 'Linking individual development and social change', *Psychological Bulletin* 44: 30–42.

Stich, S. P. (1983) *From Folk Psychology to Cognitive Science: the Case Against Belief*, Cambridge, Mass.: MIT Press.

Stigler, J. W., Lee, S.-Y. and Stevenson, H. W. (1987) 'Mathematics classrooms in Japan, Taiwan and the United States', *Child Development* 58: 1272–85.

Stigler, J. W., Nusbaum, H. C. and Chalip, L. (1988) 'Developmental changes in speed of processing: central limiting mechanism or skill transfer?', *Child Development* 59: 1144–53.

Stigler, J. W., Schweder, R. A. and Herdt, G. (1990) *Cultural Psychology: Essays on Comparative Human Development*, Cambridge: Cambridge University Press.

Strauss, M. S. and Curtis, L. E. (1981) 'Infant perception of numerosity', *Child Development* 52: 1146–52.

Strayer, F. F., Moss, E. and Blicharski, T. (1989) 'Biosocial bases of representational activity during early childhood', in L. T. Winegar (ed.) *Social Interaction and the Development of Children's Understanding*, Norwood, NJ: Ablex.

Stuart, M. (1990) 'Factors influencing word recognition in pre-reading children', *British Journal of Psychology* 81: 135–46.

Stuart, M. and Coltheart, M. (1988) 'Does reading develop in a series of stages?', *Cognition* 30: 139–81.

Stubbs, M. (1980) *Language and Literacy: the Sociolinguistics of Reading and Writing*, London: Routledge & Kegan Paul.

Styles, M. (1989) *Collaboration and Writing*, Milton Keynes: Open University Press.

Sugarman, S. (1981) 'The cognitive basis of classification in very young children: an analysis of object ordering trends', *Child Development* 52: 1172–8.

Sugarman, S. (1983) *Children's Early Thought: Developments in Classification*, Cambridge: Cambridge University Press.

Super, C. M., Herrera, M. G. and Mora, J. O. (1990) 'Long-term effects of food supplementation and psychosocial intervention on the physical growth of Colombian infants at risk of malnutrition', *Child Development* 61: 29–49.

Super, C. M., Clement, J., Vuori, L., Christiansen, N., Mora, J. O. and Herrera, M. G. (1981) 'Infant and caretaker behaviour as mediators of nutritional and social intervention in the barrios of Bogota', in T. M. Field, A. M. Sostek, P. Vietze and P. H. Liederman (eds) *Culture and Early Interactions*, Hillsdale, NJ: Erlbaum.

Sutton, A. (1983) 'An introduction to Soviet developmental psychology', in S. Meadows (ed.) *Developing Thinking*, London: Methuen.

Swanwick, K. (1988) *Music, Mind and Education*, London: Routledge.

Swift, J. [1726] (1985) *Gulliver's Travels*, Harmondsworth: Penguin Books.

Sylvester-Bradley, B. (1985) 'Failure to distinguish between people and things in early infancy', *British Journal of Developmental Psychology* 3: 281–92.

Tager-Flusberg, H. (1992) 'Autistic children's talk about psychological states: deficits in the acquisition of a theory of mind', *Child Development* 63: 161–72.

Taylor, E. (1980) 'The development of attention', in M. Rutter (ed.) *Scientific Foundations of Developmental Psychiatry*, London: Heinemann.

Taylor, E. (1984) 'Diet and behaviour', *Archives of Disease in Childhood* 59: 97–8.

Taylor, E. (1985) 'Syndromes of overactivity and attention deficit', in M. Rutter and L. Hersov (eds) *Child and Adolescent Psychiatry: Modern Approaches*, Oxford: Blackwell.

Taylor, M. (1988) 'The development of children's understanding of the seeing–knowing distinction', in J. W. Astington, P. L. Harris and D. R. Olson (eds) *Developing Theories of Mind*, Cambridge: Cambridge University Press.

Taylor, M., Cartwright, B. S. and Bowden, T. (1991) 'Perspective taking and theory of mind: do children predict interpretive diversity as a function of differences in observers' knowledge?', *Child Development* 62: 1334–51.

Teale, W. H. (1984) 'Reading to young children: its significance for literacy development', in H. Goelman, A. Oberg and F. Smith *Awakening to Literacy*, London: Heinemann.

Teasdale, T. W., Fuchs, J. and Goldschmidt, E. (1988) 'Degree of myopia in relation to intelligence and educational level', *The Lancet* 8264: 1351–3.

Tees, R. C. (1986) 'Experience and visual development: behavioral evidence', in W. T. Greenough and J. M. Juraska (eds) *Developmental Neuropsychology*, New York: Academic Press.

Teyler, T. J. and Fountain, S. B. (1987) 'Neuronal plasticity in the mammalian brain: relevance to behavioural learning and memory', *Child Development* 58: 698–712.

Tharp, R. G. *et al.* (1984) 'Product and process in applied developmental research: education and the children of a minority', in M. E. Lamb, A. L. Brown and B. Rogoff (eds) *Advances in Developmental Psychology*, vol. 3, Hillsdale, NJ: Erlbaum.

Tharp, R. G. and Gallimore, R. (1988) *Rousing Minds to Life: Teaching, Learning and Schooling in Social Context*, Cambridge: Cambridge University Press.

Thatcher, R. W., Walker, R. A. and Guidice, S. (1987) 'Human cerebral hemispheres develop at different rates and ages', *Science* 236: 1110–13.

Thomas, G. V. and Silk, A. M. J. (1990) *An Introduction to the Psychology of Children's Drawings*, Brighton: Harvester.

Thomas, G. V. and Tsalimi, A. (1988) 'Effects of order of drawing head and trunk on their relative sizes in children's human figure drawings', *British Journal of Developmental Psychology* 6: 191–203.

Thomassen, J. W. M. and Teulings, H.-L. H. M. (1983) 'The development of handwriting', in M. Martlew (ed.) *The Psychology of Written Language*, Chichester: Wiley.

Thompson, L. A. and Massaro, D. W. (1989) 'Before you see it, you see its parts: evidence for feature encoding and integration in preschool children and adults', *Cognitive Psychology* 21: 334–62.

Thompson, L. A., Fagen, J. F. and Fulker, D, W. (1991) 'Longitudinal prediction of specific cognitive abilities from infant novelty preference', *Child Development* 62: 530–8.

Thompson, R. A. (ed.) (1990a) *Socioemotional development: Nebraska Symposium on Motivation, 1988*, vol. 36, Lincoln, Nebr.: University of Nebraska Press.

Thompson, R. A. (ed.) (1990b) 'Emotion and self-regulation', in R. A. Thompson (ed.) *Socioemotional development: Nebraska Symposium on Motivation, 1988*, vol. 36, Lincoln, Nebr.: University of Nebraska Press.

Thomson, G. O. B., Raab, G. M., Hepburn, W. S., Hunter, R., Fulton, M. and Laxen, D. P. H. (1989) 'Blood-lead levels and children's behaviour: results from the Edinburgh Lead Study', *Journal of Child Psychology and Psychiatry* 30: 515–28.

Thorpe, K. J. (1988) 'Metacognition and attribution for learning outcome amongst children in the primary school', unpublished Ph.D thesis, University of Bristol.

Thorstad, G. (1991) 'The effect of orthography on the acquisition of literacy skills', *British Journal of Psychology* 82: 527–37.

Thurber, J. (1953) 'The secret life of James Thurber', in *The Thurber Carnival*, Harmondsworth: Penguin Books.

Tierney, R. J., Soter, A., O'Flanahan, J. F. and McGinley, W. (1989) 'The effects of reading and writing upon thinking critically', *Reading Research Quarterly* 24: 134–73.

Tizard, B., (1986) 'The impact of the nuclear threat on children's development', in M. P. M. Richards and P. H. Light (eds) *Children of Social Worlds*, Cambridge: Polity Press.

Tizard, B. and Hughes, M. (1984) *Young Children Learning*, London: Fontana.

Tizard, B., Philps, J. and Plewis, I. (1976) 'Play in preschool centres', *Journal of Child Psychology and Psychiatry* 17: 251–74.

Tizard, B., Schofield, W. and Hewison, J. (1981) 'Collaboration between teachers and parents in assisting children's reading', *British Journal of Educational Psychology* 52: 1–5.

Tizard, B., Hughes, M., Pinkerton, G. and Carmichael, H. (1982) 'Adults' cognitive demands at home and at nursery school', *Journal of Child Psychology and Psychiatry* 23(2): 108–17.

Tizard, B., Blatchford, P., Burke, J., Farquhar, C. and Plewis, I. (1988) *Young Children at School in the Inner City*, Hove: Erlbaum.

Torrance, E. P. (1962) *Guiding Creative Talent*, Englewood Cliffs, NJ: Prentice Hall.

Torrance, E. P. (1988) 'The nature of creativity as manifest in testing', in R. J. Sternberg (ed.) *The Nature of Creativity: Contemporary Psychological Perspectives*, Cambridge: Cambridge University Press.

Torrey, J. W. (1979) 'Reading that comes naturally: the early reader', in T. G. Waller and G. Mackinnon (eds) *Reading Research: Advances in Theory and Practice*, vol. 1, New York: Academic Press.

Trabasso, T. (1975) 'Representation, memory and reasoning: how do we make transitive inferences?', in A. D. Pick (ed.) *Minnesota Symposium on Child Psychology*, vol. 9, Hillsdale, NJ: Erlbaum.

Trabasso, T. and Nicholas, D. W. (1980) 'Memory and inferences in the comprehension of narratives', in F. Wilkening, J. Becker and T. Trabasso (eds) *Information Integration by Children*, Hillsdale, NJ: Erlbaum.

Tramontana, M. G., Hooper, S. R. and Selzer, S. C. (1988) 'Research on the preschool prediction of later academic achievement: a review', *Developmental Review* 8: 89–146.

Trevarthen, C. (1978) 'Communication and cooperation in early infancy', in M. Bullowa (ed.) *Before Speech*, Cambridge: Cambridge University Press.

Trevarthen, C. (1980) 'The foundations of intersubjectivity: development of interpersonal and cooperative understanding in infants', in D. R. Olson (ed.) *The Social Foundations of Language and Thought*, New York and London: Norton.

Trevarthen, C. (1982) 'The primary motives for cooperative understanding', in G. Butterworth and P. Light (eds) *Social Cognition: Studies of the Development of Understanding*, Brighton: Harvester.

Trevarthen, C. (1988a) 'Brain development', in R. L. Gregory (ed.) *The Oxford Companion to the Mind*, Oxford: Oxford University Press.

Trevarthen, C. (1988b) 'Universal cooperative motives: how infants begin to know language and skills of culture', in G. Jahoda and I. Lewis (eds) *Ethnographic Perspectives on Cognitive Development*, Beckenham: Croom Helm.

Trevarthen, C. and Hubley, P. (1978) 'Secondary intersubjectivity: confidence, confiding and acts of meaning in the first year', in A. Lock (ed.) *Action, Gesture and Symbol: the Emergence of Language*, London: Academic Press.

Trevarthen, C. and Logotheti, K. (1989) 'Child and culture: genesis of cooperative knowing', in A. Gellatly, D. Rogers and J. A. Sloboda (eds) *Cognition and Social Worlds*, Oxford: Clarendon Press.

Tucker, D. M. (1992) 'Developing emotions and cortical networks', in M. Gunnar and C. A. Nelson (eds) *Developmental Behavioral Neuroscience: Minnesota Symposium on Child Psychology*, vol. 24, Hillsdale, NJ: Erlbaum.

Tucker, N. (1981) *The Child and the Book*, Cambridge: Cambridge University Press.

Tulving, E. (1972) 'Episodic and semantic memory', in E. Tulving and W. Donaldson (eds) *Organisation of Memory*, New York: Academic Press.

Tunmer, W. E., Herriman, M. L. and Nesdale, A. R. (1988) 'Metalinguistic abilities and beginning reading', *Reading Research Quarterly* 23(2): 134–58.

Turiel, E. (1983) *The Development of Social Knowledge*, New York: Cambridge University Press.

Turner, G. and Jacobs, P. (1983) 'Marker (X)-linked mental retardation', *Advances in Human Genetics* 13: 83–112.

Uttal, D. H. and Wellman, H. M. (1989) 'Young children's representation of spatial information acquired from maps', *Developmental Psychology* 25: 128–38.

Uzgiris, I. (1964) 'Situational generality of conservation', *Child Development* 35: 831–41.

Valentine, E. R. (1982) *Conceptual Issues in Psychology*, London: George Allen & Unwin.

Valsiner, J. (1984) 'Construction of the zone of proximal development: the socialisation of meals', *New Directions for Child Development* 23: 65–76.

Valsiner, J. (ed.) (1988a) *Child Development within Culturally Structured Environments*, vol. 1, *Parental Cognition and Adult–Child Interaction*, Norwood, NJ: Ablex.

Valsiner, J. (ed.) (1988b) *Child Development within Culturally Structured Environments*, vol. 2, *Social Co-construction and Environmental Guidance in Development*, Norwood, NJ: Ablex.

Valsiner, J. (1989) 'Collective coordination of progressive empowerment', in L. Winegar (ed.) *Social Interaction and the Development of Children's Understanding*, Norwood, NJ: Ablex.

Vandenberg, B. (1990) 'Play and problem solving: an elusive connection', *Merrill-Palmer Quarterly* 36: 261–72.

Van der Veer, R. and Valsiner, J. (1988) 'Lev Vygotsky and P. Janet: on the origin of the concept of sociogenesis', *Developmental Review* 8: 52–65.

Van der Veer, R. and Valsiner, J. (1991) *Understanding Vygotsky: a Quest for Synthesis*, Oxford: Blackwell.

Van Geert, P. (1991) 'A dynamic systems model of cognitive and language growth', *Psychological Review* 98: 3–53.

Vaughan, H. G. and Kurtzberg, D. (1992) 'Electrophysiologic indices of human brain maturation and cognitive development', in M. Gunnar and C. A. Nelson (eds) *Developmental Behavioral Neuroscience: Minnesota Symposium on Child Psychology*, vol. 24, Hillsdale, NJ: Erlbaum.

Vellutino, F. R. and Scanlon, D. M. (1987) 'Phonological coding, phonological awareness and reading ability: evidence from a longitudinal and experimental study', *Merrill-Palmer Quarterly* 33(3): 321–63.

Vernon, P. A. (1985) 'Individual differences in general cognitive ability', in L. C. Hartlage and C. F. Telzrow (eds) *The Neuropsychology of Individual Differences*, New York: Plenum Press.

Vernon, P. E. (1972) 'The distinctiveness of field independence', *Journal of Personality* 40: 366–91.

Victor, J. B., Halverson, C. F. and Montague, R. B. (1985) 'Relations between reflection-impulsivity and behavioral impulsivity in preschool children', *Developmental Psychology* 21: 141–8.

Volet, S. E. and Chalmers, D. (1992) 'Investigation of qualitative differences in university students' learning goals, based on an unfolding model of stage development', *British Journal of Educational Psychology* 62: 17–34.

Vosniadou, S. (1987) 'Children and metaphors', *Child Development* 58: 870–85.

Vosniadou, S. and Ortony, A. (1983) 'The emergence of the literal–metaphorical–anomalous distinction in young children', *Child Development* 54: 154–61.

Vosniadou, S, and Ortony, A. (eds) (1989) *Similarity and Analogical Reasoning*, Cambridge: Cambridge University Press.

Vosniadou, S., Ortony, A., Reynolds, R. E. and Wilson, P. T. (1984) 'Sources of difficulty in children's understanding of metaphorical language', *Child Development* 55: 1588–606.

Voss, J. (1989) 'Problem solving and the educational process', in A. Lesgold and R. Glaser (eds) *Foundations for a Psychology of Education*, Hillsdale, NJ: Erlbaum.

Vuchinich, S., Vuchinich, R. and Coughlin, C. (1992) 'Family talk and parent–child relationships: towards integrating deductive and inductive paradigms', *Merrill-Palmer Quarterly* 38: 69–94.

Vurpillot, E. (1976) *The Visual World of the Child*, New York: International Universities Press.

Vuyk, R. (1981) *Overview and Critique of Piaget's Genetic Epistemology, 1965–1980*, vols 1 and 2, London: Academic Press.

Vye, N. J., Delcols, V. R., Burns, M. S. and Bransford, J. D. (1988) 'Teaching thinking and problem solving: illustrations and issues', in R. J. Sternberg and E. E. Smith (eds) *The Psychology of Human Thought*, Cambridge: Cambridge University Press.

Vygotsky, L. S. (1960) 'The development of higher mental functions', quoted in J. V. Wertsch (1985a) *Vygotsky and the Social Formation of Mind*, Cambridge, Mass.: Harvard University Press.

Vygotsky, L. S. (1962) *Thought and Language*, Cambridge, Mass.: MIT Press.

Vygotsky, L. S. (1971) *The Psychology of Art*, Cambridge, Mass.: MIT Press.

Vygotsky, L. S. (1976) 'Play and its role in the mental development of the child', in J. S. Bruner, A. Jolly and K. Sylvia (eds) *Play, its Role in Development and Evolution*, Harmondsworth: Penguin Books.

Vygotsky, L. S. (1978a) *Mind in Society: the Development of Higher Psychological Processes*, ed. M. Cole, V. John-Steiner, S. Scribner and E. Souberman, Cambridge, Mass.: Harvard University Press.

Vygotsky, L. S. (1978b) 'The prehistory of written language', in M. Cole, V. John-Steiner, S. Scribner and E. Souberman (eds) *Mind in Society: the Development of Higher Psychological Processes*, Cambridge, Mass.: Harvard University Press.

Vygotsky, L. S. (1981) 'The genesis of higher mental functions', in J. V. Wertsch (ed.) *The Concept of Activity in Soviet Psychology*, Armonk, NY: M. E. Sharpe.

Vygotsky, L. S. (1986) *Thought and Language*, new edn, ed. A. Kozulin, Cambridge, Mass.: MIT Press.

Waber, D. P. (1977) 'Biological substrates of field dependence: implications of the sex difference', *Psychological Bulletin* 84: 1076–87.

Wachs, T. D. (1987) 'Specificity of environmental action as manifest in environmental correlates of infants' mastery motivation', *Developmental Psychology* 23: 782–90.

Waggoner, J. E. and Palermo, D. S. (1989) 'Betty is a Bouncing Bubble: children's comprehension of emotion-descriptive metaphors', *Developmental Psychology* 25(1): 152–63.

Wagner, D. A. (1982) 'Ontogeny in the study of culture and cognition', in D. A. Wagner and H. W. Stevenson (eds) *Cultural Perspectives on Child Development*, San Francisco: Freeman.

Wagner, D. A. and Spratt, J. E. (1987) 'Cognitive consequences of contrasting pedagogies: the effects of Quranic preschooling in Morocco', *Child Development* 58: 1207–19.

Wagner, R. K. and Torgeson, J. K. (1987) 'The nature of phonological processing and its causal role in the acquisition of reading skills', *Psychological Bulletin* 101: 192–212.

Wahler, R. G. and Dumas, J. E. (1989) 'Attentional problems in dysfunctional mother–child interactions: an interbehavioral model', *Psychological Bulletin* 105: 116–30.

Walkerdine, V. (1988) *The Mastery of Reason*, London: Routledge.

Walkerdine, V. (1989) *Counting Girls Out*, London: Virago.

Walkerdine, V. and Lucey, H. (1989) *Democracy in the Kitchen*, London: Virago.

Wall, P. D. (1984) 'Pain and no pain', in C. W. Coen (ed.) *Functions of the Brain*, Oxford: Clarendon Press.

Wallach, M. A. (1971) 'Creativity', in P. H. Mussen (ed.) *Carmichael's Manual of Child Psychology*, 3rd edn., vol. 1, New York: Wiley.

Wallach, M. A. and Kogan, N. (1965) *Modes of Thinking in Young Children: a Study of the Creativity-Intelligence Distinction*, New York: Holt, Rinehart & Winston.

Wallas, G. (1926) *The Art of Thought*, London: Cape.

Wapner, J. G. and Connor, K. (1986) 'The role of defensiveness in cognitive impulsivity', *Child Development* 57: 1370–4.

Ward, S., Wackman, D. B. and Wartella, E. (1977) *How Children Learn to Buy: the Development of Consumer Information-processing Skills*, Beverly Hills, Calif.: Sage.

Wardle, J. (ed.) (1992) 'Nutrition and I.Q', special issue of *The Psychologist* 5: 399–413.

Warnock, M. (1976) *Imagination*, London: Faber.

Wason, P. C. (1977) 'On the failure to eliminate hypotheses', in P. N. Johnson-Laird and P. C. Wason (eds) *Thinking*, Cambridge: Cambridge University Press.

Wason, P. C. and Johnson-Laird, P. N. (1972) *The Psychology of Reasoning*, London: Batsford.

Watson, M. W. (1984) 'Development of social role understanding', *Developmental Review* 4: 192–213.

Waxman, S. R. and Hatch, T. (1992) 'Beyond basics: preschool children label objects flexibly at multiple hierarchical levels', *Journal of Child Language* 19: 153–66.

Weatherford, D. L. (1982) 'Spatial cognition as a function of size and scale of the environment', in R. Cohen (ed.) *New Directions for Child Development: Children's Conceptions of Spatial Relationships*, San Francisco: Jossey-Bass.

Weikart, D. (1978) *An Economic Analysis of the Ypsilanti Perry Preschool Project*, Ypsilanti: High/Scope Educational Research Foundation.

Weinstein, C. S. (1991) 'The classroom as a social context for learning', *Annual Review of Psychology* 42: 493–525.

Weissberg, J. A. and Paris, S. G. (1986) 'Young children's remembering in different contexts: a reinterpretation of Istomina's study', *Child Development* 57: 1123–9.

Weisz, J. R., Yeates, K. O., Robertson, D. and Beckham, J. C. (1982) 'Perceived contingency of skill and chance events: a developmental analysis', *Developmental Psychology* 18: 898–905.

Wellman, H. M. (1983) 'Metamemory revisited', in M. T. H. Chi (ed.) *Trends in Memory Development Research*, New York: Karger.

Wellman, H. M. (1985a) 'The child's theory of mind: the development of conceptions of cognition', in S. R. Yussen (ed.) *The Growth of Reflection in Children*, New York: Academic Press.

Wellman, H. M. (1985b) 'The origins of metacognition', in D. L. Forrest-Pressley, G. E. MacKinnon and T. G. Waller (eds) *Metacognition, Cognition and Human Performance*, Orlando, Fla.: Academic Press.

Wellman, H. M. (1988) 'First steps in the child's theorizing about the mind', in J. W. Astington, P. L. Harris and D. R. Olson (eds) *Developing Theories of Mind*, Cambridge: Cambridge University Press.

Wellman, H. M. (1990) *The Child's Theory of Mind*, Cambridge, Mass.: MIT Press.

Wellman, H. M. and Estes, D. (1986) 'Early understanding of mental entities: a reexamination of childhood realism', *Child Development* 57: 910–23.

Wellman, H. M. and Woolley, J. D. (1990) 'From simple desires to ordinary beliefs: the early development of everyday psychology', *Cognition* 35: 245–75.

Wells, C. G. (1981a) 'Pre-school literacy related activities and success in school', in D. R. Olson (ed.) *The Nature and Conseqences of Literacy*, Cambridge: Cambridge University Press.

Wells, C. G. (1981b) 'Some antecedents of early educational attainment', *British Journal of Sociology of Education* 2: 181–200.

Wells, C. G. (1982a) 'Influences of the home on language development', in A. Davies (ed.) *Language and Learning in School and Home*, London: SSRC, Heinemann.

Wells, C. G. (1982b) *Language, Learning and Education*, Bristol: Centre for the Study of Language and Communication.

Wells, C. G. (1985) 'Preschool literacy-related activities and success in school', in D. R. Olson, N. Torrance and A. Hildyard (eds) *Literacy, Language and Learning: the Nature and Consequences of Reading and Writing*, Cambridge: Cambridge University Press.

Wells, C. G. (1986) 'Variation in child language', in P. Fletcher and M. Garman (eds) *Language Acqusition*, Cambridge: Cambridge University Press.

Wells, G. and Gutfreund, M. (1987) 'The conversational requirements for language learning', in W. Yule and M. Rutter (eds) *Language Development and Disorders*, London: MacKeith Press and Oxford: Blackwell Scientific Publications.

Werner, H. (1948) *The Comparative Psychology of Mental Development*, Chicago: Follett.

Wertsch, J. V. (1978) 'Adult–child interaction and the roots of metacognition', *Quarterly Newsletter of the Laboratory of Comparative Human Cognition* 2(1): 15–18.

Wertsch, J. V. (1979) 'From social interaction to higher psychological process: a clarification and application of Vygotsky's theory', *Human Development* 22: 1–22.

Wertsch, J. V. (ed.) (1981) *The Concept of Activity in Soviet Psychology*, Armonk, NY: M. E. Sharpe.

Wertsch, J. V. (1985a) *Vygotsky and the Social Formation of Mind*, Cambridge, Mass.: Harvard University Press.

Wertsch, J. V. (ed.) (1985b) *Culture, Communication and Cognition*, Cambridge: Cambridge University Press.

Wertsch, J. V. and Sammarco, J. G. (1985) 'Social precursors to individual cognitive functioning: the problem of units of analysis', in R. A. Hinde, A.-N. Perret-Clermont and J. Stevenson-Hinde (eds) *Social Relationships and Cognitive Development*, Oxford: Clarendon Press.

Wertsch, J. V. and Stone, C. A. (1985) 'The concept of internalisation in Vygotsky's account of the genesis of higher mental functions', in J. V. Wertsch (ed.) *Culture, Communication and Cognition*, Cambridge: Cambridge University Press.

Wertsch, J. V., McNamee, G. D., McLane, J. B. and Budwid, N. A. (1980) 'The adult–child dyad as a problem-solving system', *Child Development* 51: 1215–21.

Wetherford, M. J. and Cohen, L. B. (1973) 'Developmental changes in infant visual preferences for novelty and familiarity', *Child Development* 44: 416–24.

White, K. R. (1982) 'The relation between socioeconomic status and academic achievement', *Psychological Bulletin* 91: 461–88.

Whitehurst, C. J., Falco, F. L., Lonigan, C. J., Fischel, J. E., De Baryshe, B. D., Valdez-Menchaca, M. C. and Caulfield, M. (1988) 'Accelerating language development through picture book reading', *Developmental Psychology* 24(4): 552–9.

Whittaker, S. (1983) 'Memory development in 3 to 6 year-olds: learning how to learn', unpublished Ph.D. thesis, University of St Andrews.

Widdowson, E. M. (1951) 'Mental contentment and physical growth', *The Lancet*, 16 June 1951: 1316.

Wilkening, F., Levin, I. and Druyan, S. (1987) 'Children's counting strategies for time quantification and integration', *Developmental Psychology* 23: 823–31.

Wilkinson, J. (1988) 'Context effects in children's memory', in M. M. Gruneberg, P. E. Morris and R. N. Sykes (eds) *Practical Aspects of Memory: Current Research and Issues*, vol. 1, Chichester: Wiley.

Willats, J. (1977) 'How children learn to draw realistic pictures', *Quarterly Journal of Experimental Psychology* 29: 367–82.

Williams, J. M., Watts, F. N., Macleod, G. and Mathews, A. (1988) *Cognitive Psychology and Emotional Disorders*, Chichester: Wiley.

Williams, M. (1989) 'Vygotsky's social theory of mind', *Harvard Educational Review* 59(1): 108–27.

Wilson, C. and Nettelbeck, T. (1986) 'Inspection time and the mental age deviation hypothesis', *Personality and Individual Differences* 7: 669–75.

Wilson, C., Nettelbeck, T., Turnbull, C. and Young, R. (1992) 'IT, IQ and age: a comparison of developmental functions', *British Journal of Developmental Psychology* 10: 179–88.

Wilson, D., Esterman, A., Lewis, M., Roder, D. and Calder, I. (1986) 'Children's blood lead levels in the lead smelting town of Port Pirie, South Australia', *Archives of Environmental Medicine* 41(4): 245–50.

Wilson, R. S. (1983) 'The Louisville twin study: developmental synchronies in behaviour', *Child Development* 54: 298–316.

Wimmer, H. (1980) 'Children's understanding of stories: assimilation by a general schema for actions or coordination of temporal relations?', in F. Wilkening, J. Becker and T. Trabasso (eds) *Information Integration by Children*, Hillsdale, NJ: Erlbaum.

Wimmer, H. and Hart, M. (1991) 'The Cartesian view and the theory view of mind: developmental evidence from understanding false belief in self and other', *British Journal of Developmental Psychology* 9: 125–38.

Wimmer, H. and Perner, J. (1983) 'Beliefs about beliefs: representation and constraining function of wrong beliefs in young children's understanding of deception', *Cognition* 13: 103–28.

Wimmer, H., Hogrefe, G.-J. and Perner, J. (1988) 'Children's understanding of informational access as source of knowledge', *Child Development* 59: 386–96.

Winegar, L. T. (ed.) (1989) *Social Interaction and the Development of Children's Understanding*, Norwood, NJ: Ablex.

Winick, M. (1976) *Malnutrition and Brain Development*, Oxford: Oxford University Press.

Winner, E., Rosensteil, A. K. and Gardner, H. (1976) 'The development of metaphoric understanding', *Developmental Psychology* 12: 289–97.

Winograd, T. (1972) 'Understanding natural language', *Cognitive Psychology* 3: 1–191.

Witkin, H. A. (1977) *Cognitive Styles in Personal and Cultural Adaptation*, Worcester, Mass.: Clark University Press.

Witkin, H. A. and Goodenough, D. R. (1981) *Cognitive Styles: Essence and Origins*, New York: International Universities Press.

Witkin, H. A., Goodenough, D. R. and Oltman, P. K. (1979) 'Psychological differentiation: current status', *Journal of Personality and Social Psychology* 37: 1127–45.

Wittgenstein, L. (1976) *Philosophical Investigations*, Oxford: Blackwell.

Wohlwill, J. F. (1973) *The Study of Behavioral Development*, New York: Academic Press.

Wolters, G., Beishuizen, M., Broers, G. and Knoppert, W. (1990) 'Mental arithmetic: effects of calculation procedure and problem difficulty on solution latency', *Journal of Experimental Child Psychology* 49: 20–30.

Woo, S. L. C. (1991) 'Molecular genetic analysis of Phenylketonuria and mental retardation', in P. R. McHugh and V. A. McKusick (eds) *Genes, Brain and Behaviour*, New York: Raven Press.

Wood, D. J. (1980) 'Teaching the young child: some relationships between social interaction, language and thought', in D. R. Olson (ed.) *The Social Foundations of Language and Thought*, New York: Norton.

Wood, D. J. (1981) *Working with Underfives*, London: Grant McIntyre.

Wood, D. J. (1988) *How Children Think and Learn*, Oxford: Blackwell.

Wood, D. J. and Middleton, D. J. (1975) 'A study of assisted problem solving', *British Journal of Psychology*, 66: 181–91.

Wood, D. J., Bruner, J. S. and Ross, G. (1976) 'The role of tutoring in problem solving', *Journal of Child Psychology and Psychiatry* 17(2): 89–100.

Wood, D. J., Wood, H. A. and Middleton, D. J. (1978) 'An experimental evaluation of four face-to-face teaching strategies', *International Journal of Behavioural Development* 1: 131–47.

Wozniak, R. H. (1987) 'Developmental method, zones of development, and theories of the environment', in L. S. Liben (ed.) *Development and Learning*, Hillsdale, NJ: Erlbaum.

Wynn, K. (1992) 'Children's acquisition of the number words and the counting system', *Cognitive Psychology* 24: 220–51.

Yang-Feng, T. L. (1991) 'The chromosome: its anatomy, and its aberrations', in P. R. McHugh and V. A. McKusick (eds) *Genes, Brain and Behaviour*, New York: Raven Press.

Yaniv, I. and Shatz, M. (1988) 'Children's understanding of perceptibility', in J. W. Astington, P. L. Harris and D. R. Olson (eds) *Developing Theories of Mind*, Cambridge: Cambridge University Press.

Yates, G. C. R., Yates, S. M. and Beasley, C. J. (1987) 'Young children's knowledge of strategies in delay of gratification', *Merrill-Palmer Quarterly* 33: 159–169.

Young, J. Z. (1978) *Programs of the Brain*, Oxford: Oxford University Press.

Young, J. Z. (1985) 'What's in a brain?', in C. W. Coen (ed.) *Functions of the Brain*, Oxford: Clarendon Press.

Young, J. Z. (1987) *Philosophy and the Brain*, Oxford: Oxford University Press.

Yuill, N. and Perner, J. (1988) 'Intentionality and knowledge in children's judgment of actor's responsibility and recipient's emotional reaction', *Developmental Psychology* 24(3): 358–65.

Yule, W. and Rutter, M. (1985) 'Reading and other learning difficulties', in M. Rutter and L. Hersov (eds) *Child and Adolescent Psychiatry: Modern Approaches*, Oxford: Blackwell.

Yule, W., Gold, R. D. and Busch, C. (1981) 'Long-term predictive validity of the WPPSI: an 11-year follow-up study', *Personality and Individual Differences* 3: 65–71.

Yussen, S. R. (ed.) (1985a) *The Growth of Reflection in Children*, New York: Academic Press.

Yussen, S. R. (1985b) 'The role of metacognition in contemporary theories of cognitive development', in D. L. Forrest-Pressley, G. E. MacKinnon and G. T. Waller (eds) *Metacognition, Cognition and Human Performance*, Orlando, Fla.: Academic Press.

Yussen, S. R. and Levy, V. M. (1975) 'Developmental change in predicting one's own span of short-term memory', *Journal of Experimental Child Psychology* 19: 502–8.

Yussen, S. R., Mathews, S. R., Buss, R. R. and Kane, P. T. (1980) 'Developmental change in judging important and critical elements of stories', *Developmental Psychology* 16: 213–19.

Zabrucky, K. and Ratner, H. H. (1986) 'Children's comprehension monitoring and recall of inconsistent stories', *Child Development* 57: 1401–18.

Zahn-Waxler, C. and Kochanska, G. (1990) 'The origins of guilt', in R. A. Thompson (ed.) *Socioemotional development: Nebraska Symposium on Motivation, 1988*, vol. 36. Lincoln, Nebr.: University of Nebraska Press.

Zahn-Waxler, C., Radke-Yarrow, M. and King, R. A. (1979) 'Child rearing and children's prosocial dispositions towards victims of distress', *Child Development* 50: 319–30.

Zahn-Waxler, C., Cummings, E. M., Iannotti, R. M. and Radke-Yarrow, M. (1984) 'Young offspring of depressed parents: a population at risk for affective problems', in D. Cicchetti and K. Schneider-Rosen (eds) *New Directions for Child Development: Childhood Depression*, San Francisco: Jossey-Bass.

Zajonc, R. B. (1983) 'Validating the confluence model', *Psychological Bulletin* 93: 457–80.

Zajonc, R. B. and Marcus G. B. (1975) 'Birth order and intellectual development', *Psychological Review* 82: 74–88.

Zaremba, J. (1985) 'Recent medical research', in D. Lane and B. Stratford (eds) *Current Approaches to Down's Syndrome*, London: Holt, Rinehart & Winston.

Zelniker, T. and Jeffrey, W. E. (1976) 'Reflective and impulsive children: strategies of information-processing underlying differences in problem-solving', *Monographs of the Society for Research in Child Development* 41(5), serial no. 168.

Zelniker, T. and Jeffrey, W. E. (1979) 'Attention and cognitive style in children', in G. A. Hale and M. Lewis (eds) *Attention and Cognitive Development*, New York: Plenum Press.

Zinchenko, V. P. (1985) 'Vygotsky's ideas about units for the analysis of mind', in J. V. Wertsch (ed.) *Culture, Communication and Cognition*, Cambridge: Cambridge University Press.

Zingg, R. M. (1940) 'Feral man and extreme cases of isolation', *American Journal of Psychology* 53: 487–517.

Zurer Pearson, B. (1990) 'The comprehension of metaphor by preschool children', *Journal of Child Language* 17: 185–204.

# Name index

Abelson, R. 111
Abrahamsen, A. 234
Acredolo, C. 69
Ades, A.E. 286
Ainsworth, M.D.S. 127, 360
Aivano, S. 56
Alexandra, H. 328
Allen, G.L. 100
Anastasi, A. 308, 359
Anderson, J.R. 70, 82, 188, 218
Anderson, K.N. 98
Anderson, M. 51, 53, 54, 90, 101, 157,
    160, 161, 162, 163, 165, 166, 167,
    168, 169, 170, 171, 175, 176, 212,
    219, 229, 253, 255, 356
Ankenbauer, M.R. 125
Anooshian, L.J. 98
Antell, S.E. 37
Aristotle 74
Armbruster, B.B. 339, 341
Armour-Thomas, E. 323
Arnheim, R. 93
Arrieta, R. 297, 299
Arsenio, W.F. 328
Ashcraft, M.R. 41
Aslin, R.N. 273, 284
Asplund-Carlsson, M. 26
Astington, J. 147, 148, 149, 150, 151,
    152, 154
Atkinson, R.C. 50, 213
Attili, G. 126
Augsbach, L.H. 61

Bachevalier, J. 53, 54, 63, 278, 282
Bacon, C. 150
Baddeley, A. 14, 49
Badgio, P.C. 187
Bailey, C. 276

Baillargeon, R. 108, 123, 198, 200, 205,
    210, 211, 349
Bairstow, P.J. 28
Baker, L. 26, 114
Baker-Ward, L. 339
Baldwin, J.M. 235
Baldwin, L. 6, 13
Balfour, G. 39
Bandura, A. 343
Banks, M.S. 10, 273, 274, 278, 279
Barker, P. 323
Barnard, K.E. 316
Barnes, W.S. 13
Baron, J. 54, 68, 187
Baron-Cohen, S. 152
Barrett, D.E. 295, 296, 297
Barrett, K.C. 357
Barrett, M.D. 94
Barrow, R. 361
Barsalou, L. 105
Bartlett, Sir F. 61
Barwick, J. 93
Bates, E. 311
Bateson, P. 351
Beach, D.R. 56
Beard, R. 211
Bearison, D.J. 343
Beasley, M.G. 286
Bechtel, W. 234
Bedi, K.S. 294
Bee, H.L. 316
Beech, J. 10
Beilin, H. 198, 200, 208, 210
Beinart, H. 125
Bellack, D.R. 61
Bellinger, D. 292
Benbow, C.P. 48
Benjamin, G. 116, 124

Kogan, N. 185, 186, 187, 191, 193
Kolstad, V. 98, 100
Koluchova, J. 321
Konner, M. 286
Kontos, S. 313
Korkel, J. 66
Kosslyn, S. 54
Kozulin, A. 106, 235, 241, 243, 244, 245, 246, 250
Krasner, S.M. 125
Kremer, K.E. 119
Kreutzer, M. 79
Kristeva, J. 35
Kuczynski, L. 328
Kuebli, J. 63
Kuhn, T.S. 81, 154, 202
Kumar, R. 328

Laboratory of Comparative Human Cognition 205, 236
La Frenière, P.J. 359
Lakoff, G. 102, 104, 106
Landau, M. 36
Lane, H. 320
Lang, A. 320
Lange, G. 56
Langston, C. 68
Lansdown, R. 116, 124
Large, B. 13, 14, 17, 18, 20
Larkin, J. 90
Laszlo, J.I. 28
Laurendeau, M. 118
Lave, J. 321, 331, 333
Laxen, D.P.H. 291
Laxon, V. 12, 13, 18, 26
Lazar, A. 116, 124
Lazarus, R.S. 357, 358
Lea, S.E.G 140
Leach, P. 140
Lebrun, Y. 312
Lee, B. 246, 249
Lee, S.-Y. 48
Leekam, S. 152
Lefevre, X. 44
Lehman, D. 341
Lempert, R.O. 341
Lenat, D.B. 194
Leonard, C. 79
Lepper, M.R. 342
Lesh, R. 36
Leslie, A.M. 129, 152, 153
Levin, J.R. 56
Levine, S.C. 41

Levinson, P.J. 71
Lewis, J. 162
Lewis, M. 240, 290, 292, 360
Lewis, V. 113
Lewontin, R. 181, 182, 183
Leyland, J. 313
Liben, L.S. 97
Liberman, A. 12
Liberman, I.Y. 12
Lieven, E.V.M. 309, 311, 338
Light, P.H. 94, 96, 126, 146, 211, 346
Lindauer, B.K. 23
Linn, M.C. 90, 99
Lipian, M.S. 127
Livesley, W.J. 130
Lloyd-Still, J.D. 298
Lock, A. 187, 240, 311, 312
Lockman, J.J. 99
Loehlin, J.C. 287, 288
Long, G. 193
Longeot, F. 211
Longuet-Higgins, H.C. 220
Lorch, E.P. 61
Lord, A.B. 243
Lowe, J. 321
Lozoff, B. 293, 294, 296, 297, 300
Lucey, H. 141
Lunneborg, C. 162
Luria, A.R. 54, 115, 249, 250
Luster, T. 180, 316, 317
Lycan, W. 155, 256
Lynn, R. 281

McAnulty, E.H. 125
McCabe, A.E. 39, 211, 216
McCall, R.B. 281, 306
McCartney, K. 283, 303
McCauley, E. 286
McClaskey, C.L. 359
McClelland, J.L. 105, 233
McCloskey, M. 91
Maccoby, E. 99
McDermott, J. 90
McGillicuddy-Delisi, A.V. 318
McGinley, W. 21
McHugh, P.R. 283
Mackay, D. 21
McKee, E. 127, 139
Mackintosh, N.J. 165
McKusick, V.A. 283
McLane, J.B. 247, 314
McLaughlin, B. 312
Maclean, C. 319

# Subject index